D0252855

B   COHEN, William S.
COH   Love in Black and White
             By William S. Cohen

AMADOR COUNTY LIBRARY
530 Sutter Street
Jackson, CA 95642
(209) 223-6400

5/07

DEMCO

6

LOVE IN BLACK AND WHITE

328.73092
COH

LOVE IN BLACK AND WHITE

A Memoir of Race, Religion, and Romance

WILLIAM S. COHEN
WITH JANET LANGHART COHEN

ROWMAN & LITTLEFIELD PUBLISHERS, INC.
Lanham • Boulder • New York • Toronto • Plymouth, UK

ROWMAN & LITTLEFIELD PUBLISHERS, INC.

Published in the United States of America
by Rowman & Littlefield Publishers, Inc.
A wholly owned subsidary of The Rowman & Littlefield Publishing Group, Inc.
4501 Forbes Boulevard, Suite 200, Lanham, Maryland 20706
www.rowmanlittlefield.com

Estover Road
Plymouth PL6 7PY
United Kingdom

Distributed by National Book Network

Copyright © 2007 by William S. Cohen

All rights reserved. No part of this publication may be reproduced, stored in a
retrieval system, or transmitted in any form or by any means, electronic, mechanical,
photocopying, recording, or otherwise, without the prior permission of the publisher.

British Library Cataloguing in Publication Information Available

Library of Congress Cataloging-in-Publication Data

Cohen, William S.
  Love in black and white : a memoir of race, religion, and romance /
William S. Cohen.
    p. cm.
  ISBN-13: 978-0-7425-5821-2 (cloth : alk. paper)
  ISBN-10: 0-7425-5821-5 (cloth : alk. paper)
    1. Cohen, William S. 2. Cohen, Janet Langhart, 1941–   . 3. Legislators—
United States—Biography. 4. Cabinet officers—United States—Biography.
5. Television journalists—United States—Biography. 6. African American women
authors—Biography. 7. Married people—United States—Biography. 8. Interracial
marriage—United States —Case studies. 9. Interfaith marriage—United States—
Case studies. 10. United States—Race relations—History—20th century.
  I. Title.
  E840.8.C635A3 2007
  328.73092—dc22
  [B]   2006028886

Printed in the United States of America

∞™ The paper used in this publication meets the minimum requirements of American
National Standard for Information Sciences—Permanence of Paper for Printed Library
Materials, ANSI/NISO Z39.48-1992.

"When they have abolished slavery, the moderns still have to eradicate a much more intangible and tenacious prejudice—the prejudice of race. Differences [between races] have lasted for centuries, and they still subsist in very many places; everywhere they have left traces which, though imaginary, time is hardly able to obliterate. I see slavery is in retreat, but the prejudice from which it arose is immovable."

—Alexis de Tocqueville,
Democracy in America (1835)

"For I am my mother's daughter, and the drums of Africa still beat in my heart. They will not let me rest while there is a single Negro boy or girl without a chance to prove his worth."

—Mary McLeod Bethune
(July 10, 1875–May 18, 1955)

Chava: "Papa, I know Fyedka is not Jewish, but I love him."
Tevye: "A bird may love a fish, but where will they make their home?"

—From *Fiddler on the Roof*

To Anne and Emmett

CONTENTS

Acknowledgments   ix

Preface   xi

One
A Capitol Idea   I

Two
The Shamrock and the Dreidel   13

Three
Up South   35

Four
Hancock Street   49

Five
Lockefield Gardens—Eden   65

Six
Destination Unknown   85

Seven
Hoops and Dreams   123

Eight
Law School and Other Maladies   141

Nine
The Windy City   155

Ten
Law and Politics   179

Eleven
Bean Town and Busing   207

Twelve
Impeachment   217

Thirteen
A Doctor in the House   235

Fourteen
The Rest of the Bastards   241

Fifteen
Of Polo and Poetry   255

Sixteen
Color Codes   265

Seventeen
Who's Coming to Dinner?   273

Eighteen
The Darndest Things   283

Nineteen
Lucky and Lucy   291

Twenty
A Call to Serve   299

Twenty-One
SecDef   309

Twenty-Two
First Lady of the Pentagon   319

Twenty-Three
A Song of Songs   335

Annex: *Anne and Emmett,* a one-act play by
Janet Langhart Cohen   343

Index   365

ACKNOWLEDGMENTS

I am indebted to many people who helped bring this book into being.

First, my enduring thanks go to Jed Lyons, the brilliant President of Rowman & Littlefield Publishing Group. Jed's confidence and cheerfulness—so evident during his days as a Bowdoin College student when he helped insure that my six-hundred mile walking campaign across Maine's Second Congressional District was successful—has only intensified over the years. Without his focus and persistence, this memoir would have remained but a memory.

Stephen Driver is surely a descendant of Job, for he suffered sustained assaults upon his time and patience throughout the editing of the manuscript. During the course of countless meetings and consultations, including precious weekends away from his wife, Deanna, and daughter, Ella, Stephen displayed uncommon grace and understanding. He assisted me and Janet sift through a massive amount of information and served as a positive force for coherency in the face of sheer entropy.

Christopher Anzalone and Sheila Burnett offered wise counsel in helping to highlight those experiential moments that readers could identify with and find of interest.

Piper Wallis was singularly creative in designing the cover of the book.

I'm grateful to our dear friend, Sambo Teng for providing the photographic portrait for the cover.

A word of thanks to my sons Kevin and Christopher who helped retrace some of their father's early steps in his climb into the world of politics. In fact, without their sacrifice, there would have been no climb!

Finally, I am truly blessed to have the hand and heart of my wife Janet, who brings great intelligence, creativity, and passion to every endeavor. It has been her life's mission to transcend the trivial, to reach out and touch that part in each of us that longs for justice and fair play. In envisioning Anne Frank and Emmett Till meeting somewhere in time and allowing their conversation to be included in this book, she ingeniously has reminded us how important it is to seek the triumph of hope over hate and the need to hold onto our humanity through understanding and tolerance.

PREFACE

My wife Janet and I entered this world under dramatically different circumstances. She is black and I am white. I was born in Bangor, Maine, and she in Indianapolis, Indiana. I, the oldest son of a Jewish father and a Protestant Irish mother, spent my early years living on the third floor of a tenement building located on a street that bordered on what was known as "The Devil's Half Acre"—the red-light district of a small city. It was a street filled with immigrant families that hailed mostly from Ireland, Italy, Greece, Poland, and Russia. There was only one black family in the neighborhood, and not more than a handful in the entire city of nearly forty thousand people. These "Negroes" were accepted by the community, provided, of course, they "stayed in their place."

Janet spent her youth under the watchful eye of a single-parent mother, a Southern Baptist woman who, when not living in the homes of white people for whom she worked as a domestic, was forced to move from one boardinghouse to another, until she was able to enter a segregated government housing project reserved principally for blacks who had family members serving in the armed forces. While there were no overtly racist signs posted in public places in Indiana, except for the occasional sign that read "restricted," blacks were systematically denied access to opportunities that were extended to whites as a matter of right. Education, housing, and employment opportunities were limited in quality and scope. Mixing in movie theaters was strictly prohibited. Prime seats on the first floor of the theater were for whites, while those for blacks were put in the remote balconies. Miscegenation laws (prohibiting the mixing of races) were deeply ingrained in the social structure and culture. Blacks and whites were said to be different, and "never the twain should meet." Under no circumstances were they permitted to marry, and surely, never in a place of hallowed significance or with the blessing of the ruling political establishment.

What a difference six decades makes.

Neither one of us ever imagined that we would one day move from the narrow streets of our youth to places of prominence in our chosen professions, deliberately ignore the social taboos of our times, get married in the Capitol of the United States, and go on to serve and represent our country and our armed forces around the world. It remains a testament to the promise of America that justice may be delayed, but cannot be denied; that rank prejudice cannot flourish in the sunlight; and that anything is possible when the heart is released from the chains of ignorance.

Today, racially mixed couples and families, while not yet the rule, no longer are considered a rarity. The face of America is changing. To some who long for a return to the yesteryear of white, European dominance, this evolution is seen as tragic. The Miniver Cheevys and children of scorn are doomed to see diversity as dilutive rather than enriching. The alloy has proved stronger than the ore, however, and the tide that runs toward greater racial integration is unlikely to be reversed.*

The role that racism has played in America's history is ugly. The fear, hatred, and murderous violence it has generated may be traced to some primordial cellular structure. We leave discovery of racism's origin to social scientists.

All of us today can see proof that, whatever their origin, crimes against humanity no longer enjoy a socially safe harbor. This is not

---

* See "Miniver Cheevy" by Edward Arlington Robinson.

to say that the struggle for equal rights has been achieved or that we have seen the end of racism, as some have declared. The eagerness to strike out against those who are different in color, race, or creed in times of physical danger or economic distress remains ever present. The profiling by law enforcement officials of those not seen as "one of us" is practiced, even though denied. But dragging our darkest and worst instincts into the open offers us a hope that we will continue the search to reconcile our practices with our professed ideals.

Janet has written a wonderful memoir, *From Rage to Reason: My Life in Two Americas,** chronicling her remarkable personal and professional journey. It would be impossible for me to replicate the power and poignancy of her story here, but with the generous permission granted by Kensington Publishing Corp., I have drawn upon some of her experiences to explain how some of the defining moments in our lives gave us the strength to challenge convention in our careers and in our love.

---

* Where direct quotes from Janet appear, they are taken from our daily conversations or from selected portions of her memoir, *From Rage to Reason.*

One

A Capitol Idea

February 14, 1996

I didn't make an entry into a journal, as I had done on the same day seventeen years earlier during my first year as a United States Senator. Then, the news was bleak and would soon become bleaker. "The American Embassy in Iran has been stormed by Iranian leftists. The Ambassador and seventy Americans were taken into custody. Two Marines were wounded. Latest reports indicate that the Americans have been released and are now safe. . . . The American Ambassador to Afghanistan was murdered last night by unidentified terrorists."

Much history had flowed beneath the bridges that span the Potomac River since I first took my oath of allegiance as a new member of the United States Senate. The Shah of Iran had been overthrown, the Soviet Empire had crumbled, the Berlin Wall had been leveled, President Ronald Reagan had survived the Iran-Contra scandal, and Saddam Hussein's military had been forcibly removed from Kuwait and chased back to Baghdad. While the World Trade Center towers in New York City had been the target of terrorists, the attack was assumed to be the work of a few wild-eyed fanatics. The depth of Al Qaeda's hatred and capabilities would not be known for another five years.

As I approached the Capitol that Wednesday morning, I wasn't consumed with the ebb and flow of geopolitical forces. Today, I was going to enter the building where I had spent much of my adult life, not to engage in the give-and-take of legislative debate, but to take a very different kind of vow. I was going to marry the woman who had seized my heart so many years earlier.

Janet and I had been engaged for several years, but she was reluctant to marry me out of fear that an interracial union would harm my career. When our engagement had become public, we had been on the receiving end of the disapproval of bigots. It was not as intense as either of us had anticipated, but it remained a concern for her.

I've always had a gothic preoccupation with time. An hourglass always seemed to be turning in my mind, the sands running inexorably to their conclusion and mine. Perhaps it was the influence of the French existentialist Andre Gide, whom I had studied in college: "It is the foreknowledge of the finality of things that destroys bliss at its very apex." Or maybe it was my father who shaped my habits by working eighteen hours a day, six days a week until the day he died in his small bakery shop at the age of eighty-six. In fact, it was my father's death four months earlier that served to reinforce how little time any of us have on Earth to pursue our dreams.

I was entering my twenty-fourth year of public service in Congress. It had become over time an increasingly unfulfilling place to labor. The art of government, of necessity, involves willingness to compromise. Yet the word "compromise" had become an object of ridicule or contempt, signifying either weakness or the lack of conviction to true-blue believers. Political leaders drew battle lines each day across a partisan divide.

Set speeches replaced genuine debate, as members became even more acutely aware that their potential opponents were recording their every statement that was being broadcast on C-Span. Although senators remained generally decorous in their behavior toward each other on and off the Senate floor, friendships across political lines were hard to forge and harder to find. Historically, senators left office either through defeat or death. But many now were signaling that the rewards of public service were no longer enough to outweigh the burdens. There were too many demands and pressures; too little time to reason and reflect; too much criticism of their efforts; the hair-trigger presumption of guilt at the mere whisper of impropriety; the schizophrenia of a public that wanted less government spending, more government services for their parochial interests, and lower taxes; the unyielding demands of proliferating single-issue constituencies; and a drumbeat of support for a mandatory imposition of term limits, since seniority of service was now seen as contributing to a calcification of the political process.

Although I had accumulated a considerable war chest for a campaign against an unfunded and virtually unknown opponent, I decided that I would join the ranks of those departing public service.

In January, I traveled with Janet to Bangor, my hometown in Maine, and announced my retirement. It was not easy to decide to give up something that I had worked so hard to achieve, but I no longer had the heart for the high honor that was becoming more of a job. I knew that if I stayed another term, I would reach the age where I would have no alternative but to hold on to the position because few options would exist for a life beyond public service. It would always be just one more race, one more time.

Shortly after returning to Washington, Janet and I began to plan the time and place of our wedding. I thought June, but she said February.

"Why February?" I asked, thinking it was much too soon.

"Think about the fourteenth," she said gently, passing over the opportunity to pour a pail of cold water on my head for being so obtuse.

"But there's not enough time." (Was I getting cold feet already?)

"There is if we start right now."

"Where should we hold it?" Neither of us belonged to a local church or place of worship.

"The Chapel," Janet said. "The one in the Capitol. We can ask the Reverend Jim Ford to preside."

It was obvious that Janet had given the time and place of our marriage a good deal more thought than had I. The Reverend James Ford, who served as the chaplain in the House of Representatives, had once been the chaplain at West Point. He had been introduced to us by our friend Pete Dawkins, the Heisman Trophy winner who had been West Point's scholastic and athletic superstar. We bumped into the Reverend Ford at a White House Christmas party five years earlier. As we passed under some mistletoe, he pulled out a small camera. As we posed and he snapped our picture, he said, "I now pronounce you man and wife."

The thought that his informal blessing would now become a reality, I found exciting. Frankly, the prospect of holding the ceremony in the Chapel was also attractive. Neither Janet nor I wanted a large wedding, and the Chapel would absolutely preclude space for more than a dozen or so people. The very next day we arranged to meet with the Reverend Ford to explore just how many people could be squeezed into the room, allowing for the placement of flowers and a photographer. Just enough for our family members and one or two friends, we concluded. Perfect!

Well, not quite. Word had spread quickly about our plans. Soon, we were besieged by our friends who insisted that they had to attend the wedding. As a result, our search for a room took on greater urgency. I spoke with Senator Mark Hatfield of Oregon, who was chairman of the Appropriations Committee. He offered a large hearing room in the Capitol. It looked as if it would be fine for our needs. But more calls continued to flood my office. The list of friends and colleagues kept growing. Soon it exceeded more than a hundred people. The Appropriations Committee Room would never do.

Senator Hatfield had another thought: The Mike Mansfield Room, named after the former Senate Majority Leader. It was located just off the Senate chamber. This was the room where Republican senators gathered every Tuesday to scope out our policies and legislative agendas. It was no small irony that we huddled under the watchful gaze of a full-length portrait of Mansfield, one of the most beloved leaders of that august body, a Democrat from Montana.

In the days leading up to the wedding, I noticed Janet's moods seemed to shift between those of sheer excitement and sober reflection of what this marriage would mean to her. There had been so many barriers strewn in her path during her life, virtually all of them involving her race. The verbal slights and body slams had come from so many different directions, and, almost always, from the least expected sources.

As we walked around the Capitol that week, we kept reflecting on our country's history. This great edifice of hope, this citadel of democracy, was the place where our nation's laws were fashioned—laws that were not always ones America could point to with pride. The Fugitive Slave Act of 1850, which made a criminal of anyone who helped escaping slaves, was a stark reminder that laws were not to be equated with justice. Before that law was passed, any slave who managed to make it to a free state was a free person. But the 1850 law reached out to stop the abolitionists who were helping runaway slaves. Bounty hunters were allowed to enter free states and capture fugitives. Any U.S. Marshal who refused to return a slave would be fined $1,000. Any black person, free or not, became fair game for law enforcement officials and other hunters. Skin color was an ineradicable tattoo, an identifier that was often the equivalent of an automatic jail sentence. A simple declaration of "that's my slave" was enough to secure an apprehension and arrest!

Interestingly enough, the Irish frequently were used by the ruling Protestant power structure to help capture slaves. Although the Catholic Irish were an oppressed race in Ireland who had to face a caste system that reduced them to a social and material position that was comparable to those of an American slave, they managed to "become white" and part of an oppressing race in America.*

The Capitol Building itself had been built on the backs of slaves. Long before air-conditioning had been invented, slaves had

---

See Noel Ignatiev, *How the Irish Became White*, (Routledge, 1995).

been used to wave fans over big blocks of ice deposited in a tunnel that ran under the Capitol, sending cool air into the Senate chamber. We wondered how weary and dispirited they must have been. What was it like for them to know that the words "freedom," "justice," and "equality" that they were forced to chisel into the gleaming marble were not meant for them? Could any of them possibly have imagined that one of their daughters would one day join hands as an equal with a white man under those words? That one aspect of Dr. Martin Luther King's dream ("One day, little black boys and little black girls will be able to join hands with little white boys and little white girls and walk the streets as brothers and sisters") was about to be realized?

When Valentine's Day finally arrived, Janet and I departed separately for Capitol Hill. As I walked up the steps of the Senate, my eyes drifted up to the dome of the Capitol glistening in the sun. I have always been awestricken at its breath-catching architecture and symbolism. There stood the nineteen-and-a-half-foot, fourteen-thousand, nine-hundred-and-eighty-five-pound cast-iron statue of Freedom, one of America's most enduring symbols. Freedom's left hand rests upon the shield of the United States while holding a laurel wreath that symbolizes victory and honor. In her right hand is a peace symbol, a sheathed sword, ready to be withdrawn if threatened with harm. Freedom had stirred controversy in her time. The sculptor, Thomas Crawford, originally had the statue crowned with a Phrygian cap like those worn by freed slaves in ancient Rome. But Secretary of War Jefferson Davis, who was in charge of the Army Corps of Engineers constructing the Capitol, protested that the symbolism would inflame the debate over slavery. The sculptor yielded, giving Freedom a helmet that carried an eagle's head and feathers surrounded with stars. From a distance, her headdress resembles that of an Indian warrior.

Today represented something of a milestone in American history. Fifty years ago, we would have been arrested for violating laws that prohibited miscegenation (from the Latin *miscere*, "to mix," and *genus,* "race"). State miscegenation laws, which went back to at least 1661, faded away in 1967, after the U.S. Supreme Court took up the case of Mildred Jeter, an African American, and Richard Loving, a white man.

They were legally married in June 1958 in the District of Columbia, not far from where work had just started on the extension of the Capitol's East Front—the extension that would include the Mike Mansfield Room. They went to live in Virginia, and soon after their marriage, they were arrested for violating the state's miscegenation law and sentenced to a year in jail. The trial judge suspended the sentence for twenty-five years, providing the couple leave Virginia. "Almighty God," he ruled, "created the races white, black, yellow, malay and red, and he placed them on separate continents. And but for the interference with his arrangement there would be no cause for such marriages. The fact that he separated the races shows that he did not intend for the races to mix."

The couple eventually challenged the Virginia law and the case—wonderfully called *Loving v. Virginia*—came before the Supreme Court. In a unanimous opinion written by Chief Justice Earl Warren, the court struck down the law as unconstitutional, saying that "the freedom to marry, or not marry, a person of another race resides with the individual and cannot be infringed by the State."* The ruling thus also wiped out similar laws in fifteen other states.

But taking a law off the books did not mean that the issue disappeared.

Less than two years before our wedding day, the issue of black-and-white marriages arose in a high school in Wedowee, Alabama. The white principal of Randolph County High School called an assembly of seniors and juniors. Sixty-two percent of the students were white; the rest were black. The principal wanted to know whether anyone was planning to attend the prom "with someone who was not of the same race." When several students said they did, he threatened to cancel the prom.

---

*See *Loving v. Virginia,* 388 U.S. 1 (1967).

The president of the junior class asked what this meant for her, since her father was white and mother black. The principal replied that her parents had made a "mistake," which he hoped he could keep his students from making. In the uproar that followed, the school was set afire and the principal was suspended with pay, later to be reinstated.

Now, on our wedding day, in just a few hours, in the presence of Senator Strom Thurmond, once an archsegregationist, and Majority Leader Trent Lott (who would later lose his position for praising the racist campaign of a young Strom Thurmond), we would seal with a kiss the coming of an America that was worthy of its professed ideals.

I felt neither heroic nor courageous. I was simply filled with pride that I lived in a nation continuing to evolve in its quest to reach the "better angels of our nature." Two people from different races, different states, and different cultures and experiences could meet, fall in love, and go tell it on the tallest Hill in America.

While I switched into formal attire for the occasion, my thoughts moved to more mundane considerations. I knew that Janet had attended to every detail of the wedding, leaving me little to do. She had ordered white roses, star lilies, and orchids to be placed on the mantle over which was the portrait of George Washington. In addition, she had arranged for a trio of cello, violin, and flute musicians to play classic chamber music.

Nearly a dozen of my Senate colleagues had gathered in the Mansfield Room as I, with my sons Kevin and Christopher at my side, anxiously awaited Janet's arrival. Senator John Chaffee of Rhode Island, an American hero who fought at Guadalcanal during World War II and fought again in Korea, kindly offered Janet the use of his Senate "hideaway" office as her dressing room. There, she primped as brides are likely to do, not quite sure that everything was quite right or under control. I knew that she would worry whether I had remembered to bring the wedding rings or had seen to it that proper protocol had been followed in the seating of the guests.

When the large double doors to the room finally opened and Janet appeared, I felt my chest tighten. Beautiful as she was the day I first saw her more than twenty years earlier, she was even more breathtaking to behold. As she entered the room and the musicians played "Here Comes the Bride," Janet turned to look at Senator Thurmond, who was sitting in the last row. I knew exactly what she was thinking: protocol dictated that he should be sitting in the front row as the Senate's president pro tempore, its most senior member.

Janet paused briefly, bent down to whisper to him, and then walked toward me with all the grace and confidence of the runway model she once had been. I tried to ignore the bank of network television cameras that hovered behind me, seeking to record every moment of this special occasion. When she finally reached me, we turned to face Reverend Ford, who was wearing his perennially cherubic smile. He proceeded with his ceremonial comments and led us through the ritual pledges of love and devotion. I slipped on Janet's finger the gold wedding band I had purchased and she, in turn, guided onto my finger the diamond ring that my father had given to me as his final gift. When Reverend Ford finally said to me, "You may now kiss the bride," I embraced Janet and kissed her as modestly as the circumstances dictated.

Janet let out an audible sigh, which produced a genuine wave of laughter from our many friends in the audience. We then turned and walked out of the room, buoyed by their applause and heartfelt good wishes.

We jumped into a waiting limousine and headed off to the Hay Adams Hotel, which sits just across Lafayette Park in full view of the White House. Once there, we hosted a reception for our guests, who were now close to one hundred and twenty-five in number. There, we moved among our closest friends, who were clearly in a high-spirited and celebratory mood. We clinked glasses, cut cake, and luxuriated in the warm embrace of the moment. My father had passed away, and my mother was unable to travel. Janet had no idea where her father was or if he was still alive, and her mother was also unable to travel to be with us.

My two sons, Kevin and Chris, who had served as best men, were there, along with their wives, Chantel and Kerry. Next to them was Janet's sister, Myrna, and Janet's friend from Chicago, Millicent Proctor. Former secretary of state and U.S. Senator from Maine, Edmund Muskie, and his wife, Jane, joined in the festive mood, as did Senator-astronaut John Glenn and his wife Annie. The chief of naval operations, Admiral Mike Borda, was also a guest. There were many so-called black "firsts" there as well: former secretary of the army, Clifford Alexander, and his wife Adele; former chairman of the joint chiefs of staff, Colin Powell, and his wife, Alma; Bill Coleman, former secretary of transportation, and his wife, Lovida; Ron Brown, former chairman of the Democratic National Committee and secretary of commerce, and his wife Alma; and Bob Johnson, the founder of Black Entertainment Television. We stayed as late as possible, savoring the laughter and love. It was our best Valentine's Day ever!

Years later, while looking through the photographs in our wedding album, we would be touched with joy at seeing so many happy faces. And we would feel the twinge of melancholy, as well, in noting how many friends we lost after the wedding, such as Admiral Borda, Ron Brown, Senator Muskie, Katherine Graham, Elliot and Anne Richardson, and Reverend Ford.

Unlike most newlyweds, we did not rush off to some exotic location on a honeymoon. There would be time enough for a romantic excursion after I left the Senate.

Or so we thought.

Later that evening, we stepped out onto the terrace of our apartment at 701 Pennsylvania Avenue, Market Square. Janet had slipped into an apricot cashmere robe and was wearing her mother's favorite cologne, Tabu, the fragrance her mother wore the night she had met Janet's father.

Scanning the horizon, we could see the Capitol's magnificent dome, luminous as the moon against the dark sky. Located directly across from us was the National Archives Building, its columns and pediment replicating the structure and spirit of ancient Rome and

Greece. Off to the right was the Justice Department and beyond it, in the distance, rose the gleaming Washington Monument. Below our terrace we could look onto the Navy Memorial and the statue of the Lone Sailor, dressed in classic bell-bottom trousers, a sea cap, and a peacoat. There he stood, hands in the pockets of his coat, the collar turned up against the back of his neck, gazing across the granite globe sculptured into the expansive surface of the memorial. In his vigil, he symbolized both adventure and loneliness.

I went back into the apartment to open a bottle of champagne, and when I returned I noticed Janet staring at Pennsylvania Avenue. She said she had been thinking about how much of her people's history and heartbeat once throbbed along this historic site. Just off to the left, we could see the place where slaves had once been sold in front of a tavern at Seventh and Pennsylvania Avenues. Today, people lined up each morning to buy Starbucks coffee instead.

We stood on the terrace in silence, taking in the sweep of this grand vista, still lost in the thoughts of how much had changed in our lives and in this country.

Then, Janet said, "I really do feel like Cinderella. I have no mean stepsisters or glass slippers. But you are my Prince Charming."

I slipped my arm around Janet and we stood there wrapped in the ecstasy of the moment.

"Could we have ever dreamed that we would be standing here, together?" I whispered.

Janet closed her eyes. "No," She said. There was never a moment when I thought I would ever be this happy, so loved."

I looked up and began to sing the lyrics: "Fly me to the moon and let me play among the stars, you are all I asked for. . . ."

We both broke into laughter. Frank Sinatra, I was not.

We raised the gold-rimmed champagne glasses that Janet had selected for the wedding, touched them, and kissed, this time much longer than we had done in the Mansfield Room.

We had both arrived at a place far beyond the streets of racism and bigotry of our childhoods. In our hearts we believed that our union was meant to be, but to this day we remain unsure how much of our lives have been governed by chance, choice, or the hidden hand of Providence.

Was it all predetermined, as the ancient Greeks believed, our fates woven by the gods? How do we explain the decisions, and their revisions, the improbabilities of circumstances that led us into the presence of each other and the magnetic field of love? What forces of character allowed us to challenge convention and the fear of social rejection?

Robert Frost wrote that he would be telling his story ages and ages hence and that his choosing of the road less traveled by had made all the difference.

So it has been with us.

Two

THE SHAMROCK AND THE DREIDEL

It was my father, Reuben Cohen, who insisted that I have the benefit of a Jewish education. It was a reasonable enough request to the first born son of a Jewish baker. Even my mother, Clara Hartley, thought it was a good idea.

Wait. Clara Hartley? Sounds Irish.

Indeed.

And that really was my beginning.

They had met at a dance hall in 1937 at a place called the Auto Rest Park, located just a few miles outside of Bangor's city limits. Clara Irene Hartley was just sixteen. Her mother had died when she was a young child and she was raised by a father who had a touch of wander lust. He moved her, her sister, Lena, and brother, Donald, from small town to small town in rural northern Maine before finally locating in Bangor.

She was five feet five inches in height, but stood so erect that she seemed a half a foot taller. Blond, blue-eyed, and stunningly beautiful (my father would always recount how her cheeks were the color of apple skins), she captured his heart immediately. Within weeks after my father met her, they were married. She obviously didn't marry him for his money. At the time, he was making a grand total of six dollars a week at the bakery. While they were not poor, there were few material conveniences they could afford to purchase.

I can still recall my mother washing our clothes on a scrub board in a cast-iron bathtub. A modest level of prosperity did not enter our lives until the war ended

Their marriage was kept a secret from his father, Harry Cohen, for months. When he learned that my mother was pregnant with my sister, Marlene, he did not greet the news of his impending grandfather status with great enthusiasm. My father had crossed a bright red line that divided Jew from Gentile. The mixing of bloodlines was a great taboo, and he had broken it. There were consequences to follow his transgression, but at the time, love had overwhelmed all fear.

There's little doubt in my mind that my father was trying to please Granpa by showing him that his son would carry on the revered Jewish tradition.

I was only five years old at the time, and it was not clear to me exactly what "Jewish" meant at the time, but I was to find out that it meant that I was not "Catholic."

One day, two of my neighborhood friends, Karl and Paul, pleaded with me to accompany them to St. John's Catholic Church. They explained to me that in addition to the pews inside the church where you could kneel to pray, there were confessional booths where you could unburden your soul. First, I wasn't convinced that I had ever sinned. Sure, I had dispensed a few choice expletives while jousting in the streets. And, yes, I had occasionally stepped on a crack in the pavement and had "broken my mother's back," according to the superstition then in vogue. But that hardly condemned me to a one-way ticket to damnation. Moreover the very thought of whispering to a man called "Father," who was not my father, that I had indulged in sinful conduct was out of the question.

After assuring me that I could skip the confessional booth, my pals finally persuaded me to venture into the cavernous interior of the church—just to watch.

Upon entering the church, I saw the vaulted ceilings and the worshippers kneeling in prayer and felt immediately uncomfortable. The atmosphere was totally alien to anything I had experienced. The church was dark, mystical, intimidating. I followed my friends to a pew and tried not to look out of place. When I saw Paul and Karl drop down on their knees, I followed suit with some hesitation. The act of kneeling was baffling to me, simply because I had never observed anyone doing it at the Jewish synagogue.

I was confused and embarrassed, much as I had been in my first grade classroom in the Abraham Lincoln Elementary School. I had always refused to pray in public school, and when my teacher and the other students asked why, I explained that I was Jewish and we recited different prayers. I would later discover that my answer was only half true. In any event, the answer seemed satisfactory to everyone but me, because I still didn't understand the harm in reciting the Twenty-third Psalm in the Bible.

There were, in fact, many things that I didn't understand. I had started to learn simplified versions of the Old Testament. I could not comprehend how God could erupt with such emotion whenever someone displeased him. Sending forth locusts, frogs, famine, and other forms of ingenious punishment seemed, well, un-God-like. Moses, after spending forty years in the desert, strikes a rock in a moment of frustration, and he gets to see the Promised Land from a mountaintop! And precisely why was it that we could never spell the word God but had to omit the letter "o"? Was it really irreverent to spell the full name of our Creator? If so, why were we allowed to say the word itself? Was it sacrilegious for me to have these doubts or express these thoughts? What were the penalties for doing so?

At the end of the service I watched as people proceeded, single file, toward the front of the church, where a priest awaited them. I hesitated at first. The priest had a somber mien about him that struck me as uninviting and unfriendly. Surely he knew that I was not a young Catholic boy! The idea of participating in this activity absolutely terrified me. "I'll stay here," I whispered. Paul and Karl wouldn't hear of it. "Come on, Billy," they whispered. I protested further but stopped short of creating a disturbance. Playground pressure won out and I followed them to the altar. I completed my visit to St. John's with a consecrated wafer and a smudge of ash on my forehead.

While walking home I had no idea that I'd just celebrated the first day of Lent and that now I was supposed to go through the next forty weekdays until Easter in a period of fasting and penitence. I felt no guilt or shame for my entry into forbidden territory, that is, not until later that evening, when my grandfather spotted me with the identifiable smudge on my forehead. That bit of ash I was sporting caused my grandfather to turn menacing toward me for the very first time. Out of his anger came one demand after another.

"Where have you been? What have you done? We're Jewish," he scolded me. "Don't go to St. John's ever again."

This was how I learned that being Jewish excluded any notion that I might also be Catholic. No one at the time thought it necessary to explain to me the fundamental tenets of each religion. I was left dangling in a dark void to ponder the significance of my transgression. My grandfather was content to strike my heart with fear. His reprimand worked. Until I reached adulthood, I never stepped inside another church.

By the time I was seven, I was ready to begin in earnest the process that would instruct me in detail what it meant to be Jewish. In Hebrew school there would be meaning attached to the customs and traditions that separated me from my peers. Unfortunately, my experience at Hebrew school, which I attended three times per week after public school, proved to be more exasperating than anything I had anticipated.

From the very beginning of my religious instruction, I felt like the proverbial odd man out. I had friends who attended both of the schools with me, so it was not a question of my being surrounded by strangers. The problem lay in my lineage. My mother's genes had proved dominant over my father's. I was constantly reminded that my face was the very map of Ireland. My blond hair stood in stark contrast to the darker Semitic look of nearly everyone else.

I felt most self-conscious about my appearance during the High Holidays. I was five when I first started going to the Beth

Abraham Synagogue with my father. There were three synagogues in Bangor at the time, all located in the same area as St. John's Catholic Church: Beth Abraham, Beth Israel, and Toldoth and Yitzchak. The three synagogues represented the Conservative, Reform, and Orthodox philosophies. I never understood the distinction except that Beth Israel was more elegant in design, with its stone and cement-block construction, ornate columns, and domed superstructure. It made the two other nearby wooden-framed buildings look like poor second cousins. The men and women who worshipped at Beth Israel were noticeably different in appearance. Their dress, manner, and confidence seemed, well, superior. In fact, it was a class distinction that separated Beth Israel from the others. Its members traced their lineage to German and Baltic states rather than to Poland or Russia. They were mostly professionals—doctors, lawyers, accountants, entrepreneurs. Their counterparts at the other synagogues consisted of the butchers, bakers, and the candlestick makers—small shop owners, peddlers, and junk dealers, men whose hands bore the calluses of manual work, lower-middle-class people who had not yet crossed the lines that marked the gentile neighborhoods.

It was only during Rosh Hashanah and Yom Kippur that my father closed the bakery. While the orthodox members would walk to the synagogue, my father placed a higher premium on convenience. Surely, he would not disturb the universe by driving his automobile during the High Holidays. His only concession to convention was to park the family car several blocks away from the synagogue and then walk the remaining distance so as to not make a flagrant display of his disregard for tradition.

From my very earliest moments in the synagogue, the strongest emotion I experienced was a sense of alienation. The men who attended the services were mostly dark complected. They dressed in dark suits, complemented with dark, broad-brimmed hats. Their hats were replaced with yarmulkes and silk "tallises" (shawls) as they entered the synagogue. Once seated, many of the men would take a pinch of snuff (aromatic tobacco) from small boxes, make a fist, place the snuff in the area formed by the thumb and forefinger, and then inhale it. (Many years later I would witness German chancellor Helmut Schmidt do precisely the same thing during a private meeting in his office.) Some of them would wrap teffilin (black straps containing prayer boxes) tightly around their arms in preparation for prayer.

I had apparel of my own, of course. I had a tallis and yarmulke that I kept in a soft maroon-colored felt bag with the Star of David embroidered on it in gold thread. But while clothes make—or conceal—the man, these religious accoutrements could not transform me into something I clearly was not.

Beth Abraham was a modest building that accommodated a series of benches on one level and a balcony above. I was particularly struck by the fact that in the synagogue men and women were not allowed to mix together in the pews. The women were all seated upstairs. It struck me as odd, but my father had a unique opinion, which he shared with me. "You don't want the women seated with the men," he explained. "Women are a distraction, see?"

I learned later that under Jewish law, women were considered to be "unclean," and were forbidden to be seated in close proximity to the men. It was in retrospect a form of "separate but equal" segregation, albeit one that I suspected lasted only during the religious ceremonies of the day.

In contrapuntal response to the presiding cantor, the men would recite passages from prayer books while standing and "dovening" (bending slightly and rhythmically) at the waist. Up in the balcony, women were wailing in grief over the loss of their loved ones. I found the sound of the ram's horn (shofar) that was being blown amusing, but inexplicable. In fact I thought the ceremonies were just as strange and incomprehensible as anything I had witnessed at St. John's Catholic Church on Ash Wednesday.

During the course of the day, there would be periodic breaks from the service and the men would gather on the street outside and engage in animated discussions. I would stay close to my father's side while he either joked with the others or offered his opinions on politics, business, a neighbor's health, or the state of international affairs. He seemed to relish the interaction, slipping periodically into Yiddish, oblivious to my discomfort.

The fact that I clung to my father and that I could recite a few words of the Jewish prayers was insufficient to acquire a stamp—or even a glance—of approval. Occasionally, a comment would be directed my way. "Who's that little goyim?" someone would ask. "That's Ruby Cohen's son. Ruby's married to the Irish broad that won't talk to anyone."

Part of the problem that I faced was that my father was not able to communicate to me a strong belief in the Jewish religion. It was obvious to me that he attended the services out of a sense of duty rather than belief. He was firmly committed to the moral code contained in the Ten Commandments, but found the rituals of religion to be of little appeal. No student of theology, he was a model of inconsistency.

During an evening at the dinner table he would say, "No, Billy, I just don't buy any of the nonsense that organized religion pumps out. When it's over, it's over. Just like when you turn the lights out, it just goes dark. Leading a good life is its own reward." A few days later, without conceding any contradiction, he would suggest that a higher, albeit indefinable, intelligence had to have constructed the miraculous chain of life. "I mean, how else can you explain it? Everything in existence serves a higher purpose. It couldn't have happened by accident. Someone or something had to have created it."

I concluded that he was a cautious agnostic: not sure that an Old or New Testament God existed, but unwilling to take any chances that one did not.

My mother rarely engaged in any disputations. She shared my father's disdain for the ceremonious aspects of religion, but held to a simple faith in the existence of an afterlife, the location of which was determined by one's thoughts and actions while alive.

The only explanation for my father's insisting that I attend Hebrew school to study the history, language, and customs of his forebears was that he was convinced that most Jews lived by a superior code of conduct that helped carry them into the higher realms of professional excellence and was an association that I would benefit from. I suspected that deep down he wanted to persuade his peers that he had, after all, produced a nice Jewish boy.

I spent the next six years attempting to prove my commitment to the Jewish faith. While I was an excellent student, things did not go well for me in Hebrew school. Rabbi Saul Brown, a man who was conservative in appearance and manner, had a problem with me. Frequently, he would seek to embarrass me in front of the other students by insisting on a show of hands as to whether our parents kept a kosher house. Predictably, my hand would not be among those that shot up. He publicly upbraided me one day after he had driven by our house and seen a Christmas tree in the window. My mother had joked to me that it was just a Chanukah bush, but Rabbi Brown was not amused.

Knowing of Rabbi Brown's dislike for me only intensified my desire to achieve the highest academic grades each year. My goal was to win the top prize of attending Camp Lown during the summer months. I knew that my parents could not afford the incidental costs associated with the camp, but I wanted the recognition for my achievement anyway. Instead of the invitation to enjoy a summer at the camp, I received a gold-plated mezuzah that contained a small piece of parchment inside with words taken from Deuteronomy. At first, I thought it was an oversight. On the second occasion, I recognized it as outright rejection. It was unacceptable to Rabbi Saul and the school's directors that the best student was not a real Jew.

I was suspended between two worlds. Every day at public school I proclaimed myself to be Jewish, refusing to recite the Lord's Prayer. Yet in Hebrew school I was treated as a non-Jew. I sought refuge from the confusion and an outlet for my anger by joining the YMCA. Yes, the Young Men's Christian Association.

Ever since the days when I sat on my father's lap watching high school basketball games, I dreamed of the time when I would exhibit my skills before thousands of fans. I asked my father permission to attend practice one Saturday each month with the promise that I would attend religious services on the other three weekends. I knew that his love for basketball would overcome any doubts he had about my absence from the synagogue. But my passion for the sport intensified with each incident of rejection at Hebrew school.

Soon I was playing organized basketball two Saturdays a month, then three. While I continued to excel in my Hebrew school studies, I eventually stopped attending Saturday services entirely. This created a problem for me at Hebrew school because the teachers insisted that all students attend Saturday services. Records were kept as to which classes maintained the best attendance. Classes with the best attendance were awarded gold stars and prizes at the end of the year. My absences bred a good deal of resentment. Occasionally, the resentment would erupt into scuffles in the playground area outside the school. Because I was bigger and eager to fight, the scuffles didn't last very long. I knew it was selfish of me to choose basketball over my classmates' aspirations, but because I knew that I was not considered one of them, I was not going to let them force me to accept either their rules or their goals.

Pride is said to go before the fall, but I was completely surprised to learn what Rabbi Brown had in store for me as I approached my thirteenth birthday and the prize of being bar mitzvahed. I was about to commence my studies for the upcoming ceremony. I had already practiced my ability to read Hebrew and committed prayers to memory, but the studying process itself would take several months of intensive training with my rabbi. Before my studies commenced, however, Rabbi Brown called me into his office after class one evening and explained that there were certain preconditions I had to fulfill before he could prepare me for my official entry into manhood. A quiet foreboding, cool as fog, began to roll up the back of my neck.

"You see, Zev," he began, his accent thickening with each word, "there's a ceremony that must be performed before you can be bar mitzvahed."

"What kind of ceremony?" I asked suspiciously.

"Your mother is not Jewish."

"So?"

"Either your mother must convert to Judaism—"

He paused, knowing the impossibility of such a prospect. My mother had never once displayed any interest in becoming a member of any church, religious organization, or community. She professed a simple faith in God and a profound disaffection for any attempt to pressure her into social conformity. While she never voiced any opposition to my attending Hebrew school, she refused to give any consideration to entering a synagogue with my father. She was Irish, a proud, if not practicing, Christian who had no intention of engaging in a theological conversion.

"Or what?" I pushed to have my reluctant mentor spell out my options, layering a certain pugnacity to my voice as a sign that I knew that the goalposts were about to be moved for me once again.

"Then you must undergo a conversion ceremony."

"Which consists of what?" It was not really a question, but rather a demand that he spell out exactly what further concessions I'd have to make. His answer exceeded the bounds of my worst suspicions.

I would have to be submerged in a pool of holy water. Whether it ran from the tap of Rabbi Brown's home or was to be imported from the Sea of Galilee remained unclear, but holy it would be. My submersion would be witnessed and presided over by a small group of Jewish community elders. Now the thought of undergoing a baptismal dunking of sorts was not particularly intimidating. After all, I had spent the last five years leaping naked into the chlorine-laced waters at the YMCA under the watchful eyes of its adult employees. There, of course, I was among peers and I was not seeking acceptance or approval, only perfecting the art of survival.

Had the ceremony consisted only of this one symbolic act, I would have accepted it. But there was more. It seemed that from me more would always be demanded, in endlessly creative ways, to compensate for having a gentile's blood in my veins. A drop of that blood, Rabbi Brown informed me, would have to be extracted from my penis.

I was dumbstruck, first with horror, then with undiluted anger. Why hadn't this been explained to me in the very beginning? Why did I have to endure six years of instruction, of perfecting my ability to read Hebrew, of receiving mezuzahs and medallions, of being chided for living in a nonkosher home, of . . . ?

I managed to trap a stream of expletives behind tightly clenched jaws. I turned away from Rabbi Brown and walked, slowly at first, then burst through the door and ran down the stairs and out into the street. I ran without stopping for nearly two miles until I reached home.

Out of breath and choking back tears, I shouted, "I'm not going to do it. I'm not going to do it."

When my father came home that evening, I explained to him what had happened at school and repeated that I wouldn't agree to participate in any conversion ceremony.

"You don't have to, Billy," he said with a profound sadness. He had been looking forward to witnessing his eldest son's proficiency with the words and ways of his Jewish forebears, but at that moment, after seeing the anger in my mother's eyes, he knew that the dream had vanished. To this day, whatever measure of independence I display, I owe almost exclusively to her rock-solid pride and resolve.

My father's disappointment quickly evolved into resentment over the retroactive application of rules that had never been made clear to him. "They wouldn't act this way down in Boston," he fumed. "I could take you down to Dorchester and get you a bar mitzvah with no questions asked!"

For the very first time, I sensed that he finally understood the acts of discrimination I had been experiencing all along. He was so upset over the treatment I had received that he never returned to the synagogue again.

For my part, I slept fitfully that night. I couldn't get out of my mind a sign I had once seen at the entry gate of a private golf club. It large letters, it read NO DOGS ALLOWED. Someone had added the words OR JEWS in bright red paint. The club owners never removed the paint.

I was bedeviled by dreams of gates being slammed in my face. No dogs or Jews allowed. No goyim either. No entry into the land of manhood for me. But I wondered exactly what powers and responsibilities would this ancient custom bestow upon me that were not mine for the taking in any event? Regret was jousting with rationalization.

Deep inside, under all the anxiety and ambition, lay an unvarnished truth. I had attended the bar mitzvahs of several of my classmates. I wasn't as impressed with their rhetorical skill as I was by the large attendance of their relatives. They had come in scores, from distances as far away as Boston, New York, and Chicago. They brought with them lavish gifts, presents to the newly crowned princes. They toasted, they drank, they danced at the postceremonial receptions for these newly minted men who were worthy of special recognition and treatment by the world.

Amid all of the merriment of these celebrations, I inevitably felt a wave of melancholy sweep over me. I knew that few of my father's relatives would trek to Bangor to pay tribute to my achievement. There would be no songs, gifts, or dancing. Still, I wanted to cross that religious threshold, to demonstrate my facility with the Hebrew language, to show that a non-Jew could compete with their sons even when the playing field was uneven. Just as I had wanted the award of Camp Lown, knowing that I could not attend, I wanted the honor of a bar mitzvah, knowing that it would not alter my life's course by a single degree.

The next day, I was still brimming with anger as I scuffed along the railroad tracks that ran parallel to my father's bakery on Hancock Street. I moved closer to the banks of the Penobscot River, kicking up mounds of dirt, unafraid of the rats, big as full-grown cats, that would slide behind piles of rocks and abandoned railroad ties.

Finally, I snapped off a tubular-shaped miniature mezuzah that I wore around my neck—one of the prizes I had received for academic excellence—and hurled it as far as I could into the polluted river.

"No more," I swore. "No more."

I would never again have to worry about measuring up to the standards of those who felt I was unworthy of them. I had been released from an obligation I never really wanted. I no longer had to pursue a prize that had never been mine for the taking. I no longer had to pretend. The Jewish community would not change its rules to accommodate me, and I would not yield to gain its acceptance. Call it a Celtic standoff. It was a valuable lesson.

In retrospect, it was also a puerile act. I had no real sense of the Jewish history of struggle and persecution. Yes, I could recite almost verbatim the Old Testament stories of the pharaohs and plagues, of Moses staring from a distant hill into the land of milk and honey. But I knew nothing of the pogroms in Poland, the Holocaust in Germany. I was completely unaware of the slights suffered by prominent Bangor Jews over the years at the hands of the Protestant majority— how the gentiles turned to them to use or exploit their brilliance at finance, medicine, and law only to then exclude them from membership in professional and social organizations and clubs. In truth, I knew neither the historic successes nor the sufferings of the Jews.

I would soon learn that it was easier to break a chain from my neck than it would be to break away from the bigotry of others.

During the war years, my parents' hard work (coupled with my father's success at the card tables of the local Elks Club) enabled them to save enough money to move off Hancock Street into a nearby middle-class neighborhood. In 1948 they paid $6,900 for an old house that was exactly one mile from the doorstep of the small apartment where I'd been born; but in terms of the social reality, it was a continent away. We were no longer a part of the swirling masses sharing walls and ceilings with others. We had privacy and stability, quiet neighbors, a front porch, and what would soon become a fenced-in yard. No more street fights or touch football played on a cinder field next to the railroad tracks for me.

Even in the near silence of the night, the difference was obvious. Gone was the harsh clanging of railcars coupling and uncoupling, the screech of the iron wheels on rails, the bellow of the engine's smokestack. No longer were there the haunting sounds of men shuffling overhead or the raucous laughter of late-night revelers.

Now, over the treetops, the train whistle came soft, as if wrapped in cotton, with a musicality that I imagined was the universe blowing on a wind instrument.

Almost from the day we moved into the house, my mother single-handedly undertook a beautification process. I was always astonished to see her at the top of a twenty-foot ladder, slapping a broad paintbrush against the clapboards that had withered under the harsh winters. Frugality might have prompted her to risk her safety by climbing to the peak of the house, but I'm convinced it was her stubborn independence and her conviction that she could do the job faster and better than anyone claiming to be a professional.

She used most of her spare moments landscaping and planting flowers in the backyard. Each day after returning from school, I would find her out attending to her grove like some imperial priestess. It was in her garden that I witnessed her physical stamina and spiritual grace merge in natural fluidity. With her perfectly coiffed hair wrapped in a protective bandanna and her upper lip beaded with perspiration, she would alternately stand in contemplative silence, and then move with the precision of a surgeon, slicing here, transplanting there. Occasionally, I would catch her in a meditative pose and be transfixed by her beauty and strength of character. She could well have been the model for the "Rosie The Riveter" posters that captured the can-do spirit of America during the war years.

My journey into the realm of the middle class (braces, a Schwinn bike, and piano lessons), however, did not pass without traveler's remorse on my part. I felt a strange mixture of relief and regret. I had the vague but powerful sense that I was escaping to a better life; yet, I was touched by an equally indefinable but persistent guilt that my good fortune had somehow come at the expense and the bad luck of others.

Some of my Hancock Street friends continued to circle on the periphery of my new existence. Grim, disapproving, and resentful, with manipulative cunning they reminded me of my promise to remain one of them. It was not long before I decided to break that promise.

It was a common practice by some of the toughs to go down to "Hobo Junction" during lunch breaks at school. There, they would taunt the derelicts who gathered at the edge of the railroad tracks. The hobos would sit around campfires drinking beer, the alcohol strained from canned heat, or any other substance that would help free them from the pain of their miserable existence. They were ragged men who traded jokes, hopped aboard slowing freight trains, and rode to neighboring towns and back again. Frequently, they would roam along Hancock Street and beg for dimes or a slice of bread from our bakery. In their stupor, they posed a threat only to themselves.

On a dare, I foolishly joined one of the forays down to their crude gathering place. As I ran down the slopes toward the Penobscot River, I felt anxiety begin to stir in my chest. What would these men do when they saw us? Did they have knives or razors? Would they smash bottles and come at us to slash our throats? And what exactly did we have in mind for them? To laugh and jeer at their plight? Could we really inflict any greater humiliation on them than they already knew, or rob them of any pride? To what end?

The anxiety of entering foreign territory slipped quickly into regret. We found the men lolling in the weeds and tall grass. They looked at us, first in befuddlement, then in fear. They had seen my friends before. They rose shakily to their feet and started to curse us. Suddenly rocks were flying in both directions. The name-calling became more energized, hysterical. Finally, the men took flight. I refused to join in the laughter and self-congratulatory delirium. It was a pathetic display of brutishness against the hapless, and I felt only shame for having been a participant. I never again felt the need to prove that I still shared a common bond with those whom I had left behind.

I decided that if I ever had to prove my superiority, it would be in athletics. Ever since the days when I sat on my father's lap and watched high school basketball, I vowed that I would one day be out on that court. The YMCA became my refuge. I went there each day after school and played against boys who were three and four years older. There was only one basketball hoop in our neighborhood, located in the yard of Mrs. O'Leary (whose son Charles "Chick" O'Leary would one day become the head of Maine's AFL-CIO), where older boys regularly gathered to play. Long after the scrimmage games ended, I would stay to shoot hoops for hours into the night even during the winter months. The ball would simply plop down into the snow after each shot, and I would dutifully retrieve it and continue to shoot until my ears ached so painfully from the cold that I would go home with tears frozen to my cheeks.

Practice is said to make perfect, but humility was not perfection's companion. During a championship game at the "Y," working with a tremendous teammate, David Schiro, I scored 43 points while my team crushed our opponents as we ran up the score to 112 to 48. The director of the "Y" was furious. While he was lodging a complaint to our coach for lack of sportsmanship, I was still caught up in the afterglow of the moment. On my way to the locker room, I sought out my father, who had watched the game from the seats next to the coach. Having scored the most points ever in a single game, I was expecting to bask in new depths of praise.

"What'd you think, dad?"

"If you hadn't missed those two foul shots, you would've scored 45."

He was no ogre with a whip in hand, lashing me for imperfection. I knew by the little laugh he gave and by the lightness of his arm around my shoulders that he was quite pleased with my performance. In fact, he had only expressed my thought at the time. But it was a thought that I had wished had gone unspoken.

I was deflated for the moment, but the sting to my pride soon passed and I made my father's drive for perfectionism a personal standard. From that moment on, I spent hours practicing free throws. Five years later, I would win a high school foul shooting contest held at the University of Maine, sinking forty-eight out of fifty. While I was still "two shy of perfection," I would go on to play high school and college basketball and be named to the New England All-Star Hall of Fame Team, and receive awards from the National Association of Basketball Coaches and the NCAA.

While I took refuge in athletics from the slights I had experienced at the hands of the Jewish community, I discovered that my name would continue to provoke overt displays of anti-Semitism throughout much of my life. I achieved the distinction of pitching the first no-hitter in Maine's Little League baseball history. I had a strong arm and all of the accuracy of an unguided missile. Few of my opponents ever dug in at the batter's box.

During a game in a nearby coastal town, my erratic pitching offended one man in the stands so much that he started to harass me verbally. After I had hit two batters in a row (I protested weakly that they were crowding the plate), a red-faced man in the stands threw a beer can at me from the stands and yelled: "Send the Jew boy home!"

He followed this up with shouts of "Jew bastard," and every other epithet that was associated with being a Jew.

I wanted to scream back at the man. But scream what? Should I yell back that my mother's name was Hartley and that I wasn't Jewish? I was tempted to toss an obscenity in his direction, but both of my parents were in the stands at the time, and the memory of my mother's reaction to foul language had not faded. I continued to pitch, holding back the thoughts that smoldered inside.

Later in the game, I hit a home run that soared over the centerfield fence and smashed through the windshield of one of the cars that had been parked there. As I circled the bases, my heart was pumping with joy, and I kept hoping that the car belonged to the Jew hater in the stands.

This incident came to symbolize the internal conflict that would serve as my constant companion. A non-Jew carrying one of the most celebrated Jewish names.

Once during a high school basketball game against an archrival, I went on a scoring spree in front of more than six thousand fans. The next day, the *Bangor Daily News* ran a headline on the sports page, in print size normally reserved for declarations of war, celebrating my performance.

The problem was that my name in the headline was spelled COYNE. The newspaper was flooded with angry callers who complained that the *News* had slighted the Jewish community by deliberately misspelling my name. I considered it to be an honest mistake, as a player named Dudley Coyne was playing ball for the University of Maine at the time. But I was also confused about the furor. Where were these callers when I needed them? Why was it that they could be proud of my athletic skills and yet reject my membership into their ranks?

At the time, I was unaware how the local papers had marginalized their contributions in the past. The names and faces of Jewish leaders rarely found their way into print. Once, for example, in 1941, the Bangor Jewish Community Center had invited Eleanor Roosevelt to visit the city. While the several leaders of the Jewish community, in the company of many others, were photographed greeting Mrs. Roosevelt, the caption and story line accompanying the picture omitted the word "Jewish" in the name of the sponsoring organization. To the city's Protestant majority, Jews were to be tolerated but not embraced.* To the KKK, which maintained its Maine headquarters in the neighboring city of Brewer, the Jew, along with the Catholic and the Negro, was a scourge who needed to be purged from the area, preferably from existence.

On more than one occasion, my father had suggested that I might fare better in the world if I changed my last name. I took him to be sincere. He was not one to engage in the subtle testing of one's loyalties. He knew that while there was much to be proud of in the name Cohen, there was pain to be found in the name for me, and it was the pain he wanted me to avoid. I resolutely refused to entertain the thought, as much out of defiance as out of loyalty. It was a determination that did not go untested.

While attending Bowdoin College during my sophomore year, I wanted to get a summer job with my roommate, Charlie Wing, at

---

*See Judith S. Goldstein, *Crossing Lines: Histories of Jews and Gentiles in Three Communities* (New York: William Morrow and Company, Inc., 1992).

Sebasco Estates, an exclusive resort located on the Atlantic shore-front little more than a half hour's drive from the campus in Brunswick, Maine.

"Don't bother applying," he forewarned me.

"Why?"

"Because the man running the place doesn't like Jews."

"But I'm not considered Jewish."

"Half is half too much as far as he's concerned."

With a summer at Sebasco foreclosed, I decided to go in a different direction. I applied to serve as a basketball instructor at Camp Kohut, a camp in western Maine that catered to the sons of wealthy Jewish families.

Once there, I struck up a friendship with Peter Chester, the swimming instructor. At the end of the season, I decided to spend a few days at Peter's home in Greenwich Village. On our way to New York City, we stopped off at the home of Peter's aunt in Scarsdale. Within moments of being offered coffee and sandwiches, Peter's aunt said,

"So tell me again, what's your last name?"

"Cohen," I responded, sensing no malice.

"How do you spell it?" she persisted.

I looked at Peter, who had turned away. Speaking very slowly and with exaggerated enunciation to signal my growing irritation at the interrogation, I spelled my name, making certain that she could not mistake the "e" for an "a."

"But you're not Jewish," she insisted.

"Why do you say that?"

"Because you've got the map of Ireland all over your face," she declared triumphantly.

The thought occurred to me that I might point out to her that however Irish I looked, I would not have enjoyed the alleged luck of the Irish had I lived in Hitler's Germany just two decades earlier. I would have been carted off to have lampshades made from my skin despite any protest that "You don't understand, I'm not really Jewish."

I decided, instead, to let the moment pass, contemplating the lyrics in the Song of Bernadette: "For those who understand, there is no need to explain. For those who do not understand, there is no explanation."

Perhaps it's the reason that I reacted with such calm when my youngest son, Christopher, called me one evening to advise me that upon his marriage, he was going to change his name.

"What's it going to be?" I asked, surprised at my matter-of-fact tone.

"It's going to be Irish, Dad."

I launched no protest or attempt to dissuade him. He was not asking permission, but declaring his independence. His bride-to-be, Kerry Cox, was Irish. He saw no need to carry a prominent Jewish name when he, his wife, and their future children could never be accepted as Jews.

The reaction of my Jewish friends was anything but calm, however. They thought it disrespectful to me. How could he possibly give up the name of his father?

"But you know he's not Jewish. Come now."

"It doesn't matter," they retorted. "It's an insult."

I concluded that they were concerned less about my feelings than about their own. How, they seemed to be saying, could anyone deliberately reject a name that carried such a rich heritage?

But to me, it remained of little importance. After all, Chris had simply done what, years earlier, my father had suggested would be a wise course for me.

My friends' reaction to Chris' decision became linked in my mind with the vigorous response by members of the Bangor's Jewish community when my name was misspelled in the reportage of a basketball game.

Some thirty-five years later, I would gain a deeper understanding of the schizophrenic pride that Jewish people took in my accomplishments.

As I walked with Janet through a mall in Arlington, Virginia, a small rotund man lifted his head like a radar scanner that had just locked onto an identifiable object. I was anxious to leave the mall and tried my best to ignore him and pretend that I hadn't seen his efforts to gain my attention. He ran after me, calling out, "I know you. I know you."

I continued to walk away from him, not being in the mood to acknowledge a stranger at that moment.

"You're . . . you're . . ."

"Jerry West," I lied as he caught up with me. West is one of the greatest basketball players of all time for whom I am frequently mistaken.

"No. You're . . . Cohen. Senator Cohen. I see you on television all the time."

Identity exposed, I finally conceded that I had indulged in a bit of frivolity. The old man, an Austrian Jew, turned serious, however. Both of his parents had died at Treblinka. He was spared the Nazi death camps and crematoriums.

"I know that you're not Jewish," he said solemnly, "but you have no idea what it means to me when I hear the name Cohen, Senator Cohen." His eyes began to well up with tears. I think it was at that moment that I understood that even while I could never be accepted as a member of their brotherhood, Jews the world over could in the very center of their souls feel a quiver of pride that someone who bore one of their most celebrated surnames could reach the highest circles of influence in the world's most powerful nation.

I felt the flush of embarrassment creep up my neck.

"You know," he said, an impish grin breaking into a full smile. "You shouldn't try to fool an old man like me."

He had forgiven my mischief.

I refused to show it at the time, but I was nearly moved to tears when I looked into the eyes of this humble stranger and saw so much pain and so much pride.

Later that night when we returned to our apartment, I opened up my jewelry box where I kept a silver ring that my friends, Joel and Linda Abromson, had given me on my first trip to Israel in 1979. The name, ZEV, had been engraved in large, Hebrew letters on the face of the ring. I slipped it on that night and have worn it ever since.

Rabbi Saul Brown did not consider me to be Jewish enough to be bar mitzvahed. In response I threw away the mezuzah I wore as a necklace.

That day, a survivor of the Holocaust looked at me with unqualified admiration and said it was enough that I willingly bore a quintessentially Jewish name and carried it with me to the United States Senate.

I was Jewish enough for him.

And for me.

Three

Up South

Janet, like me and so many others of our generation, was born at her mother's home and not in a hospital. Home for Janet was Indianapolis, Indiana.

Janet's parents and grandparents were from Tennessee and Kentucky respectively. They thought that greater freedoms and better jobs could be found to the north, only to find upon their arrival that many of the same prejudices and racists policies they thought they had left behind were practiced in Indiana but less overtly.

Indianapolis had served as the regional headquarters of the Ku Klux Klan, perhaps the most vicious home-grown terrorist organization ever allowed to take root and flourish in America. Klan members were—and remain to this day—a group of sociopaths who hate Jews, Catholics, and, most especially, blacks.

Most people associate the Klan's activities with "Down South", but Janet said Indiana was just "Up South."

In Indianapolis, the racism was not the obvious brand that you would see in the South. It was as deep, but a bit more subtle. There were no "White Only" or "Sundowner" signs (meaning: "Niggers don't be caught here after sundown"). Fear was a constant companion in the lives of black people. "Don't" was the most frequent four-letter word they heard in virtually every venue. There were streets they could not walk; restaurants where they could not eat; rest rooms they could not use; clothes they could not try on in stores; jobs and dreams they could not have. Long after they were supposedly emancipated, released from their chains, they still were bound to rules that were a manifestation of institutionalized and officially sanctioned racism.

"Look, dear, you're a little colored girl, and there are people in this world who won't like you simply because you are colored." The words were those spoken by Janet's mother, Louise Gillenwaters.*

Gillenwaters was the anglicized version of the Shawnee Indian name given in school to Janet's great-grandfather James. His real name was Toad Fish-in-Water, although family members called him "Grandpa Toad," "Grandpa," even "that Injun," while others in the neighborhood and neighborhood called him "Uncle Toad." He used to sit Janet on his lap and tell her stories of less glorious chapters in America's history. His mother was an African slave and his father was a Shawnee Indian. They had come up from the South on the Underground Railroad in the area of Ohio, Kentucky, and Indiana. He took after his father, it seems, since he was very light-skinned and had Indian features. That characteristic has been passed through all the Gillenwaters offspring.

Grandpa Toad not only looked Native American, but acted it as well. Every morning he would go outside, crouch on the ground while facing the rising sun, and chant *Huh-yuhyuh-yuh.* Janet's affection for Grandpa Toad may explain in part why she always rooted for the Indians when watching the movies at the local Lido theater where her mother worked selling tickets.

Janet's mother was an orphan raised by her mother's brother, George, and his wife, Leola, after her own emotionally fragile mother was committed to a mental institution.

When Janet's mother was only sixteen and technically, still, a ward of the state, she gave birth to Myrna, Janet's older sister. She was unable to care for her baby, and the state prepared to place her

---

*See Janet Langhart Cohen, *From Rage to Reason: My Life in Two Americas* (New York: Kensington Publishing Corp., 2004). All citations in this book refer to the 2005 trade paperback edition.

for adoption. Uncle George would have none of it and intervened. He agreed to raise Myrna as if she were his own child.

"My mother," Janet said, "met my father at St. Parrens Baptist Church in the spring of 1941. He had been drafted into the army, and during a romantic courtship that involved dining out at restaurants and dancing nights away at the USO canteen at Camp Atterbury, Mother became pregnant. Before they were married, he was redeployed for training out of the state. Although he tried to stay in touch with Mother, his attempts to communicate with her were unsuccessful.

"Mother did not want to have me out of wedlock. She hoped that if she got married and established a household, she might one day be able to have Myrna returned to her.

"Fortunately, Russell Floyd was in love with Mother and proposed to her. She advised him that she was pregnant, but he was unrelenting in his desire to marry her. He insisted on only one condition—that she never tell anyone that I was not his child. He wanted me to be raised as his very own, which is how I became Janet Floyd. The marriage didn't last, however, and by the time I was three, Mother and I were on our own."*

To provide for her family, Janet's mother worked as a "domestic." She cleaned the houses, did laundry, and cooked meals in the homes of her white employers. She took pride in her work, and never allowed anyone to treat her with disrespect. Anyone who tried to disrespect her—particularly in front of Janet—had to confront a woman of fierce pride.

Once, a white woman for whom Janet's mother worked, tried to slap her because she was dissatisfied with the manner Janet's mother had ironed the laundry. The woman thought she could do so with impunity. After all, "Negroes" were supposed to be totally submissive.

Janet's mother stunned her employer when she blocked her arm as the blow was coming and issued a stern warning: "Don't you ever try to strike me again—especially in front of my child!"

---

* See *From Rage To Reason*, p. 14.

She then promptly gathered up Janet and stormed out the door.

No matter how economically strapped she was, she never allowed poverty to rob her of her pride and dignity.

During her early years, there were times when she and Janet lived in the homes of her mother's employers. It was called "living on place." Much of her earlier years, however, were spent moving among various boardinghouses that were described as "shotgun houses" owned by poor black families. These had rooms all in a single row; you could shoot a bullet in the front door and it would exit out the back door. On other occasions she would live with relatives who were able to take in her and her mother. One such home belonged to her Uncle Robert and Aunt Laureen. A key to the house was never necessary to gain entry, as one or more of the twenty-six people who lived there were sure to be home.

"Mother and I used to spend nights listening to the radio. Among our favorites were: *The Fat Man, Inner Sanctum, Beulah, Amos 'n' Andy,* and *Life with Riley. The Shadow* always offered a good mystery and a chance for us to have a bit of fun in school. When one of my elementary school teachers would ask us a question, 'Who knows?' one of my classmates would say, 'Only the Shadow do!'

"This would prompt the teacher to silence the outburst of collective laughter by rapping her ruler on the desk. 'Now you know that is improper English. You must use the singular: Only the Shadow does.'

"We all would just keep laughing."

Janet's mother worked very hard to instill in her the value of getting a good education and the virtue of being kind in a world that was going to be unkind to her. She was a devoted Christian, and her teachings reflected her religious convictions. She knew that if Janet responded to hate with hate, it would poison her soul, turn her bitter, and pull her into a backwash of hopelessness.

On the day that Janet's mother cautioned her about having to live in an unfriendly world, Janet had just completed her first piano lesson.

"Mother wanted me to become educated and successful. Her dream was for me to one day to play piano at Carnegie Hall. She wanted to celebrate the occasion by shopping for small personal and household items along Monument Circle, located in the center of Indianapolis. We had stopped at a local restaurant to get something to eat. There we sat in a small booth and waited endlessly for a waitress to come and take our order."

No one came.

Finally, in a moment of total frustration and disgust, Janet's mother got up abruptly, accidentally knocking over a silver napkin dispenser. Everyone in the restaurant fell silent momentarily. Her mother quickly replaced the dispenser and grabbed Janet by the hand.

"Come on, Janet," she said, tugging her along.

"I was confused." Janet told me. "I thought that I had done something wrong and that Mother was angry with me."

"'No, child, it's not you,' Mother said. 'They were never going to wait on us.'"

People who had come in long after they had were seated and served quickly while they were totally ignored. They had been treated as "nonpeople" or simply "invisibles."

Janet was only seven years old at the time of this incident and she wasn't quite sure what her mother meant when she forewarned her of the hardship that awaited her because she was "colored." Janet was only vaguely aware of what being "colored" meant. She had lived in the homes of white people without incident for the most part. When she lived in boardinghouse rooms or with relatives, most of the people in her young life looked like her. Some were different shades of dark to be sure, but she associated nothing negative with skin color at the time. There were some people who had shops in the neighborhood who looked different. And there were insurance salesmen who knocked on their doors, along with policemen who seemed to appear only when someone was fighting. They were white, but again, she did not understand that they disliked her or meant to do her any harm.

While Janet's mother was trying to prepare her daughter for a world of racial prejudice, she also was determined to instill in her the need to practice tolerance.

"Janet, it's wrong to dislike people simply because of their color," her mother said. "What you look like isn't important. It's how you behave and treat people that matters. You must be aware of the hateful people, but you must not hate or judge people on color or any differences. In God's eyes, we're all equal. You've got to promise me that you'll never do that. Never dislike people because of their color or for something they can't help."*

Colored and *White* took on a new meaning for Janet at that moment. Even though she promised to obey her mother, for the first time Janet felt the faint flickering of anger at the notion of being judged by people who didn't even know her.

That anger would burn even stronger when she heard her father talk about how he had fought for his country in Europe and yet feared for his life at home.

Janet was born on December 22, 1941, fifteen days after the Japanese had bombed Pearl Harbor. From the beginning, life seemed to have its complications for her. Her mother tried to give her the name "Jeanette," because she admired actress Jeanette MacDonald. The Navy doctor who delivered her instead wrote "Janet" on her birth certificate, and to compound matters, mistakenly checked the box designating her race as "white."

The first time Janet saw her father was in the early fall of 1948, shortly after President Harry Truman ordered the desegregation of the military.

Sewell Bridges had just recently received his honorable discharge. He was coming for a visit on the way to see his family in Kentucky. He had become something of a mythological figure for Janet. She had seen so many handsome men on posters and in movie newsreels in their Army and Navy uniforms that the very thought

---

*From *Rage to Reason*, pp. 8–10.

that her father might have been among them filled her with pride. The sight of older people on buses giving up their seats for those in uniform was, to her, evidence of the pride and gratitude that America felt about those who had gone off to war.

Although Janet had been told that she looked just like her father, she had difficulty visualizing his face. She only knew that he was handsome and wore a mustache, or at least he did the last time her mother had seen him before he went off to war. Janet had fantasized about him incessantly, trying to imagine how tall he was, how he walked and talked. She kept looking at photographs of other soldiers, hoping to see anyone who might have resembled her.

When she learned that he was coming home from Europe and was planning to visit Indianapolis, she could barely contain her joy.

She got up at sunrise on the day he was to arrive and sat at a window in the boardinghouse where she and her mother had been renting a room. Then she left her post at the window and stood on the porch of the house, watching every person and every car that passed by that morning. Finally, she saw him. She was sure that he had to be the man approaching in the distance. He was tall and walked with an erect military bearing. He had a large duffle bag slung over his shoulder.

When he finally turned in front of the house and walked toward the front porch, Janet bolted from the porch and ran out to the street.

It was a Cecil B. DeMille moment. She ran as fast as she could and when she finally reached him, he dropped his duffel bag and scooped her up in his arms.

"You must be my little Janet," he said. "Give your Daddy a big kiss."

He hugged her tight, and she still recalls the feel of his uniform's rough texture against her cheek, and the scent of spearmint on his breath.

He carried Janet onto the porch, gave her another kiss, and then greeted her mother. They went into the house and sat in the living room, where other members of her family, along with several other boarders, had gathered to listen to her father discuss his experience in the Army and the war in Europe. It was a special occasion to have a military man in their midst.

Janet said, "I didn't understand everything he spoke about that day, but I learned years later, while meeting my father's family members at a reunion, that he had served in the 761st Black Panther Tank Battalion, the first black armored force to go into combat in World War II, when Army units were segregated. Nearly all of the officers in the 761st were white. One of the few black officers in the battalion was Lieutenant Jackie Robinson. But he was transferred to another black unit after his refusal to sit in the back of a bus led to a court-martial."

Robinson was eventually acquitted. He would become major league baseball's first black player.

When the Black Panthers arrived in Europe, Lieutenant General George S. Patton, Jr., called the troops together. Patton's speech became famous among Black Panther veterans: "Men, you're the first Negro tankers to ever fight in the American Army. I would never have asked for you if you weren't good. I have nothing but the best in my Army. I don't care what color you are as long as you go up there and kill those Kraut sons of bitches. Everyone has their eyes on you and is expecting great things from you. Most of all, your race is looking forward to you. Don't let them down and damn you, don't let me down!"*

The Panthers made Patton proud, knocking out German tanks, killing and wounding thousands of German soldiers, and living up to their motto, "Come Out Fighting."

What Janet does recall with absolute clarity was her father's fear about returning to Kentucky to visit his mother. He had no fear about fighting the Nazis, but black veterans were being beaten and murdered in the South for wearing their uniforms in public.

"It burns me up," Janet remembers him saying, "but I don't know if I want to attract attention to myself on that long bus ride.

---

*Joe Wilson, *The 761st "Black Panther" Tank Battalion in World War II* (Jefferson, NC: McFarland & Company, 1999), p. 53. See also Kareem Abdul-Jabbar and Walter Anthony, *Brothers in Arms: The Epic Story of the 761st Tank Batallion, WWII's Forgotten Heroes* (New York: Broadway, 2004).

I think I just might pack this uniform away and ride quietly in the back. I figure that way, I just might get there in one piece. White folks is a bitch."

Aunt Leola signaled her agreement with Janet's father. Janet silently agreed with her father and Aunt Leola. Her father was good enough to fight in die in a war but couldn't wear his uniform in Kentucky? Something was terribly wrong. While she couldn't articulate her emotions at the time, she felt a surge of anger inside her. Over the years, that rage would flare up at every hypocrisy and injustice she saw or encountered. While that emotion served to propel her to heights that were once unimaginable, it also caused her to burn many of the bridges she had hoped to cross during her professional career.

Janet's mother scowled at Aunt Leola and Janet's father. It was a withering look that warned Aunt Leola not to go into one of her patented rages against white people. She strongly disapproved of any expression of racism or bigotry whether it came from white or black people. "None of that talk in this house," Janet's mother said. "White people need some humanity, but we can't start acting or thinking like *them*."

Janet's mother had always practiced what she preached. There was an older lady in their neighborhood who owned a small dry goods store. All of the kids called the woman JewBessie. Janet honestly believed that was her name and thought it consisted of one word and not two. One day, she was on her way out the door, when her mother asked, "Just where are you going, young lady?"

"Down to JewBessie's," she said innocently.

"Her name is not JewBessie, and I don't ever want to hear that out of you again. Bessie is her name and she's a nice woman. She happens to be Jewish, but I won't have you be disrespectful. From now on, you call her Miss Bessie. Do you hear me?"

Janet had not intended any harm or slight, since she didn't know what Jewish meant, but her mother was determined to instill in her the need to treat others with decency and respect.

Janet's Aunt Leola, while a good lady, was less forgiving. Janet recalled the time when Aunt Leola came home one day holding a white baby that she was caring for. "She laid the baby on the couch to nap. I saw the baby and was mesmerized by her sparkling, blue eyes. I stepped closer to get a better view. The baby started to whimper and reach out to me, signaling that she wanted me to pick her up. I lifted the baby up and cradled her in my arms. Just then, Aunt Leola stormed into the room.

"Put *that thing* down," she shouted. "Don't start to feel anything for that thing because as soon as she grows up from looking like your little baby doll, she's going to call you a nigger. They call us names and say that we're lazy, but they hire us to do all the work that they're too lazy to do. They claim to be superior, but they know that they're not. There's just more of them and they're more ruthless. What else would you call a race of people who would go all the way to Africa, snatch people from their homes and families, bring them here, rape them, lynch them, and treat them like animals? No, don't you ever get close to them or let them get close to you."

"I was really stunned by Aunt Leola's vehemence at the time," Janet said. "But I was even more impressed by my mother's teachings of the need for tolerance and forgiveness. You know, Honey, if I had listened to my aunt instead of my mother, I would have missed you and the love we now share. I just wish that my aunt could have lived to witness your love and devotion—and your blue eyes!"

Janet's father left for Kentucky the next day and never returned to Indianapolis. Sixteen years would pass before Janet would see him again.* While there was no father in their home, there was a man, and an extraordinarily good one, in her family: Uncle George, her grandmother's brother.

"He always made my birthday special by making that the day we'd go out to find our Christmas tree. It became a family tradition. Uncle George taught me to save, giving me a dollar every time he came to visit, and a silver dollar on my birthday."

---

*See *From Rage To Reason: My Life in Two Americas*, pp. 10–13.

"'If you spend it,' he would say, 'I want an accounting of how you spent it. And if you save it, I'll double it on your next birthday.'"

He always kept his promise, but Janet didn't always save all the money. Nevertheless, she did learn the fundamental value of saving for things that were important—especially for education. Savings accounts and wise spending were to be her salvation, a way out from being poor and powerless.

Janet said that while her Uncle George taught her the importance of saving, her mother insisted that she should always be charitable and generous to the less fortunate.

"Once when we passed a man who had no legs, sitting on the sidewalk holding a cigar box that contained pencils he was selling, Mother reached into one of the gloves where she kept a few coins for bus fare and pulled out a nickel. She dropped the nickel into the cigar box. Then she reached into her glove again and pulled out a penny and pressed it into my hand and nodded for me to do what she had just done. I never forgot her lesson about the importance of giving. Whenever I'm able to help someone else out, it also enriches me."

Uncle George was definitely from the old school of survivors. At the time, it was customary for blacks to address whites, even those who were peers, as "Mr." or "Miss." Janet remembers hearing of an incident involving her sister, Myrna, who was living with Uncle George and Aunt Leola in their home. One day, when Myrna answered the phone, it was the son of the people that Uncle George worked for. He was the same age as Myrna, and they had even played together as children.

Myrna called out to Uncle George, "Daddy, Stephen's on the phone!"

Uncle George came to the phone quickly, snatched the receiver from Myrna, and while clamping his hand over the receiver whispered to her that now that Stephen had turned twenty-one, she must address him as "Mr. Stephen."

Myrna was having none of it. Indignantly, and in a voice loud enough to overcome Uncle George's attempt to muffle the receiver, she declared, "Stephen and I are the same age. I'm twenty-one, too. I'll call him Mr. Stephen when he calls me Miss Myrna."

Both Myrna and Janet thought that Uncle George was far too subservient to white people. Then again, they could afford to be brazen and critical. They didn't have the responsibility to provide for an extended family, to pay the rent, food, and clothing bills in a racist environment.

One time, when Janet was nine years old, she and Uncle George boarded a bus together. "As he deposited the coins into the toll box, I dashed to take one of the two open seats left on the bus. Uncle George continued to stand even when I motioned for him to sit down. I was concerned that the seat would be taken by someone else during the next stop.

"He kept shaking his head 'No.'

"When we stepped off the bus, I asked him why he refused to take the seat.

"'A white woman was in the next seat. I'm not sitting next to any white woman. I don't trust white people. You never know when they're going to turn on you and accuse you of doing something wrong.'"

Janet didn't comprehend fully what he meant, but in time she would learn how white women would blame blacks for what other white people did—or even what they might have done themselves.

Our history books are littered with hundreds of cases of black men being falsely accused of crimes because they were such convenient targets for prevailing racist sentiments. Often they were lynched by rabid mobs. If they escaped the rope or other physical atrocities, they could expect to spend years in prison with little hope of ever being released. Uncle George knew from personal experience what white people were capable of. His nephew, Jimmy (Janet's cousin), was lynched when he was only seventeen years old.

A more recent case in point is that of Charles Stuart, a furrier in Boston, who murdered his pregnant wife and blamed a nonexistent black man for the crime. The police conducted a furious and unlawful search throughout the black community in an attempt to locate and arrest the phantom murderer. Stuart actually identified an innocent black man as the culprit. Before the case went to trial Stuart's brother revealed that it was Stuart himself who had committed the crime so that he could collect on an insurance policy he had taken out on his wife's life.

Few can ever forget Susan Smith, the mother who drowned all of her children and claimed that it was a black man who had committed the horrible crime. Or Jennifer Wilbanks, the so-called "Runaway Bride," who abandoned her would-be groom several days before the wedding, and claimed to have been kidnapped by a "Hispanic man."

"No," Janet said in remembering Uncle George, "he knew exactly what he was doing when he refused to sit next to a white woman."

Even though in coloring Uncle George was what was called "questionable black," he lived in something of a racial no-man's-land. His skin was lighter than that of most blacks and his hair was straight. He had Caucasian features, derived no doubt from Indian and Scots-Irish bloodlines that were mixed with his African blood. Many people thought that he was either Italian or Spanish.

He worked as a chauffeur, butler, and all-around handyman for a white family. Many times he would bring home their leftovers—filet mignon, nuts, fancy fowl, all kinds of sweets. One day, while cutting the lawn in front of the white family's home, a truckload of white teenagers drove by and yelled out, "Hey, Mister. You're the only one in the neighborhood who doesn't have a nigger to cut his grass." Uncle George kept rolling that old lawn mower, which was always breaking down.

There were countless other times when he and other members of Janet's family might have "passed" for being something other than black. To their credit, none ever attempted to do so.

Even though Janet's lighter-skinned relatives generally received more favorable treatment from whites, they harbored resentments that were as strong as those of the darkest members of their race. "On one occasion," Janet said, "my Aunt Leola did something reminiscent of Alex Haley's character Kizzy in *Roots*. When she overheard her employers saying cruel, hateful things about black people, she would spit (sometimes worse) in their food. I learned right at that moment to never start an argument or offend the person who was preparing your food."

Despite how he was treated, Uncle George always found a way to transform tragedy into goodness. When his fourteen-year-old nephew killed his father (Uncle George's oldest brother), Uncle George fought to keep the boy from going to the penitentiary and experiencing the horrible life of a prisoner. He vouched for him to the court and became more than his brother's keeper: He offered forgiveness and was the keeper of his murdered brother's son.

George Washington Gillenwaters was named for the president who could not tell a lie. He knew the story of George Washington and the cutting down of the cherry tree. He had even planted a cherry tree in his own backyard. It was at the foot of the tree where he died of a heart attack, on July 2, 1974, cutting his own grass on a hot Indiana summer's day. He was the kindest, most generous, most God-loving man Janet has ever known. He didn't go to church. The church lived in him. He didn't preach kindness and gentleness; he lived it, a life of the golden rule.

And, by following his example, so did his family.

Four

HANCOCK STREET

"Someday, Billy, someday, you'll understand." The heavily East European–accented words were spoken by my grandfather as he handed me an Indian Head nickel. It was a weekly ritual whose meaning completely escaped me at the time, as I would invariably rush off to purchase a package of gum or candy. No doubt, he wanted to impress upon me how hard he had to work to acquire money to support his family, and that I would need to save it for possible hard times in the future. Sound advice that nearly sixty-five years later I have yet to fully heed.

My grandfather was old when I knew him. Gray and bald, he was remarkable only in that his nose and ears seemed disproportionately large. He usually wore a short-sleeved shirt and khaki pants held up by a pair of suspenders. He was slight in stature and frequently stooped due to a double hernia that he refused to have surgically repaired until shortly before his death. He had, indeed, known hardship. He had emigrated, I was told, without a kopek or penny in his pocket from Russia in the early 1900s. His homeland, however, remains something of a mystery to me. I heard my father speculate once that "grandpa" may have been born in Bialystok, Poland, where deadly pogroms were underway. Wherever he was born, he was drawn, like so many others from Russia and Eastern Europe, by the promise of freedom and opportunity in America.

When I was older, I often wondered whether he had crossed Europe on foot or by rail. Or was it a steamer that he had boarded along with hundreds of others and sailed off in to a foreign land? What did he think when he saw the Statue of Liberty holding up the flame of freedom to the tired, the poor, the huddled masses? What were his thoughts as he passed through Ellis Island and took or was given a new name, a new beginning? Was it a method to protect himself or family members left behind from any retribution (Czar Alexander III was not known for his compassion toward Jews) or simply that he wanted a new identity, as he began a new life in a new country? He became Harry Cohen. I never knew his real name. My father once said that he thought that it might have been "Heinz," but I thought it improbable that he would have a name of German origin. I had so many questions that went unanswered. My father had not received the answers either, as he could never offer any clarifications. My family's code of conduct was quite Spartan. Work long. Study hard. Say little. These might have been words to weave on a coat of arms, if we had had one.

America may have been the land of opportunity, but my grandfather did not meet with early success. Jobs were not plentiful for those with limited education and virtually no facility with the English language. He moved to Boston, but found no employment. Finally, he decided to locate in Bangor, Maine, which had become a magnet for so many immigrants.

Bangor, known as the "Queen City" in the mid-nineteenth century, was the largest inland lumber port in America. Henry David Thoreau had described the city as being "like a star on the edge of night." Timber barons, merchants, bankers, woodsmen, and river drivers took up residence in pursuit of the dream of making the city an enduring and economic cultural center.

By the end of the century, however, the dream had started to fade. The arrival of the railroads sped the decline of the merchants' shipping activities. Many of the entrepreneurs and industrialists had decided that fortunes would be made elsewhere. But the flow of English Protestant stock out of Bangor, like the tide of the Atlantic itself, brought something back into the city—immigrants. My grandfather, like most of the newly arrived of little means, took up residence on Hancock Street.

The neighborhood might have been plucked out of the Bowery or any urban setting that attracted immigrants. Most of the business establishments were located on the first floor of the tall, flat-topped tenement buildings. A few pitched-roofed houses were interspersed along the street, and had there been a skyline, it might have resembled an uneven, chipped set of dentures. Butcher shops, bars, salvage yards, variety stores, barbers, shoe cobblers, tailors, and Dolly Jack's whorehouse—all were located within the circumference of a few hundred feet.

Those who lived on Hancock Street were as diverse in origin as the commerce itself. They seemed to be little more than the world's pocket change, emptied there like so many unpolished pennies. They came from Ireland, Scotland, Lebanon, Turkey, Poland, Russia, Italy, Greece, and Syria. They bore the names of Caruso, Butera, Pysinski, Khoury, Karam, Byorick, Pelky, Dresnan, Gopin, Desposito, Rolnick, Wagman, McSimmick, Murray, and Cohen. There was at once a tangible, engaging vibrancy to the street, a mixture of optimism for tomorrow's promise for some, and an acceptance by others that their horizons would forever remain flat and low.

I was born, all eleven and three-quarters pounds of me, in my mother's bed in a three-story tenement house above a meat market and a barber shop. I lived there with my father, mother, and older sister, Marlene, and younger brother, Bob, in a room on the third floor. My grandfather Harry and his daughter, Gertrude (Aunt Gittle), lived on the second floor.

The tenement house was owned by Mrs. Wanda Soloby. She rented out a room on the top floor to a group of Polish immigrants that ranged between six and twelve men at any given time. At the age of four I became acutely aware of these men. I would lie in bed at night listening to them walk back and forth in the rooms above. They walked slowly and deliberately and they walked all night long.

Most of the Polish men were rough, strong-limbed men who worked for weeks or months at a time in the woods. And when the weather turned bitter or the demand for timber declined, they would spend their days drinking whiskey, gathering in small knots of fellowship along the street, or simply walking around aimlessly. They were not menacing, but always there was a sense of contained violence about them, like warriors without a war, boxers without a ring. There were others on the street who never bothered to look for work. They were known as "canned heaters," forlorn and lost men who would hover over small containers of canned heat. They would squeeze the purple gelatin through their handkerchiefs and drink the extracted alcohol that was the equivalent of lighter fluid. Occasionally, I would sneak up on them and watch the ceremony, mystified by the beet-red color of their faces.

My grandfather was no lumberjack and possessed no tradecraft. After briefly trying his hand in the purchase and sale of cows, he began a small bakery in 1929, the year of the "Great Crash." The bakery was located on Hancock Street, just a few hundred feet from where we lived.

Somehow, throughout the Depression he managed to provide for his two sons and daughter. My father became the force who made the business marginally profitable. His brother, Richard, had been drafted into the Army. Dad's color-blindness precluded him from serving in the military, and so he became the one who had to make, bake, and deliver the rye bread and bulkie rolls during the war years. Although he stood only five feet eight inches tall and was wiry in build, my father possessed large forearms and fingers that were big as bananas. He was dark complected and combed his thinning black hair straight back. A fingernail clipper had never been made that could cut through his unusually thick nails. In high school, he was a championship wrestler and loved playing basketball and the saxophone. While he was no Coleman Hawkins or Stan Getz, he was good enough to play in a small band that traveled around the state playing at weekend dances—all of which ended when his father said it was time for him to put away his childish ways. His total work experience had been limited to that of a saxophonist and a shoeshine boy before he was put to work as a baker.

While the work was not physically hard (although my father would routinely lift one-hundred-pound bags of flour and dump them into a large mixer), the hours were long. The entire work force consisted of my grandfather, father, Aunt Gittle, my uncle (once he returned from service), and my mother, Clara.

I have many recollections about my father's daily work routine, but what I remember most clearly about the small bakery was the noise—a huge mixer churning, a bread slicer rattling like a Gatling gun, three men and one woman talking (yelling, actually), usually in English, sometimes in Yiddish. There was constant motion inside. Flour bags stacked everywhere. Eight hands at a bench flattening dough the size of baseballs, then folding it over the thumb of the left hand followed by a karate chop by the right. Then another fold with the forefinger, another chop, the process repeated again until the dough looked like a puffy white sand dollar.

I would watch with fascination as my uncle sprayed water from the hose to create steam and then shoved a huge wooden board into the coal-fired brick oven and snapped it back, just like Zorro withdrawing his sword, leaving every roll in just the right position along the hot bricks.

I was confused by what sounded like angry exchanges among my father's family. They constantly fought over whose bread products should be delivered to which customers and in what order. Because the volume of bread and rolls was limited, a change in the order by any customer set off an immediate row. And when a first-time customer walked into the bakery and asked for three or four dozen rolls, the conversation went as follows:

GITTLE: "You want what? Three dozen rolls! I've got a half dozen, a dozen maybe."

CUSTOMER (stunned): "But, you seem to have plenty of rolls. Look at those boxes, bags. They're full."

GITTLE: "Those are on order. Besides, they're regular customers. We have to take care of them first. They buy every day. They buy every day, not just once a year."

CUSTOMER: "What's the matter? My money not good enough?"

GITTLE (looking surreptitiously over her shoulder): "Okay. I can steal an extra dozen from one of them. But that's the best I can do."

She would do this periodically to ingratiate herself with retail customers only to walk to the back of the shop and run into a firestorm.

"You did what?" my uncle would yell. "You stupid *schmegegge*. Those were mine. . . . Ruby, I'm going to take them from your customers."

"Like hell you are," my father would yell back.

Each day, the angry ritual was the same. Sometimes it got out of hand, and they began to throw pieces of dough at each other. Customers who knew them used to smile and take it all in stride. Strangers must have thought they had entered a madhouse. For my part, when the cursing started, my mother would usher me to the front of the store while yelling at them to stop yelling.

From the very beginning, my mother assumed the role of the family's enforcer. While beautiful as a Hollywood movie star, she had a spine (and hand) of solid steel. She was a strict disciplinarian who brooked no challenge to her authority or moral code.

She kept a tight watch on me most of the time, whenever her attention wasn't occupied by the bakery. She was already working the cash register and bagging rolls, but when my Uncle Dick was drafted to serve in the Army during World War II, she was prevailed upon to drive the delivery van even though she did not possess a license.

Babysitters were sought out to corral my mischievous behavior. Grandpa Cohen was my first overseer, but he proved a somewhat dubious choice. With all of Hancock Street's activity, he considered it to be a waste of time to stay indoors for something as unimportant as my nap. My parents would come home from the bakery expecting to find me asleep and learn instead that Grandpa and I were out socializing with neighbors across the street.

Grandpa's successor was Annie Caruso, the daughter of the Italian family who owned the spaghetti house we frequented. Annie was a superior guardian but lacked the authority to govern my behavior, or so I believed as a four-year-old. One day on our walk to the bakery I chose an unfortunate moment to test her. Of course my mother had warned me about looking before I crossed the street, but Annie, doubting my obedience quotient, kept a firm hand over mine on every corner. I tolerated such coddling for several streets, but at the last corner, I decided to proclaim my independence and make a break for freedom. With the bakery in sight, I wriggled from Annie's grasp and bolted across the street, escaping death from an oncoming vehicle by no more than a hair.

I walked the rest of the distance to the bakery with none of my newly claimed independence. I was shaken by the near miss but was even more apprehensive that the incident was going to be relayed to my mother. Common sense told me that I needed to turn my witness into a confidante, but Annie was still fuming over my defiance and not open to any solicitations from me. It was clear from that very moment that I was not destined to become an intelligence operative or poker player. My effort to conceal my guilt by slinking off behind a rack of warm bulkie rolls trumpeted my misdeeds to all. When I heard Annie say, "Well, we almost lost him this time," the bread in my mouth turned to cement.

After dispensing what I considered to be an overly enthusiastic spanking, my mother advised me that her watchful eye was not going to blink—ever!

As in any community, peer pressure dictated that we sons of immigrants form a fraternity of sorts. It was something akin to "The Bowery Boys," rather than a street gang. There was a hierarchical order to it all. The older and bigger boys assumed leadership roles. Younger ones were expected to wait their turn. The only dues that had to be paid were displays of courage. You had to be willing to fight back against anyone regardless of his age or size. The opportunity to do so was abundant. We played our games of touch football either on the sidewalks or on a narrow stretch of rock- and cinder-strewn land located between parallel sets of railroad tracks a stone's throw from the bakery. Usually, what started out as a test of athletic skills quickly descended into a minor brawl.

The fights began over silly matters. A tease that went on too long, turning into a taunt. Then, the taunt would quickly shift into loud words of abuse. A shove was sure to follow. At this stage there was no graceful, face-saving way out. Diplomacy would be seen as cowardice. There was only one option and one rule: be sure to throw the first punch directly into the nose or mouth of your opponent. The first to draw blood usually gained an immediate psychological advantage, particularly if you could put some of the other boy's teeth on the ground. Like all general rules, there were exceptions, but the combination of surprise and courage to attack was usually enough to prevail. Even if you miscalculated and only succeeded in enraging a larger or stronger opponent who pummeled you into the ground, you nonetheless established a reputation for being unafraid—and that was worth a punch or two all of its own. Not exactly the stuff of the Crips and Bloods, but those were the days when the only weapons of choice were fists, not guns or knives.

Once, after being on the receiving end of a cheap shot taken by a street tough who ran off before I could respond, I yelled out an obscenity worthy of a one-eyed pirate. I had no idea of the meaning of the word, and was simply repeating what I had heard from others. I failed to communicate my innocence to my mother, however, who to this day can still hear a tree fall in the Brazilian rain forest.

While I was reflecting on the success of my curse, I suddenly found her standing directly behind me. Somehow she had heard me from the third floor of the tenement house. There in the street she slapped me hard across the face. My seasoned toughness was no match for her fury. I cried and pleaded over and over, "What did I say? What did I say?"

"Don't you ever say that word again" was her only response.

While my vocabulary of obscenities has enlarged over the years, I've scrupulously avoided that insult even if a continent away from my mother's earshot.

My father, by contrast, was quite willing to allow my mother to assess crime and inflict punishment. He enjoyed playing the role of benevolent provider.

My uncle told me in confidence one day that, while my father always preached nonviolence ("Billy, you have to kill people with kindness"), he had practiced something quite different in his youth. He described an incident that took place in 1927. A young man named Jimmy Rist challenged my father to a fight. Even though Rist was taller and bigger, my father went after him with the ferocity of a pit bull. With a few quick punches, he knocked Rist down and bloodied his nose. Rist quickly conceded defeat.

The story took on significance because Jimmy Rist went on to become one of gangster Mickey Cohen's bodyguards. Whether my uncle had initially embellished the story or I had suddenly elevated my father to hero status by virtue of the account, I can't verify. That the fight occurred before Jimmy Rist had added another six inches in height and one hundred pounds in weight, and carried a semiautomatic handgun, did not seem particularly relevant to me at the time. To me, the man and the myth were one.

Whether it was a boxing match, a pool hall, or a basketball game, my father always seemed to be in his element at sporting events. I remember accompanying him to a variety of these events as a child. He usually would place me in his lap and put my legs through the spokes of the steering wheel of the car and allow me to "drive." Things would go smoothly until we had to make a right or left turn and I started to tip over. One of his favorite activities was playing pool. The pool halls attracted a menagerie of odd characters. Some of the men wore wide-brimmed Beau Brummel hats and sharkskin suits. Other wore slacks and open-necked shirts. There were fast-talking hustlers and quiet, mean-looking men who did not consider pool to be a game. I was fascinated by a man named Arthur Dinian whose raw arthritic fingers curled up so radically that it was almost impossible for him to hold a cue stick, and yet, he shot with the dexterity of a professional.

My father had a soft touch at pool. He played position well, always looking two or three strokes ahead of his immediate shot. On one of my birthdays, he took me to a dark lair where cigarette smoke curled around intense, Runyonesque faces. That night he won a porcelain clock shaped in the form of a horse. He stuffed a five-dollar bill in the horse's tail and presented it to me as a gift. Actually, after swaying in all directions for several hours, coaxing his combinations and bank shots to drop, I considered myself to have been his silent partner, the clock being my half of the evening's take. But I was thrilled with my gift and glad to be in my father's company.

My father's favorite pastime was basketball. He never missed a high school game on Friday nights. With the band beating their drums, cheerleaders rushing up and down the floor, the smell of popcorn and hot dogs wafting in the air, and the sound of yelling mixed in with the whistles of the referees, a Friday night game was an exhilarating experience.

Tickets in those days were sold on a first-come, first-serve basis. Since Fridays were always busy days at the bakery, there were times when he wouldn't arrive at the auditorium until a few minutes before the game started and he would find it sold out. He was not deterred. Even if there wasn't a seat left in the house, he had a vast arsenal of tricks at his disposal to gain entry to the event. The terrifying part was when he convinced my mother and me to take part in his schemes.

If my father took my mother to a sold-out game, he bluffed his way in by pointing out some man standing in line who supposedly held the tickets. He just kept walking and never gave the admissions people time to verify his claim. Once he got to his favorite seats along the balcony, he would tell the ushers that his friends with the tickets were lost. If there was any doubt on the part of the ushers, a quick look at my mother's beauty convinced them otherwise. Usually two seats were provided for my mother and father at once.

Whenever he took me to a sold-out game, the deception became a bit more involved. Since I was only four years old, he used my size to his advantage and hid me next to him inside his long tweed coat. If he had one ticket, he would wait until the crowds had jammed the tunnel leading inside and then press us right along with them. If my father didn't have tickets for either one of us, he would wait by an exit door for a crowd to come out, then walk us in backwards as though he had been inside all along and had just momentarily stepped out. It was an early and awkward version of Michael Jackson's "moonwalk."

For me, it was like being in a cocoon. I couldn't see anything through his coat except for our two sets of feet. I was terrified that someone would look down and notice the extra set of legs. The idea that we might get caught scared me, but my father was completely nonchalant. He assumed that he could talk his way past anything or anyone. Scared as I was, I loved him for his daring and for his wanting me to be with him.

Once inside, the tweed coat was opened and the two of us rushed to the gallery upstairs. There my father sat me on his knee and pointed out the coach and players whom everyone was cheering for. I would watch the Bangor Rams and say to myself that someday I would be out there playing for that team.

I would prefer to think that the warmth of my father's arms, the smell of popcorn and hot dogs, the beat of a bass drum, the blare of a trumpet, and the roar of the crowd were the external stimuli that prompted me to pursue the dream of becoming one of the Bangor Rams. But there was more.

According to the poet Robert Bly, every boy suffers a blow from one of his parents that damages his "princehood" or "infantile grandiosity."* The blow may be a physical one, or consist of a sharp criticism, the absence of love, or simply the absence of the parent. But it is a wound that throbs for years. Mine came at the age of four.

---

*See Robert Bly, *Iron John: A Book about Men* (New York: Addison-Wesley, 1990).

In addition to being a great fan of basketball, my father played in games frequently at the YMCA. The games were in the evening and were mostly between a few Jewish friends. I either sat and watched the games, or sought out the former high school wrestling coach who served as a trainer at the Y. The big, bald-headed man would reach around and stretch my back for me and make me feel as though I too were part of the athletics going on.

Something about watching my father play basketball made me long to be a part of it. He had a two-handed set shot that worked well for him but looked too difficult for me to attempt at that point. Instead, I chose to demonstrate my prowess another way. I had only picked up a basketball once or twice in my life but came to the conclusion that ball handling was my strongest suit. At the end of one of my father's games, while everyone was toweling off, I took a basketball and dribbled it all the way from one end of the court to the other. I knew everyone was watching me and the fact that I had an audience spurred me on even more. I ran as fast as I could and didn't miss a dribble until I got to the very end of the court, where I bounced the ball off my foot and out of bounds. I turned around expecting congratulations on having made it down the court so successfully.

I had never put two dribbles together, let alone a fast break like that. Instead, I found that my father and the other men were laughing at me for bouncing the ball off my foot. It almost put me in tears. I was so stunned by the laughter that I angrily decided no one was going to make fun of me again. I started practicing on my own from that time on, promising myself the day would come when I would be able to play this game so well that instead of laughter I would hear cheers of approval.

The need for approval at times became a test of endurance. Once, while I was with my father on a delivery run, I made the mistake of investigating the cigarette lighter in our 1940 Packard. I was waiting in the car while my father delivered an order of rolls to an invalid woman who lived on Essex Street. I had been warned never to touch the cigarette lighter and, given my track record with such warnings, had even been made to promise not to do so. Well, there

I was all alone in the car. I didn't start with the idea of handling the lighter. All I did was push the lighter knob into its dashboard receptacle.

Most children have difficulty understanding the laws of cause and effect when the results are not immediate. I was no exception. When the knob finally popped back out, it seemed to do so all on its own. *Well, now, what was this?*

Then, of course, I had to determine if our lighter was hot enough to inflame a cigarette. Perhaps our cigarette lighter was faulty. The only scientific thing to do was test it. I took the lighter and looked at it with a critical eye. I hadn't yet grasped the idea that colors could be associated with heat. Otherwise, I never would have tested that red-hot coil on my thumb.

While I may have started out as an ace detective, I ended up as a little boy in a lot of pain. Smoke and the smell of burnt flesh permeated the car. My thumb was yellowish white, imprinted now with concentric circles from the heating coil of the lighter. The pain was bad enough. But all I could think about was how to keep my father from knowing what had happened while he was gone. Tears were certain evidence of wrongdoing. So I stopped crying. Between sniffles I rolled the passenger side's window down, hoping to clear the air.

With a bit more time and a stiff breeze that day, I might have maintained the secrecy of my experiment. But a few stray tears and a lingering odor of singed flesh raised my father's suspicions when he returned from his delivery. Reluctantly, I showed him my crusted thumb and weathered a strong reprimand that I could have anticipated word for word. The pain of the scolding lasted beyond that of my fried thumb.

Characteristically, my father's anger quickly dissipated as he looped the Packard down Center Street, then onto Oak, and headed for the Getchell Brothers ice house. During the summer, he would regularly pick up a five- or ten-pound block of ice, chip it up with an ice pick, and dump it into the dough bin in order to prevent the dough from rising ("proofing") too quickly. That day, the ice had a dual mission—to cool the dough and my thumb.

There were innumerable times when I might have provoked even the Dalai Lama to anger, but my father never saw it fit to put me over his knee for a spanking. The only time he came close to striking me occurred during the weekly driving lessons that began eight years later, when I was twelve. The problem was with the clutch! I could never master the damn thing. I would push it in, awkwardly ram the gearshift from first to second, then try to ease the clutch back out while stepping on the gas pedal.

"You're giving it too much gas," my father would say, clearly exasperated.

"Okay, dad," I would respond, feeling the tension start to permeate the front seat of our delivery wagon. While taking my right foot off the gas pedal, I managed to keep the clutch half-depressed. The wagon's engine voiced its displeasure, a tremor rising from its very depths.

"Billy, take your foot off the clutch!" he would shout.

Immediately, I lifted my left foot and let the clutch pop out. The horses under the wagon's hood turned angry and launched into a wild, furious bucking motion that stopped momentarily only to lurch forward again, threatening to toss the both of us into the street.

"Gas, Billy! You've got to give it gas!" This time the shout came with a hard slap on my right knee.

"Dad, I'm giving it gas," I shouted back, tears welling up, humiliated because I could not control the mechanical beast. Finally, the wagon picked up speed, ending its protest over being driven by the infant cowboy.

This scene was repeated many times, none more frightening than when we stopped at the top of one of Bangor's many hills. Fear would inevitably wrap an ice pack around my heart as the overhead traffic light turned red. As we sat waiting for the light to turn green, my father would warn me not to allow the wagon to roll back. The warning was redundant, for without fail, a line of cars would pull up inches behind me, their drivers unaware that they were in dire risk of receiving a bash in their bumpers or headlights.

I was so terrified that I would jam the accelerator and "pop" the clutch in a Mario Andretti maneuver that left my father in a state of chronic despair.

My father and mother rarely shared their innermost thoughts or feelings. Both remained stoic when dealing with private disappointments or tragedies. I saw my father cry only once during his life, and that was for just a few seconds at his brother's funeral. As we entered a small nondenominational chapel, he turned away, sniffled, and blew his nose. He said to me, "I'm going to miss him." He dried his eyes and went back to work immediately after the burial ceremony. He never spoke about his loss again.

My parents, while not rigid authoritarians, refused to bend to my entreaties on matters involving personal honor. As a five-year-old, my battered Japanese rifle, a war trophy given to me by a returning veteran, meant more to me than anything in the world. My friend Benny Gopin, who was three years older, favored it, too.

With the solemnity of international commodity traders we met on Hancock Street to discuss the relative advantages of a trade. In exchange for my prize rifle, Benny offered me his pair of binoculars. Benny must have put together quite a sales pitch because I readily traded my rifle. It didn't take long for doubt to set in, and soon I was convinced that I had been had and wanted my rifle back.

Surely my parents would see the injustice of the deal. But when I told my story at supper, my parents informed me that "a trade's a trade."

That I had been the victim of superior salesmanship meant little to them. I had lost my rifle and had hopefully learned a lesson. The suggestion that I bring the binoculars to the next basketball game came up, but that was extent of the help I received from my parents.

There was little to fear in our neighborhood, other than an outbreak of fire. The old wood-framed buildings offered little resistance to a candle or match that was handled haphazardly. Occasionally, the night would be pierced by a shrill siren, announcing an air raid drill. Morris Slep, the butcher whose shop was just below us, would don a white "Doughboy" helmet, strap on a white shoulder harness and belt, and bark through a megaphone: "Turn out the lights in your apartments. Turn out all the lights." Although the war was an ocean away, civil defense was taken very seriously.

Entertainment options were not plentiful then. We could, and usually did, go to a movie on Saturday afternoons. We had four theaters to pick from: the Bijou (where I would one day work as an usher at the age of twelve); the Park Theater; the Opera House; and last and certainly least, the Olympia, better known as "The Rat Hole," because of the presence of large river rats that would slither under the hard wooden seats during the shows. Competition among the theaters was fierce, prices ranging the full gamut between ten and twelve cents per movie.

The only other entertainment available was the radio. Except for air raids, the only time I can recall ducking for safety was with my sister, Marlene. If our parents were late coming home or went out for a few hours at night, we would sit in the kitchen, turn out the lights, turn on the small box radio, and tune into our favorite programs: *The Lone Ranger, The Green Hornet, Inner Sanctum, Mr. and Mrs. North,* and *Johnny Dollar.* The signature music and sounds of these programs always provoked a reaction in us. Whether it was the "William Tell Overture" (*The Lone Ranger*) or the creaking sound of a crypt being opened (*Inner Sanctum*), we responded with the predictability of Pavlov's dogs. Sometimes the programs were so frightening that we hid under the table until the imagined danger had passed.

Early habits are not easily erased. Marlene to this day still loves to watch horror movies. Fortunately, she no longer watches them from under a table.

Five

Lockefield Gardens—Eden

As I've indicated, Janet lived a rather nomadic life during her early years, as she and her mother had to move periodically into the homes of accommodating aunts and uncles and then into the less inviting environs of rooming houses. So, even as a very young child, she was used to hearing the word "moving." But one day her mother said the word so happily that Janet immediately knew this move was going to be different.

This time, they were moving not out, but up. Her mother had found a way to get Janet and her newly born brother, James, a one-bedroom apartment in a large federal public housing project called Lockefield Gardens. Lockefield Gardens had been built in the 1930s as part of a New Deal program to provide low-rent housing for blacks by clearing out slums and replacing the shacks and tenements with decent modern apartments. President Franklin Roosevelt allowed federal housing to be segregated. But that did not hurt him politically among black people, who overwhelmingly continued to support him.

It was 1949, the year that Janet's brother was born. The family was able to qualify for an apartment because priority was being given to veterans and Russell Floyd had served in the Army. Indiana Congressman Andrew Jacobs, Sr., who continued to be a source of assistance throughout the years, helped Janet's mother manage to track down enough information to complete the required forms and get them into their new home. Out of respect and gratitude for his kindness, Janet's mother would maintain a scrapbook filled with newspaper accounts about Jacobs' activities in Congress.

It is one of the many happy coincidences in life that I would serve in Congress with Andrew Jacobs' son "Andy."

When Janet and her family first moved into their new home, they lived at 633 Locke Street, a solidly built brick building that stood four stories high. There were a number of similar structures throughout the complex. Each had an entrance leading into a court-yard. The buildings were arranged so that there was space for play-grounds, gardens, and an elementary school.

Amenities that most white people took for granted were some-thing of a novelty for them. Janet remembers, for example, the time they were living in a rooming house owned by a black woman they called "Miss Maggie."

"There were no indoor plumbing facilities in the house. Mr. Mays was an eighty-year-old man who wore a plaid shirt and baggy corduroy pants that were held up by frayed suspenders. He walked on a wooden leg. He would pump water from a well and climb three flights of stairs to empty 'slop jars' and pour water into a large tin basin that served as a bathtub. My family had to limit baths to once a week, since it was such a chore for Mr. Mays to carry the water."

It was something of a cultural shock when Miss Maggie arranged to install indoor toilet facilities. "It was really quite amaz-ing," Janet said, "all the neighbors on the street rushed to Miss Mag-gie's house to watch the toilet being flushed. But old and gentle Mr. Mays thought it was unclean to have a toilet in the house.

"'Just what will they think of next?' he would say, shaking his head."

In Lockfield, three apartments were located on each floor of the building, sharing a large concrete reception area that the tenants were expected to take turns cleaning once a week. One of Janet's neighbors was quite elderly and unable to perform this chore, and so Janet's mother volunteered to do it for her.

Janet's mother had two mantras: "Cleanliness is next to Godliness" and "A place for everything and everything in its place."

"Mother had a day for everything. Monday was her laundry day, when she washed the clothes in a Maytag washing machine, ran them through a hand-turned wringer on the side of the machine, and then hung the laundry on the backyard clothesline. She used Tide detergent for both the laundry and 'luxury' bubble bath. It was a wonderful treat, provided we rinsed extremely well!

"Tuesday was ironing day. Mother always pressed our sheets. She believed that whatever little luxuries she bestowed upon white families she would bestow upon us.

"Wednesday and Thursday were free days, if one could call taking care of a busy household being free of work. Friday was fish market day. I didn't know many people who were Catholic until I went to high school. But I did know that Catholics couldn't eat meat on Fridays, and that became something of a secular tradition in Lockefield. Most ate fish on Fridays: catfish, buffalo fish, sunnies, perch, and whitefish. The fish-on-Friday tradition was also based on a simple culinary wisdom: Friday was the day the markets had the most—and the freshest—fish.

"Saturday was the day that we cleaned our home from floor to ceiling, room by room, foot by foot. I admired Mother's rigid discipline and determination to remove anything that would mar her quest for perfection, but questioned whether she needed to tax herself so physically. She always washed and waxed the floors on her hands and knees. I wanted her to use a mop. But she refused, insisting that you couldn't get into the corners and crevices with a mop.

"'If I get down on my hands and knees to clean a white woman's house,' she said, 'I can certainly do it for my own.'

"Mother would take a white cloth and go around the moldings and baseboards, making sure she said that 'everything was spic and span.' That was the name of the cleaning powder she used, and it served as the official description of a perfectly cleaned house.

"After moving into Lockefield, everyone was required to bathe every day—not just on Saturdays, as in our earlier days when plumbing was not available. On Saturday night, Mother began preparing Sunday dinner and getting her children's Sunday clothes ready.

"On Sunday I had a choice: Sunday school or the 11 a.m. service, when the minister really let loose with a mighty sermon and the ladies in the congregation would shout."

Janet's mother loved hearing the gospel songs and the black church music. Two of her favorite songs were "The Last Mile of the Way" and "His Eye Is on the Sparrow."

> *Why should I feel discouraged?*
> *Why should the shadows come?*
> *Why should my heart feel lonely?*
> *And long for heaven and home*
> *when Jesus is my portion*
> *My constant friend is he*
> *His eye is on the sparrow*
> *and I know he watches me.*

After church on Sunday, the family went home to feast on a formal dinner as a way of honoring the Sabbath. The meal consisted of baked chicken, macaroni and cheese, and mixed greens: mustard greens, kale, turnip greens, and collards. While collards are not everyone's favorite food, Janet told me that she loved them because of their texture and flavor. "Not until I became an adult," Janet said, "did I realize how 'collards' was spelled. I, along with most people in my neighborhood, called them 'colored greens,' thinking that they were greens for colored people."

It was a family tradition to say grace at every meal. After Janet moved away from home, that expression of gratitude fell into disuse. When her mother discovered this one evening while visiting her, she rebuked her.

"Janet, don't you say grace anymore? I brought you up to be grateful and reverent. Now you don't thank the Lord for the bounty that He's given and provided for you?"

Not wishing to feel like a heathen in her mother's presence, Janet relented.

"One of my mother's favorite blessings was, 'Dear, Lord, we wish to thank you for the food we're about to receive for the nourishment of our bodies to benefit mankind. And thank you, Dear Lord, for this day and this bounty. We ask this in Jesus' name. Amen."

"My brother, James, had to say 'thank you' and 'please,' not only to people outside their home but also in talking to each other. We used to joke that Mother was a drill sergeant or that we lived in a boarding school. Actually, she was no martinet, just a mother with rules about values, traditions, expectations—and limits. She might forgive an act of disobedience with a lecture, but if she felt that a pattern of defiance was developing, she could be a swift and very convincing disciplinarian."

Janet was perplexed about the depth of her mother's religious convictions and tried, unsuccessfully, to test them against the force of logic.

"During the first Christmas when James was serving in the Navy during the Vietnam War, Mother visited me in Chicago. We were about to enjoy the dinner we had prepared together when Mother said, 'Janet will you pray with me? My heart is heavy. I'm worried about James and all the young people affected and injured in this war . . . on both sides.'

"We knelt, and while my head was bowed I heard Mother speak to God as if she knew Him. Her words were beautifully spoken and clearly from her heart and deepest soul. It was a wonderful side of Mother that I had never seen before. Even in her humility there was strength. She first spoke of her respect for the Lord, thanked Him, not leaving out a person or thing that she loved. Then she began telling God how mighty He was and would He please use His mercy and power to protect her son James as he goes in to unknown and dangerous areas. She remembered the sick, people in despair, the elderly, widows and orphans, and asked Him to keep us all healthy, safe, and happy, with food and shelter 'and always with gratitude to you, Oh Lord.'"

Janet's mother lived with the constant concern about what would happen to her children if she died or became unable to take care of them. Would they be shifted here and there? Would they be abused, left without love and nurture? Would their relatives be resentful or abusive?

The Bible served as a lifesaver in a sea of turbulence and uncertainty. She would frequently remind Janet and James of the less fortunate on Earth.

"One day it would be Biafra. 'Think about the starving people in Biafra,' Mother would say. By pointing to some of the least fortunate on Earth, she hoped to reinforce to us that our deprivations were minimal."

"Despite my meager wages," Janet remembers her saying in one of her prayers, "and despite how hard I have to work to provide a home for my children, this would not be possible without the Good Lord. So you must be grateful."

Janet was respectful of her mother's religious convictions, but she couldn't refrain from asking her, "If God is a just and fair God, why doesn't He just give them food?" Or, "If we're expected to be so grateful for our food and shelter, what does God expect the starving people to be grateful for?"

Not only did her mother not respond to her questions, but she promptly accused Janet of blasphemy. "I realized that my questions about God did not shake Mother's faith. They only succeeded in wounding her and making her unhappy."

Janet and her family remained at 633 Locke Street for four years, proud of being model tenants. As Janet was approaching her teen years, her mother wanted Janet to have a room of her own and applied for a two-bedroom apartment in what was called a group house, a two-story structure that was the equivalent of a townhouse with front and back yards. "With a backyard, we could have a dog," Janet said. Janet's mother planted flowers, kept the little front and back yards tidy, and picked up trash whenever she saw it in front of other buildings.

* * *

"I remember the day as clearly as if it were just yesterday," Janet said, "It was a slow, boring Sunday afternoon. Mother and I were whiling the time away playing one of our favorite games, Chinese checkers. It was played with marbles on a six-pointed star shaped board with holes cut out for the marbles to sit in. The game's moves were similar to regular checkers."

Janet continued, "I remember Mother was holding her chin in her hand leaning on the table, as I was contemplating my next move, when she said, 'Your Aunt Laureen's dog just had a litter of puppies.'

"I looked up and said: 'Mother! Can we have one of the puppies?'

"James, who was sitting on the floor watching TV, said: 'Yea! It would fun to have a dog.'

"Mother called our cousin and asked if he could drive over to pick us up.

"When we arrived, I couldn't wait to go in the shed where the puppies were. It was the first time I'd seen a baby dog.

"The mother looked drained from the delivery and the nursing. There were at least five or six puppies. They were all black with white paws, white bibs and bellies. But the one that caught our eye was the one who looked as though his tale had been dipped in white paint It looked like a brush. He was the one we chose. He was only a few weeks old; too young to take him from his mother, but we did anyway. We just had to have him. At the time, he was squirming and a little feisty, so we named him Tuffy. We immediately fell in love with that little guy.

"Aunt Laureen was glad to find a home for at least one of her puppies. So she wrapped Tuffy in a blanket and handed him to Mother. I couldn't stop looking at him. He was so small and sweet.

"Tuffy grew as did our love for him and his for us. He followed my brother everywhere, a classic boy and his dog, and he loved alternating his time between sleeping in James's room, then mine. He always celebrated Christmas with us, and one year he was so excited about the twinkling lights on the Christmas tree that he nearly knocked it over with his wagging tail.

"I'll never forget one Easter Sunday. Mother had a baked ham cooling on the kitchen table. When we entered the kitchen, there was Tuffy on the table feasting on the family dinner. Mother, ever conscious of the need for cleanliness, had been outdone."

"'Tuffy! You brat!! Get off the table,' Mother shouted."

"Tuffy jumped like lightning. I opened the screen door to the back yard to save him from one of Mother's flying shoes.

"Mother collected her emotions. She rinsed off the ham and sliced it for dinner. Not an Easter would pass that we didn't take great delight in telling the story about Tuffy and our Easter Ham.

"Community living had its upsides and its painful downsides. One downside was when other tenants broke the rules and we'd all end up paying. One rule required everyone to pick up after their pet; another was to keep your pet on a leash unless you were in your own backyard. We obeyed the rules. But we paid a price for those who didn't.

"Mother always had an anxiety attack every time a notice from the rental office was slipped through the slot in the front door. It always meant bad news. Either the rent was going to be raised or those who were late in their payments were being given an eviction warning or a notice of an outright eviction. Even though Mother always made sure that the rental bill was the first one she paid each month, she always seemed to shake when arriving home and seeing an envelop on the floor.

"One day I watched Mother open up an envelop. Her eyes filled with tears and she sat down, dropping the notice on the table. She just shook her head, but remained silent.

"Mother. What is it?" Janet asked, suddenly frightened to see the sorrow on her face.

"It's Tuffy," Janet's mother said, "We . . . we have to give him away."

"No! No!" Janet cried, "Tuffy's part of our family. . . . He's our baby. . . . We can't give him away!"

"I was distraught," Janet said, "I wondered who would take a full grown dog? How would Tuffy feel about this? It was a nightmare. It was so cruel."

"We told James when he came home from school. He, too, was overcome with grief. Tuffy was his buddy, his best friend. They fetched and rolled on the floor. Mother and I loved watching them rough house together."

A pall, heavy as a toxic cloud hung over their home for days. The notice said they had thirty days to "get rid" of Tuffy.

Either that or move. Some choice.

They had no place to go.

Janet's Mother had worked hard to get them that safe haven, a place with running water and heat in the cold winters. Plus, the price was manageable. If her salary went up, so did the rent. But if it went down, so did the rent. That was the upside side of government housing.

"Mother found a couple who lived by our neighborhood," Janet said, "They had a yard and agreed to keep Tuffy, but he had to be chained to a clothesline. We'd go by and see him on our way to the store. He'd see us and run toward us until he was yanked back by the shortness of the chain. We'd pet and feed him and inquire why the family wouldn't keep him inside on the hot days. There were times when I would walk by and see that there was no water for him. I noticed James stopped going by altogether. It wasn't that James no longer loved Tuffy. He just couldn't deal with the heartache of knowing that he could never have his buddy back, that he would never be able to enjoy rough housing with Tuffy again."

"I could only imagine what Tuffy thought of us. Why had we done this? Why were we leaving him there? What had he done to deserve this? He had only tried to please.

"Finally it was too hard for all of us to bear. Mother found another family that lived in the country, with a big yard where Tuffy could romp.

"Or so we hoped," Janet said.

"I will always remember the day I came home from work and found Mother with her head on the kitchen table . Her eyes were red and puffy. She'd been crying. My mother said, 'Tuffy's gone! I took him to the car, Janet. He resisted getting in. It was like he knew this was it, that he was never going to see us again. I watched as the car drove off and saw Tuffy scratch and claw the backseat window, trying to get back to me, pleading with me to rescue him.'"

"At that moment," Janet said, "I fell to the floor and wailed uncontrollably."

Janet's mother continued, "Janet, it was the hardest thing I've ever had to do. You know, when they took your sister from me, I knew she was in good hands and was loved by Uncle George. I knew that I'd always be able to see her. She'd always be within reach. But this time, Tuffy's out of sight, out of reach. He's gone forever."

"Mother got up from the table and sat down on the floor with me. I don't know how long we wept together, but it seemed like forever."

It was difficult for Janet to lose Tuffy, but especially hard for her mother. She had been given away as a child because of her own mother's illness. She had her first daughter taken away. Now another separation, another goodbye.

Over the years, Janet and her mother would weep whenever they talked about Tuffy, even when they'd recall the Easter Ham story.

As Janet said, "A loss like that, well, you weep forever. It's been almost fifty years since that day. Mother's gone on . . . and I still weep, alone for now, the only one left to remember that day."

Lockefield was a ghetto. Admittedly, a modern and quite intelligently designed one, but a ghetto nonetheless. The cluster of apartment buildings that housed some seven hundred families became the heart of an immense black neighborhood that was like a small town in many ways. There were well-to-do, upwardly mobile black families in the area who owned the businesses, from grocery stores and restaurants to beauty parlors and funeral homes. There were black churches nearby, and in the summer, when the windows were open, everyone in the neighborhood could hear the choirs filling the Sunday morning with sweet music.

Indianapolis's most famous black woman was Madame C. J. Walker, who left the cotton fields of the South and settled in Indianapolis around 1910. Madame Walker was the first American woman, white or black, to become a self-made millionaire. She did so by devising a method of straightening hair. She also founded the city's black YMCA. A building named after her contained a movie theater (where Janet went to movies on Saturdays for nine cents) and offices that were occupied by doctors, dentists, and lawyers. There were educators and entrepreneurs, such as the Stuart family that owned a major storage and moving company, along with a prominent funeral home. Members of that family looked white, but they never tried to pass, the way some others did. The owner of the company, Marion ("Mayday") Stuart, would tell stories about white businessmen who assumed that he was white and constantly used racial epithets in his presence when referring to blacks.

According to Janet, "Mayday once overheard a mayor who was campaigning for reelection in the area say to an aide, 'Let's get the hell out of here. These niggers are never going to vote for me anyway.'

"Mayday would even see members of the KKK exit from a nearby church wearing Klan robes with their hoods pulled off. It was unclear whether they removed their hoods because it was so hot inside during the summer or because they simply were so comfortable and confident of their power that they didn't give a damn about who saw them. Their contempt for blacks had been long-standing."

Indiana, which had a large black population by the early nineteenth century, may not have been a slave state, but it was not much of a free state, either. The first black settlers could not vote or appear in court either as jurors or witnesses against whites. When a white man was brought before the court in Indianapolis for beating up a young black man, the judge dismissed the case because all the witnesses were black and, "therefore, incompetent." But black men of Indiana were good enough to fight and die for the Union Army. About two hundred and fifty of those Civil War veterans are buried in Crown Hill Cemetery in Indianapolis.

Janet attended Public School Number 24, where she was taught by teachers who saw their work not so much as a job as a calling.

They put their students on the path of learning, making them understand, even as young children, that they had to try extra hard to make it in the world beyond their restricted neighborhood. There, she learned more than how to read and write. The teachers reinforced the same core values that her mother had insisted upon: punctuality, orderliness, self-discipline, and respect for her elders and especially for herself. Above all, she learned why it was important to strive to do her very best.

Somehow Janet's mother knew that the world was going to change, and she told Janet that she had to prepare for that change, not through rebellion or resistance but through education and self-discipline. While whites were determined to confine blacks and define the limitation of their rights, her mother refused to acknowledge their power or privilege by accepting any acts of condescension. Insults, Janet learned from her, could come in many forms, including intended compliments, such as the time a little white girl said to her, "You're pretty—for a colored girl."

Prior to moving into Lockefield Gardens, Janet lived in a neighborhood, right across the street from a dairy company, Polk Milk. Part of the block-long dairy building consisted of two big milk bottles about four stories high. Between them was a huge sign: Polk's Best. Polk milk bottles had distinctive caps and seals, which helped boost the dairy's advertisements about keeping the milk clean and safe. The caps had a special meaning to black children. If they collected enough of them, they could present them to the ticket collectors at Riverside Park, a white-only amusement park, which had a roller coaster, Ferris wheel, and all the usual attractions of amusement parks. With or without bottle-cap currency, black children could gain admission to Riverside on only one day a year, "colored people's day."

As the day neared, Janet's mother realized that Janet had been saving up the bottle caps for the "colored people's day." While she was sad that she had dashed Janet's hopes, she refused to allow Janet to go with her friends. She considered the "special" day for "coloreds" an insult and would simply not allow Janet to feel grateful to anyone who treated her with disdain.

Reluctantly, Janet gave the bottle caps to her friends. She felt as if she were handing over jewels. Those caps, in fact, were really a kind of treasure, according to archaeologists who recently discovered some while excavating in her old neighborhood in a belated effort to explore the black experience in Indianapolis.

Janet and her mother never went to Riverside Park even after it was integrated years later.

Janet and I were watching television one evening and found it interesting that Academy Award winning actor, Morgan Freeman, while appearing on CBS' popular "60 Minutes'" raised a similar objection to designating February as "Black History Month." He asked host Mike Wallace, "If February is Black History Month (incidentally the shortest month in the year), when is White History Month?"

Wallace appeared stunned by the directness and simplicity of the question.

Janet said, "Bill, of course, he has no answer because white people have always considered blacks to have had a separate and unequal part in American history. Tell me, why is our calendar segregated? Black history is the struggle of blacks to overcome the legacy of slavery in America. Since slavery existed, there must have been slave masters. Did they enslave blacks for only one month a year? Why isn't the legacy of America overcoming its racist past the history of all Americans—white and black? Blacks have contributed to this country's greatness, and we continue to do so, every day, every month, every year, and the notion that we should receive 'special recognition' for one month should be rejected as an act of pure condescension.

"You know, when my mother rejected 'colored people's day,' she was well ahead of her time."

By 1954, change was coming to America in terms of race relations, and that change happened to coincide with the timing of a decision that Janet had to make about what high she should attend.

In 1954, the U.S. Supreme Court ended official segregation in public schools with its historic decision in *Brown v. Board of Education*.

The decision was a major chapter in the long story of the black struggle for equality and the desegregation of all public institutions and accommodations.

Prior to 1954, the schools in Indianapolis had been largely segregated. In fact, the idea of an all-black high school was first raised back in the 1920s at the instigation of the Ku Klux Klan. The KKK had always been a powerful political force in Indiana. In 1924, Klansman, Edward Jackson, had been elected governor of the state. At that time, there were reports that more than forty percent of the white males in Indianapolis were members of the Klan. They dominated the city council, the school board, and the board of county commissioners.

It was only after a series of scandals had enveloped the Klan that popular support for its xenophobic and racist hatreds started to decline. One of the most prominent scandals occurred in 1925. It involved David Stephenson, the Grand Dragon of Indiana and fourteen other states. Stephenson was convicted of the rape and murder of Madge Oberholtzer. During the trial, the prosecution revealed that Stephenson had ripped away a portion of Oberholtzer's vagina with his teeth and had caused her to bleed to death. One witness said she looked as if she had been "chewed by a cannibal."

By the time Janet was growing up, the Klan was still active in Indianapolis, even though its profile was less visible. She remembered once, when she and her mother were "live-ins" in a white family's home, being taken by two white girls to a large clearing, where they laid on their stomachs on a small hill. At dusk, a parade of cars began to pull up. Out spilled men, women and children, many of them dressed in white robes and hoods. They soon gathered around a tall wooden cross at the end of the field. When the cross suddenly burst into flames, Janet kept watching, at once fascinated and bewildered by the sight.

She didn't tell her mother about what she had seen until years later, long after she had realized that she had seen a Klan rally.*

---

*See *From Rage To Reason*, pp. 3-4.

"My first recollection of the cross is one that is burning. The sight of the Klan burning the cross has stayed with me to this day. Even though I was raised as a Christian, I could never wear a cross, not even the gold one Mother had given me as a graduation gift. She used to ask me why I never wore the cross and the necklace. I told her that the cross meant religion to her but racism to me. She got upset and said that I was being blasphemous and that it was against Christ for me to even think such a thought. I told her it was blasphemous for Christians to allow the Klan to burn the cross."

At the time that the Klan had first proposed constructing an all-black school, there were many black families who supported the idea because at that time blacks in Indianapolis's predominately white schools were tolerated, more than they were taught. Black students were barred from most extracurricular activities, which left them with little meaningful social life. Athletic teams were segregated, as was the seating in many classrooms. There were no black teachers in those high schools, so the black students had to depend upon white teachers who at best were indifferent about teaching blacks. Many of them were convinced that black students were intellectually inferior and we had little potential for meaningful employment. Others were pure racists who simply despised the idea of educating blacks and made no attempt to conceal the hate and burning crosses they carried in their hearts.

There was also, a group described as "progressive colored citizens" who protested the Klan's efforts, insisting that black children deserved the right to the same quality of education given to white students. Those were brave colored citizens, indeed. The Indianapolis school board rejected their complaints and voted unanimously to construct the school. They proposed naming it after a famous slave owner—Thomas Jefferson. This, too, proved controversial. Under pressure from the black community, whose members had petitioned for a more appropriate designation for the school, the board agreed to name the school after the first man to die in the Revolutionary War against the British, a black man, whose name was Crispus Attucks.

Janet is always amazed that virtually every white American knows the name of the Bostonian silversmith, Paul Revere, who rode through the streets of Lexington and Concord, proclaiming that the British were coming! Yet virtually none know the name of the man who was the first to die in the fight to establish our independence from the British Crown. Crispus Attucks.

It was no small irony that the Klan's efforts to force black students into separate and unequal schools actually resulted in providing them with superior educations.

Some of the teachers at Crispus Attucks had doctoral degrees. All of them had enough education and training to teach in college. But the traditional black colleges had few vacant positions for new teachers and so they came to Crispus Attucks, more qualified than most of the teachers in the white schools. At least two teachers were lawyers and many were World War II veterans, including a Tuskegee Airman and two members of the Golden 13, as the Navy's first black officers were called. They were among those who blazed the path to the nonviolent protest demonstrations that Dr. Martin Luther King, Jr., would lead in the 1950s and 1960s. Those teachers were in the ranks of the blacks who sang the first freedom songs and first chanted, "Hey, Joe, whaddye know; Ole Jim Crow has got to go!"

Janet had always intended to attend an all-black high school. Frankly, she knew that her temperament would not serve her well in an integrated school. She had absolutely no doubt that if a white student ever hurled a derogatory name at her, she'd respond by beating the hell out of him or her. Even though she was being raised as a good Baptist, she never subscribed to the ethic of "turning the other cheek." Her attitude was simple: "Insult me and be prepared to pay the price."

Janet also knew, however, that if she did respond to such taunts, she'd be the one to pay a price, that of running the very real risk of expulsion from school. That could put her on the path to truancy, possibly on the road to prison—a destination for too many people of color.

The Supreme Court's decision in *Brown v. Board* helped dispatch Ole Jim Crow, and Janet briefly flirted with the idea of attending Short Ridge High School so that she could be with her sister, Myrna, who was enrolled there. But something happened in 1955 that told her where she had to go. Any thoughts she had about attending an integrated school vanished.

His name was Emmett Till. He was Janet's age, a fourteen-year-old boy from Chicago. He was visiting his relatives in Money, Mississippi. Although he was said to be a nice young man, according to some reports, as a result of having suffered infantile paralysis as a child, he sometimes whistled when he tried to talk. Whether he had a speech impediment or was being flirtatious that fateful day remains unclear. Clearly, he had forgotten that he was in Mississippi, the heartland of hate. Accounts differ on whether he had entered a local store to make a purchase or in response to his cousin's dare. Standing inside the store was a white woman who claimed that when he spoke, she heard a whistle. That became his alleged "crime": He appeared to have whistled at a white woman.

She was the wife of the store owner. Three days later, two relatives of the store owner went to the house of Emmett's great uncle, pulled the boy from his bed, stripped him, beat and mutilated him, shot him, wired a 100-pound factory fan around his neck, and dumped his body into the Tallahatchie River. There never was a mystery about who did it. After being acquitted in a trial that was a travesty, the two killers confessed to a journalist who quoted their confession in *Look* magazine.

When Emmett's body was returned to Chicago, his mother decided to have his coffin opened and allowed the black-owned magazine *Jet* to publish the horrific photographs of what had been done to him. When Janet saw the photographs of Emmett Till's mutilated body in *Jet*, she knew that she could never attend a white school. She knew that she would be fighting to control her rage there instead of preparing her mind for the cruel world ahead.

Years later, Janet would become a friend of John H. Johnson, publisher of *Jet* and *Ebony*. "There were people on the staff who were squeamish about the photographs." Mr. Johnson said. "I had reservations, too, but I decided finally that if it happened it was our responsibility to print it and let the world experience man's inhumanity to man."

That issue of *Jet* sold out immediately and, Mr. Johnson believed, "It did as much as any other event to traumatize Black America and prepare the way for the Freedom Movement of the sixties."

Emmett Till's murder in Money, Mississippi, burns in Janet's soul today, every bit as painful as the sight of Klansmen torching a cross as the symbol of their evil.

Despite all the hardship and adversity Janet's mother had to confront in her life, she had great faith in the future of America.

"By the time you are a woman," Mother said to me more than once, "you'll be able to do things we can't do now. You've just got to be prepared." She gave me a lasting motto: *Reach for the stars even if you have to fall through the tree tops.**

She insisted that Janet practice her English, perfect it. "Speak clearly and with confidence," she would say. "Always remember, education is the one thing that they can't take away from you."

It was an expression that Janet had heard before, but she didn't know who the "they" were that she referred to. "I simply was unaware of the history behind her words at the time." She discovered the meaning soon enough. Her ancestors had been taken away from their homeland, their families, their language, their freedom. Knowledge and education could unshackle blacks from slave owners and permit them to succeed. It was precisely because slave owners understood the fierce desire that black people had for freedom that motivated them to prohibit their "chattels" from learning to read and write, and then in an act of supreme hypocrisy, to criticize them for being ignorant and uneducable. They had spared no effort to keep blacks down and in a position of servitude.

---

*See *From Rage To Reason*, p. 19

Blacks may have been emancipated, but they were never truly free. The land they owned and tilled was taken from them at gunpoint by Klansmen who threatened to kill them unless they abandoned all that they possessed.

"Janet," my mother insisted, "you've got to keep your grades up and your dress down. You'll be attracted to boys, but if you want to see just how much hardship not taking my advice can bring you, just look at me and my life."

"I took her words to heart. I studied hard, practiced abstinence, and played the piano with the hope that I could one day fulfill Mother's dream for me to play in a concert hall.

"My teachers created classroom discipline by making us realize that every minute of our lives was a minute we should be using to the best of our ability. We were told that Negroes were thought to be lazy and never got anywhere on time. This, our teachers said, was a bit of prejudice we could wipe out simply by being determined to be punctual. Our principal, Russell Lane, a majestic figure, stood at the front door in the morning, making us move along to class. When the five-minute bell rang, you went to your classroom. The halls were empty by the time the class bell rang—except for the principal, Mr. Lane, waiting to pounce on any unfortunate latecomers.

"We admired all of our teachers. There was one, however, our gym teacher, who was very light-skinned and obviously color conscious. When she lined up kids for a performance, she always put the less talented but lighter-skinned students in the front row. The blacker you were, the farther back you were placed."

Although Janet never quite mastered the piano as an instrument, she did learn to play the flute. That happened when she and her girl friend April Brown decided to try out for majorette of the band. The music teacher, Russell Brown (no relation to April), said no one could even begin competing until they had learned to play an instrument. He handed Janet the mouthpiece of a flute and said, "Come back when you can get a sound out of it."

"Well," Janet said, "April became a majorette and I wound up playing in the marching band and in the orchestra. Regrettably, I never did learn how to march and play at the same time. I would hold the flute to my lips and parade down the field. Nobody ever missed not hearing my flute."

The schoolbooks were old and marked up—hand-me-downs from the white high schools. Many of the mathematics books had a dividend: the answers to problems scribbled in the margins. Luckily, Janet learned more from her teachers than from her books.

There was no "Black History" for Janet and her classmates, though there was a Negro History Week. In her books she read about an America that was described as a "melting pot," but her teachers described a different kind of America, one that chronicled the struggle of her people to secure an education and equality.

It was an America that she would come to know well.

Six

Destination Unknown

My father's work defined the circumference of our existence. Sundays, my mother insisted, was for family, and it generally involved a trip to a nearby lake or out to my Aunt Gittle's camp on Pushaw Pond. On special occasions, we might venture for a picnic to Fort Knox in Bucksport, some twenty miles away, or to Perry's Nut House in Belfast to pick through a treasure trove of small trinkets and curios. And if the weatherman predicted a truly hot day, we might be treated to a trip to Sandy Beach near Bar Harbor, where we could frolic in the Atlantic's frigid water.

Swimming was pretty much out of the question, unless you were partial to the thought of soaking in a tub filled with ice cubes. So we would dash, skinny legs kicking up sand on the blankets of fellow beachgoers, headlong towards the surf, our lips sealed tight so as not to swallow gallons of seawater, until we hit the force of an unfriendly wave and were slammed hard into the sand. Then, screaming with joy and more than a touch of terror at the ocean's power, we would run back to the warmth of the family blanket, all goose-bumped, shivering, and slightly blue around the lips.

Our preferred resort area was Green Lake. Not only was the lake water, while cold, still swimmable, but there was a large float there that served as a special attraction. The adults liked to swim out to the float and dry off in the sun, letting the waves gently rock beneath them. The challenge for the kids was more daring.

For us, the float was a place of games and adventure. It was a life raft for an imagined shipwreck on some days, and then at the word "Go," it was a diving board for crazy jumps into the water. When we had the float to ourselves and the lifeguards weren't looking, each of us would try to keep the others from coming aboard until one of us reigned as King of the Hill over all the rest. If the adults were spread out on the float, we continued our games under water.

The bold thing to do was to dive off one side and swim the length of the float underwater until you were able to surface on the other side. I did this right along with the others until I learned there was real danger involved. Some years later, Joel Paine, the brother of my first law partner, played this game and got so tangled up underneath the float that he drowned. After Joel's death, we played our games above the water whenever we neared the float.

My father's voice, a voice worthy of a Shakespearean actor, echoes through my memories. It was his voice—and his irrepressible spontaneity—that often sparked controversy over the years. Once in 1950, while we were delivering rolls in the Atlantic Sea Grill Restaurant on Exchange Street, the owner, Mr. Vomvouris, asked him whether he was going to attend the Boston Celtics exhibition game that night. Several of the Celtics players were seated at nearby tables, along with Coach Red Auerbach.

In a voice that no one has ever characterized as *sotto voce*, my father boomed, "Why? Why would I want to spend to money to see that game? It's fixed. They're all fixed."

This was too much for Auerbach, who nearly choked on the coffee he was drinking. He slipped away from his table and rushed over to my father. With his jaw jutting out, he approached my father. "Who the hell are you to tell people that we're a bunch of crooks?" he demanded. Auerbach spun around to Mr. Vomvouris, saying, "Who is this jerk, anyway?" Mr. Vomvouris, caught between his famous (but one-time) customer and his steady supplier of bread, chose not to pick sides. Instead, he just urged Auerbach to calm down while I tugged at my father's coat sleeves and urged him to leave. Outside, I cautioned him to be more careful. "Dad," I said, "you shouldn't say things like that, especially not in front of them."

He just laughed it off, apparently not aware of his voice's wattage. "I'm telling you, Billy. The games are in the bag. Just like those with the Globetrotters."

Not once did he ever express regret over a comment that others found offensive or simply too blunt. He was without malice and without forethought. Honesty had always been his guide, but never his guard. Years later, during the impeachment hearings of President Nixon, a CBS correspondent asked him what he thought would happen. In Miller's Restaurant, among the presence of several dozen members of the national press corps, he boomed out, "He's guilty as hell. No question he was involved in the cover-up. Congress is going to impeach him. No doubt about it." He was right, of course, but at that moment I just shook my head in silence as I bolted for the door. Red Auerbach, Richard Nixon, it didn't make any difference.

My parents had not provided me with much sex education. In fact to this day I don't remember receiving a single word of advice. The closest I ever came to one of *those* talks was when my father handed me one of his sweeping, all-purpose suggestions. "Stay away from girls," he told me. "Stick to basketball instead."

If they lived interior lives, my parents rarely revealed it. My father was strangely lacking in all curiosity about his roots, the village in Poland or Russia that his father had abandoned to escape a hated czar, or the name he had acquired as he was processed through Ellis Island. Surely, there were stories to be told, stories of danger, adventure, hardship, and heartbreak. But the past seemed to be devoid of a single event of interest to him.

My mother's past was creased with poverty and the perpetual motion of her family traipsing from rural town to rural town in the tow of a rootless father. Her frequent relocations were the most she would discuss, as if nothing else in her childhood had ever happened or her father's grim ghost had simply closed off the past for her and her siblings.

So we lived in the hard-working present, holding out for ourselves the vague promise that a string of tomorrows would render unnecessary any reflection upon the sorrows of yesterday.

Our dinner table conversation usually involved a recitation of, or reaction to, events at the bakery that day, of what transgression Uncle Dick or Aunt Gittle had indulged in once again or whose orders and deliveries had been delayed to accommodate a customer of lower priority. We tossed words on the surface of things, and they skipped like flat stones along the glass surface of lake water.

While the subject of sex was taboo, occasionally my father did discuss religion, usually in a more serious vein than when he stopped at Mama Baldacci's restaurant every day on his delivery route. All the Baldaccis are strong Catholics and Democrats. My father maintained that the two were synonymous. Each day they would gather their daily customers, set up a round of beers, and await my father's arrival. Then for forty minutes or more they would bait him about the economy, politics, and religion.

"Ruby," they would ask, "what do you think about alimony?"

"Don't say alimony. It's all the money."

"Jesus? What do I think of him?" they'd persist.

"Well, I think he was a smart young man."

"Smart?" they would retort, laughing at his irreverence, and not quite sure they wouldn't be punished for doing so.

"Sure," he would say, making no effort to contain a wide smile. "You see, you believe Jesus walked on water. I'm telling you he was smart because he knew where all the rocks were."

At this point those at the table would burst into laughter, not wishing to condone his blasphemy, but relishing the bravado in the agnostic before them. They would glance around to make sure no priests were in the restaurant at the time. "That's our Ruby," they would say. "Thank God, there's only one of you!"

There was one topic my father would raise periodically—his fear of doctors and hospitals. In his eighty-six years, he had been a hospital inpatient on only three occasions: first, when he fell down a flight of stairs in a restaurant while delivering his bread, sustaining a concussion, broken teeth, a broken shoulder, and several broken ribs; second, when he suffered a stroke following an automobile accident; and third, when he nearly died from congestive heart failure. At no time did his confinement to a hospital bed extend beyond three days. Bruised and bandaged, he would rush back to his beloved bakery, dismissing his condition with a supplicant yielding-up of his palms. "What will my customers do without my bread?" was his standard rationalization.

By contrast, my mother placed an abiding faith in the man who had delivered all of her three children. It was a faith that was for the most part well placed. But not always.

Dr. George Horton was regarded as a saint by his patients, many of whom were poor. He carried his Hippocratic Oath beyond the walls of his office and the hospital to the people in the countryside. There were few homes that he considered too remote or inconvenient to visit with his black medical valise in hand. With his white hair, which he kept cropped in a short crew cut, and a manner that was genial and compassionate, he inspired a loyalty that was unmatched by any in the local medical community. Of course, it helped that many times, he simply didn't charge his patients for his services. If a patient was short of money on a given visit, he would say in a deep, raspy voice, "That's okay, Mrs. Smith, don't worry about a thing." He never added the obligatory "You can pay me later when things are a little better for you." If he knew that a patient couldn't afford the cost of a prescription drug, he would hand out a week's supply (sometimes more) of sample medication that had been furnished to him by one of the drug manufacturers trying to encourage him to promote their products. This practice of dispensing drugs from his office would years later place him in professional jeopardy with the medical authorities.

Dr. Horton's expansive generosity was not always matched with corresponding medical skill. He was, after all, a general practioner, and specialists at the time were a rarity in Bangor. From early childhood, I had difficulty breathing through my nose. Dr. Horton, after staring intently up my nasal passages with the aid of a cold metal prong, arrived at a diagnosis. He handed me a plastic inhaler that I was to fill with penicillin. For years, I inhaled the antibiotic powder, only to discover four decades later that I had a deviated septum that was in need of a surgeon's knife.

Somewhere between my mother's faith and my father's fear lay the answer. It's called a second opinion.

I had made quick friends with a boy named Barry Shuman, who had moved to Bangor from Dorchester, Massachusetts. Barry was only a year older than me, but he was streetwise far beyond any measure. His father was a salesman at a used-car dealership. Barry, I concluded, had been sent on a mission of mercy. Although, thanks to my father's knee-slapping driving instructions, I had obtained a license at the ripe old age of fifteen, I did not always have access to my mother's car. Barry, as I saw it, was there to fill the vacuum: Double dates at the "passion pit" drive-in theater (to hell with the smell from the adjacent pig farm); trips to Boston, where we first experienced the intoxicating qualities of alcohol.

When I did get my hands on the steering wheel of my mother's Oldsmobile convertible, I would drive down Main Street, top down, rev up the rpms, then drop the gears into low and wait for the growl from the glasspak mufflers that I had outfitted the car with to ricochet against the shop windows.

Bangor, the state's third largest city, with a population of thirty-five thousand, was Small Town U.S.A. It was a sleepy city that tolerated little misbehavior. Inevitably, after my mother's car emitted its signature growl, Morris Thurston, a Bangor police officer, would pull us over, and demand that I turn down the radio, which was inevitably playing either Elvis's "Jailhouse Rock" or Jerry Lee Lewis' "Whole Lotta Shakin' Goin' On."

"Come on, Morris, you know we aren't doing anything wrong."

"You guys been drinkin'?"

"Nope. You want us to walk the line?"

Stony silence while he picked through the back seat of the car. "Okay. But cut the noise. If I catch you poppin' those glasspaks again, I'm gonna give ya a ticket."

"Okay, Morris," we laughed, relieved that he did not force us to open up the trunk of the car, where on occasion, he might have found a bottle of Budweiser. Unopened, of course, but still illegal in the possession of those under twenty-one years of age.

My years in high school passed quickly and, relatively speaking, without major incident. I emphasize the word "relatively" because I twice narrowly missed entering the local obituary column. One incident involved a head-on collision with a drunk driver during a severe snowstorm. I escaped with a bruised chest, while the passenger in the other vehicle was launched through the windshield. The second came during a weekly fishing expedition with Barry Shuman on Graham Lake—about a forty-five-minute drive from Bangor.

One cold spring morning, shortly after the ice had melted in the lake, we were trolling for trout when I managed to get my line wrapped around the boat's motor. Not only had I rendered useless a perfectly good fishing line, but I also had put the engine out of commission. The remedy was to tip the motor out of the water and unravel the line.

At the time, I was wearing a long winter overcoat, but the 45-degree cold cut through it as if it were little more than a T-shirt. While leaning over the engine and unraveling the line, I was suddenly catapulted head over heels into the lake when the engine tipped back into the water. I was being pulled down by the weight of my waterlogged overcoat. Luckily, the boat was not moving when I performed my somersault routine. But I had drifted quickly to one of the small floating islands on Graham Lake that had been created when sections of wetlands along the old river had been cleared to make way for the lake reservoir. These islands were unstable and not strong enough to support a person's weight. Worse though, the islands were a tangled mess of roots and vines below the water line. To get entangled underneath was to risk drowning, much like my friend Joel Paine had done under the float at Green Lake.

Fortunately, Barry's long arms were strong enough to pull me out of the freezing water and into the boat before I slipped below the surface. I'm not certain whether Barry's rescue efforts helped to shape his career path, but he continued his life-saving duties as one of Maine's outstanding state troopers.

In the spring of 1958, as high school graduation approached, I was unsure what path to follow into the future. The words that accompanied my photograph in the school yearbook captured this lack of clarity: "Destination unknown."

My father, no doubt influenced by the high cost of orthodontic braces, expressed the hope that I pursue a career in dental medicine.

"You see, Billy, they make big money and there's no heavy lifting involved in fixing teeth. You don't want to become a schlepper like me."

In addition, he wanted me to attend the University of Maine, located just eight miles from the doorstep of our home. I could continue to live at home and save the costs of a private college. He could also enjoy watching me play basketball at the collegiate level for the next four years. I knew that basketball was more important to him than the financial concerns. My father never missed a game of mine from the time I was twelve years old. He even extended his interest to my practice sessions.

Each afternoon while he was on his delivery route, he would stop by the gymnasium to urge me on—or yell when I made a mistake. The other players asked me to tell him not to come because he was a distraction. I wasn't sure how to break the news to him diplomatically. I attempted to convey the notion that a matter of equity was involved, hoping he would see his presence was giving me something of an unfair advantage.

"Dad," I said, "the other players' fathers aren't able to attend our practice sessions, and it makes it a little difficult for me when you stop by."

He was hurt by my awkward request but simply pretended that it was of little interest to him and that he stopped by only because the gym was on his delivery route.

I had held my head down when I spoke. I didn't want to see the pain in his eyes as he tried to dismiss my anxiety with indifference.

He didn't come by the gymnasium for several weeks. One day, during a bad snowstorm, I was dribbling down the court when I felt someone's eyes watching me. It was dark outside, but the lights from the gym picked up a silhouette in a window. I looked up and saw my father's face peering through the window with his hands cupped around his temples. His hat was covered with snow. He had been standing on a railing outside the gym watching the entire practice session. The baker man, covered with flour, covered with snow, standing in the freezing cold. I felt a sharp pang of guilt for having asked him to not come to the gym. I also felt a deep sense of pride that he came anyway and watched in dark silence. I never told him that I saw him that afternoon and all those that followed. But I played each day knowing he was there, and I tried just a little harder for that face in the window.

Much as I wanted to accommodate my father's wishes, I found my mother's advice more persuasive. She thought that I should secure the best education possible, whatever the costs. I decided on a compromise of sorts. I would select the college with the best academic credentials but remain in Maine so that my father could on occasion catch one of my basketball games. I selected Bowdoin College, a small, all-male, highly acclaimed liberal arts college located in Brunswick, just one hundred miles south of Bangor. Bowdoin offered me a partial scholarship, which I was able to supplement by washing dishes nights and on weekends at the Psi Upsilon fraternity house, which I had pledged to and then joined after submitting to a month-long exercise in hazing.

It became clear quite early that I was not prepared to cope with the intellectual demands of the school or with a newfound freedom from parental supervision. While I had been an honors student in high school, I found that many of my new peers had had the benefit of a preparatory school education and simply were more advanced academically. Moreover, the Psi U fraternity, an early version of "Animal House" where most of the football and basketball players congregated, hardly constituted a study-friendly environment.

During the first few weeks, there were many challenges on campus, one being my assigned dormitory—an arena for the primal male quest for territorial domination and leadership. I quickly found myself in an unavoidable confrontation with a tackle on the football team. He was apple-cheeked and stocky, with shoulders wide as the wingspan of a B-1 bomber. Though he wore a perpetual grin, he never conveyed a sense of mirth. His eyes, filled with dancing light, said, "Challenge me, and you will feel pain." And it was clear to all that he had decided that he was to be the imperial power of Winthrop Hall.

One of his favorite tactics was to throw one of his powerful shoulders into your ribs as you tried to slip past him in the corridor. In one of his more frivolous moments, he would, while stripped down in his shorts, adopt a three-point stance and dare anyone within shouting distance to get by him. This was a challenge that I foolishly failed to resist. It was the equivalent of a doe bucking heads with a buffalo.

Word spread quickly throughout the dorm's four floors. Bets were laid, and the odds were very long. I tried to bolster my confidence and that of my roommates who, out of loyalty, had wagered on me with some sharp-tongued bluster: "Your mouth is almost as big as your ass. You've been stuffing lasagna in your butt so long, you look like a sumo reject."

I quickly discovered that it was not wise to provoke a young man who outweighed me by at least fifty pounds with this kind of verbal abuse. He charged and battered me back, prompting the betting spectators to shout victoriously. Using his forearms for leverage, he alternatively drove them into my chest and then lifted them up sharply, nearly separating my head from my neck.

I had never desired to assert myself over others, to either rule or ruin them. But there is in me a pride, and more than a touch of self-righteousness, that refuses to accept anyone else's need to dominate. Being another man's victim or serf is not a station that I was willing to accept. But pride carries its price. What began as a display of blustering, infantile machismo quickly turned to something more serious.

Knowing that I could not hope to push Sumo backwards, I used enough resistance to entice him to exert maximum force. Then, using a tactic that would have made the Chinese philosopher and author of the *Art of War,* Sun Tzu, proud, I stepped quickly to the side and pushed Sumo's head down. He went sprawling down on his knees to the delight of my supporters, whose number had suddenly swelled.

The joy of the moment was just that, a moment. Enraged at his awkward display of raw power, Sumo caught me with enough force with his shoulder to reinjure the collarbone that I had broken six months earlier. We rolled around on the floor, screaming obscenities at each other until the dorm proctor finally raced in to break up the fight, rescuing me from further injury. But in that momentary confrontation, the myth had taken root that Sumo had met his match.

The college expected its students to work hard to meet its high academic standards. Most of the students did so, but, in turn, they expected the college administrators to look upon their weekend activities with the benign forbearance of an overly pliant parent. At times, the college found it a difficult bargain to keep.

What might begin as a bit of innocent frivolity could quickly degenerate into action akin to anarchy. During prefootball rallies, it was customary to light a bonfire behind the school library. The night before the Homecoming game, someone decided that it might be exciting to extend a torchlight parade beyond the campus boundaries—in fact, right into the heart of Brunswick's business district. Soon, a phalanx of students, armed with burning torches, descended upon the town. The local police lowered the railroad crossing gates just below the crest of the hill on Maine Street. The students responded by chaining the gates closed, thereby tying up vehicular traffic for several hours. Protests were lodged, but no arrests were made. The antics of the privileged, treated as "boys will be boys" adolescent mischief, would have been considered far more dangerous or sinister if they had been carried out by the poor or working class.

While most students did not abuse their privileged status, there were others who assumed an arrogant contempt toward those they considered intellectually or socially inferior.

During another weekend celebration, my fraternity house, in violation of the college's rules, arranged to have a band play at the house on a Sunday afternoon. I had volunteered to secure the band, a rock 'n' roll group that played at a rough-and-tumble bar in Bangor called the Silver Dollar Cafe. Curtis Johnson, the lead guitarist and vocalist, arrived at the fraternity house with my high school friend Robert "Ziggy" Zoidis in the front seat of his big red Cadillac convertible.

Ziggy had helped persuade Curtis to bring his band to Bowdoin for the party and decided he would like to enjoy this feature of college life as well. In the past, Ziggy had made his presence known through a combination of flashy clothes and hip talk. He had recently returned from the Navy and a side stint with a singing group. The group, who originally called themselves "The Viceroys," had switched to "Brother Z and The Decades." Ziggy was tall and dark, and wore his hair in a momentous "duck's tail" that made Elvis Presley's look like a crew cut. He had inimitably stylish dance steps and spoke a language that was as foreign as that of the Zulus. Ziggy's nickname came from his childhood tendency to dart around in zigzag fashion. Needless to say, he had not outgrown his name or habit by the time he arrived at the Bowdoin campus. On the day of the party, Ziggy's unconventional look and language provoked a small riot.

The problem started when Ziggy encountered a conservative stalwart who held a dim view of Ziggy's presence. Ziggy was listening intently to Curtis Johnson and the band, and was eager to express how much he liked the music. Next to him was a tall Psi U alumnus who seemed to be appreciative of the band as well.

"Pretty good music," Ziggy said. "Do you dig rock 'n' roll, man?"

The alumnus looked at Ziggy as if he were a foul substance and said, "No, I don't *dig* it, I enjoy it." A few more crass words followed, and Ziggy found himself being told to find the door.

A bit stung, Ziggy came over and found me. "Some cat's screaming on my sky," Ziggy complained. Translation: Somebody was giving him a hard time. He told me what had happened, that the alum had looked at him and demanded an explanation. "Who in the world ever let you in this place?"

"Did you tell him I invited you?" I asked Ziggy.

"Yeah, man. He just told me to get the hell out."

I was furious. "Where is this guy?" I asked.

"He's a big cat, man," Ziggy answered. "A big cat."

"I don't care how big he is. Point him out to me."

Ziggy led me through the party, which was in high gear. The specialty drink that day was a milk punch full of rum and ice cream. We wound our way around the semi-inebriated mass of fraternity brothers and alumni until we found the man who'd been so insulting to Ziggy.

The alum was six-foot-two, a former captain of the swim team who'd blossomed out to about 220 pounds. Physically, I was no match for him. I decided not to engage in any verbal chest pounding. I would just walk up, with Hancock Street rules in play, and punch him.

"Step out of the way," I told Ziggy. "I'll take care of this."

Ziggy must have misunderstood me because, before I could do anything, he had approached his antagonist and pointed me out. "This is my friend Billy Cohen," Ziggy said. "He's the one who invited me."

I knew that I had found trouble. Fear gave way to self-righteousness, which was now standing at rigid attention. Ziggy's hairstyle, clothes, and language had clearly excluded him from the rank of student. But what troubled the alumnus was Ziggy's "lower-class" status—and, by implication, that of the man who was taste-less enough to have invited him.

While I had never considered myself to be either downtrodden or an underdog, I nonetheless identified with those who had been looked down upon, locked out of the circles of acceptability by those who considered themselves more worthy because of their bloodlines or bank accounts.

The alumnus glared at me as if I were some long-jawed piece of white trash who had defiled the honor of the college by slipping through the cracks in the admissions system. My presence was quite offensive enough, but exactly what was this rockabilly band doing here? And this loathsome creature called Ziggy? Let one in and there goes the neighborhood. . . . It was all there in his eyes—the disdain, the contempt.

"Cohen," he said pugnaciously, "it's very discouraging to see what has happened to the college when I see an asshole like you here."

Every voice of prudence counseled me to walk away from this confrontation. In the momentary hiatus between thought and action, between the idea and the consequence, I could hear my father's wise advice: "Billy, you've got to kill 'em with kindness." But his was never a constant voice of passivity. Without acknowledging the contradiction, he would then suggest that if I was ever trapped and had no option but to fight, then I should emulate the style of his hero, Joe Louis.

"Remember, keep your chin tucked to your chest. No long, looping punches. No wild swings. They're telegraph punches. Too easy to avoid and counter. Short, straight punches. The left hook is the deadliest. You can set it up with a right jab."

I chose to disregard his preferred path to peace and decided on the Joe Louis approach to supremacy. I turned as if to walk away from my tormentor, spun around while screaming, "Asshole? *You're* the asshole!" and unleashed the biggest roundhouse right of my life. My fist landed solidly on the bridge of his nose, slicing it open. He went down on his knees, whether from the force of the blow or astonishment at seeing his blood flowing profusely.

I had no intention of letting him up and proceeded to pound him while he was still dazed. His date rushed to his rescue. Ziggy tried to pry her from off my back.

It may have been the music, the milk punch, or just the sight of blood that triggered something of a free-for-all. Suddenly, fists and objects were flying everywhere. The band played on without missing a beat. The drummer began to scream with delight. "Goddamn, Curtis," he kept shouting, "this is just like the Silver Dollar Cafe!"

The melee lasted only a matter of minutes, but it was long enough for someone to have reported the incident to the college administration. The next morning, I was summoned to meet with the dean of students. Dean Nathaniel Kendrick made it clear that he did not consider my conduct exemplary. Not only had I brought a band into a fraternity house on a Sunday, but I'd also been the catalyst for a brawl. Dean Kendrick suggested I was a prime candidate for dismissal from the college.

There wasn't really very much I could offer in my own defense. I did not even bother with the customary apologies.

I admitted that I hadn't been exactly Gandhiesque in my actions, but I suggested that the college didn't have much to be proud of either if it was busy churning out snobs like the ex–swim team captain.

Even though I managed to avoid a suspension, Dean Kendrick, who had a habit of tugging on his right ear while lecturing a student, left me with much to ponder. Could I really justify my quick resort to violence? Had I placed loyalty to a friend above decorum and a sense of civility? Why hadn't I tried to determine the nature of my friend's comportment before confronting the alumnus? Better yet, why hadn't I simply ignored the verbal insult?

It was clear that my high school diploma did not mark a transition to emotional maturity. It was also clear that I was not up to Bowdoin College's standards. "Son," the Dean intoned, tugging his ear again, while averting his eyes, "you're going to have to work a lot harder if you hope to stay in this college."

It was not an idle warning. I knew that I was in over my head almost from my first week of classes. It was obvious that many of the young men had come to Bowdoin from privileged homes. More than a few had had the benefit of a college preparatory education at schools such as Choate, Andover, Exeter, and Deerfield. The quality of their clothes, their speech and mannerisms, their confidence in the classroom and in social settings all set them apart. True, there were also a number of students who came from families whose means were far more modest than my own, but it was clear to me that I would have a hard time competing with those considered to be Bowdoin's finest.

By the end of December I was beginning to doubt that I could continue at Bowdoin. It was not due to a lack of effort on my part. Rather, it was a case of the spirit being willing, but the mind being weak. Every evening I would study for several hours and then listen to music until midnight or one in the morning. I would mix the soul of Nancy Wilson and Dakota Staton with the jazz of Earl Bostic, Gerry Mulligan, Dave Brubeck, Thelonious Monk, and the Modern Jazz Quartet.

After my roommates retired, I would undertake to study again, sometimes paging through the dictionary until five in the morning in an attempt to improve my thin vocabulary. I did not want them to see how ill prepared I was for college and how desperate I was to succeed. But the sheer volume of hours devoted to reading did not translate into comprehension.

Academically, I was in a free fall, my grades plummeting in virtually every course. Even history, my best subject in high school, was proving to be a disaster. I had a vertical appreciation of the flow of time, but lacked any horizontal vision. I could recite the long list of events in England from the days of William the Conqueror, but I could not comprehend the interrelationship among the events, say, of 1415–16 A.D. when John Huss and Jerome of Prague were burned at Constance for heresy, while Britain's Henry V defeated the French at the battle of Agincourt and Spain's Alfonso V became King of Aragon and Sicily.

Professor, could you repeat that once more and just a little bit slower?

What I lacked in history, I thought I might make up in English. But I struggled through the thicket of Chaucer's *Canterbury Tales* and flailed blindly at Milton's *Paradise Lost*. And when Professor Leroy Greason (who later became president of the college) reminded me that it was mandatory for his students to compose a sonnet, I thought he didst demand too much!

Real athletes didn't eat granola, and surely, they could not be expected to write poetry!

Nothing seemed to be working as I had hoped. Even basketball did little to redeem my spirits. As a team, we were usually over-matched, and the sport itself, unlike football or hockey, generated little enthusiasm among the student body. I enjoyed a successful scoring season, moving one sportswriter to proclaim grandiosely that I could "score forty points on a good night and twenty on a bad one." The accolade, other than allowing me a moment of narcissis-tic pleasure, only prompted every team we played during the re-mainder of my college years to make me eat that writer's words.

While basketball provided the principal diversion from my studies, I also managed to spend a considerable amount of time in the pool room that was located in the basement of the student lounge. Ever since my father had taken me to watch him play in the local pool halls he frequented, I had remained fascinated with the game. There I discovered a slightly built black man named Ed who wore a Frank Sinatra–style felt hat and possessed a voice as high-pitched as Smokey Robinson's. Ed was an absolute magician with a pool cue in his hand. He could put more "English" on a ball than most of us could on a midterm exam. With a deft stroke, he could make the ball drag, hang, and carom off three cushions before en-gaging in "kissing" combinations that left everyone watching slack-jawed with awe.

Here was a man my father just had to meet.

I was unaware that racism existed in Maine. In fact the word "racism" was not to be found in my limited vocabulary. I knew of discrimination from personal experience, but I had no understand-ing of the degrees of evil it reflected or just how insidious had been its application to blacks in America. I assumed that discrimination was an unpleasant but unalterable fact of the human condition.

On Hancock Street there was one black family (called Negroes at the time) among the residents. The family's oldest son was ac-cepted as "one of the gang," but I noticed that whenever some cri-sis surfaced, or some external enemy could not be located, the gang always seemed to turn on him first.

Then too, when we were not playing touch football or spoil-ing for fights, we would, over their protests, inject ourselves into our sisters' recreation of skipping rope on the sidewalks in front of our houses. And, yes, inevitably we would, between the double ropes, catch our breath and shout:

Eeney meeny miny moe
Catch a "N—" by the toe,
If he hollers, let him go,
Eeney meeny miny moe.

We intended no malice, no harm. After all, we had heard Italians called "Wops" and "Ginnies"; Jews, "Kikes" and "Hebes"; and Irish, "Harps" and "Micks." But not one of us bothered to ask why it was the "N—" we always wanted to catch by the toe, not the "kikes" or the "wops."

While one might expect ethnic people, many of whom had to fight their own battles against prejudice and discrimination, to be more sympathetic toward the most readily identifiable minority in our society, no white person then—perhaps even now—could ever appreciate the venom, the savage malevolence that lay behind that epithet.

Throughout my school years, I saw or knew only a handful of black students. Invariably, they were outstanding athletes or super-achievers in the classroom. I never witnessed any overt acts of discrimination against them, but there was always a silent understanding within the community that they should "keep to their kind" and "know their place." That was French for "not in my neighborhood."

It was one thing for us to live in relative harmony with a community's "own," but fear and suspicion was directed toward blacks from "away." These were the servicemen who were stationed at Dow Air Force Base, the Strategic Air Command facility that infused the local economy with millions of dollars each year. The men always seemed to travel in groups of five or six. They were tall and usually dressed in dark clothes when out of uniform. Some of them moved with an effortless, fluid grace, while others walked with an exaggerated gait that looked as if they might be dragging an artificial leg. And always, to a man, they wore sunglasses, even at night.

"What are they trying to hide?" my father would always ask me upon seeing them.

I had no answer. Today, I would tell him, "Their rage, Dad, their rage."

I felt a curious, inexplicable bond with these mysterious men. Perhaps it was because they had welcomed me into the circle of their friendship.

During my high school years, I frequently drove out to Dow's gymnasium to watch them play basketball. Inevitably, they would invite me to join one of their teams. I would be the only white boy on the court. I thought nothing at the time of this exclusivity until years later when Walter Fauntroy, the District of Columbia's nonvoting delegate to the United States Congress, invited me to join the Black Congressional Caucus for an exhibition game at Howard University, an historically black institution.

"Your 'membership' in the Caucus," Walter laughed, "has to be revoked at the conclusion of the game."

When I took the court that evening, I experienced jeers and catcalls of disapproval based on nothing more than the color of my skin. I gained that night just a small appreciation of the pain that black people have had to endure—and continue to endure—in a white-dominated society.

No thoughts of racism were on my mind as I stood with my schoolmate, Ed, along Route 1 with our thumbs extended.

I had hitchhiked home on many previous occasions and had always managed to secure a ride within ten or fifteen minutes. On that day, more than two hours passed and there were no takers. Ed knew what had to be done. Over my objection, he walked off the highway's shoulder and hid behind a clump of bushes. It worked, at least temporarily.

Once a car stopped and I entered the passenger's door, I would tell the driver that my friend was responding to nature's call and he would be with us momentarily. Did he mind? No, was the answer, of course not.

That is, not until the driver would see Ed.

Suddenly a phony apology would be offered.

"Sorry, I can't take you to Augusta. Only going to Bowdoinham" (which was on the way).

Or, "Did you say you were going to Bangor? Sorry, I'm heading for Topsham and then Lewiston. Sorry."

It may have been my imagination, or just a matter of coincidence, but I found it strange, indeed, that it took us almost three hours to travel just thirty miles that day.

During the long, exasperating wait, Ed had dipped into his duffel bag, where he kept a bottle of Jack Daniel's bourbon. It all started out as "just a little taste." Before long, the taste turned into a giant thirst. I had indulged more moderately than had Ed in the slaking of that thirst, so that when we finally reached the bridge that extended across the Kennebec River in Augusta, Ed was in no shape to walk. I had to carry him, fireman's style, over my shoulders, along with both of our bags.

By the time I traveled across the bridge, I was practically on my knees with fatigue. I had no choice but to pick Ed up and carry him up into the surrounding hillside out of view of the general public. We rested in the tall grass with the afternoon sun beating down on us for not more than twenty minutes when I heard the sound of sirens approaching. The police. They were coming for us!

Some neighbors had seen two strange men hiding out in the hillside. They appeared to be running from something. Maybe they were fugitives. Maybe dangerous.

"Come out of there with your hands up!" a voice demanded.

This was bizarre.

"Officer, don't shoot. We're Bowdoin students!"

I'm not exactly sure what prompted me to think that this declaration would grant me immunity from being shot. I gave consideration to saying, "We're your children," but under the circumstances I didn't think that they would find it amusing. I emerged from the underbrush with my hands over my head like some prisoner of war I used to imaginatively capture in my childhood.

"Where's the other one? There's two of you. Where is he?" A different voice demanded.

The reference to Bowdoin did stop bullets from flying but not intolerance. My budding powers of persuasion were only half successful. I was free to go but my companion had to be locked up.

"He only needs a few hours of rest," I argued. "He's coming to visit my family. He's—"

"No, s'r. He's going to jail."

"Well, you'll have to take me, too."

So I went with my friend and sat just outside a holding cell. I thought that the gendarmes would relent. They didn't.

About nine o'clock that evening, I finally screwed up my courage and called my mother to explain that I needed her to drive to Augusta to extract us from our predicament. Without hesitation or complaint, she did exactly that. With my sister Marlene as her companion and co-conspirator, she pulled us from the grip of the lawmen and had us home before midnight—just before my father trudged off to work.

My father never did get to meet Ed or witness his wizardry at the pool tables. I thought we might have too much explaining to do the next morning.

Whatever innocence I possessed about the absence of racial discrimination in Maine had been shattered by our hitchhiking experience. I decided that we should return quickly and safely back to Bowdoin the old-fashioned way—by bus.

We both rode in the front seats of the bus and not those in the rear.

My grades, already on the decline, would take a precipitous drop when I ventured to Fort Lauderdale, Florida, during the annual spring recess with a carload of compatriots.

After a few days of overexposure to the sun and Fort Lauderdale's nightlife, we were ready for a change. One afternoon in the Elbow Room someone suggested, "Hey, what the hell. Let's go to Havana." A "why not?" response was sounded, and the decision was made without a dissenting vote.

We drove to Key West from the Elbow Room and parked the car, and each of us bought a ten-dollar plane ticket to Havana, where the ink had yet to dry on the pamphlets and banners of the new communist regime. The attraction that the island nation held for us had nothing to do with the freshly won revolution. Rather, we were counting on Havana to live up to its reputation as a wide-open town.

I don't think any of us were prepared for the kind of adventure that we had talked about. What we found upon our arrival was what we should have expected, a small country in the midst of transition from old to new.

We were excited about Havana, but none of us stopped looking over our shoulders. After all, Castro had brought a country to its knees with a peasant revolution fostered in the hills. No one had expected him to succeed. Now that he was in, what form would the change take in Havana? Should we worry that the casinos might be razed and freshman students from small private colleges hung from hacienda bell towers in a show of fervent excitement for the new government?

After realizing that the talk of change still was more talk than reality, we relaxed, and our initial insecurity turned to bravado. There was strength in numbers after all. We were five college guys from Bowdoin College, and we were going to have a hell of a time.

Wine, song, and, yes, beautiful women. Everywhere. Fidel Castro had not yet snuffed out Havana's nightlife.

After three or four days, the adventure began to wear thin for everyone but me. I waved good-bye to my friends as they left the hotel and headed for the airport. I promised to see them back at Bowdoin soon.

I spent the next few days at La Concha Beach getting dark, loving the warm feel of the sun. Every now and then I worked my way around the liquor shops, pretending I was interested in their wares. The owners offered samples to encourage one's purchase, and I enjoyed letting them prove to me how distinct the taste of apple liqueur was from that of apricot. We were all aware of the cat-and-

Happy days on Hancock Street, Bangor, Me., (1943). *Courtesy of University of Maine*

My mother, Clara (1948).

My father, Reuben (1927).

Sister Marlene, me, and brother, Bob, Easter Sunday (1948).

Janet's mother, Louise, with sister, Myrna (left) and Janet, Easter Sunday (1943).

Janet and Mother in Chicago (1966).

Janet's father, Sewell Bridges (1938).

Janet's uncle, George Gillenwaters (1941).

My father, Reuben (holding trophy), captain of his 8th grade basketball team.

Scoring against Stearns High School (1959). *Courtesy of* The Bangor Daily News

Slipping past a defender as co-captain of Bowdoin College Basketball Team (1960). *Courtesy of* The Portland Press Herald

Shooting hoops at Kosovo refugee camp after defeat of Slobodan Milosovec (1999). *Courtesy of Dept. of Defense*

Janet and her friend, April, graduating Crispus Attucks High School, June, 1959. *Courtesy of April Brown Searcy*

Janet's brother, James, and his wife, Debbie, on their wedding day.

Janet with her mother and brother in Rome (1981).

Janet meeting my mother and father for the first time in 1992.

My mother and father in front of the Bangor Rye Bread Company.

My sons, Kevin (left), me, and Chris in Boston at Faneuil Hall (1981).

Me serving as a constable in Old Lyme, Conn., (1962).

Janet modeling for the Boston Ballet Charity Ball (1978).

Janet playing polo with her pony, Delta.

Taking a break in Houlton, Me., during my 600-mile walk across the state (1972). *Courtesy of* The Bangor Daily News

Celebrating the 60th anniversary of my father's bakery. My brother, Bob (left), me, Dad, Mom, and sister, Marlene (1989).

Janet celebrating her mother's 50th birthday (1973). Her sister, Myrna (left), Janet, Uncle George, Janet's mother, and brother, James.

mouse game that was being played. As an American, I was presumed to have money and to be likely to spend it if I was properly lubricated. I, in turn, let a few store owners try to convince me to buy a few bottles of liqueur for later consumption.

In the nightspots I spoke with women who were angry about Fidel Castro and how he wanted to shut down their love-for-money activities. "How are we going to survive?" they complained.

As it turned out, I, too, was on the verge of being left to my own devices. After all, I was not some guy with Roman numerals behind my name with a trust fund in the Chase Manhattan Bank. None of this, of course, seemed very pressing in the feel-good environment of Havana. What did it matter that my cash was dwindling? There was sun on the beach, and that carried no price tag.

I finally realized that I might be in for trouble when my explanation to the hotel manager that I'd run out of money did not go over in the endearing manner that I intended. "Perhaps the next time you're in Havana you'll be able to stay longer," was the reply I heard as I was shown to the door.

I didn't have to worry about carting around much in the way of belongings. Besides jeans, a blue shirt, and a trenchcoat, the only clothes I had at my disposal were a couple of changes of underwear that I carried with me in a drawstring bag. As souvenirs I had a cheap conga drum for myself and two sacks of liqueur for my mother when, or I might say if, I saw her again. The drum and liqueur fit into the drawstring bag. Voila! There I was, the measure of a man.

Unfortunately in the days and nights that followed I was the measure of an American man. Correction: a penniless American man. This was the way I described myself, at least to the disbelieving Cubans who couldn't help but notice me. Americans were earmarked for attention because we presumably had money. A poor American in Havana? Protests notwithstanding, I was peppered constantly with offers. I heard, "Hey mister, my sister?" every time I ventured close to the street. I leaned up against stucco walls for a lower profile, but after I had dishwater dumped on me from a terrace overhead, I revised my strategy. Thinking I'd be safer in the light, I slept under street-lamps, my head propped up on my arm to make myself seem less vulnerable, as if I were simply dozing and not fully asleep.

In the nightclubs, I occasionally confronted the newly empowered members of Castro's ragtag militia. If it wasn't someone trying to talk me into supporting the revolution, it was a thirteen-year-old boy walking in and slamming his machine gun down on the bar. I quickly realized guns, alcohol, adolescence, and politics did not balance out in my favor. It was time for me to leave.

Luckily, I ran across an American who was willing to loan me ten dollars for the flight back to Key West. From there I hitchhiked to Miami Beach, where I thought I might be able to find some relatives. I had never even met the Weisners, my great uncle and great aunt. All I knew was that their bakery was located on lower Collins Avenue, near the beach.

I found a small bakery called The Paramount, and I knew that it was the right place. I stood outside the bakery and practically broke down crying. I hadn't eaten in three days. The smell of fresh bread almost brought me to my knees.

Apparently the odd appearance of a grimy young man in a trenchcoat and jeans attracted some attention from those inside. When I walked in, a gruff older man had his eye on me, wanting to know what I had been up to, standing outside his store.

"I'm Billy Cohen," I said. "My father is Reuben."

My Uncle Louis looked at me in a rather dismissive fashion. "Well, that's good," he said. "Say hello to your father when you see him." Then he excused himself and turned his attention back to his ovens.

I'm not sure what I was expecting. Perhaps something along the lines of "Hey, come on and meet the family."

Outside the store, I slung my drawstring bag over my shoulder and was about to wander off in despair when the door opened and my Aunt Julia rushed over to me. She asked if I wouldn't stop and come back inside. I was led to the back room and offered food to eat. "So you're Ruby's boy," she smiled.

Thank God for that woman's gracious heart. Given the awkward circumstances, I tried to act polite and not devour the food she gave me. Observing my transient appearance, she asked if I had a place to stay. "Not really," I answered. Without a moment's hesitation she said, "Well then you must stay with us."

My unannounced arrival there was obviously more than an impromptu vacation, and so I gave her a sanitized version of what I had experienced. I explained that I had been attending school but that I was unhappy there. "I was captain of the basketball team," I told my relatives over dinner, "but other than that I don't have much to go back for."

"Would you like to try the University of Miami instead?" Aunt Julia asked.

I loved the idea. This was a new direction for the future, and I seized upon it with almost as much hunger as I had for the meals she provided. I would simply leave Bowdoin and continue my studies in Florida.

Less than a week passed before I reconsidered the thought of taking up residence in the Sunshine State. Dean Kendrick had managed to send me a message that "I was being missed up there."

Rather than ask for a loan from Aunt Julia to return to Bowdoin, I elected to hitch a ride back home. I was no doubt suffering from sunstroke at the time because I thought that the fastest and least traveled route was straight through the center of the state. A big mistake. I needed to get at least to Georgia, and the man who stopped to pick me up assured me, "Yep, I'm goin' straight on through."

We started the journey in the late afternoon so that by nightfall we were still in the Everglades. The route dwindled from highways to a simple two-lane road. The night was pitch black except for our headlights. We passed cars so infrequently that we may as well have been lost on some unmarked road. It was a dismal drive, a journey through a wasteland. "If I'd known I had to go through the Everglades I would have gone up the coast instead," I chided myself.

Suddenly the man who had offered me the "straight on through" ride stopped his car. There were no engine problems. We weren't lost either, because the man didn't ask for the map. "This is where I'm turning off," he said.

I looked up in disbelief. Turning off? There wasn't even a cross-road in sight.

"Hey, what you told me was—" I started to protest. "Get out of the car," the man said.

Realizing now that this man was crazy, I came to the conclusion that I was probably safer outside of the car than in it. I grabbed my drawstring bag and got out.

Apparently, he somehow derived pleasure in abandoning me in no man's land. So there I was.

I didn't see more than five or six other vehicles all night long. Every time a car approached, I tried to flag it down. But in the glare of the headlights I obviously didn't look like Dobie Gillis. What the hell was someone doing out in the middle of the swamps? Some guy in a trenchcoat with no car? I must have looked like a nightmare.

The problem with being stranded in the Everglades was that the place was profoundly unsuited for pedestrians. Graded steeply, the road was really nothing more than a hot-topped bridge. Ten or so feet down on either side was a swamp that I assumed was full of snakes, alligators, and all kinds of creatures from the lagoon. To step near the shoulder was to risk plunging down to an entanglement of pepperwort and sawgrass. One might thrash around in the vegetation a bit, but it was a certain, watery grave. Or so my mind said.

My options were limited further by the sheer darkness that enveloped me. I found myself in a moonless night under a canopy of marshland trees. It was so dark I couldn't even see the white stripes of the centerline. In fact, I couldn't see my hand when I held it up *six* inches from my face.

My options came down to just one. I had to stand in one spot the entire night. From ten until dawn, for seven long hours I stood in place. It was a night of terror and prayer. I lost count of how many times I said, "Please, God." I discovered the meaning of the saying "There has never been an atheist in a foxhole." Each car that passed seemed like another sure sign that I would not survive the night.

To pass the time I pulled out my little conga drum and tapped out a pleasant rhythm. Then in a sudden panic I put my souvenir down. What was I doing, drumming away in the middle of the jungle? I may as well have been ringing a dinner bell for all the alligators and snakes. They were probably lining up at marsh central, sorting out which creature would get first dibs on me.

The slightest sound sent a tremor through my body. If leaves rustled, twigs snapped, or water lapped, I reacted as though I'd heard a death knell.

Can the creatures smell me? I wondered. *Can they smell fear?* I thought I'd been through the worst of things in Havana: thinking I was going to be murdered by a gringo-hating cabbie, sleeping on sidewalks overnight with the water from dirty dishes still drying behind my ears. Now here I was standing immobile, waiting for daylight, convinced utterly that there was nothing quite as precious as life at Bowdoin College.

Finally, at dawn a family traveling north saw my desperation and gave me a ride to Georgia. A few rides later I was back at Bowdoin.

I was treated as the prodigal son upon my return. The fraternity gave me a hero's welcome and threw a small party for me. The dean's office gave me a slightly less favorable reception. I was sure I would be expelled from school but, mercifully, I received only an extension of my probation.

Nathan Dane II, my Latin professor, decided to intervene and help pull me out of the quicksand that was now chest high around me. Nate was a fan of our luckless basketball team. So naturally he had followed the progress of the new crop of freshman players. I had impressed him both in the classroom and with the skills I displayed on the court. He took me under his protective wing. "You have a great opportunity at Bowdoin," he reminded me. "Besides that the basketball team needs you."

With Nate's encouragement I started to gain the confidence that I obviously had been lacking. While my grades did not reflect a student of marked ability, I managed to pass all of my courses. For the first time, I felt I just might survive there.

The academic free fall during my freshman year was not quite as traumatic as the physical one I nearly experienced in the summer of 1959. I had secured a job with the Hughes Brothers Construction Company, helping to lay pipes for a new sewer system in Bangor. The trench for the sewer line was supported by a series of pilings that had to be set with the use of a crane. Attached to the end of the crane's boom was a metal slat on which I would sit and do my job while suspended sixty feet above the ground. Once the steel pilings were positioned vertically, I had to unhook by hand the bolts that passed through the pilings. When I had finished this rather menial task, I was lifted aside while a giant hammer pounded the pilings into the soft earth below.

Convinced of my immortality, I gave no thought to the danger involved—until my third week on the job, when I slipped off the slat and found myself dangling by one arm sixty feet above the ground. When I looked down, I saw nothing but steel girders waiting to impale me. I twisted about frantically, catching only a glimpse of the crane cab, which to my astonishment was vacant. The men below were all on a coffee break! My screams eventually attracted someone's attention on the ground. A man rushed into the cab and lowered the crane's boom. I was completely shaken by the experience and decided that the minimum wage was not worth the maximum risk.

I resumed my sophomore year with best of intentions but quickly turned onto a paved road that headed straight for hell raising. I had the opportunity to live at the fraternity house and to select my roommates. Good judgment yielded to good times when I agreed to room with a dangerous duo known as "Tommy and Eyeball."

Tommy, a tall slender man, was of Germanic descent and had a characteristic proclivity for order and efficiency. Eyeball, by contrast, was short and slightly stocky, and he was an advertisement for entropy. Whereas Tommy would always fold his clothing neatly in drawers or hang his slacks with just the right crease in closets, Eyeball would toss his clothes into a heap in the center of his room and then pull out a sweater here and a pair of corduroys there with little regard as to whether they matched or carried last week's body odor. It seemed as if Eyeball had taken it as his mission in life to torment Tommy, and Tommy, in turn, understood that he had been sentenced to endure the pain with a display of humor and grace. Prometheus, cast out from the heavens for giving the gift of fire to mankind and then lashed to a rock while a bird of prey picked at his liver, could not have suffered more.

Eyeball was the co-captain of the basketball team, and while he stood only five-foot-seven, he could launch a jump shot from twenty feet or more with deadly accuracy. His nickname had been derived not from his peripheral visual acuity on the court, but rather from his uncanny ability to spot the correct answer on a fellow student's exam from ten paces. Eyeball's antics included cutting up one of Tommy's newest suits in order to fashion himself a pair of beachwear cutoffs; regurgitating a bad meal on the sheets of his friend's bed; and, as a hoax, saying he had just totaled Tommy's mother's car during a severe snowstorm and that the police were demanding a statement from Tommy, as was the dean because Tommy was on scholarship and was not allowed to have a car on campus. There were screams of anguish, threats of bodily harm—and ultimate forgiveness.

I never understood their relationship or why I wanted to share three rooms on the top floor of the Psi Upsilon house with them. Particularly after the time I returned to find that Eyeball, seized with an artistic impulse, had decided to paint all the walls in the suite completely black. Oh, he did manage to break the monotony of the darkness with flecks of orange paint that he had sent flying toward the walls with a flick of his brush. And to ensure that our freshly decorated living accommodations had just the right bohemian touch, he appropriated the two speakers from my stereo system and hung them from the ceiling in a fishing net that no doubt once had belonged to a lobsterman.

When Dean Kendrick, a Psi U alumnus who was more than familiar with the temptations and bacchanalian traditions of the fraternity, discovered my selection of living accommodations and associates, he decided to intervene. The line that separates liberty from license is readily identifiable to mature and responsible adults. It was clear to him that I did not possess such a discerning eye. My tenancy at the fraternity house would expire at the end of the semester, and the dean would personally select my new living arrangements.

When first introduced to my new roommate, I thought that my punishment had exceeded my crimes. Charlie Wing lived on the third floor of an apartment house just yards away from the dean's residence. The room itself was a model of asceticism—a bed, a makeshift bookcase consisting of cinder blocks and pine planks, and a small table covered with a red-and-white-checkered cloth. And Charlie could have passed as the son of the Dalai Lama. He sported a crew cut that had to have come at the hands of an ex-Marine. He sat on his bed, frequently in a lotus position, reading books on quantum physics and advanced calculus as if he were flipping the pages of an L. L. Bean catalogue. And he never underlined or starred a paragraph once! I was convinced that he was an extraterrestrial who was just visiting.

Embarrassed over my profligate ways, I began to adopt Charlie's disciplined study habits. My grades improved almost immediately. I felt confident enough to contribute to *The Quill*, the college's literary magazine. By the end of the year I was named to the Dean's List for academic excellence. Dean Kendrick's plan was working— or at least half of it. He had failed to realize that I might have an influence on Charlie's habits. Call it behavioral reciprocity.

It began when I noticed a small conga drum sat passively in a corner of the room. (I assumed that he used it on full-moon nights to send signals to other aliens.) After my foray to Cuba, I decided that I had something of a Latin beat in my soul and I purchased a handsome set of bongo drums, which I played with a skill comparable to an infant banging out "Chopsticks" on the piano. To my amazement, Charlie could play those drums so brilliantly that Count Basie, who brought his band to one of our homecoming weekends, invited Charlie to play in his band for the entire evening.

I couldn't believe that this little E.T. failed to see the social opportunities that his talent could open up. I persuaded him to teach me the art of playing the conga drum and then encouraged him to take our duo on a circuit of campus parties and local bars. It was a mutually beneficial deal. Charlie helped pull me up scholastically and I liberated him from a social life that was more appropriate for a Tibetan monk. But not everyone agreed that the scales of equity were in full balance.

Although there were many nights that were filled with adventure and occasional stark terror during our years of friendship, two remain vivid.

One evening, following a display of our talents on the drums at a local night spot, Charlie and I met two sisters from a neighboring city. Talk turned to quick friendship, and thoughts of amorous entanglements, we believed, were sure to follow. We made arrangements to meet again the following week at the State Hotel, a bar that generally catered to local patrons ("townies") and enlisted men and officers from the U.S. Naval Air Station in Brunswick. Both the bar's local patrons and the Navy held a decidedly negative opinion of "Bowdoin Boys."

It was our misfortune to arrive at the hotel late for what we hoped would prove to be a romantically rewarding evening, only to discover that two Navy airmen had purchased several rounds of libations for our dates before we crossed the bar's darkened threshold. As we joined our companions and suggested that *six* people at the table constituted an unwelcome crowd, there was little doubt that we were about to make an exit that was less grand than our entry.

Charlie, being the smaller contestant on our side of what quickly was evolving into a tag team match, became the focus of our rivals' attention. The two aviators were about to separate him from consciousness when Charlie's date reached into her leather bag and extracted a knife. Not a penknife or letter knife, mind you, but a razor-edged hunting knife worthy of Crocodile Dundee. Lowering it to a menacing level, she engaged in the gentle art of persuasion. "Anyone try to touch my Charlie," she screamed, "and I'll cut your balls off!" Not eager to engage in hand-to-groin combat under the circumstances, our antagonists hurled some choice epithets and beat a bitter retreat.

While initially touched by the thought that a woman just might kill to save him, Charlie was so unnerved by the sight of the gleaming blade that all intimations of a blooming romance disappeared as quickly as did the danger.

The other memorable moment began innocently enough. The town of Topsham, located just a few miles north of the college, each year hosted a country fair that drew hundreds of people from the surrounding communities. Along with the cotton candy, mechanical rides, the three-eyed man, and the snake lady, there were sure to be one or two "girlie shows." I suggested to Charlie that we might spice things up by playing the drums for one of the bump-and-grind routines. The shows, charitably speaking, were not exactly fit for family viewing. In fact, in order to protect the sensitivities of the clientele, the proprietors erected a large tarpaulin screen inside the tent in order to separate the sexes.

Charlie and I approached a stripper whose stage name was "Jamaica Ginger" with an offer to add some rhythm to her well-honed routine. It was an offer that she did not refuse.

As the crowd gathered in front of the tent, we climbed a platform facing the midway, while a honky-tonk barker attempted to lure prospective customers inside with salacious promises that that was where the "real show" would begin. As Ginger began to bump her way across the stage to our drumbeat, Charlie, his eyes closed and a big cherubic smile on his face, sat cross-legged in a chair, rolling his thumbs and fingers on the drumheads. I looked out into the gathering crowd and realized that we were becoming quite an attraction. I noticed that out on the periphery of the circle of people who were gathering at the foot of the stage were several Bowdoin professors and their wives. They stared up at us from the midway in disbelief. I knew that they were lamenting this sad turn of events, wondering what in the world was happening to Bowdoin's number one student.

When the show was finally over, we decided that we, if not Jamaica Ginger, were going to continue into the night. We returned to the campus and headed for the Walker Art Museum. Facing the quad on either side of the museum like bookends were a pair of stone statues that we proceeded to mount. From our perch on top of two grand lions, we started to play our drums again. Some of our fraternity brothers were roused by our performance and brought torches out to the quad. It was a transcendent, communal event that lasted for hours, almost until dawn. Of course reality came screaming in the next day.

It screamed a bit louder for Charlie.

This was the day when all James Bowdoin Scholars were to be recognized for their academic achievements. Charlie's mother had driven up from Baltimore to witness the honor that, unfortunately, was not bestowed upon her son that day. Charlie, exhausted from the previous night's activities, had overslept, missing the event entirely.

A guest lecturer, the president of Oberlin College, singled out Charlie (and me indirectly) in his speech that morning by stressing the importance of maintaining ties to the local community. "I understand that at least two of your fellow students maintained very strong ties last night," he noted sardonically.

It was only a momentary embarrassment. There simply were no external forces that could keep Charlie from graduating at the top of his class two years later. He would go on to earn his doctorate in oceanography at MIT in two years. His friendship—and his example of academic excellence—had encouraged me to become a more serious-minded student. I studied philosophy and poetry, majored in Latin, and was awarded a research fellowship to translate an obscure elegiac poet into English.

There were other lessons in store for me at Bowdoin. Because I was the high-scoring co-captain of the basketball team, I assumed that my professors would be inclined, if not eager, to give me special treatment on occasion. My English professor, Leroy Greason, quickly dispelled this delusion. He had assigned each member of the class to compose a sonnet. My only exposure to poetry was reading portions of *Hamlet* during a diction class in high school. Understanding poetry was difficult; writing poetry would be impossible. Besides, I had little time to devote to an enterprise I thought was reserved for effete intellectuals.

I approached Professor Greason with the sob story that the basketball team's travel schedule precluded me from undertaking the assignment.

His response was direct and delivered, I thought, with a certain theatrical panache: "Your athletic gifts and schedule are of little importance to me, Mr. Cohen. You will compose a sonnet or you will fail the course."

I couldn't conceive how a failure to complete one assignment would result in a failure of the entire course, but I was unwilling to take the chance. I struggled for days trying to string words together to form a fourteen-line lyrical message. After suffering multiple high-anxiety attacks, I turned in my handiwork.

Can Season Be the Reason?
Winter freezes summer blood to ice,
And chills the passions that await the spring;
The lover suffers seasoned sacrifice,
At Altars bleak with crystal covering.

What heart can hold a love in winter's time,
When even Nature slacks her passioned pace,
When minor creatures flee the upper clime,
For warmer realms of borrowed, burrowed space?

But spring has courage to oppose the cold,
And passes on to those in love the same;
The sounds of life and future birth take hold,
Of human ears that closed at winter's name.

Yet is it fair to unimpassioned reason
To say that love depends upon a season?

William Shakespeare was under no threat.

Even as I was learning not to associate poetry as the preserve of the effete, my conduct on the basketball court did not reflect that I was evolving into a more sensitive being. Our team, to put it bluntly, was mediocre on a good night and quite horrid on a bad one. My competitive spirit had lost none of its zeal, and on more than a handful of occasions I engaged in exchanges with opposing teams that resulted in my being evicted from the game. Despite my frequent resort to fisticuffs, I was selected to be one of the five best players in the state.

When I received a call to meet with Malcolm Morrell, the athletic director, I assumed that he was going to reveal to me that I had been awarded the Paul Nixon Award for Leadership, which was normally given to the outstanding player on the team.

As I looked into Mr. Morrell's face, I knew immediately that my expectations were unwarranted. He began the conversation in a friendly and cordial manner, floating soft inanities mostly. I kept listening for the whisper of the ax. It was not long in coming.

"Son, we all know that you're the best player on the team . . ."

I knew the classic "but" was coming. I had been there years before, in Rabbi Saul Brown's classroom, as he explained why I would not be receiving the top prize.

"But what? Mr. Morrell," I interjected, not allowing him to soften the blow with any ingratiating words. "But what?"

"But the Administration has declined to award you the Nixon trophy."

I stared at the director but said nothing. Rage, my old friend, was running up my spine.

"We don't believe that your conduct on the court was in the best traditions of the college. Frankly, we thought it was unbecoming."

I was dumbstruck.

"Unbecoming? You mean because I wanted to win too badly, because I fought so hard to bring victory to the team, you're going to penalize me?"

"I'm sorry, son, we want victory, but not at all costs. We expect more from you here at Bowdoin. There's a code of conduct that is the essence of leadership."

Admittedly, I was no Boy Scout out on the court. During most of my time at Bowdoin, I usually drew a "double team" from opponents in an effort to prevent me from scoring. I had to play more aggressively just to touch the ball. If anyone shoved me, I shoved back, believing in the golden rule that I should do unto others as they were doing unto me. During the seven years that I played in high school and college, I suffered a twice-broken jaw, a broken collarbone, and three broken ribs as a result of diving for loose balls, running into hard picks, and taking sharp elbows to my face. Despite my injuries, I missed only three games during that entire period. In my desire to win, I cast prudence to the wind, ignoring the threat of reinjury. I was from the Vince Lombardi school: "Winning isn't everything. It's the only thing."

Bowdoin thought otherwise.

There was little sense in pleading the merits of my case. The decision was irreversible. As I turned to leave the meeting, Mr. Morrell attempted to assuage my anger.

"You shouldn't be too disappointed," he said. "You still have a chance to win it next year."

"Next year?" I sputtered, and headed for the door. "You tell the college fathers that if they think I was bad this year, they haven't seen anything yet."

I knew that I was going to regret the words before they even left my mouth, but I didn't give a damn. It was baffling to me how the school officials could turn my desire to take on all competitors, however big or strong, and not give any quarter into a negative, a lack of class, unbecoming.

I simmered for months over this decision. I even considered taking revenge by simply not playing the next season. It was an empty threat. My anger cooled over the summer. I began to read about the life and lore of Joshua Lawrence Chamberlain, one of our greatest Civil War heroes.

Chamberlain was born just a few miles from where I grew up. He had been a professor of rhetoric at Bowdoin when he volunteered to serve the cause of preserving the Union. His bold and brilliant decision to charge and rout the Confederate forces on Little Round Top at Gettysburg after his troops had run out of ammunition remains one of the most celebrated war stories in history. General Ulysses S. Grant selected Chamberlain to receive General Robert E. Lee's sword at Appomattox, where the Confederate soldiers were to surrender. Equally impressive as Chamberlain's brilliance and bravery on the battlefield was his sense of respect for the vanquished. As the defeated warriors surrendered their arms, Chamberlain issued an order for his men to salute them.

It was an act of grace and generosity to a defeated enemy. This was the code that Director Morrell was referring to: the legacy that Bowdoin men (and soon women) were expected to measure up to. I took the lesson to heart.

The next year I was granted the coveted leadership award.

Seven

HOOPS AND DREAMS

Of the many interests that Janet and I share, the love of basketball is high on the list. I'm forever watching college and professional games on television. But, as an Indiana "Hoosier," Janet's no basketball widow. She grew up with Oscar Robinson bouncing a ball as a young boy in the playground adjacent to the housing project where she lived. The "Big O" became the best all-around ballplayer in the history of the game.

On one occasion, Janet joined me to watch Michael Jordan put on a dazzling display of his talent during his final year as a professional with the Washington Wizards. I, like virtually everyone else on the planet, admired Jordan's grace and incredible athleticism, but most compelling to me was his incomparable competitive spirit. After the game, I mentioned to Janet my less-than-glorious moments on the court, including the time I once provoked an official to call a technical foul against me for smiling at him. "Nice call," I said, handing him the ball. The referee knew that a compliment was not intended and nearly ejected me from the game.

Upon hearing a recitation of my exploits, Janet said, "You never could have played for my high school team, the Crispus Attucks Tigers."

Quick to nurse any wound to my pride, Janet added, "It's not because you weren't good enough. It's your attitude. Our coach would have benched you for fighting or showing any sign of disrespect for an official."

Crispus Attucks High School, as I mentioned earlier, was constructed in order to prevent black and white students from attending classes together. While the school itself was well built, the basketball auditorium was small. Architecture, like much of life in Indianapolis, was bounded by race. According to articles published at the time the school was opened, the town fathers had decided that "Since the traditions of the Negro race are deeply founded in music, that art has been especially emphasized in the new building." The auditorium was designed to serve as a combination stage and gymnasium, with a seating capacity of just eight hundred.

In other words, it was never designed to accommodate the large crowds that I played before in high school because Negroes were said to be more interested in music than sports. Left unsaid was the assumption that black ballplayers would never draw crowds of any significance in Indianapolis. Consequently, their teams were forced to play official home games at Butler University, which would later become Janet's alma mater. The Crispus Attucks Tigers never enjoyed a home court advantage because they never had a home court.

Also hampering its teams was the fact that for many years, the school was not allowed to belong to the Indiana High School Athletic Association. The reason? Crispus Attucks had no white students and thus was deemed not to be an open-admission public high school. Segregated schools were constructed to keep blacks separate from whites—and then their segregated status was used to prevent them from enjoying equal opportunities! As a result, the Crispus Attucks Tigers had to travel to distant towns to find other black schools to compete against.

Having the rules stacked against them was not a new phenomenon for black people. It had always been so. For years, they were prohibited from learning to read or write. White society then used the mandated disability to declare that they were ignorant, uneducable, not quite human, not entitled to the rights guaranteed to others under the Constitution.

According to Janet, Russell Lane, the principal of Crispus Attucks High School, reinforced a dictum that had been handed down to blacks through generations: They would always have to be twice as good to receive half as much as their white counterparts. He and Ray Crowe, the athletic director and coach of the basketball team, imposed a rigid discipline in the classroom and demanded of students nothing less than a total commitment to their studies. They had to excel in every aspect of their lives. Coach Crowe insisted that his basketball players devote as much time to their studies as they did to basketball. They were going to be students first and athletes second. He was a very tough taskmaster and wasn't afraid to hand out flunking grades in his mathematics course. Janet attested to this from personal experience!

After 1950, when Ray Crowe became coach, basketball fans—that would include just about everyone in Indiana—marveled at seeing an all-black team show up in a town. The Tigers were likened to the Harlem Globetrotters—without the clowning. Soon they were playing to standing-room-only crowds. White teams could lay no claim to greatness unless they were willing to face black athletes and win against them. Eventually, shame and peer pressure helped to break down the racist barriers that the Klan had erected.

While the black players were allowed to compete on the courts against whites, off the court, they still had to play by Jim Crow rules. They could not stay at a white hotel or motel, could not eat in a white restaurant or diner, and, in many places, could not use a public restroom. No one was allowed to complain. Lane insisted on living by the rules, though he had been the one who led the campaign to get Crispus Attucks admitted to the state high school athletic association.

Coach Ray Crowe imposed Lane's rigid discipline on the court. The game was not going to be fair. That was a given. They were going to be playing against seven people, counting the two officials. He would tell his players that the first ten points were needed to offset what were certain to be egregious calls by the officials. Protesting, however, would only invite the officials to impose technical fouls, or worse, eject them from the game. He tolerated no exceptions, not even from Oscar Robertson, whom he pulled from a game once when Oscar started to argue with an official.

How well did the Lane-Crowe philosophy work? During the seven years Ray Crowe served as coach, the Tigers won 179 games and lost 20. They lost only one game in two seasons and never had a technical foul called against them.

The Crispus Attucks Tigers made history in Indiana on more than one occasion. Once, during a game against the Evansville high school team, all of the white players had fouled out. Suddenly, the Crispus Attucks fans on its side of the auditorium stomped and shouted, letting out a deafening roar.

"What happened?" Janet asked her date. "Nobody scored."

"Oh yes, we did," he responded. "Look."

She looked up at the scoreboard and saw that the score was unchanged. She was still confused. "What? What are you talking about?"

"All the white guys on the other team have fouled out. For the first time in Indiana basketball history, all the players on the floor are black!"

Janet looked over to the other side of the auditorium. The white fans just sat there stunned. But the black fans who had been supporting the Evansville team were on their feet cheering too. Everyone in attendance that night, black and white, had just witnessed history.[*]

In 1955, the Tigers entered the state playoff tournament with a record of 20–1. They beat every competitor, including the state favorite, Muncie High. Crispus Attucks became the first all-black high school in the nation to win an open state sports championship and the first Indianapolis school, black or white, to win the state title.

How were they treated by the white community during the postvictory activities? Traditionally, winning teams climbed onto a fire truck and rode into downtown Indianapolis for a celebration.

---

[*]See *From Rage to Reason*, pp. 22–23.

This time, the fire truck, following a route established by worried city officials, sped halfway around Monument Circle, a major landmark, and then dashed to the black section of the city.

Oscar Robertson said, "I guess they felt black people would tear up downtown. I was part of Indiana basketball history. I wasn't an asterisk on the side, and neither were the other guys on the Crispus Attucks team. We were a part of the Indiana High School Athletic Association, and we shouldn't have been treated that way."*

Janet shared Oscar's sentiments and, no doubt, it was the reason she felt disappointed when Hollywood decided to make the film *Hoosiers*, starring Gene Hackman. The movie told an inspiring story of David fighting Goliath: Milan, a small school of only one hundred and sixty-one students, managed to beat Muncie High, whose student body numbered twenty-two hundred, for the state championship in 1954. It was described as a miracle.

"I was disappointed," Janet said, "not because of Hackman's performance, which was characteristically brilliant, but because the Crispus Attucks Tigers had produced a miracle as well. Sure," she said, "it's always good to see the triumph of the underdog. But the Crispus Attucks Tigers were the real underdogs. They had to overcome years of blatant, state sanctioned racism. They had to cope with the denial of athletic facilities and fair play, and face hatreds and hardships that white players never had to experience or endure. They played harder and jumped higher because they had more to play for. Their honor and sense of self-worth."

The celebrated achievements of Crispus Attucks athletes, combined with the passion and sacrifice of those engaged in the civil rights movement, no doubt contributed to breaking down the wall of Indiana's racist policies. In the late 1960s, for example, the Indianapolis School Board transferred black teachers to white schools and sent white teachers to Crispus Attucks. Bob Jewell, a Tigers star, went on to graduate from Indiana Central, and in 1957 Eli Lilly, one of Indianapolis' major employers, hired him as one of their scientists.

---

*See Tracy Dodd, "Champions for Change," *Indiana Star*, February 27, 2005.

He was the first black scientist to work for Lilly. Edgar Searcy, who later married Janet's best friend, April Brown, became a certified public accountant and later an attorney who was also hired by Eli Lilly. Oscar Robertson became not only one of the NBA's superstars but also a highly successful businessman in Cinncinati, Ohio.

The Crispus Attucks miracle had spread beyond the basketball courts. That was the movie Janet wanted to see.

Janet's teachers insisted that their students hold high hopes as well as hoop titles. One of her English teachers was fond of quoting Langston Hughes:

> Hold fast to dreams
> For if dreams die
> Life is a broken-winged bird
> That cannot fly

Dreaming was one thing; studying was another. Janet did both.

Her dedication to her studies was rewarded with a scholarship to Butler University, a venerated Indianapolis institution. Butler had started out in 1850 as North Western Christian University, the vision of Indianapolis lawyer Ovid Butler, who had drawn up the charter and presented it to the Indiana State Legislature. Later, the university was renamed to honor Butler.

In 1922, while the Ku Klux Klan still ruled much of Indiana, seven black women—six of them teachers—founded Sigma Gamma Rho Sorority, the only historically black sorority founded on a predominantly white campus. From that start at Butler, the sorority grew to some four hundred chapters with more than eighty thousand members.

Although integration was not new at Butler, it was a new experience for Janet. Initially, she had trouble adjusting.

When she was registering at the university, the form asked for her race and gave three choices: White, Black, and Other. Next to that it read, "if Other, please explain." That third choice bothered her. What exactly is an Other?

The Africans on both sides of Janet's family lived in the eastern Tennessee area around the 1840s. Whether they arrived there by choice or force is unclear. At the time, white settlers were pushing Native Americans from the east Ohio Valley region to the West. Although the Indians were being persecuted, they nonetheless were free. African people frequently lived among and mixed with Indians in the region. Whites' nocturnal lust or rapist urgings often prompted them to mix with Africans. That part of the South had been settled by people from Scotland, which likely accounts for the names of Scotsville, Glasgow, and Bowling Green, Kentucky. Interestingly, the songs her mother would sing, in addition to hillbilly numbers, were *Auld Lang Syne*, *Danny Boy*, and *My Bonnie Lies Over the Ocean*. Her features, while clearly African, showed traces of Indian blood as well.

As best as Janet can determine, she has Scots-Irish, Shawnee Indian, and African blood flowing through her veins. Did that make her an "Other?" The question still vexes her.

There were no outward signs of hostility directed toward Janet and her friend, April, at Butler, but there was always a quality of "otherness" about their relationship with the white students.

Once, when they were walking down a set of icy stairs, April slipped and fell to her knees. A nice young man rushed over to help her to her feet. It was a very kind act on his part. They learned later, however, that several of his classmates had chastised him for "helping that nigger up."

Also, there were a few young white men who had asked to date them. Initially, they were flattered and were tempted to accept until they learned that they could not enter the fraternity house for the parties held on weekends, and that they'd have to meet off-campus. In other words, Janet and April were objects of desire, but only in the dark where no whites would be seen as mixing with "undesirables."

During lunch breaks, the black students would gravitate toward tables that were separate and apart from those of the white students.

One young student, thinking that Janet was one of those practicing racial segregation, asked her why she didn't mix with whites.

"It's nothing personal," Janet assured her. "We've never been asked to join you. You're welcome to sit with us."

She politely declined, and she never extended a comparable invitation.*

Janet found that bigotry came in different shapes and sizes. When she was a senior in high school, she had purchased a necklace with a pendant in the form of two inverted triangles. It held no particular symbolic significance to her. She just was drawn to its beautiful design.

While she was at Butler, some of the white male students badgered her to take it off. "That's a Jewish symbol," they sneered. "It's sacrilegious for a Christian to wear it."

"At the time," Janet said, "I had no idea why being 'Jewish' was considered to be something contemptuous, but by their tone, they clearly intended the word to be a slur. I knew something about being on the receiving end of slurs and continued to wear the pendant out of defiance."

Ironically, it was during the study of religion that she would be exposed to the history of the Jewish people. Her professor, a Talmudic scholar who lectured about the Old Testament, liberated her from an intellectual straightjacket that had been wrapped around her mind. She had been taught to accept the Bible literally. But from the very beginning of her religious instruction, she found it difficult to abandon all reason in reading the Bible and accept all that it contained as a matter of blind faith. The God described in the Old Testament, for example, struck her as being more human than divine. He seemed petulant, vindictive, and punitive. These were not the characteristics she found worthy of admiration.

Janet's professor said that she needed to consider the historical context of the time period involved. The Jews, like most people at

---

*See Beverly Daniel Tatum, Ph.D., *Why Are All the Black Kids Sitting Together in the Cafeteria? And Other Conversations about Race* (New York: Basic Books, 1997).

the time, were exposed to the elements and forces of nature that were beyond comprehension. They, as we do today, stood in awe of the extraordinary beauty and terrible power of the natural world. When they were frightened by storms or afflicted with drought or disease, they assumed that they had offended their all-powerful Creator. Since they could not fully grasp the concept of infinity, they looked at the universe through the prism of mortal eyes and ascribed to this unseen power in their lives human attributes.

"Remember," her professor said, "much of the Bible was handed down orally. The Gospels, for example, were not written until long after Christ died. Many see the Bible as the Word of God, but you should view it as a history book. Like many history books, it is written from the subjective view of the one telling the story. You need to consider the knowledge available to the people at the time, their political views, and the various languages from which they are translating or interpreting the text of the story. For example, many religions admonish us to 'Fear God,' but in some languages, it is written that we should 'Revere God,' to honor and respect the infinite, indefinable, all powerful force that has given us the precious gift of life."

When Janet heard this explanation, she felt as if a giant rock had been lifted from her shoulders. She didn't live in fear of any person and she didn't want to live in fear of God. She didn't have to suspend logic or reason from all discourse about religion.

"I always wanted to know why church elders considered it blasphemous to ask questions of God," Janet said. "Why did they claim that God had cured a woman of cancer and then consider it a sin for me to ask why God had allowed the woman to get the disease in the first place? They called me impudent, a troublemaker who was headed straight for hell and damnation if I continued to think and ask questions. I knew that logic couldn't provide answers to existential questions that exceeded the bounds of human comprehension, but I no longer had to accept all of the rituals and liturgies of the church as divinely inspired and dictated. I could love God and not be afraid to challenge dogma that I found unbelievable or irrelevant."

"When I revealed to my professor my growing ambivalence about the role of religion in my life, he suggested that I read a number of books written by theologians. In addition he thought that I should read *The Diary of Anne Frank*, the story of a brilliant teenage Jewish girl who had had to hide from German authorities in the attic of her home. Anne had spent her days writing about her life, holding out hope until the day came when she was taken away to a concentration camp, where she died.

"I couldn't put the book down.

"As a young girl, I also had kept a diary, locking away my innermost thoughts. I never had to fear the coming of the Nazis, but I could never forget the tone of my father's voice when he told my family that he couldn't wear his uniform in the South, or the time when I was visiting relatives in Kentucky and was forced to lie flat on the floor as Klansmen on horseback rode past the house threatening to fire shotguns into it as they had done in the past."

She could identify with Anne in so many ways. Anne had revealed the existence of a tug-of-war that took place within her. She lived two lives: an exterior one that was social, light-hearted, flippant, and superficial; the other, a sad, solitary, and profound one that she refused to display to others for fear that she'd be seen as artificial and pretentious.

While in high school, Janet had read W. E. B. Du Bois' *The Souls of Black Folk*. DuBois had captured another kind of duality that many black people experienced:

[We were] born with a veil and gifted with second sight in this American world. . . . It is a peculiar sensation, this double consciousness, this sense of always looking at one's self through the eyes of others. . . . One ever feels his twoness—an American Negro; two souls, two thoughts, two unreconciled strivings; two warring ideals in one dark body, whose dogged strength alone keeps it from being torn asunder.*

---

*W. E. B. Du Bois, *The Souls of Black Folk* (New York: Modern Library, 2003), p. 5.

Anne also had come to question the trappings of religion:

People who are religious should be glad, since not everyone is blessed with the ability to believe in a higher order. You don't even have to live in fear of eternal punishment; the concepts of purgatory, heaven and hell are difficult for many people to accept, yet religion itself, any religion keeps a person on the right path. Not the fear of God, but upholding your own sense of honor and obeying your own conscience.

Somehow throughout her entire ordeal, to her very last entry, Anne had held on to her ideals:

It's difficult in times like these: ideals, dreams and cherished hopes rise within us, only to be crushed by grim reality. It's a wonder I haven't abandoned all my ideals, they seem so absurd and impractical. Yet I cling to them because I still believe, in spite of everything, that people are truly good at heart.

After reading Anne's *Diary*, Janet wore the pendant out of pride more than defiance. Years later, she would carry the name "Cohen," one of the most celebrated names in the Jewish faith, with the same pride with which she wore that Star of David.

Although Janet found the intellectual experience at Butler liberating, she was also liberated in other ways. The discipline that she had maintained while a student at Crispus Attucks waned. Her grades began to slip in direct proportion to her social agenda. At the end of her sophomore year, she lost her scholarship and had to drop out of Butler.

She and April fell from scholastic grace simultaneously. They found employment as telephone operators at Indiana's Ma Bell. Janet worked there during the day, and attended Indiana University in Indianapolis at night, hoping to restore a grade average that would allow her to reenter Butler's scholarship program. But at the end of a year, she had lost interest in completing college and fulfilling a dream she had once had of becoming a missionary.

She wanted to enter a line of work that no college could prepare her for.

While Janet was a student at Crispus Attucks, a white representative from a local modeling school appeared during annual "Career Day," to explain some of the opportunities that awaited the students upon graduation. Excited over the prospect that she might perfect her manners, prepare elaborate dinner tables, and walk gracefully with a book balanced on her head, Janet went to the business office of the school filled with excitement and expectation. Instead, the very same woman who earlier had appeared at the high school showed her the exit door with the explanation that she'd be wasting her money. She said that the school didn't do Janet's kind of hair, and the skills they offered to perfect in others would be of little benefit to her. The message was clear—blacks need not apply. Modeling and manners were reserved for "whites only."*

Janet burned with anger as she was escorted out the door, and vowed that she was never going to accept the notion there was anything beyond her reach. She didn't know at that moment, however, that in just three years, she would enter a world that exceeded the bounds of her imagination.

Janet decided to enroll in a different school and face a different kind of challenge. She was going to become a student in Cordie King's Castle.

Cordie King was a remarkable woman and a wonderful role model. Born in Mississippi in 1924, she spent her early and teenage years working in cotton fields. Somehow, she managed to go to school while taking on jobs as a baker, a dishwasher, and a newspaper seller. She grew into a stunning beauty.

Her poise and beauty were discovered in 1949 by *Ebony* magazine, which featured her in an article titled "What Men Notice Most About Women." Next she entered a beauty pageant sponsored in Chicago. Competing against more than forty contestants, she was chosen as one

---

*See *From Rage to Reason*, pp. 28–31.

of three models, breaking the racial barrier that had kept black women from fashion runways and out of TV commercials. Cordie pitched goods that included Schlitz beer, Fuller brushes, and the black hair and beauty products of the Madame C. J. Walker Company.

Cordie became known as the Singing Model, and her pals in the whirlwind of show business included Frank Sinatra, Ava Gardner, and Sammy Davis, Jr., to whom she was briefly engaged. She was told by Peter Lawton's wife, Pat (John F. Kennedy's sister), that running with the "Rat Pack" would not prove to be a long-distance race for her, she returned to Indianapolis and settled down with Marion ("Mayday") H. Stuart, a member of one of the most prominent black families in Indianapolis. They were married in 1956. She soon founded Cordie's Castle.

Cordie took Janet under her wing, turning an awkward teenager who couldn't make majorette into a runway model.

In 1962, under her tutelage, Janet successfully auditioned to become a model in the Ebony Fashion Fair, which had been established in 1956 by the late John Johnson, founder of the Johnson Publishing Company, publisher of *Ebony* and *Jet* magazines, and his wife, Eunice W. Johnson. The Ebony Fashion Fair was an event that drew the crème de la crème of black celebrities—Sidney Poitier, Bill Cosby, and Muhammad Ali among them. The fair, traveling to sixty-two cities in a chartered Greyhound bus, became a showplace for black designers and a bazaar for African-American women.

The clothes were always expensive and sumptuous, designed by Rudi Gernreich, Givenchy, Balenciaga, Bill Blass, and Oscar de la Renta. Johnson always purchased the clothes instead of borrowing them, as fashion show entrepreneurs traditionally do. No one then would loan a dress to a black person. This was at a time when most department stores would not allow black customers to try on clothes.

On the tour, the models had to stay in black motels and dine in black restaurants. There was always a color line, and, glamorous as they might have been, they were never allowed to cross it. In case they needed a written reminder, restaurants—even greasy-spoon diners—put signs in their doors saying "We Reserve the Right to

Refuse Service." The sign artists in Mississippi were more direct, painting two words: "Colored Only" or "White Only." Often they did not have to use these designated black accommodations because they were welcomed into the luxurious homes of black doctors, lawyers, and businessmen who belonged to charities or organizations that were among the sponsors of the fair.

Usually, though, they had no choice but a rundown black hotel or motel with bad plumbing and peeling wallpaper. San Antonio's accommodations were typical: The black motel was on one side of the street; the white hotel was on the other side. But something untypical happened. All the models but two checked into the shabby motel. "I could hear the bugs running when I turned the lights on," Janet remembers.

The two rebellious models were not American. One was from Brazil. She was light-skinned, and, in terms of color, she could have been Janet's sister. The other model was from Haiti. She also had fair skin and gray eyes, but was obviously black.

"We don't have to take this insult," the Haitian model said. "In our countries, we are not considered black." She and the Brazilian walked across the street, and, speaking with heavy accents, checked into the "Whites Only" hotel.

They had urged Janet to come with them—and remain silent so that the desk clerk would assume she too was a foreigner. Janet refused. She was angry about the treatment they routinely received. She also resented her two "foreign" associates for not staying with the rest of them.

Janet's city-to-city tour began just a year after the 1961 Freedom Riders trip: two buses, with black passengers sitting in front and whites in the back. As a test of a new Supreme Court decision that outlawed segregation in bus terminals, the riders planned to disregard the segregated restrooms and lunchrooms along the way from Washington to New Orleans. They never made it. One bus, luckily empty, was firebombed. Riders were beaten by mobs or jailed by local judges. The reaction was especially violent in Alabama, where there were threats of martial law.

The Ebony Fashion Fair models never ran into trouble because they were not considered to be civil rights activists. They had to play by Jim Crow rules, much as they hated them. They were on a mission not to tear down unjust laws, but to change unflattering images and instill pride in black people.*

Janet's desire to see her father again started to surface more intensely during the time she traveled with the Ebony Fashion Fair. Part of her motivation stemmed from curiosity. Another part was pure anger, and a third part was a desire to show him how successful she had become without him or his love.

After the one visit he paid to her when she was seven years old, Janet never heard from him again. No phone calls. No Christmas cards. No Happy Birthdays. He cared little whether she or her mother were well or ill, alive or dead. Janet could never understand how he could have abandoned his family. Why did he feel so free of responsibility for either of them?

When she heard that he was serving as an associate pastor in a Los Angeles church, she felt compelled to try to see him again to find answers to questions that she had forced into dormancy for sixteen years.

At first, she called him, declaring that she was an operator with a long-distance call for him. When she heard his voice acknowledging that he was Sewell Bridges, she inexplicably hung up the receiver. She simply didn't know what to say at that moment.

She waited several days and placed a second call. This time, she pretended to be a distant cousin of her mother's, who was traveling to Los Angeles and was interested in visiting with a family member. She engaged in this masquerade because she didn't want to alarm him or cause him to think that she was seeking any financial support.

Initially, he professed not to know any Louise Gillenwaters. Janet was so angry with him that she terminated the call without saying anything more.

---

*See *From Rage to Reason*, pp. 39–41.

She waited several days and called again. This time she let him know that she was his daughter and that he had once held her in his arms upon his return from the war. She said that she was going to be in the Los Angeles area with the Ebony Fashion Fair and wanted to see him again.

Her high expectations for a joyful daughter-father reunion were quickly dashed. He had a conflict. It was bowling tournament time and he was booked for the two nights that she was in the city. He suggested that perhaps they could meet on the second night after the game was completed. Janet insisted that they meet the first night, as she suspected that he would somehow manage to arrange to miss the meeting at the conclusion of his bowling activities.

The atmosphere of the bowling alley did not exactly lend itself to an intimate conversation.

She was determined to get answers to her questions, so she waited until he and his friends had finished bowling. After excusing himself from the group, her father went to change. He returned wearing a minister's collar. When Janet saw the collar, she was stunned. It was but another example of her view that rampant hypocrisy existed in the church and in those who professed to be religious.

They went to a nearby restaurant and after a few minutes of cordial preliminaries, Janet chastised him, "a man of the cloth," for abandoning his family.

His response was weak. He blamed his neglect in part upon Janet's mother having married while he was in Europe, and upon the war itself and his long effort to cope with the experience while in a VA hospital.

He made some effort to reconnect with Janet, who was in no mood to accept his rationales or his sudden display of affection. He asked her to celebrate both her birthday and Christmas with him, but Janet declined, noting that it was a tradition for her to spend those days with her mother and brother.

Suggesting that he at least give Janet something for her birthday, he reached into his pocket and pulled out a single bill. As Janet slipped it into her purse, she saw that it was a one-dollar bill! She wasn't asking anything from him, but a dollar bill for a daughter he hadn't seen for sixteen years?

Nevertheless, she thanked her father and kissed him good-bye, certain that she would never see him again.

He did attend the fashion show the following night. After the show she found in her dressing room a beautiful bouquet of roses with a card that read, "From Your Father. You Looked Beautiful Tonight."

That was the last time Janet saw her father. He would write occasionally to tell her that he had seen her picture in a newspaper or a magazine. He would send her clippings and tell her how proud he was of her. But they never met again.

It was only after Janet published her memoir that she met her father's relatives at a family reunion in Bowling Green, Kentucky. Floyd Bridges, her paternal cousin, explained to her that Janet had misconstrued the significance of the dollar bill her father had given her. It was simply part of the family tradition to give family members a dollar bill on their birthdays. It was meant as a token of love.

She felt a twinge of regret that she had failed to appreciate the significance of the dollar bill, but no token could ever compensate for all of those lost years. One day years later, she sensed that her father had died. She placed a call to the Los Angeles Directory asking for his telephone number, just as she had done when she had first contacted him. There was no listing.

She left it at that.*

---

*See *From Rage to Reason*, pp. 43–49.

Eight

LAW SCHOOL AND OTHER MALADIES

In 1962, as I approached graduation, the future continued to remain shrouded in fog. The Vietnam War was seen as a low-level conflict at the time, and it seemed to be a remote factor in my life. There was a draft, but the military was not yet demanding large numbers of young men to fill its ranks. As a student, I was given a deferment. While in high school, I had won the individual command and response competition in ROTC, and I had enrolled in Bowdoin's ROTC program during my freshman year. It was a hedge. If called to serve, I wanted to have some advance preparation. When I discovered the amount of time I'd have to devote to the program, however, I quickly dropped it.

In prior years, I had held two equally improbable visions for my future life. I thought I would live in Europe, ride a motorcycle while touring the continent, and write novels. Less romantic was the notion of pursuing a career as a professional basketball player. While I could shoot with some of the best players in the NBA (I played and scored against Celtics great Bill Sharman and the New York Knickerbockers' Richie Guerin during summer scrimmages), I was not big or fast enough to be physically competitive with them.

During the summer recess of my junior year, I had met and fallen for Diana Dunn, a beautiful young woman from the neighboring town of Bath. I experienced a new grounding in reality. We would be married at the end of my senior year, and I would either continue my education or enter the workforce.

Although I would graduate with honors, my ability to read and recite Latin (considered to be a "dead language") was likely to limit my career to that of teaching. An attorney friend from Bangor, Norman Minsky, suggested that a better plan would be for me to attend law school. "The study of law will sharpen your mind by narrowing it," he said, quoting a familiar dictum. "Even if you never decide to practice law, the experience will give you enormous flexibility for the future."

I held no particular interest in the study of law at that moment, but the prospect of possessing a wider range of employment opportunities had great appeal. I thought that my father would approve of my decision to attend law school.

He didn't. "Lawyers are a dime a dozen, Billy. I'm telling you, you should be a doctor."

Once again, he had given me good advice, which I, of course, rejected.

At the end of my senior year, Diana and I were married, and we made our way, with the help of my classmate and friend, Christian Peter Potholm, to Old Lyme, Connecticut, to work and save for my entry into Boston University's School of Law. Diana obtained work as a waitress in nearby Niantic, while I worked construction during the day and served as a pistol-packing (.38 snub-nosed revolver) constable at night. By the end of a long, hot summer, I concluded that I was more fit to study and practice law than to try to enforce it at the end of a gun barrel.

I was in for another revelation. Diana was with child. I was going to be a father, a role that I was no more suited for at that time than that of law enforcement officer.

The maturation process that had begun during my senior year accelerated once I entered that gray-columned two-story brick building at 3 Joy Street on Beacon Hill, the home of the Boston University Law School. The street's name was a misnomer. It should have been called Misery.

My first year at law school stripped away whatever romantic notions I once held of traveling throughout Europe, gathering experiences that I might one day turn into the stuff of poetry and novels. Gone were the blue jeans, white sneakers, and black leather jacket that served as my uniform at Bowdoin. One suit, two sports jackets, and two slacks, along with several button-down cotton shirts, hung on a wooden pole that provided a makeshift closet in our bedroom. Actually, the bedroom itself was a closet masquerading as a place to sleep. Since I did not own a car, it made sense to lease an apartment within walking distance of the law school. It was anything but a renter's market, and we ended up on the first floor of a shabby three-story tenement building on Myrtle Street. For the princely sum of ninety dollars a month plus utilities, we had a hovel to call our own. It could not be called luxury living.

The bathroom was separated from the apartment by a hallway and was equipped with a pull-chain flush toilet. A window inside the bathroom provided a scenic view of an interior airshaft, down which the tenants on the second and third floors invariably dumped their garbage. All of the windows in the apartment were single-pane and they kept neither the cold nor the soot from entering at will. The landlord, a cigar-chomping scoundrel, had, over the years, covered the warped kitchen floor with several layers of linoleum, each layer more hideous than the previous one.

Two elderly English sisters lived on the first floor next to us. While they exuded an air of absolute rectitude, I discovered that they were nipping into something more than the cooking sherry each afternoon. The other neighbors were, well, not neighborly. A beefy man who drove a motorcycle lived with a tall German girl on the third floor. Two or three evenings a week—and every Saturday night—they hosted a noisy party that inevitably involved their guests tossing beer and whiskey bottles out onto the street below. And just as inevitably, when the drunken guests departed, they would roll empty bottles down the rear steps until they came to the first floor landing. Spotting a door, they would mistake it for an exit to the street. When the floor refused to budge, they put their shoulders into it and tried to break it down. Unfortunately, it happened to be the door to our bedroom that they were battering, and the early morning hours usually ended in a shouting match, with me threatening to commit mayhem.

I had thought my hazing days as a fraternity house pledge in college were over, but I could feel a familiar tingling sensation on the first day of law school.

Along with approximately 150 students, I filed into a large, dimly lit room on the second floor of the school. After a brief welcome by the dean of students, who reminded us of the hallowed traditions of the school, Professor Paul Siskind (he would later become dean) paced somberly before us.

Siskind's specialty was contract law. He was a solid, bulldog-faced man whose permanent scowl reinforced the impression that he was to be taken very seriously. He wore a dark blue suit, white shirt, and bow tie. He spoke knowingly of the need for preparation. It was the key to success in the classroom and in the courtroom. He fore-warned us to read at least three of the cases in our textbooks prior to each class, five if possible. "Know the facts, remember the issues," he repeated several times. "At the end of each week, go back to the first page and start all over again. . . . There are only three elements to a contract: an offer, an acceptance, and consideration. What's consideration you ask? (none of us had). It's a peppercorn. It's a hat, a hawk or a horse." One hundred and fifty pairs of eyes could be heard clicking as we glanced at each other, some nervously giggling. What in hell is the man talking about?

But Siskind had more than a lecture on his favorite subject to deliver. In deep, measured tones, he spoke about the need for independence and integrity. "Never limit yourself to a single client," he advised us. "If you do, you become a captive. You will forfeit your objectivity because if you lose that client, you'll jeopardize your ability to survive financially.

"And most importantly," he said, scanning the innocent faces before him, "never, under any circumstances, compromise your honor for anyone, no matter how powerful, for any price no matter how high. If you do, you'll spend the rest of your life trying to buy back the one thing you'll never be rich enough to afford—your reputation."

Siskind spoke with such power and precision that he could just as well have been God burning a commandment into a stone tablet.

Sufficiently forewarned, we had started to gather up our notes and books, when he said, "There's one other thing. I want each of you to look to your right and then to your left because one of you will not be here at the end of the year."

His words struck like a thunderclap. It was a dramatic restatement of a statistical truth: one-third of the class was destined to fail or drop out by next June. As we filed out of the classroom, most of us had a sheepish grin locked on our faces. In reality, it was a mask of anxiety. I left the room slightly shaken, not quite sure why I had ever decided to pursue a law degree. As I walked back to the apartment that day, I felt as if my shoes were full of cement.

In any new beginning, there is an inevitable sorting out. As in any other contest, there would be a struggle to demonstrate superior strength. In this case, strength would consist of a razor-sharp analytical ability and facile tongue. But what made this contest unique was the absence of trial runs, the cushion provided by quizzes, or the opportunity to build academic success slowly. It was going to be hit or miss. One exam only in each class, nine months away—except for Criminal Law, which was the only one-semester course. For the first time in my academic life, there would be no safety net and no second chance.

I had spent four years mastering Latin elegiac poetry, and studying the rise and ruin of ancient Greece and Rome, with classes often conducted over wine and cheese at Professor Nate Dane's saltwater farm. Now I had crossed a threshold and entered a wholly mystifying new world.

There was no protective campus to stroll languidly about, inhaling a sense of institutional history; no friendly advisors to massage bruised egos in a book-lined study. We were all on our own.

Scanning the faces of my competitors, I could tell not many came from the ranks of privilege and wealth. They were distinctly middle-class achievers who lacked either the family connections or perhaps the LSAT scores to gain admission to Harvard, Yale, or Columbia. They were no easy marks to be sure. A few were identifiable scholar types who puffed on pipes and smelled of the lamp. Some were fast-talking streetwise personalities who were destined to be deal makers or criminal defense attorneys. Most were very much like me—ostensibly able, but wracked with doubt over our choice to attend law school and fearful that we were going to be the ones to the left or right who were not going to make it.

The pressure to succeed intensified for me. I was going to become a father the following spring. The thought of becoming a parent, when coupled with the fear that I might be part of that third who would fail, stirred me to adopt study habits comparable to those of my old friend Charlie; I remembered I compared him to a Tibetan monk. Now I was one.

Each professor would assign three to five cases for the following class. Each case might run five, or even eight or ten pages, in books that could double as five-pound dumbbells. The print was small, the cases complex, the language lifted from seventeenth-century England. Contracts. Torts. Civil Procedure. Criminal Law. I had to memorize every word in every case, every day—and be prepared to be plucked from the anonymity of the faceless herd, forced to stand up before the entire class and be filleted by an unsmiling, razor-tongued inquisitor.

There were no assigned seats, but neither was there a place to hide. One was just as likely to be called upon sitting in the rear of the room as in the front row. And woe be unto him (or her) who came to class unprepared. The slightest pause or hesitation in response to a question sent the hands of the other students shooting up for recognition, thereby magnifying the pressure and the humiliation.

The law defined the rights and obligations of a society's citizens. One person's right meant another person's obligation. Someone had to win, someone to lose. Law school was simply the boot camp that forced everyone who entered to strip away all of the excess weight, the degrees, honors, and glories of yesteryear. No judge or jury would be impressed that your college sheepskin was stamped "cum laude" or that you once had a great jump shot. No. We were to learn the martial arts of survival. He with the sharpest and quickest blade would win. Provided, of course, he had the heart. And that heart was to be tested daily.

Each professor engaged in his unique version of the Socratic method: asking questions in an ever-narrowing circle of refinement until the logic of a court's ruling was seen as inexorably sharp or shallow. Paul Liacos, who would become the chief justice of the Supreme Judicial Court of Massachusetts, taught Criminal Law and Evidence. I thought that Liacos, a tall, dark man, could have doubled as a Peter Lorre character. His classes were always a joy. He provided insight in a playful manner, never seeking to intimidate or embarrass a student.

LIACOS: Suppose A pushes B off the top of the Empire State Building. What crime has A committed?

STUDENT: Murder, obviously, because B is going to be reduced to jelly.

LIACOS: But what if C is on the fifty-fifth floor target practicing with a high-powered rifle and strikes B in the head on the way down? What is A guilty of? What about B?

STUDENT: A is guilty of attempted murder. B is guilty of manslaughter.

LIACOS: But what if B miraculously survives the fall and the gunshot wound and lies broken and bleeding in his final moments of life? D comes along and sees B in excruciating pain begging to be put out of his horrendous misery and D drives a wooden stake through his heart. B had only three more seconds to live—

Not every professor was quite so light-hearted. All of us had heard horror stories of Henry Monahan's brilliance and brutality. If we were fortunate enough to survive the first year, he would be waiting in his black hood at the top step of the guillotine. Henry was a Yale Law School graduate who had a passion for shooting basketball hoops and humiliating those he thought his intellectual inferiors—virtually everyone in the universe.

His tactic was to shout a student to attention, and demand a recital of a case's facts, issue, and holding. No matter how proficient the recitation, he inevitably would shred either the court's ruling or the student's analysis. And then, after hacking away at his bleeding victim, he would dismiss him (he showed an equal level of disdain for the few female students in our class) by shouting, "If you think that, you're an idiot!"

Henry always managed to stir one's anger. Good was never sufficient. Excellent was not good enough. Perfection was reserved for . . . Henry. I was never sure whether it was just a clever, but tough teaching tactic or the ranting of a scholar with a serious personality problem, but I always came to his classes prepared.

The pressure that I'd internalized finally took a physical toll. I developed severe eyestrain and began to suffer disabling headaches. Sunlight only intensified the migraines that began to overwhelm me. Studying in the afternoons was prohibitively painful. Relief seemed to come only late at night. Most afternoons I simply left school and went home to bed and then hit the books in the middle of the night.

Anxiety soon led to a separate ailment. I developed gingivitis, a common and treatable condition, but I lacked sufficient funds to seek treatment from a dentist. I wound up at Tufts Dental School as a volunteer guinea pig for dental students.

It was difficult to tell whether I had placed myself in the hands of A+ or D- students. At one point, I was in the operating chair and had three students peering into my mouth, which had been pried and held open with what appeared to be a car jack. I had been pumped full of Novocain, but I could still feel a sudden slicing movement along my gums. When I heard one of the students say "whoops!" I immediately broke into a cold sweat. Sterile gauze pads were quickly jammed under my upper lip as an instructor was summoned to see (repair) the handiwork of Freddy Krueger.

I soon learned that by signing on as a volunteer, I had about as much clout as a lab rat. I spoke up one day when a technician was busy preparing his zillionth X-ray of my jaw. "I think I've had enough for one day," I said finally. "I'm told that X-rays aren't high in nutritional value."

The technician, unimpressed with my attempt at levity, looked at me as though one of his rats had just bitten him.

"You're either in the program or you're out," was his stiff reply.

After that exchange I decided to opt out of the program. I concluded I'd be better off flossing with barbed wire than I was in the hands of the aspiring dentists.

Not so surprisingly, my health didn't do much for my temperament. The minor inconveniences I had to fend off seemed like cogs in the overall conspiracy that had been set in motion once I'd made it clear I wished to attend law school. At night there were a few times when the migraines dissipated, but invariably whenever I tried to take advantage of this luck and drift off into sleep, the partygoers on the upper floor rolled empty bottles down the stairs. The hollow CLINK! CLINK! CLINK! against each stair and the final THUD! upon our door at the landing was impossible to shut out of my head. Long after the noise had faded I would stew in my bed, daring the upstairs tenants to make more noise.

One night I released months of pent-up frustration at the bowling alley sounds of the rolling empty bottles. Rather than bottles of Thunderbird or Wild Turkey, two drunks had come tumbling down the stairs and crashed right through our kitchen door.

I was in an absolute rage. This wasn't about sleep anymore. My privacy and that of my pregnant wife had been invaded. I came out of the bedroom with my snub-nosed .38 leading the way. I pointed the gun at the intruders, who were still fighting with each other on the buckled linoleum floor. Luckily for all, the gun was not loaded.

I knew that. They did not. "Get out of here," I shouted, "before I blow your fucking heads off!"

Both men, certain that I was going to make good on my threat, struggled to their feet and scrambled awkwardly down the hall and out of the building.

After they left, I was so concerned about my response, that the next day I shipped the pistol to my brother, Bob, who lived in Maine, a state that looked more favorably on gun ownership and theories of self-defense in one's household. I was convinced that if the gun had been loaded, I would have committed manslaughter that night. Not exactly a great way to begin a career in the law.

The pressure of impending fatherhood continued to weigh heavily on my mind. I decided that it would be prudent to explore employment opportunities as a hedge against failure during final exams. Recruiters had been circling the law school for weeks, waiting like so many predators to move in and grab those who were in the grips of doubt about a career in the law.

I agreed to be interviewed by a representative from New England Telephone & Telegraph. Had the man conducting the interview not made conformity such an unappealing prospect, I might have agreed to enter the field of communications.

The interview proceeded at a slow pace, with the recruiter pausing between questions to tap his pen in a most serious manner.

BOW TIE: But why do you want to work for New England Tel & Tel?

ME: I'm not sure that I do. I came to find out what opportunities your company has to offer.

BOW TIE: Why do you want to leave law school?

ME: Frankly, I haven't made that decision yet (the school may make it for me). I'm going to be a parent soon and I may not be in a position to support my family for the next three years. I'm simply exploring other options in the event I decide to leave at the end of the school year.

This sort of fencing went on for four or five minutes. Obviously the man knew that a percentage of first-year students (Siskind's one-third) were ill suited for the law, and various companies wanted to weed out the talented but disenchanted from the misfits. Finally, the man said, "Describe to me the happiest moment in your life."

I started to laugh. Had it come down to a verbal Rorschach test? What kind of a question was this?

"I'm not sure I know what you mean by happy," I said. "Coming from a school like Bowdoin College, I might ascribe a multitude of connotations to that word. There are happy hours, happy weekends, happy times."

"I think you should define what happy means to you," he replied.

I knew the answer—or at least the type of answer—that he was looking for. It was a free throw. I could have said it was the moment when I received my degree from Bowdoin College, marking the culmination of four years of study, competition, hard work. Or the day that I was married and assumed the responsibilities of a husband. Or . . . but I rebelled. I kept looking at this organization man and thinking that I would be entering something akin to Jean Paul Sartre's version of hell—locked in a room with an infinite number of bow-tied replicas and forced to engage in an attitudinal test.

"I experienced happiness when Bowdoin beat the undefeated University of Maine's Black Bears basketball team. I was elated when I aced a religion exam without an hour of preparation. I was overjoyed to make it safely through the Everglades on a spring break trip (I skipped the expedition to Havana)."

After several *hmms* and *harrumphs* while scanning the biographical information I had furnished, Bow Tie said, "Mr. Cohen, looking at your résumé, I don't think you would be happy working for New England Tel & Tel."

Of course it was not my résumé that disqualified me. It was my answers. More specifically, my attitude.

Freed from pretense, I replied that he was a man of remarkable insight and that I agreed it was unlikely that I would find employment in his company to be a rewarding experience.

Shaken by the future that lay waiting outside the doors of law school in corporate America, I returned to my studies with a near-frenzied enthusiasm.

My fear of failure proved unwarranted. I did well enough on my final exams to be invited to join the *Law Review*, which would add another fourteen hours (and additional eye strain) to my weekly workload. In addition, I became the proud father of our first son. We named him Kevin.

The law proved, in the words of Supreme Court Justice Oliver Wendell Holmes, Jr., to be a "jealous mistress." She demanded an all-consuming devotion. I found external events in the world to be of no interest except one.

"The President's been shot. In Dallas, Texas, the President's been shot." The news hit the law school with hurricane force, blowing away all of our comfortable assumptions about the inviolability of America's leader. Shock waves followed. At first, there was disbelief, then rage. "Who would dare?" "Why?" "How badly is the President hurt?" "A head wound? How bad?"

I bolted from school and rushed home. I stayed glued to the television and radio reports until our grimmest expectations were confirmed. At the time, I was only vaguely aware of national events and didn't identify with either political party. But John Kennedy held a special appeal for me. I took quiet pride in the youthful and vigorous image that Kennedy projected. I loved the humor he displayed during his televised news conferences, the easy rapport he enjoyed with national correspondents, and the apparent goodwill they seemed to hold for him. I welcomed his acceptance of responsibility for the Bay of Pigs fiasco, and admired him for he strength he displayed in confronting the Soviet missile challenge in Cuba. I still experience a spinal shiver whenever I see reruns of his speech in West Berlin (just as I do with President Reagan's speech calling upon Mr.

Gorbachev to "tear down this wall"). The fact that he was a Democrat was of little concern to me.

November 22, 1963, would have a more profound impact upon me than I realized at the time. Presidential assassinations were not unprecedented in America, but at the time I held on to the illusion that we Americans were somehow invulnerable to the violence that afflicted other nations. In less than five seconds that illusion had been shattered. On a more personal level, I was reminded that if death could take away the youthful, rich, and dynamic John Kennedy in the flash of a gunshot, then my own life's expectations could be cancelled without notice.

There were deeper and darker thoughts lurking in my mind that had their roots in my study of ancient mythology. Somehow we had offended those mercurial gods who play, rage, and fornicate on Mount Olympus. Surely this crime of such horrible dimensions would satiate their anger. Whatever hubris or false pride we had displayed as a nation had been paid for by the blood of our leader. The future should hold no further agonies.

Regrettably, neither James Earl Ray nor Sirhan Sirhan believed in myths or prayers.

On November 22, 1963, the same year that I was attending Boston University Law School and interviewing for a job at the New England Telephone and Telegraph Company, Janet was working in Indianapolis for AT&T as a telephone operator. On that day, she was on the three-to-eleven afternoon shift. Janet was entering the elevator of the office building when she first heard that President Kennedy had been shot. She and her co-workers were in a state of shock and disbelief. *My God*, she thought, *the President's been shot! How bad was he hurt? What kind of a wound? Was it mortal? What about Jackie?* Others asked, "How could this have happened? Where was the Secret Service? Why hadn't they protected him?" The elevator conversation had all the nervous anxiety of a disrupted bee hive.

"I rushed to the switchboard, which was completely lit up. I put on my headphones and began connecting calls by plugging cables into the multiple receptors. At the time, people had the option of placing person-to-person calls (which were more costly) or those that were designated as station-to-station calls. For person-to-person calls, I had to stay on the line until the person who was called answered the phone. I then got off the line. A light on the switchboard would signal when the call was completed. I'd then throw a lever, terminating the connection. While in the process of connecting several of the calls, I lingered on the line, listening to the television broadcasts in the background of the callers.

"One of callers was desperate to make contact with Robert Kennedy in Washington. Another caller was a mother who reached her son in the Capital. She expressed her disbelief that something so tragic could have happened and wanted to know if he was safe. And she then added, 'This won't affect your job, will it?'

"By the time I arrived home that evening I was completely shattered and depressed. While the country was in a state of grief, a young man who lived in the apartment across from mine and who had approached me on several occasions for a date, knocked on my door and inquired if I had heard the news.

"He had boasted to me on an earlier occasion that he was a proud Republican. His political party affiliation was not particularly relevant to me at the time. But I was stunned when he gloated that night that 'Kennedy got just what he deserved.'

"For what? I asked.

"For being a liberal, a troublemaker. He had no business stirring up the entire South, sending federal troops to Mississippi."

"You mean for trying to treat us as equals?" I slammed the door in his face and told him never to bother calling me again—ever.

"I saw the Zapruder film played over and over, in excruciatingly slow motion, in the years that followed, and each time President Kennedy was hit, my head would snap back as if I was recoiling from the shots fired by Lee Harvey Oswald."

Many Americans associated John Kennedy with the mythical land of Camelot, and for them the myth and the music died that day in Dallas.

It would not be long before America would lose a King as well.

Nine

THE WINDY CITY

Janet joined the Ebony Fashion Fair again in 1964, after an interval back home in Indianapolis. The Fair was already on the road. One of the models had dropped out, and John Johnson had called her to ask if she could fill in. She enthusiastically accepted the invitation and was soon on the runway again. That second tour with the Fair did it for her. The Fair, along with the encouragement of Cordie King, had given her the desire to move on to a new life.

She had made up her mind that she was going to move to Chicago. She had traveled there several times with Cordie King to audition for various modeling jobs and had fallen in love with the city. It was also the headquarters of Johnson Publishing, and being close to John Johnson and his widely read publications seemed like a good career move.

Janet's mother disapproved of her decision, convinced that Chicago was simply a gangster city. But seeing that Janet was determined to leave, she finally relented.

Janet moved to Chicago and found that it was, as Frank Sinatra used to croon, "[her] kind of town." It was big, muscular, dynamic, and integrated, with a politically active and influential black population.

There was a song that said it all: "Sweet Home Chicago."

Oh, baby, don't you wanna go
Back to that same old place?
Sweet home Chicago.

She loved Chicago. Even its founding was special. The first set-
tler was a black man named Jean Baptiste Point du Sable, who hailed
from Sainte-Domingue, as Haiti was then known. He built the first
permanent settlement, not far from where one of her favorite
Chicago landmarks, the mighty Michigan Avenue Bridge, stands today. Forty years after Janet began her career in Chicago, she received
the History Makers Award from the institution named for him: the
DuSable Museum of African-American History.

Janet had never seen such a sight as Lake Michigan, as big and
blue as an ocean and in winter as windswept and icy as an arctic
wonderland. She never had a problem with the cold weather when
"The Hawk"—Chicagoese for high winds—was out. She found
Studs Terkel's radio interviews fascinating, and loved seeing the
Chicago River flow green on St. Patrick's Day (thanks to some dye
donated by the Pipefitters Union).

In Chicago she felt an energy and spirit of the city that said:
Anything is possible. And for her it was. Just about every celebrity
she had ever admired or even merely heard about passed through the
Windy City. Lena Horne. Count Basie. Duke Ellington. Louis Arm-
strong. Malcolm X. Jackie Robinson. Quincy Jones. Bill Cosby.
Mort Sahl.

Janet loved the food of Chicago. She was an Indianapolis girl
who had never tasted Serbian, Czech, or Polish food or frequented
the great cabarets—the London House, Mr. Kelly's, the House of
Blues, and Flukies on the South Side.

She was only twenty-five years old and standing in tall cotton.

It was not until Janet attended a reunion of her father's family
in Kentucky in 2005 that she learned that she was following the
path taken by a famous cousin, Willa B. Brown. Willa was born in
Glasgow, Kentucky, the same town as Janet's mother, but was raised
in Indiana. At the age of twenty-six, she moved to Chicago, and began taking flying lessons, inspired by the pioneer black pilot Bessie

Coleman, a 1920s air show star known as Queen Bess—the first black woman to fly and the first to earn an international pilot's license.

Willa earned a master mechanics certificate at Chicago's Aeronautical University and then obtained a master's degree, along with a pilot's license. She married Cornelius Coffey, and together they trained nearly two hundred pilots, including some of the famed Tuskegee Airmen of World War II.

Willa had been a trailblazer at many levels. She was described in a *Time* magazine article as a "cream and coffee-skinned Negress."* She became the first black member of the Civil Air Patrol and the only woman in America to hold simultaneously a mechanic's license and a commercial pilot's license. In addition to breaking racial barriers in the field of aviation, in 1946 she became the first black woman to run for Congress.

Janet was equally ambitious and she too would become a trailblazer. She was the first black woman on Chicago television. Maybe it was in the genes.

When Janet moved to Chicago, she was fortunate to have been welcomed by John H. Johnson. While few people in the white community may have ever heard of Johnson, to black people he was an icon, a giant who rose from poverty in rural Arkansas to become one of the most successful media magnates in the twentieth century.

More important to Janet than his wealth and fame was his wisdom and the strength of his character. He saw every obstruction in his path not as an impediment but as an opportunity. He dared to shatter the negative image that those in power in promoted, of blacks as violent, drug-crazed, immoral members of society.

His magazines displayed the beauty, talent, and strength of blacks in high gloss. He placed Lena Horne and Sidney Poitier on the cover of *Ebony* and *Jet*. He celebrated the music of Sam Cooke,

---

*See *Time*, September 25, 1939. See also Tonya Bolden, *The Book of African American Women* (Avon, Massachusetts: Adams Media, 2004), p. 203.

Otis Redding, and Chuck Berry. He extolled the cool of Shaft and Isaac Hayes. If *Time* or *Look* showed blacks in cotton-picking overalls, Johnson displayed them in haute couture.

They were not the stereotypical "Negroes" that Hollywood and Madison Avenue always portrayed them as being. They were beautiful, sophisticated, and sassy.

Johnson had spent years trying to persuade General Motors to place ads in his magazines. Interestingly enough, blacks were never allowed to appear in GM's ads. It finally occurred to the GM executives that not all black people were on welfare and that they were professionals and had good jobs. They consumed products just like white Americans. They bought Cadillacs and other luxury cars. It was the smell of money that persuaded GM's executives that Johnson's magazines offered them opportunity to fatten their balance sheets. He wanted to demonstrate "black power" not with a fist raised in defiance, but in the corporate boardrooms, where he was as fast, agile, and ruthless as any competitor of any color.

It was Johnson who gave Janet her start in the world of fashion and allowed her to walk down those glittering runways with confidence and panache. She was only twenty years old when she first started, but just knowing that he had chosen her allowed her to "strut her stuff" with a souciance that said, "I am somebody."

Among those who embraced Janet in Chicago was Mahalia Jackson, the great gospel singer. She allowed Janet to stay in her home until Janet could find an apartment of her own.

It was an extraordinary experience having breakfast where Mahalia Jackson would greet the morning by humming "Take My Hand, Precious Lord" or "Move on Up a Little Higher."

"It took me several days to adjust to the reality that I was living with the Queen of Gospel Song, a Chicago landmark as famous and solid as the Tribune Tower," Janet said.

Mahalia told her that when she first came to Chicago as a teenager, she kept herself alive by doing housekeeping. She was the daughter of a preacher, and so it was natural for her to join the

Greater Salem Baptist Church and sing gospel. She never sang anything other than gospel, refusing to sing any other kind of music, unlike many singers who started out with gospel and switched to rock 'n' roll. One of Jackson's accompanists, keyboardist Billy Preston, did just that, going on to fame as a rhythm and blues star.

"When you sing gospel," Mahalia once said, "you have a feeling there is a cure for what's wrong."

She helped find that cure by turning her home into a civil rights headquarters. She had been involved in the movement since the 1955 Montgomery bus boycott. Reverend Dr. Martin Luther King, Jr., a frequent guest, was awed by her voice.

Virtually everyone who either lived in or passed through Chicago and was involved in the civil rights movement at some point appeared at a gathering in her living room. It was there that Janet first met Andrew Young, who would one day become a United States congressman, ambassador to the United Nations, and mayor of Atlanta, Georgia.

Dick Gregory, the brilliant comedian who turned his satire to political activism was another luminary that Janet spent time with in Chicago. Janet had first met Dick in 1956 when she was fifteen years old. It was just a year after Emmett Till had been murdered. She and her friend April Brown were working at a Dairy Queen. He invited them to hear him lecture at a local church. The title of his speech was "It's Open Season on Negroes in America." With razor-sharp wit, he shredded the notion that black people enjoyed equal rights and protections under the law. In fact, he made the case that deer and rabbits enjoyed more rights than blacks did. Hunting was a highly regulated sport. By contrast, killing Negroes was an unrestricted one.*

You didn't have to be living in Mississippi to understand the naked truth beneath the fig leaf of Gregory's humor. Few whites had been charged with murder for killing blacks, and even fewer ever convicted.

---

*See *From Rage to Reason*, pp. 35–36.

Dick Gregory's comments resonate today as powerfully as they did fifty years ago. In New Orleans, months after hurricane Katrina had ravaged much of the city, Janet and I watched the evening news and saw several policeman beat a sixty-year-old black retired teacher while another officer mounted on horseback blocked bystanders and camera crews from seeing or filming the beating. As recently as 2006, a black man in Florida, wielding a hunting knife, was trapped in the center of a circle comprising thirteen police officers who were all armed with automatic weapons. Rather than disable him with a Taser gun, or shooting him in the arm or leg, they simply opened fire and killed him. Thirteen armed men against one man with a knife—and they had no alternative but to kill him?

What made this scene so Kafkaesque was that about a week after this incident, police in another state had to face a different kind of threat, one that arguably posed greater harm to them and others. The incident was also captured on television.

A moose was roaming the streets of a quiet neighborhood in a small town. The police fired a tranquilizing dart into the animal, and gently carted it off so it could be released to return to life in the forest.

The fact that the police could be so humane in saving the life of an animal and so contemptuous toward the life of a black man speaks volumes about the value with which blacks are held by those who are theoretically dedicated to upholding the rule of law.

Nearly forty years would pass before Janet received a call from her comedic genius friend. Gregory had read in her memoir that her cousin Jimmy had been lynched years ago.

Dick Gregory had been involved with Washington attorney Mark Planning in an effort to have the U.S. Senate offer a public apology for failing to stop the heinous practice of lynching in America. Gregory had the additional goal of having the Senate change the name of the Russell Office Building, named after Richard Russell, whose racist sentiments are well documented in his tape-recorded conversations with President Lyndon Johnson. He realized, however, that removing Russell's name was just a bridge too far.

Janet agreed to help promote the passage of a simple resolution expressing the Senate's apology. Frankly, she found it stunning that any senator could object to such a simple and long-overdue act.

"Bill, how can any of the people you served with refuse this simple resolution?"

I found the rationales offered by dissenting senators to be weak or disingenuous. More than four thousand men, women, and children had been murdered. Many had been disemboweled, their limbs and sexual organs amputated. Some had even been set on fire as they hung from trees. These acts of sheer terrorism had been carried out not just by mobs but also by "town fathers" who had arranged the savagery to serve as Sunday after-church entertainment during picnics.

Janet couldn't fathom how any person of reason or conscience, of any faith, could possibly tolerate such barbarism, such pure evil. They not only tolerated it, they sanctioned it under the cover of "states' rights." It was noteworthy that some of my former colleagues who refused to express any regret for past atrocities committed against blacks had done so for Native Americans and Japanese-Americans. And it was not happenstance that most of the dissenting senators were from the South. They managed to prevail upon the Senate leadership to schedule a vote on the antilynching resolution on a night when few senators would be in the city. They also insisted that the vote be cast by voice only so that the country would not see who lacked the moral courage to condemn acts unworthy of a nation that claimed that "all men were created equal and entitled to certain inalienable rights."

Janet couldn't restrain her fury. At a press conference held prior to the vote in the Mansfield Room where we had been married, she was asked to comment on the actions of those who had refused to allow a recorded vote by the Senate and thought an apology to be a waste of time and too insignificant to merit their attention.

She declared on national television ABC's Brian Ross that they were cowards, hiding behind the anonymity of a voice vote just the way they used to wear hoods to conceal their identities while they terrorized blacks.

I joined Janet later that evening in the Senate's Family Gallery to listen to the "debate." While she was clearly disappointed, she took heart that the two chief sponsors of the resolution were both white Southerners: Republican George Allen of Virginia and Democrat Mary Landrieu of Louisiana.* But hope turned to disappointment when Senator Allen, during the course of his 2006 reelection campaign for the senate, singled out S. R. Sidarth, a young American citizen of Indian descent, as a "Macaca." The word Macaca may have multiple meanings (one being monkey) and connotations, but it clearly is not a term of endearment. It appeared to have been used to embarrass Sidarth, who was working for Allen's challenger, by suggesting he was something of an alien in the midst of "real" Virginian voters.

After watching the incident that was broadcast on national television, Janet shook her head.

"You know, Bill," she said, "it's really hard to believe that Senator Allen could resort to using a racial slur, particularly after he stood on the Senate floor and read my words on the evil of racism."

I agreed and added, "As a potential presidential candidate, he should also have known that the camera never blinks."

"Wouldn't matter if it did." Janet added, "Character is supposed to be something you do or say when the camera's not on. . . . Some people, some things never change. This episode is just another reason why blacks are always skeptical about even the most well-meaning white people. I was willing to give him the benefit of the doubt over his past displays of the Confederate flag and the noose he kept in his office when he was Governor, but now this. More distrust, more doubt."

More shoes were to fall.

When Janet first learned that Senator Allen's mother was Tunisian, the thought occurred to her that perhaps the reason he had been so strong in his support for the anti-lynching resolution

---

*See *From Rage to Reason*, pp. 312–314. See also Philip Dray, *At the Hands of Persons Unknown: The Lynching of Black America* (New York: Random House, 2002).

was because he might have some African roots in his family tree.

Not quite.

In fact for several years, rumors had circulated that Senator Allen might have Jewish ancestry—rumors he either ignored or simply denied.

But the rumors persisted until he finally disclosed that his mother had recently confided to him that she was Jewish. While he expressed pride in his newly discovered ethnic heritage, Senator Allen was also quick to publicly declare that he still enjoyed feasting on ham sandwiches and pork chops.

I, of course, was fully aware of the irony involved that I carried a celebrated Jewish name and had spent six years in Hebrew school but was unable to qualify for membership in the Jewish faith because of the primacy of matrilineal rule under Jewish law. I quipped, "I tried, but George denied."

Sadly, further allegations surfaced alleging that Senator Allen, on multiple occasions during the 1970s, had frequently referred to blacks with the "N" word. Senator Allen stated that he couldn't recollect ever having used the racial slur.

It was at Mahalia Jackson's that Janet got to know Dr. Martin Luther King, Jr. Her first encounter with the famed civil rights leader was far from glorious. In March 1964, while attending a Chicago Freedom Movement Rally, she was jostled by a man in the packed crowd, causing her to spill the Coke she was carrying on the beautiful black mohair suit worn by the man in front of her. The crowd of men around the man suddenly turned aggressively, almost menacingly, toward Janet. The man she had just victimized held up his hand, signaling for calm.

She recognized the man's rich voice immediately. It was that of Dr. King, who remained calm, almost serene. Without a hint of annoyance, he allowed that he was "pleased to meet" her.

Dr. King was a regular guest at Mahalia's home and never failed to regale the others gathered there about that first encounter.

Like so many millions of Americans, Janet came to idolize Dr. King for his courage to face down the George Wallaces and Bull

Connors of the world and risk his life to force America to begin to live up to the ideals it so proudly professed and practiced so little.

Mahalia treated Dr. King as a son. She worried and fretted about his safety, once even venturing out of her sickbed to drive to a demonstration area where a hostile crowd was hurling bottles at him. Mahalia was right to be worried. Tensions were running high in the summer of 1966.

Chicago's Southside and Westside ghettoes were seething with discontent over extensive unemployment, inadequate housing, and poor educational opportunities for many blacks. Although the police were on hand, they did little to protect the protesters who gathered in Gage Park, Marquette Park, and Cicero. White crowds gathered to hurl stones, bottles, bags of urine, and trash with virtual impunity.

There were other civil eruptions of violence in Chicago. Riots had broken out in the Puerto Rican community when twenty-year-old Cruz Arcelis was shot by police. Fifty buildings were destroyed, sixteen people injured, and forty-nine arrested. Property damage amounted to millions of dollars. During the three days of rioting, Puerto Rican representatives refused to allow Dr. King to serve as a mediator between them and the police.

There were other forms of violence. Senator Charles Percy's daughter, Valerie, was bludgeoned and stabbed to death in the family's mansion in an exclusive Chicago suburb, a crime that was never solved. Richard Speck slaughtered eight Filipino women in their condominium unit. Only Corazon Amurao survived to describe how Speck had turned their home into an abattoir.

"While I never feared for my own life," Janet said, reflecting on that time in Chicago, "I was reminded constantly of danger, even several years later, when I lived on the twenty-seventh floor of a spectacular building that soared over Lake Shore Drive. It was then the largest apartment building in the world, a city within a city complete with swimming pools, a skating rink, and a theater big enough to seat 1,700 people. Architectural beauty, however, didn't always translate into safety. I was disturbed by the sight of a cardboard sheet that had been used to cover a missing window in the John Hancock skyscraper located near my apartment building. A young woman had fallen—many people believed she had been thrown—out of the window above the fiftieth floor. I kept the shade to my window that faced the office building closed so that I didn't have to contemplate the horror of the woman's death."

Janet was overjoyed to be in the company of Dr. King and was eager to join him in the civil rights movement. Unfortunately, she did not share his belief in nonviolence. "I was far more militant in my views, which were more closely aligned with those of H. Rap Brown and the Student Nonviolent Coordinating Committee (SNCC), along with Malcolm X, who declared that blacks should take 'all means necessary' to secure the rights guaranteed to all American citizens."

While Dr. King understood Janet's desire to become involved in the movement, he refused to allow her to march with him. After posing a series of questions about how she would respond if jeered or attacked during a demonstration, he was convinced, upon hearing her eye-for-an-eye philosophy, that she would be unarmed, but dangerous.

"Janet," he said, "with your attitude you'll get us all killed. This is a nonviolent movement. You have to remember, they have all the weapons, all the bullets. We have to use our brains. We will shame them into giving us our rights."

Janet recounted to me the night that she, Bernard Lee, the Reverend John Thurston, Chauncey Eskridge, and Jackie Jackson (Jesse Jackson's wife), were at Trader Vic's Restaurant in Chicago. They had just toasted Dr. King, pledging to him how they were all willing to join him, to fight and die in the crusade for justice and equal rights. As they started to exit through the restaurant's revolving glass doors out into the street, several of them were still carrying their thin-stemmed souvenir champagne glasses.

They were shuffling through the doors, jammed tightly against each other, when the pressure caused one of the glasses to pop, sounding for all the world like gunfire. They dropped to the ground—all except Dr. King, who laughed at the display of their fear.

"Let me just assure you, you are all safe. When that bullet comes, it's coming for me."*

Soon after Janet arrived in Chicago fortune started to shine brightly on her. First she won the Miss Chicagoland Beauty Pageant, a significant victory for her personally and symbolically. For a black woman to win the crown was something of a breakthrough, especially while at the same time blacks were fighting for fair housing and equal educational opportunities. Louis Armstrong performed at the crowning ceremony while Tony Bennett joined them on the stage at McCormick Place, Chicago's mammoth convention center. She began to move in charmed circles, dancing one evening with Duke Ellington, who, mischievously, claimed he had written *Satin Doll* for her.

She would meet other heroes of the black community, including Jackie Robinson, Floyd Patterson, and Jesse Owens. She found each of these superathletes to be genuinely kind and modest; and, given their accomplishments, their modesty was one of their laurels. For Janet, however, the most memorable celebrity was Muhammad Ali, regarded as the greatest heavyweight boxer of our time, perhaps ever. Modesty, of course, was not a word easily associated with Ali.

After Janet's photo appeared on the cover of *Jet*, she received a call from Chauncey Eskridge, her attorney who also represented Ali and many other African Americans in Chicago, including Dr. King. Like everyone else in America, she knew the charismatic boxing champion as Cassius Clay.

After Cassius Clay joined the Nation of Islam, he changed his name, and Chauncy forewarned Janet that when Muhammad called her, she was to be sure to call him by his adopted Muslim name. She was so excited when she received the call that she promptly forgot Chauncy's admonition and blurted out Muhammad's "slave name,"

---

*See *From Rage to Reason*, p. 59.

as he called it. Despite her misstep, they became quick friends. Muhammad would flirt with her, but it was always playful, and the relationship that evolved was closer to that of brother and sister. In fact, Muhammad treated her as a member of his family, inviting her once to accompany his parents to his fight with Ernie Terrell in Houston, Texas.

Muhammad Ali was beautiful and brash, poetic and powerful. The boxing world had never seen such a big man who moved with such grace and fluidity. He mocked and toyed with his opponents mercilessly, defeating them psychologically before ever stepping into the ring. He dazzled the sports world with his bravado and backed it up with his brains and brawn. Many white people were put off by this sassy, uppity Negro who boasted, "Ain't I pretty?" and said, "I can float like a butterfly and sting like a bee." He once tried to explain the ceaseless talking that earned him the nickname Mighty Mouth: "Where do you think I'd be next week if I didn't know how to shout and holler? I'd probably be down in my hometown washing windows and saying *yassuh* and *nossuh* and knowing my place."

When I told Janet about my childhood experiences and how I reacted to my frustration over religious rules by throwing my mezuzah into the Penobscot River, she recalled something that had happened to Ali. After winning the gold medal for boxing at the 1960 Olympics, he went home to Louisville, Kentucky, and, with the medal swinging on his chest, walked into a restaurant to buy a cheeseburger. He was refused service. He was so angry that he threw his medal into the Ohio River.

Ali made faces, recited doggerel, and pounded everyone in his path to the canvas. They hoped that big, bad Sonny Liston would punish Ali in the ring. Or Floyd Patterson. Or Ernie Terrell. Someone! Anyone! But it took the federal government to strip him of his title.

It happened on April 28, 1967. Muhammad had refused to be drafted into the Army. Ironically, on two prior occasions before he had become champion, the Army had declared that his aptitude test scores were so low that he was not fit to serve in the military. The war in Vietnam continued to rage on, and after he became the reigning heavyweight champion of the world, the Army reversed itself and insisted that his service was needed.* Muhammad declared that the war contravened his religious beliefs. More colorfully he said: "Why should I, a black man, go kill a yellow man for a white man who stole land from a red man? I'm not going to kill a yellow man for that white man who's oppressing me. That yellow man ain't done nothing to me. He ain't burned no crosses on my lawn. I ain't got no problem with them Viet Cong. They ain't never called me nigger."

Shadowed continually by reporters seeking his reasons for being against the war, Ali said, "I'm not going 10,000 miles from home to help murder and burn another poor nation simply to continue the domination of white slave masters of the darker people the world over. . . . I have nothing to lose by standing up for my beliefs. So I'll go to jail. So what? We've been in jail for 400 years."†

He was stripped of his title and sentenced by an all-white jury to five years in prison and a $10,000 fine. He never had to spend a day in prison, however. Three and a half years later, in 1971, the United States Supreme Court overturned his conviction. The Court ruled that as a conscientious objector, he was not guilty of draft evasion.

Dr. King had openly supported Muhammad's decision not to serve in the U.S. Army. Muhammad's long legal struggle came at a time when Dr. King was crusading against the Vietnam War. He arranged meetings with a number of celebrities and activists to rally support for Muhammad. In fact, the first time Janet met Harry Belafonte was at Belafonte's apartment in New York City. Dr. King had invited Janet to accompany him, but her presence provoked something of a controversy, as Belafonte had expressly indicated that the meeting was for "men only." Dr. King insisted that Janet be allowed to stay, and Belafonte, after noting that he had even sent his wife away for the evening, finally relented.

---

*See Remnick, David, *King of the World*, Vintage (1999), p. 285–86.
†Zirin, Dave, "What's My Name, Fool?" in *Sports and Resistance in the United States*, Haymarket Books, Chicago, Ill. (2005), p, 66.

That night, all in attendance exchanged views on how and where they might meet to avoid the prying eyes and ears of J. Edgar Hoover. Phone calls were out, as were meetings in hotels and places where Hoover's men could set up listening devices. They discussed meeting in Central Park, where they could see anyone close enough to monitor their conversations. They wanted to help Ali, but their agenda also included the causes of achieving racial justice and ending the war in Vietnam.

Danger has always been the unwanted companion of black people in America. But for Dr. King the danger zone had no geographical or physical limits.

In a sermon in April 1967 he said that the war was "taking the black young men who had been crippled by our society and sending them eight thousand miles away to guarantee liberties in Southwest Asia which they had not found in southwest Georgia and East Harlem." In the wave of condemnation that fell upon Dr. King, even the NAACP condemned him for making a "serious tactical mistake."

Three months after Dr. King's sermon, the Long Hot Summer of 1967 began. On July 13, police in Newark, New Jersey, arrested and beat up a black cab driver. When rumor spread that he had been killed, black tenants of a public housing project jammed the streets, confronting club-swinging police. Before rioting ended on July 17, the National Guard had been called out and twenty-six people were dead—all but two of them black.

Cities exploded with violence from New Haven, Connecticut, to Atlanta. In Detroit on July 23, police made a routine raid on an after-hours place. Patrons fought the police officers. The small melee quickly grew, encompassing much of the city and triggering one of the most deadly race riots in modern American history. National Guardsmen and U.S. Army troops finally quelled the rioting four days later. Forty-three people—most of them black—were dead, two thousand buildings had been burned down and seventy-five hundred people—again, most of them black—had been arrested.

Dr. King saw racial and economic injustice as the root causes of the violence, but he did not veer from his faith in nonviolence. He worked through the summer and into the fall on the Poor People's Campaign, which he described at a press conference in December 1967. The SCLC (Southern Christian Leadership Conference), he said, would "lead waves of the nation's poor and disinherited to Washington, D.C. next spring to demand redress of their grievances by the United States government and to secure at least jobs or income for all. We will go there, we will demand to be heard, and we will stay until America responds. If this means forcible repression of our movement we will confront it, for we have done this before. . . . But we hope with growing confidence that our campaign in Washington will receive at first a sympathetic understanding across our nation followed by dramatic expansion of nonviolent demonstrations in Washington and simultaneous protests elsewhere."*

One day, Muhammad drove Janet to the airport for a flight to San Francisco, where Dr. King was to make a major speech. While on the plane she was approached by a man who said he was a reporter and wanted to talk to her about Muhammad. When he started to probe about where she had met Muhammad and how long she had known him, she grew suspicious and cut the interview off.

Around the time Janet met Dr. King in Chicago, the Federal Bureau of Investigation had him under intense surveillance. Dr. King and all of those around him suspected that he was a target at the time, but it would be many years before the FBI would be forced to release its reports under the Freedom of Information Act.

The surveillance apparently began in earnest in 1962, when J. Edgar Hoover, director of the FBI, began passing to Attorney General Robert Kennedy reports that linked Dr. King and the SCLC to the U.S. Communist Party. This fed into the "red scare" mentality that assumed that if one had any association with communists, he or she had to be a tool of Moscow. The link had been forged by FBI communist hunters who had been tapping the

---

*See Taylor Branch, *At Canaan's Edge: America in the King Years, 1965–68* (New York: Simon and Schuster, 2006).

phone of a suspected white communist who was in touch with Dr. King.

FBI files show that Robert Kennedy first considered ordering phone taps of Dr. King and the SCLC. According to some accounts, Kennedy later changed his mind, but, without Kennedy's knowledge, the FBI launched what a Department of Justice statement later called "an illegal counter-intelligence program directed to discredit and neutralize the civil rights leader." That Department of Justice report, incidentally, was not issued until 1977, five years after Hoover's death.

There's little doubt that anyone associated with Dr. King in the 1960s was considered by J. Edgar Hoover to be a member of a communist conspiracy. Even paranoids are said to have enemies. Well, Janet and her friends were paranoid at the time, and they had enemies. Now, so many years later, the public can look at a document that states that on August 23, 1963, the assistant director of the FBI's Domestic Intelligence Division presented a seventy-page report to Hoover saying that the Communist Party had tried to infiltrate the civil rights movement but had failed.

Hoover was not satisfied with the dismissal of the charge of communist collaboration against Dr. King. In addition, noting that because Dr. King had a friendship with Bayard Rustin, a homosexual, Dr. King must be a homosexual as well. To add another dimension to Dr. King's transgressions, Hoover had arranged to film King in the company of other women and then send the film to King's wife, Coretta. But Coretta King would have no part in Hoover's attempt to discredit her husband, and she refused to watch or acknowledge anything that was designed to smear him.

Hoover, again refusing to accept the findings of his own department that Dr. King had no involvement with communists, continued to ask Robert Kennedy for authorization to tap the phones of Dr. King and the SCLC. This time, Kennedy approved, and intense surveillance of Dr. King began with the wiretapping of his phones and the planting of microphones at places where he was known to be, such as at SCLC meetings in Chicago. Janet was convinced that she was caught up in that surveillance.

* * *

In San Francisco, she mentioned to Dr. King her encounter on the plane with the man who held himself out as a reporter. "He was no reporter," Dr. King said. "In all probability, he was an FBI agent and he was following you on your trip out here. In fact, you should assume that your phones are all wiretapped. They're trying to dig up anything they can on Muhammad and me."

Years later, Janet asked the FBI for any records it had maintained pertaining to her association with Dr. King and Muhammad Ali. She was told none existed. Really?

She had traveled with both friends frequently. Tens of thousands of pages had been complied by the FBI revealing Hoover's obsession with both men, yet not a single word about a high-profile model? Could it be that she was too small and insignificant to be caught up in Hoover's dragnet? Or was there a Rose Mary Woods (of Watergate fame) who hit a delete button?

Dr. King campaigned relentlessly for the poor and disadvantaged. On April 4, 1968, he was in Memphis, where he was to lead a protest march in sympathy with striking garbage workers. He and some aides were to have dinner in a supporter's home. Dr. King was staying at the blacks-only Lorraine Motel, where Cab Calloway, Nat King Cole, and Count Basie had stayed in their day. As he was leaving his second-floor room, he paused on the balcony and was fatally shot.

When that time came on the infamous day in Memphis, no one was there to take the bullet for him, just as he had once said in jest—or was it a prophecy?

Janet was in New York on April 4, 1968, working as a model for Kaiser Jeep at the New York automobile show being held at the Columbus Circle Coliseum. That evening she went to see the all-black version of *Hello, Dolly!* The show starred Pearl Bailey and Cab Calloway, who had come out of retirement to play Horace Vanderbilt. She had met Cab earlier, when she was traveling with the Ebony Fashion Fair. He was always highly energetic and entertaining. That night, however, he seemed out of sorts, terribly sad and lethargic.

Janet concluded only that he was starting to feel his age. It also struck her as odd that when Pearl Bailey came out onto the stage to take a bow, she lingered for a long time and said, "I could feel your love come over these footlights all during the performance. I love you back. We love you back, and now more than ever we need love in this country."*

It was not until Janet was making her way back to her hotel that she learned that Dr. King had been assassinated. She completely lost all composure and restraint. On her way to the elevator, she hoped that she wouldn't encounter any white people at that moment, as she believed it was their silence that enabled racial hatred to flourish in America and that made them complicit to Dr. King's murder.

Janet had planned to fly to Memphis for Dr. King's funeral, but she received a call from her mother. Another shooting! The victim was "Little Myrna," daughter of a neighbor who had been a close childhood friend. A man had walked into the church where she was singing in the choir and begun shooting. One of the bullets hit her, blowing away part of her head.

Janet flew home totally devastated. She had lost two people she had dearly loved. While Janet was picking out a casket for Myrna, she heard a television set playing somewhere in the funeral home. Mahalia Jackson was singing a eulogy for Dr. King. For Janet, words do not exist that can describe the ineffable sadness in Mahalia's voice.

Many black Americans remain convinced that Dr. King had been assassinated in a government conspiracy directed by the man who insanely hated him, J. Edgar Hoover. Although multiple investigations have concluded that Ray was the lone gunman, for Janet, Hoover's spirit was in James Earl Ray's racist heart even if his finger wasn't on the trigger.

Thirty-five years passed before Janet traveled to Memphis to promote her memoir. While there, she visited the Lorraine Motel,

---

*See *From Rage to Reason*, pp. 86–87.

the place where Dr. King had been assassinated. The tour guide who escorted her had once worked for President Clinton's secretary of commerce, Ron Brown, another hero to black people who had died too soon. She asked if Janet wanted to go out on the balcony to see where Dr. King had been shot. Reluctantly, Janet agreed to do so. She touched the wrought iron bars on the balcony and looked across to that spot to see where Dr. King's cowardly assassin had lain in wait. She could almost see the violent scene in her mind. Every fiber in her being was enraged at the thought of what had happened. She broke down and cried. Finally, after collecting herself, she arranged with the guide to have a memorial wreath, with fresh flowers, displayed over the balcony twice a year: once on the day of Dr. King's birth; the other on the date of his death.

After Memphis, Janet traveled on to visit the Martin Luther King, Jr., Historic Site in Atlanta. It was there where she was stunned for a second time. In a display case were the items found in Dr. King's possession on the day he was murdered. There she saw a small wallet that she had bought Dr. King for his last birthday in January 1968. She had intended it as a lighthearted, gentle reminder that he needed to break his habit of rarely carrying cash. When she saw that small gift with the special gold letters of his initials embossed on the wallet, she felt that she remained connected to him to the very day he died. Once again, she broke down and began to weep.

Martin Luther King, Jr., was only thirty-eight when he died, but he was wise beyond his years. Those who thought they could silence him failed to understand that the power of his message for a better and more just America could not be stopped by a bullet.

It was Dr. King's assassination that opened doors that had previously been closed to blacks. The federal government and corporate leaders, whether from shame or fear, decided that people of color should be given new opportunities.

Marshall Field, Chicago's biggest and most famous department store, broke its color barrier when it allowed Janet to model fashions in a place where black men and women once were not allowed to try on clothes. It was considered revolutionary to let this black woman wear the bridal gown in their fashion shows. Her modeling appearances made her highly visible, especially for television executives who were looking for ways to put a few black faces on screen.

In the summer of 1969, she was asked to be the weathergirl for a local UHF station that offered "A Black View of the News." She knew virtually nothing about weather forecasting or television reporting, but was mindful of the advice offered by Gypsy Rose Lee, the vaudeville star and stripper: "A girl's gotta have a gimmick."

Chicago was suffering from a ninety-degree heat wave at the time. She decided to tease the viewing audience by wearing a mink coat during the broadcast, promising to reveal what she was wearing beneath the coat after a commercial break.

She came back on to do a straight report of the weather, and gave the appearance that she was going to wrap up the report and ignore the promise she had just made minutes earlier. Then, as if it was an afterthought, she opened the coat and revealed that she was wearing a bikini.

Well, Gypsy Rose Lee was right. The gimmick worked. The switchboard lit up with calls from people who were watching the program. Not everyone approved, but her beauty and brazenness caught the attention of the executives of the CBS network affiliate. She was hired to do the weather (without any more gimmicks) and quickly demonstrated that she had a natural ability to conduct interviews with prominent personalities, such as Woody Allen, Sidney Poitier, Harry Belafonte, and Topol, the Israeli actor and star of *Fiddler on the Roof.*

At the same time, requests for modeling assignments suddenly multiplied. *Jet* magazine published a saucy photo of her on its cover. The photograph drew a good deal of attention, resulting in more requests for modeling assignments.

In 1973, in addition to doing the weather and interviews in Chicago, she was hosting her own television show five days a week in Indianapolis called *Indy Today with Janet Langhart.*

It was a happy, exhausting, and career-building year. And when she received an offer from a major television station in Boston, momentum and ambition tugged her eastward.

Still, she cried when the plane lifted from O'Hare and she looked down on Chicago's beautiful skyline and lakeshore. She thought about all the incredible people she had met in Chicago: Mahalia Jackson, Dr. King, John H. Johnson, Muhammad Ali, just to name a few.

Janet would never forget Muhammad when she saw him standing alone in a crowd during a Bud Billiken Day Parade in Chicago.

As Miss Chicagoland in the parade, Janet was sitting in the rear seat of a convertible, waving to the thousands of people who were cheering as she rode by. Muhammad, now without his title, had no entourage with him, none of the usual hangers-on. She could feel tears start to well up in her eyes. Muhammad waved to her and signaled that he would meet her at the end of the parade route. When she finally arrived, he was waiting in his car. They took a drive along Lake Shore Drive.

Janet was distraught over how Ali had been abandoned. He was completely nonplussed, however. "They've taken everything from you," she said.

"No, they didn't. They didn't take everything from me. They didn't strip *me* from me. I got *me*. I got my dignity. As long as I got that, they can't take anything."

Janet started crying. "Muhammad, they took your title. That's how you make your living."

"Let me tell you something, Janet. I've got my dignity and that's all you ever need to make it in life. I know you want to be somebody . . . but don't ever want something that only *they* can give you. . . . You're a poor black girl; you want a lot of things you don't have. And there are a lot of things out there in the world to take. But don't want those things more than you love or want yourself. Never want anything that badly, because that's when they can take *you* from you."*

---

*See *From Rage to Reason,* pp. 83–85.

They took away Muhammad's prime years of boxing, but they could never strip him of his principles and pride. It was a lesson Janet's grandmother had offered her years earlier: "Never sell more of yourself than you can buy back later."

As the plane climbed above the cumulus clouds that looked as soft as cotton candy, Janet had little idea that the *they* that Muhammad had warned her about would be so many in number and so cunning of mind.

She looked out the window, feeling her eyes start to mist up, and murmured to herself, "Good-bye, Sweet Home Chicago."

Ten

Law and Politics

The bromides about law school almost proved true: "The first year, they scare you to death; the second year, they work you to death; and the third year, they bore you to death." By my third year, I had mastered the law's language and art of legal analysis. And I felt rather superior to the fresh faces entering the school's doors for the first time, much as a war-weary veteran might view the innocence of new recruits and sympathize with the forthcoming pain they were about to face on the front lines of battle.

As a result of working to death that second year, I was selected to serve on the editorial board of the *Boston University Law Review*, and that left little time for boredom. In addition, in a few short months, I would become a father for the second time of a son. We would name him Christopher. Graduation and impending fatherhood concentrated my mind, forcing me to seriously consider how I was going to turn the theory of law into a livelihood.

Although I gave serious consideration to joining a Wall Street firm and possibly doing a stint at the U.S. Department of Justice, I was not convinced that I could work in either densely populated environment. Instead, I accepted a position working as the assistant to Thomas F. Lambert, Jr., editor-in-chief of the American Trial Lawyers Association. I intended to hold the position for a limited time, but the opportunity to work closely with Professor Lambert was an opportunity I couldn't pass up.

Tom had been a prosecutor on the staff of Justice Robert Jackson during the Nuremberg War Crimes trials. He became the dean of Stetson Law School in Florida at the age of twenty-seven and, subsequently, a full professor at Boston University Law School, where he lectured to standing-room-only classrooms. He was in my opinion, and that of virtually every practicing trial attorney, the most eloquent orator in America. Not one of the most talented members of the trial bar, who had won megamillion-dollar judgments before juries, would agree to follow him to a podium.

Tom possessed a photographic memory and could cite hundreds of cases by volume, page number, and specific paragraph without ever referring to a note. He was, however, far more than a legal scholar. He was so well versed in the classics that lawyers would call on him constantly for some esoteric reference or point they could make to sway juries or appellate court judges. He was, in effect, the Google of his time.

At the conclusion of each workday, I would drive him home from his office in the home of Harvard's famous dean Roscoe Pound to his apartment that overlooked the Charles River. There we would join his lovely wife, Elizabeth, sip devastating martinis, and watch sailboats dance on the water against the red glow of the setting sun. For an hour we would discuss a new novel or work of non-fiction completely unrelated to the law while classical music or light jazz played softly in the background.

Those were magical moments for me, and they reinforced my admiration for a man who was the most gifted advocate for those who were victims of negligence, malpractice, or social injustice.

On one occasion, Tom invited me to attend a speech he had been asked to deliver at the Southern Attorneys General Convention being held in Wilmington, Delaware. The setting was a scene taken out of an MGM movie. A sprawling mansion atop gently rolling hills. Black waiters dressed in white dinner jackets serving mint juleps in white-gloved hands. The exquisite sound of violins floating softly over the easy conversation of friends. It was all so, well, Southern.

Tom had been invited to give the keynote speech. His speech was titled "From Civil Rights to Civility."

While he was predictably courteous and gracious in manner, he was unwilling to sand down the edges to his message on the need to recognize that the Civil War had not ended the evil of racism in America. For well over an hour, he spoke passionately about the history of slavery, debunking Southerners' claims that they were simply defending their traditions and the concept of "States' Rights." Tom pulled no punches before this audience. The invocation of "States' Rights," he said, was little more than a mask they wore to cover their naked racial hatreds.

During the course of his remarks, several attorneys from Alabama walked out of the ballroom.

Tom was unfazed. He was also unwilling to give the North a free pass from criticism that evening. Indeed, while the South is consistently and deservedly cited for its racist practices, back in 1863 New York City dwellers engaged in one of the most violent and savage riots in New York's history. Although the imposition of a military draft to help bolster the diminished ranks of the Union Army following the battle at Gettysburg was said to be the spark that ignited the riot, the rioters, many of whom supported Southern Democratic politicians, seized the opportunity to beat, murder, and lynch nearly two hundred blacks. Tom decided to skip the past and focus on the present.

Paraphrasing the words of Dick Gregory, Tom said, "In the South, people don't care how close Negroes get to them. After all, white babies are given suckle by Negro women. They just don't want them to get too high. In the North, there is a different brand of racial prejudice. We don't care how high Negroes climb in life. We just don't want them to get too close."

When Tom finished, he was given a standing ovation. I beamed with the pride of a son rather than that of a mere apprentice.

As much as I admired Tom, I couldn't accept the notion that I would have to be beholden to the organization's board of directors. Trial lawyers are, by their very nature, self-centered, confident, and vainglorious. I had watched Tom reject any attempt (and there were many) by the top members in the organization to use his prestige and pen to glorify them by heralding their specific cases in a monthly newsletter and annual report. When he rejected their attempts to compromise his judgment, they attempted to undermine him and replace him with a crony. At one point, they in essence had handed me a knife to place in his back by promising that I would be rewarded his crown. I would have none of it and neither would the general membership of the association.

But the experience convinced me that I should never be beholden to anyone for a paycheck (Siskind's rule of never having only one client).

When I finally convinced Tom that I intended to leave at the end of the summer, he tried to persuade me to teach law. It would be a virtuous circle: I would enrich the students and they would rejuvenate me in return. He forewarned me that "the practice of law will either harden you or hurt you."

I suspected that he was right, but I was determined to prove that I could swim with the sharks and survive.

When I returned to Bangor, I decided to register as a Republican. I was little more than an ingénue when it came to politics. I had admired John F. Kennedy and thought his call to public service inspirational, and I found the Democratic Party's commitment to social justice appealing. But I also was influenced by my father's example of working eighteen-hour days to provide for his family without any assistance from the government. His hard work, frugality, and criticism of waste in the expenditure of tax dollars proved more compelling to me in my deliberations. Although he was inclined to hurl a pox upon both parties, I thought his antitax, antiregulatory rhetoric was more closely aligned with the Republican philosophy of limited government.

Before the ink on the registration card had dried, I was approached by several Republican stalwarts to manage the congressional campaign of Howard Foley, a popular, hard-nosed county attorney who had undertaken to challenge the popular Democratic incumbent, Bill Hathaway. I had little interest in politics at that moment and zero experience. I was perplexed why, with little more than four months remaining until Election Day, Foley didn't have a campaign manager. I was not reassured when told that the candidate had been serving in that capacity.

In essence, I was the only warm body in town, and the party leaders had assumed that any young man who was willing to declare himself to be a Republican had to possess all the right stuff to cope with the vicissitudes of a political campaign.

I agreed to accept the position, with the thought that I might gain the gratitude of the party establishment, such that it was, and that it might serve to balance the political activities of my future law partner, who was active in Democratic politics.

Once seated in the chair of campaign manager, I quickly discovered why there had been a vacancy in the position. Foley was not "manageable." He was extremely bright and exceptionally blunt, which was an attractive combination, but not a winning one. Howard's bluntness could easily slip into bombast.

The campaign, indeed, proved to be a learning experience. I worked out of Howard's private law office, spending most of my time studying the demographics of the largest congressional district east of the Mississippi River. There I also learned how to create television and radio commercials and purchase the best time slots for their broadcasts. As little as I knew about the makeup of the nine counties and twenty-six thousand square miles that comprised the district, I knew even less about managing people either above or below me in authority. When the campaign's fund-raising efforts started to wane, I proceeded to lecture one of Bangor's most successful businessmen on the subject of motivation. He promptly—and properly—quit as the finance chairman and bequeathed both the title and responsibilities to me in a less than ceremonious fashion.

From there, well, it was all uphill. Foley traveled north to Aroostook County, known by its hearty residents as "God's Country." One of the major issues of the campaign was a proposal by

Congressman Hathaway (and Senator Edmund Muskie) to construct the Dickey-Lincoln Dam, a large hydroelectric project on the St. John River. The county suffered from high unemployment and was in desperate need of an economic boost. The promise of hundreds of construction jobs and lower utility bills was a politically potent message to voters in the region.

Foley was totally opposed to putting the production of electricity in the hands of the federal government. Fair enough; it was a principled conservative position. Unfortunately, he could not resist resorting to a colorful articulation of his views. He proclaimed that he would provide free champagne to every resident in Aroostook County if Congressman Hathaway's promise were ever to become a reality.

Foley was, in fact, a visionary. Ultimately, after nearly a quarter century of effort, all plans for the construction of the Dickey-Lincoln dam were finally scrapped by Congress. The people of Aroostook County seized upon his prognostication as evidence that he was a tight-fisted Republican who was dedicated to depriving them of the promise of growth and prosperity.

Statesmanship has its rewards, but political victory is rarely one of them. The wheels came off the Foley campaign (the tires were already threadbare) and Hathaway rolled to a smashing victory.

As I shut the doors of the campaign office on November 15, 1966, I hoped that my venture into the practice of law would prove more successful than my foray into politics.

When I decided to return to Bangor, I spurned an opportunity to join a prominent trial firm and instead formed a partnership with Errol Paine, a former schoolmate who promised to evenly split his weekly income. He had four children at the time and I had two.

"How much are you making?" I asked.

"One hundred and fifty dollars."

"I get seventy-five dollars a week. That's it?"

"You got it."

"OK. I accept."

My first day in the offices of Paine & Cohen proved that I had much to learn about the practice of law.

Alfred Cataldo, a burly man, burst into my office with a temperament as hot as the weather was cold. He had delivered a truckload of Christmas trees to a buyer who had refused to pay him but still had control of the flatbed containing the trees.

"I want my trees back now!" Mr. Cataldo boomed.

I dropped my voice an octave and assured him that I could achieve that result. Actually, at that moment I had only a vague notion of his legal remedies. But an action of "replevin" sounded right to me. (Replevin is a legal action for recovering property.)

I advised Mr. Cataldo that my fee would be two hundred and fifty dollars, payable in advance. I had the passing thought that if I was unsuccessful in securing the return of his trees, he might consider taking out his rage on me. So I set the fee on what I thought was the high side, with the hope that he might consider it unacceptable and walk out the door.

He plunked down the fee in cash and asked menacingly, "How long will it take you?"

I lowered my voice once more, this time to a near-gravel level. "I'll have the papers ready in two hours."

As soon as Cataldo stormed out of the office, I rushed into Errol's office, completely at a loss as to where I might file a writ of replevin or find a sheriff to serve a summons.

Errol just laughed, pointed to a set of large loose-leaf books on the shelf in his office, gave me the Penobscot County Sheriff's telephone number, and said, "You only made one mistake so far."

"What's that?"

"You should have charged him four hundred dollars."

It was conventional wisdom that young attorneys were expected to labor in the vineyards for seven years, gratefully accepting whatever crumbs fell off the table of the established firms. In other words, we should take the cases they no longer would accept and be prepared to endure slim economic pickings. In addition, we should be prepared to devote significant amounts of time to community service.

Errol and I had different plans. We had no intention of waiting in the equivalent of a breadline. While we were fully prepared to toil in the vineyards, we were going to skip the lean years.

We were determined to show the legal community that we could compete at any level of law practice. There was no case so complicated or distasteful that we would refuse to undertake it. Moreover, we would not only be eager to engage in jury trials but be willing to appeal every case throughout the state and federal courts, if necessary. We were going to establish a reputation from the moment we opened our partnership doors.

There were only two ways to show that we had the talent to match our bravado. According to the ethical practices in force at the time, the only way that lawyers could advertise their talents was to perform in the courtroom and actively engage in community service activities. We were professionals, not tradesmen, and we were not to hawk our capabilities like some carnival barker.

Two years after we opened the doors of our firm, Errol ran for the office of county attorney. He was elected easily but found that filling the two assistant positions was impossible. They were all work and virtually no pay. So taking a page out of John F. Kennedy's playbook when he appointed his brother Bobby to be attorney general, Errol appointed me as his top assistant.

I thought that I was fully prepared to do battle in the courtroom. A no-nonsense trial judge showed me that I had some hard lessons to learn.

One of my criminal trials involved a rape case.

At the time, rape was almost impossible to prove unless you had a witness that was either present during the rape or was in a position to otherwise lend credibility to the victim's charge. Usually, rape—unless multiple parties are involved—is not performed for the benefit of spectators. Officers in the sheriff's department advised me that a criminal conviction would be problematic and that I should forgo prosecuting the alleged rapist. I disregarded their ad-

Welcoming Janet to Capitol Hill (1991). *Courtesy of U.S. Senate*

Janet and Muhammed Ali at the NABOB dinner in Washington, D.C. (1992).

Janet with Sydney Poitier at the home of film producer, Mike Medavoy (2004). *Courtesy of Jerry Friedman*

Harrison Ford joining me and Janet to celebrate Armed Forces Day at Andrews AFB (1998). *Courtesy of Dept. of Defense*

Janet with Richard Burton, Elizabeth Taylor, and Joan Kennedy at a Boston gala. Mayor Kevin White (left) was the host.

A reflective moment during the House of Representatives Impeachment Inquiry of President Richard M. Nixon (1974). *Courtesy of* The Washington Post

Conferring with Senator Daniel Inouye (left) and Congressman Lee Hamilton (right) during the Iran-Contra investigation (1987).

Janet conducting an on-the-street interview during the school busing crisis in Boston (1974).

Sharing my novel with former President Richard Nixon (1995). *Courtesy of U.S. Senate*

Conferring with President Ronald Reagan at the White House (1984). *Courtesy of the White House*

Vice President George H. W. Bush and Mrs. Barbara Bush offer congratulations on my reelection to the Senate in 1984. *Courtesy of U.S. Senate*

Discussing the Kosovo War with President Bill Clinton, Prime Minister Tony Blair, and Secretary of State Madeleine Albright at a NATO summit (1999). *Courtesy of* The New York Times

Janet interviewing Civil Rights icon, Rosa Parks on BET (1993). *Courtesy of Robert Brooks/BET*

Janet's cousin, Willa B. Brown, the first black woman to hold a commercial pilot's license, trained the Tuskegee Airmen. *Courtesy of the Smithsonian Institute*

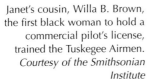

Meeting South African President Nelson Mandela at his home in Quana, S. Africa (2000). *Courtesy of the Dept. of Defense*

Janet's cousin Floyd Bridges, his daughter Mechelle, Janet, and me, joined by Senator Barak Obama to celebrate the Tuskegee Airmen (2005). *Courtesy of Alphonso King*

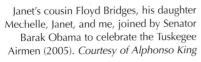

Janet and I tour a Jewish cemetery overlooking the war-torn city of Sarajevo (1999). *Courtesy of the Dept. of Defense*

Janet celebrates Senator Ted Kennedy's birthday (1978).

Janet and former Secretary of State Henry Kissinger at a White House dinner.

Opening night of *Men of Honor*, a movie celebrating Carl Brashear, the Navy's first black diver, starring Cuba Gooding, Jr. who portrayed Brashear in the movie (2000). *Courtesy of Dept. of Defense*

Sailors give the SecDef a "welcome aboard" salute (1999). *Courtesy of the Dept. of Defense.*

Janet and I attend the christening of the U.S.S. Winston S. Churchill, DDG-81 at Bath Iron Works, Bath, Me. Janet was the co-sponsor of the ship that bears her hero's name. Commander Michael Franken looks on (2000). *Courtesy of the Dept. of Defense.*

Israeli Prime Minister Benjamin Netanyahu and I inspect our troops during a formal ceremony at the Pentagon (1997). *Courtesy of the Dept. of Defense*

Janet and me meeting China's President Jiang Zemin in Beijing (2000). *Courtesy of the Dept. of Defense.*

Nyet! A friendly exchange between Russian President Boris Yeltsin and me in Senator Bob Dole's Leader's Office (1995). *Courtesy of U.S. Senate*

vice and decided that I would take my chances with a jury. The problem was that the case never reached the jury.

During the course of the trial, I asked the rape victim to identify her attacker.

"Is the man who raped you in the courtroom today?

"Yes."

"Is his name [John Doe]?"

"Yes."

"Is he the same John Doe who is the defendant?"

"Yes."

"Will you point him out for the benefit of the jury?"

The victim stood and pointed at the defendant, John Doe. "Is the man that you're now pointing to the person who raped you?"

"Yes."

I went on to ask questions of other witnesses about what treatment the victim sought and called the medical personnel who had treated her on the night of the rape. I then rested my case and expected the defense counsel to call his client to rebut the testimony or allow the case to go to the jury.

Instead, he simply stood and said, "I ask the Court for a directed verdict in favor of my client."

This was, I thought, a standard procedural motion, but to my surprise the judge said, "Request granted. The jury is dismissed."

Bang. The gavel came crashing down.

Surely, the judge was in error! To the contrary, the error was mine. I had failed to state, after the victim had pointed to the defendant, "Let the record show that the witness is pointing to the defendant, John Doe."

This was a mandatory requirement, because if the case were ever appealed by the defendant, the appellate court would have only the printed record before it, and without those magic words, the court would not know whom the witness had identified.

I was stunned. In my naiveté, I thought that in the interest of justice, the judge might have intervened to correct my oversight. No such luck. He was not going to place his finger on the scales of justice to help out the county. It was my job to present the case according to the rules of evidence, and I had failed to do so.

I later learned that the judge was convinced that I could not satisfy Maine law as it then existed without greater corroborating evidence, and he wanted to spare the county the cost of an appeal in the event the jury decided to convict the defendant. He was also sending this young prosecutor a signal not to overreach in marginal cases, no matter however odious I found the defendant or his conduct to be.

I left the courtroom angry that day. Angry with a law that placed a nearly impossible burden upon a rape victim, and angry with myself that I had made such a fundamental error.

I vowed that I would never make such a stupid mistake again. And I never did. In three years of prosecuting criminals, I lost only one other case.

As part of my prosecutorial duties, I was required to attend autopsies of murder or suicide victims and those killed as a result of someone's criminal negligence. It was important for me to witness every step taken by the county pathologist, as defense counsel were certain to allege some irregularity in the process that they could exploit to undermine the case. "If you're going to be successful in court, you have see death up close," Errol counseled me. "A numb feeling will pass through you when you see it, and that numb feeling is what you have to relate to the jury."

Frankly, I had little intellectual curiosity about how the thighbone was connected to the hipbone. Most importantly, I held no desire to see a human body systematically eviscerated with hacksaws, rotary blades, and rib cutters and watch brains and internal organs pulled out and dropped like so much garbage into a plastic throwaway bag. But I went, time and again, and hated every moment of it.

Shotgun-in-the-mouth suicides, automobile accidents, and negligent homicides. Each time I attended an autopsy, I felt almost as violated as the victim lying on that cold metal table. And I could never feign the pathologists' cavalier, ho-hum, just-another-piece-of-meat matter-of-factness.

The experience increased my level of competence as a prosecutor, but it also made me more rigid and zealous in my approach to punishing society's miscreants. I would discover on occasion that there was no such thing as an open-and-shut or "slam dunk" case. More than once I encountered what trial lawyers call "jury justice." I had successfully convicted a drunk driver who had killed a sixteen-year-old girl as she walked along the side of the road on her way home one evening. During the course of the autopsy performed the night of her death, I had watched the pathologist move with brutal efficiency in carrying out his task. I was thankful that the girl's parents were not present to see what a complete stranger was doing to her body. The pathologist did something that struck me as macabre. He draped a small towel over the young woman's pubic area as if to protect it from the prying eyes of the law enforcement officials surrounding the table. I could not suppress the thought of how absurd was the attempt to provide a measure of decency in an abattoir.

The absurdity haunted me for weeks and served to reinforce an already unyielding approach I had displayed toward those who climbed behind the wheel of an automobile while under the influence of alcohol.

Shortly after the negligent homicide case, I was asked to prosecute an Air Force sergeant who had been arrested for driving on the wrong side of the highway. He failed miserably to pass the standard field tests for sobriety. He couldn't walk a straight line or touch his finger to his nose without the risk of poking out his eye. What solidified the case in my judgment was the observation of a young Air Force captain who had been sent to bail out the defendant some five hours after the arrest. The captain testified that the sergeant was completely incoherent, unstable, and disoriented when he observed him in his jail cell.

With the image of the dead young girl still fresh in my mind, I was determined to send this man to the slammer. It has been observed that there isn't a more ineffective lawyer than one who is passionately convinced of his client's innocence. I found the corollary to be true as well. I was passionately convinced of the sergeant's guilt; the jury was less so.

I paraded a series of witnesses before the jury: the bartender who had served the sergeant; the arresting officer; the officer on duty at the police station; and finally, the captain who had come to bail out the defendant on the morning after his arrest. The captain was, I thought, a superb witness. Clean-cut. Well groomed. A spit-and-polish, by-the-book young man who clearly was on a positive career path.

By contrast, the sergeant looked the part of a decadent boozer. He had a whiskey-soaked voice that sounded like bark being peeled off a tree. He was red-faced and had eyes that were clouded and sad. The testimony that he offered in his defense was patently false. He had weaved in the road because he was trying to avoid hitting a cat that had scurried in front of this car. He may have had three or four drinks but that was before he had eaten a full-course meal.

"Could you explain why you seemed to have so much difficulty walking a straight line for the police officer?"

"Oh, yes, that was because I had suffered serious wounds to both knees while serving in Vietnam."

He failed to explain just exactly how he acquired his war wounds while serving as an aircraft mechanic far from enemy lines.

"And about that nose-to-finger test where you nearly poked out your eye?"

"Just a little case of the nerves."

And so it went.

I had trouble concealing my contempt for his tale of woe, and I tried to infuse the jury with my absolute conviction that the defendant was drunk on the night he was arrested but had lied under oath while testifying.

After three hours of deliberation, the jury returned a verdict of "Not Guilty."

Why? I asked the jury afterwards. The answer was that they didn't like the young captain. He was too smooth, too arrogant, too willing to testify against a common man, one who may not have had the privileges of wealth or schooling. After all, he had served his country in a time of war, and he looked as if life had not treated him with a gentle hand.

After the loss that day, I felt another one of Professor Paul Siskind's warnings touch me with the heat of a branding iron: "Just remember, any connection between law and justice is purely coincidental."

The lesson I learned that day didn't diminish the zeal with which I prosecuted criminal defendants. But it did force me to look at each case through a prism that was not so quite so perfect in its size or shape as I had once thought.

Together Errol and I were a formidable team. Errol was the fist of iron; I was the velvet glove. During the convening of each grand jury, we would secure roughly seventy to ninety criminal indictments. Our message to defense counsel was simple: have your client plead guilty to the charges or go to trial. We stacked cases back to back and tolerated no delaying tactics. Once the trial started, there would be no deals to allow a pleading to a lesser offense.

Since we were considered to be part-time civil servants, we also were allowed to maintain our civil or noncriminal law practice. In a single year we tried two landmark cases in contract and real estate law. Although we lost both cases at the trial, we appealed them to Maine's Supreme Judicial Court, where we were successful in overturning hundred-year-old precedents. The fact that most trial lawyers had considered the cases to be unwinnable, and that we were prepared to spare no effort on behalf of our clients, gave us enormous negotiating leverage from that point forward.

It was not long before our reputation spread beyond the city of Bangor. Soon our firm would have six lawyers and nine secretaries.

The confidence I had gained in appearing before juries on an almost daily basis carried over to my civil practice. A judge of Maine's highest court appointed me to review the issues involved in a case where a wealthy individual wanted to develop a ski resort on a portion of the real estate that had been left in trust for the benefit of his children. Everyone assumed I would give it a cursory review and endorse the transaction. I concluded that the proposed development would not serve the interests of the children and sued the father; the bank that was serving as the trustee of the real estate; the state agency that was to finance the development costs; and the father of my best friend, the chairman of the bank's board of directors, who had once offered me the position of general counsel of his oil company.

At one point, I looked across the courtroom to see seven attorneys at the defense table. I received a warning at one point from the lead defense attorney that my career as a lawyer was finished. The threat only caused me to vow to fight the case through to Maine's Supreme Court. Although after four years of litigation, the proposal to develop the land was finally approved, I wanted to send a message to the most established firms in the state that I could not be intimidated.

I also began to understand the truth contained in Tom Lambert's forewarning: success would not come without costs. In addition to dealing with the disposition of the community's criminals, I also handled numerous bankruptcy and divorce cases. They were not particularly lucrative, but they did pay the bills. And as we continued to add more attorneys and secretarial help to our firm, those bills continued to balloon. But more than economic factors were involved. I was dealing almost daily with other people's failures—in their business pursuits and in their lives. I watched with dismay as love dissolved into hatred, and children were treated as little more than pawns in the hands of parents who were seeking to increase or reduce weekly support payments. I was dealing with society's underbelly, and what I found there was not life-enhancing.

The world's slow stain was starting to touch me and I felt unclean.

I had been away from Bangor less than eight years pursuing my education, but upon my return I was struck by the changes that had taken place during my absence. I had always been proud that I had been born and raised in Maine's "Queen City," but the city now had about it a curious air of ruin and expectation. The Defense Department had announced that it was closing Dow Air Force Base. The decision sent shock waves through the community. Millions of dollars would be lost to the local economy, and more than eleven hundred housing units were to be thrown onto an already depressed real estate market.

But not only had money been taken from the city's treasury. Dutch elm disease had stripped the major streets naked of their stately trees. The great homes along the major thoroughfares were either falling into disrepair or being converted into professional offices. The merchant shops and bars situated on the commercial streets sagged and buckled with age. The structures that had once accommodated the prosperous city during the timber-booming years were now a decaying eyesore. City planners, intoxicated with the promise of "urban renewal," decided that radical surgery was called for. No attempt was made to preserve historic landmarks, such as the local railroad station terminal or the City Hall tower that had been constructed in 1894. Both were carted off, with nearly half of the entire downtown area, to the dustbin of history. Those who were concerned about preserving some of the city's past were steamrolled by the promise of a new beginning, a rebirth marked by new housing, streets, and an industrial park to serve as the home for old and new commercial enterprises.

The past seemed to be no contest for the future, but that future proved to be a long time in coming.

With the exception of a few bank buildings, much of the land remained vacant for years. Upon seeing much of the empty space utilized for parking lots, I thought of the remark that Thomas B. McCauley made about John Dryden: "His imagination resembled the wings of an ostrich. It enabled him to run though not to soar."

When some of the same community leaders who had asked me to manage Howard Foley's congressional campaign suggested that I seek a seat on the city council, I was initially hesitant. In addition to prosecuting criminal cases and carrying on a law practice, I was also teaching a three-hour course in business law each week at the University of Maine. I was assured that the council business was not overly demanding and that a highly visible role in the community's affairs would be beneficial to my law firm. It was economics rather than ego or altruism that proved persuasive. Fourteen candidates would vie for three council seats in the nine-member body. I considered my chances remote, but I knew that three important factors weighed heavily in my favor: my days as a high school and college athlete; my father's popular rye bread and rolls; and a large campaign budget. I raised the vast sum of twenty-five hundred dollars and was immediately attacked by one of the populist candidates as being a tool of the business community who would balance the city's budget on the backs of the working men and women.

Why, he demanded to know, would I spend so much for a position that paid only four hundred dollars a year? A good question, one that is asked frequently of presidential candidates. Why would anyone spend $500 million for a position that pays $400,000 a year? The answer is simple: politics is not about money, but about power. The power to formulate policy means the power to influence or alter lives; raise or lower taxes; build better roads, schools, or waste treatment centers; hire more police and firemen; attract better teachers to enhance education—in short, the power to make decisions that will have an impact on the quality of life of a community's or a country's citizens.

Anyone who enters the world of politics for the money will leave it either disappointed or dishonored. The hours are long; the workload heavier than advertised; the schedule erratic; the challenges guaranteed to exceed the solutions; and the constituency, in numbers larger than you hoped, bound to be dissatisfied with your performance. And it does not take long to discover that the toll taken on one's family life can never be adequately reimbursed.

As I struggled to build our law practice and contribute to the affairs of the city, I slipped quickly into the habits of the workaholic. In order to help offset the ever-expanding costs of our secretarial pool in the law firm, I had agreed to teach a course in business law at the University of Maine, the campus of which was located only eight miles from Bangor. Classes started at 8 a.m. and ended at 9:30 a.m., which left me just enough time to rush to the courthouse to take up my prosecutorial duties. I would set aside early afternoons to interview clients or prepare for the next day's trials and then reserve an hour or two for work on the city council's finance committee, of which I had been named chairman.

I was running late one Tuesday afternoon in 1970 and called Diana at home to say that I would have to skip dinner in order to attend the council's executive meeting at 7 p.m.

"But the boys are looking forward to seeing you," she said. "They missed you last night. Can't you come home long enough just to tuck them in bed?"

"Ummm. Okay. Sure . . . but I can't stay long."

I rushed home and performed a largely perfunctory task of stepping into their bedroom and reading them a Dr. Seuss story. Then, oblivious to a marriage partner's responsibilities, I was off, racing to the city council's chambers. I arrived twenty minutes late to discover that others had plans for me that I had never contemplated or wanted.

On the agenda for that evening was a discussion of the reappointment of a prominent physician to serve on the school board. Tensions had always existed between the elected city council members and those whom they appointed to serve on the school board. Inevitably, money proved to be the root cause of that tension. The school board was responsible for helping to formulate and oversee local educational policy. The board would submit a budget request to the council that reflected the funding needed to support the schools' educational, sports, and maintenance programs. The council, which had the taxing power, could—and usually did—reduce the budget, but could not dictate how those reductions were to be achieved. The school board, in retaliation, would reduce maintenance, say by cutting lawns less frequently, or scale back popular programs, such as driver's education, and then blame the council when parents complained.

Relations between the council and board had reached the point of outright hostility that year. The board had approved the implementation of a "model schools program"—an innovative approach to education that sought to discard the traditional notion that all students, if not created equal, must proceed along the educational curriculum in a lockstep manner at an arbitrarily calibrated learning pace. Under this new approach, students would be allowed to establish a personal timetable for the achievement of certain academic goals, negotiate contracts with their teachers, and take exams when they felt prepared (rather than be ordered) to do so.

The program was a disaster.

Among other problems, school officials had decided to implement the changes at the high school level rather than phase them in at the elementary grades. Students who had been dictated to from their kindergarten days were released from their bondage. But liberation, rather than tapping into their creative spirits, led instead to anarchy. The teacher-student contracts were made and broken. Exams were not taken; grades not given. Seniors could not produce satisfactory academic records for college applications. Parents were ready to riot. Something drastic had to be done.

I arrived at the council's executive committee meeting twenty minutes late to discover that indeed something drastic was about to be done. The school board member who was to be reappointed, a prominent physician, was involuntarily retired. Bill Nealley had submitted my name instead. I thought he was joking. The council members quickly approved the nomination. I was both stunned and flattered. My peers had just polished my ego, and I accepted their compliment without consideration of the consequences.

Late that night, I crawled into bed with all the confidence of a man about to walk a gangplank. "You won't believe what happened to me tonight," I whispered in the dark.

Diana greeted my revelation with a stony silence. She knew that my new responsibility would only diminish our shrinking private lives. There would be fewer trips to Green Lake, fewer meals together, and more missed moments with our sons. She realized long before I did that politics, as Justice Holmes cautioned about the law, was going to be a jealous mistress.

Her resentment was directed at the city council for putting a man with a young family into such a time-consuming position. She felt some lingering anger toward me as well. Couldn't I have waited before accepting their vote, at least to consult her? I was living out the work ethic of my father—day trips instead of vacations, family dinners rather than family time.

It was difficult for her to take on the burden of family cheerleader all alone. My guilt about my neglect came out as an apology one day, defensiveness another. Some days I went out of my way to prove I wasn't an absentee parent. On other days, leisure time was economized. Sure enough, there were fewer trips to Green Lake and less time for bedtime reading to the kids. I scanned the Sunday paper while I tried to snatch a few glimpses of a ball game on television.

It was the beginning of public life.

My wife was not the only one who had questions about my presence on both the city council and the school board. The superintendent of schools was encouraging but nonetheless quite practical about the difficulty I was getting myself into. In an article by John Day published in the *Bangor Daily News* on December 31, Wendell Eaton said, "I think we have to bring up the question of the ability of anybody to function adequately on two policy-making bodies that meet in excess of 24 times a year. It will take a superhuman task to serve both adequately."

Wendell went on to say that if anybody could do the job, I could probably be the one to do it. Having been my elementary school principal, Wendell smoothed the waters for me the best he could. Still, the only welcoming I remember from the board itself was its boycott of me during my first two meetings.

The only way the school board would tolerate my presence with anything more than the silent treatment was if I went along with their budget recommendations. I made it clear that I wasn't going to just rubber-stamp a budget I had not had a chance to examine. Given the cold shoulders all around me, I could have built an igloo on my side of the dais. But eventually the conflict healed over.

The first issue I had to evaluate on the school board, other than my right to be there, was the incendiary "model schools" program. This was a fairly new concept in education, and parents didn't know what to make of it. Open classrooms, homework contracts with teachers, students taking exams at their own pace—all of it was a radical departure from the rote methods of the past. Fifteen hundred parents showed up at one school board meeting to voice their opposition to the program.

Upon examining the way the program was implemented, I came down against it. I might have considered the benefits of a progressive program if it had started in elementary school. But this particular system was being thrust upon students in high school. Seniors were being adversely affected, with the loose guidelines causing them to fall at least a year behind students learning through more conventional methods.

Over the next year I became an active board member, showing the others what areas I thought they could cut back in and what areas needed higher allotments of money. Although the city council decided to end the experiment of "Our Man in Education" with me, the experience of dealing with such a broad range of public policy issues proved to be the catalyst that led me even further down the political road.

Initially, I thought that after completing my stint on the school board I would be able to shift my primary focus back to the law firm's business. But I found the resolution of public conflict far more stimulating than engaging in courtroom battles. When the opportunity presented itself, I jumped at the chance to become one of the youngest mayors in the city's history.

My candidacy would not go uncontested. Robert Baldacci, a prominent businessman who owned and operated a popular Italian restaurant, was eager to hold the honor. Bob was not only one of my father's best friends; he was also one of his best customers. Blood, however, was thicker than bread and my father encouraged me to run. The council, no doubt grateful that I had been doing double duty on the school board, gave me its confidence, and I proceeded to preside over council meetings and perform the ceremonial obligations of the office.

During my tenure on the council I had started to develop an interest in international affairs. That interest became more intense when President Richard Nixon decided to pay a stopover visit to Bangor in the summer of 1971. The Vietnam War was still raging and demonstrators were determined to attend the rally at the airport to voice their dissent. Their protest was peaceful until the Secret Service started ripping up their signs. I was in the group receiving the president and was shocked to see how the agents moved through the crowd and destroyed all the posters. At the time, they offered the lame excuse that the demonstrators were on private property and had no right to be there. They also claimed that the very existence of posters obscured their view and posed a security threat to the president.

It was absurd. The protestors were standing on public property. The protestors were far removed from the president and posed no obstruction to the Secret Service's line of vision. I thought their motivation was to prevent the television cameras from photographing the antiwar posters and said so during the public hearing that followed the president's visit. President Nixon was quoted as being "disgusted" by the activists. I, in turn, was troubled by the sight of federal security personnel trampling on the right of citizens to express their dissent.

I had no idea at the time that I would have a different rendezvous with President Nixon.

The only other political figure I encountered in Bangor was California congressman Ron Dellums. He was tall, striking man, who stood ramrod straight (he was a former Marine) and sported a huge Afro. He looked to be nothing less than an African warrior king, distinctly out of place walking the streets of an almost exclusively white society. He had come to promote support for the poor and disenfranchised living in Bangor, reminding us that Dr. Martin

Luther King's dream of justice, equality, and decency was not reserved for blacks alone, but for all Americans.

I had watched Alabama's governor, George Wallace, sneeringly pledge to defend his "State's Rights" and the "traditions" of the South. The only things missing, I thought, were a Nazi armband and Hitlerian salute. What, I wondered, did Wallace's words about tradition mean? Was he defending grand mansions and mint juleps or plantations, slavery, and racism?

While I had viewed Dr. King's historic speech delivered on the steps of the Lincoln Monument in Washington on multiple occasions and was moved by his passionate rhetoric and total commitment to the nonviolent civil rights movement, I had failed to appreciate that disdain or disregard for the poor and socially disadvantaged was a twin sister of racism.

I joined Congressman Dellums on a march through the main streets of the city to a local Baptist church that was serving as a shelter for the homeless. There I spoke with people who had been living on the thin edge of existence, people who were unlikely to attend city council or school board meetings, people who suffered pain in the shadows of neglect. The experience served to remind me that my belief in the virtue of a free market economy should not ignore the health, welfare, and basic human needs of those who were being left in the backwash of a competitive world. And it also served to solidify a friendship with a firebrand congressman with whom I would, on occasion, disagree but a man of character whom to this day I respect and admire. In fact, years later, I awarded Ron a Public Service Medal at the Pentagon for his years of service, not only as a Marine but also as chairman of the House Armed Services Committee.

I might have remained a small-town lawyer with a long-term commitment to community affairs but for one person: Robert Augustus Gardiner Monks. His was an imposing name for an imposing man with an intellectual capacity and generosity of spirit to match his six-foot, five-inch frame. Bob's family was extraordinarily wealthy. Bob lived on a two-hundred-acre estate on southern Maine's Cape

Elizabeth. He was married to Millicent Sprague, a member of a distinguished family that had acquired wealth in the oil business. He might have chosen a life of leisure, clipping coupons, enjoying the high life on the Riviera or some other exotic retreat. Instead he wanted to shake up Maine's political system. He single-handedly was responsible for pushing through a referendum that abolished the "Big Box" that forced Maine voters to vote a straight party line ticket when they went to the polls. He is one of the most ethical men I've ever known. No doubt he inherited his moral code from his father, a prominent Episcopal minister.

Bob had decided to run in a primary contest against Senator Margaret Chase Smith, one of Maine's greatest political institutions. The incumbent congressman, Bill Hathaway (who had so handily defeated Howard Foley six years earlier), was going to vacate his seat to challenge Senator Smith in a general election. Bob had concluded that Hathaway would defeat Senator Smith, but if he was the Republican candidate, he could save the Senate seat for the party.

Bob had much to offer as a candidate. He was a Harvard graduate, a Rhodes Scholar, and at the age of thirty-eight a successful attorney and entrepreneur. Few people believed that he was on anything but a kamikaze mission, an act of political suicide, in seeking to dethrone one of Maine's icons. No amount of nay-saying, however, could diminish his enthusiasm and self-confidence. In addition, he thought that the right kind of Republican could take back Hathaway's congressional seat—and, he believed, I was that Republican.

I didn't share Bob's confidence in my prospects. Beyond Bangor, I was virtually unknown. The second congressional district's twenty-six thousand square miles were inhabited by more trees than people. I had no ties to the Republican establishment other than my brief experience as Howard Foley's campaign manager. When I consulted several party leaders about my potential candidacy, I was told, "With a name like Cohen, you can't get elected." I was not entirely surprised by the comment.

The congressional district was largely rural. Prejudice against Jews was hardly a thing of the past. I was convinced, however, that, if the people of Maine could elect an Edmund Muskie (who was a Polish Catholic) to be governor and United States Senator, they wouldn't reject me because of my name. Even if they hated half of my heritage, I'd win them over with the other.

From February to the middle of June I traveled some twenty-six thousand miles across the state by car and plane. Most of my appearances were at party functions, rallies, or public events with high visibility. I covered a good deal of territory but had little contact with voters, one on one. My opponent, a commercial airline pilot and strong conservative who had made a previous, unsuccessful run for Congress, didn't have much more personal contact with the voters, however. We were both running conventional campaigns that meant addressing voters at teas, coffees, or wherever else the interested electorate congregated to hear us speak. Of course, the voters, ultimately, were the ones who spoke the loudest. I won the June primary by a comfortable margin, but not by enough to ease my mind about facing a popular state senate leader in the general election.

A Bowdoin College student who had been added to the staff through Chris Potholm, my campaign manager, came up with a recommendation that proved to be of vital importance. The student suggested the idea of a walk across the state as a way to reach the people who fell through the cracks, the voters who were put off by showy politics but who still had an interest in how government affected their daily lives. He had worked on Illinois governor Dan Walker's successful campaign, which was how he'd been able to recommend the idea of a walk.

Lawton Chiles, or "Walkin' Lawton," as he came to be known, in 1970 had also used a walk crisscrossing Florida in his successful run for the U.S. Senate. There was no denying the effect of a walk in terms of bringing politics to the people. Quite simply, a walk was an attempt to bridge the gap between government and the people most in need of its help. It was a chance to listen to the people rather than talk at them. After all, what better way to represent the voters than to learn their concerns firsthand?

All of these strong reasons aside, I initially resisted the idea of a walk across the state. I worried about how much time it would take away from "the real campaign." I couldn't get beyond the idea that the whole task would be written off as some kind of gimmick. I dragged my heels, but after much prodding from Chris and the rest of the staff I consented to give the walk a try. My route was planned so I would reach the most populated sections across the district. Because of the hilly and winding secondary roads, we thought it prudent to have an advance car in front of and behind me at all times. The lead car would have signs reading "Bill Cohen Up Ahead— Honk and Wave." The cars were for advertising purposes, not transportation. The walk would be conducted on foot the entire distance. From Gilead on the New Hampshire border I would walk to Houlton, and then later even farther north to the Canadian border at Fort Kent.

On July 19 the journey began.

The walk didn't feel right to me when I started out that first day. Chris and about ten staff people had joined me in the small town of Gilead, located on the border of New Hampshire. We started out together. Soon, though, I was quite literally dragging my heels. It felt like I was part of a caravan or a sideshow, surrounded by too many people. I was too embarrassed to go on.

The walk wasn't about a group of like-minded young people roaming the countryside, looking for converts. The walk was serious. If it was going to really mean something, it had to rest on the shoulders of one, not the many. I decided after the first day that there would be no more staff tagging along, no carnival atmosphere providing moral support. I didn't even want to be able to see the pace cars. I couldn't go another step unless I did it alone. Only at that point did the walk down all those long roads become honest for me. I caught my shadow every so often. There I was once again, I realized, an Outsider.

And for the first time, it felt right.

There was much that followed over the next six weeks, a six-hundred-mile odyssey. The few mishaps I experienced along the way were picked up by the media. It was reported that I had been bitten by a dog near Smyrna and coaxed onto a horse that ran away with me for a wild ride in the countryside around Sherman. The journey was a matter of physical endurance. On two occasions I had to seek medical relief for the severe blisters I developed during the walk. But the experience of meeting people face-to-face proved unforgettable.

I walked an average of twenty-two miles a day and talked with people while they were going about their lives, at homes, in stores, or even in cars that pulled up along the road. At night I slept on the pull-out beds and sofas of anyone who was kind enough to put me up. Of course, in Democratic strongholds such as Lewiston and the St. John Valley, it proved challenging for me to find a place to stay. Yet I was always cordially received.

Along the way, I was accommodated by a wide cross section of Maine residents: plumbers, farmers, lumberjacks, doctors, lawyers, and yes, even Indian chiefs. In Old Town I stayed with Penobscot chief Bruce Poolaw on Indian Island. We reminisced about how he used to put a hex on my basketball team's rim whenever the Rams played the Old Town Indians.

The walk itself became an issue in the campaign, and it made the difference for me in the minds of the voters. It didn't matter that I had started out as an unknown. Someone who would make that kind of effort to hear the concerns of the people was not practicing some gimmick, but rather was pursuing an honest exchange of ideas. I had the assistance of two young women who helped me along the long trek—Olympia Snowe and Susan Collins, both of whom lived in largely Franco-American areas of the state—and both of whom would one day become United States Senators.

Important as the long walk was, perhaps the most poignant, and memorable, moment in the campaign occurred when I was filming a commercial along the Maine seacoast and was joined by my two young sons, Kevin and Christopher.

With the cameras rolling, Kevin looked up at me, and totally unscripted, asked me, "Dad, if you get elected, will you still have time to play with us?"

I was left speechless for several seconds. I looked over at Chris and his eyes told me that he too was concerned about whether I would be too busy to make time for them.

It was one of those moments that touched the lives of virtually everyone who saw the commercial that contained that question. During the course of the entire campaign I received this question more than any other: Are you making sure to look after your sons?

I remain convinced that it was the innocence and spontaneity of that question that more than anything else opened the hearts and votes of my constituents.

I won the race easily.

Without having the benefit of any prior legislative experience, I set out to move to Washington, filled with high hopes and equally high anxieties. Before arriving there, however, I, along with Barbara Jordan, Alan Steelman, and Yvonne Braithwaite Burke, was invited to attend the John F. Kennedy Institute of Politics to participate in a program designed to demonstrate how new members of Congress could become effective early in their careers. In addition to the intellectually stimulating presentations delivered by Professors John Kenneth Galbraith and Daniel Patrick Moynihan, I was given some very practical advice by the director of the program, Mark Talisman: "If you want to serve on a particular committee, don't list it as your first priority; list it last."

"Why?" I asked, thinking that the advice was counterintuitive.

"Because your elders don't know you and frankly, they're not prepared to trust you with membership on the most important and powerful committees. They'll want to test you and see how you perform on committees of lower importance."

Peculiar as I thought Mark's advice, I followed it. Out of five possible choices, I listed the Judiciary Committee as last in my order of priorities. Every knowledgeable person on Capitol Hill advised me to avoid that committee assignment because there was no political mileage to be gained there, nothing that I could translate into visible benefits for my constituents. In fact, I would toil endlessly on such politically charged issues as abortion and prayer in public schools, leaving me with nothing to show to the people of Maine as a reason to send me back to Washington when my contract was up for renewal in two very short years. If I persisted in my misguided effort to serve on this committee, I would find little but hard work—and heartbreak.

Their warnings proved prophetic, but the heartbreak was not to be mine alone.

Eleven

BEAN TOWN AND BUSING

J anet arrived in Boston on September 16, 1973, full of excitement and expectation. Boston was the city known as America's Athens, the cradle of liberty. Crispus Attucks had died here, a black martyr of the American Revolution. She could walk the red bricks of the Freedom Trail and find the spot where he fell, struck by two British musket balls. She soon discovered that some in Boston had other targets in mind.

In 1971 the U.S. Supreme Court upheld the idea of achieving integration of public schools by transporting white or black students from their neighborhood schools to other schools. The decision brought a new word—busing—into American education and tore Boston apart, making the city for a time as notoriously racist as Birmingham and Biloxi.

Busing came to Boston in 1974, when Federal District Court Judge W. Arthur Garrity, Jr., ruled that the city's school committee, led by Louise Day Hicks, had "intentionally brought about and maintained racial segregation" in Boston's public schools. The judge ordered the school committee to develop a temporary desegregation plan. When the committee failed to do so, the judge set his own plan for ending school segregation by ordering the busing of students to produce racial balance in Boston's public schools.

The plan paired Roxbury High, in the heart of Boston's black ghetto, with South Boston High, whose white students were the sons and daughters of Southies—Boston's tough, working-class whites, most of whom were Irish Catholics. Black students bused from Roxbury made up about half of South Boston High's sophomores, and virtually all of South Boston's juniors were bused to Roxbury High.

The order shattered the city and produced the nation's most brutal antibusing counterattacks. The hate and rage that descended on the city was captured in Stanley Forman's Pulitzer Prize–winning photograph of a white man ramming a black man with a flagpole flying the American flag during a riotous antibusing demonstration at ironically Boston City Hall's Freedom Plaza.

It was into this social climate that Janet entered and became the first black woman to cohost a morning show in Boston. *The Good Morning Show* was one of the first live morning shows in the country. The ninety-minute public service program consisted of a potpourri of light-hearted banter, interviews relating to national and local current events, and those involving the scores of entertainment stars who paraded through Boston. The *New York Times* proclaimed *The Good Morning Show* to be the best local morning show in America, and the *Boston Globe* described Janet as: "A black free spirit . . . who sparked the interest of viewers throughout New England with her glamour, intelligence and spontaneity."

Janet also managed to generate considerable controversy by condemning the mothers who with one hand were stoning the buses transporting black schoolchildren while holding rosaries in the other. In addition, she refused to ignore the conspicuous silence of Cardinal Humberto Medieros and the Catholic Church toward the daily scenes of violence and confrontation. After failing to gain a private audience with the Cardinal, she felt compelled to speak out publicly on live television, calling for Cardinal Medieros to condemn the stoning of children. For Janet, it was not only a moral obligation for her to use her visibility to speak out, but one that she considered a matter of personal survival. If the children were being stoned because they were black, then she felt the only difference between her and the children was that they were there and she wasn't. So, she thought she was at risk in the city as well. Sophisticated as Boston might be, she longed to be in a place more like her home town where the racism was more subtle, less overt and violent in expression.

In expressing her sentiments about the Church so openly, Janet was echoing the searing words of her mentor and friend. In his famous "Letter from Birmingham Jail" written on April 16, 1963, Dr. Martin Luther King Jr. responded to the criticism of eight clergymen from Alabama who had called his activities "unwise and untimely."* He wrote that among his many disappointments was that with religious leaders.

> I must make two honest confessions to you, my Christian and Jewish brothers. First, I must confess that over the past few years I have been gravely disappointed with the white moderate. I have almost reached the regrettable conclusion that the Negro's great stumbling block in his stride toward freedom is not the White Citizen's Counciler for the Ku Klux Klanner, but the white moderate, who is more devoted to "order" then to justice; who prefers a negative peace which is the absence of tension to a positive peace which is the presence of justice; who constantly says: "I agree with you in the goal you seek, but I cannot agree with your methods of direct action"; who lives by a mythical concept of time and who constantly advises the Negro to wait for a "more convenient season." Shallow understanding from people of good will is more frustrating than absolute misunderstanding from people of ill will. Lukewarm acceptance is much more bewildering than outright rejection. . . .

> Let me take note of my other major disappointment. I have been so greatly disappointed with the white church and its leadership. . . . I do not say this as one of those negative critics who can always find something wrong with the church. I say this as a minister of the Gospel, who loves the church; who was nurtured in its bosom; who has been sustained by its spiritual blessings and who will remain true to it as long as the cord of Rio shall lengthen.

> When I was suddenly catapulted into the leadership of the bus protest in Montgomery, Alabama, a few years ago, I felt we would be supported by the white church, felt that the white ministers,

---

*The letter was written over several days. often on scaprs of paper that had been smuggled out of jail to his supporters, which accounted for the spelling errors.

priests and rabbis of the South would be among our strongest allies. Instead, some have been outright opponents, refusing to understand the freedom movement and misrepresenting its leader era; an too many others have been more cautious than courageous and have remained silent behind the anesthetizing security of stained-glass windows.

In spite of my shattered dreams, I came to Birmingham with the hope that the white religious leadership of this community would see the justice of our cause and, with deep moral concern, would serve as the channel through which our just grievances could reach the power structure. I had hoped that each of you would understand. But again I have been disappointed.

I have heard numerous southern religious leaders admonish their worshipers to comply with a desegregation decision because it is the law, but I have longed to hear white ministers declare: "Follow this decree because integration is morally right and because the Negro is your brother." In the midst of blatant injustices inflicted upon the Negro, I have watched white churchmen stand on the sideline and mouth pious irrelevancies and sanctimonious trivialities. In the midst of a mighty struggle to rid our nation of racial and economic injustice, I have heard many ministers say: "Those are social issues, with which the gospel has no real concern."

Janet found irony in the parallels of Dr. King's cry from the Birmingham jail to the local clergy to support the quest for justice and her plea to the Catholic Church for support in the busing conflict in Boston. In each case, the faithful had failed them. She wondered whether the sound of their silence was a product of fear or a not-so-subtle signal of support for the racial injustices toward her people. Both she and Dr. King discovered that the church was not always a place of sanctuary for blacks.

She felt that the church leaders had failed the very teachings of their religion, and therefore had failed God.

The response to Janet's call to conscience was immediate and predictable. The station's switchboard lit up with racist sentiments, urging Janet to make a journey back to Africa. Her producer cautioned her to stay away from racial politics and that "black stuff."

If Janet thought that the black community would rally to her support, she was mistaken. The sound she heard was that of the proverbial one hand clapping. In fact, she discovered that she was not quite black enough to suit some. When her cohost was questioning Bobby Seale about the Patty Hearst abduction and membership in the SLA (Symbionese Liberation Army), he mistakenly assumed that Seale's Black Panthers and the SLA were one and the same. The black community interpreted his confusion and inability to distinguish one black group from the other as symbolic of whites saying that all blacks look alike.

His error prompted a number of protest calls from the black community to the studio. On the air the following day, Janet allowed that it was an "understandable mistake" on his part, and by doing so, validated his innocence. For this transgression she was summoned to a meeting with a group of black staff members and criticized for being too soft or forgiving to suit them. They were not prepared for the profane tirade that she unleashed on them in response. They were not the first or last to learn why one magazine had described her as "a cupcake with a razor blade inside."

Janet was torn by the pull and tug of racial politics being played out. Mrs. Melnea Cass, a black woman in her early eighties who was known as the First Lady of Roxbury, offered Janet wise counsel.

"Don't just talk to the black people of Boston," she said. "And don't just talk to the white people of Boston. Talk to the good people of Boston. I know Boston. The only minority are the haters. America will change, and we'll be ready for that change."*

Another extraordinary woman who helped Janet find her way through the minefields of Boston's social and political worlds was Mrs. Mildred Albert, a grand dame in speech and demeanor. She

---

*See *From Rage to Reason*, pp. 123–131.

was only a little more than four feet tall, but she could take over a room with her grace, style, and subtle command for respect. Mrs. Albert was knowledgeable on subjects that ranged from high fashion to history and race.

She had described to Janet how the Jewish people were first treated in Boston.

"The people here used to be strongly anti-Semitic. Some still are. But we knew what we had to do to survive and prosper. We kept a low profile, tried not to stand out. We worked hard and made education our highest priority. Now? We're doing quite well thank you."

Looking for guidance, Janet asked Mrs. Albert what people thought about the comments she was making on the *Good Morning* show. "What will people think?"

"Janet, dear," Mildred responded in a lilting voice that hinted of a British accent with a mid-Atlantic touch, "half the people only think about themselves. And the other half, well, they don't think at all."

Her thoughts on fashion?

"Everyone appreciates beauty. But one has to be a lady, a lady who lives with grace and style."

Despite Janet's involvement with the busing controversy, the people of Boston embraced her. *Boston Magazine* put her on its cover. *U.S. News & World Report* used her photo in its national advertising campaign, and the local Jewish community's Hadassah named her "Woman of the Year."

There wasn't a place in the city that she could not go, including South Boston.

Stage and screen stars, authors, and politicians lined up to appear on *Good Morning*, including Marion Anderson, Gloria Swanson, Lauren Hutton, Betty Freidan, Richard Burton, Dan Rather, and William Loeb, the publisher of the *Manchester Union Leader*, a conservative newspaper in New Hampshire. Inexplicably, became her devoted fan and personal friend.

Yul Brynner, the charismatic movie star who appeared in *The Ten Commandments*, *The Magnificent Seven*, and countless other films, gave

Janet advice that proved to be of immense help to her at the time. She had interviewed him while he was in Boston performing on stage in *The King and I*. She was intrigued by his philosophy: he insisted on keeping his mind and body in harmony. Clear the body of detritus, he urged her. Do the same for the mind. Drink pure water, exercise vigorously, and meditate. To make certain that she followed his prescribed regime, he sent her an exercise bicycle.

I had been invited to appear on *Good Morning*, and I eagerly accepted. Boston was a convenient stop on my routine visits back to Maine each Friday. An appearance on the show would be seen all over New England by thousands of Maine voters and provide me with an opportunity to discuss my views on the House Judiciary Committee's examination of whether Richard Nixon had committed impeachable offenses, and so I accepted the invitation.

I was not in the best physical condition at the time. My system had started to break down from the daily pressure and lack of sleep. I was suffering from a serious cold and had considered canceling my appearance on the show and simply staying in bed for the day. But the political pressure to explain the mechanics of the committee's deliberations trumped all concerns about health.

Just before moving into the studio, I took the opportunity to blow my nose. At that moment, I locked eyes with a striking black woman who was walking toward the door leading onto the studio set. My friend, Congressman Tom Railsback, had mentioned that once, several months earlier during a trip to speak at Harvard, he had appeared on *Good Morning* and had met a beautiful black woman. Tom joked that she had undoubtedly found him "fascinating." It was a standard line he used with everyone he met. It was pure Railsback: gregarious, fun-loving.

Only a second or so passed, but during that instant, I could sense an energy and intelligence that was magnetic. I had never seen the program and surmised at the time that she must be associated with the broadcast. She simply nodded at me as she passed by. Following my interview with her co-host John Willis, I had started to leave the studio when she stopped me and introduced herself. She

213

indicated that she hadn't realized who I was at the time she passed me in the hall corridor, and that her friend Congressman Andy Young had suggested that I was someone she should talk with about the various Watergate personalities who were appearing on the program she was cohosting. Her eyes expressed sympathy for my condition, but there was laughter in them as well. No doubt she found the sight of a sneezing congressman a touch amusing.

I was careful not to shake hands, not wanting to pass on my cold. I had played some basketball with Congressman Young in the House gym, but didn't know him well. I told her that Tom Railsback was a big fan. I didn't say that Tom thought she had found him "fascinating."

I gave little thought to our chance encounter at the studio until I caught her interview with Elia Kazan, the Hollywood director who gained notoriety during the McCarthy era for naming names of his colleagues who allegedly sympathized with the communist philosophy. Kazan had written a novel called *The Understudy*, which I had read. I thought Janet had conducted a truly insightful interview, interweaving questions about the novel and Kazan's personal life with great sensitivity and sophistication.

Wow! I remember thinking at the time. This lady has much more going than a pretty face.

Several months passed before I was scheduled to be in Boston again. This time it was for a fund-raising event. In the meantime, Congressman Young and I had spoken, and he indicated that Janet was a close personal friend who had been involved with civil rights issues and that she was a good person for me to know, given the popularity of her show. I called WCVB's studio and asked to speak with Janet. Once patched through by her producer, I invited her to have lunch at a prominent restaurant. I had concluded from seeing her interview with Kazan that she was an avid reader. For some inexplicable reason, I thought that she'd find Lawrence Ferlinghetti's poetry to be of interest, and I presented her with a copy of *A Coney Island of the Mind*. While she accepted the gift with great grace, I later thought she must have considered it to be the equivalent of me asking her to listen to Bill Haley and the Comets instead of Miles Davis or Lena Horne.

It was not until the publication of *The Double Man*, the 1985 novel that I co-authored with my senate colleague, Gary Hart, that I returned to the *Good Morning* show (by then, renamed *Good Day*). It was something of a novelty for two senators to indulge in the writing of fiction, doubly so for us to represent different political parties.

Janet wanted our segment to be somewhat light and to avoid at all costs the descent into senate-speak for her morning audience. After extracting from us the motive that compelled us to write the novel and the method we used to collaborate, she asked playfully,

"Okay, now which one of you wrote the sex scenes?"

Gary and I laughed (sheepishly) and then pointed to each other as the culprit.

A year would pass before I saw Janet again. This time it was to talk about *A Baker's Nickel*, my second volume of poetry.

The subject of poetry had been the subject of some concern during my first campaign for the senate in 1978. Most of my campaign had counseled me not to publish my first volume (*Of Sons & Seasons*) prior to the election, judging it to be too much of a distraction from the serious business of politics.

I was undeterred by their warnings. I had been in office for six years and had found that even in the most rural and impoverished parts of the state, Maine people responded positively to my speeches that were laced with literary references. They wanted me to look up to them, not down on them. I was proved right. In a five-man race for the senate (there were three who ran as Independents), I won by fifty-six percent of the votes cast.

Janet was interested in exploring the relationship between politics and poetry (indeed, if there was one). I usually deflected such questions by quoting Shelley who said that, "The poets are the true legislators of the world." Shelley, of course, had a conflict of interest. Of the many poems that I'd written, it was clear that the one Janet most wanted to discuss was "Clara's Eyes," the one that described my mother's determination never to yield to the pressure to conform to the demands of others. While I had no knowledge of Janet's background, I knew that she was a successful black woman in television, and that meant that she had faced more than her share of society's obstacles and rejections.

The interview went well. Janet was completely professional. She didn't attempt to score any points or play the "gotcha" games that some journalists are inclined to do. I didn't feel it necessary to go into an intellectual crouch or parse my words. I felt completely at ease with her, sensing that she had been touched by life in ways that were somehow similar to my own.

Of course, I was not immune to the magnetic power of her beauty and personality. In those few moments, I felt the vague stirrings of an emotional connection that would go undefined and unfulfilled for five years.

Twelve

IMPEACHMENT

"**S**on of a bitch!"

The curse came from a nearby colleague and was accompanied by the loud thwacking sound of the sheaf of papers in his hand striking the dais.

As the chairman of the House Judiciary Committee, Pete Rodino, announced the vote of twenty to eighteen that favored rejecting President Richard Nixon's offer to provide the committee with the edited transcripts of secretly taped conversations that had taken place in the Oval Office, another congressman leaned over from the dais' upper tier and spoke to me.

It was Chuck Wiggins, a brilliant lawyer from California who was Nixon's most ardent and effective defender on the committee. Everyone who witnessed Wiggins' action assumed that he was castigating me. Just the contrary.

"Bill, he said, "you're going to come under a lot of pressure after this. Just remember to keep your cool." He spoke with the gravity and gentleness of a father providing advice to his son.

At that very moment I was anything but cool. I was hot with anger. I felt my eyes start to tear up and decided to bolt through the rear door of the hearing room to avoid the crush of journalists who were rushing toward the dais to capture the comments of committee members on this historic occasion.

It was a crucial point in the impeachment process that had been underway for several months. In the summer of 1973, following the disclosures before the Senate's Watergate Committee that the break-in into the headquarters of the Democratic National Committee had been something far more serious than a "third-rate burglary," Congressman Robert Drinan, a Jesuit priest, introduced a resolution to impeach President Nixon.

Drinan was viewed as an intractable foe of Nixon, and few treated his legislative efforts as anything but another manifestation of his liberal orthodoxy. But as the Senate continued methodically to strip away the lies and deceptions from the story that only a handful of unguided zealots had been engaged in a bit of innocuous skullduggery, the country began to see that something far more serious had been underway.

Under increasing political pressure, President Nixon agreed to appoint a special prosecutor to investigate the alleged abuse of his office. He selected Archibald Cox, a Harvard professor who had served as Lyndon Johnson's solicitor general. Cox was to serve under the aegis of the attorney general and at the pleasure of the president—meaning that he could be dismissed by Nixon with or without cause. Skeptics of this arrangement nonetheless feared that the president could not easily rid himself of this nettlesome professor.

President Nixon, no doubt, had assumed that Elliot Richardson, a fellow Harvard man and member of Boston's intellectual elite, would ride herd on Cox. But the more Cox learned about the activities of the Watergate burglars, the more information he demanded from the White House. Nixon was convinced that Cox had embarked on the political agenda of the Democrats. He had gone too far. He had to be fired. Richardson refused to dismiss Cox, as did his deputy, Bill Ruckleshaus. Both men resigned. Robert Bork—who would, fifteen years later, achieve another dimension of notoriety—was called upon to notify Cox of his dismissal from office.

Elliot Richardson had campaigned on my behalf during my congressional race, and I had maintained a close personal friendship with him while he served as attorney general. President Nixon's treatment of him bothered me personally. Elliot was a handsome man, with a square jaw and chiseled face. His horn-rimmed glasses added distinction to his face rather than detracted from it. There was, however, an impenetrable quality to his character and, for some, a formidable one. His conversation was as intricate as his doodles, which became collector's items. He did not talk, he parsed. Sentences would emerge from him full-blown, and then he would pause as if to enable listeners to see for themselves that each semicolon was properly placed and he had left no participle dangling. His manner may have been too aristocratic for some, but no one ever questioned his reputation for total integrity. His dismissal was a shot heard round the nation.

Suddenly, the word "impeachment" was no longer the shibboleth of liberal Democrats. There was a scent of blood in the air. The House of Representatives instructed its Judiciary Committee to initiate an investigation to determine whether articles of impeachment should be brought against the president.

The committee's staff began to compile a historical analysis of the impeachment process that reached back into seventeenth-century English law. Only once before had the Congress of the United States attempted to impeach a president. I took note that it was a Republican senator from Maine, William Pitt Fessenden, who saved Andrew Johnson from impeachment. Now speculation bloomed almost immediately that a Republican congressman from Maine might be willing to assist the Democratic majority and impeach another president.

At that point, I had served in Congress less than a year and had not diverged radically from Republican policy positions. It may have been the presumption that Republicans from Maine were independent-minded. Margaret Chase Smith's "Declaration of Conscience" speech during the poisonous McCarthy days was testament enough to Maine's insistence that ethical standards were not reserved for ministry students. More likely, it was my comments during Congressman Gerald Ford's confirmation hearing to become vice president that caused my Republican colleagues to be doubtful.

I thought back to the moment, only a short time before, when Spiro Agnew had resigned as vice president after pleading no contest to a charge of income tax evasion. President Nixon, under the Twenty-fifth Amendment, appointed Congressman Gerald Ford. That was when my first breach of the rules came.

When Gerald Ford appeared before the House Judiciary Committee during confirmation proceedings for the office of vice president, I thought that the Republican members were taking the proceedings too lightly. They knew Ford from his long years in the House and as the minority leader. They liked him and trusted him and had no desire to press him on any serious issues beyond his age, citizenship, education, and law practice. Several Democratic members were pursuing his ill-conceived attempt to impeach Justice William O. Douglas, but their attacks smacked of political partisanship and carried very little weight.

When my turn came to ask the nominee questions, I inquired as to what he thought about the reports that the Nixon administration had offered the FBI directorship to Judge Matthew Byrne while he was still presiding over the Daniel Ellsberg trial. He dismissed that as a case of bad judgment and then added, "Actually, it was not a promotion, but a demotion."

It was a good throwaway line and provoked general laughter throughout the hearing room. We were operating under a five-minute rule for each member of the committee, and I was unable to follow up on his answer, since I had several other questions to which I wanted responses.

The next day, I proceeded to give Ford a lecture on the subject of ethics:

"In 1968, at a Lincoln Day speech, you made a statement that 'Without truth in government'—this was in reference to the Johnson Administration at that time— 'without truth in government, there can be no confidence in government. Without confidence in government, the nation finds itself in great peril.'

"I believe that statement is as relevant today as it was in 1968," I said, "and I raise it because yesterday, when I inquired about the ethical and legal ramifications of inviting the presiding judge of the Ellsberg trial out to San Clemente [Nixon's "Western White House"], you indicated that at the very least there was a lack of discretion and perhaps poor judgment. . . . I appreciate the note of levity that you injected in considering the FBI directorship as a demotion rather than a promotion. But I refer to that incident because I would like to express my own reaction to this: that it is one of the most singularly destructive acts of the judicial process that I can think of because I think it was calculated to influence the impartiality and neutrality of the presiding judge in one of the most historic cases of the decade.

"I think it is important to state that the Administration officials who secretly met with a judge to find out if he was interested in joining a law-enforcement team while that team was prosecuting a case before that very judge violated our fundamental notions of due process. I think it would have been reversed on due process alone, and I think you share that view. It brought to my mind yesterday another question.

"Several years ago, John Mitchell [the attorney general] stated, 'Watch what we do and not what we say.'

"Taking it at face value, many of us accepted that statement as a paraphrase of the quote 'Deeds often speak louder than words.' But over the years it has come to be viewed by many as a rather cynical expression of calculated duplicity, that our deeds are going to be, indeed, different from our words, and I think this is perhaps the frustration that I feel, that many people in Congress feel, and I know many millions or American people feel, that there seems to be a great disparity between what we profess and what we practice.

"I just want to say that one of the strongest consolations I have is that we have in you a man who does believe in the rule of law. And I am satisfied from my experience with you and what I have heard today and yesterday, and reading over your records, that these activities will never take place with you as Vice President or as President of the United States."

My colleagues were aghast. "Who in hell does he think he is?" "What's he trying to prove?" In retrospect, I think they were justifiably outraged with me. It was not so much what I said, but the manner in which I said it. I was too strident, too self-righteous, too eager to lecture the leader of our party, the next vice president of the United States, possibly the next president. I was flaunting my disrespect for the rules of the game and team membership.

I didn't consider myself a maverick, but that's the label with which I was smacked. Reputations are made quickly in politics, and they are not easily erased.

Now, as the impeachment crisis simmered, the maverick label was being applied again. And a spotlight of scrutiny began to shine on virtually every public statement and appearance that I made. I was, at once, both flattered by and uncomfortable with the attention, and not at all prepared for the criticism that accompanied it.

Republican Party activists who had raised funds for my campaign began to flood my office with mail. There were office visits, telephone calls. Insistence quickly descended to anger. My simple declaration that I would keep an open mind until all the evidence was presented had been taken as an incipient sign of disloyalty. They demanded an unqualified commitment that I would support the president. Anything less and they would put the mark of Cain—or that of Benedict Arnold—on my brow. Letters containing nickels and dimes ("Thirty pieces of silver for Judas") or small stones began to arrive. The trickle of hate mail turned into a river. The mailbags were stuffed with vile ramblings and threats. A few writers were clever in the expression of their contempt.

One man from Spokane, Washington, wrote: "Dear Congressman Cohen: May a thousand camels relieve themselves in your drinking water.

"(Signed) A conservative Republican and supporter of Richard Nixon."

(Thirteen years later, the same man, pained to see me sitting on the committee to investigate the Iran-Contra scandal, wrote again, although in a less poisonous tone: "Dear Bill, The dromedaries are still waiting at the oasis, all one thousand of them saddled up and ready to go.")

The external pressure was intensified by that generated from within. Weekly meetings were arranged, ostensibly so that Republican members of the committee could keep the leadership apprised of any new developments. The real purpose, however, was to attempt to bond us together so that we might form a stone wall of opposition to what was clearly an attempt by the Democrats to reverse Richard Nixon's triumph over George McGovern.

There were times when I felt we were all supposed to clap hands in unison and shout, "Let's go out there and win one for the Gipper" (even though the Gipper was actually a character played years before in a football movie by another up-and-coming Republican, Ronald Reagan). But throughout the early weeks of the investigation, I simply attended the meetings and maintained my silence—until the night when we had to decide to confront the president.

The committee had requested President Nixon to furnish it with all taped conversations that had been held in the Oval Office. Nixon refused, but in a dramatic, nationally televised announcement from the White House, he said that he would turn over a score of volumes containing transcripts of conversations that had been edited to exclude "irrelevant matters."

"Never have conversations so private been made so public," he intoned. It was his hope that these documents would satisfy the public that he was cooperating fully with the committee and thus satiate the appetite of the most partisan ideologue.

Nixon was right; it was an unprecedented act to divulge the substance of private conversations. But the offer was not nearly as open or generous as he had attempted to portray it as. Yet, the drama of the moment and the sheer power of even a wounded president issuing a statement from the hallowed Oval Office were enough to cause the members of the Judiciary Committee to pause, scurry about, and then retreat to our partisan camps.

The next morning's newspapers carried banner headlines reminiscent of declarations of war. Editorial opinion divided along political lines. The Judiciary Committee's deliberations were postponed for a day.

I called Peter Rodino, the chairman of the committee.

"Peter," I asked, "what do you intend to do at tonight's meeting?"

"The transcripts aren't sufficient," he said. "No one on our side will vote to accept them. I'm going to propose that the committee send a letter to the president, rejecting his offer and reaffirming our request for the tapes." Rodino's voice was the sound of sandpaper on soft wood.

"And if he doesn't agree to produce them?"

"Then I'm sure that we'll issue a subpoena and take whatever action is necessary to enforce it."

President Nixon, like other presidents before him, may have had contempt for Congress, but Congress attempting to hold a president in contempt of its process was guaranteed to make its way to the top of the Supreme Court's docket.

I ended my conversation with Rodino and left to attend a caucus that had been called for the committee's Republican members. It was the equivalent of a war council where the tribe's elders debate the merits of tactics against an attacking enemy. The substance of President Nixon's proposal was not at issue. The politics of the confrontation was.

The edited transcripts were clearly deficient. The written word does not always convey the true meaning of a remark. The tone and tenor of one's voice can turn a mirthful phrase into a menacing one. And what were we to make of the "expletive deleted" passages? Was it concern for the tenderness of our ears that caused the pen of the White House's censor to stir? What truths would be lost among the many ellipses? And who was to judge whether certain conversations were irrelevant to our inquiry? The man under investigation?

None of these questions were deemed worthy of serious consideration.

"Listen," I was told, "these guys are out to get our president. They lost the election and now they're trying to steal it back. We've got to stand together and support the president."

I remained unpersuaded. Yes, there were some Democrats who were "Nixon haters," and they liked vengeance served hot or cold.

But I thought we should be concerned about the merits of the issue raised by the president's refusal to release the tapes of the conversations.

I had another question: "What if Rodino only wants authority to send the president a letter outlining the objections that our own counsel [Chicago trial attorney Bert Jenner] has spelled out for us?"

"You don't understand," several senior members responded almost in unison. "The letter is going to be used as a partisan attempt to embarrass the president."

"But what if I write the letter, setting forth in an objective and respectful way the reasons that the transcripts are insufficient?"

"There'll be no letters," Congressman Ed Hutchinson, the ranking Republican on the committee, admonished me.

Hutchinson was a short, portly man who wore rimless eyeglasses and had a penchant for grey vested suits. He looked like a small-town auditor or accountant. Life to him seemed to pretty much be a series of columns and bottom lines. And one stood on one side of the line or the other. Republicans and Democrats. Right and Wrong.

He and others had long chafed under the rough collar of minority status in the House. The procedures, as established by the Rules Committee, were always stacked against Republicans. The votes were stacked against them, too. It was rare when Democrats joined a Republican in a spirit of bipartisanship on a legislative initiative. Only when the majority was faced with the loss of southern conservatives on a fiscal or social issue did they ever invite Republicans to be principal cosponsors. No, the Democrats called upon every card-shuffling trick to prevent Republicans from either being successful or appearing to be successful. And so the resentment had deep and well-nourished roots.

And yet, what if the Democrats would never do onto their own what they were asking Republicans to do onto ours? I doubted that they would ever have initiated impeachment proceedings against Lyndon Johnson under similar circumstances. And it was pure folly to even speculate whether they would have tried to bring down John

Kennedy whatever his transgressions. But I was convinced that I wasn't sent to Washington to enforce the golden rule of reciprocity. I knew that whatever private views the members had, they were not going to express them at the meeting.

Republican leaders began to doubt my loyalties when I refused to agree that the phrase "high crimes and misdemeanors" found in the Constitution required Congress to find that the president had engaged in criminal misconduct before he could be impeached. The suspicion deepened when, after firing Archibald Cox, President Nixon appointed Texas lawyer Leon Jaworski to serve as special prosecutor. Democrats were furious. They concluded that the presidential power to appoint had been abused and that Nixon could not be trusted to appoint a truly independent prosecutor.

Even though Jaworski had been appointed and was in the process of continuing the investigation, the committee was on the verge of passing a bill that would call upon the federal court of appeals to appoint a new special prosecutor, one who could not be fired by President Nixon. The *Washington Post* had editorialized in favor of such an action. Republicans were adamantly opposed to any congressional effort that sought to diminish the president's powers. They threatened to fight such an action all the way to the Supreme Court.

Looming constitutional challenges did not deter the enthusiasm of the bill's supporters. They had anticipated that the bill would pass both the House and Senate and then be vetoed by President Nixon. The veto would be sustained and, in the meantime, Jaworski would continue his efforts to prosecute those who had engaged in criminal conduct. If he succeeded, he would be praised by all. If he failed, proponents of the bill could maintain that they had stood tall in the pursuit of justice, while opponents had succeeded in frustrating the search for the truth.

But I assumed a different scenario, one in which certain White House advisors advised the president to allow the bill to become law without his signature and then challenge its constitutionality in the courts. The result would have been months of delay and confusion and confrontation. Jarworski could not have continued his activities because congressional action would have superseded his appointment. The president would have been under no obligation to fully cooperate with a court-appointed prosecutor whose powers were under challenge. The quest for truth would have been delayed or possibly even derailed.

I wrote an article outlining these arguments for the *Washington Post*. On the day the House was scheduled to take action, the *Post* reversed its editorial position and supported Jaworski's continuation in office. The power of the *Post* exceeded the majority's zeal. The vote on the legislation to create an independent prosecutor was indefinitely postponed.

While Republicans saw the result as a temporary victory (thinking that Jaworski would be less antagonistic to Nixon than Cox had been), my reasoning that Jaworski had become a "prisoner of Cox's staff" proved worrisome to many. Mine were not the words of a party loyalist. I was to be watched and monitored. A steady stream of party officials began to visit me in Washington to plead for my allegiance to the president.

Now, in Hutchinson's office, I could sense that he was about to ask the group to take a pledge that we all agree to oppose any proposals offered by the Democrats at the public hearing scheduled to begin at eight o'clock that night. Who among us would stand tall with the President? Who among us would trace his lineage to Judas?

Without saying a word, I walked out of the room.

As soon as I arrived at my office, I drafted a letter that was unadorned with partisan rhetoric and then placed a call to Peter Rodino:

"Peter, I need your help. There's strong opposition on our side to any letter drafted by you. I know you've tried to keep this thing nonpartisan so far. And there's a way for you to continue to do this. I've drafted a letter that sets forth the reasons why the edited transcripts are insufficient. Will you support me on this?"

"I can't," the chairman replied in his raspy voice. "I've got a coupla guys on my side who want to impeach Nixon right now.

They're unwilling to go along with me. If I support you, I might lose everybody on our side. But what I will do is agree to recognize you first to offer your language as a substitute for mine. That's the best I can do."

It was not the answer that I had hoped for, but I knew was the best I was going to get. I photocopied my letter and placed one copy on each of the thirty-eight desks on the dias just before eight o'clock that night. As the members took their seats, Congressman Hutchinson spotted my letter and boomed, "I thought we'd agreed that there'd be no letters."

"Bullshit, Ed," Tom Railsback retorted. "Cohen's doing the right thing. I'm going to support him." One of the two mentors that I looked to for guidance in my first year was Tom Railsback. The other was John Anderson. Both were regarded as "moderates" from conservative districts in Illinois.

There was a good deal of harrumphing and muttering as Rodino gaveled the committee to order.

The chairman outlined the chronology of events that had brought us to that evening. His tone was flat and unemotional; his rhetoric, quasi-judicial. The Republicans were buying none of it. After a brief period of partisan debate, I raised my hand and was granted recognition for the purpose of offering my substitute. When the roll was called, the clerk gave a disappointing tally. Eleven in favor, twenty-seven opposed.

Then the long roll call vote began on Rodino's motion to approve the sending of his letter on behalf of the committee. An extraordinary silence pervaded the hearing room. As the count began, Jerome Waldie and John Conyers voted against Rodino. There were twenty-one Democrats and seventeen Republicans. If every other Democrat supported Rodino and every Republican opposed him, we were headed for deadlock. The motion would fail.

My stomach was churning. Maybe Henry Smith of New York would vote with Rodino. "No." Surely Railsback would support him. His "No" cracked like a rifle shot in the silence. Hamilton Fish: "No."

The rush of the "Nos" picked up speed until the clerk's nasal voice called my name. I hesitated momentarily, and then voted with Rodino. The silence in the room was broken. Papers fluttered as if lifted by a sudden gust of wind. A nearby colleague cursed me. Reporters gathered their weapons of art and charged the dais, their microphones fixed like bayonets, as the official vote tally was announced.

I was angry with Railsback and others who knew that the edited transcripts constituted not only partial, but potentially misleading evidence, and yet had voted to accept them. I realized that I was in no frame of mind to discuss my vote with reporters.

I stepped quickly out the rear door of the committee room and ran down the long, marbled corridor, the click of my heels ricocheting off the walls sounded like rifle shots. I took an elevator to the garage level of the labyrinthine Rayburn Building and burst out onto D Street, desperate to be alone.

As I walked up D Street, heading for the Longworth Building, my anger began to cool. Like some Rambo character, I had been firing mortal thoughts in a wide arc of outrage at everyone in sight: Smith, Railsback, Fish. . . . But they had given me their vote. They had signaled the White House that the transcripts were inadequate. But they had also affirmed that they were unwilling to partake in any Democratic power plays. They were the battle-scarred veterans of the political wars that were waged on a daily basis in the House. They understood that when you were down in the trenches, unit cohesion and morale would prove even more important than numerical advantage (or abstract theologies of right or wrong).

I had acted with the naiveté and arrogance of a new recruit fresh out of basic training, armed with gleaming thoughts of truth, justice, and the American way.

I did not doubt that I had cast the "right" vote that night. But I knew intuitively that I had crossed a line that would define the rest of my career in Congress—which at the moment I believed would be of limited duration. There are many rooms in the mansion of power politics, but I knew there was something inside of me—an impetuosity, a resistance to conformity to what others considered to be acceptable conduct—that would place me outside the gates of that estate.

As I tried to enter the rear entrance to the Longworth Office Building, I discovered that the doors had been locked. I pounded in vain on the doors for several minutes, hoping to attract the attention of an attendant or police officer inside.

A man passed behind me in the darkness and said, "Maybe they're trying to tell you something."

He had no idea that his words came at me with the sharpness and weight of stones.

I made my way to the front entrance to the Longworth Building and stepped onto an elevator. Congresswoman Barbara Jordan joined me just as the doors were about to close. We had not spoken since our "boot camp" days together at the Kennedy Institute of Politics. We rode in silence for several seconds. Then, as the elevator arrived at the floor where Barbara's office was located, she turned toward me as she stepped into the corridor and spoke in her powerful and clipped manner of speaking.

"Bill, one day history will vindicate you."

She turned and walked away without waiting for any response from me. It was the only time she spoke to me during the entire investigation. Barbara was not one to engage in small talk or stroke one's ego or pride. While I appreciated her comments, they offered little consolation to me at the moment.

Washington is said to be a city of marble surrounded on four sides by reality. Following my vote to reject President Nixon's offer, I found what "real Americans" thought of me. The hate mail turned truly vicious. Nazi swastika stickers laced obscene and violent messages in the letters: "Hitler should have burned all of you Jews" was a common theme. Bomb threats interrupted committee hearings. I received death threats against my sons. Republicans in Maine, while respectful, were no less disenchanted. In fact they were furious.

While it was too late to sponsor a credible primary opponent to oppose me, they made it clear that they would never support me in the general election. A popular Vietnam War veteran had announced his candidacy as a Democrat. Political pundits were already speculating about my political demise. I was convinced that if Republicans stayed home during the election, my career as a congressman was going to be short-lived.

After the U.S. Supreme Court ruled that Nixon had to release the tapes containing conversations in the Oval Office, I devoted days to listening to the tape recordings. I compared the voices, word by word, to the edited transcripts President Nixon had supplied to the Judiciary Committee. I committed to memory the testimony of the witnesses who had appeared before the Senate Watergate Committee. During the course of taking the testimony of witnesses behind closed doors, Democratic members would frequently offer to yield portions of their allotted time to me to pursue lines of examination—which did not sit well with my Republican colleagues. While I had not made a final judgment on whether President Nixon had committed impeachable offenses, I was determined to eliminate the spurious and speculative in my search for the truth.

It was not until the Judiciary Committee was about to begin public debates on whether to bring articles of impeachment that I discussed my thoughts with other members on the committee.

Tom Railsback called and said that he was asking a few people to come to an 8 a.m. meeting in his office for coffee and donuts, and invited me to join him.

"Who else is coming?" I asked, wary that it might be an attempt to lock me into a meeting with the Republican leadership.

"I don't know," was his answer.

"Okay. I'll be there."

When I arrived in Tom's office the next morning, I was truly surprised to see Democrats Jim Mann of South Carolina and Walter Flowers of Alabama, along with Republicans Caldwell Butler of Virginia and Henry Smith of New York.

Tom opened the meeting and said that he wanted to see if we should discuss our thoughts before the Judiciary Committee began its public sessions. Tom, I had noticed over the last few months, was losing his voice. He would eventually undergo several surgical procedures, but his voice was never restored to its original tenor vibrancy. According to physicians who treated him, his voice impairment was due to stress.

Walter Flowers, in a strong southern drawl, said, "I just think we need to toss everything up in the air and see what shakes out. Whether there is anything that all of us can agree on." Flowers had developed bleeding ulcers during the course of the hearings. Richard Nixon was enormously popular in Alabama, and the criticism of Flowers' seeming lack of commitment to Nixon was taking its toll.

We spent several hours reviewing the key parts of the evidence that we had heard. We concluded that the evidence was clear that President Nixon had abused his power and that he should be put on trial in the Senate, and if convicted, removed from office.

After a vigorous debate, the Judiciary Committee voted to send two articles of impeachment to the full House for deliberation and decision. Republican leaders originally declared that they were prepared to fight this issue all the way to the Supreme Court. But then one of the missing tapes surfaced and revealed that President Nixon had been deeply involved in the cover-up of the Watergate burglary and had lied to the American people.

A group of Republicans, including Barry Goldwater, met with Nixon, and advised him that they could no longer offer him support. Nixon saw that the fight was over. He gathered his staff in the East Room of the White House and, in a very emotional manner, announced his resignation.

I watched his speech with little joy. I had voted for him and believed that he was the best person to lead our nation through some very difficult times. Even as I had listened to all of the cynical and depressing conversations held in the Oval Office, I was convinced that if President Nixon had come forward, explained to the American people the nature of the pressure he was under as a result of the war in Vietnam and the potential conflict in the Middle East, and accepted full responsibility for the misdeeds he had set in motion, if not directed, he could have survived. Time and time again, the American people had demonstrated a capacity for forgiveness and a belief in redemption.

Regrettably, President Nixon continued to indulge in deceit and defiance until he was left with only the prospect of political rejection by his own party.

Once Gerald Ford assumed the presidency, the tide of political opinion shifted dramatically in favor of my decision that President Nixon had abused the power of his office and had violated the public's trust. While I won reelection easily, my colleagues in Washington made it clear that any aspirations I might hold for a leadership position within the party were finished. Since they could never again count on my support for the party's position, I would never be able to count on theirs.

Never.

In a way, I found my exclusion from the circles of power to be quite liberating. I was mindful of what Thomas Jefferson had written: "Whenever a man has cast a longing eye on office, a rottenness begins in his conduct."

Throughout my career in politics, I would witness individuals who were seeking a leadership position indulge in conciliatory, very nearly obsequious behavior, when soliciting my support. I considered their gestures of outreach to me patently insincere. The purchase price for achieving influence was too high.

I was prepared to remain an outsider in the insider's game of politics.

Thirteen

A DOCTOR IN THE HOUSE

Although the popularity of Janet's television show continued to grow, she was having difficulty containing her rage over the busing controversy and racial tensions that existed in Boston. Outwardly, she projected an appearance of being a light-hearted, fashion-conscious professional journalist, full of panache and goodwill toward the world.

Inside, the anger was beginning to affect her health. She started breaking out in hives, and then developed a case of acne. She felt constantly agitated and aggressive. She consulted an endocrinologist who diagnosed her condition as Stein-Levanthal Syndrome, a hormonal imbalance resulting from an insufficient production of estrogen and an overproduction of testosterone. She was told that it was stress-related. Repressed anger doesn't dissipate. In swallowing it, it literally started destroying her inside. Surgery was a likely option.

Janet kept thinking about Anne Frank and the "good Anne" that she kept safely out of the view of others, the one that was serious, more reflective, and profound.

"I knew that I needed to let go of the rage and try to use the power of reason and moral suasion to bring out the humanity in people, to shame them into decency, as Dr. King had always advised. But emotion prevailed in the struggle with reason. I couldn't ignore or accept displays of racism and injustice."

Her condition continued to deteriorate. Finally, a friend rec-ommended that she consult Dr. Robert Kistner, one of the coun-try's most renowned gynecologists. Dr. Dr. Kistner concluded that she needed to have her uterus and one ovary removed. This would result in her not being able to have children. After witnessing how hard her mother's life had been, she had resolved to forgo the re-sponsibility of raising a family. Still, she did not want to rush to make such an irrevocable decision.

"I experienced an indefinable sense of extinction," she said. "There would be no genetic continuity of my being. No child to care for or to care for me. But I didn't want to live with the contin-uing discomfort. I made the decision to go forward with the surgery. The date happened to coincide with the death of Elvis Presley, Au-gust 16, 1977."

During the time Janet was recovering from the anesthesia, Dr. Kistner had checked in on her several times, something that was highly irregular for him. Then, on the day of her discharge from the hospital, he personally insisted upon driving her home. Instead of returning to her apartment, however, he wanted to show her his mansion, located in Milton, a Boston suburb. She suspected that he might be a touch taken with her, but what she didn't realize was that he had been nursing a serious crush on her for several years. Actu-ally, it was more than a crush. He wanted to marry her.

Every woman is said to fall in love with her doctor, and Janet was no exception. Intrigued as she was with the thought of being married to this brilliant surgeon and author, she wanted to think about it. Long and hard.

She thought about the fact that Kistner was wealthy. But she was not poor; in fact, she was making a comfortable living. She owned her apartment, had money in the bank, and was providing full support of her mother back in Indianapolis. Also, she treasured her freedom and independence.

Kistner was twenty-five years older—and he was white. She knew that "color" was going to sit like some giant bird on her shoulder and caw incessantly. How could she claim to be so outraged over the treatment of black people and then marry a white man?

It angered her to think that people continued to see her as a color and not as a person. They saw just the surface of who she appeared to be. They couldn't see that her rage over racism had nothing to do with the whiteness of one's skin, but the wickedness in one's heart. Marrying a white man wouldn't erase her experience as a black woman. It wouldn't make her white. It would mean that she was not a racist, a hater; that she would be practicing what her mother had preached—not to judge people by their surface appearances.

So she rationalized.

Still, she wanted the advice of the people she trusted most. She turned to Mrs. Melnea Cass. "What if they ask me why I married an older—and wealthy—man?"

"Don't explain," she replied. "You don't owe anyone an explanation. Simply say, 'Because I love him. Why do you ask?'"

Janet's father had something of a different reaction when he learned that she was planning to marry out of her race. He indicated his disappointment in one of his letters: "How could you, a prized flower of our garden, give this beauty and strength to a race that has suppressed us?" The fact that Dr. Kistner was a Catholic was doubly offensive to him. As the letter had come from the very man who had abandoned her and her mother, Janet tossed it in a circular file. She delayed her decision for a year and finally discussed it with her mother.

Janet's mother liked Bob Kistner. She was very direct: "If you don't marry him, I will."

Mrs. Cass, the woman that Janet so admired and considered her mentor agreed.

Originally, they had planned to hold the wedding in Acapulco, Mexico, but when Janet learned that Mrs. Cass, suffering from cancer, was too ill to travel, she decided that the wedding ceremony would take place in Roxbury—right in Mrs. Cass's bedroom. Janet was touched by Mrs. Cass's courage and determination to put on her finest clothes for the occasion and sit through the entire ceremony although she was in great pain..

A month later she passed away and all of Boston, including Mayor Kevin White, Speaker Tip O'Neil, Senators Ted Kennedy and Ed Brooke—even residents of South Boston—turned out for her funeral to pay their respects and say goodbye.

For the next several years, Janet continued to expand the range of her interviews on the morning show. She was ambitious, however, and anxious to move up to work on national television. She learned to her dismay that an opportunity to do so had been blocked by her station manager, Bob Bennett. He was not going to let his "cash cow" move on to greener pastures.

She jumped at the next opportunity to perform on network television. It was not without risk. If you do well on local television, you basically have a job for life. Network and nationally syndicated television are pretty much riverboat gambles. She decided to roll the dice.

She took a job as cohost on NBC's *America Alive* with Jack Linkletter and Bruce Jenner, who earned the title of "World's Greatest Athlete" by winning the gold medal in the decathlon at the 1976 Olympic Games in Montreal. The show failed to seize the public's imagination and went off the air.

She then moved to cohost *A.M. New York*, a show that was the precursor to *Live with Regis and Kathy Lee*. She loved the show because it gave her an opportunity to interview major political figures as well as the personalities who dominated the tabloids.

Once again, however, her passion overruled all prudence. When U.S. Ambassador to the United Nations Andrew Young was forced to resign because he had met with a representative from the Palestinian Liberation Organization (PLO) without authorization, Janet raised questions on air as to why this constituted a firing offense.

Even though the show was doing well in the ratings, beating Phil Donahue, she was shown the exit door. Supporting Andy Young was not the popular thing to do in New York.

After Janet's departure from *A.M. New York*, she returned to Boston. And when WCVB offered to hire her for a show called *Sunday Open House*, she accepted.

Bob Bennett, the station manager, harbored great anger toward her for leaving the station to go to New York. An agent of Janet's once counseled her to always leave the discussion about money to the last item during a negotiation. In fact, she should always leave it to the agent.

As she was signing the contract with WCVB, before the ink was even dry, Bennett said, "I got you back dirt cheap."

He intended his comment as an insult but what Bennett didn't know was that she was prepared to do the show without compensation just to be back on television. Bennett's comment, however, served as a mighty lesson for her to never undersell her talent.

Once again, when the opportunity to participate on a nationally syndicated program arose, Janet took it. This time it was *The New You Asked For It*, a revival of the show that had been hosted by Jack Smith and Art Baker during the 1950s and 1960s. Almost immediately, Janet, along with other correspondents, became globetrotters, jetting off to cover safaris in Africa, climbing Masada in Israel, shooting the great pyramids in Egypt, and riding horses through the narrow streets of the Camargue in the south of France.

Exciting as it was, the work was only part-time. Ever open to new experiences (in Africa, it was landing in a hot air balloon into a pride of lions and drinking a witch doctor's nasty brew), Janet decided to take up the sport of polo.

As a child visiting relatives in Kentucky, she was once forced to get down on the floor and blow out the lamp in the bedroom when a group of Klansmen rode past the house, threatening to shoot their shotguns into the house. From that time on, she had always associated horses with a profound sense of danger. Once she overcame that sense of fear, she embraced polo ponies and the game with passion.

Janet met Lord Patrick Beresford, the younger brother of the Duke of Waterford, while he was playing in the polo matches being held in Massachusetts. Patrick enjoyed being the keeper of the Queen's horses in England. He became a close friend who instructed her on the finer points of polo. In addition, after she and Patrick had ridden on Windsor Grounds, they paid a visit to a friend's house where she was introduced to Princess Anne. Janet was polite to Princess Anne who was quite pleasant and approachable, but she fumed over the host's fawning attitude toward royalty.

"You must be overjoyed at having met Anne," he said to Janet.

"I was offended by the very notion that one's social or economic class should be considered superior to anyone not in their ranks. People of wealth and lineage claim an entitlement to power and privilege the same way that racists claim superiority on the basis of skin color.

"It no doubt sounds arrogant, but damn, I thought, given all that I'd had to encounter in life, Princess Anne should have been honored to meet me. All she had to do was drop out of a royal birth canal and just be."

Fourteen

THE REST OF THE BASTARDS

The title congressman or congresswoman manages to carry sway in Washington and in one's home district, and most people are convinced that the lifestyle enjoyed by those who hold it is one of relative comfort and ease. The reality, however, is quite the opposite. While congressional salaries far exceed those of most Americans, the expense of living in Washington, maintaining two homes, and attempting to balance family responsibilities with constituent service create hardships that few people would find attractive. The hours devoted to legislative work are long and erratic; the demands of constituents insatiable; the chase for campaign donations constant; and time for one's family limited. Still, the psychic rewards in helping to shape national policies and programs more than compensate for the hardships and punishing schedules.

Following my role during the Judiciary Committee's deliberations, the psychic rewards faded quickly. Democrats continued the practice of marginalizing Republican members' initiatives, while conservative Republicans viewed moderates with increasing disdain. I decided that if I were to continue a life in politics, it would have to be in the Senate, where I would have greater independence and the opportunity to shape public policy.

Just twelve years after my first entry into the political world as a campaign manager for congressional hopeful Howard Foley, I defeated Senator Bill Hathaway, the very man who had crushed my candidate.

"Just remember, when you get to the Senate, don't become like the rest of those bastards."

The admonition came from my friend, Congressman Tom Railsback. Tom said this in his usual light-hearted manner, but he reflected a sentiment that was deeply rooted in the culture of the House of Representatives.

Congressmen viewed senators as pompous, self-inflated asses who attempted to convey profundity and failed miserably. In turn, senators considered congressmen to be a cut above used-car salesmen, legislators who possessed little substance, or as the Texans like to say, were "All hat and no cattle."

I could sense a change almost immediately in how I was treated by members of the press. As a congressman, my views on any major policy issues were rarely sought. Suddenly, without an appreciable increase in knowledge, I was contacted almost daily for an opinion on issues that ranged from foreign policy and arms control to the macroeconomic impact of actions taken by the Federal Reserve.

The House operated under the harness of the Rules Committee, which set both the agenda and strict time constraints under which debate would be conducted. In the Senate, all business was conducted by "unanimous consent." In other words, if a single senator objected to allowing a bill to be brought to the floor for debate, or to permitting a final vote to occur, or refused to accept any time limits on the debate itself, he or she could tie the Senate up in procedural knots for days. Each senator represented a sovereign state, and the vote by a senator from Texas, New York, or California carried no greater weight than that of a senator from Maine, Vermont, or Rhode Island.

Although I had pledged to remain loyal to my House friends, particularly those with whom I had played basketball regularly in the House gymnasium, I knew it was a pledge that I was bound to break—just as I had broken the one that I had made to my friends on Hancock Street when I moved up to a middle-class neighborhood.

My staff director had sent me a memo reminding me that, other than Bill Bradley and Nancy Kassebaum, I would be one of the best-known freshmen members by virtue of my exposure to the media during the impeachment proceedings. Reputations in the Senate, once established, were not easily erased. Senate elders would be watching carefully to determine if I intended to be a workhorse or a showhorse. I decided I would be the former.

The test came quickly. I received a call from Senator Howard Baker's office. The Senate minority leader was asking me to join a small delegation consisting of John Glenn, Sam Nunn, and Gary Hart to travel to China and other parts of Asia. I eagerly agreed. It was a trip that would shape my career in the Senate and beyond.

We traveled first to Thailand, then to China, Japan, and South Korea. In China, we were scheduled to meet with Deng Xiaoping in the Great Hall located in Tiananmen Square. There was only one major hotel in all of Beijing at the time, and it was worthy of a page in a Stephen King novel. What was most striking was the presence of bicycles—millions of them! There were no private cars in the streets, only military vehicles and buses that were crammed tighter than a can of sardines. All the people were dressed in Mao suits. Men and women did not hold hands in public. Women wore no makeup. The people were obviously poor, and yet, there was a detectable sense of expectation and optimism in their manner. It was if they knew that tomorrow was going to be far better than today.

I, the most junior member of the CODEL (congressional delegation), was assigned the responsibility to raise the issue of human rights. I wasn't sure whether the others had a touch of mischief in mind or were just testing me to see how well I handled a sensitive subject.

I broached the topic with the diminutive, chain-smoking Chinese leader with some preliminary attempts at diplomacy, which I'm sure were lost in the translation. He dismissed my questions with a declaration that the winds of change and respect for human rights would continue to blow throughout all of China.

It was, of course, nonsense; but just by raising the issue, we sent a message that our concerns were high on the list of the concerns of the American people.

On our trip back to Washington, we stopped in South Korea to meet with President Park Chung Hee. He was very concerned that President Jimmy Carter was going to carry out a campaign pledge to reduce our troop level by five thousand men. This, he argued, would be a dangerous signal to the North Koreans and could possibly precipitate a war.

Once back in Washington, we arranged to brief President Carter about Park's warning. Carter, who struck me as rigid and uncompromising, seemed singularly unimpressed with the dire prediction. Ultimately, he yielded to the gentle prodding of his fellow Democrat from Georgia, Senator Nunn, and agreed to renege on his campaign promise.

During the entire trip, I was both entertained and besieged by a young Navy liaison officer, Captain John McCain. McCain had been held a prisoner of war in Vietnam for more than five years. He had been beaten and tortured on a regular basis and had spent much of his ordeal in solitary confinement because he had proved so nettlesome to his captors and so inspirational to his fellow prisoners being held in the "Hanoi Hilton."

What I found so compelling about John was his good humor and unshakable optimism. Throughout the long trip, he continued to pressure me to join the Armed Services Committee. Until then, I was intent on serving on the Government Affairs and Judiciary Committees. But once I saw the men whom I had traveled with— along with John's persistence—I agreed to request an assignment on the committee that would provide for and oversee our military and its global operations.

The differences between the House and the Senate were stark. Ralph Waldo Emerson, while standing in the gallery of the House and pointing to a gaggle of congressmen on the floor below, reportedly said, "There, Sir, is a standing insurrection!"

The Senate, by contrast, was quiet and more dignified. The seating in the House was arranged in a large semicircle; each congressman could sit in an unoccupied leather chair. Senators were the proud possessors of individual desks and chairs. Propping up the desk's lid, one could see the names of those Senators who had once occupied the desks, carved and then inked into the wood.

Congressmen tended to dress in gaudy polyester suits and carry on voluble side conversations during proceedings, and they frequently had to be gaveled to silence by the presiding officer. Senators dressed in dark business suits and consciously—almost unctuously—referred to each other as "My good friend" or "The distinguished gentleman or gentlewoman" even though they might hold that senator with a minimum of high regard.

Initially, I found these flatteries simply false and time consuming. But it was not long before I came to appreciate the need for the forced courtliness. The House operated under the hammer of the powerful Rules Committee. In the Senate, however, virtually all legislative business had to be conducted by unanimous consent. Necessity, therefore, dictated that every effort had to be made to accommodate the needs and egos of individual members.

One hundred senators were expected to cover the same legislation as the four hundred and thirty-five members of Congress. The upshot was that while senators appeared to be more thoughtful and statesmanlike in the conduct of the nation's business, congressmen actually were more well-versed in the details of legislation. Senators enjoyed the reputation of looking at the forests, while congressmen were scurrying about counting all the trees.

The demeanor of senators was also quite different from that of their counterparts in the House of Representatives. Silly as it is, the procedural etiquette required one to avoid referring to the House of Representatives other than as "the other body."

I was immediately impressed with the talents of Abraham Ribicoff, Edmund Muskie, Henry "Scoop" Jackson, Daniel Patrick Moynihan, Lloyd Bentsen, John Glenn, Sam Nunn, Robert Byrd, Howard Baker, Jacob Javits, Charles "Mac" Mathias, John Tower, and John Danforth. These were men who revered the Senate's custom of courtesy and deference to one another even as they engaged in vigorous and, at times, heated debate. What was most notable and instructive was the absence of any personal animus. They were mature men who could leave the passions of the debate in the Senate and then dine and drink together the same evening. In the House, members tended to view each other through the prism of a gunsight, as might the Hatfields and McCoys.

I continued to play basketball with Tom Railsback in the House gymnasium on weekends. One day, Tom asked me how I found the Senate, and I said, "Rails, I think you misunderstood us bastards all of these years."

On the Armed Services Committee, I immersed myself in the intricacies and arcania of arms control issues, complex weapons systems, and cumbersome procurement and budget accounting rules. I came to admire the talent and tenacity of Senator John Tower, with whom I started to travel extensively on trips to military facilities throughout the world. Barry Goldwater seemed impressed with my grasp of security issues and arranged for me to join him on the Intelligence Committee.

I also joined an informal group of Senate and House members, including Gary Hart and Newt Gingrich, which called itself the "Military Reform Caucus." We were determined to explore whether the military needed to change its doctrine, training, and procurement practices. To my amazement, the Pentagon put together a "watch group" and assigned uniformed officers to follow our speechmaking activity in our home states and then rebut our comments or observations about the need to change the status quo.

This was the first time that I had to confront the possibility that my government was monitoring my words and actions—although I had had my tax returns audited during the time I served on the House Judiciary Committee when it was deliberating on whether to bring impeachment proceedings against President Nixon. At the time, I passed it off as a coincidence rather than harassment or intimidation.

The Pentagon monitoring me, however, was no coincidence. Nor was it a case of happenstance when the FBI paid me an unexpected visit.

Congressman Pete McCloskey had arranged for a congressional basketball team to play an exhibition game against a Soviet Embassy team at Georgetown University. CBS agreed to film the game and then show the highlights on the evening news. The game could be seen as a metaphor for playing out the Cold War with less catastrophic consequences or simply as an effort on the part of congressmen to help provide a breakthrough in our relations.

While we had a very good mix of talent, the Soviet Embassy had at least one, and possibly two, former members who had played on past Olympic teams. The odds were not with us.

In fact, it proved to be no contest. We blew the Russians away that night.

According to our agreement, the losing team had to buy the winners a dinner at Clyde's Restaurant in Georgetown. During the course of the dinner, as the MVP of the game, I was given a T-shirt emblazoned with CCCP in large red letters. I also managed to be on the receiving end of a diatribe about the superiority of the Soviet Union. The conversation turned rather heated at one point and I decided to leave before my temper got the best of me.

The next day, the player who was badgering me (the Olympian) called my office and asked to speak with me. I assumed that he wanted to apologize for turning the evening into a verbal slugfest.

I waited several days and then returned the call. I was told that he (I'll call him Yuri) was out and would call me back.

A day passed and Yuri called again. This time, I was unavailable.

A day or two passed before I received a call. This one was from the FBI. The caller asked if I'd be willing to meet with a counterintelligence unit that afternoon. I agreed to a meeting, but I grew suspicious that this was not going to be a social meet-and-greet, let's-get-to-know-you visit. I immediately called Howard Liebengood, the Senate's sergeant of arms, and asked him to sit in on the meeting.

Right on schedule, two FBI agents came to my office. They looked like Eliot Ness clones. Dark suits. Short hair. Polished wing-tip shoes. One of the agents had a briefcase that he laid flat across his lap. I suspected that it contained a recording system.

The agents, not pleased that Liebengood was in the room, asked him to leave. I indicated that there would be no conversation without him.

I assumed that the bureau might be interested in what we learned from the Russians during and following the ball game, but the agents had a different agenda.

"The word is out all over town that you and Yuri are close buddies," one of the agents said.

I was stunned by the allegation and the agent's tone in delivering it.

"I played against the Soviet team the other night. You can check with CBS. They filmed it. There was a postgame dinner at Clyde's. That's the only contact I've had with any Russian."

"That's not what we hear. We've got good information that the two of you are pretty tight. You guys are in constant contact with each other."

Now, I really was hot. "You're either tapping the Soviet Embassy's phones or mine. Either way, your records will show that in fact I've never had a conversation with Yuri or anyone else. I returned a phone call that was made to me. Period. So stop trying to bullshit me."

As it turned out, the FBI was testing me to see if I was in covert contact with Yuri. It seemed that Yuri had been making a number of calls to people on Capitol Hill. He might have been trying to pad his credentials with his superiors to show that he had multiple political contacts. This could be helpful to him now or in the future if he wanted to be rotated back to Washington after completing other assignments.

The FBI had something else in mind. They wanted me to continue to contact him and consider setting up a dinner meeting. Apparently, they thought that they might be able to compromise him and turn him into an asset.

I agreed to help, provided that a written record was created and signed off by Howard Liebengood. The last thing that I wanted was to be photographed in the company of a Soviet spy and run the risk that the photo could be used to compromise or discredit me.

Nothing ever came of the dinner plans. Yuri dropped out of sight and never tried to contact me again.

I tried for several years, including during my tenure as secretary of defense, to see the file that the FBI maintained on the case. The FBI said that it had no record of any contact it had with me in connection with Yuri or anyone else.

Just as Janet had discovered in her request to the FBI for any information they had collected on her as a close friend of Dr. Martin Luther King, Jr., someone had hit the delete button.

During my eighteen years in the Senate, I worked with Democratic and Republican colleagues to reform our outdated procurement rules (Competition in Contracting Act); to create, over the objections of the Pentagon, the Special Forces Command led by a four-star general, along with a civilian office of Special Operations and Low Intensity Conflict (SOLIC); and to reform the power and procedures of the Joint Chiefs of Staff (Goldwater-Nichols Department of Defense Reorganization Act). This was also opposed by the Pentagon. We also passed legislation to overhaul the intelligence community's operations and to force the executive agencies to organize their information technologies in a rational and comprehensive fashion (Clinger-Cohen Act).

During President Ronald Reagan's second term, a scandal erupted when the administration was exposed as having lied when it declared the United States would never trade arms to seek the release of American hostages. In fact, the administration had authorized the sale of weapons to the Iranians at inflated prices and diverted the excess profits from the sale to support the Nicaraguan Contras, who were waging an insurgent war against the Sandinistas. At the time, I was serving as the vice chairman of the Intelligence Committee, and I was appointed by Senator Bob Dole to serve on the Joint Congressional Committee to investigate what became known as the Iran-Contra scandal.

While the word "impeachment" rarely surfaced, there was genuine concern that the sale of weapons to Iran in exchange for the release of Americans being held hostage in Lebanon, and the use of proceeds from those sales to fund an insurgency against Nicaragua's Sandinista government, constituted a grave threat to our democratic system.

As charismatic Marine Lieutenant Colonel Oliver North proudly boasted during the hearings, the administration had created a stand-alone, off-the-shelf, self-sustaining entity to conduct covert operations. Stripped of their lyrical ring, North's words meant that the president of the United States could completely bypass Congress, secure millions of dollars through the sale of U.S. assets, and conduct secret operations to undermine or overthrow foreign governments. This scheme struck at the very heart of our constitutional system.

The Joint Committee's public hearings unleashed ugly passions that flooded the offices of committee members. Senator Daniel Inouye, who had lost his right arm to a German grenade during World War II, became a favorite target of racist hate mail. Inouye's heroism on the battlefield (for which he would receive a Medal of Honor) was given little weight by rabid partisans. Senator Warren Rudman, a tough, battle-hardened veteran of the Korean War, denounced the racist smears. To make clear his disgust for several of the witnesses who invoked patriotism as a defense of their actions, Rudman declared, "I'm tired of people who wrap themselves in the flag and go around spitting on the Constitution."

Arthur Liman, the Senate's chief counsel, came under frequent assault. Liman was constantly referred to as that "New York lawyer," which translated to "New York Jew." When several committee members tried to limit his interrogation time or criticized his examination technique, I intervened to oppose any effort to place "a gag rule" on him.

Arthur sent me a wry, appreciative note: "But why does your name have to be Cohen?" The anti-Semitic slurs were full-throated and they were not reserved for Liman alone.

Once again, I had drawn the animus of those who insisted that I place loyalty of party over principle. I was accused of betraying President Reagan; I was called a "Judas," and a "disgusting, self-loathing Jew." The incantation of Hitler's name and praise for his "final solution" became commonplace. Ironically, a Jewish man also found me disgusting and disloyal. "You, sir, are an asshole. You have caused me and my family great embarrassment. Please change your name!"

"Ordinarily," I wrote back, "I don't respond to the idiosyncrasies of people who write me. But in your case I have I decided to make an exception and agree to your request."

I signed the letter, "Samuel Cohen."

Although President Reagan continued to remain personally popular with the American people, I could not absolve him from responsibility for the lies, deceptions, and lawbreaking that his subordinates had indulged in as a result either of his encouragement or neglect. Even though his intentions may have been noble, our Founding Fathers decided that unchecked power would be arrogantly used and inevitably abused. If secrecy and speed of action were to be the central values of government, they would have embraced a king and not created a Congress.

Lies admittedly had been told to the American people, but they were justified on the basis that they were necessary in order to save lives. I didn't accept this or any of the other rationales that were offered. I was convinced that creating a secret fund to finance covert operations was in violation of legislative restrictions. There had been no consultation with Congress, which has the constitutional responsibility to appropriate funds for authorized purposes. This posed a serious threat to our democratic form of government. Whether President Reagan knowingly authorized the activities remained unclear. President Reagan, however, delivered a public address in which he accepted the findings of the investigation even though in his heart he did not believe he had traded weapons for hostages. This public declaration stood in stark contrast to that of President Richard Nixon during the Watergate scandal.

While Ronald Reagan's presidency had survived, my twenty-four-year marriage did not.

My wife, Diana, had been longing to return to Maine and sink roots in the soil of her childhood. I, by contrast, was still addicted to a life of public service. Our sons were grown and pursuing their own careers. Difficult as any parting is, we decided that our respective needs dictated a divorce.

Once the news became public, I was deluged with calls from friends expressing sympathy and support. One call took me by complete surprise.

It was from Janet.

Janet said that she was surprised and sorry that I was divorcing after so many years. She succeeded in bolstering my spirits with her expression of concern for my well-being. Over the period of thirteen years since I had first met her, I had completely lost track of her whereabouts or activities. Although Boston remained her base, she had been traveling a great deal. She brought me up to date on her travels in Europe, Egypt, and Kenya.

Life, it seemed, was going well for her. The reality, however, was less positive.

During all of Janet's travels, she and Dr. Kistner managed to have a healthy marriage. He was completely dedicated to his profession and consumed with his duties as surgeon, lecturer, and author. He was totally supportive of her television commitments and newfound passion for polo.

At the time, Janet owned two ponies and kept them sheltered at a farm on the outskirts of Boston. She was concerned about the impact of the cold winters on their health, and while talking with a friend, discovered that she could keep them at the Palm Beach Polo and Country Club. There, they would be better cared for, and at less expense.

While on a visit to a spa in Fort Lauderdale, she went to see her ponies and to satisfy herself that they were being properly looked after. During the visit, she saw a number of attractive villas at the country club. When she returned to Boston, she suggested to her husband that it would be a good investment to acquire one of the villas. He readily agreed, as he had been a devoted sun worshipper his entire life, and jumped at the chance to spend weekends away from Boston's gray overcast weather.

He would frequently slip down to the villa on weekends. Janet would either join him or meet him there and participate in some of the polo matches.

Then in 1985, trouble began to brew in paradise. Age began to take a toll on Dr. Kistner physically. He developed arthritis in his fingers, making it impossible for him to wear surgical gloves or perform surgery. His eyesight started to deteriorate. He became depressed and easily agitated. He then developed skin cancer and had to reduce his time in the sun.

Slowly, Dr. Kistner started to slip into a deeper state of depression. He would speak to her of his fear of becoming incapacitated and make Janet promise never to keep him on a life-support system. He hinted that he might consider suicide one day rather than wait for his body to fall apart. In the months that followed, he became increasingly distant.

Finally, one day, Janet received a letter telling her that he wanted a divorce. She was stunned. She flew to Florida immediately and found him in a state of anger and barely contained rage. He said that he never wanted to see her again.

Janet returned to Boston dejected, suffering from her own brand of depression. Misery decided it wanted to pile on: Janet also had a falling out with her mother. And she was without a job.

During this time, WCVB called and offered her an opportunity to earn a six-figure salary to do nothing more than pick out a lottery number every evening at the station. It was an offer she intended to refuse. She had spent years honing her ability to interview important people, to question and examine their views, and to help bring the full bloom of their personalities to her viewers. Spinning a lottery wheel was tantamount to being an Italian organ grinder's monkey. She wasn't going to do it.

During a small gathering with a few friends at the apartment, Janet was asked whether the rumor about the lottery offer was true. She acknowledged that it was, and added, too cavalierly, that she had no intention of becoming "Vanna Black." That smart-aleck remark made its way into the following day's *Boston Herald*.

Her former benefactors at WCVB didn't think the comment was so clever.

She never worked in Boston again.

Fifteen

OF POLO AND POETRY

It came as a shock when I read that the internationally renowned Dr. Robert Kistner had committed suicide. I called Janet to express condolences and offered any emotional support I could give at the moment.

It was in early January 1990 when Janet first learned that her husband had attempted to commit suicide by taking an overdose of sleeping pills. The woman he was dating discovered him unconscious and was able to foil his suicide. Then in February, she received a telephone call from the sheriff of West Palm Beach. Dr. Kistner had slit his wrists and bled to death in the bathtub. The news hit her like a sledgehammer. She extracted every gory detail that she could from the sheriff and then attempted to reach her husband's sons.

The reception she received from his family, who had once been so friendly to her, was colder than a New England ice storm.

Dr. Kistner's medical colleagues suddenly treated her as if she were invisible. She tried to rationalize that some of their animosity was understandable. Grief can turn a heart sad or hard, and fixing blame can be a convenient excuse to avoid finding fault within.

But nothing prepared her for the hatred that her deceased husband's attorney held for her. Not only did this celebrated Bostonian try to strip her of the inheritance that she was legally entitled to, but his racist sentiments were so strong that he scuttled any attempt to resolve the legal dispute on an amicable basis. In fact, having previously represented her husband as a divorce attorney, he appeared to have switched law firms just so he could handle the estate.

It was Janet's good fortune to have famed trial attorney F. Lee Bailey as a friend. Lee offered to help her resolve her dispute with her husband's family. During the course of negotiations with Lee and in the presence of several other people, Kistner's estate attorney had said, "The black bitch has gotten more than she deserves. She got the pleasure of being with Dr. Kistner, and she's not entitled to a damn thing. She's gotten all she's going to get. I took the case to make sure of that."

Up to that point Janet had been willing to compromise her claim, even though she was convinced there was no need to do so. But the "black bitch" comment hit her rage button. She had never swallowed her pride for anyone, and as much financial stress as she was under at the time, she told Lee to call off all negotiations. "I want the whole estate or nothing at all," she said. "Let's roll the dice."

"You could end up with nothing," Lee cautioned. "Let's sleep on it."

But her mind was made up. It was all or nothing. Thanks to Lee's brilliance, it turned out to be all. After the court ruled in Janet's favor, she met with Lee in New York to discuss with him how she wanted to proceed. She had proved that she was right in her claim. Now, she wanted to show that she also knew how to be fair. She gave Bob's family 40 percent of the estate—the same percentage she had been willing to agree to from the beginning.

Lee said, "That's why I love you. You've got brass balls, and you've got character."*

There's an old expression: "When someone tells you that it's not about the money, it's about the money." Once the Kistner estate attorney referred to her as a "black bitch," money, as much as she needed it at that time, no longer was the issue. Now it was principle—and more. Now it was personal.

---

*See *From Rage to Reason,* pp. 207–209.

During much of Janet's life, white society had tried to place limits on her: where she could eat; where she could sit; what she could do; who she could be. The warning "Stop! Do not enter" was the equivalent of a watermark they tried to imprint on the tissue of her mind. She might not be wearing chains, but she was expected to continue to live on a plantation, obeying rules that were made for people like her, people of color.

Several years after her courtroom battle, our friend Adele Alexander, a noted historian, told Janet the story of Alice Jones and Leonard Rhinelander. The two had married after dating for some three years, despite efforts by Rhinelander's father to break up the relationship. The father had opposed his son's amorous activities, not simply because Jones came from a very modest family, but because the blood of Alice Jones' father was not completely white. One drop of black blood, and behold, you were black!

The Rhinelanders were a family of enormous wealth, and not only would Alice Jones be the first black woman to be entered into the New York's *Social Register,* but she stood to be a beneficiary of the huge fortune that her husband would one day inherit. The national newspapers and scandal-seeking tabloids had a field day with the story of young Leonard marrying the daughter of a "colored man."

Shortly after the media frenzy was unleashed, Leonard filed an annulment petition with the court. During the course of the trial, Rhinelander's attorney portrayed Alice as a low-class sexual predator who had lured and duped Leonard into marrying her, concealing the fact that she was "colored." During the trial, he accused Alice of trying to "pass as white" by attending religious and social functions that were exclusively for whites. In one of the most memorable racist comments uttered in a New York courtroom, Rhinelander's attorney made a desperate appeal to the basest instincts of the jury: "There isn't a father among you who would not rather see his own son in a casket than to see him wedded to a mulatto woman."*

---

*See Mark Kittrell, "Love On Trial: an American Scandal In Black and White," *Journal of Law and Family Studies,* 331 (2001).

Alice's attorney had conceded from the start of the trial that Alice had "colored blood." In fact, he went further and had her disrobe in front of the judge and jury to demonstrate that Rhinelander had to know that she was colored. Who were they going to believe? Rhinelander or their own eyes? The tactic proved successful. The jury did rule against Rhinelander, but it was shameful that Alice had been forced "to strip to conquer."

Alice eventually agreed to a divorce in exchange for a very modest financial settlement. For her, it was not a question of the money. It was principle.

And it was personal.

Whenever I think back on my chance encounter with Janet in 1974, I'm forced to question whether life is all just a roll of the dice. The day we met at the television studio, for example, I was in terrible physical condition. I had considered canceling my weekly trek back to Maine and my scheduled appearance on *Good Morning* in Boston.

Was it sheer persistence on my part to climb on the Delta flight and head north, or was it simply destiny asserting itself?

While I had talked politics with Janet periodically over the intervening years, I knew very little about her background or life experiences; nothing of the poverty of her childhood, the perils of her profession, or the trauma behind her husband's suicide. All I knew was that I was determined on our next meeting to make a far better impression than I had on the day on which I presented her with a copy of Lawrence Ferlinghetti's poetry.

I waited months before I called her again. I had tickets to a Broadway play. Thinking that she might be in the mood for something spiritually uplifting, I invited her to join me. After the play, we stopped at a small French restaurant near Janet's apartment. In the darkness of the room, with candlelight flickering in her eyes and the play's musical score still dancing in my mind, I found myself staring at Janet. At the time, I didn't know that the famed photographer Francesco Scavullo had deemed Janet to be one of the most beauti-

Wedding day, February 14, 1996. Vows were exchanged in the Senate's Mansfield Room. *Courtesy of Jerry Friedman*

Under the mistletoe at a White House Christmas party (1991). *Photo by Reverend James Ford*

Arriving in Kosovo under heavy guard (1999). *Courtesy of Dept. of Defense*

On a flight to visit our forces in the Persian Gulf, Senator Daiel Inouye (left), Congressman John Murtha, and me (1999). *Courtesy of the Dept. of Defense*

Janet taking country music star Clint Black on her Citizen's Patriot Tour in Bosnia. Maj.-Gen. Blum was the host. *Courtesy of the Dept of Defense*

President Bill Clinton and Mrs. Clinton host a White House Christmas party (1998). *Courtesy of the White House*

President Bush and Mrs. Bush greet us at a White House Christmas party (1991). *Courtesy of the White House*

Senators Sam Nunn (Left) and John Warner (center) join me in con-
gratulating General Norman Schwarzkopf for achieving success in
driving Suddam Hussein's forces out of Kuwait during Desert
Storm (1991). *Courtesy of U.S. Senate*

John Shalikashvili, Chairman of the Joint Chiefs
of Staff, discusses issues with me and Senator
John McCain at my Pentagon office. *Courtesy of
the Dept. of Defense*

Presenting former Congressman (now Mayor of
Oakland, Calif.) Ron Dellums his Public Service
Award. *Courtesy of the Dept. of Defense*

Bringing Holiday greetings to our soldiers in Bosnia (1997). *Courtesy of the Dept. of Defense*

Janet in my Pentagon office (2000).

Marion "Hutch" Hutchisson, one of the Navy's first WAVES, touring the Pentagon (2000). *Courtesy of the Dept. of Defense*

My son, Kevin, and his wife, Chantel, with their two sons, Jordan (left) and Connor (right)

My son, Chris, and his wife, Kerry, with their daughter, Lilia, and son, Jacob. Their dog, Ace, is in the foreground.

Janet and me with our Maltese puppy, Lucy (2006). *Photo by Sambo Teng*

Taking the Oath of Office in the Oval Office of the White House. Vice President Gore administered the oath while President Clinton and Janet look on (January 17, 1997). *Courtesy of the White House*

Janet and me during the playing of our national anthem at our farewell ceremony at Comny Hall, Ft. Myer (2001). *Courtesy of the Dept. of Defense*

Wedding-day kiss. *Courtesy of Jerry Friedman*

Last dance at the White House. *Courtesy of the White House*

ful women in the world. That much, even Stevie Wonder could see. But her physical beauty was transcended by a generosity of spirit that set her above anyone I had ever known.

One glass of Absolut vodka on the rocks eased my normal Maine reserve. "Janet, you are beautiful." Such compliments, I assumed, were commonplace to her, but she accepted it gracefully.

After a second vodka, I said, "You *really are* beautiful."

This time, she broke out in open laughter. "One more," she teased, "and you'll be proposing."

Embarrassed that I was acting like a schoolboy out on his first date, I laughed in return. "Trust me. It's not the booze."

This was the beginning of a romance that would catch fire and flourish throughout the year. I started reducing my trips to Maine to just two a month. The other two weekends Janet and I would spend together in New York, shopping or going to movies. Frequently, while walking along Fifth Avenue, we'd stop in St. Patrick's Cathedral to pray or simply meditate in the exquisite silence. These visits marked the end of my grandfather's prohibition against my entering a church. I was struck when I saw how many of the faces in the church seemed so troubled and in need of some signal that their pain did not go unnoticed by their Creator. Invariably, we would end the day at what became our favorite Italian restaurant, Bravo Gianni's on East Sixty-third Street.

Janet was a highly visible television personality in the city and attracted a good deal of attention. But for the most part, people either ignored us or respected our privacy. On one occasion, an older couple approached us during dinner and invited us to join them for a drink at their apartment on Park Avenue. Sensing that they were sincere in their gesture of friendship, we agreed.

Not everyone was quite so well-meaning. On another occasion, two couples were sitting at a table directly behind us at Bravo Gianni's. It became obvious that we had become the subject of their conversation throughout the evening. When we got up to leave, they rose up from their table simultaneously. As Janet and I started for the door, one of the men started to engage me in conversation. I assumed that he simply wanted to introduce himself and say something about politics or the media. He had something else in mind.

"It must be very hard for you," he said.

"Excuse me?"

"I mean, you're a politician and you have to be careful."

"About what?" His tone had started to irritate me.

"Well," he said, looking at Janet disapprovingly, "what you do in public."

Fortunately, Janet was several paces ahead of us and had her back to the man. He was rude and racist. What enabled him to approach me and make a statement like that? Had I not been a senator, I might have allowed my emotions to prevail over my judgment. But the politician in me checked in. Any physical response was out of the question if I wanted to avoid becoming an item in the New York tabloids.

"Mister, I'm free, single and over twenty-one."

I might have expected such an encounter in rural America or the South, but not in cosmopolitan New York, which simply proves the point that racism is not a matter of geography or region.

There were few such open displays of bigotry. In fact, other than some ugly letters from constituents who had learned that I was dating a black woman, most people embraced us warmly and unconditionally.

One incident did occur after we were married, when a prominent talk show host asked, "What's it like being married to a black woman?"

I was momentarily stunned by the question.

Janet had told me of an incident that involved one of her cousins, who was serving in the Army during World War II. While relaxing in a Paris bar, he was approached by a woman who asked if she could see his tail! (Little seems to have changed in sixty-five years, as European soccer fans routinely hurl bananas at black players and indulge in monkey calls.) After risking his life to help liberate France, he was in no mood to tolerate the racist insult. He erupted with anger. A brawl ensued, and he was arrested for disturbing the peace and confined to a brig!

I was tempted to rephrase the question as "You mean what's it like to be in love with an extraordinary woman?" or "What are some of the interests we share?"

To these, I would have answered, "Let me count the ways."

When I look at Janet, in Carole King's words, "I feel the earth move under my feet." We love music (I play the piano and Janet the flute). We enjoy listening to classical music, Mozart, Brahms, and Schubert, but we also like recording artists such as Newell Oler, Phil Driscoll, Celine Dion, Eva Cassidy, Michael McDonald, Luther Vandross, and Patti LaBelle being among our favorites. We dance, read books, watch movies, and devote endless affection to Lucy, our Maltese puppy. On special occasions we send each other Hallmark cards and (using the respective code names our pentagon security detail used for us, Joshua and Firebird) stay in constant touch with each other through a stream of e-mails.

Instead of responding in this fashion, I let the moment pass, knowing that the talk show host was not engaging in any malice with his question. I responded simply by saying that we had encountered little societal discontent and had been embraced by our many friends.

As we walked out of the studio, Janet looked at me and said, "Did you hear him say what I heard him say?"

"I did, but I let it go. I don't think he realized what he was saying."

He may not have understood the implications of his question, but one of his producers must have. The program had been taped for broadcast later that evening.

Janet and I watched television that night to see if the camera caught my reaction to his question. We watched in vain. The host's question had disappeared, edited out! Actually we were at once disappointed and relieved.

"Bill, I hate it when supposedly sophisticated people continue to see color and assume that we have to be different."

I agreed. Few people are prepared to engage in an enlightened discussion about racial attitudes and stereotypes. It produces anger in some and embarrassment in others.

"This country," Janet went on to say, "needs to have an open dialogue on racism. America likes its history in fairy tale form. The founders and leaders of the country are portrayed as good and noble individuals with a few character flaws. It we point out their personal failures, then we're said to be 'ungrateful' or that we've got 'chips on our shoulders.' We're not allowed to dwell on black history. That's airbrushed out because it contradicts the 'grand story.'"

What most people fail to understand about Janet is that, successful as she's been, a quiet rage still runs through her. From outward appearances, she reflects a serenity and generosity of heart—which are real—but beneath those calm waters is a powerful current of anger that will burst to the surface whenever she sees a display of prejudice, injustice, or hypocrisy.

"I still don't understand why white people act the way they do towards blacks and other minorities."

"All white people?" I asked defensively.

"No, Honey," she said, giving me a hug around my shoulders. "I know you can't answer for others, only for yourself. But that's one of the major differences we have. Black people have a collective history of oppression at the hands of whites and that enables me to express their feelings because we've all had virtually the same experience."

"What you're saying is that as whites, we never have to think about our whiteness."

"Exactly. Your lives have never been affected by *our* decisions—unless we managed to escape from the plantations or took to the streets to demonstrate for freedom and equal rights. And then all those who brutalized and exploited us over the years start crying, 'there goes my everything!'

"Think about it. All the stories we're seeing now about the 'out-sourcing' of jobs and the flood of illegal immigrants coming into the country. 'The Asians and Latinos are stealing our jobs' is the latest battle cry. Funny, they didn't seem to be complaining when blacks were taking their jobs during slavery. They didn't have to pay us anything. They just insisted that we 'tote that barge, lift that bale,' keep smiling, while they went off to the bank."

"Janet, you know that I think about these issues all the time. I've got grandchildren who are bi-racial."

"You know," she teased lightly, "it still only takes one drop of black blood."

"Yes, but I'm still hopeful they won't have to be twice as good to get half as much."

As I suggested, this is not the type of conversation that most people are eager to have, but it's one America needs to hear.

One moment during our courtship remains especially vivid in my mind. I had decided to accompany Janet to West Palm Beach and watch a polo match. Polo is principally a male sport—and, I discovered, a rather dangerous one.

I watched in awe as high-spirited ponies raced back and forth across the polo field, bumping each other for position while at full gallop, pirouetting on a dime to change direction and race off after the ball. It was the equivalent of hockey on horseback.

That afternoon, Janet decided to suit up, but just to practice a little stick and ball. As I watched how she handled her pony and swung her mallet while at a full gallop, I saw in her another dimension. A woman of strength and daring, unafraid to mix it up with men on their turf, in their game, by their rules. I concluded that polo was but a metaphor for much of her extraordinary life.

Janet wore a gardenia in her hair that evening. Just before we sat down to a candlelit dinner, I wrote a few lines about how the sight of her joy, her spirit, and zest for life had affected me.

A cry,
a gull song,
wings white against
a liquid sky;
palm trees sway in a wind
suddenly warm with rage;
horses race in the distance,
polo fields shudder
under hooves that whip and whirl

in pirouettes of mammoth grace.
Was it you,
the one with gardenias
in your hair
who reached out and touched me?
Were those your tears or mine
that salt-licked their way into an
invisible wound?
Or was it, instead,
imaginary horses whirling now
wet with heat
trackless in the
wild-headed sea
drowning me in the perfume
of crushed flowers?

Sixteen

COLOR CODES

In 1991, I had encouraged Janet to move to Washington so we could spend more time together. She had already been contacted to cohost a syndicated television show, *America's Black Forum*, with civil rights leader Julian Bond. The opportunity to work with Julian had great appeal to her, and she agreed to leave New York, a city she had come to love, and take up residence in the nation's capital.

I knew that a weekly show would not be enough to satisfy Janet's desire to be in the mix of things, and I suggested that I call our mutual friend, Bob Johnson, the founder of Black Entertainment Television (BET), to ask if she could work for his network. I had met Bob back in 1973 when he had served as chief of staff for Walter Fauntroy, the District of Columbia's nonvoting delegate to Congress. Janet had mixed emotions about my request.

Two years earlier, Bob had offered Janet her own show on BET. Unfortunately, *Entertainment Tonight* (*ET*) was pursuing her at the same time. I encouraged her to place a higher priority on *ET*, since she was likely to reach a much wider audience there. Janet was convinced that she could handle both jobs and had instructed her agent to seek a nonexclusive contract with *ET*. Regrettably, either *ET* would not agree to a nonexclusive arrangement or the agent did not take her request seriously. She ended up signing an exclusive deal that precluded her from working for BET.

It turned out to have been a bad decision. Janet's stint with *ET* was short-lived. After having been encouraged by her producers to be more sharp-edged in the interviews she was conducting during the Cannes Film Festival, Janet asked movie star Arnold Schwarzenegger about the role his father had allegedly played in the Nazi Party during World War II.

Although Schwarzenegger had raised no objections with CNN's Larry King, who had first mentioned the subject, he was furious with Janet. He walked away from the interview and warned everyone that if she appeared at the hotel the next day to conduct interviews, he would grant none to anyone. Janet was effectively blacklisted during the remainder of her time at Cannes. Sylvester Stallone did grant her an interview, but she decided to conduct it in the basement of the hotel so as not to jeopardize opportunities for other journalists working the film festival.

Schwarzenegger was able not only to blacklist Janet at the film festival but also to put an end to her career with *ET*.

When Janet returned to the United States from Cannes, she discovered that *ET* executives, after previously pursuing her so vigorously, suddenly had a problem with the quality of her English. Notwithstanding her more than twenty years as a popular talk show host, they thought she needed speech therapy and sent her off to the Magid Institute, a school in Iowa where she was asked by a twenty-four-year-old white man to repeat individual words slowly and endlessly. *How now, brown cow?*

Indeed.

When this obvious insult failed to provoke Janet to quit, they finally advised her that she was being terminated because her English wasn't up to par. Apparently, when it came to the English language, the "Kalifornia" Terminator had set the bar too high for her to reach.

Janet called me immediately after she walked out of the paramount Building on Columbus Circle in New York.

I was upset, "Two Jewish executives fired you for raising questions about the allegations about Nazi activities of Schwarzenegger's father during WWII?"

"Ironic, isn't it?" Janet asked.

"At the very least. Maybe there's more to it. . . ."

"No. It's not about race. It's about power."

"Like the Godfather said, 'it's not personal, just business?'"

"Exactly."

It would come as no smaller irony that ten years later, *ET* would ask her to serve as both producer and on-air correspondent during a tour she had organized to entertain our troops serving in Bosnia, Kosovo, Macedonia, and Italy after the September 11 attacks.*

In any event, Bob Johnson of BET was not a man to nurse grudges. *ET* was a thing of the past to him. He hired Janet to host a show called *Personal Diary with Janet Langhart*, in which she interviewed prominent blacks who had achieved extraordinary success in life. Among the many luminaries she showcased were Rosa Parks, Quincy Jones, Congresswomen Barbara Jordan and Shirley Chisholm, Spike Lee, Earl Graves, Geoffrey Holder, Carmen DeLavallade, Clifford and Adele Alexander, Billy Eckstein, Ramsey Lewis, Betty Carter, Faye Wattleton, and General Benjamin O. Davis.

While Janet was thrilled to have the opportunity to meet many distinguished and accomplished men and women in Washington, and to celebrate their lives during this time in her career, she also discovered that there were limitations on what she could say and do.

On *America's Black Forum*, for example, she was in the process of interviewing the Reverend Louis Farrakhan when her producer slipped her a handwritten note, reminding her to be sure not to go easy on Farrakhan. He was controversial, to be sure, and Janet didn't subscribe to all of his views, particularly those he holds toward Jewish people and their faith. But he is, nonetheless, revered by millions of black people for his efforts to rekindle a sense of pride in who they are and what they can do as a people committed to self-help rather than waiting for handouts from others. Janet had watched

---

*See *From Rage to Reason*, pp. 213–215.

interviews conducted by white interrogators, and they usually did everything they could to discredit him.

She was stunned to discover that the employees of a black-owned program felt obligated to remind her that she had to be tough on him. And she couldn't help but think back to her days in Boston when her producers warned her not to be overly aggressive during her interview with David Duke, former leader of the Ku Klux Klan, lest she appear "biased."

"I had always tried to extend an even hand to my guests," she said, "but I resented the note because it reflected a plantation mentality. Blacks still had to please the masters, the advertisers, lest we fall out of favor."

Janet was equally disappointed to learn that despite her professional accomplishments, she was still subject to being pulled back down into the crab barrel. Bob Johnson, entrepreneurial genius that he is, had decided to create a cosmetic makeup line called, ironically enough, "Color Code," and was using many of the on-air personalities at BET to advertise the products. The ads were directed to black women of all shades. When Janet asked why he had not used her for any of the ads, given her modeling background, he said that he had been unaware that she was interested. He also revealed that he had a problem at the studio. He was receiving complaints from viewers who accused him of using too many light-skinned people. He had to use more dark-skinned people on the air.

Being recognized as a black celebrity gave Janet a confidence she had never had before. But she also felt rage. She could never get the "Colored Only" signs of the past out of her mind. Nor could she ever forget that day when her Haitian and Brazilian modeling colleagues played their race card. Is that the way it was to be? She had read that when Lena Horne became an actress under MGM contract, Hollywood image-makers decided she was too light. So they made her darker, calling in makeup genius Max Factor to smear her face with the same caramel shade that he had used to make Hedy

Lamarr look black enough to play Tondelayo, an exotic, racially mixed native in the 1942 movie *White Cargo*.

The "color code" has long been known among blacks. It is a reflection of just how pernicious and damaging racism has been in their lives. The story is as old as America. One drop of black blood—and presto, you were considered black. If you were classified as black, then in the white world it followed that you were, considered, inferior, immoral, ignorant, uneducable, and shiftless. Such qualities, however, didn't prevent the morally minded white slave masters from slipping into black beds, subjecting their "property" to activities that ranged from rape to common-law (unwritten) marriage. These illicit couplings produced babies of mixed color. The lighter offspring were seen as more attractive and acceptable to whites and, accordingly, received special treatment. The darker blacks were shunted to the rear and treated with disdain. It didn't take long for this reward system to take root in the black consciousness. Some black parents encouraged their children to marry spouses with lighter skin. If society said the lighter you were, the better shot you had in life, then most parents saw this as a matter of survival. Skin color could determine whether your children climbed up the ladder or stayed in the crab barrel.

But as favors were dispensed to fairer-skinned blacks, those who were darker grew more resentful. Rather than support those who had an opportunity to escape hardship, they turned on them and tried to pull them back into the barrel. Janet was more than familiar with the doggerel about color when she was growing up:

If you're White,
you're alright.
If you're black,
get back.
If you're yellow,
you're mellow.
If you're brown,
stick around.

And, when she was older, she heard stories about "color tax" parties run by black fraternities at all-black colleges. The blacker the fraternity brother, the higher his admission price to the party. Some black men put it this way: They want a woman who is "light, bright, and nearly white."

Revelations about the color code were featured in Spike Lee's movie *School Daze.* In the film, set in an imaginary black college, light-skinned students struggle against dark-skinned students. As a critic noted, "For every light-skinned, affluent sorority girl affecting blue contact lenses, there's a darker-skinned, poorer, less artificially coiffed classmate who bitterly resents such aspirations." In a musical number, dark and light students argue about the virtues of hair-straightening.

"Whether black men admit it or not," Lee said in an *Essence* magazine interview, "they feel light-skinned women are more attractive than dark-skinned, and they'd rather see long hair than a short Afro, because that's closer to white women." Lee blamed the phenomenon on the fact that black men are bombarded by media images that portray "the white woman as the image of beauty." In the movies, the color code called for dark-skinned black actors and light-skinned actresses, preferably with features more Caucasian than African.

"Historically," Janet said, "Hollywood has had much to do with the negative stereotyping of blacks. It still does. For far too long, black actors who were allowed to appear in movies or on television were cast only as clowns, criminals, and crack addicts. Strong and handsome males were seen as too threatening, and beautiful females were relegated to secondary roles. Those who held the power to display the beauty of our race chose to pick weeds in our gardens rather than flowers."

Several years ago, much was made over Hollywood's awarding of Oscars to Sidney Poitier, Denzel Washington, and Halle Berry. I could see that Janet took enormous pride when she watched those three elegant people, with grace and emotion, accept what had been denied to so many for so long. But she couldn't suppress a twinge of regret that of all the positive and uplifting roles that Denzel had portrayed on film, he was rewarded for playing a corrupt, drug-dealing cop, and Halle received her Oscar not for her performance in *The Dorothy Dandridge Story*, but for portraying a prostitute who was sleeping with a racist bigot in *Monster's Ball*.

She finds it equally discouraging to see what music is now celebrated as a reflection of black culture.

As we watched the Oscar Awards night on television, Janet said, "Once again, those who dispense our entertainment choose the negative over the good. The culture that gave America spirituals, soul, the blues, and jazz is only a memory. Today, what we expect from black rappers is the Three 6 Mafia giving 'It's Hard Out Here for a Pimp' to an Oscar night audience. Look at this performance: black women dressed as prostitutes and black men stomping around, win the group an Oscar." Some critic observed, watching the Three 6 Mafia was like watching a minstrel.

There are some prominent blacks who are vocal in their criticism of those who are content to place the blame on others for the problems that afflict the black community. Bill Cosby, for example, has been making news in recent years, not for his comedic talents but for his commentaries on the crude language that is becoming commonplace among the young in the black community and for the failure of parents to make education a top priority for their children. While many praise his courage and candor, others resent him for washing the community's dirty laundry in public. Such public displays, they are convinced, will only serve as weapons to be wielded by others against African-Americans.

In addition, Michael Eric Dyson, a well-known scholar and social critic, argues that the ability to rise up from the floor of grinding poverty and discrimination is not easy when those who hold political power have a foot on your neck.*

Cosby's critics also insist that the younger generation's language and attitudes are merely a reflection of black culture. Janet abhors the denigration of women as "bitches" and "ho's" in music. "It doesn't

---

*See Michael Eric Dyson, *Is Bill Cosby Right? Or Has the Black Middle Class Lost Its Mind* (New York: Basic Civitas Books, 2006).

enhance or uplift our culture, it only fattens the coffers of the music industry."

"The culture of my generation," Janet said, "was not to yield to the bigotry of others, but to contest and overcome it—on the battlefields, in the classrooms, in the courtrooms, and in the board-rooms. We did it through education and effort, self-love, and self-discipline, and through the sheer determination to prevail."

There is more than a generational divide at issue. During the long struggle for civil rights, countless heroes risked life and limb to erase the cruel vestiges of slavery and racist stereotypes. It is dis-heartening to watch young people forfeit their futures or indulge in slurs that were once the epithets hurled by slave masters and segre-gationists.

As *New York Times* columnist Bob Herbert has written: "It's time to blow the whistle on the nitwits who have so successfully pro-moted a values system that embraces murder, drug-dealing, gang membership, misogyny, child abandonment and a sense of self so diseased that it teaches children to view the men in their orbit as niggaz and the women as hoes. However this madness developed, it's time to bring it to an end."*

To this, Janet and I both offer an Amen.

---

*Herbert, Bob, "Blowing the Whistle on Gangsta Culture," *New York Times*, December 22, 2005. See also Juan Williams, *Enough: The Phony Leaders, Dead-end Movements and Culture of Failure That are Undermining Black America—and What We Can Do About It* (New York: Crown, 2006).

Seventeen

WHO'S COMING TO DINNER?

During the time that Janet worked at BET, I would pick her up at her apartment and drive her to and from the studio. We made no secret that we were dating. I knew that Washington gossip columnists were bound to report us as an "item," and I suggested to Janet that I should consider telling my parents about her and not have them guess who was coming to dinner.

Frankly, I didn't know quite what to expect in terms of their reaction to Janet.

Neither of my parents could be said to be worldly. My father had always had the hope that I might marry a "nice Jewish girl." I was quick to remind him gently that he had not exactly set the standard. While I had never heard either my father or mother utter a racial slur, they had had absolutely zero contact with black people during the course of their lives.

I called home and spoke first with my mother, telling her that I was bringing a special friend to meet them. I alerted her that Janet was an African American. I wasn't sure that she understood what the term meant, but I thought that saying she was black might create unwarranted anxiety. I remained somewhat apprehensive during our journey north to meet my parents.

My apprehensions proved to be baseless. Ironically, Janet had far greater insight into my parents than I did. She used to listen to my weekly conversations with them while I had them on speakerphone. She knew intuitively that they had good hearts and didn't have a trace of bigotry in their bones. My mother didn't flinch when she saw Janet. There were no awkward moments, no silences, no subtle signals of disapproval. Janet spoke with my mother about gardens, flowers, and clothes. She traded views with Dad on food (they both loved chopped liver, sardines, cow brains, and beef tongue), philosophy, and current events. She said that my father was just as she had imagined him. She had once interviewed the actor Topol, the star of the classic play *Fiddler on the Roof*. She told me, "Your father is Tevye, the wonderful man of philosophical wisdom. He loves food, books, music, dance, and all things living. He is 'old world' in every good sense of the words—physical, honest, and uncalculating."

"Isn't it ironic," Janet said to me later that evening as she recounted how much she enjoyed discussing food with my father, "that I know more about Jewish food than you do?"

It was not really a question. Janet, while her mother worked as a domestic, had lived in the homes of Jewish people. She ate the same food as they did for the simple reason that her mother often prepared the meals there. In fact, her mother would continue to cook the same meals when she and Janet were living in their own home.

I, by contrast, had a Jewish father, attended Hebrew school, but ate ethnic food that was mostly of Irish or Italian origin.

Whatever the reason, Janet connected with both my parents. In the short time we were together, they understood—and welcomed—the fact that Janet and I were going to marry. They embraced her as if she were their own daughter.

Janet's race did not present any problem for them. For example, one day a gossip magazine called my father while he was at work to seek his reaction to my romance "with a black woman." Apparently, the mixing machines were roaring at the time and the question had to be repeated several times. The reporter, in exasperation, practically shouted the words "BLACK WOMAN!"

Dad, thinking that the reporter was trying to provoke a negative reaction from him, shouted back, "SHE'S NOT THAT BLACK!"

and slammed the receiver down. He knew nothing about the perverse notion of color coding, but simply had lived at a time when black people were called "colored." He had concluded that the reporter, in calling Janet a black woman, was insinuating a negative: that she was not worthy of his son's affection or his approval.

To this day, my mother refuses to think that anyone would treat Janet any differently than they would a white woman. Her solution if Janet ever runs into trouble? "Just put on a little rouge and no one will know the difference."

Ah, if it were all so simple!

Shortly after I took Janet to meet my parents in Bangor, I traveled to Los Angeles to see my older son, Kevin, who was pursuing a writing career in Hollywood. We were standing on a corner on Little Santa Monica Boulevard and about to enter a coffee shop. It became obvious to me that Kevin had something on his mind other than his work as a screenwriter.

"Dad, there's something I need to tell you."

"Something serious?"

"I think so. I've been dating a girl and I like her a lot. Her name's Chantel."

"So?"

"She's black." Kevin said, somewhat tentatively, waiting to judge my reaction.

I started to laugh, and it confused him. Was I making light of his new love? Derisively mocking him?

"Kevin, you don't have to worry. It just so happens that I'm about to become engaged to Janet Langhart."

"Who?"

"A black woman. You may not remember, but you were with me the day I appeared on her television show to discuss one of my poetry books."

It was Kevin's turn to break into laughter. "Maybe we should have a double wedding," he exuded.

As it turned out, both Kevin and Christopher would beat me to the wedding altar.

While I may have been somewhat apprehensive over how my parents would react to Janet, Janet also had to consider how her mother and other black people would see our engagement.

"The first time I considered dating a white boy occurred while I was a student at Butler University. I wanted to broach the subject with Mother before agreeing to go out with him. I began the evening discussion by asking Mother whether she had ever dated a white man.

"Mother looked up from her dinner plate, starred at me rather quizzically, and proudly said, 'No.'

"I paused, not wanting to move too quickly into a combat zone, and asked simply, 'Why not?'

"Mother paused in return, knowing that more questions were likely to follow, 'Janet, you're a young girl. You shouldn't go out of your own race. White boys only want one thing from us. They think that we're loose. A self-respecting black woman's not likely to want to be seen with one of them unless she's slinking off in the shadows.'

"Seeing that Mother was building a major case against any foray into the white world, I decided to tell her why I was asking the questions: 'One of the white students at Butler, a boy whose name is Tom, has asked to take me to the Tee Pee (a popular hamburger restaurant near the Indiana State Fair Grounds). What do you think? May I let him take me out?'

"The next few minutes were something straight out of Tevye in *Fiddler on the Roof.*

"'Why would you want to go out with him? The dating can't lead to anything good. There's no future with him.'

"'Future? Mother, I'm only seventeen. I'm not planning a future with him. Just dinner in a restaurant.'

"Mother finally relented, but insisted on meeting him. Correction: Interrogating him. Frankly, I never thought that Tom would dare to venture into a black neighborhood, but he was undaunted by the prospect.

"When Tom arrived, Mother questioned him with the thoroughness of detective Jack Webb of *Dragnet* fame. Where was he from?

What did his parents do? What plans did he have for the future? Then, she demanded, 'Be sure to have my daughter home before 11 p.m.'

"I dated Tom several times. One night, Mother asked if I was getting serious with him. I assured her that the answer was 'No.'

"'Good. Remember, no matter how many times you cross the color line, this side is home. You can dance and play over there, but when the music stops, he'll go home. It's us, your people that you'll always have to come back to. They'll never accept you as an equal."

"I took Mother's words to heart and eventually dropped Tom from my social agenda.

"My mother had no reservations about my marriage years later to Bob Kistner once she met him and saw how much he loved me. And when she met you, well, she understood the challenges you were prepared to face to have my hand."

When black people see Janet and me together, Janet says that they tend to reflect a range of emotions. To some, Janet may appear to symbolize a rejection of their identity, their history, their blackness. Is she a "sister" who is a "wanna-be" white, crossing over to leave her black identity on the other side of town?

Of course once they see or hear her on television or read how she's spent a lifetime speaking out against bullies, racial intolerance, and injustice, their doubts are quickly removed.

"I understand their feelings," she confided to me one evening at dinner. "There's an inevitable resentment, a picking at a psychic wound whenever one of us chooses to be with one of the very people who held us down and back for so many centuries. But you aren't keeping me down. You're lifting me up to stand beside you, not like some exotic toy or trophy, but as an equal, a partner. Some may find it difficult to understand that when I marry you, it won't erase my history or memory of our experience. It won't make me white. It'll just make me Mrs. Cohen."

Curiously, while I had anticipated that black people might hold some measure of hostility for me being *The Man* who stepped into their garden and picked one of their most beautiful flowers, their reaction has been just the opposite. They understand that I chose to cross the color line, not as a display of power, but because of the power of love for a woman who happened to be one of them.

How have I been accepted by the black community? Recently, Janet and I attended a Washington Wizards basketball game as guests of Raul and Jean-Marie Fernandez; Raul is part owner of the Wizards, the Washington Mystics basketball team, and the Washington Capitals hockey team. As we left the game, I was practically mobbed by black men coming over, embracing me and giving me the "black handshake" (fist-to-fist followed by a thumb-to-thumb roll), and pleading with me to return to public service. When they finally turned to acknowledge Janet, one of them eager to pay respect to her, said, "Hey, we've got to get his wife back there, too!"

Although I had proposed to Janet on several occasions, she said that she didn't want to be a Senate wife. I assumed what she really meant was that marrying me might have a negative impact on my career and she didn't want that responsibility.

Actually, I had been pondering for some time retiring from the Senate. I thoroughly enjoyed the give-and-take of the legislative process. I had been the author of significant achievements in military and intelligence reforms, and had helped streamline our government's procurement and business processes and investigate executive branch scandal and abuses of power. But the joy that I had once known had begun to evaporate. A poisonous partisanship had started to infiltrate the Senate's actions and deliberations. The great issues of the day were obscured or obliterated by both political parties moving away from the center and to their extremes. Those of us who considered ourselves "moderates" were scorned.

I had once asked Congressman Bill Hungate why he was retiring from Congress. In response, he said, "You know how when you first get here and all your constituents hand you a plate of horse shit, and ask you to eat it. You eat it and then you say, 'Oh, thank you, can I have seconds?' Well, Bill, I just can't bring myself to ask for seconds any more."

I laughed at Hungate's rough Missouri humor at the time. I had always said it a different way. When I stopped having fun and public service became a job, then it would be time for me to leave. We were both saying the same thing. The people of Maine needed someone who had a hunger to serve them.

Yet it was hard for me to let go of something that I had spent so much of my life devoted to.

A phone call that came shortly after midnight one night resolved any lingering doubts about just how I wanted to spend the rest of my life.

I had been watching my father's slow decline on my return trips home. Each Saturday, I would join him at the bakery, helping him bake, bag, and deliver his product to the local restaurants. Each week, he became harder of hearing, his walk a little slower, and his body thinner. Several months before he died, I received a call at three in the morning from my brother, Bob. Dad had fallen and couldn't get up from the floor. An ambulance had been called but he had refused to go to the hospital. When I spoke with him on the phone, he tried to dismiss his condition as nothing more than a leg cramp. I badgered him to go to the hospital, forewarning him that I would catch an early flight to Bangor and see him there. He finally relented.

I arrived at St. Joseph's Hospital to see him stretched out on a bed with various tubes and wires attached to his body. He had suffered a stroke, but was determined to return to work to finish delivering rolls to his customers. I offered to complete the work for him, but he would have none of it. More than twenty years earlier, while delivering bread to a local restaurant, he had opened the wrong door and fallen a full flight of stairs down into a basement. He shattered his teeth, and broke his nose, arm, and several ribs, but was back at work within three days. "What will my customers do without bread?" he would lament to me as I chastised him for risking his health. He was a man who truly loved his work—and hated hospitals.

So it came as little surprise when my phone rang again. This time it was my mother on the line.

"Dad's gone," was all she could say. I learned that Bob had found him lying on the floor shortly after midnight. He died while mixing his last batch of dough. Once again, I headed home, this time to handle the funeral arrangements.

More than five hundred people attended the service, which was held at the Beth Israel Synagogue—the Beth Abraham had been destroyed by fire. I fought to hold back tears by poking fun at all of my father's idiosyncrasies: his irreverence, his wretched driving habits, and his inability to censor whatever politically incorrect thought would enter his mind—the very things that endeared him to the community. They loved him for all of his faults, but especially for his humanity. There was no man whom he feared or envied. He cared little about either success or wealth. He was a terrible businessman, refusing to raise his prices while his costs for flour, yeast, and sugar continued to soar over the years. When I chastised him for imposing irrational price caps on his products, he would simply brush off my concerns. "What will my customers do without bread? They're not rich people."

"But neither are you. You don't have to be afraid of losing them. You have no competition. They have no place to go."

He would offer a familiar rejoinder, "But they still need bread. I can afford it better than they can."

It was an argument that I could not win. But more than I ever conceded openly to him, I loved him for his concern for the well-being of people who were struggling. While he had little sympathy for those who could work but didn't, he never once turned down those who lived on the ragged edge of life and asked only for his bread. I decided to recite a poem that I had written when I finally accepted the fact that I would one day lose him. It was when I reflected on how much joy he took in his work that I finally resolved the path I needed to follow in my own life.

Time ticked slow
for me when I was young,
it took so long to grow
("Come measure me,

will I be tall as a tree?")
until that moment
in reaching to outreach
my father, I found him old.

I am larger, Father, taller
But you seem to grow smaller
each day, as if nature,
once engaged in play,
suddenly turned
to complete her course
and take you back to an aged infancy.

The wheel of time
weighs like a stone
upon your back,
the signs are in your eyes
but how you do pretend
that age knows no circumference!
Infinity will one day add your dust
to its boundless bin,
but how you do contend
with a wink and grin
that you will always
catch each dawn
breaking through the window
of your work.

That moment will come
When the night will shake
With our mother's cries,
tears will fill her eyes,
but you will be gone,
beyond prayers or promises.

Father, I would join
you now in eternity
but my sons still
look to outreach me;
I cannot fall,
not until they are tall
and I am small

and the cycle
complete.

One day we may again
share the same horizon,
perhaps conscious, perhaps not,
but knowing now the sun
was ours once then.
And with the blade
of having been,
took reluctant leave
from our shrinking selves,
carving a mark
into the bark
of an ancient tree.

Eighteen

The Darndest Things

"You know, Bill, it's been my experience that whenever the subject of race is raised, most white people's body language shrinks back, as if to say, 'Oh, no. There you go again. First, it's slavery, then lynching, affirmative action, and soon we're bound to hear the drumbeat for reparations. Slavery was long ago and far away. We had nothing to do with it. We are not racists. Look at Colin Powell, Condoleezza Rice, Oprah Winfrey, and Barack Obama. Who is dominating the sports world? Blacks have their own entertainment channel. Check out the CEOs of Merrill Lynch, American Express, and Time-Warner. How bad can it be? And for God's sake, when are they going to get over it? And by the way Mizz Cohen, what's your problem? Looks to us like you're living large.'

"True enough. Those individual success stories are all well and good. Yes, a few celebrities of African American descent have been allowed to break through the barriers that have been designed to keep them back and down for more than three centuries. But the future for an increasingly large number of blacks—particularly males—has never looked bleaker."

As usual Janet has a point, some academicians and politicians who insist that we have witnessed the end of racism in America, that blacks are now living, working, and competing on an equal playing field. They argue that today it is morally wrong to give any additional consideration to those who've had to struggle with limited educational and employment opportunities, who've had to grow up and survive in dangerous, unpatrolled, and unprotected inner-city neighborhoods, while their white counterparts are safely ensconced behind walled communities and wired to the Internet. Foes of affirmative action argue that three hundred years of legalized oppression have been offset by thirty years of affirmative action!*

America is now color-blind? Remarkable!

Television shows devoted endless coverage to the story of a single white woman missing in Aruba, but for years barely mentioned the genocide in Darfur, where tens of thousands of black people were being raped and slaughtered. Was it simply a matter of coincidence that prominent white actors, such as George Clooney and Angelina Jolie, were the ones desperately trying to stir the world's conscience over genocide in Africa, and not equally popular and influential black television and film stars? Is it not the reality that white society will view an issue as being monumentally moral when their stars become its advocates, whereas advocates of African American descent, however powerful and prominent, will find the same issue dismissed by white society simply as *their* problem?

During the evenings when I'm not traveling, Janet and I usually sit around the dinner table and discuss the day's events. Inevitably, our talk turns to politics, race, or religion.

"You know," Janet said to me recently, "I'm thinking about writing another book."

"About what?"

"I'm going to call it, *People Say the Darndest Things.*"

"Such as?"

"Well beginning with the comment of that twelve-year-old white girl who once said that I was pretty for a colored girl. Or perhaps I could start with Barbara Bush's (former first lady) statement when she saw thousands of New Orleanians who had been displaced (and turned into refugees by some commentators) by Hurri-

---

*See Ira Katznelson, *When Affirmative Action Was White* (New York: Norton, 2005).

cane Katrina and forced to survive for days in the Houston As-
trodome: 'They're doing alright. After all, they didn't have much to
begin with.' *Au contraire!* They had homes (meager though they may
have been), families, pets, jobs. What they didn't have was the attention and protection of their government."

"Would you include Kanye West's statement that George Bush
hates black people?"

"I could, but what he said wasn't obtuse. He was stating a fact
that black people are always last in line when it comes to any help
from the government and Katrina was a classic example of it. You
saw those pictures. They were abandoned for days. And who were
the first people evacuated? Those staying in hotels. Now do you
think they were white or black?"

"But that doesn't mean that Bush hates black people. Race was
not the defining issue with Katrina. It was class, poverty."

"Bill, just who are the majority of poor in this country?"

"Statistically, white people are."

"And who was it who said that there are lies, damn lies, and
then there are statistics?"

"It was Mark Twain."

"Statistically you may be right. Okay, white poor outnumber
black poor. Spike Lee even said that when he went to see the devas-
tation of Katrina and was surprised to see just how many whites had
been hit. But you don't have to have a math degree to calculate the
odds of black people getting out of poverty in this country."

"Okay," I said, knowing I was not going to win this argument.
"Enough. What else are you going to say in this book?"

"Well, I thought I would include the comment made by one
of your former senate colleagues who thought that one of my parents had to be white. That that had to be the reason I was so intelligent!"

I winced as she reminded me of the incident.

"I rest my case," Janet said triumphantly. "I don't know whether
it's a question of ignorance or malice, but people in high places have
given me enough material to fill two or three books."

I had to concede defeat. Once, when Janet and I attended the annual Kennedy Center Awards night to witness Sidney Poitier being honored for his stellar career in the movies, Paul Newman was asked to offer commentary on Sidney's life. Newman peered into the darkness from the stage, looked up to the balcony where Sidney was sitting with the other honorees, and said, "Smile, Sidney, so I can see you."

Janet muffled a gasp. It was a lousy joke, one that played to the racial stereotypes that had been in vogue for too many years. Whenever she heard it, she would point out that she found it offensive, only to be told that she was "too sensitive" or had a "chip on her shoulder." No one said anything about it that night, and not a word of it appeared in the reviews in the next morning's papers. Maybe they were too embarrassed. Maybe they didn't care.

On another occasion, when I was asked to testify before the 9/11 Commission, a popular radio host in Boston mentioned my appearance and, to remind his hometown audience about my connection with Janet, blurted out, "Mandingo!"

Mandingo is the name of a proud tribe in Africa, but the term is used by whites in America as a racial slur in referring to mixed race couples. *Mandingo* was the title of the black sexploitation film of the early '70s in which the wife of a slavemaster had an affair with one of his slaves, who was boiled alive when the affair was discovered. Was Janet's skin color the sum total of who she was, and the contributions she had made to Boston community? The radio host was a contemporary of hers who had once been on the opposite side of the busing debate. While they had disagreed, was Janet not to be seen as a serious professional?

Janet wasn't the one called to testify before the commission. I'm half Jewish and half Irish. Why, I wondered, if he wanted to offer a slur, had he not uttered the derogatory words "Hymie" or "Mick"? Why use Janet's race and not my ethnicity, since I was the one testifying, not Janet?

Once in Indianapolis, while Janet was working at Ma Bell, a coworker threw a newspaper on the table in front of her and pointed to a story about a black man who had been arrested for committing murder. "Don't you think that he's a discredit to your race?" she asked, seeking to provoke Janet.

"Was Hitler a discredit to yours?" Janet responded, her tone more declarative than inquisitive. She was tired of having the misdeeds of any one black person laid at the feet of the entire race, while white people absolved themselves of any association with white monsters and miscreants.

William Bennett, the former Republican education secretary and energy czar and author of *The Book of Virtues*, managed to stir controversy and the ire of many when he said, on his nationally syndicated radio program, that, hypothetically, one way to reduce crime in America would be to abort all black male babies. Admittedly, Bennett was drawing upon the book *Freakonomics* for his insight, and he took great offense that his musings could have been misconstrued by anyone. He did say that racial cleansing would be impossible to carry out today and that the very thought was morally reprehensible, but, in theory, it would work.

One wonders, however, how he found it so easy to hypothesize about a "final solution" for black males to reduce crime in America, the mere discussion of which would likely reinforce a subliminal association of blacks and crime and sanction the brutal and disparate treatment they often receive at the hands of police. If some British commentator had suggested that the best way to prevent the Northern Irish IRA from blowing up Harrod's department store in London or the Queen's horses in Hyde Park would be to abort Irish male babies, would Bennett have used this hypothetical example and agreed to its plausibility, unthinkable though it might be?

Several years ago, a liberal acquaintance of Janet's disclosed to her that a Bush cabinet member's wife was upset with the manner in which the subject of slavery was being taught to one of her grandchildren. Apparently, the child, who was enrolled in an elite private school in the Washington area, had been taken on a field trip to the historic home of Frederick Douglass in a large black neighborhood, the Anacostia section of Washington. The child returned from the

excursion troubled by the atrocities that their ancestors had perpe-
trated against African Americans during slavery.

This prominent woman was said to have been outraged. This,
she believed, was a distortion of history, and she visited the school
to try to ensure that a balanced historical account of slavery be
taught. Reportedly, she asserted that slavery wasn't as bad as many
blacks had made it out to be. Many Africans, in fact, were far better
off for having been dragged from their homeland and carted off to
be enslaved rather than live in the primitive jungles of Africa. In
other words, the slave traders had done the Africans a favor!

Noblesse oblige. History revisited. History revised. Quite noble of her ancestors to be so thoughtful of Janet's.

The most deeply disturbing comment was one offered by a
woman who, upon learning that Janet was completing a memoir
about living in two Americas, said, "Well, I hope you're not going
to play the victim!"

Janet slow-counted to ten. She was tempted to respond, "I'm
not a victim. I'm a survivor."

But angry as she was at the moment, she let it pass. It's true,
Janet is a survivor, but she knew the significance that the word *survivor* would hold for the woman. She didn't want to diminish the
magnitude of what the Jewish people have had to suffer over the
centuries. The Holocaust was a terrible crime against humanity. She
never will forget the depths to which mankind can sink and the
level of barbarity practiced by the Nazis at Auschwitz, Buchenwald,
and Baden-Baden. Her father had fought to liberate those concentration camps, only to receive the reward of being forced to ride in
the back of a bus, dressed in civilian clothes, in his home state.
Janet had been named Hadassah Woman of the Year in Boston. She
had been active in the sale of Israeli Bonds. She had traveled with
me to Israel to visit Yad Vashem. She had wept at the grave of
Yitzhak Rabin and embraced his widow. Topol, the brilliant Israeli
actor, had serenaded her in the Knesset while she sat next to Ariel
Sharon. No, she would never say anything unkind or disrespectful
about Jewish people.

When Janet arrived home, she was still burning. "Isn't it possible for more than one people in history to be victims? As a black woman, am I not entitled to tell the story of my people, of their suffering, degradation, and horrific deaths and how these oppressive acts had shaped me?"

Janet thought of the entry in Anne Frank's diary where Anne revealed that she had two personalities at war with each other. There was one that was open, light-hearted, and nonserious. The other was silent, reserved, and profound. The latter one, which she described as the "good" one, she never revealed to others.

She wondered, *What would Anne Frank have said to Emmett Till?* The question itself inspired her to write in the form of a one-act play, an imaginary dialogue between two of history's most famous victims of institutionalized terrorism.

She thought that in this play, she might provide an answer to the woman's question.*

---

*See Annex, *Anne and Emmett*.

Nineteen

LUCKY AND LUCY

Much as Janet and I loved each other, I'm not sure that our wedding would have arrived quite as soon but for her accidental encounter with a dog that had been either lost or abandoned.

Janet was working at BET at the time. When she stepped outside during a lunch break one day, she discovered a group of her colleagues standing in a circle. Something had obviously caught their attention. Peering over their shoulders, she saw a hairless dog that looked very much like a large rat chasing and biting its tail. It was racing around and around, prompting some of those watching the spectacle to laugh.

Janet was horrified. The dog had sores all over its body and looked emaciated. It was in obvious distress. She called Dr. David Brown, the veterinarian who had treated her two cats, Tony and Cleo, during the last stages of their lives. Dr. Brown's clinic was located more than forty minutes away, but he agreed to come and pick up the dog.

When Janet checked back that night to determine the condition of the dog, Dr. Brown informed her that it had been on the verge of starving to death. A day or so longer and it would have died.

When Janet inquired what kind of dog it was, Dr. Brown said, "It's a Maltese."

We laughed. It had a better lineage than either of us.

After it had spent a week at his clinic, Dr. Brown arranged to have the dog placed with a woman who was a member of the local Maltese Society. We had no idea that such a thing existed.

When we went to visit the dog Janet had saved, we met a gruff-talking eighty-two-year-old woman with beautiful white hair. Her name was Marion "Hutch" Hutchisson. She had served as a Navy WAVE during World War II. Janet fell in love with Hutch immediately. She was an unmarried, independent, self-supporting sweetheart who loved food, gardening, and dogs. Hutch was what the Israelis would call a "Sabra"—tough on the outside and sweet on the inside.

While Janet suggested that the dog be given some exotic name that invoked its homeland of Malta, Hutch would have none of it. She said his (not its) name should be "Lucky." He had been found on Friday the 13th, and it had turned out to be his lucky day.

So, "Lucky" it was.

It all might have ended with an agreement on his new name, but Hutch proceeded to tell us that she was too old to care for him. Hutch had spent much of her life devoted to caring for her pets. In fact, she had retired from the Navy rather than accept an assignment to a place that would not permit her to bring her dog. "I'm eighty-two and I want my freedom," she declared.

We left Hutch's home disappointed and uncertain of what to do.

Later that night, Janet returned to Hutch's home in Falls Church, Virginia, and picked up Lucky. Hutch was determined not to keep him, but Janet knew that Hutch would find a good home for him. Still, she was haunted by the memory of her mother being forced to give away their dog, Tuffy, when they lived in Lockefield Gardens.

"I would always wonder whatever happened to Lucky," she said, "and I didn't want to do that."

Janet had a major problem on her hands. She had just purchased a new condominium in Crystal City, Virginia, and had moved in all of her furniture. At the time she purchased the unit, she didn't give any consideration to the rules that prohibited tenants from having pets, since both of her cats had died.

Now, she had a real dilemma. She felt an inexplicable tie to Lucky even though she had had little contact with him since the day she found him. But what to do?

She had vowed never to live with a man unless she was married to him, but she was unwilling to have anyone else adopt Lucky. She had never forgotten how distressed her mother was when she described the look on their dog Tuffy's face as he was taken away by a new family. She knew that she couldn't live with the thought that she would be abandoning Lucky to an unknown fate.

Janet arrived at my new townhouse in Rosslyn, Virginia, located just across the Key Bridge from Washington's historic Georgetown.

I was faced with a dilemma as well. I had just sold my condo unit to my friend Senator John McCain. I had been in my new home less than a month and wasn't eager to have my white carpets become a "target-rich environment" for a dog whose household habits were problematic.

But when I saw Janet holding Lucky in her arms while standing on my doorstep, looking like two little orphans, I laughed and embraced them both.

I knew I was a very lucky man.

Lucky became the center of our attention and love. For the next ten years he traveled everywhere with us, including Texas, California, and western Europe. We adopted Hutch as a surrogate mother and made her a part of our family, hosting her ninetieth birthday at the Pentagon and having her meet President Clinton.

As Hutch approached the age of ninety-two, she began to fail. It was painful to see someone who had been so vital, independent, and full of life decline in health. But we provided for Hutch until her final days, when she died of congestive heart failure.

We would lose Lucky, too. We kept him alive through sonograms, MRIs, and stomach surgery, but finally had to face the reality that it was cruel to force him to continue the battle against a spreading cancer.

I held Lucky in my arms while Dr. Mark Johnson, Hutch's favorite vet, administered the lethal injection.

Once outside in the car, Janet and I both cried, vowing that we would never again go through such agony. No more pets!

Over a period of ten months, my resolve began to weaken. Something was taking place in the universe.

As her last Christmas gift to us, Hutch had given us a set of wind chimes to hang in our garden. One night, while I was traveling, Janet was really missing Hutch. She heard her chimes playing softly in the breeze and stepped outside on the terrace. She looked up into the sky that was alive with bright stars and said, "Oh, Hutch. I wish you were here with me now."

Janet was convinced that Hutch's spirit had touched the chimes. She grasped the wooden tongue tied to the ringer and saw the word Aria printed on it. Curious, she went back into the apartment and turned on her computer. She typed in the name Aria and up popped a reference to a company in Ohio, the state where Hutch was born. She then decided to type in Hutch's full name.

Janet was stunned!

Music started to play and stars started to cascade across the computer's screen, much as the stars had looked just a few moments before out on the terrace. Then a photograph of Hutch and Janet appeared in full color. The picture had been taken by one of Hutch's closest friends, a woman named Linda Coleman, who raised Maltese puppies professionally and who had traveled with them to the annual Westminster Dog Show in New York.

Linda had died of brain cancer several years earlier, but her husband, Len, had decided to carry on her business. On his web site were recent photos of a litter of puppies.

Janet met me in New York several days later. We happened to stroll past a popular pet shop on Lexington Avenue. I wanted to look at two Coton de Tulear puppies that I had spotted in the window. Janet played with them for five or ten minutes, and while she thought they were cute, she felt no connection to them.

Later that night, she told me about her extraordinary experience with the chimes and how they had led her to Len Coleman.

I generally believe in coincidences; Janet does not. She believes in fate, in kismet, that all was meant to be. The thought had occurred to me that Janet might be slipping into a fantasy world, but I decided to turn on my computer as a reality check. To my surprise, up popped the image of Len Coleman and his new litter of puppies.

While I pretended to be working on a speech in an adjoining room at the Regency Hotel, I placed a phone call to Coleman and asked him to send more photos of the puppies. I was particularly interested in looking at a female, as I didn't want to have to compare a male with Lucky.

Well, the photos came. I fell in love with a little one. Two months later we drove about twenty miles beyond Pittsburgh to acquire a new family member. On the way, our driver, Sambo Teng suggested that we call her Lucy because it was the same name as Lucky without the "k."

Initially, Janet was unimpressed with the puppy that I had selected because she seemed timid and weak, hanging back from participating in the roughhousing of her siblings. Janet then received assurances from a woman named Becky, whose Maltese was the mother of the litter, that little Lucy was tired because she had been raising hell for hours and that, contrary to all appearances, she was anything but meek. In fact, she usually instigated all of the action. Janet remained dubious, but I insisted that Lucy was to be the chosen one.

When Janet finally concurred, Lucy's mother came over to Janet, who was holding Lucy in her lap, and started licking her little girl's face. She had seen so many strangers come and take away her babies, one by one, from the three litters she had birthed. She knew we were going to take Lucy, and in Janet's mind, she was saying good-bye and, in a most tender way, telling us to take good care of her baby.

On the way home (after a moment of panic when we thought we had taken her male brother by mistake), Janet bonded with our new family member whom, weighing only two pounds, we could hold in the palm of one hand. She looked more like a tiny white bird than a puppy.

Whenever Janet kisses Lucy, which is often, she thinks of Lucy's mother's last gesture. Janet will nibble on her little ear, which folds back, revealing bright pink skin. During these moments, Janet thinks of the stories told through the generations of how children were ripped from the bosoms of their mothers during slavery and sent to faraway places, never to be seen again. She has read the poignant story told by Frederick Douglass of how his mother, a slave, was forced to work on a distant plantation when he was a child. She would walk miles each night in the darkness to hold and comfort him and then, just before daybreak, rush back to her slave master's plantation. Douglass never saw his mother's face in the light. Janet believes that the animals we are so fond of calling "dumb" are spiritually much more highly evolved than many humans she knows. In this regard, she is very much like my mother, who is fond of saying, "They're your best friends. They don't talk about you and they're always glad to see you. They have feelings like us; they just can't talk."

They may not talk, but they see, hear, and feel things that are beyond our reach. They know our moods, and they can sense when we are approaching home long before we arrive and wait patiently for us to cross the threshold to greet us. They know when we're in pain and will touch that very place of pain more lovingly and with more curative power than any physician or medicine known to man.

While Sambo had suggested we call her Lucy because it was close to Lucky, there was more involved in the selection of her name.

Hutch had been born during the week of Saint Lucia—the saint who wears a candelabra on her head to show the way with her light. We were driving during a snowstorm through the night on our way back to Washington. It was December 11, the week of Saint Lucia. I continued to insist that it was all a matter of coincidence.

Janet remains convinced, however, that Hutch talked to her through the chimes that night in September when the sky was filled with stars that looked like diamonds.

What's in a name is important, but we also found that it sometimes can provoke an interesting response from other people.

One evening following a Kennedy Center Gala, we were in the process of being picked up by our family driver, Sambo Teng, a Cambodian who once served in the Cambodian military and who, unlike most of his family, managed to survive the Khmer Rouge's "Killing Fields." His oldest daughter is now serving in the U.S. Army and has completed two tours of duty in Iraq.

Our friend Bob Johnson, the founder of Black Entertainment Television (BET) spotted us getting into the car. He rushed over and asked if he could borrow a cell phone so he could call his chauffeur.

Reflexively I yelled out, "Sambo, can I have your phone?"

Bob, whose head was halfway into the open rear door window, pulled back in shock and disbelief. He thought that I had a black chauffer and had used a blatant epithet in his presence.

I had some quick explaining to do. "No, Bob. It's okay. Sambo is Cambodian. That's his name—Sambo Teng."

Bob continued to look at me skeptically. He wasn't sure that I wasn't putting him on. Finally he stuck his head back in the car to verify my story.

"Okay," he said, taking the phone Sambo had handed him, "but I'm going to call him Mister Teng!"

We laughed at the incident all the way home. There are moments when we find the need to see humor in the dark side of our history. There are other occasions when we enjoy poking a finger at our nation's pretensions about equality for all.

Sambo usually drives us to every meeting and errand during the course of the week, but although Janet disapproves, I love to drive on weekends. I always insist that Janet sit in the back seat whenever we take our Maltese puppy, Lucy, with us. I worry that if I have an accident an the airbag releases in the front seat, it very likely will kill Lucy.

While driving Janet and Lucy, I'm mindful of one of our favorite movies, *Driving Miss Daisy*, which features Morgan Freeman serving as a chauffeur and handyman to Jessica Tandy, a white woman. In one of the movie's most memorable scenes, Freeman is driving Tandy, who is sitting in the backseat of her Cadillac as they move across state lines in the deep South. Freeman is stopped by two racist policeman for no reason other than he is a black man driving an expensive car. After seeing Tandy in the backseat and satisfying himself that this elderly woman is not a kidnap or rape victim, one of the cops allows Freeman to drive on.

When the cop returns to his vehicle and is asked about the incident by his partner, he says, "Oh it was just some nigger driving an old Jew."

Much has changed since the time frame reflected in the film. Still the sight of a white man driving a black woman, holding a white Maltese puppy in the rear seat of a luxury sedan might strike some as a bit odd—even funny.

As we coast along the highway, I glance back frequently in the rear view mirror and see Janet smiling at me. I tip my imaginary cap and imitate Morgan Freeman's voice: "Oh, officer, I'm not driving Miz Daisey. I'm just driving Miz Lazy."

Twenty

A CALL TO SERVE

As I approached my final days in the Senate, I was eager to move on to a new career and a new life with Janet. I had had business cards printed and had just signed a letter of intent to lease office space in downtown Washington.

Then I received a phone call that proved to be life-altering. This one came from the White House. Would I be willing to meet with President Clinton?

Yes. Of course.

While I was flattered to have received the call, I was not completely taken by surprise. A few weeks earlier, Defense Secretary William Perry had advised me that he was going to submit my name along with several others to be a potential candidate to succeed him, unless I had objections.

Frankly, I dismissed the notion as farfetched. I indicated that I was determined to leave public service, but I also didn't want to slight Secretary Perry, whom I considered one of our finest public servants, by in any way intimating that I didn't value the position to which he had brought such great distinction.

I met with President Clinton in his private quarters at the White House. He arrived twenty minutes late, which, I was forewarned, was not unusual. We sat for more than an hour engaging in a broad discussion of issues facing the country. He solicited my views on Russia, China, and other international issues. He wanted to explore my reasons for leaving the Senate and what I thought about the state of politics today.

This was the first time in four years that he and I had exchanged more than a passing greeting. While I admired his political gifts, I had on more than one occasion been critical of some of his policies. In fact, just two months earlier, I had engaged in a debate with my friend and retired colleague, George Mitchell, the former Senate majority leader, at the Council on Foreign Relations in New York. I was an open and vigorous critic of the president's conduct of foreign policy.

The meeting was intended as a test of our personal and philosophical compatibility. No mention was made of the Department of Defense, but it clearly was the elephant sitting in the center of the room.

About a week later, we ran into each other in Bangkok, Thailand. I was there to give a speech to the U.S.–Thai Business Council, and President Clinton was attending ceremonies celebrating the birthday of King Bhumibol Adulyadej. We exchanged a few lighthearted remarks, but nothing more. I met with my friend, Malaysian Deputy Prime Minister Anwar Ibrahim, during the trip and then returned to Washington. I received another invitation to meet with President Clinton.

This time the president wanted to talk about specific issues: defense reform, NATO expansion, combating terrorism, budget priorities, and missile defense. At the end of our conversation, he indicated that he was going to give serious consideration to asking me to be his secretary of defense because he thought it was necessary to build bipartisan support for a national security policy. He hadn't made a final decision, but wanted to know whether I would accept the position if it were offered to me.

I said that I would upon one condition—that I would be totally responsible for running the Department of Defense and that I would not be called upon to attend or participate in any partisan political deliberations or discussions. In return, I made a pledge to the president:

"Mr. President, if you offer me the position and I accept, you'll never have to worry that I'll be going backdoor to my former colleagues on the Hill. I will maintain the confidence of all of our discussions. You have my word on that."

We shook hands and I left to return to my Senate office. I slipped out of the West Wing undetected by the White House press corps.

Once back on Capitol Hill, I went to my hideaway office in the Capitol. I needed time to reflect upon the meeting I had just left. It was one thing to be knowledgeable in military matters, to understand budgets and weapon systems, to improve organizational efficiencies. But it was quite another to be responsible for making daily decisions that involved putting people in harm's way. I remembered the time shortly after the Vietnam Memorial was opened to the public when I took my two sons Kevin and Chris with me to visit it. I wanted to locate the name of Alan Loane, the young man who had served with me as co-captain of the Bowdoin basketball team. Alan had died in Vietnam, having developed spinal meningitis after he had been seriously wounded.

As I walked down the paved walkway to the memorial, I passed a kiosk where a uniformed National Park Service employee stood behind a counter, leafing through a large bound volume, helping an older couple who had come in search of their son's name. Behind the kiosk, about fifty feet or more, a man stood on crutches. He was dressed in faded green and black camouflage fatigues and a soft Ranger hat that was tied up rakishly on one side. His right pant leg was folded up and pinned in the back. There was a mixture of hostility and pride in his face. He stood there like a watchdog at the gates of hell.

Approaching the memorial, I saw that it was cut below the earth, forcing us to descend symbolically into a mass grave. It was V-shaped, the angles of the black marble slabs as sharp and brutal as a knife wound. Then the names started to come at me like a blizzard of blood, names that spoke of young men and women whose bodies had broken and bled into this stone. I kept searching for Alan's name, but was unable to find it. The names had been etched into the marble at random, not by alphabet, but by date of death. War's booby trap.

I watched others standing at the wall, tracing longitude and latitude lines, as if they were searching for a piece of geography, until they came to what they were looking for. One woman held her granddaughter in her arms and stood there weeping for her son. A young man touched the wall and closed his eyes. He was praying for his father.

At the foot of the memorial there were bouquets of flowers, stick flags, photographs, and dog tags. I stood there mesmerized by my reflection on the polished marble. The silhouette was shaped like me, but in the fading light had no features. It was just a dark, anonymous shadow that stared back at me like a shrouded question mark. Finally, I found Alan's name and touched the marble. It was a cold day, yet the marble had absorbed the sunlight's warmth. It felt strangely warm, almost at body temperature.

When I looked into the innocent faces of my sons, I could not hold back the tears.

Memory of this experience, along with other emotions, kept tugging at me during the rest of the day.

I was at once excited and ambivalent. First, I was by no means convinced that President Clinton could induce insider Democrats to believe that it made sense to bring a Republican into the inner circle of his cabinet. Second, I wondered how congressional Republicans would react to my joining a Democratic administration. Wouldn't they see my acceptance as a sellout? Would they still love me in the morning? Not a serious question of love, since I enjoyed so little. But would they subtly work to undermine my efforts and impair my effectiveness? Would I actually be contributing to our national defense or weakening it?

Initially, I thought some might consider me a defector, but I was convinced that any ill feelings would dissipate over time, particularly as they witnessed the efforts I would undertake to strengthen our defense capabilities.

More important to me than these political questions was the worry that I'd be breaking my promise to Janet. We had spent hours outlining plans for a new life together. Much as I was excited over the prospect of serving as the second in command of the finest military in the world, the job would be incredibly demanding. I would be mastering budgets and bureaucratic turf battles, testifying before Congress, and traveling the globe. There would be virtually no opportunity to share quality time together. I would be falling off the wagon I had pledged to climb onto and would be returning to the addictive behavior that had consumed virtually all of my time over the past twenty-seven years.

I could feel ambition start to quicken my pulse rate. Family needs, friendships, privacy, quiet moments for reflection, time to simply collect time—all would be sacrificed. I had struggled to maintain a larger perspective on life. I sought wisdom in the writings of philosophers who warned of the fragility of existence, the folly of reaching for the brass ring of power.

That evening, Janet was perplexed about my apparent lack of enthusiasm at the prospect of becoming the next secretary of defense.

"This would put all of our plans on hold for four years."

"So?"

"How much time do you think we have left to be together?"

"There you go being Irish again. This is an opportunity of a lifetime for you. Our plans can wait. We'll find ways to be together."

"Listen," I jested, "This is just your way of trying to get me into the Democratic Party."

Clearly, I had underestimated Janet. I thought that she'd be disappointed and exasperated with me. Had she expressed the slightest doubt about my remaining in public office, I would have advised President Clinton that I could not serve him. Once I saw her enthusiasm, the dark cloud hovering over me vanished.

Still, I didn't want to become too excited. The president hadn't made a decision. There were other candidates in the running.

Moreover, there was considerable risk in his turning to another politician to run the department.

He had selected Congressman Les Aspin to serve as defense secretary during his first term. Les had been one of Robert McNamara's "whiz kids" back in the 1960s. He had been elected to Congress and became chairman of the House Armed Services Committee. Les had become a lightning rod for his role in constructing a compromise on the issue of gays in the military. The uniformed military was adamantly opposed to allowing gays to join or remain in the military if they engaged in homosexual conduct or declared themselves to be gay. President Clinton, under pressure from his political base, wanted to change the status quo but not lose the support of the military. Aspin proposed the policy of "Don't Ask, Don't Tell." In other words, if gays stayed in the closet and remained silent, they could gain entry to, and remain in, the military. The compromise managed to anger both the right and left.

After our peacekeeping mission in Somalia came under fire in the battle of Mogadishu, the commanding general was faulted for a feckless military operation that lost eighteen Army Rangers and dozens more wounded. Aspin's leadership was called into question, as was President Clinton's concern for the welfare of American soldiers. Shortly after that battle, Les retired for health reasons, dying prematurely at the age of fifty-six. The commander in chief simply could not afford his defense secretary making another mistake.

This consideration alone caused me to curb my enthusiasm.

With each passing day, I became more convinced that I should continue with my plans to form a private strategic consulting firm. Then, early in December, Janet and I attended a White House Christmas party. As we wound slowly through the receiving line, Vice President Al Gore discreetly pulled me aside and asked if I would take a call from the president the next morning between eight and eight-thirty.

I said, "Of course," forgoing any visible display of excitement, and slipped back in line just as easily as I had slipped out.

Later that night, Janet and I talked about the significance of the call that would come in the morning. In truth, I had prepared myself for President Clinton to say that after careful reflection, he concluded that it could not work. Too much opposition from Democrats; too little enthusiasm from Republicans.

Janet, by contrast, was convinced otherwise.

The next morning, the clock ticked past the witching hour.

"I'm going to take Lucky out for a walk."

"But what if the White House calls while you're out?"

"Don't worry," I assured her, "it will only be the White House operator on the line. She'll call back. Trust me, it's no big deal. The president won't be left hanging on the line."

Janet remained unimpressed with my attitude. It wasn't arrogance or disrespect on my part. My indifference was a protective mechanism. When the call didn't come through on time, I assumed that the decision was negative.

When I returned to the apartment, Janet informed me that I had missed the president's call.

I called the White House switchboard and was patched through to the president. It was a brief conversation.

"Bill, I want you to serve as my defense secretary."

"Mr. President, I accept. I look forward to serving you subject to the conditions we discussed."

"Agreed. We're faced with some challenging issues. We have a chance to do some great things together." President Clinton then clicked off the line.

Janet was intrigued. "What conditions did you discuss?"

"That I would never be involved in political discussions or decisions."

Janet set down the pot of coffee she had just brewed and we hugged each other for a long time.

We knew that we were both about to enter a very different world.

On January 21, 1997, I was sworn into office in the Oval Office of the White House by Vice President Al Gore.

After a few celebratory moments with the invited guests, we left the White House, entered a black, armored limousine and headed for the Pentagon. Janet was still beaming. She was clearly thrilled to see President Clinton standing behind me as I swore to up hold the Constitution and to defend the country against all enemies. She had always admired the President's brilliance, compassion and sense of humanity, but she was even more enthralled that he had had the boldness to ask me to be part of his administration. While holding onto my Republican Party affiliation, I nevertheless agreed with her assessment. Bill Clinton was an extraordinary human being.

While heading toward the Pentagon, we passed Arlington National Cemetery and looked out at all the white stones that filled the soft rolling hills. Janet seemed momentarily lost in thought.

"What is it?" I asked her.

"I was just thinking about our Constitution. How special it is to live in a country where the military has answer to the people and not the other way around. How we also insist that there be a separation between church and state. I felt something that was very spiritual when you held your hand on the Bible. You're going to lead a mighty army, but I think you're also going to need the help of the Almighty."

As we moved toward the River Road entrance to the Pentagon, I had to beat back a number of thoughts that were fluttering about my mind. I was confident that I was well versed in the strategic and foreign policy issues that I was likely to face. But the knowledge was all academic. I had no experience in managing a large bureaucracy and was not steeped in the military's culture. How, I wondered would the Joint Chiefs of Staff and senior military officers respond to me? How would the lower ranks relate to me? And what about President Clinton's political appointees and the career civil servants who had seen so many secretaries come and go? How eager would they be to test me?

By the time we pulled up to the entrance to the Pentagon, I had cleared these doubts away.

I had some of the major issues I wanted to tackle. First was the so-called Revolution in Military Affairs, the transformation of our fighting forces in doctrine, training, equipment, and deployment. It was a transformation initiated by Bill Perry, one that I wanted very much to continue. I knew that this had to be an evolutionary process and was not likely to be completed during my term. I also wanted to accelerate the introduction of "best business practices" to the Department of Defense so as to take advantage of the new technologies and processes that enabled the private sector to become more efficient and productive.

I thought of the bombing of the Khobar Towers Complex in Dhahran, Saudia Arabia, that had occurred the previous summer while I was still serving in the Senate. The bombing killed nineteen American soldiers and injured hundreds more. I was determined to make force protection one of the department's highest priorities.

The level of defense procurement had slipped dangerously low and would have to be increased, although I had been forewarned by the Office of Management and Budget (OMB) that I would not be receiving any increases in budget allocations. I was also concerned about the too-frequent deployments of our forces. They were being stretched too thin, and as a result, we had to be concerned about a decline in retention and recruitment.

These and an endless number of issues would have to be addressed, along with containing Saddam Hussein in Iraq and trying to capture or kill the man who would mastermind the September 11, 2001, attack on the United States—Osama bin Laden.

Bill Perry had forewarned me that my job was going to entail an enormous amount of travel to visit our forces in the field. The travel objectives—hands-on, touch-the-metal knowledge and meeting the men and women of the Armed Services—would serve two objectives: to see our military in action and assess their readiness and requirements; and to lift the morale of the troops, who were always eager to meet their civilian leader and take his measure.

Of all the duties I had, this would prove to be the most re-warding. When it came to boosting morale, I knew I had a powerful secret weapon in Janet.

She was holding my arm as we exited the limousine and started to walk up the front steps of the Pentagon, passing the honor guard standing there to welcome us. The entire day had a surreal quality to it. The pace of events seemed to accelerate beyond my ability to cal-ibrate it. I was about to assume an enormous responsibility that I did not seek, one that I could not refuse.

Maybe Janet was right to believe in fate, I thought at that very moment, that we're all in the hands of Providence.

Twenty-One

SecDef

From the moment I climbed the front stairs of the Pentagon, I knew that I had to demonstrate that my days as a legislator were far behind me.

The diversity and complexity of the issues that I had to contend with during the next four years as Secretary of Defense (SecDef) would require a lengthy book. Here, I only hope to provide a general sense of the scope of my responsibilities.

As a senator, I tried to be open to competing ideas, willing to accept those that I considered superior to my own, and strive to develop a consensus that could be fashioned into a responsible compromise. As secretary of defense (SecDef), my carriage and manner had to be quite different.

The military is a mission-driven institution, one that demands and accepts direction. Compromise and consensus building are not concepts that fit easily into its culture. Command presence is required of anyone who seeks to lead this great institution. That presence need not consist of a pompous display of chest-puffing confidence. A willingness to listen to professionals and treat those offering it with respect is essential. But one has to take care to maintain an appropriate distance from the military as well. Get too close and one can be perceived as having been co-opted; stay too removed and the men and women of the military will feel that they are being ignored.

I was mindful of the advice that my friend Tom Lambert had once given me: "Wise leaders should always be willing to doubt their first principles."

This was but a shorthand expression that one should always remain open to questioning one's deeply held assumptions. Remaining firmly attached to flawed analyses or dogmas is not a sign of strength, but one of folly.

True enough.

I was willing to have my personal opinions examined and dissected by military and civilian experts. That analytical process, however, would take place behind closed doors. During all of my public appearances, I spoke without displaying any doubt or hesitation about the direction in and the speed with which the Defense Department needed to head.

While I retained most of the civilian personnel that my predecessor Bill Perry had collected as his team, I brought in Bob Tyrer and Jim Bodner, two young, brilliant men who had been with me for most of my political career. Bob would serve as my chief of staff, and Jim as my principal policy analyst and advisor. In addition, I asked Lieutenant General James Logan Jones, a three-star Marine officer whom I had first met in 1979 when he was serving as the Marine Corps liaison officer to the Senate, to be my senior military assistant. Jim and John McCain were the equivalent of Butch Cassidy and the Sundance Kid on Capitol Hill, and they were in constant demand by senators to serve as travel escorts and confidants on visits to military facilities around the world. The position of military assistant usually called for a one-star officer, but I knew that I was going to need more firepower and that Jim could deliver it.

On my first day in the office, an aide asked me whether I wanted to continue to have the portrait of war hero and statesman par excellence George Marshall hang on the wall behind the massive desk that had once belonged to General John "Black Jack" Pershing. Pershing, the commander of the American Expeditionary force in World War I, subsequently became the Army chief of staff. He acquired the nickname "Black Jack" because he had commanded a black cavalry unit in Montana after graduating from West Point in 1886.

Someone suggested that I might consider bringing out the portrait of the first secretary of defense, James Forrestal. I was never quite sure whether the suggestion was offered in a spirit of innocence or sly malice. Forrestal had lost his mind here in the job. He saw Russians pursuing him everywhere, even at the Bethesda Naval Hospital, where he jumped to his death from the sixteenth-floor window in 1949. I had heard some speculate that he might have been pushed, but whatever the cause of his plunge, I quickly rejected the thought of having Forrestal's visage staring down on me during moments of solitude or crisis. Maddening as the job might prove to be, George Marshall was going to stay with me.

I did want to add the image of another hero to my walls, that of Joshua Lawrence Chamberlain, the man still revered not only by his and my alma mater, Bowdoin College, but also by virtually every person with even a rudimentary knowledge of Civil War history. Anyone who entered my office would be greeted by a huge portrait of Chamberlain.

There was no such thing as on-the-job training, for handling the issues that came before me was the equivalent of drinking from a fire hose. The issue of gays in the military somehow made its way back onto the front burner. The Kelly Flynn affair, in which the first female pilot of a B-52 bomber had a romantic relationship with a married enlisted man, touched off a heated debate on the question of maintaining "good order and discipline" in the military. Charges of sexual harassment by service drill instructors also prompted endless stories about "sex and the military."

I had to select and recommend to the president a successor to General John Shalikashvili, the chairman of the Joint Chiefs of Staff. My choice was General Hugh Shelton.

Shelton was, as they say, a general's general. From the first time I interviewed him, I could see why he enjoyed the unqualified support of his comrades in arms. He stood six feet, five inches tall, walked ram rod straight and spoke with a no nonsense directness.

He was a warrior of few words and those he offered carried the weight of great experience and wisdom.

He enjoyed the benefit of having the best "wing man" of all time to serve as his Vice-Chairman—General Joseph Ralston, a veteran Air force combat pilot.

I wanted Generals Shelton and Ralston to help me to drill home a message contained in three simple words: Recruit, Retain, Reconnect.

It was important to the "readiness" of our forces to continue to recruit bright, highly motivated young people. Secondly, it was critical to retain them, to provided incentives for them to re-enlist so that our forces remained competent and had continuity. Finally, the American people needed to feel connected to and deeply committed to those who were prepared to sacrifice life and limb for them. I had just the people to do the job.

The first major issue for me to confront, however, came in the form of a direct challenge to my authority. General Ron Fogleman, a distinguished combat pilot who served as the Air Force chief of staff, had made it clear to me and others that my review of the multiple investigations into the Khobar Towers bombing could have only one acceptable outcome. If I were to hold one of the Air Force's rising stars, Brigadier General Terryl Schwalier (who was serving as the base commander at the time of the bombing), in any way accountable for the deadly attack, then General Fogleman would have no choice but to resign.

Everyone in the chain of command, from the Chairman of the Joint Chiefs to the soldier in the field, would be watching and take my measure in how I resolved the issue. This was not an easy call. The bombing of the tower, used as quarters for Air Force personnel in Dhahran, Saudi Arabia, had happened in 1996, while I was serving in the Senate. Three separate reports had been launched. The young officer involved had a very promising career, and I didn't relish making a decision that would constitute an expression of no confidence in his performance and effectively terminate his military career. On the merits, however, I concluded that the steps taken to protect those under his command were deficient. General Fogleman, true to his pledge, submitted his resignation. He did so quietly, and I thought, with a great deal of professionalism.

In addition to establishing a command presence at the Pentagon and maintaining control over the agenda, I also had to persuade those in the White House that a Republican was prepared to be a team player in a Democratic administration.

While President Clinton, Vice President Al Gore, National Security Advisor Sandy Berger, and Secretary of State Madeleine Albright seemed completely at ease with me, other members of the president's cabinet initially were more tentative. It didn't help that during discussions in the Situation Room, I would venture an opinion by saying, "Sandy, the President's problem is . . ." or "Your problem is. . . ."

Sandy would remind me that his patience, while a virtue, was not eternal. "Bill," he finally said after six weeks or so, "when are you going to say, OUR problem is?"

In truth, I had no problem serving in President Clinton's administration. He had kept his pledge never to involve me in a discussion of partisan politics. He agreed to virtually all of my requests, including substantially increasing the defense budget and providing the largest pay raise in nearly two decades to our military personnel. He also supported my recommendation to sustain an air war campaign against Slobodan Milosevic, even though he was receiving heavy pressure to wage a ground war.

The biggest challenge to my leadership came, not from the Pentagon or the White house, but from Capitol Hill.

It was December 16, 1998.

"You need to get up here right away!" The caller was Newt Gingrich, the soon-to-resign Speaker of the House. Earlier his successor-to-be, Congressman Bob Livingston, had issued a similar call. The House was in an uproar. President Bill Clinton, with my support and recommendation, had ordered a military strike against Saddam Hussein in Iraq.

The timing was suspicious. The House was scheduled to debate the articles of impeachment that the Judiciary Committee had recommended. Republicans smelled what they thought was a rat: Our military was being used to divert attention from the president's predicament. The commander in chief had sacrificed the nation's security to save his political hide. It was *Wag the Dog* time, the cynical exploitation of America's military to manipulate public opinion, as captured in the Hollywood movie starring Robert De Niro and Dustin Hoffman.

Only it wasn't true. None of it. But the burden had now shifted to me, as President Clinton's secretary of defense, to disprove the allegations.

At precisely 7:00 p.m., I entered the chamber of the House of Representatives. It was packed to full capacity. No journalists or television cameras were permitted. I walked over to the podium facing the Republican majority. The atmosphere was sulfurous. A seething anger was visible on the faces of the members. I had not prepared any notes for my remarks. This was going to be straight from the heart. No rehearsal was possible or necessary. Twenty years had passed since I had stood behind that very podium. I never expected or wanted to be there again. I looked directly at the Republican leadership.

Resentment stared back.

The facts were that during the fall of 1998, Saddam Hussein stopped cooperating with the UN inspection team (UNSCOM) that was scouring Iraq in search of weapons of mass destruction. Saddam's men had the inspectors under constant surveillance and routinely delayed or completely obstructed them from carrying out their responsibilities. In October, the inspectors were pulled out of Iraq, and we made preparations to attack a number of facilities, particularly a missile production factory and Republican Guard headquarters and barracks.

I was flying over Wake Island in the Pacific Ocean, heading toward Hong Kong, when I received a call from the White House to return to Washington immediately.

Upon my return, I was briefed in the Situation Room and instructed to touch base with our allies and all countries we would need to call upon for assistance. I visited eleven countries in three days, laying out to each nation our intent and general plan of attack. It was by no means an easy sell to the Gulf States.

Finally, we were ready to launch our attack. Then, as some of our aircraft were in the air, Saddam sent a signal that he was ready to allow unimpeded inspections to occur. The UN sent a team headed by Ambassador Richard Butler to determine whether Saddam had, indeed, had a change of heart.

After two weeks of intensive effort, Ambassador Butler determined that behind the new Saddam was the old Saddam. Butler filed a negative report on his inspections effort, and when President Clinton returned from his trip to the Middle East, we met in the Situation Room to discuss our options. He ordered us to proceed with the attack.

I was determined to prove that President Clinton's difficulties over the Monica Lewinsky affair had nothing to do the either the decision to attack or its timing.

For three hours, I stood in the well of the House chamber and laid out in detail the factors involved in our decision. Congressman Tom DeLay, known as "The Hammer," seemed the most distressed and energized. He asked numerous questions and even slipped notes to other members to do the same. When he asked me whether the House should delay taking any action against the president, I demurred, saying that was a decision only they could make. As I stood in the well responding to questions, I was struck by the irony that twenty years earlier I had stood in the very same chamber, preparing to recommend that a Republican president should be impeached. That night I was defending the actions of a Democratic president who was about to be charged with having committed "high crimes and misdemeanors."

Although I privately thought that the allegations of presidential misbehavior were serious, I didn't believe they measured up to the threat that President Nixon's actions had posed to our Constitution.

But that was not an opinion that I had any intention to offer that night. My goal was to convince the members that political factors had played no role in the president's decision.

I concluded my remarks by saying that I was prepared to lay all of my years of public service on the line to defend the military action we were taking.

By the end of a long session, most members were on their feet and signaling their approval with applause.

I had few regrets during my four years at the Pentagon. Serving as defense secretary was the most exhilarating, exhausting, and rewarding experience of my life. The one profound regret I had, however, was our failure to capture or kill Osama bin Laden, who masterminded the attack on the USS *Cole* in October 2000 and the September 11 attacks against the World Trade Center towers and the Pentagon nearly a year later.

We came close to killing bin Laden when we attacked a terrorist training camp in Afghanistan, but we were hampered by the lack of any access to base facilities or personnel anywhere in the region. We had to attack from a long distance, which posed something of a logistical challenge, not to mention the danger that the operation posed to two major nuclear-armed countries in South Asia: India and Pakistan. Any military operation that traversed the territory of Pakistan could be mistaken for an attack being launched by India. This in turn could set off retaliation, which conceivably could escalate into a nuclear exchange. The problem was we could not afford to provide any advance notice to anyone without compromising the mission itself.

I had asked General Joseph Ralston, the Vice Chairman of the Joint Chiefs and a veteran combat pilot who had flown 152 missions over Vietnam, to arrange a dinner meeting with his counterpart in Pakistan.

None of us knew how the Pakistanis would react if they detected the missiles. Would there be a break down in the chain of command? Would passion override reason? Would they think that

General Ralston was there to delay a response that might prove vital to Pakistani's security and give an advantage to the Indians? Would General Ralston be in any personal danger? General Ralston never raised any of these questions. As a fighter pilot, he faced far greater dangers than those involved in this assignment.

Fortunately, the Pakistani radars did not detect our missiles. During the course of the evening, General Ralston glanced at his watch and knew that the missiles had passed through Pakistan's air space and by that time had hit their intended target in Afghanistan. He then excused himself from dinner.

Being the consummate warrior/diplomat, before leaving for the airport, General Ralston disclosed to his host what had transpired during the course of the dinner. He explained to the general that if he had advised him of our plan in advance, the general would have been duty bound to report the operation to his superiors, and that would have risked compromising the mission. If the general had failed to notify his superiors, he might have placed in jeopardy more than just his military career.

I was so impressed with General Ralston that I would later recommend to President Clinton that he replace General Wesley Clark, whom I retired early, as Supreme Allied Commander Forces Europe (SACEUR). I had enormous confidence in his can-do attitude, but most importantly, with his judgment.

While General Ralston succeeded in his mission in Pakistan, unfortunately, our cruise missiles failed in theirs. They did hit their target with great precision. The problem was that Osama bin Laden had left the area some hours before they arrived.

We continue to this day to see just how elusive Osama bin Laden remains, as thousands of U.S. and allied soldiers are on the ground in Afghanistan, and we have yet to be able to capture or kill him.

Twenty-Two

First Lady of the Pentagon

J anet had passed by the Pentagon on many occasions. She considered its geometric design to be an architectural marvel. It spoke of power, simplicity and solidity. She also found the building to be strangely fascinating. There was a certain ominous quality about it, one that conveyed the message to stay away—this property was strictly off limits to ordinary citizens!

As of January 17, 1997, it was no longer off limits. The Pentagon had rolled out a red carpet for us.

My security detail pulled open the heavy doors to our limousine almost before the car stopped. The uniformed men awaiting our arrival said, "Welcome, Mr. Secretary. Welcome, Ma'am" We were escorted quickly up to my office that was located on the Eisenhower Corridor of the E-Ring. The moment we entered the reception area, the people inside rose and snapped to attention.

The military's culture was, indeed, different from that of the political world.

One young soldier who, after providing a brief orientation of the huge office and conference room, pointed out the historic significance of each piece of furniture in the room. He proceeded to tell a story that occurred during the time when Robert McNamara had served as secretary of defense.

"A father who had lost a son in Viet Nam," he said, moving to one of the windows and pointing to an area outside, "set himself on fire to protest the war."

It may have been a bit of lore that he dispensed to visitors as a routine matter, but it had an impact on Janet. She could never look out that window without thinking about the father who had engaged in an act of self-immolation as an expression of grief and rage.

It was not long before it became clear that it was time to get to work. Janet decided to walk along the E-Ring to acquaint herself with some of the offices located there. Before departing the building, she stopped at a restroom and discovered something that struck her as odd. She had a choice of a door to the left or a door to the right, both marked Women. There were two ladies rooms.

Why?

When construction of the Pentagon began in September 1941, the uniformed armed forces and the civilians who worked for them were all segregated. So the contractors, following Virginia's Jim Crow law of the time, built two sets of restrooms for the Pentagon's prospective male and female workers: one that would be labeled Colored and one that would be labeled White. The blueprints called for 284 restrooms, 142 for Colored and 142 for White.

As the Pentagon was nearing completion, the construction orders mysteriously changed: There would be no restroom discrimination. It was too late to cut back to 142 restrooms, so the double-set pattern remained—but without the Colored and White labels.

How did it happen?

President Roosevelt personally supervised plans for the Pentagon, making sure, for instance, that the view of Arlington Cemetery from Washington was not obscured. Legend has it that Eleanor Roosevelt happened to see the Pentagon plans on the President's desk and noticed the Jim Crow restroom layouts.

As the administration's self-appointed champion for civil rights, she argued that the federal building did not have to conform to Virginia restroom laws. The President supposedly agreed. Perhaps

Mrs. Roosevelt was trying to compensate for her husband's failure to order the racial desegregation of our military.

The history of how the military had treated blacks was not a proud one.

During the time Janet worked at BET she had the opportunity to interview Lieutenant General Benjamin O. Davis, Jr., a hero in so many ways.

During his four years at West Point, the other cadets refused to speak to him. When Janet asked him if any other famous officer was in his class, he mentioned General William C. Westmoreland, who was commander of U. S. troops during the Vietnam War and later served as Army Chief of Staff.

"Did Cadet Westmoreland (who hailed from South Carolina) ever speak to you?" she asked him.

"No," Gen. Davis said, signaling that he did not want to talk about it any further.

While Janet was doing research for that interview, she learned that Lieutenant General Davis' father was the first black general officer in the U.S. Army. The elder Davis had begun his service in the Spanish-American War. As a brigadier general during World War II, his assignment, first in the United States and then in Europe, was the handling of what the Army called "Negro problems."

The problems tracked back to 1925, when the U.S. Army War College published a report that labeled African Americans as ignorant, immoral, and "a subspecies of the human family." That effectively kept black men out of the Army. But in 1940 Congress approved the nation's first peacetime draft, and the draft included black and white men. Young black men who had grown up in the North found themselves in training camps near small towns in the South. No one had ever told them to step off the sidewalk when a white person approached. They may have experienced prejudice in the North, but they never had experienced the fear of being lynched.

The elder Brigadier General Davis toured those southern camps during the war, assessing "Negro problems." In a report you can find today in the National Archives, General Davis said, "The colored officers and soldiers feel that they are denied the protection and rewards that ordinarily result from good behavior and proper performance of duty. The colored man in uniform receives nothing but hostility from community officials."* He suggested that black troops not be stationed in the South.

There was no chance for integration. Secretary of War Henry L. Stimson firmly believed in a segregated Army. "I hope to Heaven's sake," he wrote in 1940, after the draft began, "they won't mix the white and the colored troops together in the same units, for then we shall certainly have trouble." Stimson had his way. The mix never occurred in World War II.

But black soldiers did get a chance to fight—as Janet's father did—and some got a chance to fly as Tuskegee Airmen, pioneers of what was called the "Tuskegee Experiment," an Army Air Corps program to train black volunteers to fly and maintain combat aircraft. The story of the Tuskegee Airmen began in 1941, when President Franklin Roosevelt ordered the creation of an all-black flight training program. He did so one day after the NAACP filed a lawsuit on behalf of a Howard University student and others to force the Defense Department to accept black pilot trainees. The Tuskegee Institute, an historic all-black college in Alabama, was selected because it already had facilities for aeronautical training.

One of those trainees was Lieutenant Colonel Charles W. Dryden, and if one wants to know what the Negro problems were during World War II, read his book, *A-Train, Memoirs of a Tuskegee Airman.* He could not enter all-white officers clubs. When 101 black officers tried to enter an officers club (in good old Indiana), they were all arrested. And he remembered how German prisoners of war "could use all the facilities at the post exchange at Waterboro, South Carolina, and I, an American citizen who had fought the Nazis to defend America, could not."†

---

*Memorandum from Brig. Gen. Benjamin O. Davis to General Peterson, November 9, 1943.

†See Dryden, Charles W., *A-Train: Memoirs of a Tuskegee Airman,* University of Alabama Press (1997), p. 391–93.

While Brigadier General Davis was stubbornly working to change the racist mindset of the Army, his son was training Tuskegee Airmen. Young Davis became the first black officer to solo in an Army Air Corps aircraft. He later took command of the 99th Pursuit Squadron and then the 332nd Fighter Group, assigned to escorting bombers over North Africa, Sicily, and Europe. They never lost a bomber to an enemy fighter. In the group's most famous mission—a 1,600-mile escort to Berlin—Davis and his Tuskegee Airmen downed three German jets, a new weapon that had stunned American fliers. In total, the Tuskegee Airmen flew 15,553 combat sorties and 1,578 missions. They destroyed 261 aircraft, and damaged another 148. Sixty-six of their pilots died and thirty-three were shot down and captured as prisoners of war. German pilots both respected and feared them. White American bomber crews referred to them as "Redtailed Angels" because of the bright red paint on their tail assemblies.

As a child watching cowboy movies, Janet found herself rooting for the Indians. "While I never sympathized with the Japanese or Germans in war movies or newsreels, I resented it when those in the audience screamed out 'Japs' or 'Kraut heads,' knowing that they were the same people who would call me a 'nigger' or go out on 'coon hunts' whenever they wanted to terrorize us."

She also saw how race had been injected into the war when American citizens of Japanese ancestry were rounded up and placed in internment camps. Those of German ancestry in Indiana and elsewhere, however, were never criticized and, of course, not interned. As Colonel Dryden noted, even German prisoners of war, our sworn enemies, received better treatment than the black soldiers who had fought and bled to defeat them.

Janet said, "I will never forget how the USO had banned Lena Horne from performing with the organization after she refused to sing as long as black soldiers were relegated to the rear of the performance area while German prisoners enjoyed front-row seats."

Janet had always envied white people for being able to pledge allegiance to the flag and to sing the national anthem and feel the tingling of a spinal shiver. Whenever she sang the lyrics "O'er the land of the free, and the home of the brave," her voice was thin and hollow because she didn't really believe she enjoyed the same liberties as other Americans.

"Ironically," she told me, "the only time I felt that I was ever treated as a complete American was when I traveled abroad, and then I was considered to possess all of the negative characteristics ascribed to our culture. When the locals would learn that she was from the United States, they would say, 'You Americans! Why do you act like you own the place when you come here? Why are you so arrogant?' I would find myself feeling like a battered child, forced to defend a hateful parent because it was the only one I had."

The feeling of being disconnected, an alien in her own country, was about to change, although she had no idea just how life transforming that experience was about to be.

America had changed and the military had been at the forefront of that change. It had become the most integrated institution in the country, where people were judged on merit and not color.

In short, it was not her father's military anymore.

Soon after I started my job, I spoke with David O. ("Doc") Cooke, whom everyone called the mayor of the Pentagon. Doc had been at the Pentagon almost as long as the building had been there. Doc arranged for Janet to have access to a small office about a five-minute walk from mine.

The Pentagon is a city all unto itself. The building was completed just sixteen months after construction was started. It covered twenty-nine acres of land and more than six and a half million square feet of space. But Janet began to feel very much at home there, even though twenty-four thousand people moved through its corridors every day. There was a tangible sense of energy in the building that she found stimulating. Soldiers, sailors, airmen, and Marines strode along in their smartly pressed uniforms and spit-shined shoes, their ribbons and medals conveying their accomplishments. They walked erect and ramrod straight. No slouching permitted there.

They all moved with a sense of mission. They might have been off to an important meeting, to the restaurant or other service facility in the building, the Metro station, or perhaps out to the open area called "Ground Zero," at the very center of the Pentagon. Whatever their destination, they walked with a no-nonsense pep in their step that Janet found impressive.

The building itself was christened on September 11, 1941, the year that Janet was born (a date that did not acquire particular significance until sixty years later when Al Qaeda jihadists plowed a Boeing jet into the side of the building that had just been renovated). The more that Janet learned about it, the more she felt a sense of kinship with it. The doors, floors, moldings, and radiators were similar in design and material to those used in the construction of the federally built Lockefield Gardens she had lived in as a child in Indianapolis.

There were nights when Janet would stay late and walk the long corridors, listening to the click of her heels on the polished floors, the sound bouncing off the walls. She would wander through the many exhibits: African-Americans in Defense; Buffalo Soldier Exhibit; Hall of Heroes; Hispanic Medal of Honor Display; Military Women's Corridor; Native American Display; Navajo Code Talkers Display; POW/MIA Corridor. She found it noteworthy that even our heroes were separated according to race, gender, and ethnicity. She'd pass by the banners under which various regiments had fought and find herself nodding, as if she was saluting them all.

One day, while she was giving our beloved "Hutch" a tour of the building, Hutch excitedly pointed to a display cabinet.

"Look! That's my Navy uniform," Hutch said. "It's the one I donated when I retired."

Janet marveled at the coincidence. She had been delivered by a Navy doctor. Her brother, James had served in the Navy. We had adopted a Navy woman as our godmother. One of my very first pictures was taken in a sailor's uniform, and there was Hutch's old uniform on display.

Hutch gently poked Janet in the shoulder and joked, "I was a lot smaller then."

* * *

I had to travel a great deal, both domestically and internationally. In fact, I covered more than eight hundred thousand miles during my tenure. Janet was with me much of the time. I wanted her to serve as my eyes and ears to learn about issues that were unlikely to reach me during the course of my travels.

Initially, Janet thought that the men get to discuss war and peace, and the women talk over tea and crumpets about cooking, kids, and cleaning. She learned very quickly how right—and wrong she was. Bill Perry's wife, Lee, had spoken to her about her devotion to quality-of-life issues. Janet didn't realize it at the time they spoke, but these are issues fundamental to our national security.

If housing, health care, schooling, or home finances are inadequate, they will have a major impact upon the recruitment and retention of our soldiers. These are not abstract matters. In an all-volunteer force, if a spouse and family are not well cared for or are unhappy, it can not help but affect the focus and mind-set of the warrior.

The spouses of flag officers have always been concerned with quality-of-life matters, but they might not always have the opportunity to press their observations or recommendations to the highest levels in the chain of command. As "First Lady of the Pentagon," however, Janet could make sure that their views could go right to the top. This was the message that Lee Perry had passed on to Janet.

With my support, Janet proceeded to organize the First Military Family Forum at the Pentagon, bringing together the top military leaders, including the chairman and vice chairman of the Joint Chiefs of Staff and the Supreme Allied Commander of Forces Europe (SACEUR), and enlisted men and women from all over the country. She presided over a full-day, closed-door session, where warriors and their spouses were able to express their views on what issues mattered to them most. Once everyone saw that this was not a media publicity stunt, they opened up to express their genuine concerns. It proved to be a big morale booster.

Janet said, "I was convinced that we had to use every tool available to boost the military's efforts to recruit and retain high-quality people to serve our country. I wanted to use the power of television to demonstrate to our young people that their personal and family needs were being heard by decision makers, including President Bill Clinton, who agreed to be a guest on a television program I instituted."

It was called *Special Assignment with Janet Langhart Cohen.* The program was broadcast worldwide over the Armed Forces Network each week and was designed to send the message to the military rank and file about the Pentagon's commitment to their well-being and that of their families.

General Carl Mundy (Ret.), who had served as the commandant of the Marine Corps, asked Janet to join the board of directors of the USO, a congressionally chartered nonprofit organization whose mission it is to help build and sustain the morale and general welfare of our military.

Janet agreed to do so. "After making several trips with the USO to the front lines where our troops were deployed and seeing the impact of our visits, I thought it would be important to do two things: establish a USO liaison office in the Pentagon and create an interactive display of the USO's activities, reminding all who passed by the corridor leading to the Metro station how important the USO was to our military."

Not everyone in the Pentagon shared her enthusiasm for the project. A lawyer buried somewhere in the bureaucracy suggested that she had a conflict of interest and could be charged with a criminal offense if she pursued this goal.

Incredible!

"I had to pay to become a member of the USO Board. I served as a volunteer without compensation to further the goals of a congressionally chartered organization to help our soldiers. And that was a crime?"

Well, Charles Dickens had Mr. Bumble say in *Oliver Twist:* "If the law supposes that, the law is a ass—a idiot."

Doc Cook swiftly overruled the lawyer's opinion and authorized the project to go forward.

Janet organized a ribbon-cutting ceremony that was attended by Football Hall of Famer Terry Bradshaw, actors Mickey Rooney and Gerald McRaney, and Ross Perot, all of whom were major supporters of the USO.

During the holidays, my office would organize USO-supported trips to visit our forward-deployed troops. We were joined by musicians Mary Chapin Carpenter, Carole King, David Ball, Shane Minor, and Jon Carroll; comedian Al Franken; and football stars Mike Singletary and Terry Bradshaw.

Janet worked with Terry to persuade the FOX Sports team of Jim Brown, Howie Long, and Chris Collingsworth to broadcast their NFL color commentary from the deck of the USS *Harry Truman*, which was sailing in the Mediterranean. These musical and athletic superstars were a big hit with our kids.

During her years in Boston, she had developed a close friendship with Arthur Fiedler, the conductor of the Boston Pops Orchestra. After seeing just how popular our holiday visits were, Janet suggested that we create a Pentagon Pops and have them broadcast over the Armed Forces Network so that all members of our military could enjoy seeing these stars and the musical talent within the military itself. And where else to hold the musical tribute than Constitution Hall—the hallowed place that the Daughters of the American Revolution had prohibited the internationally famed Marian Anderson from performing?

Tom Brokaw agreed to serve as master of ceremonies for the evening, and we proceeded to put on a show that was second to none in quality. We showcased the enormous talent of our military men and women, ranging from big band and country music to opera and the 104th Airborne Chorus. In addition, jazz spiritualist Phil Driscoll blew his trumpet with the power of Gabriel; R&B singers Peabo Bryson and Ruth Pointer infused the hall with soul; and keyboard genius Jon Carroll rocked it to the rafters.

But the biggest stars of these events were always the Medal of Honor recipients. Each year we held a special reception for them. When our heroes walked out onto the stage, the audience burst into a standing and sustained ovation, bringing tears to our eyes.

It was during one of my first trips abroad, to Bulgaria, that Janet had the opportunity to help put our "soft power" in action. The Soviet Union's planned economy had been a disaster for the countries under its domination.

Although Bulgarian students always scored at the top of scholastic aptitude tests, their intellectual capital was squandered. The country remained poor and underdeveloped. Janet was told that patients were often forced to bring their own beds, even their own hypodermic needles, to some of the medical facilities. Once we returned to Washington, she immediately contacted CARE and arranged to have medical supplies and equipment shipped to Sofia. The doctors organized a press conference praising the humanity and generosity of the American people.

It took so little to build so much goodwill for our country.

Janet couldn't get that thought out of her mind whenever we visited our troops in the field. How little they asked for—how much they gave. These brave young people hailed from Appalachia, the Bronx, inner-city ghettoes, the barrios, the suburbs. Their motives in enlisting in the military were as varied as their socioeconomic, racial, and geographic backgrounds. Some joined to follow family tradition; others to escape a dysfunctional family situation, or to please a loving parent. Most were anxious to acquire an education and elevate their prospects for the future. All were prepared to sacrifice for their country and the preservation of our way of life.

It was during the Thanksgiving and Christmas holidays that Janet was most touched. She would see them standing in the cold, the snow, the mud, standing guard duty. She would see them conducting maneuvers in the deserts of Saudi Arabia and Kuwait, always but a bullet or land mine away from extinction. She would hold the hands of orphaned children, embrace the sorrows of widows at funeral ceremonies, and stand next to a mother who would bury just a few fragmentary bones of a son who had been lost in Vietnam some thirty years before.

Janet wept when we lost men and women in the bombings of our embassies in East Africa and at the ceremonies honoring those who died when the USS *Cole* was attacked in the Yemeni port of Aden.

Little did she know then that she would one day volunteer to serve as an Army Arlington Lady and attend the funerals of those who would be buried at Arlington National Cemetery. Or that, as the former first lady of the Pentagon, she would walk the corridors of the Army's Walter Reed Hospital and embrace the severely wounded men and women who, she was convinced, had been sent to fight against a dictator who posed no imminent threat against anyone but the Iraqi people.

"I knew," Janet said to me, "that they would receive adequate medical treatment and rehabilitative services at Walter Reed, and I could see that some were strong, like Tammy Duckworth, a beautiful young helicopter pilot who lost both of her legs and went on to seek a career in politics. There were others, however, who, with little family or financial support, will face a future of psychological and economic hardship when they return to their homes, whether in 'red' or 'blue' states, to find their sacrifice treated as a memory by some or as a mistake by others."

It was when Janet discovered how good and great these men and women were that she finally saw the American flag in a different perspective. It was not just a flag, a piece of beautiful bunting. It was the symbol of a great, moving experience in human history. When she saw just how democratic our country could be when we stopped judging people by color, when black and Latino soldiers could command whites, or be commanded in turn by them, in a spirit of patriotism, committed to defending one America and not two—that was the moment when she finally felt that the flag was hers as well, that she could truly feel that America was her country, too.

I learned that there were times when Janet would slip into my office when I was away. She would go behind my desk, touch the flag, and say a prayer. She would ask God to protect all who served under it, pray for the souls of those who had sacrificed their lives, for the heroes who still stood on duty and for those who remained at home, worried that they would receive a letter from the front or dreading the moment when a car ominously approached the driveway bearing two officers, who, with their words, would break their hearts forever.

Janet had hoped to continue working with the USO to serve those who were serving us, but the USO decided that when my term of office ended, her assistance was no longer needed. "The king is dead," she was told by one official.

"But the queen isn't," she retorted.

It was no use. Realizing that the USO's decision was final, Janet decided to find other ways to serve.

The code name she had chosen for use by my security detail was "Firebird," a phoenix that would always rise up from the ashes. She formed the Citizen Patriot Organization, a nonprofit organization through which she could continue to lift the morale of our servicemen and servicewomen. With the help of several major corporations, film giant Steven Spielberg, Canadian businessman David Ho, and others, Janet was able to tour our bases in Europe following the September 11 attack, bringing the music of superstar Clint Black, the beauty of the New England Patriots cheerleaders, and the comedic talents of Al Franken to our troops. *Entertainment Tonight*, the same program from which she had been fired ten years earlier because her English was deemed professionally inadequate, asked her to both produce and anchor the week-long tour.

History, it seems, has its curious and cunning passages.

Janet strongly opposed going to war with Iraq in the Spring of 2003, but felt that she needed to support our military. She was outraged that the American people were not allowed to see the flag-draped coffins that carried the remains of our soldiers who had been killed in Afghanistan and Iraq. If she couldn't go to Dover Air Force Base and offer some consolation to the families who had lost their loved ones, well, she was going to find some way to honor those who had answered the call to duty.

She asked, in fact, pleaded to become an Army Arlington Lady. As a member, she attended nearly twenty funerals held for those who were to be buried at our National Cemetery. In addition, she felt compelled to travel out to Walter Reed Army Medical Hospital many evenings to try to comfort the young men and women who were coming home with terrible wounds. She'd return late at night, emotionally drained, but filled with rage over what had happened to them.

"Bill," she would say, "this war is wrong. You've got to come out with me to see what this war is doing to our kids. Tonight, I met a beautiful Army Reserve Blackhawk helicopter pilot. Her name's Tammy Duckworth. She lost both of her legs and part of her arm. I asked her how she was doing. She said, 'I'm fine ma'am,' and then proceeded to tell me that she was going to fly again. She wasn't going to let those who had shot down her helicopter determine her future. She's got more guts than any of those hawks who sent her off to war."

"Janet, I can't start going out there without it appearing that I'm playing politics with this issue."

"You can go with me at night. There aren't any cameras around when I go there."

"If I start going out there, it won't take long for the story to get out and then the cameras will be there. I think it's great what you're doing, but frankly, I think you need to ease up and take a break. Don't go out so often."

I was worried about what all the visits were doing to her. She would come home and recount to me every detail about the injuries the soldiers had received. What they said to her and how she responded. Some could only squeeze her hand. Others couldn't respond at all. She would lie awake in the darkness for hours thinking about what had happened to them and what their lives were going to be like once they returned to small town America.

Janet said, "Bill, when I go out to walk the halls at Walter Reed, I see a lot of poor, rural white kids from Appalachia, lying alongside those black and Latino kids from the cities. They're missing arms and legs. They got serious brain injuries, post-traumatic stress. A lot of them joined the military for the same reason the other kids do: escape poverty, get an education, have a better future. Sure they're patriotic. But our system doesn't give them much more than it gives to blacks and Latinos.

"One day these white kids are going to forget about color and realize that they've been had by all the politicians and pundits who've been telling them that they're from red states and that they're the true patriots and warriors and the people from blue states are pacifists and appeasers.

"The poor whites of this country are like a sleeping giant and one day they're going to wake up. If they can ever get beyond their false pride or the delusion they're somehow superior because they've got white skin, that's when they'll realize that we're all in this together, that we're all red, white, and blue Americans.

"It's what Dr. King once said, 'We may not have come here on the same ships, but we're all in this boat together.'

"That's when America is going to be the dream it was meant to be."

Eventually, to my relief, Janet began to space out her visits to Walter Reed. Although she was moved profoundly by the pain and suffering she saw on the faces of our young heroes, she was also inspired by them.

Tammy Duckworth wouldn't fly again, but she would run. Run for the United States Congress.

Win or lose, she would inspire her fellow veterans and countrymen by demonstrating that one could overcome any loss or hardship.

Twenty-Three

A Song of Songs

My, or I should say *our* tour of duty, ended too quickly. Janet and I knew the day would come when we would have to take our leave. Both of us felt sadness and a measure of relief. I had averaged roughly four and a half hours of sleep each night during those years, and even those hours were frequently interrupted by phone calls alerting me to some crisis or tragedy. Janet's nights were consumed with her sending hundreds of e-mails to soldiers in the field or to their families here at home. We could now enjoy a slower pace of life and look back more reflectively on all that we had experienced and accomplished.

I wasn't quite sure how to express my feelings during the retirement ceremony that was to take place the next morning. I had always considered brevity to be key to a successful speech, but I had so much that I wanted to say about the meaning of America, about the promise and peril of the future that was rushing at us. There were so many moments, large and small, that had touched me profoundly.

One occurred during a visit to a base in Bosnia while I was moving through the chow line in the dining hall. A young Russian soldier, so excited and proud to be serving alongside his American counterparts as part of a peacekeeping force, rushed over to me and presented me with his slightly worn blue beret. I gave him one of my official secretary of defense coins in exchange.

I later pondered the significance of what had transpired in that moment. As a young boy, I used to attend movies on Saturday afternoons for the price of ten or twelve cents. On my way home, I would climb an old, gnarled tree located on a slope across the street from a bowling alley. I would hide in the tree and pretend that I was a sniper killing German and Japanese soldiers. During that time, returning veterans would bring back hats and helmets (and in my case a Japanese rifle) as war booty that they had snatched from dead or captured enemies.

That day, a soldier, who just a few years before had been a Cold War enemy, had handed me something very special—a gift of peace. I was not naïve enough to think that all swords were being beaten into ploughshares or that the world had turned away from its war-making ways. But in that small gesture, I felt that hope was like the poet's bird "that feels the light and begins to sing when the dawn is still in darkness."*

I thought also of the significance of passing out the coin that bore the seal of my office. One of the most rewarding aspects of meeting troops in the field was to press into their hands that special token. It was a long-standing tradition in the military for superior officers to hand out a unit's coin to those who were being singled out for special recognition. Over the years the circle of privilege had been significantly expanded, and so I had several thousand of them minted. Also, part of the tradition required that the recipient of the coin carry it with him at all times, or risk having to purchase a beer should he be caught by the donor without it. It's impossible to capture in words the sense of human connection and those fleeting seconds of joy when the transfer occurs and words of mutual respect and gratitude are exchanged.

Whenever I looked into the eager faces of our young men and women, I would think of my grandfather handing me an Indian Head nickel each week whispering, "Someday, Billy, someday, you'll understand."

---

*Rabindranath Tagore, *Fireflies* (New York: Collier Books, 1928), p. 203.

There was so much that I still did not understand, particularly the strange and wondrous way the universe had unfolded.

Consider Independence Day 2000. Janet and I were hosting a celebratory event on the deck of the USS *John F. Kennedy*, one of our magnificent aircraft carriers that had sailed into New York's harbor. From the deck of the carrier, we watched hundreds of tall ships, bearing the flags from countries the world over, sail past the Statue of Liberty, whose torch-bearing hand is held high to light the path of freedom for those brave enough to seek it.

As the day darkened into a perfect, moonlit night, I held Janet tightly around her waist, as we both stared at Lady Liberty, bathed in light. I wondered what my grandfather thought when he first saw her? Could he have ever imagined the little boy he used to coddle would one day stand on the deck of a mighty warship as secretary of defense and celebrate the fiery birth of our nation's freedom? That by stepping into the darkness of an unknowable future, he had stirred the winds of fortune to blow in such a favorable direction? The answers, of course, are unknowable, but my grandfather's experience offered a lesson for all who come to, or are lucky enough to be born in, America. This is a country where anything and everything is possible. A country where no dream is beyond any who have the heart to reach for it.

I wanted to say all of this and more, but I was overwhelmed by the task. I couldn't write and I couldn't sleep. Janet, finally seeing me sitting in a chair at 4 a.m., offered me some simple, heartfelt advice. "Bill, just tell them what you feel."

The next morning, before we left to attend the farewell ceremonies being held in Comny Hall at Fort Myer, Janet slipped into my office at the Pentagon and had her last moment with the American flag that stood behind my desk. She had touched it lightly on many previous occasions. This time, she did more than just touch it. She embraced it. She had spent so many years wandering in an emotional diaspora until coming to the Pentagon and serving those who served us. She wept and whispered: *America the Beautiful. God Bless America. My Country 'Tis of Thee.*

She dried her eyes and then headed with me for our last ride in the SecDef's limousine. The past four years had been telescoped into just minutes, minutes that had proved life transforming for both of us.

We passed Arlington Cemetery on our route to Comny Hall. Seeing all of the white crosses marking the graves of those who answered the call to duty caused us to clasp and squeeze our hands together. So much blood had been shed to secure our freedom.

As we rode along the highway, so many memories started flashing past. We thought of all of the young men and women whose dedication and idealism had touched us to the core. They asked for so little and gave so much.

We thought back to that brilliant, sunshine-filled day in Bath, Maine, when Janet became cosponsor of the guided missile destroyer, *USS Winston S. Churchill* DDG-81, named after her hero. Lady Soames, Churchill's last surviving daughter, joined her there. Together, they smashed champagne bottles against the bow of a mighty warship that would bear the name of one of the giants of the twentieth century, and sent her off into the sea to defend freedom.

We would never forget the moment when President Bill Clinton, during his final State of the Union Address, praised Janet's efforts on behalf of all those who wear our nation's uniform. Dressed in one of her beautiful red dresses, she was overcome with emotion when the entire Congress stood and began to applaud. For the lady in red, there was no holding back the tears.

Our future, and that of America, would not be filled with roses. Janet would lose her mother, the woman who had to cope with so many disadvantages and yet had managed to instill in Janet a sense of self-worth and tolerance and the courage to challenge every convention, black or white. Her last years were filled with pain and paralysis, and yet she was able to face the end with grace and dignity.

Janet's adopted "godmother," Hutch, and her beloved mentor, Cordie King, would pass as well. Two more strong women who refused to bend to the will of others.

My brother, Bob, would die, and then Lucky, the lost waif we had embraced and treated as our son, would succumb to cancer.

Janet and I would take comfort in words spoken at a eulogy for Tom Lambert's wife, Elizabeth, by one of her closest friends, Ann Bonin:

> The light we live in is inhabited by shadows. We live among ghosts, always, everywhere. People, animals, butterflies, have all traversed every place on earth before our time. Their footsteps and passions and heart beats and wing beats have smoothed the way for ours. Their in-breaths and their out-breaths have sweetened and charged the air for us. We live in their shadows, and create our own shadows for all who are to come. . . .
>
> Sadness is a cloak we can take off and pack away with a loved one's things. We are not meant to mourn for very long. We are meant to remember, but not to mourn. Better by far that we should forget, and smile, than that we should remember and be sad.

Shortly after we were seated in the large hall, Janet slipped a note into my hands and nodded for me to read it. It was in her handwriting.

> Alas, Joshua, we cannot live our dreams.
> We are lucky enough if we can give a sample of our best,
> and if in our hearts we can feel that it has been nobly done."
> > Nobly done, my love.
> > Firebird

She had quoted the words of one of our greatest Supreme Court Justices, a veteran of the Civil War, Oliver Wendell Holmes, Jr.

I closed my hand over Janet's and held it tight for a few moments. I felt my throat go a little dry. As the honors ceremony began, the lights in Comny Hall dimmed and we sat shrouded in darkness, feeling a mixture of pride and sadness. This was our farewell to arms. It was in almost every aspect identical to the ceremony held for us four years earlier, except now the military was going to be saying good-bye instead of hello.

I love to give Janet surprise gifts, and I had one more in store for her. When the time came for me to "troop the line"—to pass and review the honor guard units and inspect them—General Hugh Shelton, the chairman of the Joint Chiefs of Staff, called for Janet to come forward and troop the line with me. This was an unprecedented honor.

Joined by General Shelton, she walked—no, glided—along the grandest runway in the world, one that no modeling or finishing school could have ever prepared her for.

She looked into the handsome faces of the young men and women standing at attention. The faces were black, white, brown, and yellow in color. They were proud, patriotic faces. They were the faces of one America.

When the time came for me to walk to the podium in the center of the hall to give my final address to the parade units of the respective services and the large audience gathered in the stands, I followed Janet's simple advice. I spoke of what I felt.

So what do I feel? I feel honor, to be sure, but most of all, an unqualified sense of awe. When I'm in the presence of men and women who serve and sacrifice themselves and their families for our freedom, I am in awe. I've had the privilege of meeting with kings and queens, and presidents and prime ministers, and princes and sultans and emirs, and yes, parliamentarians the world over. But nothing has ever been more rewarding than to visit our troops in Bosnia, in Kosovo, Korea, Kuwait, or Saudi Arabia; to land on a carrier in the Gulf where the temperatures can run 120, 130, 140 degrees, and to see our sailors and Marines carrying out their duties in that heat; to watch our Air Force put steel on target or deliver humanitarian relief to helpless victims of hurricanes, earthquakes, or other natural disasters; to witness our Coast Guardsmen protecting our shores or rescuing those who are caught up in those perfect storms.

I marvel at your raw courage and your willingness to constantly train and prepare to fight the wars that can't be prevented. And I am touched to the core when I visit you at Christmas time, knowing what a special moment it is for you, how far away you are from your families, what spirit you show in your very loneliness as you're surrounded by your comrades, what pride you take in knowing that you save lives, that you've touched hearts of total strangers, and that you've given them something more precious than gold.

And as I reflect on the swift passage of time these past four years, all of these moments and memories come rushing at me with a terrifying velocity. But I'd like to share one of my earliest with you.

On our visit to Eagle Base in Bosnia on Christmas Eve three years ago—as we have done every holiday since that time—we joined hundreds of soldiers to share songs and love and levity and laughter, and to bring them just a touch of home. As we left around midnight, we passed along the perimeter and came across three young soldiers for whom Christmas Eve meant manning a security post that was fashioned from wood. They were out there in the mud, in the cold, in the darkness, standing guard in the night.

As we expressed our gratitude for their service and conveyed our sorrow that they couldn't be home with their families, one of these soldiers looked at Janet and he offered a response that we will never forget, so eloquent in its simplicity, so profound in its sincerity, "That's all right, ma'am. Somebody has to do it. And besides, I think we're making a difference here."

Men and women of the United States Armed Forces, for the past four years, we've been blessed to serve with you as you stand guard in the night, and as you continue to make an extraordinary difference the world over. Because of your patriotism and professionalism, because of your dedication and your daring, more people today sleep under the flag of freedom than at any time in history. . . .

On countless occasions I've been asked by foreign leaders, "How can our military be more like America's?" I'll repeat here today what I've said time and time again. It's not our training, although our training is the most rigorous in the world. It's not our technology, although ours is the most advanced in the world. And it's not our tactics, although ours is the most revolutionary in the world. We have the finest military on Earth because we have the finest people on Earth, because we recruit and we retain the best that America has to offer.

So as I prepare to leave public office, I want to take this final occasion to remind all of America: take a look at the leadership that we have, take a look at what you see arrayed before you here. Be inspired by their character and their devotion to duty. Stand in awe of their courage and their professionalism and their ability to maintain bravery in the midst of tragedy and loss.

When we stood on the tarmac at Andrews Air Force Base to welcome home the flag-draped coffins of those that we lost in our embassies in East Africa, when we stood on the pier in Norfolk with the wounded sailors and the families of those who perished in the *Cole*, when we learned of those who were lost aboard the Osprey, and whenever the phone rang at midnight or in the early morning hours telling me of an accident that would not make the headlines but would rip a hole in the hearts of the families who were affected, then we understand why these brave men and women and their families truly are patriots among us—the pride of America, the envy of the world.

I'd like to close with the paraphrased words of the poet Tagore:

"When one comes and whispers to me, 'Thy days are ended,' let me say to him, 'I have lived in love and not in mere time.'

"And he will ask, 'Will thy songs remain?'

"And I shall say, 'I know not, but this I know. That often when I sang, I found my eternity.'"

ANNEX

Anne and Emmett
A One-Act Play
By
Janet Langhart Cohen

PREFACE

Dr. Martin Luther King, Jr., said, "[T]he arc of the moral universe is long, but it bends toward justice." Our history books would seem to validate Dr. King's vision. Still the ugly, twin heads of anti-Semitism and racism continue to lurk just below the surface of civility, eager to seize upon and exploit our fears and differences.

I have struggled to understand the genesis and reason for man's capacity to hate. I continue to be baffled at how seemingly civilized and sophisticated societies, filled with intelligent human beings, can resort to the most barbaric displays of cruelty—particularly toward those who are seen and treated as "minorities."

To help me to understand and articulate the need to find harmony in the world rather than hate, I have turned to an imaginary vision of two historic and tragic victims of institutionalized terrorism meeting somewhere in time. They are forever destined to remain suspended in the netherworld and locked in a repetitive conversation until the chain of mankind's evil is broken by the grace of illumination and knowledge. The young voices that I hear and call forth remind us of our history, the commonality of their experiences, and the need to be mindful of those who hope to steal our humanity.

The imaginary conversation that follows is offered with the hope that it will appeal to all audiences, but most specifically to those of Anne and Emmett's age, lest they never know—or are allowed to forget.*

The stage lights come up. ANNE, a young girl about fifteen years of age, is dressed in a pretty wool skirt, dark sweater, and white frilly blouse. She is in a loft (stage right), sitting at a desk and writing on a note pad.

A street sign outside the house reads "Prinsengracht." The numerals 263 are on the door of the house.

A large projection screen is located center stage. We see newsreels of goose-stepping soldiers, Adolph Hitler speaking to mass audiences who salute, shouting, "Heil Hitler."

We hear loud pounding on a door off stage. Before the elderly man has the chance to answer the door, a Nazi SS sergeant (the swastika armband clearly visible) and members of the Dutch Security Police in plain clothes enter and they begin to search the house. The soldier begins to tap the walls of the house with the butt of his automatic weapon. He detects a hollow section. He reaches behind the books, and discovers a small protruding object. It is the handle to a door that is hidden behind the wall of books. They pull the façade away and rush up the stairs that lead to an annex.

Upon seeing the men, Anne cringes, raising her arm to fend them off. They pull Anne from her desk, descend the stairs, and cart her off the stage.

On the screen we see and hear the answer with more news clips. This time, they are of men, women, and children being herded like cattle aboard sealed railroad cars, dumped into mass graves, and

---

*It is no small irony that it was the parents—Otto, Anne's father, and Mamie, Emmett's mother—who were left to tell the world the stories of their children; stories that have touched me profoundly.

shoved into gas chambers and crematoriums. Railcars can be heard screeching, along with the bellow of a locomotive's engine.

A spotlight illuminates a stage prop crematorium. Smoke billows from the chimney and wafts ominously across the stage.

The stage goes dark momentarily.

When the lights slowly come back up we see EMMETT, a young teenage black boy who is dressed in a white shirt and a pair of trousers held up by suspenders. He's wearing a brown, snap-brimmed hat and a wide smile. He's in the company of several other young KIDS who approach a small store where, on the benches just in front of the store, there is a small cluster of boys playing checkers. The sign over the store, braced by Coca-Cola advertisements, reads "BRYANT'S Grocery & Meat Market."

There is a sun-faded decal of the Confederate flag in the store's front window. Emmett speaks to a young white woman who is standing behind a counter. He purchases a small item and walks back outside, stopping just outside the open door.

KIDS: What 'cha buy Emmett?

EMMETT: Just some bub . . . bubb . . . (*He pauses, clearly frustrated by a speech impediment. Finally, he holds up a piece of bubble gum and whistles.*)

The young woman who sold him the gum is exiting the store when she hears the whistle. She is angry and points a condemning finger at him.

The stage lights go semidark.

Emmett and the Kids turn the revolving store front face and reveal a small house. An older man, Emmett's great uncle, Papa Mose, is sleeping in a large chair. Emmett is visiting his relatives. He jumps into bed.

It is night. Two men come for Emmett. They enter the small house, armed with guns. They order everyone out of bed. Pointing their flashlights into the eyes of each family member, one by one, finally, they settle on Emmett and drag him from the house over the protests of Papa Mose. Outside is the young woman from the store and she confirms that Emmett is the one who whistled. The men whisk Emmett away in a pickup truck.

The scene shifts to a remote area where there is a tall barren tree stage prop. Next to the tree stands an ethereal figure dressed in a white sheet and hood, the garb of the Ku Klux Klan. He is holding a large wooden cross in one hand and a rope in the other. His arms are folded, striking a casual pose, as if he has been there many times before. He loops the rope over the lowest branch of the barren tree as the men proceed to beat Emmett with hammers, shovels, and an ax. They shoot Emmett, then tie him up with wire to a cotton gin fan and lift him above their shoulders.

The lights are cut, and the stage again goes into darkness.

The sound of a loud splash can be heard, along with the harsh laughter of the men. Suddenly, the wooden cross bursts into flame as the laughter continues to reverberate. The smoke from the burning cross wafts across the stage, as did the smoke from the smokestack in the earlier scene.

Once again, the stage goes dark.

Seconds pass before the lights come up, slowly, replicating a sunrise. When they do, Anne is sitting at a desk in her loft, writing on sheets of paper.

Emmett appears from behind the barren tree and moves to a tree stump near by. He sits on the stump, his head bowed. Anne, suddenly aware that someone else is on stage, is startled. She looks down and sees Emmett.

ANNE: Who are you?

EMMETT (*Looks up, his eyes meeting Anne's. He's hesitant, on guard.*): My name's . . . Emmett. . . . Who are you?

ANNE: My name's Anne.

EMMETT: Why are YOU here?

ANNE : It's a long story. I was born in Frankfurt, Germany, but when the Nazis came to power we moved to Amsterdam to escape their hatred. It didn't work. Germany invaded and conquered the Netherlands. The Nazis took me away. They murdered me and millions like me.

EMMETT: But why?

ANNE: Because we're Jewish.

EMMETT: Jewish. That's it? You've got a different religion? They murdered you for that?

ANNE: Yes, and because we're Jewish, they blamed us for everything that was going wrong in Germany. Said that we were the reason that Germany lost World War I. They called us vile names. They restricted us to ghettoes and made us wear armbands and patches with the yellow Star of David on them, identifying us as Jews. They cut off all the hair of the women and girls and used it as stuffing for mattresses. . . .

EMMETT: Wait. They cut off your hair? My mother always said that a woman's hair was her crowning glory. They took that from you?

ANNE: More than that, Emmett. They tattooed our skin. Stole all our property. They even took all the gold from our teeth. . . .

EMMETT: Gold. We were called Black Gold! We created real wealth for whites.

ANNE: They treated us as sub-human animals. Took us off to concentration camps in railroad cars. . . .

Here the screen shows scenes of Hasidic Jews being mocked; Jewish stores being smashed and burned during Krystallnacht; gold teeth extracted; shoes and hair of Jews being collected.

EMMETT (*emotionally sympathetic*): Sounds familiar. White people came and shackled us. Shipped us to America in the stinking bowels of slave ships. They robbed us of our names, family, country. Sometimes they branded us, but the color of our skin was brand enough. They sold us off on auction blocks and treated us as only three-fifths human. Can you believe that deer and rabbits had more rights than we did? They used to say, "We shoot rabbits, but we hang our niggers." We were slaves for three hundred years in the land of the free.

The screen center stage shows photographs and drawings of slave ships and blacks being auctioned off, forced to work as laborers in cotton fields, and lynched at the whim of the plantation masters.

ANNE: We Jews have a slave history too. We were slaves a long time ago in Egypt. Later, we had to face the Inquisitions. They tortured us, making us confess to crimes we never committed. Even blamed the Black Plague on us and burned us at the stake. Then, after so many years of suffering, we had to face the Germans who decided they had a "Final Solution" for us.

The screen shows film of German leaders at a conference deciding how each agency and department could participate to expedite the extermination of the Jewish people.

ANNE: Their solution was to exterminate us. To send us into their gas chambers and crematoriums . . .

Film clips appear on the screen of Germans engaging in mass executions, herding their victims into gas chambers and ovens.

Anne chokes up with emotion. She decides to shift the focus to Emmett.

ANNE: I'm curious, Emmett. Why did they hate you?

EMMETT: Different color skin. That simple, I guess.

ANNE: shakes her head in disbelief. (*A beat*): You know it's all just one big paradox.

EMMETT: Paradox? Meaning what?

ANNE: I'm white but Jewish . . .

EMMETT: Yeah. I'm Christian but black. It wasn't a question of religion for us. It was color.

ANNE: Yet they came for both of us. I guess haters love to hate anyone or anything that's different.

EMMETT (*nods his approval*)

ANNE: I could never understand it. We have given so much to the world. Medicine. Art. Music. Law . . . What, I always wondered, would the world be like without us?

On the screen, we see photographs of Albert Einstein, Marc Chagall, Arthur Rubenstein, Benjamin Cardozo, Felix Frankfurter, Itzhak Perlman, Irving Berlin, Saul Bellow, and Steven Spielberg.

ANNE: Think of Jonas Salk and his discovery of the vaccine for polio. . . .

A picture of Jonas Salk appears on the screen.

EMMETT: Man (*expressing awe*), he came a little late for me. I was born with polio. It affected my speech . . . made me stutter.

ANNE: I didn't realize polio could cause stuttering. But you're okay now. . . .

EMMETT: It only happens when I'm nervous. Here (*he smiles*) everything is okay, Anne. (*A beat.*)

But you raise a good question about what your people have given the world.

You know, I'm proud of what my people have given the world too, despite what we've had to overcome. What would America have been, or be today, without our strength, our culture, our minds and music?

On the screen appear photographs and film of Dr. Charles Drew, George Washington Carver, Frederick Douglass, W. E. B. Du Bois, Jesse Owens, Dr. Martin Luther King, Jr., Justice Thurgood Marshall, Marion Anderson, Rosa Parks, Harriet Tubman, Dr. Ben Carson, Muhammad Ali, Benjamin Bernacker, and Quincy Jones.

EMMETT: They stole everything from us and when we complained, started marching and demonstrating and demanding to be treated as equals, they said that if we niggers didn't like it we should go back to Africa!

ANNE: We didn't have a place to go back to then, Emmett. Imagine, during the time that the Nazis began to persecute us, a German ship, the *SS St. Louis*, carried more than nine hundred Jewish passengers who were trying to immigrate to Cuba.

A photograph of the *SS St. Louis* appears on screen.

ANNE: But the fascists in Cuba revoked their visas and allowed just a few people to get off the ship. The rest had no place to go. They begged to be allowed to dock in America, but President Franklin Roosevelt refused. Said he had a strict policy on admitting refugees. They had to return to Europe where they were taken to the Nazis' death camps.

EMMETT (*shakes his head, stunned*): An American president treated white folks like that? Sent them back to Europe knowing it was a death sentence? I remember our folks saying that Roosevelt was a good man, especially considering how Herbert Hoover treated us. Hoover used to say, "All a poor man needs is a dollar a day and a deck of overalls." Most of our people never forgave him and refused to vote for his party for a long time. Hard to believe, though, that an American President would send your people back to certain death.

ANNE: Yes, Emmett. It was shameful, unspeakable! Most Americans have no idea what happened. And if they did, they didn't care.

EMMETT: You said you had no place to go then. And now?

ANNE: Now we have our own country. Israel. A place that's ours. Where Jews can live as Jews. Practice our traditions and worship God.

EMMETT: God. You still believe in God? After all that's happened?

ANNE: Yes. Some good has come out of all that evil. I still believe that there is goodness in people. That there's redemption in the world. That evil doesn't win in the end. God will never forsake us. I know this.

EMMETT: I'd like to agree with you, Anne. My mother had your strong faith.
     But take a look around. Things don't look so great to me. We always seem to be the ones left behind, the forsaken ones.

On the screen are scenes of thousands of blacks left stranded in the aftermath of Hurricane Katrina.

ANNE: I won't give up, Emmett. The time will come when we'll be seen just as people, not singled out as Jews.

EMMETT: Well, it might be easier and come sooner for you. I'd like to be seen as a person, not a color. Just because I'm a black male, doesn't mean I should be treated as a threat or someone to be scared of. But I don't think we blacks will ever be treated just as people, as equals. . . .

On screen are film clips of Rodney King being beaten. Headline clips of Haitian Abner Louima sodomized by New York City police; Amadou Bailo Diallo, an unarmed man, shot at forty-one times and hit with nineteen bullets; other acts of police brutality toward minorities.

ANNE: Don't despair Emmett. I understand why you're down. There were times that I felt the same way and ended up snapping at everyone. People have no idea what it was like to live with eight people all crammed into a small place. There was no privacy. We couldn't move around, make any noises or do anything that might let the Nazis know we were there. It was maddening. We lived in total fear. It was like being in a tomb. When someone got sick, we couldn't call a doctor. Then the plumbing stopped. It was just, well . . . I used to write just to find some place where I could go to be alone and talk to the one person who would never break any confidence and talk about me. When we fled from Germany, I had to leave my cat, Moortje, behind. I really loved Moortje. She was my best friend. I wrote all of the letters in my diary to Kitty. In fact, I called my diary, Kitty.

Anne catches herself, realizing this is no way to pick Emmett's spirits up.

ANNE: But I realized that we had suffered for centuries but somehow managed to keep on living. The suffering made us stronger. Made us survivors. You've got to have faith, Emmett. Courage, determination, solidarity. That will defeat all the oppressors.

EMMETT (*Shakes his head, unconvinced.*): Slavery has really messed with our solidarity, dividing us against each other over the years: field slaves against house slaves; light skin against dark skin; those in a crab barrel pulling back those trying to climb out. We can't seem to get a break even when white folks try to do the right thing.

ANNE: How so?

EMMETT: Well a lot of folks believed that when the U.S. Supreme Court declared that black school children were entitled to an equal education, it provoked a backlash by white people, and not all of them were in the South. They wanted to teach us a lesson. The law wasn't going to make us equal or protect us because THEY were the law.

On screen are film clips of Thurgood Marshall, Jr., the NAACP, and the Brown v. Board of Education case; James Meredith entering the University of Mississippi; Charlayne Hunter Gault with her attorney Vernon Jordan entering the University of Georgia; and Ernie Green and the Little Rock Nine, under the protection of the Army National Guard and the Army's 101st Airborne Division, being escorted to Central High School in Little Rock Arkansas.

ANNE: But didn't that make them lawbreakers?

EMMETT: Yes, but they were the ones wearing the sheriff's badges and carrying the guns.

ANNE: Then what changed their attitude?

EMMETT: Well, after my murder, (*he shudders*) black people decided to protest, to start a movement. In Montgomery, Alabama, a brave lady named Rosa Parks refused to give up her seat on a bus in to a white man. The bus driver had her arrested.

On screen is a photo of Rosa Parks.

ANNE: For not getting up?

EMMETT: Yup. But then that caused black people to boycott the local bus company. Lasted nearly a year.

ANNE: Did it work?

EMMETT: Helped inspire more protests, marches, and sit-in demonstrations. Took ten years of being beaten up, bombed, attacked by dogs and fire-hosed, but Congress finally passed a Civil Rights Act.

The center screen shows Alabama church bombings, German Shepherd dogs attacking blacks who were demonstrating for equal rights, and helmeted police turning fire hoses on them.

EMMETT: Kinda ironic to think about it. But my murder helped spark the Civil Rights Movement and the murder of Rev. Martin Luther King, Jr. sort of ended it.

ANNE: I'm not sure I understand what you mean by "ended it."

EMMETT: It didn't end racism, which just changed its form. It just marked the end of the Civil Rights Movement. White people were so ashamed of what they had done and scared of what we might do, they finally started giving us some opportunities, to let us in places, open up jobs, treat us the way the law said they were supposed to—sort of like the end of Aparteid in South Africa.

ANNE: So no more riding in the back of the bus?

EMMETT: Mostly. But there's been some backsliding. Even fifty years later, there were still some bus drivers in Louisiana trying to make black children ride in the back of the bus, so whites could sit up front. It's like anti-Semitism, I guess. The hatred is always there, hiding just below the surface. It's like Fannie Lou Hammer used to say about racism being so tiring. "I'm sick and tired of being sick and tired." (*Emmett rubs his head*)

ANNE: You know, Emmett, whenever I start to feel down, I think about people like Elie Wiesel. A Holocaust survivor. He's been able to cope with all the horror of the death camps, the murder of his family and now he's touched the conscience of the world. (*A beat*) And music. I listen to Shalom Alechem's

354

Fiddler on the Roof. His Tevye is so wonderful. So wise. He always has an answer to his own questions. "Why do we Jews always wear hats? Because we never know when we might have to leave." He finds humor in the struggle. Has so much joy. Oh, Shalom Alechem, thank you for Tevye.

Screen shows clips of Tevye.

At this point, the Fiddler score starts to play in the background. "If I was a rich man..."

EMMETT (*Tips his hat to Anne*): We've had great writers too. James Weldon, Paul Lawrence Dunbar, W. E. B. DuBois, Langston Hughes, James Baldwin, August Wilson, Alice Walker, Toni Morrison. They're wise too. But they tell a different story. And if you listen to our music, the Blues, then you'll understand why I'm sad.

The Fiddler music stops and we hear Billie Holiday sing some of the lyrics to "Strange Fruit." A picture of Billie Holiday, wearing a gardenia in her hair, appears, followed by those showing blacks who were lynched swinging from trees. Then the mood and melody shift briefly.

ANNE: Oh, Emmett that's horrible. Sad. (*She is consoling with her words and manner*)

(*A beat*) (*the faint sounds of a different song can be heard*)

ANNE: Listen. . . . It's a beautiful musical written by George and Ira Gershwin about the lives of *Porgy and Bess.*

The music continues to play. "Summertime and the livin' is easy . . ."

EMMETT: Yeah. *Porgy and Bess.* It's been called America's first opera. But I don't like the song, "Summertime."

ANNE (*disappointed*): Why not?

EMMETT: Because it was the summertime when they came for me in Mississippi.

Screen shows the newspaper headline and the date August 28, 1955.

EMMETT: I was living in Chicago and went to visit my relatives. That's when they tortured me and then threw me in the Tallahatchie River.

I was beaten so badly, the only way they could tell it was me was because I was wearing my father's silver ring. It had his initials, LT on it. It broke my mother's heart to see what they had done to me.

On the screen, Emmett's mother, Mamie, is seen crying over his casket. Then *Jet* magazine's photograph of Emmett's mutilated body lying in an open casket appears. Emmett looks at the screen and sees the photograph of his mother weeping at his funeral. The music stops abruptly.

ANNE (*recoils in horror at the sight*): Oh, Emmett! (*a beat*) You know they came for me in the summertime too—

The screen shows the date August 4, 1945, the date of her last entry in her diary.

ANNE: But I still love that song.

EMMETT: I know, but the livin' has never been easy for us.

ANNE: I'm really sorry, Emmett. Didn't anyone warn you to be careful in Mississippi, that it was more dangerous for black people in the South?

EMMETT: Oh sure, I was told I had to be afraid, be careful to mind my ways when it came to white folks in the South. Not look them in the eye. Be sure to call them sir and ma'am. Shuffle and scrape. Look like a "happy Negro" just as if we were on a plantation serving the "Masa." Negroes there lived in fear all the time. Just as well might have had a chain and collar around their necks. (*Mockingly*) "Yassa. I's just an Uncle Tom." Well, in Chicago, we didn't have to do any of that stuff and I was going to show my cousins that I was from the North and I wasn't afraid of anything.

ANNE: Did you know that your murder made the papers in Germany?

EMMETT: You're kidding! I know it was a big story in America, but Germany? Now that's something.

ANNE: I think the story ran in the Düsseldorf papers with a big headline: "In America, A Negro's Life Isn't Worth A Whistle."

Screen shows headline.

EMMETT: Well, they got that pretty much right.

ANNE: What's interesting is that during WWII, the Nazis used to point to how America's South treated Negroes as being a confirmation of their belief in the superiority of the Aryan race.

EMMETT: Well, as my mother used to say to me, "The devil can quote scripture to serve his ends. "

Emmett goes silent. Stands, shoves his hands in his pockets and starts to pace about. Struggles to contain his emotions but remains silent.

ANNE: Emmett, what's wrong? What are you thinking?

EMMETT: I was just thinking about what you said about what the Nazis did. . . . The cutting of your hair, taking gold fillings from your teeth, the concentration camps, the gas chambers, the Nazis' experimentations on you, their determination to exterminate you. . . . My father was in Europe during WWII. He was killed over there. The Army sent his ring to my mother. Nothing else, just the ring, with no explanation how he died. Did you know that black soldiers, fought to defeat Hitler? That they helped liberate those concentration camps, but that our own government treated German prisoners better than us?

On screen are photographs of black soldiers staring at the unspeakable evil of Hitler's "Final Solution."

ANNE: How so?

EMMETT: Think about it. The Tuskegee Airmen, all-black squadrons of fighter pilots. They protected American bombers all over North Africa, Sicily, and Europe. They never lost a single bomber to German airplanes. . . .

Screens shows Tuskegee Airmen, Willa B. Brown, and General Benjamin O. Davis, Jr.

ANNE: Amazing.

EMMETT: What's amazing is that German prisoners of war were invited to eat and drink in our Officers Clubs and black officers were arrested and tossed in jailed for demanding the same rights. Even court-martialed!

ANNE: You mean that those who were destroying us were granted privileges in the Army above the black American soldiers? It's too twisted to contemplate. It's impossible to believe.

EMMETT: Believe it. They even threatened to put baseball great Jackie Robinson in an Army prison for speaking out. And when Lena Horne protested that Nazi P.O.W.'s were sitting in the front rows during her performance for the USO, while black soldiers had to stand in the back, the USO, instead of moving the blacks up front, refused to let her perform again. Basically, they banned her. They let her know that she was still on the plantation. They didn't know Lena Horne. She went on entertaining all the troops and paid for it herself. She didn't need them. She was going to play by her rules, not theirs.

On screen, we see film clips of Jackie Robinson in his Army uniform and then facing jeering crowds when playing baseball. Film of Lena Horne also appears while singing in front of a USO sign.

ANNE (*shakes her head*): Two separate evils were playing out for both of our peoples at the same time.

EMMETT: Right. That was the other side of what we all call the "Greatest Generation," the one most white folks don't like to talk about. The fact that blacks could fight and die for America, but they couldn't wear their uniforms in public in the South when they returned.

Every time any of our leaders spoke out demanding freedom and justice, they risked their lives. Many of them had to die just for demanding that we be treated as equals. Would you believe that the United States Senate allowed people to lynch us? Hang and mutilate us in front of white people who were all dressed up in their Sunday best as if they were attending a picnic?

The sound of Senator Richard Russell's voice is heard. His photograph is seen on the screen. Fragments of his Senate speeches flash on the screen, along with some of his colloquies with President Lyndon Baines Johnson, who urged the passage of the Civil Rights Act of 1964. The names of those U.S. Senators who in 2004 refused to sponsor a bill apologizing for the Senate's historic opposition to banning lynching in America scroll across the screen.

EMMETT: We asked for a simple apology—not justice—but a simple apology for the Senate's historic failure to stop all the lynchings. Not all one hundred senators would sign the resolution. Those who refused to sign, the "dirty dozen," had some phony excuse that it was too trivial and unimportant.

You know, when as many as a dozen or more members of the U.S. Senate refuse to say they were sorry for what had happened, then every black person has reason to fear that they're still not safe.

ANNE (*shakes her head once again in disbelief*): Seems like there wasn't too much daylight between some Germans and some Americans. I suppose you know that the Germans gassed black people in Europe, too. Along with gypsies, homosexuals, handicapped people. Anyone who didn't fit into their plans for the "master race." Joseph Mengele, the so-called "Angel of Death," and others performed experiments on us, Emmett. Jewish children were put into pressure chambers, castrated, tested with drugs and frozen to death. . . . It was horrible.

Photographs of Mengele's victims appear on screen.

EMMETT: They experimented on us too. Used us as guinea pigs in syphilis experiments. It was called the Tuskegee Experiment. Not to be confused with the Tuskegee Airmen. That's why we still don't trust the health system in America. (*A beat.*)

White men in their lab coats examining black men afflicted with syphilis are on screen.

EMMETT: By the way did you know that they lynched some Jewish people in America? In fact, now that I think about it, they lynched a man named Leo Frank—just like your name.

On screen we see the photograph of Leo Frank.

ANNE : Yes . . . I heard about him. I don't believe we were related. There were a lot of families with that name.

EMMETT: Given everything that has happened to you, I still can't figure out why you said that you still believe in the goodness of people.

ANNE: (*more upbeat*) Well, a lot of people are really sorry for what the world allowed the Nazis to do to us. Did you know that it's now a crime in some parts of Europe to promote anti-Semitism or to insist that the Holocaust didn't exist, was a myth? You can go to jail just for saying that. I'd call that progress.

EMMETT: That's progress, I guess, but Malcolm X said that "You don't stick a knife in a man's back nine inches and then pull it out six inches and say you're making progress."

On Screen we see a film clip of Malcom X.

ANNE: I'm not saying that things are great, just that . . .

EMMETT (*emotional now, interrupts*): In America, the Ku Klux Klan can march down Main Street in any city, praising Hitler, condemning Jews, blacks, and Latinos. And it's all protected under the Constitution. They marched twice in Skokie, Illinois, the city with the largest number of Holocaust survivors in America! And they had police protecting their right of "free speech."

On screen are film clips of the KKK marching in Skokie, while Jewish groups protest.

EMMETT: The Klan's no different than the Nazis. But they get to wrap themselves up in both the Confederate and American flags. They burn a cross, knowing that's the symbol of white terrorism and claim they're just doing what they're entitled to do. Exercising their rights in direct denial of ours . . .

ANNE: I'm sorry, Emmett. I just meant that things were getting better for us. All those companies who stole our property and profited by using our labor and taking our lives have had to pay the families of the victims. Reparations, if you can ever repay for anything so horrible, is what they're making.

EMMETT: Funny, when it comes to black people, no reparations. White folks say that slavery happened too long ago. Statute of limitations ran out. Claim they can't figure out who to pay or how much. So they tell us to shut up and just forget about it. It's history!

Oh, they can keep writing books on Jefferson and not mention he was a great slave owner himself. Let's just forget about that history. Get over it. After all, he was just a man of his times. . . . What I want to know is when does *our* time ever come. How long do we have to wait for equality, for justice?

ANNE: They're wrong, Emmett. Time can't erase a crime. It's never too late for justice. And if scientists can figure out how many years ago God created the universe, it seems to me, they could figure out how much your people are owed.

EMMETT: Yeah, well, not much hope for that. I'd be happy just to see every black family receive free health care, or a college education for everyone who wanted one. That'd be cheap compared to what they really owe.

He hears something off in the distance.

EMMETT: Anne, I th . . . th . . . (*starts to stutter*) think you need to be ca . . . ca . . . carereful. I hear that the sk . . . sk . . . skinheads and neo-Nazis are be . . . bec . . . becoming bolder, especially in Eu . . . Europe.

ANNE: I don't think we have to worry, Emmett. That's all something in the horrible past.

EMMETT: Ah! If only that were tr . . . true (*collects himself*).
Anne, what are you doing up there? What are you writing?

ANNE: Oh, I'm just working on a few more entries into a diary. I'm telling Kitty about some fairy tales, and the play I keep thinking I should write one day. Maybe I'll tell the world what I've learned since the last time the Nazis came for me. Maybe I can write a play about meeting you, Emmett! (*A beat.*)
Emmett, why don't you come up here so I can show you?

EMMETT (*Visibly shrinks back at the suggestion.*): No. I can't. . . .

ANNE: Why not?

EMMETT: You're a white woman. I ca . . . can't . . .

ANNE: Oh, nonsense, Emmett. You don't have to worry any-more.

Seeing that he won't climb to her loft, Anne prepares to descend down the stairs.

In the distance, we hear the subtle sounds of someone approaching. Then, the sound of a door being busted open is heard, and a gust of wind blows Anne's note pages off her desk, causing them to cascade down onto the stage.

At this moment four Nazis wearing SS uniforms and polished black leather boots enter from stage left and goose step across the stage.

An equal number of hooded Klansmen emerge stage right and march toward the SS troops while carrying burning torches. Both groups salute as they cross, shouting "Sig Heil"and "White Power."

In the background the barren tree with the hanging rope reappears. The crematorium's smokestack emerges directly opposite it, its gray smoke floating across the stage, mingling with that coming from the torches.

The Nazis drag Anne by her hair from the stage. She reaches out to try to touch the hand of Emmett as he is being carried off and beaten by the Klansmen. Their hands almost touch.

The stage lights start to dim when on the center screen a large cross suddenly bursts into flame.The cross burns and morphs into a charred swastika.

Anne's voice can be heard as the image of the swastika fades from the screen.

ANNE: "I still believe in the goodness of people. I still believe."

On the screen appear Elie Wiesel's words:

"To forget would be not only dangerous but offensive; to forget the dead would be akin to killing them a second time."

THE END

Index

Abromson, Linda, 33
Adulyadej, Bhumibol, 300
Agnew, Spiro, 220
Albert, Mildred, 211–12
Albright, Madeleine, 313
Alexander, Adele, 10, 257, 267
Alexander, Clifford, 10, 267
Ali, Muhammad, 166–70, 172, 176–77
Allen, George, 162–63
America Alive, 238
America's Black Forum, 265, 267
A.M. New York, 238–39
Amurao, Corazon, 164
Anderson, John, 228
Anderson, Marion, 212
Anne and Emmett, 345–62
Anti-Semitism, 23–24, 29–31, 230, 251. *See also* racism
Armstrong, Louis, 166
Aspin, Les, 304
A-Train: Memoirs of a Tuskegee Airman, 322
Attucks, Crispus, 80. *See also* Crispus Attucks High School
Auerbach, Red, 86–87

Bailey, F. Lee, 256
Bailey, Pearl, 172
Baker, Art, 239
Baker, Howard, 243–45
A Baker's Nickel, 215
Baldacci, Robert, 198–99
Ball, David, 328
basketball, 123. *See also* sports
Bennett, Bob, 238–39
Bennett, Tony, 166
Bennett, William, 287
Bentsen, Lloyd, 245
Beresford, Patrick, 239–40
Berger, Sandy, 313
Berry, Chuck, 157
Berry, Halle, 270–71
Beth Abraham Synagogue, 16–17
Beth Israel Synagogue, 280
bin Laden, Osama, 307, 316–17
Black, Clint, 331
Black Congressional Caucus, 103
Black Entertainment Television (BET), 265, 267, 273, 291, 297
Black History Month, 77
Black Panthers, 211
Bly, Robert, 59

Bodner, Jim, 310
Bond, Julian, 265
Bonin, Ann, 339
Borda, Mike, 10
Bork, Robert, 218
Boston University Law Review, 179
Bowdoin College, 30–31, 93–100,
    104–5, 109–11, 118–20, 141,
    151, 202, 311
Bradley, Bill, 243
Bradshaw, Terry, 328
Bridges, Floyd, 139
Bridges, Sewell, 37, 41–43,
    65–66, 137–39
Brokaw, Tom, 328
Brooke, Ed, 238
"Brother Z and the Decades,"
    96–99
Brown v. Board of Education, 78, 81
Brown, Alma, 10
Brown, April, 83–84, 128–29,
    133, 159
Brown, David, 291
Brown, H. Rap, 165
Brown, Jim, 328
Brown, Ron, 10, 173
Brown, Saul, 20–23, 34
Brown, Willa B., 156
Brynner, Yul, 212–13
Bryson, Peabo, 328
Burke, Yvonne Braithwaite, 205
Burton, Richard, 212
Bush, George W., 285
busing, 207–8, 235
Butler University, 124, 128, 133
Butler, Caldwell, 231
Butler, Ovid, 128

Butler, Richard, 315
Byrd, Robert, 245
Byrne, Matthew, 220

Calloway, Cab, 172
Camp Kohut, 31
Camp Lown, 20
Capitol Building, 5–6
Carpenter, Mary Chapin, 328
Carroll, Jon, 328
Carter, Betty, 267
Carter, Jimmy, 244
Caruso, Annie, 55
Cass, Melnea, 211, 237–38
Castro, Fidel, 106
Cataldo, Alfred, 185
Chaffee, John, 8
Chamberlain, Joshua Lawrence,
    121, 311
Chester, Peter, 31
Chicago, 155–56, 164, 166
Chiles, Lawton, 202
Chisholm, Shirley, 267
Clark, Wesley, 317
Clay, Cassius. *See* Ali, Muhammad
Clinton, Bill, 292, 299–300,
    302–5, 313–15, 327, 338
Clooney, George, 284
Coffey, Cornelius, 157
Cohen, Christopher, 9–10, 32,
    179, 205, 275, 301–2
Cohen, Clara Irene Hartley
    (mother of William), 13–14,
    21–22, 26, 54–55, 87–88,
    279–80
Cohen, Harry (grandfather of
    William), 14, 16, 49–50, 54–55

Cohen, Janet Langhart, 252; *Anne and Emmett* (play), 345–62; birth, 35, 40; career, 134–36, 153, 155–56, 158, 166, 174–75, 208, 254; childhood, 82–83; education, 84, 128–33; family history, 129; Lockefield Gardens, 65–66, 67–69, 71–74; and the Pentagon, 319–30; political role, 332, 338, 341; racism, 76, 80, 130–31, 257, 323; religion, 68–69, 79, 130–31, 132; meeting William Cohen, 257–62, 275; wedding to William Cohen, 2–11

Cohen, Kevin (son of William), 9–10, 152, 204–5, 275, 301–2

Cohen, Marlene (sister of William), 14, 64, 105

Cohen, Mickey, 57

Cohen, Reuben (father of William), 61–63, 87–88, 92–93, 279; career, 52–54, 85–86, 89; death, 2; marriage, 13–14; religion, 17–19, 23; sports, 28, 57–59, 60

Cohen, Richard (uncle of William), 52, 54

Cohen, Robert, 339

Cohen, William: birth, 51; career, 141, 152; and Catholicism, 14–16; childhood, 25–26, 56–57, 85–86; college, 92–99, 100–1, 111–120; education, 13, 16–17, 18–20; law practice, 184–89, 190–92; law school, 144, 145–48, 179; marriage to Diana Dunn, 141–43; meeting Janet Langhart, 257–59, 260–62, 275; name change, 30–31; political career, 194, 195–98, 231, 233, 241, 249; racism, 101–5; religious identity, 14–22, 23–25, 32–34; retirement, 3, 335–37, 340–42; as Secretary of Defense, 300–306, 309, 312, 316; sports, 20–21, 27–30, 60, 92–93, 101; wedding to Janet Langhart, 2–11. *See also individual family members*

Coleman, Bessie, 156–57

Coleman, Bill, 10

Coleman, Len, 294–95

Coleman, Linda, 94

Coleman, Lovida, 10

Collingsworth, Chris, 328

A Coney Island of the Mind, 214

Congress, culture of, 2–3

Conyers, John, 228

Cooke, David O. "Doc," 324, 327

Cooke, Sam, 157

Cordie's Castle, 134–35

Cosby, Bill, 271

Count Basie, 115

Cox, Archibald, 218, 226–27

Coyne, Dudley, 30

Crawford, Thomas, 6

Crispus Attucks High School, 124–27, 134

Crowe, Ray, 125

Dane, Nathan II, III, 145
Danforth, John, 245
Davis, Benjamin O., 267, 321, 323
Davis, Jefferson, 6
Davis, Sammy, Jr., 135
Dawkins, Pete, 4
Day, John, 197
DeLavallade, Carmen, 267
DeLay, Tom, 315
Dellums, Ron, 199
The Diary of Anne Frank, 132–33
Dole, Bob, 249
The Dorothy Dandridge Story, 271
The Double Man, 215
Douglas, William O., 220
Douglass, Frederick, 287–88, 267

Eskridge, Chauncey, 165–66
Essence, 270

Farrakhan, Louis, 267
Fauntroy, Walter, 265
Federal Bureau of Investigation (FBI), 247–49
Ferlinghetti, Lawrence, 214, 258
Fernandez, Jean-Marie, 278
Fernandez, Raul, 278
Fessenden, William Pitt, 219
Fiddler on the Roof, 274
Fiedler, Arthur, 328
Fish, Hamilton, 228–29
Flowers, Walter, 231–32
Floyd, Russell, 37, 66
Flynn, Kelly, 311
Fogleman, Ron, 312

Foley, Howard, 182–83, 193, 201, 241
Ford, Gerald, 219, 220
Ford, Jim, 3–4, 9–10
Forman, Stanley, 208
Forrestal, James, 310–11
Frank, Anne, 132–33, 235, 289
Franken, Al, 328, 331
Freakonomics, 287
Freedom of Information Act, 170
Freeman, Morgan, 77, 297
Freidan, Betty, 212
Frost, Robert, 12
Fugitive Slave Act (1850), 5

Galbraith, John Kenneth, 205
Garrity, W. Arthur, Jr., 207
General Motors, 158
Gide, Andre, 2
Gillenwaters, George (great–uncle of Janet Langhart), 36–37, 45–47
Gillenwaters, James (great–grandfather of Janet Langhart), 36
Gillenwaters, Leola, 36, 43, 44
Gillenwaters, Louise (mother of Janet Langhart), 36–38, 67, 71–74, 82–83, 237; and racism, 43–44; religion, 68–70, 79
Gillenwaters, Myrna, 36–37, 45–46, 81
Gingrich, Newt, 246, 313
Glenn, Annie, 10
Glenn, John, 10, 243, 245
Goldwater, Barry, 232, 246

The Good Day Show, 215. *See also The Good Morning Show*
The Good Morning Show, 208, 213
Gopin, Benny, 63
Gorbachev, Mikhail, 152–53
Gore, Al, 304–5, 313
Grant, Ulysses S., 121
Graves, Earl, 267
Greason, Leroy, 100, 118
Gregory, Dick, 159–60, 181
Guerin, Richie, 141

Haley, Alex, 48
Hart, Gary, 243, 246
Hartley, Clara Irene. *See* Cohen, Clara Irene Hartley
Hatfield, Mark, 4
Hathaway, Bill, 183–84, 201, 241
Havana, 105–8
Hayes, Isaac, 158
Hee, Park Chung, 244
Herbert, Bob, 272
Hicks, Louise Day, 207
Ho, David, 331
Holder, Geoffrey, 267
Holmes, Oliver Wendell, Jr., 152, 197
Holocaust, 288
Hoover, J. Edgar, 168–70, 173
Horne, Lena, 157, 268, 323
Horton, George, 89
Howard University, 103, 322
Hughes, Langston, 48, 128
Hughes Brothers Construction Company, 112
Hungate, Bill, 278–79
Hussein, Saddam, 307, 315

Hutchinson, Ed, 225, 227–28
Hutchisson, Marion "Hutch," 292, 296, 325, 338–39
Hutton, Lauren, 212

Ibrahim, Anwar, 300
Indiana, 75–76, 128
Indiana University, 133
Indy Today with Janet Langhart, 175
Inouye, Daniel, 250
Iran–Contra, 250

Jackson, Edward, 78
Jackson, Henry "Scoop," 245
Jackson, Jackie, 165
Jackson, Jesse, 165
Jackson, Mahalia, 158–59, 163, 173, 176
Jacobs, Andrew, 65–66
Javits, Jacob, 245
Jaworski, Leon, 226–27
Jefferson, Thomas, 80, 233
Jenner, Bert, 225, 238
Jet, 82, 135, 157, 166, 175
Jeter, Mildred, 7
Jewell, Bob, 127
Jim Crow, 80–81, 125, 137, 320
Johnson, Bob, 10, 265, 297
Johnson, Eunice W., 135
Johnson, John H., 82, 157–58, 176
Johnson, Lyndon, 160, 225
Johnson, Mark, 293
Jolie, Angelina, 284
Jones, Alice, 257, 258
Jones, James Logan, 310
Jones, Quincy, 267

Jordan, Barbara, 205, 230, 267
Jordan, Michael, 122
Judaism, 16–18

Kassebaum, Nancy, 243
Kazan, Elia, 214
Kendrick, Nathaniel, 99, 109,
 114
Kennedy, John, 152–54, 182,
 225–26
Kennedy, Robert, 154, 170–71
Kennedy, Ted, 238
King, Carole, 328
King, Cordie, 134–35, 155, 338
King, Coretta, 171
King, Larry, 266
King, Martin Luther, Jr., 5–6, 80,
 154, 159–65, 169–72,
 199–200, 209–10, 235, 249;
 death, 172–74
Kistner, Robert, 236–37, 252–53,
 255–56, 277
Ku Klux Klan (KKK), 30, 35, 75,
 78–80, 125, 128, 209, 268

Lamarr, Hedy, 268–69
Lambert, Elizabeth, 339
Lambert, Thomas F., Jr., 179–82,
 309, 339
Lane, Russell, 83, 125
Langhart, Janet. *See* Cohen, Janet
 Langhart
laws. *See* miscegenation laws
Lee, Bernard, 165
Lee, Robert E., 121
Lee, Spike, 267, 270
Lewinsky, Monica, 315

Lewis, Ramsey, 267
Liacos, Paul, 147
Liebengood, Howard, 247, 249
Lilly, Eli, 127
Liman, Arthur, 250
Linkletter, Jack, 238
Liston, Sonny, 167
Live with Regis and Kathy Lee, 238
Livingston, Bob, 313
Loane, Alan, 301–2
Lockefield Gardens, 65–68,
 71–75
Loeb, William, 212
Lombardi, Vince, 120
Long, Howie, 328
Lott, Trent, 8
Louis, Joe, 98
Loving v. Virginia, 7
Loving, Richard, 7
lynching, 160–62

Malcolm X, 165
Mandingo, 286
Mann, Jim, 231
Marshall, George, 310–11
Mathias, Charles "Mac," 245
McCain, John, 244, 292, 310
McCauley, Thomas B., 193
McCloskey, Pete, 247
McGovern, George, 223
McNamara, Robert, 319–20
McRaney, Gerald, 328
Medieros, Humberto, 208
Milosevic, Slobodan, 313
Minor, Shane, 328
Minsky, Norman, 142
miscegenation laws, 6–7

Miss Chicagoland Beauty Pageant, 166
Mitchell, George, 300
Mitchell, John, 221
Monahan, Henry, 148
Monks, Robert Augustus Gardiner, 200–201
Monster's Ball, 271
Morrell, Malcolm, 119, 121
Moynihan, Daniel Patrick, 205, 245
Mundy, Carl, 327
Muskie, Edmund, 10, 184, 202, 245
Muskie, Jane, 10

Nealley, Bill, 196
Negro History Week, 84
The New You Asked For It, 239
Newman, Paul, 286
Nixon, Richard, 87, 199, 213, 217–23, 226, 231–33, 315
North, Oliver, 250
Nunn, Sam, 243–245

Oberholtzer, Madge, 78
Oberlin College, 117
O'Leary, Charles "Chick," 28
O'Neil, Tip, 238 ·
Oswald, Lee Harvey, 154
Owens, Jesse, 166

Paine, Errol, 86, 91, 184–85, 188, 196
Palestinian Liberation Organization (PLO), 238
Parks, Rosa, 267

Patterson, Floyd, 166, 167
Patton, George S., Jr., 42
Paul Nixon Award for Leadership, 119
Percy, Charles, 164
Percy, Valerie, 164
Perot, Ross, 328
Perry, Lee, 326
Perry, William, 299, 306–7, 310, 326
Pershing, John "Black Jack," 310
Personal Diary with Janet Langhart, 267
Planning, Mark, 160
Point du Sable, Jean Baptiste, 156
Pointer, Ruth, 328
Poitier, Sidney, 157, 270, 286
Polk Milk, 76–77
Poolaw, Bruce, 204
Potholm, Christan Peter, 142, 202–3
Pound, Elizabeth, 180
Pound, Roscoe, 180
Powell, Alma, 10
Powell, Colin, 10, 283
Preston, Billy, 159
Proctor, Millicent, 10
Psi Upsilon, 113–14, 93

The Quill, 114

Rabin, Yitzhak, 288
race relations, 78–80, 130, 283. *See also* racism
racism, 35, 36, 38–40, 43–46, 76–78, 83, 101–4, 136, 161,

255, 260, 274–75, 287–88. *See also* anti-Semitism, lynching
Railsback, Tom, 213–14, 228–29, 231–32, 242, 246
Ralston, Joseph, 311–12, 316–17
Randolph County High School (Alabama), 7–8
Rather, Dan, 212
Ray, James Earl, 153, 173
Reagan, Ronald, 152–53, 249, 251–52
Redding, Otis, 157
religion, 14, 68–70, 210
Reserve Officers' Training Corps (ROTC), 141
Revere, Paul, 80
Rhinelander, Leonard, 257–58
Ribicoff, Abraham, 245
Rice, Condoleezza, 283
Richardson, Anne, 10
Richardson, Elliot, 10, 218–19
Rist, Jimmy, 57
Robertson, Oscar, 122, 125
Robinson, Jackie, 42, 166
Rodino, Pete, 217, 224–25, 227–29
Rooney, Mickey, 328
Roosevelt, Eleanor, 30, 321
Roosevelt, Franklin D., 65, 322
Ross, Brian, 161
Roxbury High, 207–8
Ruckleshaus, Bill, 218
Rudman, Warren, 250
Russell, Richard, 160
Rustin, Bayard, 171

Sartre, Jean Paul, 151
Scavullo, Francesco, 258–59

Schmidt, Helmut, 18
School Daze, 270
Schwalier, Terry, 312
Schwarzenegger, Arnold, 266
Seale, Bobby, 211
Searcy, Edgar, 128
Shalikashvili, John, 311
Sharman, Bill, 141
Sharon, Ariel, 288
Shelley, Percy Bysshe, 215
Shelton, Hugh, 311–12, 339
Shuman, Barry, 90–91
Sidarth, S. R., 162
Singletary, Mike, 328
Sirhan, Sirhan, 153
Siskind, Paul, 144–45, 191
Smith, Henry, 231
Smith, Jack, 239
Smith, Margaret Chase, 201, 219, 229
Smith, Susan, 47
Soloby, Wanda, 51
The Souls of Black Folk, 132
South Boston High, 207–8
Southern Christian Leadership Conference (SCLC), 170–71
Special Assignment with Janet Cohen, 327
Speck, Richard, 164
Spielberg, Steven, 331
sports, 20–21, 27–30, 57–60
Sprague, Millicent, 201
Stallone, Sylvester, 266
Steelman, Alan, 205
Stephenson, David, 78
Stimson, Henry L., 322
Stuart, Charles, 47
Stuart, Marion "Mayday," 75, 135

Student Nonviolent Coordinating Committee (SNCC), 165
Sun Tzu, 95
Sunday Open House, 239
Swanson, Gloria, 212
Symbionese Liberation Army (SLA), 211

Tandy, Jessica, 297
Teng, Sambo, 295–97
Terrell, Ernie, 167
Thurmond, Strom, 8–9
Thurston, John, 165
Thurston, Morris, 90–91
Till, Emmett, 81–82, 159, 289
Topol, 274, 288
Tower, John, 245–46
Truman, Harry, 41
Tufts Dental School, 148
Tuskegee Institute, 322–23
Tyrer, Bob, 310

U.S. Communist Party, 170
The Understudy, 214
University of Miami, 109
USS Cole, 330
USS Harry Truman, 328
USS John F. Kennedy, 337
USS Winston S. Churchill, 338

Vashem, Yad, 288
Vietnam War, 157, 168, 199, 301

Wag the Dog, 314
Waldie, Jerome, 228
Walker Art Museum, 117
Walker, C. J., 75
Walker, Dan, 202
Wallace, George, 200
Warren, Earl, 7
Washington, Denzel, 270
Wattleton, Faye, 267
West, Jerry, 33
West, Kanye, 285
Westmoreland, William C., 321
White, Kevin, 238
Wiggins, Chuck, 217
Wilbanks, Jennifer, 47
Willis, John, 213
Winfrey, Oprah, 283
Wing, Charlie, 30–31, 114–17, 146

Young Men's Christian Association (YMCA), 20–21, 60, 75
Young, Andrew, 159, 214, 238

Zoidis, Robert "Ziggy," 96–99

Introduction

The issues that surround the general problem of investigating the nature and extent of human knowledge are known collectively by philosophers as the problems of epistemology. It is very important to realize from the beginning that epistemology is never undertaken from a completely naïve position. By the time any philosopher comes to reflect on the problem of what human beings can be said to know, he has already acquired a reasonably formidable education and some degree of sophistication. It is impossible for a philosopher to discover what he knows by simply thinking back to the time when nothing was known to him (if there was such a time) and then slowly tracing the acquisition of his knowledge. Indeed, another question must be answered first: what is described when one speaks of human knowledge? Unless this question is answered, a study of epistemology is totally useless, since it would not be possible to distinguish those moments which represented the acquisition of knowledge from those moments which represented, for example, the acquisition of nonsense.

The philosopher who is interested in epistemology is thus forced to begin in the middle of things by examining the results of what would normally be called his education. He will surely say a variety of things which might be cast into the general grammatical form 'I know that ———.', where the blank space is filled with a phrase describing some item of information. Among these statements the following examples, or claims of a similar nature, may well occur:

1. I know that $3 + 5 = 8$.
2. I know that it will rain this afternoon.
3. I know that something caused the water to stop running.
4. I know that the Dodgers will win the pennant.
5. I know that I left the back door unlatched.

The grammatical similarity of form which the statements of this list exhibit

1

is not taken by any important philosopher to represent a single sense of the word *know*, since we feel quite differently on reflection about the certainty of the various things that are said to be known on any complete list which would be an extension of the list of statements just given. In some intuitive sense, we surely feel less secure about some of the items than about others.

One question often asked of someone who says 'I know that ———— .' is 'Are you sure (that ————)?'. With reference to the list, someone uttering all of the examples at various times might feel that 1–3 are all true, but that 4 and 5 are open to doubt and may in fact not be true if some check were to be made. In this case, he may say that he *knows* (in some stronger sense) only the items of information referred to in the first three sentences. The point is that when we are asked what we know in a situation where we must defend against possibly hostile criticism, we are likely to be more cautious in our claims to information than we would be at other times. And in the face of sustained criticism, we may often want to retreat to the position that we *know* only those things which are not open to any reasonable objection.

A great deal of technical philosophical epistemology has been developed by philosophers who have subjected the results of their own formal education or official schooling to severe and hostile criticism in an effort to winnow out those claims which will stand against any reasonable doubt. A philosopher may suddenly discover that he says that he knows many things of palpably differing certainty, or even that some of his information is contradictory. An obvious way of proceeding at this point to answer the question of the extent of his knowledge is to pick from it some examples he is certain are most defensible in some intuitive sense. Studying these examples, he can then look for some qualities that distinguish them from examples that he feels can be or should be questioned, if not dropped outright from the information that he wishes to take as defensible knowledge. On the basis of this investigation, a philosopher usually ends by giving a definition of *knowledge*, as distinct from *opinion* or *belief*. *Knowledge* then constitutes those claims that he thinks are ultimately defensible, while *opinion* or *belief* constitutes those claims for which *some* justification is possible, but not a complete defense. This way of looking at the start of epistemological investigations stresses the investigator's *feeling* of certainty about some of his knowledge claims. Because of this, it would not be surprising that different investigators should select different examples of knowledge as the basis of their definitions. Indeed the notion of *reasonable* objection is subjective to the point that we would expect major philosophers to disagree over the examples that may be accepted as paradigm or model instances of human knowledge. We will look at the basic epistemological problem not as that of discovering the *true* extent of human knowledge, but as that of *deciding* which of our ordinary knowledge claims can properly be called examples of human knowledge, and then of investigating the difference between these examples and examples of opinion in an effort to *justify* the decision. We will consider seven major philosophers who have chosen differently the paradigm cases of knowledge, and we will do this in an effort to determine how epistemology may enable us to make a consistent theory of knowledge out of the confusing class of purported claims to knowledge that accrue when we listen to those who profess to know something. In epistemology one does not try to build a system of knowledge from nothing, but one tries to *select* some relatively clear examples of knowledge in order to discover what else may reasonably be considered knowledge. On such a basis it is possible to create a consistent and useful account of all human information.

It should be immediately clear that the epistemological problem is one of the most basic problems of philosophy. An answer to it must be either found or presupposed before one can answer the more specific questions "What can I know about the world? (science)" or "What can I know about behaving in a moral fashion? (ethics)" or "What can I know about beauty? (aesthetics)" or any of the other questions that occupy philosophers with specialized interests.

Our survey of different positions with respect to some of the basic problems of epistemology will be made by considering seven major philosophers of the Western philosophical tradition. We shall do this by considering these seven philosophers in the order of their historical appearance, although biographical information about these philosophers will be almost totally suppressed. For our purposes they will be treated as contemporaries, that is, as though their basic positions could still be maintained by present-day philosophers. As a matter of fact, variations of these seven positions are taken by present-day philosophers (as well as other positions which we will not consider), although a present-day Platonist, for example, would have to defend against more subtle criticisms raised by other philosophers than Plato had to defend against. This has resulted in modifications of some of the positions which major historical figures seem to have argued for.

Of the seven philosophers, the first two, Plato and Aristotle, are distinguished by their appearance in Greek culture over two thousand years ago. In broad outlines, they established the problems that have occupied epistemologists to the present day, subject only to the more sophisticated problems that some recent discoveries in the natural sciences have raised. For this reason, they occupy a particularly important place in the history of Western philosophy. Plato and Aristotle, along with some other Greek philosophers, may be looked on as the beginning of epistemology as we have characterized it, and this appearance of epistemological problems in Greek thought unpreceded by any other epistemological reflection is worth some detailed consideration.

Perhaps the most important characteristic of Greek philosophy, that which may ultimately be judged to be the most important reason for its continuing influence, is its dependence upon human reason for the solution of problems. This statement raises a tangle of problems that are difficult to deal with. The first of these is the question of what is meant by human reason. Rather than attempting an answer to this question here, in view of the immense problems which the question of the nature of human reason has raised in philosophy and psychology, we can make useful progress without controversy by simply identifying it with what many people refer to when they speak of the human mind as an instrument for evaluating and organizing human experience. Exactly what this suggests is a matter of dispute, but it may make enough initial sense for us to say that the Greeks *thought as we do in many important respects,* and that they considered thought to be a process associated with the *human individual.*

The significance of the latter remark may not be clear without some reference to history. Prior to Greek philosophy, if thought was discussed at all, it was evidently supposed that the ideas in the mind and thought associated with them were explicable, not in terms of the individual thinking, but in terms of some god (or some sort of being beyond the influence of direct human control) who *caused* the human to have the ideas and the thought processes in order to direct his activity. This view of man as being in the control of higher agencies seems to predominate in cultures earlier than Greek culture whenever anything like thought is referred to. It is even in the early view of the Greeks, exhibited in Homer's *Iliad* and *Odyssey,* where we find instances of thoughts being implanted in the minds of the heroes of those epics by gods desirous of influencing the outcome of events. Between 600 and 300 B.C., however, which is the period that produced the important Greek philosophy which is still studied, many Greek philosophers and scientists (the distinction was not explicitly made by the Greeks) adopted the view that reason was something under individual control. This view, that reason is a process associated with human individuals, and in important respects a process under their control, has had important consequences for philosophy. For example, in ordinary moral judgments we do not consider the person who has made a bad moral choice in quite the same way as a person who has acted similarly but who cannot be said to have made a choice because he was compelled to act as he did. A psychotic is simply not morally culpable (he is *compelled* by insanity to do the act in question) as is a sane individual who deliberately chooses his action from among moral alternatives. This distinction is reflected in the way that the two cases are treated separately in courts of law. Morality, or ethics, in the contemporary sense, can only exist for individuals who have control, or choice, over their decision. Thus, the problem of which choice from among a range of choices is the best one is an ethical question only in the context of the view that human beings have control over their own actions. It is first formulated in the modern sense by the Greek philosophers, perhaps as a direct result of their views about human individualism.

Notice that it would not be correct to suppose that human individualism in the sense that each human being has control over his own thinking and action is to be necessarily equated with individualism in another sense, that of supposing that each human being is totally unlike every other and that any individual's choice is as good as any other individual's choice. On the contrary, and as we shall see in Plato and Aristotle, many Greeks supposed that the sustained use of reason would have the result that human beings could eventually hope to have a common standard of judgment, so that properly educated individuals, although each would do his thinking for himself, would have a common standard of truth in ethics and aesthetics as well as in the more obvious cases of mathematics and science. For Plato and Aristotle, individualism of the second kind is the result of lives based upon sensual pleasure rather than upon reason as a basis of choice. Not all Greek philosophers, however, would agree with Plato and Aristotle, and this point is raised here only to suggest that the mere adoption of the view that reason is under the control of the individual does not dictate the answers to the problems of philosophy, at least not until reason receives further clarification, and the philosophers have not agreed upon such a clarification, as we shall see.

Perhaps the similarity between what we call reason and what the Greek philosophers called reason (in contrast to earlier views) can best be brought out by an example, rather than by a straightforward definition or a pronouncement about intellectual history. Even the example about to be given cannot be defended as necessarily historical, but at the very least it is a charming story compatible with history that illustrates the difference that has here been claimed. Consider the so-called Pythagorean theorem from plane geometry as it is traditionally taught in school. The name of the theorem refers to Pythagoras, a Greek philosopher, although one of the historical problems is whether Pythagoras or a student of his first established it by a proof like that given below. The theorem, of course, is that the sum of the squares of the legs of a right-angled triangle is identical with the square of its hypotenuse. (The Greek influence is everywhere, as a check of the etymology of *hypotenuse* in the dictionary will confirm.) We may summarize that information by the expression '$a^2 + b^2 = c^2$', where a and b stand for the legs of some arbitrary right triangle, and c for its hypotenuse. Strictly speaking, a, b, and c stand for the *length* of the respective sides as represented by some number, although the Greeks gave this length a purely geometrical significance, as we will see in the proof given below.

The theorem of Pythagoras is not a piece of mathematical knowledge which just suddenly appeared in Greek history. Scattered mathematical information can be found in the remains of civilizations which long antedate Pythagoras, for example, in Babylonian and Egyptian documents. What is instructive in this case is to compare what the Egyptians did with mathematics with the approach that Pythagoras took, as an illustration of how strikingly modern Pythagoras's approach appears when we contrast it with what had gone before. Apparently some Egyptian, or perhaps several, had come across the following useful piece of information, perhaps entirely by accident; that is, they discovered it without consciously looking for a solution to the problem that it solves. By tying two knots in a long piece of cord or rope at some arbitrary distance apart (a relatively small distance with respect to the total length of the cord), it is possible to produce a series of equal lengths in the cord by tying more knots at the same distance from one another as the first two using the length marked by the first two as a standard. Suppose that thirteen such knots are tied, resulting in twelve equal lengths marked off on the cord or rope. Now suppose that the thirteenth knot and the first are held together, and the rope staked out on the ground by fixing the first and thirteenth knots together under one stake, and then stretching out three lengths in one direction, staking that down, and then stretching out the remainder of the rope by dividing it into lengths of four and five by seizing it at the proper point, stretching it out, and staking it down. The result would be a figure like this:

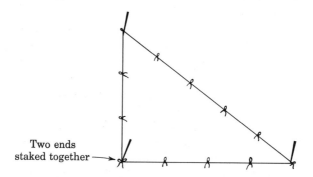

The Egyptians discovered that this device, as well as other devices somewhat like it, proved useful in surveying and building measurement, since it could be used to determine the corners of rectangular fields or buildings. Although the Egyptians were able to use these rather isolated discoveries, they do not seem to have been tormented by the problem of explaining their success. At any rate no clear and distinct record of work on problems explaining the success of these devices exists, and no systematic treatment of geometry along the lines of Euclid's *Elements* is found until the Greeks worked on the problem. In a sense, the Egyptian discoveries may be looked on as *practical* devices for solving particular problems, in contrast to the Greek penchant for theoretical knowledge and solutions to general problems as represented by the Greek philosophical tradition.

By way of contrast to the Egyptian device just mentioned, let us consider what may have been the Pythagorean proof of the theorem that the sum of the squares of the legs of a right-angled triangle is identical with the square of the hypotenuse. Consider the following two drawings:

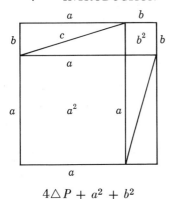

$$4\triangle P + a^2 + b^2$$

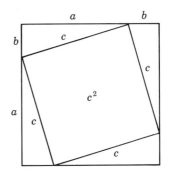

$$4\triangle P + c^2$$

Let two legs of an arbitrary right-angled triangle be represented by a and b, and the hypotenuse by c. Each of the drawings is constructed by placing the arbitrary triangle in the upper left-hand corner, extending the legs, and building up the figure by placing replicas of the triangle in various positions with respect to the original triangle and its extended legs. A brief examination of the drawings will show how this can be done without going through the tedious detail of describing it step by step here. The result of performing these constructions consists of two squares, each of side $a + b$. The area of either of these squares is identical with that of the other, namely, $(a + b)^2$. Examining what is inside these two squares is somewhat interesting. In each of the squares four of the original triangles have been used. The one square contains an area equal to c^2, and the other square contains two areas equal to a^2 and b^2, in addition to the four triangles which appear in each square. If we call the triangle with which the construction was started triangle P, then the contents of each of the squares is summarized in an obvious way by the expression under each of the squares. But we know that the area of each of the squares is equal to that of the other, so that their areas are identical, a fact which we may state by means of the expression

$$4\triangle P + a^2 + b^2 = 4\triangle P + c^2$$

where the equality sign stands for the identity of the two areas. At this point the solution is plain to anyone, but we do need some kind of justification for canceling out the expression $4\triangle P$ on each side of our identity. The Greeks took a rule like "Equals subtracted from equals produce equals." to justify this cancellation. Although this rule is not obviously true, as the Greeks thought, it does justify this cancellation and the resultant proof of the expression $a^2 + b^2 = c^2$, which is interpreted according to our previous stipulations as a statement of the Pythagorean theorem.

A present day geometer would not be entirely happy with what has just transpired, and he would insist that a number of turns in the argument be clarified, as well as that the assumptions of the argument be made explicit. We assumed, for example, that the triangle we started with was a right-angled triangle, so that one would have to understand what is meant by a right-angled triangle before he could follow this proof. Further, the dependence of the proof on the drawings which we exhibited would be dropped. Drawings are not always reliable, for they may smuggle in extra assumptions as in the classic "proof" that all triangles are isosceles, which is reproduced in many elementary geometry texts. Nevertheless, the feeling that we have in following the argument just exhibited is a comfortable one: it is just like a great many arguments that we meet with every intellectual day. As a matter of fact, it can very easily be brought up to date, and the very fact that the proof is so intuitively convincing makes it the kind of knowledge that one can build on, in contrast to the rope figure, which is just an interesting curiosity, no matter how useful it might be, as it stands. The Pythagorean theorem suggests that other theorems might be proved in a similar way, so to speak, so that it is *stimulating* in a way that the discovery of accidental matters of fact can never be.

One aspect of the Pythagorean theorem deserves special attention in this context. Notice that the theorem does not mention any *particular* triangle, but affirms that a certain relationship will hold in any right-angled triangle whatsoever. In our statement of the theorem this is handled by allowing a, b, and c to be variables which stand for the legs and hypotenuse of any right-angled triangle that one might care to start with. In using variables in this fashion, our statement really summarizes what might otherwise have to be stated by a long series of statements, each one of which would mention the legs and hypotenuse of a particular triangle. Thus, we may look at the Pythagorean theorem as an explanation of a great many particular facts in terms of some simple concepts and variables which reason manipulates to convince us that the great number of facts is true without the necessity of our checking each one individually. No matter how sophisticated this basic claim may become, and it will become a great deal more sophisticated when made by a contemporary philosopher, it is nevertheless true that without some method of explaining a wide variety of particular facts by means of general concepts and some tactical aids like variables, science and mathematics as we know them would be impossible. It is not surprising that epistemologists since the Greeks have been concerned with finding an explanation for the existence of *general* human knowledge in this sense.

Another aspect of the Pythagorean theorem is important for the history of philosophical epistemology. The Pythagorean theorem is the kind of statement which may be defended against any reasonable doubt, and hence it furnishes along with other examples of provable mathematical truths, an example of knowledge which virtually every philosopher since the Greeks has included in his paradigm cases of human knowledge. In rebuttal of criticism, a sufficiently educated geometer can defend the steps of reasoning involved by reference to principles which it is unreasonable to doubt if anything is unreasonable to doubt. As a consequence, philosophers have generally supposed that at least *some* of the properties of mathematical knowledge would have to be properties of knowledge in general. The remaining sections of this book will exhibit the profound impact of this point of view on Western philosophers.

The general epistemological problem of separating purported information into the categories of knowledge and opinion has already been introduced. It is clear that the problem of drawing such an epistemological distinction might be undertaken with respect to a very limited field of interest. One might, for example, be interested in separating knowledge from opinion about some restricted problem, such as finding the best strategy for winning at checkers. Any person undertaking epistemological clarification of any problem, no matter how restricted, can be considered as thinking along philosophical lines, provided that he makes a reasonable effort to be impartial in conducting his analysis. The major philosophers of the Western philosophical tradition, including the seven that are considered in this book, have earned their importance partly because they have attempted epistemological clarification of a very wide range of purported beliefs which are associated with various human interests. In most cases, the major philosophers have attempted to sketch out some method of distinguishing knowledge and opinion in all sustained areas of human inquiry.

PART 1
Plato

(427–347 B.C.)

The Theory of Ideas

Plato's importance for the history of philosophy is grounded in the fact that he attempted to provide a theory of knowledge which would separate knowledge from opinion in all the major intellectual controversies of his time. His continuing importance is due to the fact that the intellectual controversies of his time were in many cases concerned with problems that are still the subject of intellectual dispute, and to the fact that his solution of the epistemological problems posed by these disputes is still thought by many people to provide a justifiable and logically consistent position for present-day philosophers.

There are interesting historical reasons for the important disagreements among the Greeks that Plato considered, but exploring the historical background adequately is not a necessary prerequisite for understanding the important positions that Plato reached as a result of his philosophical activity. For our purposes we may merely note that Greek civilization had beaten off Persian invaders of overwhelming numerical superiority about a hundred years before Plato wrote his philosophical works, an event which seems to have raised for the Greeks the question of accounting for their obvious qualitative superiority. But soon after this victory over the Persians, the Greeks, who lived in small groups called city-states, which were largely autonomous in their military, political, economic, and cultural organization, found themselves fighting internal civil wars. The important Greek city-states on opposite sides of the biggest of these civil wars, Athens and Sparta, were quite distinct in terms of traditions associated with the various aspects of city-state life that have just been mentioned. Sparta defeated Athens in the war, but did not completely crush Athens. In the years after the war, Athenians raised the issue of the causes of their defeat, an issue which developed into an examination of what was best in Greek life. Part of this examination was devoted explicitly to the question of which form of city-state government was most desirable.

Plato was confronted with a welter of opinions on the matter, ranging

13

from traditional religious answers to skeptical views expressed by itinerant lecturers who were known as sophists. The religious tradition, like many religious traditions, supposed that there was divine guidance of human affairs and that wars were lost through failure to obey divine instructions. The sophists, on the other hand, who were cosmopolitan travelers and lecturers, pointed out that this kind of religious view was taken on both sides of any war and might consequently be ruled out as worthless with increasing sophistication. Sophists also urged skepticism against those philosophers who contended that some *form* of government was the secret to city-state success, arguing that human failure would corrupt any constitutional imposition of democratic or autocratic forms of government on a society. In addition to the political controversies of his time, Plato dealt with controversies over what was beautiful and what was morally good. Plato attempted to find philosophical solutions to these problems, even though it may be said that he seems to have exhibited aristocratic bias in some of his attitudes. We do not have to be concerned with this bias in discussing whether or not the solutions that he proposed were adequate.

In order to answer these special problems, Plato dealt with the more general epistemological question "What can we know?". In other words, Plato was interested in establishing what constituted human knowledge in any area, on the grounds that this would enable a careful investigator to decide which problems connected with some particular political, aesthetic, or ethical debate were definitely soluble and which were merely confusions based on conflicting opinion.

It is impossible to avoid assumptions in philosophy, but this does not vitiate philosophical investigation, since it would be unreasonable to demand that everything be proved. What is interesting to the philosopher is the question of which assumptions it would be best to adopt for some given purpose. One of Plato's assumptions seems to have been that human beings do have some knowledge. It is pretty easy to argue that this is a reasonable assumption, and Plato was given to exhibiting his assumption as true by pointing out examples of human knowledge. Some of his examples, and these are crucial examples for all of subsequent philosophy, are taken from familiar areas of mathematics. Consider two simple examples: the Pythagorean theorem of elementary geometry, which was proved earlier, and the arithmetic sum "$2+2=4$.". It is important to keep these examples in mind, since Plato uses mathematical examples to make an extremely important point: that truths of arithmetic and geometry seem to be examples of unquestionable truths, the certainty of which is sufficient to prove complete skepticism false. Plato also used other examples from ordinary skills, and he pointed out that crafts like piloting vessels and making shoes involve *knowledge*, in the sense that successful practitioners of these crafts might be said to know some things that others do not know. The pilot, for example, knows that certain areas of a harbor are too shallow for certain ships to pass over. Argument about claims made in these areas could be settled by appeal to someone with the appropriate knowledge. A skilled mathematician, for example, could settle any reasonable argument over whether the Pythagorean theorem was true by constructing a proof of the theorem. Plato's problem was whether or not all genuine human disagreements might be resolved by appeal to human knowledge, and in order to answer this special problem he had to consider the problems that we have previously characterized as epistemological.

The first clarification proposed by Plato was that something could be considered knowledge only if it could be said to be *certain*. This would rule out all guesses about the future as knowledge, on the grounds that no one can be *certain* what will happen in the future. At the same time it would preserve the examples given earlier, since it has been, is, and always will be the case, presumably, that "$2 + 2 = 4$." as well as that particular ships cannot pass over areas which are only of such and such a depth. There may be some doubt about the latter assertion, since we might argue that there might be developed a new system of propulsion which could enable a ship to pass over areas that it could not formerly pass. But then one might argue that the new system of propulsion changed the nature of the ship and that the statement of the pilot would still hold true of the particular ships that it talked about. Examples from piloting and shoemaking, however, do seem more troublesome than the examples from mathematics with respect to their certainty, and Plato had a tendency to fall back on the mathematical examples when he was pressed, since they seem to be the strongest examples in support of his contentions. We shall consider mathematical examples almost exclusively on the grounds that bona fide examples that support Plato's philosophy as strongly as possible are to be looked for if any accurate assessment of its final worth is to be made. In short, Plato's claim against skepticism that there is certain knowledge is *true* if mathematical examples *are* examples of certain knowledge. In Plato's philosophy, then, the word *knowledge* will be applied only to a claim that is certain, a claim which could not be said to be true today but false tomorrow, or even possibly false tomorrow. Mathematical statements of a sufficiently simple kind are obvious candidates for knowledge in this strong sense.

If we take it as established that human beings do have at least some certain knowledge, then in order to ask how much they might have, that is, how many questions might be capable of determinate resolution like simple mathematical claims are, we could proceed by inquiring how we came to have what certain knowledge we do have. Then, by extrapolation, we might be able to determine how much knowledge it would be possible for us to obtain by following the same process of acquisition that has worked for mathematical knowledge. This is one line of investigation that Plato probed.

The most influential theory to account for human knowledge in Plato's time was that it was acquired through the senses or by experience. This seems, of course, quite natural, on the grounds that human babies do not seem to know very much, yet learn more and more as they gradually acquire a greater range of experiences. But Plato was able to show that his test case of mathematical knowledge could not have been acquired as a result of experience. There are two arguments which show this convincingly: the first is that experience can never yield certain knowledge, and the second is that the knowledge expressed by mathematical statements is not about experienced objects.

To demonstrate the first point it is only necessary to show that sense experience often leads to unreliable impressions. It seems to follow from the frequent unreliability of sense experience that we can never be certain that sense experience has led to certain knowledge in any particular case. Many examples of mistaken sense impressions were known to the Greeks. A visual illusion such as the following will illustrate the point:

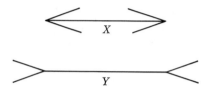

Line X appears to be shorter than line Y in the drawing. But it can be argued that they are of the same length, since measurement with a ruler indicates this to be the case. Now one might ask how the conclusion is drawn that they are of the same length, if all sense experience is taken to be potentially misleading. The point is that we ordinarily take measurement with a ruler as more reliable than sight alone in cases like the preceding, but we need not. As long as we notice that one way of determining length gives a different result than the other, it follows that sense experience alone cannot be taken as a reliable guide to knowledge. How do we know when to trust our sense impressions? The answer, in Platonic terms, is that we can never be certain when it is that they can be trusted. To express the unreliability of the senses in another way, and a way that has proved influential for the history of philosophy, it can be said that the senses yield only the *appearances* of things, but not their *reality*, so that in order to have *knowledge* about anything, we must know it through some other means than the senses. In the visual illusion, one sense experience makes it appear that Y is longer than X, the other makes it appear that Y is the same in length as X. But we know that both of these claims cannot really be true because they conflict. The existence of illusion, or conflicting reports from the senses, proves to Platonists that the senses cannot be trusted to provide knowledge in their sense.

This conclusion does not quite follow logically, since it might be the case that some sense impressions are accurate and others misleading, but Plato seems to be right that no way of distinguishing accurate from inaccurate sense experiences is readily available, and surely no way that is itself dependent upon sense experiences. If there were some sign associated with every accurate sense experience, like a funny pain in the brain, but this sign was never associated with inaccurate sense experiences, then sense experience might be a reliable guide, yielding knowledge when the pain was felt. But it is a convincing argument that no such sensed criterion of an accurate sense experience can be found when we analyze the quality of our sense experiences.

The other point in support of the claim that mathematical knowledge is not derived from sense experience is that the subject matter of the mathematical examples appears unaccessible to sense experience. Although we see a *2* quite often, we never see the number two. It is clear that *2* is not the number two since the expression '2 + 2' would show that there are at least two number twos, but we know from elementary arithmetic that there is only one number two. *2* somehow refers to the number two, and it is considered by many to be a *name* for the number two which we use to refer to the number two in the process of constructing mathematical proofs. From arguments like this, it is easy to show that neither numbers nor geometrical figures are the objects of any sense experience. As against objections that a jelly-jar lid is a circle, one can note that a jelly-jar lid does not have all of its radii equal, as a circle does. Thus, although we experience *circular* objects, we cannot be said to *experience* circles. It follows from these considerations that mathematical knowledge, being about nonexperienced objects, could hardly have been acquired from sense experiences of mathematical objects.

From the two established points that human beings have certain knowledge and that this is not acquired through the senses, Plato developed an idea that was already present in Greek culture in various religious traditions. This idea, quite simply, is that human beings remember or recollect knowledge from a past life, rather than acquire it in their current lives through experience.

You may be familiar with an idea like this in connection with the term *transmigration,* and Plato's ideas are like some of those which are normally associated with transmigration. Transmigrationists hold that souls are immortal and pass from human body to human body as these bodies die or wear out. Notice that this view holds at least implicity that human beings are made from two completely different entities, their bodies (which are mortal) and their souls (which are immortal). Now if we read *mind* for *soul,* we begin to get an impression of what Platonism is like. Historically, it is not entirely accurate to translate the appropriate Greek work as *mind,* but it seems even more misleading in view of Christian associations to translate it as *soul.* Plato's view is then that the human mind is the locus of human knowledge, and that the human body, through experience, can only provide the kind of misleading sense impressions that we spoke of earlier. We explain the fact that the human baby becomes more and more sophisticated not by the gradual acquisition of knowledge through experience, but by the mind's gradual remembrance of knowledge due to the prodding of sense experience.

It is important to realize that the Platonic explanation is compatible with the observed facts of child development. The fact that a child's knowledge increases as his experience increases does not prove that the two are causally correlated, and it certainly does not show that increasing experience is the *cause* of increasing knowledge. In fact, when human beings grow senile, their knowledge decreases at the same time that they continue to have more and more sense experiences.

An explanation of the origin of the knowledge that the mind recollects is now clearly required, since denying that knowledge originates in sense experience does not explain the origin of knowledge very satisfactorily. Plato's explanation will be presented as an analogy to begin with, since more exacting treatments of it require a great deal of detailed study of the relevant Platonic texts. The basic idea is this: just as there are objects which the senses experience, so there are objects which the mind experiences; only these objects are quite different, and they will be called *ideas* or *forms*. The mind may be said to *experience* these ideas or forms through a process which has subsequently been called *Intuition*. *Intuition* will be used as a proper name to refer to this special faculty of the mind invoked by Plato to explain knowledge of ideas, although the word *intuition* will occasionally be used to refer to our ordinary, unreflective beliefs. The notion is then this: just as the senses experience objects in the (ordinary) world, so the mind Intuits ideas or forms in the world of ideas or forms. The experiencing of objects is subject to uncertainty. In contrast, Intuition may produce *certain* information about the forms it scrutinizes, since it is concerned with forms that are (assumed) clear and unchanging. The ordinary world is called the world of becoming to emphasize the changing nature of it as it is revealed by sense experience, and the world of ideas is called the world of being, or the *real* world, which means here that it is the one that we are concerned about if we wish to have knowledge.

The structure of Plato's position is rather interesting. It is based on the powerful arguments that he can bring to bear to show that we do have knowledge and that it cannot be acquired through sense experience if it is to be certain like the mathematical knowledge exhibited in his examples. His theory of ideas (a name given to the whole conception that the mind's Intuition of the ideas is the source of human knowledge) is offered as the theory of knowledge that will save knowledge from skepticism or an inadequate grounding in sense experience. Plato's theory seems to fit the facts that he adduces to support it. But for the discerning reader there will be a number of crucial problems: what is the relationship between the body and the soul; if ideas or forms do not exist in the ordinary world of experience, then where do they exist; how can one who has never felt that he was intuiting an idea be convinced that this is what he has in fact done when he has learned mathematical theorems; and so on. The acceptability of Plato's philosophy will have to hinge on whether or not these questions can be satisfactorily answered, to say nothing of whether or not it is possible to prove that Plato's position is the only one that will explain how human beings can have certain knowledge without acquiring it through the senses.

Standards for Judgment

We have seen that Plato takes a human being to be composed of two fundamentally different kinds of entities, the body and the mind (or soul). When knowledge is taken to be certain or indubitable, and it is shown that the objects in the universe are too changing to be objects of knowledge (what is true of them today may be false of them tomorrow), it follows that for knowledge to be possible, unchanging objects like Plato's forms must be the objects of knowledge. This position is supported by the evidence that mathematics is about objects which are not found in the universe but is about ideas or forms. Plato thus proposes a view which is compatible with our commonsense observations about mathematical knowledge, and he extends his view in proposing that knowledge is only possible where there are forms. Mathematics does not exhaust the possible knowledge of forms, but only of certain mathematical forms, among which is the form of the number two. If ethical and aesthetic knowledge is to be obtained, it must be founded on the intuited existence of ethical and aesthetic forms. Our immediate problem, then, is to determine the totality of forms in an effort to discover whether ethical, aesthetic, or any kind of forms can be shown to exist, in order to justify the existence of knowledge in traditional areas of human interest other than mathematics.

Although Plato held that knowledge is to be limited to certain or indubitable statements among those which we might ordinarily say that we know to be true, he did not hold also, as he is sometimes misrepresented as holding, that complete skepticism is the only position with respect to the world of becoming. Plato did suppose that some estimates about future events in the universe, or evaluations of current events, were better than others. But he gave claims about the world of becoming the status of opinion or belief, as opposed to knowledge, because statements of opinion cannot be said to be certain. Some opinions may be better than others, but none is certain. Better opinions will be formed by those who compare their mental knowledge of the forms with their sensual knowledge of the universe, for the world of becoming and the world of being are related, somewhat like an image of an object as seen in a distorted mirror may be related to the object itself. Thus, a distorted image of a teapot may enable one to form an opinion about the qualities of the actual teapot that is more reliable than a guess based on no information at all, but it can hardly compare with the knowledge that examining the teapot itself can yield. We may now take Plato to be effecting a definition of knowledge and opinion in the following sense: he maintains that all the occasions of someone's uttering 'I know that X' are to be divided into two large groups. Those utterances which are based on sense experience and constitute an expression of opinion would go into one group, and those utterances based on intuitions of the forms or ideas would go into the other group. In this way, knowledge and opinion become *defined* terms for Platonic philosophy, and they are not used in that philosophy in quite the same way that many persons are likely to use them.

We have seen that one powerful argument for the existence of the forms or ideas is the fact of the apparent certainty of the truths of elementary arithmetic and geometry. The fact that the world of being and the world of becoming are related, however, gives some additional support to the theory of forms. Suppose, for example, that I draw the following figures:

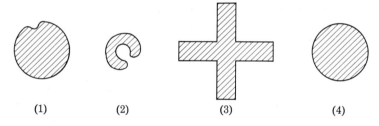

(1)   (2)   (3)   (4)

Anyone asked to arrange these figures in order of increasing circularity would no doubt order them in the following way: 3, 2, 1, 4. The Platonist might now make the following point. In order for comparisons of circularity to be made, it seems reasonable to suppose that the comparisons are made by examing each figure against some standard of circularity, and saying that that figure which most nearly matches the standard is the most circular, and so on. The standard of circularity involved is undoubtedly the circle mentioned in geometry. But geometrical circles are not to be met with in experience, as we have seen. No circular object can be said to have all its radii *identical* in length within the limits of some measuring instrument that is available. That this claim is true can be seen from the fact that only a finite number of radii could even in principle be checked by measurement, while a circle has an infinite number of radii that might be measured. But waiving such difficulties, suppose that there were a manhole cover or some other circular object, all of whose radii are equal in length so far as anyone can tell. If this manhole cover were taken as the standard of circularity, we still could not effect a comparison of the drawn figures with the cover, for they are of different sizes. We must imagine some of the figures to change size, but not shape, in order to make the comparison. This shows that the comparisons of the figures to any standard must be mental comparisons, and it shows that the drawn figures are not compared to a mental picture of a circle of any size, since the problem of comparing sizes would still remain. Platonists argue that only the idea of circularity can be a suitable standard to explain the comparisons of circularity that we are able to make. They further argue that an ordering in terms of circularity is to be explained by saying that those objects which rank higher in the ordering than others *participate* more in the form of circularity. The notion of participation, of course, needs some further clarification, but it expresses the idea that objects in the world of becoming are what they are because of their relationships to the forms or ideas.

Let us consider one more example. Suppose that several people were asked (in turn) to collect all the green objects in some room into one place, and that the possible complication of borderline objects is not present because every object in the room is clearly black, or green, or yellow, or red, and no other color, in terms of our everyday use of such words. It seems to follow from our everyday experiences that a variety of people might well select the same objects as green in such an experiment. Platonists would insist on some epistemological explanation of this uniformity. It is a simple fact of language usage that people of diverse backgrounds can understand one another by using their common vocabularies in a uniform way when they wish to describe to each other some new experiences. In reply to a request for *his* explanation of the uniform usage of *green* exhibited when a variety of people pick the same objects to be green when they are confronted with a collection they have not see before, a Platonist would reply that the uniformity could be explained because people have remembered the same form, to which each of them assigns the name *green* in conformity with linguistic practice. (We shall assume that they are all English speakers.) Confronted with the roomful of objects, they simply observe which objects participate in the form, and then they can name those objects green. Other uniformities in practice could be similarly explained.

Now suppose that someone objects to the Platonist that his argument shows only that the ideas might exist, since if they did they would account for this kind of sorting behavior, but that in fact the ideas do not exist, so that Platonism is not a tenable theory of knowledge. A Platonist can reasonably demand to know what criterion for separation of kinds could be invoked by his critic. It might be claimed by his opponent, for example, that the separation is effected by a learned verbal response, in the following sense. Perhaps objects similar or identical to those in the room have previously been labeled *green, blue*, etc., by someone who had taught us the language. The separations are then effected by applying the labels in the way that they had been previously learned. But this explanation fails to do justice to the way in which we are able to employ the word *green*. After being shown a relatively small number of objects that are called *green*, normal human beings who are developing in a culture using English as a means of communication are quickly able to extend this word in a correct fashion (by ordinary standards) to objects completely unlike the ones to which the word *green* has been applied except for the common color. To say that *green* is used to apply to any object *like* those which have been called *green* in the past encounters the difficulty that any two objects are alike in an infinite number of ways. This remark is trivially true. Two objects may be said to be alike because they are both *not* on Mt. Everest. When such likenesses are taken into account, we can see that it will be trivial to find a great number of likenesses between any group of green objects and some new object. This great number of likenesses makes it difficult to explain why people should choose likenesses in a way that would account for linguistic uniformities of usage. To say simply that we apply a word to new objects which are like those to which the word has been applied in the past must be supplemented by some account which explains the relatively uniform way in which speakers of some given language learn to use certain words. It is not true, and Platonists know that it is not, that words are always used in a uniform way by good speakers of a language. There are situations in which considerable argument may arise between speakers of a language as to which words are appropriately used. But there are simple situations in which uniformity seems to be observed, and an adequate theory of knowledge will have to account for them. Platonists would argue that the use of words in uniform fashion is explained by the ideas; application of some word to a group of objects gradually causes the mind to take that word as the linguistic name for the form which it intuits that all the objects participate in. Any suggestion that objects may be similar in an infinite number of ways along the lines just suggested would be met by the Platonist with the claim that only certain forms exist, but that it is possible to string together words to which we can assign some meaning but which do not correspond to a form. With reference to the example given above, it would be said that there is a form of greenness but not a form of not-being-on-Mt.-Everest. This explains the commonsense observation that people see green things as being green but they do not say that they see them as not being on Mt. Everest.

From these considerations it follows that the existence of the forms seems to be proved both by consideration of elementary mathematical truths and from consideration of the judgments or opinions that we can express about the world. Against this background of arguments, a question like "What is beautiful?" is ambiguous. It can be taken as a question about the world of becoming, equivalent to the question "What things are beautiful?", or it may be taken as a question about the world of being, equivalent to the question "What makes things beautiful?". The answer to the former question is a list of beautiful objects, or a description of the beautiful objects which would go on such a list. The latter question is a request for information about the form of beauty, and Plato sometimes reformulates this questions as "What is *the* beautiful?". It is the answer to this latter question that determines whether or not any answer to the first question is justifiable.

Two points that have been discussed in connection with Plato represent enduring philosophical positions that may more or less be said to begin in the Western tradition with his speculations. One of these points is the definition of knowledge that restricts knowledge to judgments or statements that can be said to be certain or indubitable. The other point is the belief, accompanied by telling examples, that sense experience cannot lead to knowledge in this defined sense because it results in judgments or statements which are not certain. Many philosophers of the Western tradition have held these positions in common with Plato. In fact, these two fundamental positions occur so frequently that it is useful to call any philosopher who adopts them a *rationalist*. It follows from acceptance of these two positions that the occurrence of human knowledge has to be explained by some means other than an origin in sense experience, and rationalistic philosophers after Plato have entities in their theories of knowledge corresponding to Platonic forms or ideas, as well as a non-sensual faculty corresponding to what has here been called Intuition that enables these entities to be known. Some rationalists have called the faculty that knows the ideas or forms in their theory of knowledge *Reason* rather than *Intuition*, which is a natural extension of the role which reasonable doubt is called upon to play in constructing answers to epistemological problems.

It will be interesting later to compare Descartes with Plato, in that both of them are rationalists, but Descartes's method of explaining the origin of certain human knowledge is different from Plato's. Philosophers who take the position that sense experience is the source of knowledge are conveniently called *empiricists*. Empiricists usually deny that there is any faculty corresponding to Platonic Intuition, and many of them have claimed that sense experience *can* lead to certain knowledge. It is clear from Plato's arguments that any empiricist who makes this claim must find some way of distinguishing veridical sense experiences that can lead to certain knowledge from sense experiences which are illusory, in that they suggest false beliefs.

Problems in Participation

Certainly the theory of ideas can provide an explanation for human knowledge, where human knowledge is defined according to Plato's technical usage. Although the theory may therefore be true, or at least adequate in some sense, the crucial question is whether or not it can be said to be superior to any alternative, and this gives rise to problems. The most important of these is whether or not the forms or ideas may be described more directly than by simply describing them as entities which must be postulated in order to account for human knowledge.

Plato ruled out the answer to the question of the form 'What is Y?' (This is different from the question of the form 'What is a Y?' as quite different linguistic terms fill the two blank spaces represented by Y.) that would be given by pointing to something and saying 'That is Y.'. Clearly an instance of Y, or an object which is Y, is not identical with Y. Things are red, for example, but we cannot point to any thing which *is* red (all of redness). Still, Plato was influenced by the implicit theory of his time that words have meaning because they refer to or name some object. Since the Y in 'X is Y' judgments names no sense object, the theory of ideas may be looked at in another way as the generation of entities that Y in such judgments can refer to, and this would in turn explain how we could understand Y. If we say "Tom is tall." and "Harry is tall.", Platonists and non-Platonists alike may agree that there is something which Tom and Harry both *are*, i.e., *tall*, but Platonists are distinguished by arguing further that there is something (some thing—a single entity) which Tom and Harry both have, or which they are both related to, in this case the form of *tallness*. Now the difficulties with the theory of ideas may in many cases be reduced to difficulties about how a single thing (tallness) may be related to many things (Tom and Harry) and to difficulties about the description or knowledge of what tallness (the form) is like. For example, tallness cannot be related to Tom and Harry by virtue of the fact that some *part* of tallness occurs in both Tom and Harry, for then tallness would not

25

be a single entity by which the participation of things could be judged. On the other hand, if tallness as an idea or form exists in a world of being completely separate from Tom and Harry who exist in the world of becoming, the relationship between tallness and Tom or Harry is something that Plato's theory of knowledge should describe in some detail. Calling it participation does not solve the problem of the relationship, since such a relationship is not *explained* by giving it a name, unless it is also specified how it can be determined that the relationship does or does not obtain in particular cases. For example, to decide whether the relationship described by 'heavier than' holds between two objects a and b, we can proceed by techniques of measuring weight that we know to be related to the problem of determining whether one object is heavier than another. Faced with the question whether a participates in the form X, no procedure for determining the answer is as yet available.

An interesting study of the possible relationship between particular red objects and the idea of redness may be made by studying the relationship between particular pound weights and the standard pound. The pound, under traditional methods of setting standards, was some fixed object kept under relatively invariant conditions in a bureau of standards. An ordinary pound weight was then defined to be any ordinary weight which would balance the standard pound. Of course, these comparisons would have to be made indirectly, but we may treat all of them as involving the weight of the standard pound. For two arbitrary objects, it would be easy to define a sense in which one would be said to be 'closer to a pound' than the other, using well-known techniques of measurement. Consequently, the status of the standard pound for determining the *poundness* of other objects has an analogy to the relation between a form and the particular sense objects which are said to participate in it.

Interesting as this comparison may seem on first consideration, it does not suffice to indicate completely what the relationship of the forms or the ideas are to particular objects in the world of becoming. To begin with, the standard pound is still something that we can see, feel, smell, etc., at least in principle, so that it is an object of the world of becoming. A form or idea, however, is not an object of sense experience. Further, because the standard pound is a sense object, we can imagine it changing over a period of time, even though it is chosen and kept in such a fashion that it changes very slowly, or remains unchanged for a long time, by comparison to other sense objects. A form, however, is defined in part to be something which is eternal, that is, something which never changes.

At this point, we can preview an argument between Platonists and non-Platonists. A Platonist takes the following question to be a sensible one: "Does the standard pound weigh the same today as it did yesterday?". In other words, the Platonist can imagine that some object whose weight remained constant might be said to become heavier (*appear* to become heavier) because the standard pound became lighter. Real weight, then, cannot be arbitrarily identified with physical standards. An empiricist, however, might argue that the question "Does the standard pound weigh the same today as it did yesterday?" is in fact nonsense, since to be a pound is to be equivalent in weight to the standard. Now if A is the standard pound, and B and C are two other objects equivalent in weight to A, and suddenly A was found to be lighter than B and C, which remained equivalent in weight, we would be faced with a question about which of the objects had changed in weight. But this is the question as to which object is to be taken as the standard. If, for example, we saw someone cut A into two pieces, we would switch to some other object (possibly B or C) as the standard. The point is that some *object* is the standard, apart from which talk of weight is nonsense to the empiricist. The perennial problem of the significance of everything doubling weight might be mentioned in this context. Suppose that all objects simultaneously doubled in weight (*pretend* that all objects are decomposable into atoms, each of which, by fiat of divinity, doubles in weight). For the Platonist, this is a legitimate possibility, so that the question "Has everything doubled in weight in the last five minutes?" is meaningful, even though it may not be answerable. On the other hand, because it is not answerable in terms of the standard weight (whose weight relationships with other objects remain unchanged), the question is nonsense to most empiricists, or at least it is a question not worth asking.

A slightly different question, namely, the question of whether the standard pound is a pound may also be asked. The question seems odd, but the oddness is difficult to trace down. Since the standard pound cannot be balanced with itself, it does not follow that it is a pound by application of the usual techniques of measurement invoked in defining a pound. Yet the standard pound must have some weight, and assigning it any weight but a pound would seem ridiculous. It surely has the same weight as it has itself, and that is the weight which we call a pound. If these considerations are transferred to forms or ideas, some difficult problems ensue. Consider the idea of Justice, which Plato explicitly mentions as an idea existing in the world of being. We may ask whether (the idea of) Justice is just. This, in effect, is to raise consideration of what we may say about the forms. If *no* properties or relations between forms may be described by philosophers, the theory of ideas reduces to the kind of visionary scheme that describes the goal for a program without giving evidence that the goal is attainable or any suggestions for a program that will enable attainment of the goal. In this case, the theory of ideas would be of little help, being at best an ex post facto justification for what knowledge we think that we have. On the other hand, if properties may be legitimately ascribed to the forms, and relations between them affirmed by philosophers, some very awkward consequences follow unless extreme care is taken in the statement of a theory of forms. Although it may seem awkward to say that the standard pound is a pound, it may seem even more awkward to deny that the standard pound is a pound. Similarly, injustice cannot be attributed to Justice (the form), since it is the standard by which examples of justice are judged. Therefore, if any properties can belong to the form of justice, *just* would seem to be among them. Any judgment like "Justice is just.", in which some property is ascribed to a form such that the form is taken to be the cause of objects in the world of becoming having a property with a similar name, may be said to be an instance of self-predication.

Examples of self-predication lead to the following problem. Suppose we take the collection of all acts, etc., which may be said to participate in Justice. These things are all said to be just because of their participation in Justice. But we cannot say, as the theory of forms seems to suggest, that a thing can be just only if it participates in some form of justice. For now, in addition to the class, call it J, of things which are just by their participation in Justice, there is the form of justice, Justice itself. We may call this form F. If self-predication be allowed along the lines suggested above, we can imagine F to be just. Consider the class J' which consists of every member of J plus the form F. Everything in J' is just. But if all these things are just, by the theory of forms there must be a form, call it F', which accounts for their being just. Continuing in this manner, an infinite series $J, J', J'', J''', \ldots$ of classes and an infinite series $F, F', F'', F''', \ldots$ of forms may be constructed. These infinite sequences conflict with the Platonic description of the world of being, particularly the Platonic description of the unity and uniqueness of the forms. This example was recognized as a criticism of the theory of forms by Plato in the dialogue *Parmenides*, and the problem of rebutting it successfully is one of the interesting features of Platonic scholarship. Apparently paradox is to be avoided by some restriction on forming any class of the kind J', or else self-predication is to be construed in some more sophisticated way, but Plato himself does not provide a clear answer to this difficulty.

The world of being is as yet unanalyzed in any fruitful way. Yet Plato did provide a partial criterion for determining whether or not particular claims made about the world of being were tenable. There are elements of mysticism in Plato's writings suggesting that a philosopher might have insight into the structure of the world of being. Accepting the possibility of these individual insights, a general epistemological problem is raised when different philosophers claim to have insights into the world of being, but their insights are different. The general criterion introduced by Plato and accepted by subsequent rationalists for resolving these disputes is that any inconsistent description of the world of being will be an incorrect description. Rationalists have held in addition that any incorrect description of the world of being will be inconsistent. Since it is not always possible to prove that something is inconsistent, this criterion is used in practice to *reject* any inconsistent description as a description of the world of being, but it does not compel the adoption of a description not known to be inconsistent as a description of the world of being. The Platonic attack on the problem of discovering true claims about the world of being is to examine rival descriptions of the world of being in order to find inconsistencies in them. The process of letting rival views clash until some consequence of one is found inconsistent with another consequence of it is reflected in the arguments occurring in Plato's dialogues and is sometimes called *dialectic*.

Claims about the structure of the world of being have important consequences for particular examples of participation. Participation is extremely important in this respect because an object may participate in more than one form. In ordinary terms, an object can be both spherical and red and hence participate in two forms. Structure in the world of being is considered to be hierarchical in that one form may be said, for example, to be higher than another. Thus Goodness may be said to be higher than Justice, which means that anything which participates in Justice will also participate in Goodness, or that anything which is just is also good. Any way in which the properties of objects are invariably related would be a result of some association between the relevant forms that they participate in. Attempts to locate structure in the world of being of this kind have been very frequent in rationalistic philosophy since Plato.

Readings from Plato

The selections which follow have been chosen for the purpose of exhibiting Plato's epistemological thought in his own writings. Identification of the selections is made by the name of the dialogue from which the selection is taken and by the initial Greek line in which the translation starts. '*Phaedo* 64+' means that selection *A* begins in Greek line 64 of Plato's *Phaedo*. Greek manuscript line numbers are accepted by convention among scholars, and they will be reprinted in the margins of most good editions. There are four selections, labeled *A*, *B*, *C*, and *D* on the pages where they begin below, and they are as follows:

A. *Phaedo* 64+
B. *Phaedo* 72+
C. *Phaedo* 100+
D. *Republic* 506+

All selections are reprinted from *The Dialogues of Plato*, 4th edition, translated by Benjamin Jowett, 1953. They are reprinted here by kind permission of The Clarendon Press, Oxford.

Both the *Phaedo* and the *Republic* are dialogues, as are most of Plato's extant writings. Philosophical dialogues are literary compositions in which two or more persons discuss a philosophical topic. In the *Phaedo*, the discussants are principally Socrates, Simmias, and Cebes. In the *Republic*, they are Socrates, Adeimantus, and Glaucon. It is the discussant called *Socrates* who expresses the views which are attributed to Plato in the preceding chapters.

The figure called *Socrates* is obviously a sketch of the historical philosopher Socrates, who had a major influence in turning Plato to philosophical speculation. Since there is no philosophical literature which can be attributed to Socrates, possibly because his social status as the son of an artisan prevented him from receiving the formal education necessary for writing literary Greek, a major problem in interpreting the Platonic dialogues is that of distinguishing the views of Plato from the views of the

30

historical Socrates. Other accounts of Socrates than Plato's exist, but they are much less flattering. This has led some commentators to suppose that Plato's account is *idealized,* but it may only reflect the fact that Plato *understood* what Socrates was saying while the others did not. A close study of the texts is sufficient to prove that both Plato and Socrates were original and important philosophers. The crucial theory of ideas as it has been presented seems to have been an insight of Socrates that Plato shaped into a comprehensive and impressive theory of knowledge. It is assumed, consequently, that Plato can be taken as the author of the theory of ideas which is discussed in the book and exhibited in the following selections. With this issue brought into the open, we are not concealing anything by taking the *Socrates* of the dialogue to represent the historical Socrates's most sophisticated epistemological reflection as interpreted by an outstanding student.

Other dialogues which the student may wish to read after reading the *Phaedo* and the *Republic* more fully are the *Meno,* the *Protagoras,* the *Euthyphro,* the *Symposium,* and the *Gorgias.* Like the *Phaedo,* these dialogues are lively discussions of philosophical topics by Socrates and other participants.

Plato's later philosophical speculation seems to have become much more technical and sophisticated. Issues in epistemology are discussed in the *Parmenides,* the *Theaetetus,* the *Sophist,* the *Statesman,* and the *Philebus.* The *Theaetetus,* in particular, may represent Plato's most sophisticated epistemological speculation. A student of Plato will have to study these dialogues closely, but they are much more difficult than the dialogues which are cited above. It is well known to Platonic scholars that the theory of ideas is somewhat differently handled in these later dialogues. For example, the argument for the theory which is presented in the *Phaedo* as depending on the notion of *recollection* becomes considerably less important, while difficulties in the notion of *participation* come to dominate many of the discussions. These differences raise the important problem (an instance of a general problem for the consideration of any historical philosopher) of whether the theory of ideas is a single theory that Plato always adopted or whether Plato started with a Socratic theory that he had to modify considerably as various objections were raised against it. This question is the question of whether all the dialogues can be taken to propose a consistent theory of knowledge or whether the dialogues propose several theories of knowledge that Plato adopted serially during his lifetime.

One must not make the mistake of supposing that if a major philosopher gives up one position for another, the newer view is necessarily the better or more defensible one. In fact, it is clear that the last view that a philosopher holds may be worse than the first one, if for no reason other than that he has become senile. This introduction to Plato tries to present some of the basic problems and insights that led Plato to suppose that some theory of ideas was a necessary part of any adequate theory of knowledge. The difficult interpretive questions which have been raised above are normally dealt with in specialized studies of Plato. Many of the books cited below can provide the student with a detailed consideration of them.

There are many editions of Plato's dialogues and a great many translators of particular dialogues. As with any translations, there are legitimate arguments about which of the translations most accurately conveys what Plato said. The *Library of Liberal Arts,* published by the Bobbs-Merrill Company, is a paperbound series that has some excellent commentaries on particular Platonic dialogues. For those who can read classical Greek, *The Loeb Classical Library* publishes editions with facing English and Greek texts. The entries in the following bibliography are those of important secondary sources and recent books for the study of Plato's philosophy.

Allen, R. E.: "Forms and Standards," *The Philosophical Quarterly,* vol. 9, pp. 163–167, 1959.

Cherniss, Harold: *The Riddle of the Early Academy,* New York, 1962.

Cornford, Francis M.: *Plato's Theory of Knowledge,* New York, 1957.

Crombie, I. M.: *An Examination of Plato's Doctrines,* New York, 1962.

Cushman, R. E.: *Therapeia, Plato's Conception of Philosophy,* Chapel Hill, 1958.

During, I., and G. E. L. Owen (eds.): *Aristotle and Plato in the Mid-fourth Century,* Göteborg, 1960.

*Friedlander, Paul: *Plato: An Introduction,* New York, 1963. (Harper Paperbound.)

*Grube, G. M. A.: *Plato's Thought,* London, 1935. (Beacon Paperbound.)

Gulley, N.: *Plato's Theory of Knowledge,* Cambridge, 1962.

Havelock, E. A.: *A Preface to Plato,* Oxford, 1962.

Levinson, R. B.: *In Defense of Plato,* Cambridge, 1953.

Lodge, R. C.: *Philosophy of Plato,* London, 1956.

Mills, K. W.: "Plato's *Phaedo* 74 b7–c6," *Phronesis,* vol. 2, pp. 128–147, 1957; vol. 3, pp. 40–58, 1958.

Ross, W. D.: *Plato's Theory of Ideas,* Oxford, 1953.

Runciman, W. G.: *Plato's Later Epistemology,* Cambridge, 1962.

Sprague, R. K.: *Plato's Use of Fallacy,* London, 1962.

*Taylor, A. E.: *Plato: The Man and His Work,* London, 1955. (Meridian Paperbound.)

Wedberg, Anders: *Plato's Philosophy of Mathematics,* Stockholm, 1955.

*Winspear, A. D.: *The Genesis of Plato's Thought,* New York, 1940.

Zeller, E.: *Plato and the Older Academy,* New York, 1962.

A   PHAEDO 64+

There is another question, which will probably throw light on our present
d   inquiry if you and I can agree about it:—Ought the philosopher to care

about such pleasures—if they are to be called pleasures—as those of eating and drinking?

Certainly not, answered Simmias.

And what about the pleasures of love—should he care for them?

By no means.

And will he think much of the other ways of indulging the body, for example, the acquisition of costly raiment or sandals, or other adornments of the body? Instead of caring about them, does he not rather despise anything more than nature needs? What do you say?   e

I should say that the true philosopher would despise them.

Would you not say that he is entirely concerned with the soul and not with the body? He would like, as far as he can, to get away from the body and to turn to the soul.

Quite true.

First, therefore, in matters of this sort philosophers, above all other men, may be observed in every sort of way to dissever the soul from the   65 communion of the body.

Very true.

Whereas, Simmias, the rest of the world are of opinion that to him who has no taste for bodily pleasures and no part in them, life is not worth having; and that he who is indifferent about them is as good as dead.

Perfectly true.

What again shall we say of the actual acquirement of knowledge?— is the body, if invited to share in the inquiry, a hindrance or a help? I mean   b to say, have sight and hearing, as found in man, any truth in them? Are they not, as the poets are always repeating, inaccurate witnesses? and yet, if even they are inaccurate and indistinct, what is to be said of the other senses?—for you will allow that they are the best of them?

Certainly, he replied.

Then when does the soul attain truth?—for in attempting to consider anything in company with the body she is obviously deceived by it.

True.   c

Then must not true reality be revealed to her in thought, if at all?

Yes.

And thought is best when the mind is gathered into herself and none of these things trouble her—neither sounds nor sights nor pain, nor again any pleasure,—when she takes leave of the body, and has as little as possible to do with it, when she has no bodily sense or desire, but is aspiring after true being?

Certainly.

And here again it is characteristic of the philosopher to despise the body; his soul runs away from his body and desires to be alone and by   d herself?

That is true.

Well, but there is another thing, Simmias: Is there or is there not an absolute justice?

Assuredly there is.

And an absolute beauty and absolute good?

Of course.

But did you ever behold any of them with your eyes?

Certainly not.

Or did you ever reach them with any other bodily sense?—and I speak not of these alone, but of absolute greatness, and health, and e strength, and, in short, of the reality or true nature of everything. Is the truth of them ever perceived through the bodily organs? or rather, is not the nearest approach to the knowledge of their several natures made by him who so orders his intellectual vision as to have the most exact conception of the essence of each thing which he considers?

Certainly.

And he attains to the purest knowledge of them who goes to each with the intellect alone, not introducing or intruding in the act of thought 66 sight or any other sense together with reason, but with the intellect in its own purity searches into the truth of each thing in its purity; he who has got rid, as far as he can, of eyes and ears and, so to speak, of the whole body, these being in his opinion distracting elements which when they associate with the soul hinder her from acquiring truth and knowledge—who, if not he, is likely to attain to the knowledge of true being?

What you say has a wonderful truth in it, Socrates, replied Simmias.

B   *PHAEDO* 72 +

Yes, said Cebes interposing, your favourite doctrine, Socrates, that our learning is simply recollection, if true, also necessarily implies a previous time in which we have learned that which we now recollect. But this would be impossible unless our soul had been somewhere before existing in this 73 form of man; here then is another proof of the soul's immortality.[1]

But tell me, Cebes, interrupted Simmias, what arguments are urged in favor of this doctrine of recollection. I am not very sure at the moment that I remember them.

One excellent proof, said Cebes, is afforded by questions. If you put a question to a person properly, he will give a true answer of himself, but how could he do this unless there were knowledge and a right account of the matter already in him? Again, this is most clearly shown when he is b taken to a diagram or to anything of that sort.[2]

But if, said Socrates, you are still incredulous, Simmias, I would ask you whether you may not agree with me when you look at the matter in another way;—I mean, if you are still incredulous as to whether what is called learning is recollection?

Incredulous I am not, said Simmias; but I want to have this doctrine of recollection brought to my own recollection, and, from what Cebes has started to say, I am beginning to recollect and be convinced: but I should still like to hear you develop your own argument.

This is what I would say, he replied:—We should agree, if I am not mistaken, that what a man is to recollect he must have known at some previous time.

Very true.[3]

And do we also agree that knowledge obtained in the way I am about to describe is recollection? I mean to ask, Whether a person who, having seen or heard or in any way perceived anything, knows not only that, but also thinks of something else which is the subject not of the same but of some other kind of knowledge, may not be fairly said to recollect that of which he thinks?[4]

How do you mean?

I mean what I may illustrate by the following instance:—The knowledge of a lyre is not the same as the knowledge of a man?

Of course not.

And yet what is the feeling of lovers when they recognize a lyre, or a cloak, or anything else which the beloved has been in the habit of using? Do not they, from knowing the lyre, form in the mind's eye an image of the youth to whom the lyre belongs? And this is recollection. In like manner anyone who sees Simmias may often remember Cebes; and there are endless examples of the same thing.

Endless, indeed, replied Simmias.

And is not this sort of thing a kind of recollection—though the word is most commonly applied to a process of recovering that which has been already forgotten through time and inattention?

Very true, he said.

Well; and may you not also from seeing the picture of a horse or a lyre recollect a man? and from the picture of Simmias, you may be led to recollect Cebes?

True.

Or you may be led to the recollection of Simmias himself?

Quite so.

And in all these cases, the recollection may be derived from things either like or unlike?

It may be.

And when the recollection is derived from like things, then another consideration is sure to arise, which is—whether the likeness in any degree falls short or not of that which is recollected?

Certainly, he said.

Now consider this question. We affirm, do we not, that there is such a thing as equality, not of one piece of wood or stone or similar

c

d

e

74

material thing with another, but that, over and above this, there is absolute equality? Shall we say so?[5]

b   Say so, yes, replied Simmias, and swear to it, with all the confidence in life.

And do we know the nature of this absolute existence?

To be sure, he said.

And whence did we obtain our knowledge? Did we not see equalities of material things, such as pieces of wood and stones, and conceive from them the idea of an equality which is different from them? For you will acknowledge that there is a difference? Or look at the matter in another way:—Do not the same pieces of wood or stone appear to one man equal, and to another unequal?[6]

That is certain.

c   But did pure equals ever appear to you unequal? or equality the same as inequality?

Never, Socrates.

Then these equal objects are not the same with the idea of equality?

I should say, clearly not, Socrates.

And yet from these equals, although differing from the idea of equality, you obtained the knowledge of that idea?

Very true, he said.

Which might be like, or might be unlike them?

Yes.

But that makes no difference: so long as from seeing one thing you
d   conceive another, whether like or unlike, there must surely have been an act of recollection?

Very true.

But what would you say of equal portions of wood or other material equals? and what is the impression produced by them? Are they equals in the same sense in which absolute equality is equal? or do they fall short of this perfect equality in a measure?

Yes, he said, in a very great measure too.

And must we not allow, that when a man, looking at any object, reflects 'the thing which I see aims at being like some other thing, but falls
e   short of and cannot be like that other thing, and is inferior', he who so reflects must have had a previous knowledge of that to which the other, although similar, was inferior?

Certainly.

And has not this been our own case in the matter of equals and of absolute equality?

Precisely.

Then we must have known equality previously to the time when we
75   first saw the material equals, and reflected that they all strive to attain absolute equality, but fall short of it?

Very true.

And we recognize also that we have only derived this conception of absolute equality, and can only derive it, from sight or touch, or from some other of the senses, which are all alike in this respect?

Yes, Socrates, for the purposes of the present argument, one of them is the same as the other.

From the senses then is derived the conception that all sensible equals aim at an absolute equality of which they fall short?   b

Yes.

Then before we began to see or hear or perceive in any way, we must have had a knowledge of absolute equality, or we could not have referred to that standard the equals which are derived from the senses?—for to that they all aspire, and of that they fall short.

No other inference can be drawn from the previous statements.

And did we not begin to see and hear and have the use of our other senses as soon as we were born?[7]

Certainly.

Then we must have acquired the knowledge of equality at some   c previous time?

Yes.

That is to say, before we were born, I suppose?

It seems so.

And if we acquired this knowledge before we were born, and were born having the use of it, then we also knew before we were born and at the instant of birth not only the equal or the greater or the less, but all other such ideas; for we are not speaking only of equality, but of beauty,   d goodness, justice, holiness, and of all which we stamp with the name of absolute being in the dialectical process, both when we ask and when we answer questions. Of all this we affirm with certainty that we acquired the knowledge before birth?

We do.

But if, after having acquired, we have not on each occasion forgotten what we acquired, then we must always come into life having this knowledge, and shall have it always as long as life lasts—for knowing is the acquiring and retaining knowledge and not losing it. Is not the loss of knowledge, Simmias, just what we call forgetting?

Quite true, Socrates.   e

But if this knowledge which we acquired before birth was lost by us at birth, and if afterwards by the use of the senses we recovered what we previously knew, will not the process which we call learning be a recovering of knowledge which is natural to us, and may not this be rightly termed recollection?

Very true.

So much is clear—that when we perceive something, either by the   76 help of sight, or hearing, or some other sense, that perception can lead us to think of some other thing like or unlike which is associated with it but has been forgotten. Whence, as I was saying, one of two alternatives follows:—either we all have this knowledge at birth, and continue to know through life; or, after birth, those who are said to learn only recollect, and learning is simply recollection.

Yes, that is quite true, Socrates.

b   And which alternative, Simmias, do you prefer? Have we the knowledge at our birth, or do we recollect afterwards things which we knew previously to our birth?

I cannot decide at the moment.

At any rate you can decide whether he who has knowledge will or will not be able to render an account of his knowledge? What do you say?

Certainly, he will.[8]

But do you think that every man is able to give an account of the matters about which we were speaking a moment ago?

Would that they could, Socrates, but I much rather fear that to-morrow, at this time, there will no longer be anyone alive who is able to give an account of them such as ought to be given.

c   Then you are not of opinion, Simmias, that all men know these things?

Certainly not.

They are in process of recollecting that which they learned before?

Certainly.

But when did our souls acquire this knowledge?—clearly not since we were born as men?

Certainly not.

And therefore, previously?

Yes.

Then, Simmias, our souls must also have existed without bodies before they were in the form of man, and must have had intelligence.

Unless indeed you suppose, Socrates, that all such knowledge is given us at the very moment of birth; for this is the only time which remains.

d   Yes, my friend, but if so, when, pray, do we lose it? for it is not in us when we are born—that is admitted. Do we lose it at the moment of receiving it, or if not at what other time?

No, Socrates, I perceive that I was unconsciously talking nonsense.

Then may we not say, Simmias, that if there do exist these things of which we are always talking, absolute beauty and goodness, and all that class of realities; and if to this we refer all our sensations and with

e   this compare them, finding the realities to be pre-existent and our own possession—then just as surely as these exist, so surely must our souls have existed before our birth? Otherwise our whole argument would be worthless. By an equal compulsion we must believe both that these realities exist, and that our souls existed before our birth; and if not the realities, then not the souls.

C *PHAEDO* 100 +

... I should like to know whether you agree with me in the next step; for I cannot help thinking, if there be anything beautiful other than absolute beauty it is beautiful only in so far as it partakes of absolute beauty—and I should say the same of everything. Do you agree in this notion of the cause? [9]

Yes, he said, I agree.

He proceeded: I no longer look for, nor can I understand, those other ingenious causes which are alleged; and if a person says to me that the bloom of colour, or form, or any such thing is a source of beauty, d I dismiss all that, which is only confusing to me, and simply and singly, and perhaps foolishly, hold and am assured in my own mind that nothing makes a thing beautiful but the presence or participation of beauty in whatever way or manner obtained; for as to the manner I am uncertain, but I stoutly contend that by beauty all beautiful things become beautiful.[10] This appears to me to be the safest answer which I can give, either to myself or to another, and to this I cling, in the persuasion that this principle will never be overthrown, and that to myself or to anyone who e asks the question, I may safely reply, That by beauty beautiful things become beautiful. Do you not agree with me?

I do.

And that by greatness great things become great and greater greater, and by smallness the less become less?

True.

Then if a person were to remark that A is taller by a head than B, and B less by a head than A, you would refuse to admit his statement, and 101 would stoutly contend that what you mean is only that the greater is greater by, and by reason of, greatness, and the less is less only by, and by reason of, smallness. I imagine you would be afraid of a counter-argument that if the greater is greater and the less less by the head, then, first, the greater is greater and the less less by the same thing; and, secondly, the greater man is greater by the head which is itself small, and so you get the monstrous absurdity that a man is great by something b small. You would be afraid of this, would you not? [11]

Indeed I should, said Cebes, laughing.

In like manner you would think it dangerous to say that ten exceeded eight by, and by reason of, two; but would say by, and by reason of, number; or you would say that two cubits exceed one cubit not by a half, but by magnitude?—for there is the same danger in all these cases.

Very true, he said.

Again, would you not be cautious of affirming that the addition of one to one, or the division of one, is the cause of two? And you would c loudly asseverate that you know of no way in which anything comes into existence except by participation in the distinctive reality of that in which it participates, and consequently, as far as you know, the only cause of two is the participation in duality—this is the way to make two, and the participation in unity is the way to make one. You would say: 'I will let alone all subtleties like these of division and addition—wiser heads than

d   mine may answer them; inexperienced as I am, and ready to start, as the proverb says, at my own shadow, I cannot afford to give up the sure ground of the original postulate. And if anyone fastens on you there, you would not mind him, or answer him until you could see whether the consequences which follow agree with one another or not, and when you are further required to give an account of this postulate, you would give it in the same way, assuming some higher postulate which seemed to you to

e   be the best founded, until you arrived at a satisfactory resting-place; but you would not jumble together the fundamental principle and the consequences in your reasoning, like the eristics—at least if you wanted to discover real existence. Not that this confusion signifies to them, who probably never care or think about the matter at all, for they have the wit to be well pleased with themselves however thorough may be the muddle of their ideas. But you, if you are a philosopher, will certainly do as I say.

D   REPUBLIC 506+

Evidently, then, there are many great differences of opinion about the good.

Undoubtedly.

Is it not likewise evident that many are content to do or to have, or to seem to be, what is just and beautiful without the reality; but no one is satisfied with the appearance of good—the reality is what they seek; in

e   the case of the good, appearance is despised by every one.[12]

Very true, he said.

Of this then, which every soul of man pursues and makes the end of all his actions, having a presentiment that there is such an end, and yet

506   hesitating because neither knowing the nature nor having the same assurance of this as of other things, and therefore losing whatever good there is in other things,—of a principle such and so great as this ought the best men in our State, to whom everything is entrusted, to be in the darkness of ignorance?

Certainly not, he said.

I am sure, I said, that he who does not know how the noble and the just are likewise good will be but a sorry guardian of them; and I suspect that no one who is ignorant of the good will have a true knowledge of them.

That, he said, is a shrewd suspicion of yours.

b   And if only we have a guardian who has this knowledge our State will be perfectly ordered?

Of course, he replied; but I wish that you would tell me whether you conceive this supreme principle of the good to be knowledge or pleasure, or different from either?

Sir, I said, I could see quite well all along that you would not be contented with the thoughts of other people about these matters.

True, Socrates; but I must say that one who like you has passed a lifetime in the study of philosophy should not be always repeating the opinions of others, and never telling his own.

Well, but has anyone a right to say positively what he does not   c
know?

Not, he said, with the assurance of positive certainty; he has no right to do that: but he may say what he thinks, as a matter of opinion.

And have you not observed, I said, that all mere opinions are bad, and the best of them blind? You would not deny that those who have any true notion without intelligence are only like blind men who feel their way along the right road?

Very true.

And do you wish to behold what is blind and crooked and base,   d
when others will tell you of brightness and beauty?

Still, I must implore you, Socrates, said Glaucon, not to turn away just as you are reaching the goal; if you will only give such an explana- tion of the good as you have already given of justice and temperance and the other virtues, we shall be satisfied.

Yes, my friend, and I shall be at least equally satisfied, but I cannot help fearing that I shall fail, and that my indiscreet zeal will bring ridicule upon me. No, sirs, let us not at present ask what is the actual   e
nature of the good, for to reach what is now in my thoughts would be an effort too great for me. But of the child of the good who is likest him, I am ready to speak, if I could be sure that you wished to hear—other- wise, not.

By all means, he said, tell us about the child, and you shall remain in our debt for the account of the parent.

I do indeed wish, I replied, that I could pay, and you receive, the   507
account of the parent, and not, as now, of the offspring only; take, however, this latter by way of interest, and at the same time have a care that I do not pay you in spurious coin, although I have no intention of deceiving you.

Yes, we will take all the care that we can: proceed.

Yes, I said, but I must first come to an understanding with you, and remind you of what I have mentioned in the course of this discussion,   b
and at many other times.

What?

The old story, that there are many beautiful things and many good. And again there is a true beauty, a true good; and all other things to which the term *many* has been applied, are now brought under a single idea, and, assuming this unity, we speak of it in every case as *that which really is.*[13]

Very true.

The many, as we say, are seen but not known, and the Ideas are known but not seen.

c   Exactly.

And what is the organ with which we see the visible things?

The sight, he said.

And with the hearing, I said, we hear, and with the other senses perceive the other objects of sense?

True.

But have you remarked that sight is by far the most costly and complex piece of workmanship which the artificer of the senses ever contrived?

Not exactly, he said.

Then reflect: have the ear and voice need of any third or additional

d   nature in order that the one may be able to hear and the other to be heard?

Nothing of the sort.

No, indeed, I replied; and the same is true of most, if not all, the other senses—you would not say that any of them requires such an addition?

Certainly not.

But you see that without the addition of some other nature there is no seeing or being seen?

How do you mean?

Sight being, as I conceive, in the eyes, and he who has eyes wanting to see; colour being also present in the objects, still unless there be a third

e   nature specially adapted to the purpose, sight, as you know, will see nothing and the colours will be invisible.

Of what nature are you speaking?

Of that which you term light, I replied.

True, he said.

508   Then the bond which links together the sense of sight and the power of being seen, is of an evidently nobler nature than other such bonds— unless sight is an ignoble thing?

Nay, he said, the reverse of ignoble.

And which, I said, of the gods in heaven would you say was the lord of this element? Whose is that light which makes the eye to see perfectly and the visible to appear?

I should answer, as all men would, and as you plainly expect— the sun.

May not the relation of sight to this deity be described as follows?

How?

Neither sight nor the organ in which it resides, which we call the eye, is the sun?

No.   b

Yet of all the organs of sense the eye is the most like the sun?

By far the most like.

And the power which the eye possesses is a sort of effluence which is dispensed from the sun?

Exactly.

Then the sun is not sight, but the author of sight who is recognized by sight?

True, he said.

And this, you must understand, is he whom I call the child of the good, whom the good begat in his own likeness, to be in the visible world, in relation to sight and the things of sight, what the good is in the   c intellectual world in relation to mind and the things of mind:

Will you be a little more explicit? he said.

Why, you know, I said that the eyes, when a person directs them towards objects on which the light of day is no longer shining, but the moon and stars only, see dimly, and are nearly blind; they seem to have no clearness of vision in them?   d

Very true.

But when they are directed towards objects on which the sun shines, they see clearly and there is sight in them?

Certainly.

And the soul is like the eye: when resting upon that on which truth and being shine, the soul perceives and understands, and is radiant with intelligence; but when turned towards the twilight and to those things which come into being and perish, then she has opinion only, and goes blinking about, and is first of one opinion and then of another, and seems to have no intelligence?

Just so.

Now, that which imparts truth to the known and the power of knowing to the knower is, as I would have you say, the Idea of good, and this   e Idea, which is the cause of science and of truth, you are to conceive as being apprehended by knowledge, and yet, fair as both truth and knowledge are, you will be right to esteem it as different from these and even   509 fairer; and as in the previous instance light and sight may be truly said to be like the sun and yet not to be the sun, so in this other sphere science and truth may be deemed to be like the good, but it is wrong to think that they are the good; the good has a place of honour yet higher.

What a wonder of beauty that must be, he said, which is the author of science and truth, and yet surpasses them in beauty; for you surely cannot mean to say that pleasure is the good?

God forbid, I replied; but may I ask you to consider the image in another point of view?

b   In what point of view?

You would say, would you not, that the sun is not only the author of visibility in all visible things, but of generation and nourishment and growth, though he himself is not generation?

Certainly.

In like manner you must say that the good not only infuses the power of being known into all things known, but also bestows upon them their being and existence, and yet the good is not existence, but lies far beyond it in dignity and power.

c   Glaucon said, with a ludicrous earnestness: By the light of heaven, that is far beyond indeed!

Yes, I said, and the exaggeration may be set down to you; for you made me utter my fancies.

And pray continue to utter them; at any rate let us hear if there is anything more to be said about the similitude of the sun.

Yes, I said, there is a great deal more.

Then omit nothing, however slight.

I expect that I shall omit a great deal, I said, but shall not do so deliberately, as far as present circumstances permit.

I hope not, he said.

d   You have to imagine, then, that there are two ruling powers, and that one of them is set over the intellectual world, the other over the visible. I do not say heaven, lest you should fancy that I am playing upon the name (οὐρανός, ὁρατός).[14] May I suppose that you have this distinction of the visible and intelligible fixed in your mind?

I have.

Now take a line which has been cut into two unequal parts, and divide each of them again in the same proportion, and suppose the two main divisions to answer, one to the visible and the other to the intel-
e   ligible, and then compare the subdivisions in respect of their clearness and want of clearness, and you will find that the first section in the sphere
510   of the visible consists of images.[15] And by images I mean, in the first place, shadows, and in the second place, reflections in water and in solid, smooth and polished bodies and the like: Do you understand?

Yes, I understand.

Imagine, now, the other section, of which this is only the resemblance, to include the animals which we see, and every thing that grows or is made.

Very good.

Would you not admit that both the sections of this division have different degrees of truth, and that the copy is to the original as the sphere of opinion is to the sphere of knowledge?

b   Most undoubtedly.

Next proceed to consider the manner in which the sphere of the intellectual is to be divided.

In what manner?

Thus:—There are two subdivisions, in the lower of which the soul, using as images those things which themselves were reflected in the former division, is forced to base its enquiry upon hypotheses, proceeding not towards a principle but towards a conclusion; in the higher of the two, the soul proceeds *from* hypotheses, and goes up to a principle which is above hypotheses, making no use of images as in the former case, but proceeding only in and through the Ideas themselves.

I do not quite understand your meaning, he said.

Then I will try again; you will understand me better when I have made some preliminary remarks. You are aware that students of geometry, arithmetic, and the kindred sciences assume the odd and the even and the figures and three kinds of angles and the like in their several branches of science; these are their hypotheses, which they and everybody are supposed to know, and therefore they do not deign to give any account of them either to themselves or others; but they begin with them, and go on until they arrive at last, and in a consistent manner, at the solution which they set out to find?   d

Yes, he said, I know.

And do you not know also that although they make use of the visible forms and reason about them, they are thinking not of these, but of the ideals which they resemble; not of the figures which they draw, but of the absolute square and the absolute diameter, and so on—the forms which they draw or make, and which themselves have shadows and reflections in water, are in turn converted by them into images; for they are really seeking to behold the things themselves, which can only be seen with the eye of the mind?   e

That is true.   511

And this was what I meant by a subdivision of the intelligible, in the search after which the soul is compelled to use hypotheses; not ascending to a first principle, because she is unable to rise above the region of hypothesis, but employing now as images those objects from which the shadows below were derived, even these being deemed clear and distinct by comparison with the shadows.

I understand, he said, that you are speaking of the province of geometry and the sister arts.   b

And when I speak of the other division of the intelligible, you will understand me to speak of that other sort of knowledge which reason herself attains by the power of dialectic, using the hypotheses not as first principles, but literally as hypotheses—that is to say, as steps and points of departure into a world which is above hypotheses, in order that she may soar beyond them to the first principle of the whole; and clinging to this and then to that which depends on this, by successive steps she descends again without the aid of any sensible object, from ideas, through Ideas, and in Ideas she ends.   c

I understand you, he replied; not perfectly, for you seem to me to be describing a task which is really tremendous; but, at any rate, I understand you to say that that part of intelligible Being, which the science of dialectic contemplates, is clearer than that which falls under the arts, as they are termed, which take hypotheses as their principles; and though the objects are of such a kind that they must be viewed by the under-

d   standing, and not by the senses, yet, because they start from hypotheses and do not ascend to a principle, those who contemplate them appear to you not to exercise the higher reason upon them, although when a first principle is added to them they are cognizable by the higher reason. And the habit which is concerned with geometry and the cognate sciences I suppose that you would term understanding and not reason, as being intermediate between opinion and reason.

You have quite conceived my meaning, I said; and now, correspond-ing to these four divisions, let there be four faculties in the soul—reason

e   answering to the highest, understanding to the second, faith (or conviction) to the third, and perception of shadows to the last—and let there be a scale of them, and let us suppose that the several faculties have clearness in the same degree that their objects have truth.

I understand, he replied, and give my assent, and accept your ar-rangement.

BOOK VII

514   And now, I said, let me show in a figure how far our nature is enlightened or unenlightened:—Behold! human beings housed in an underground cave, which has a long entrance open towards the light and as wide as the interior of the cave; here they have been from their childhood, and

b   have their legs and necks chained, so that they cannot move and can only see before them, being prevented by the chains from turning round their heads. Above and behind them a fire is blazing at a distance, and between the fire and the prisoners there is a raised way; and you will see, if you look, a low wall built along the way, like the screen which marionette players have in front of them, over which they show the pup-pets.

I see.

And do you see, I said, men passing along the wall carrying all

c   sorts of vessels, and statues and figures of animals made of wood and

515   stone and various materials, which appear over the wall? While carrying their burdens, some of them, as you would expect, are talking, others silent.

You have shown me a strange image, and they are strange prisoners.

Like ourselves, I replied; for in the first place do you think they have seen anything of themselves, and of one another, except the shadows which the fire throws on the opposite wall of the cave?

How could they do so, he asked, if throughout their lives they were   b
never allowed to move their heads?

And of the objects which are being carried in like manner they
would only see the shadows?

Yes, he said.

And if they were able to converse with one another, would they not
suppose that the things they saw were the real things?

Very true.

And suppose further that the prison had an echo which came from
the other side, would they not be sure to fancy when one of the passers-by
spoke that the voice which they heard came from the passing shadow?

No question, he replied.

To them, I said, the truth would be literally nothing but the shadows   c
of the images.

That is certain.

And now look again, and see in what manner they would be released from their bonds, and cured of their error, whether the process
would naturally be as follows. At first, when any of them is liberated and
compelled suddenly to stand up and turn his neck round and walk and
look towards the light, he will suffer sharp pains; the glare will distress
him, and he will be unable to see the realities of which in his former state
he had seen the shadows; and then conceive someone saying to him that
what he saw before was an illusion, but that now, when he is approaching   d
nearer to being and his eye is turned towards more real existence, he has
a clearer vision,—what will be his reply? And you may further imagine
that his instructor is pointing to the objects as they pass and requiring
him to name them,—will he not be perplexed? Will he not fancy that
the shadows which he formerly saw are truer than the objects which are
now shown to him?

Far truer.

And if he is compelled to look straight at the light, will he not have   e
a pain in his eyes which will make him turn away to take refuge in the
objects of vision which he can see, and which he will conceive to be in
reality clearer than the things which are now being shown to him?

True, he said.

And suppose once more, that he is reluctantly dragged up that
steep and rugged ascent, and held fast until he is forced into the presence
of the sun himself, is he not likely to be pained and irritated? When he
approaches the light his eyes will be dazzled, and he will not be able to   516
see anything at all of what are now called realities.

Not all in a moment, he said.

He will require to grow accustomed to the sight of the upper world.
And first he will see the shadows best, next the reflections of men and
other objects in the water, and then the objects themselves; and, when he
turned to the heavenly bodies and the heaven itself, he would find it easier

b to gaze upon the light of the moon and the stars at night than to see the sun or the light of the sun by day?

Certainly.

Last of all he will be able to see the sun, not turning aside to the illusory reflections of him in the water, but gazing directly at him in his own proper place, and contemplating him as he is.[16]

Certainly.

He will then proceed to argue that this is he who gives the seasons and the years, and is the guardian of all that is in the visible world, and in a
c certain way the cause of all things which he and his fellows have been accustomed to behold?

Clearly, he said, he would arrive at this conclusion after what he had seen.

And when he remembered his old habitation, and the wisdom of the cave and his fellow-prisoners, do you not suppose that he would felicitate himself on the change, and pity them?

Certainly, he would.

And if they were in the habit of conferring honours among themselves on those who were quickest to observe the passing shadows and to remark which of them went before and which followed after and which were
d together, and who were best able from these observations to divine the future, do you think that he would be eager for such honours and glories, or envy those who attained honour and sovereignty among those men? Would he not say with Homer,

'Better to be a serf, labouring for a landless master',[17]

and to endure anything, rather than think as they do and live after their manner?

e Yes, he said, I think that he would consent to suffer anything rather than live in this miserable manner.

Imagine once more, I said, such a one coming down suddenly out of the sunlight, and being replaced in his old seat; would he not be certain to have his eyes full of darkness?

To be sure, he said.

And if there were a contest, and he had to compete in measuring the
517 shadows with the prisoners who had never moved out of the cave, while his sight was still weak, and before his eyes had become steady (and the time which would be needed to acquire this new habit of sight might be very considerable), would he not make himself ridiculous? Men would say of him that he had returned from the place above with his eyes ruined; and that it was better not even to think of ascending; and if anyone tried to loose another and lead him up the light, let them only catch the offender, and they would put him to death.

No question, he said.

b This entire allegory, I said, you may now append, dear Glaucon, to

the previous argument; the prison-house is the world of sight, the light of
the fire is the power of the sun, and you will not misapprehend me if you
interpret the journey upwards to be the ascent of the soul into the intellectual world according to my surmise, which, at your desire, I have expressed
—whether rightly or wrongly God knows. But, whether true or false, my
opinion is that in the world of knowledge the Idea of good appears last of
all, and is seen only with an effort; although, when seen, it is inferred to be   c
the universal author of all things beautiful and right, parent of light and of
the lord of light in the visible world, and the immediate and supreme
source of reason and truth in the intellectual; and that this is the power
upon which he who would act rationally either in public or private life must
have his eye fixed.

I agree, he said, as far as I am able to understand you.

Moreover, I said, you must agree once more, and not wonder that
those who attain to this vision are unwilling to take any part in human
affairs; for their souls are ever hastening into the upper world where they
desire to dwell; which desire of theirs is very natural, if our allegory may   d
be trusted.[18]

Yes, very natural.

And is there anything surprising in one who passes from divine
contemplations to the evil state of man, appearing grotesque and ridiculous; if, while his eyes are blinking and before he has become accustomed
to the surrounding darkness, he is compelled to fight in courts of law, or in
other places, about the images or the shadows of images of justice, and
must strive against some rival about opinions of these things which are   e
entertained by men who have never yet seen the true justice?

Anything but surprising, he replied.

Anyone who has common sense will remember that the bewilderments   518
of the eyes are of two kinds and arise from two causes, either from coming
out of the light or from going into the light, and, judging that the soul may
be affected in the same way, will not give way to foolish laughter when he
sees anyone whose vision is perplexed and weak; he will first ask whether
that soul of man has come out of the brighter life and is unable to see
because unaccustomed to the dark, or having turned from darkness to the
day is dazzled by excess of light. And he will count the one happy in his   b
condition and state of being, and he will pity the other; or, if he have a
mind to laugh at the soul which comes from below into the light, this
laughter will not be quite so laughable as that which greets the soul which
returns from above out of the light into the cave.   c

That, he said, is a very just distinction.

But then, if I am right, certain professors of education must be wrong
when they say that they can put a knowledge into the soul which was not
there before, like sight into blind eyes.

They undoubtedly say this, he replied.

Whereas our argument shows that the power and capacity of learning exists in the soul already; and that just as if it were not possible to turn the eye from darkness to light without the whole body, so too the instrument of knowledge can only by the movement of the whole soul be turned from the the world of becoming to that of being, and learn by degrees to endure the sight of being, and of the brightest and best of being, or in other words, of

d   the good.

Very true.

And must there not be some art which will show how the conversion can be effected in the easiest and quickest manner; an art which will not implant the faculty of sight, for that exists already, but will set it straight when it has been turned in the wrong direction, and is looking away from the truth?

Yes, he said, such an art may be presumed.

And whereas the other so-called virtues of the soul seem to be akin to

e   bodily qualities, for even when they are not originally innate they can be implanted later by habit and exercise, the virtue of wisdom more than anything else contains a divine element which never loses its power, and by this conversion is rendered useful and profitable; or, by conversion of

519   another sort, hurtful and useless. Did you never observe the narrow intelligence flashing from the keen eye of a clever rogue—how eager he is, how clearly his paltry soul sees the way to his end; he is the reverse of blind, but his keen eye-sight is forced into the service of evil, and he is mischievous in proportion to his cleverness?

Very true, he said.

But what if such natures had been gradually stripped, beginning in childhood, of the leaden weights which sink them in the sea of Becoming,

b   and which, fastened upon the soul through gluttonous indulgence in eating and other such pleasures, forcibly turn its vision downwards—if, I say, they had been released from these impediments and turned in the opposite direction, the very same faculty in them would have seen the truth as keenly as they see what their eyes are turned to now.

NOTES

1   Is this argument valid? Knowledge might have been *given* to the mind at birth in some fashion: this is discussed and dismissed below. The dismissal of this, and other possibilities, follows from the Platonic view of the soul. A full discussion of this argument requires that the properties of the soul be made explicit.

2   The mention of diagrams is in reference to drawings used in finding geometrical truths. In the *Meno*, another Platonic dialogue, a slave *proves* a geometrical theorem by answering questions put to him by Socrates. Notice that this passage explicitly acknowledges that the questioner's way of putting questions is important, but that in spite of this necessary skill on the questioner's part, the right answers are still possible only if the soul has had previous knowledge.

3 No other answer seems possible because of the meaning which is being given to *recollection*. This is an example of the important way in which definitions function in philosophical argument.

4 This is a difficult passage, and Plato proceeds to discuss it at great length. It seems to be a compact way of announcing his view that sense experience may prod the soul to remember true knowledge, even though the soul's knowledge does not *depend* on sense experience.

5 The following passage is extremely difficult for Platonic expositors. You can find extended discussions of it in the articles "Forms and Standards," by R. E. Allen, and "Plato's *Phaedo* 74 b7–c6," by K. W. Mills, which are cited above in the bibliography for this part. What is translated here as 'absolute equality' ($\alpha \dot{v} \tau \grave{\alpha} \ \tau \grave{\alpha} \ \ddot{\iota} \sigma \alpha$) is normally taken to refer to the form of equality and the term *equals* occurring in later lines ($\tau \alpha \hat{v} \tau \alpha \ \tau \grave{\alpha} \ \ddot{\iota} \sigma \alpha$) to actual objects which are judged to be equal. The total passage then suggests that absolute equality is equal, that is, has the property of equality. This kind of passage supports a crucial premise of the infinite regress argument against the theory of forms discussed in "Problems in Participation," namely, the premise asserting self-predication of the forms. Now the key problem of interpretation becomes that of explaining how equality, which is a relation between two or more things, can be known by a form of equality, which by the nature of forms can have no parts.

6 A familiar Platonic point! Equal things are not always equal or are not equal in every respect. On the other hand, the idea of equality remains the same. Thus our knowledge of equality cannot be reduced to knowledge of actual pairs of things, since our idea of equality has a property (invariance) which pairs of experienced equal things do not have.

7 The ambiguity of the word *see* must be considered in evaluating this argument. Although babies *see* when they are born (those that are not born blind), babies do not seem to *see* mother, *see* father, *see* danger, and so forth. Exactly what they see is extremely problematic. In terms of Plato's argument, if babies see when they are born, why do they not seem to recollect knowledge until they are older?

8 Remembrance or recollection is invoked to explain obvious differences in human knowledge. Plato rules out the possibility that these differences are due to relative *abilities* or to differing biographies. Does the claim that anyone who has knowledge will be able to render an account of it seem as obviously true as Simmias takes it to be? Or can someone know something that he cannot explain to others?

9 The *cause* of something's beauty is said to be the form of beauty. This notion of causation must be distinguished from causation as it might be understood in science. By the cause of what is beautiful Plato refers to what enables us to know or to recognize what is beautiful.

10 Natural causation is here excluded. Plato is claiming that explaining one sense experience (a beautiful flower) by other sense experiences is to explain the inexplicable by means of the inexplicable, as we do not have knowledge of *any* sense experiences. *Ingenious* is used sardonically.

11 Passages like this are indicative of Platonic difficulties in handling relations.

Let Tom, Dick, and Harry be arranged in order of relative height, with Tom as the tallest. If Tom's height relative to Dick's is explained by Tom's participation in the form of tallness, and Dick's participation in the form of smallness, how is Dick's relative tallness to Harry to be explained? Dick cannot presumably participate in both smallness and tallness. It should be pointed out that the theory of ideas has difficulty in accounting for complex relationships among a number of objects.

12   The point is that although one may wish to appear just in order, for example, to pursue political power, no one considers himself evil. This is a curiosity of moral theory. With the exception of some religious saints, most people seem to feel that they are good people (or mostly good) in terms of their own standards. Plato uses this point in support of the claim that to know the good is to do the good, by virtue of the fact that he took it to be obvious that one would not willingly fail to do what he knew to be the good thing to do.

13   Here is a succinct formulation of the Platonic point that anytime we may separate some class of objects from the rest of things in some nonarbitrary way, this separation may be accounted for by an Idea in which these things participate.

14   It is not clear what pun Plato may have had in mind. There is some suspicion that he may have been avoiding an argument from words which would support his position on the accidental etymology of the words used crucially in the argument.

15   There are some subtle difficulties in Plato's account of the divided line. See, for example, Robert S. Brumbaugh's "Plato's Divided Line," *Review of Metaphysics,* June, 1952, pp. 529–534, which shows that the figure as described by Plato cannot be constructed. Suppose a line to be divided into segments with the ratio $m:n$. Let m be divided into segments a and b, and n into segments c and d. Now by the construction, $m/n = a/b = c/d$. If r is the length of the original line, one can show $b = (m/r)n$, and $c = (n/r)m$. Consequently, b and c have the same length. But in context, the significance of the length of the segments (the clearness of the knowledge in the nontechnical sense that is represented by the segment) indicates that the segments should get increasingly longer in one direction. The problem then becomes one of deciding whether or not this discrepancy is a slip on Plato's part, or of some other significance.

16   An interesting problem is that of relating the Allegory of the Cave (which is what this section of the *Republic* is called) to the fourfold division of the line described above. Richard Robinson (in *Plato's Earlier Dialectic,* 2d ed., Oxford, 1953, p. 182), among others, has argued that there is no exact correspondence indicated in the text. In "The Line and the Cave," *Phronesis,* vol. 7, pp. 38–45, 1962, John Malcolm argues that a correspondence is intended by Plato. If the Allegory of the Cave is taken as a description of the philosopher's acquisition of knowledge, Malcolm correlates watching the shadows on the wall of the cave with the uneducated state of the common man, seeing the objects in the cave with true belief about material objects, seeing the reflections of objects in the world above with the study of mathematics, and contemplating the objects in the world above with knowledge of the forms. Most of the relevant bibliography associated with the problem of correlating the Allegory of the Cave and the divided line is cited in Malcolm's article. In view of Malcolm's conjecture, is the allegory helpful? Are the fire and the sun identical? Why should those

released from the cave look at the shadows of the world above before looking at the objects themselves?

17   The shade of Achilles in Hades said this when he was asked what he thought of life after death (Greek style). See Homer's *Odyssey*, 11: 489–491.

18   A justification for the impracticality of the philosopher in the eyes of the ordinary man and citizen.

PART 2

Aristotle

(384–322 B.C.)

Plato and Aristotle

Aristotle discerned a difference between knowledge and opinion in human thought, but he drew the boundaries of knowledge more liberally than Plato, extending the range of examples of human knowledge to cases that Plato would have rejected. Where Plato had a tendency to conflate opinion and ignorance, making uncertain information almost as inconsequential as complete ignorance, Aristotle developed analyses of subject matter where certainty was, by his own admission, impossible, but where he took the discovery of statements *true in most instances* to have important consequences for guiding human action. For Aristotle, informed opinion is a kind of knowledge. All cases of knowledge exhibited in human claims to knowledge are considered by Aristotle under two classifications, dependent on whether or not the knowledge considered represents what is always true or what is merely true in many cases, yet of value for practical action. Knowledge which represents what is necessarily true independently of human desires and hopes is called theoretical science. True statements of theoretical science are always true, and hence the range of theoretical science is quite similar to the range of *knowledge* in Plato's defined sense. On the other hand, practical science is the result of studying what is quite often true (perhaps even true in every observed case), but which need not be true if human beings should desire to bring about some change.

Practical science is the result of collecting and speculating upon observed regularities among things, taking into account information accumulated by other human beings as relevant data. Aristotle's contributions to what he called practical science range over analyses of what would now be called biology, psychology, ethics, political science, and literary criticism. His development of techniques of analysis for these areas and the acuteness of many of his conclusions constitute one of the great single contributions to human knowledge. For example, his analysis of drama into plot, character, etc., and his definition of tragedy have become staples of literary criticism in all intellectual traditions which may

57

be traced back to Greek origins. Still, Aristotle's practical science is largely to be tested by later observations of a factual kind, and its content is not as important for philosophy as what he considered to lie within the domain of theoretical science.

Theoretical science, to repeat, is the study of what is necessarily true independently of human desires. The truths of theoretical science are thus certain, and they may be taken to be those universal truths which may be deduced from what Aristotle called *self-evident* principles. Self-evident principles are defined to be those principles which no properly disciplined mind could deny. This does not mean that everyone understands them and knows them to be true, or even that anyone whose attention has been drawn to them sees them immediately to be true and universal, but it means that those who give the matter sufficient attention and take time to learn the techniques of inquiry will come to see their truth. Aristotle concludes that some knowledge of this kind is available to human beings as certain truth. This has the consequence that Aristotle is as impatient with complete skepticism as Plato is.

Two remarks about Aristotle's method might well be made before we consider the content of theoretical science. The point of these remarks may be summarized by saying that Aristotle's approach to philosophical questions is considerably more analytical than Plato's. To begin with, Aristotle often takes comparatively minor problems and examines them carefully, without particular regard in each case for consistency with what he says elsewhere. Thus, although certain points appear in a number of places in Aristotle's writings, there are likely to be discrepancies between the treatments in these places which are not always easy to resolve. This may be due to the fact that there is no dominant insight in Aristotle's writings that plays quite the same role as the theory of ideas does in Platonic philosophy. Instead, Aristotle often uses his philosophical concepts (form, matter, substance, cause, potentiality, actuality, substratum, etc.) as *tools,* to be used in any way that advances the solution of a particular problem. Tools are used at different times in different ways, and perhaps this is why it appears that some of Aristotle's tools are described differently in different contexts. Dealing with the problem of whether these varied accounts are actually consistent with one another is one of the major challenges of Aristotelian scholarship. A consequence of the differences of approach of Aristotle and Plato is that although Platonic philosophy seems to stand or fall with the acceptability of the theory of ideas, Aristotle's analyses can often be accepted or rejected independently of one another. In particular, many philosophers accept much of Aristotle's logical speculation and large amounts of his contributions to practical science, while rejecting many conclusions of his discussions of topics in theoretical science.

The other remark about Aristotle's method is that he introduced to philosophy and science an important technique that is now commonplace. Confronted with some problem, Aristotle often surveyed the answers that had already been given to the problem, as well as possible answers that had not been explicitly given but which could be given. In this way, he was often able to discuss all of the answers to some question in a general way, since it could be shown that any possible answer would be equivalent to one of the answers discussed in the survey. A good classification of the possible answers and an efficient method of working through such a classification often reveals some of the characteristics of any good answer to the problem being considered. The usefulness of this technique is enormous, as is immediately apparent from the fact that an infinite number of incorrect solutions which it is possible to formulate for some problem may be eliminated from consideration if they are all shown to be equivalent to some kind of answer that can be shown to be unacceptable. Classification of possible answers may also be used to answer the question of how many different kinds of something there are, as in the syllogism, where classification into figures, moods, etc., enables one to discover how many valid arguments of syllogistic form there are by working through a finite classification of possible forms of syllogistic argument and checking them for validity.

Consider any two classes of things, say the class of men and the class of animals. To keep the discussion conveniently abstract, we may call these classes A and B. The A's (that is, the members of the class A) and the B's may be related in a number of ways, but Aristotle proposed that they could all be analyzed in terms of four relationships which we may express in the following four *categorical* statements: All A's are B's, No A's are B's, Some A's are B's, and Some A's are not B's. Traditionally, a syllogism is any argument in which three categorical statements appear, one as conclusion and the other two as premises, such that the categorical statements are about three classes, each of which is mentioned in two of the categorical statements of the syllogistic argument. The following two arguments are syllogisms:

> All men are animals.
> All animals are mortal beings.
> Therefore, All men are mortal beings.

and

> All petunias are plants.
> All plants are living things.
> Therefore, All petunias are living things.

To begin with, it might be said that these arguments are obviously *different*, in that one argument is about men, animals, and mortal beings, and the other argument is about petunias, plants, and living things. We might express this difference by saying that the two arguments have different subject *matter*. At the same time, we might take these arguments as having the same *form*, and hence as belonging to the same classification. For example, consider the following *form* of an argument:

All X's are Y's.
All Y's are Z's.
Therefore, All X's are Z's.

This form is not an *argument* because it does not have sentences as parts, but expressions which may be turned into sentences when appropriate substitutions are made for X's, Y's, and Z's. Both of our previous *arguments* can be taken to have this *form*, since substitution of *men* for X's, *animals* for Y's, and *mortal beings* for Z's results in the first argument, while substitution of *petunias* for X's, *plants* for Y's, and *living things* for Z's results in the second argument. Since X's, Y's, and Z's could be substituted for by the names of any collections of things, it is clear that an *infinite* number of possible actual arguments might have this form.

There will be only a finite number of *forms* of syllogistic argument, since each argument has three categorical statements and three classes mentioned in it. One can make a list of these possible *forms* and work through the list checking those forms which are valid. Then when one wants to know if a syllogistic argument is valid, he can determine the form of the argument and then check the list of forms that he has constructed. This is what Aristotle attempted, and it shows the power of the analytic method. An *infinite* number of possible syllogistic arguments is analyzed by constructing a finite *classification* of such arguments such that any actual syllogistic arguments must belong to one of the classifications. Studying the classification, in turn, enables us to have *knowledge* about *all* the possible particular syllogistic arguments that we might encounter in philosophical practice.

An exhaustive classification of possible answers may also be applied to questions of theoretical science, which, as we have seen, deals with truths not affected by human desires. One question is: what kinds of entities is theoretical science about? If Platonic antecedents are taken into account, two properties of entities may be considered which, taken together, provide a fourfold classification of the possible objects dealt with by theoretical science. Plato considers objects which are sensible (known to sense experience), like tables and chairs, and objects which are not sensible, the ideas or forms. Further, we find in Plato reference to changing objects and to objects which do not change. Now in Plato's discussion, sensible objects and changing objects are correlated, as are the non-sensible and eternal objects, in that any object belonging to one of the correlated classes also belongs to the other. The possible fourfold classification suggested by the four terms (sensible changing objects, sensible eternal objects, non-sensible eternal objects, and non-sensible changing objects) is discussed by Aristotle. He finds objects in all these classes except the class of non-sensible changing objects. Physics is the theoretical science of sensible changing objects, mathematics the study of sensible eternal objects (Aristotle notes that some mathematical statements appear to speak of non-sensible eternal objects), and metaphysics or theology is the study of non-sensible eternal objects.

A comparison of this classification of Aristotle's range of certain knowledge with Plato's range of certain knowledge is sufficient to point up a marked difference between Plato and Aristotle. Whereas Plato felt that the objects of certain knowledge must be unchanging, Aristotle held that we might have certain knowledge about changing objects. Thus, a crucial difference between Plato and Aristotle is that the latter felt that an adequate philosophy would have to explain knowledge of changing things. Is there such knowledge? Evidently Aristotle felt that one could know just as certainly that some arbitrary acorn would grow, in proper circumstances, into an oak tree, as that one could know that the arithmetical sum of two and two is four. We shall see in succeeding chapters how Aristotle justified the claim that theoretical science could be about changing objects. It is worth noticing, however, that Plato's Theory of Ideas cannot provide a ready justification for physics in the Aristotelian sense, although it can provide a justification for mathematical knowledge without difficulty. The structure of the world of being, as Plato described it, has remarkable similarities to the structure of many branches of mathematics. For example, just as the relationships between the ideas never change, so the relationships between the integers can be taken never to change. An integer is eternally odd or even, prime or not prime, divisible or not divisible by some other integer. If the world of being is used in an attempt to justify knowledge about changing objects, difficulties arise. Suppose an object of sense experience to be red. As long as it stays red, one might explain its redness by saying that it participates in the idea of redness. But suppose that it turns blue, as some objects do, over a period of time. At the end of the time, this can be explained by saying that it now participates in the idea of blueness. But what of the time between? Does it participate less and less in one form, and more and more in the other? Is there a time at which it participates in neither? Problems of this kind prove difficult for Platonic philosophy. Plato seems to have considered them, but perhaps it was the difficulty in answering them which led him to deny certain knowledge of changing objects.

Since Plato and Aristotle disagree, we might inquire which of them is right and which of them is wrong. The point at issue between Platonic and Aristotelian philosophy is that of the definition of *knowledge*. It is not generally thought that definitions are true or false. Whether one definition is better than another is a question of which definition preserves certain accepted usages of the word being defined, and which definition makes it possible to communicate in the most convenient fashion. Such questions are not settled by any simple appeal to commonly agreed-upon facts. As our characterization of epistemology has shown, a basic problem of epistemology is to decide which of the knowledge claims that we make are philosophically deserving of the honorific term *knowledge*. Is it as certain that an acorn cannot grow into a lion as it is that four is the sum of two and two? The choice between philosophies which assert and deny, respectively, that the one claim is as certain as the other is somewhat difficult. While one can say that to accept *both* the Platonic and Aristotelian philosophies is to contradict oneself, to say that one of them must be false is to make a mistake. The strongest claim it is reasonable to make is that one or both of them does not define *knowledge* in a way compatible with what we consider a fruitful way of explaining human experience.

There are difficulties in completing the philosophical program suggested by either Plato or Aristotle. Attacks on the difficulties of completing one program by someone who accepts another philosopher's viewpoint do not constitute a *proof* that the attacker occupies a superior philosophical position, since the attack does not *prove* in turn that the attacker's position is satisfactory. An uncommitted person attempts to evaluate the epistemological claims of philosophers by a study of human experience in an effort to determine which definition of *knowledge* seems to fit human experience best. In such a study, there seems to be room for legitimate disagreement. In comparing Plato and Aristotle, for example, it is necessary to decide whether certainty ought to be a property of what we wish to call knowledge. This decision is not to be made simply on commonly accepted facts but is in part a decision as to how we wish to use our language.

Categories and Classification

The philosophies of both Plato and Aristotle are at least partly based on the supposition that every sentence expressing a knowledge claim can be analyzed as having two essential *parts,* which may be called the subject and the predicate. The *subject,* in this sense, is the expression designating what is talked about in the sentence, and the *predicate* is the expression which attributes some characteristic to the subject. Not every sentence has an obvious predicate expression and an obvious subject expression, for example, "John plays tennis.". The theory of analysis referred to, however, argues that any sentence which is a knowledge claim is equivalent in meaning to some sentence which does consist of a subject expression and a predicate expression between which occurs some form of the verb *to be,* normally, an occurrence of *is* or *are.* "John plays tennis." may thus be transformed into "John is a tennis player.". "John is playing tennis." would not be the appropriate equivalent sentence since "John plays tennis." may be true when it is said (because John *is* a tennis player) even though "John is playing tennis." is false at that time. With care in application, the position that all knowledge may be analyzed as being of the form 'X is Y.', where X is a subject expression and Y is a predicate expression, it true of many claims to knowledge. As we have seen, the distinctive feature of Platonic epistemology is the argument that a knowledge claim 'X is Y.' is true if X is some object in the world of becoming and Y is a form in which the object participates. The Platonic theory of knowledge implicitly assumes that 'X is Y.' is the general structure of knowledge claims.

Aristotle employed his method of classification to answer two kinds of questions about knowledge expressed in the general form 'X is Y.'. One question asks how many different kinds of Y there might be in such sentences, and the other question asks in what way X and Y might be related. The first question is answered by Aristotle in a list of ten *categories,* the Y of any particular 'X is Y.' statement belonging to one of the ten categories. The second question is answered by Aristotle in a discussion of the *predicables*, which for any particular statement of '*X* is *Y*.' form explains the relationship between the *X* and the *Y* of the statement.

In both of these cases, Aristotle discusses distinctions made *in the language* of the statement '*X* is *Y*.', so that the categories may be taken partly as a grammatical division of all possible expressions which may tke the place of *Y* in some '*X* is *Y*.' statement; and he also takes the distinctions as reflecting distinctions in being, or what exists, so that the categories may be taken to explain *what* may be distinctly predicated of some object. The categories are ten in number:

1. Substance   (what *X* is, what kind of a thing *X* is)
2. Quantity   (some measure of *X*)
3. Quality   (some qualitative property of *X*)
4. Relation   (some relationship of *X* to other things)
5. Place   (some place where *X* is)
6. Time   (some time at which *X* is referred to)
7. Situation   (some environment in which *X* is found)
8. State   (some condition in which *X* is found)
9. Action   (something *X* does or is doing)
10. Passion   (something done to *X*)

The following example may indicate how the categories are to be interpreted, since for each of the ten examples, the predicate belongs to the appropriate category in the list of categories:

1. Socrates is a man.
2. Socrates is 5 feet 7 inches (tall).
3. Socrates is wise.
4. Socrates is the husband of Xanthippe.
5. Socrates is in Athens.
6. Socrates is alive in 321 B.C.
7. Socrates is surrounded by his students.
8. Socrates is barefoot.
9. Socrates is running.
10. Socrates is defeated.

It is clear that the categories involve some problems, in that it may prove difficult to place the *Y* of some particular '*X* is *Y*.' statement into a definite category, but it is equally clear that the categories represent prima facie an interesting and fruitful classification into which we might try to place particular *Y*'s. For reasons that will be discussed shortly, the most important distinction for Aristotle is that between the category *substance* and all the other categories. Consequently, difficulties with placing a *Y* into a category are serious only if the *Y* in question seems to belong both to the category *substance* and some other category. Aristotle's theory of knowledge supposes that this difficulty will not arise, although one may have the minor difficulty of deciding between, for example, the categories *place* and *situation* in a particular analysis.

Given some particular 'X is Y.' statement and knowledge of the appropriate category of Y, the problem is still to be raised as to how X and Y are related. For example, suppose of two such statements 'X is Y.' and 'X is Z.' that X is the same in both, but that Y and Z are two predicates belonging to some one category. Could these predicates, both belonging to the same category, express differing kinds of information about X? The Aristotelian answer is that they can and indeed that there are five possible relationships between the X and Y of any 'X is Y.' statement:

1. Definition
2. Genus
3. Differentia
4. Attribute
5. Accident

Because these notions have become common intellectual coin, they are easy to understand in one sense but difficult to reconstruct in exactly the way that Aristotle meant them. 'X is Y.' is a definition if Y defines X, but in Aristotle's philosophy there is only one way of accomplishing this correctly. Y must be what X is essentially.

To see what this means, an example may prove helpful. Suppose we ask "What is a man?", anticipating a definition of the form 'A man is W.'. What will take the place of W? To answer this question, the properties of three *normal* men, say Tom, Dick, and Harry, will be compared. Any property not shared by all men would be ruled out as a possible defining property of *man*. This, for Aristotle, will not include examination of those properties of some men which have been taken from them as the result of accident, for example, the losing of a leg. To consider the definition of man, we consider the properties common to those specimens that we would pick out without reservation as men. Suppose that Tom is 5 feet 10 inches tall, but Dick and Harry are of some other height. If we put '5 feet 10 inches tall' for W in the definition, we get "A man is 5 feet 10 inches tall.". This statement, construed as "Some man is 5 feet 10 inches tall." is true, but false if construed as "All men are 5 feet 10 inches tall." Being-5-feet-10-inches-tall is apparently a property that a man may or may not have. It is consequently, an *accidental* property of any man of whom it is true. Relationship (5) above, accident, holds between an X and Y when Y is an accidental property of X, that is, a property which some X's may have, while others may not have.

It is thus necessary to restrict attention to properties shared by *all* X's. A possibility is that Y is some property shared by all X's as well as by some non-X's. For example, if we substitute 'an animal' for W, we get the statement "A man is an animal.", which is true, but which is similar to the true statements "A goat is an animal.", "A horse is an animal.", etc.

Thus Y may be predicable of each X, but also of A's, B's, etc. In this case, X and Y, if Y is predicable of each member of classes other than X, like A, B, etc., are such that Y is said to be a genus of X, and expresses the existence of some large class of things of which X is a subclass. Now, in some other 'X is Y.' statement, Y may describe the property of some genus of X which singles out the class of X's as a subclass or species of that genus. Aristotelians usually consider the class of animal to be a genus of the class of men, which is distinguished in the genus of animals by the property of rationality. Thus "A man is a rational animal." is taken to express the fact that *rational* is the *differentia* of the species man within the genus animal, since all men are rational and no animals who are not men are rational.

To this point we have considered properties which a man might or might not have, as well as properties which all men have, but other beings might have as well. (There may be other beings than man which possess the property of rationality in Aristotelian systems, God being an obvious non-animal candidate.) This has enabled us to consider briefly *accident, genus,* and *differentia*.

What is left is apparently the class of those properties which *all* men have, and only men have. It is at this point that the *crucial* notion of Aristotle's scheme becomes apparent. Of those properties of men, or of any arbitrary class X, Aristotle distinguishes between those which are considered necessary for the members of the class and those which are merely contingent. This distinction, of utmost importance to Aristotelian thought, might be considered in the following way. In the case of man, suppose that we are faced with two properties compounded of simple properties, namely, *laughing animal* and *rational animal,* which all men and only men exhibit. Aristotelians would consider the latter property an *essential* or *necessary* property of man, because it is the meaning of *man* which is defined in its terms, while the former is only an attribute, because it is conceivable that all men and only men may have laughed as animals because of historical accident. In this case, the contingent property of being a laughing animal is an attribute of man (we say that all men and only men laugh but not that this property is essential to man), while the necessary property of being a rational animal is the defining property of man. Thus "A man is a rational animal." ends the search for a definition of man, yielding a property which all men and only men have in some necessary sense. The property that defines man, or any X, is also called the essence or form of X, so that being a rational animal is the form or essence of man.

The discussion of the predicables, generalized from our discussion of 'A man is a W.', is extremely important to an understanding of Aristotle. Further, a great deal of the acceptability or unacceptability of Aristotelian philosophy may be traced to the acceptability or unacceptability of the notion of a necessary property used in describing the essence of anything. What is involved in the notion of a necessary property? It seems to rest on *two* important considerations: one of them is that there are *natural* groupings of clearly separated objects of sense experience in the world which may be called *natural kinds,* such as men, horses, etc., and secondly that these groupings are to be accounted for in some nonarbitrary fashion, that is, that there is only one correct way of dividing up the properties of members of a natural kind into contingent and necessary properties, so as to discover the essence of a natural kind. Without such an essence, as will be shown, there is no *knowledge* of natural kinds for Aristotelians. In a way, Aristotelians transfer the basis for certainty from the unchanging structure of a world of being to an unchanging structure of natural kinds defined in terms of essences or forms. These natural kinds are groupings in the Platonic world of becoming, and hence could not be objects of knowledge for Platonists.

This unchanging structure is clearly related to the difference between what is called essential and accidental predication. To see why a distinction between these two kinds of predication is called for, the following examples are useful:

A. Socrates is a man. A man is an animal.

B. Socrates is 5 feet 7 inches. 5 feet 7 inches is a height.

From (A) we may legitimately conclude "Socrates is an animal.", but (B) yields "Socrates is a height.", which is absurd. What has gone wrong? It might be claimed that the first sentence in (B) is not grammatically well formed: one wants to ask of this sentence "5 feet 7 inches *what?*" In many contexts, we know that this means 5 feet 7 inches tall. But it *may* mean 5 feet 7 inches from the door, or almost anything. Now, if this sentence and the other one are made explicit, something like (B′) can be obtained:

B′. Socrates is 5 feet 7 inches tall. 5 feet 7 inches tall is a height.

It is clear that (A) and (B′) are not exactly grammatical parallels in several ways. To see this, note that the paraphrase "Any entity which is a man is also an entity which is an animal.", which is suitable for the second sentence of (A), results in nonsense of the following kind for (B′): "Any entity which is 5 feet 7 inches tall is an entity which is a height.". A more Aristotelian way of marking the difference is to note that in the examples given above for Socrates, sentences 2–10 are of the kind that are true at some time for Socrates but not necessarily true at all times. On the other hand the first sentence is true at all times for Socrates and is consequentially an essential predication since we could not imagine it otherwise, while 2–10 are accidental predications. In terms of traditional English grammar, sentences like the first are completed with a common noun in the place of *Y*, and the rest of the sentences are completed with different kinds of predicate expressions.

Reflection indicates that any '*X* is *Y*.' statement in which *Y* is related to *X* as genus, or as differentia, or as definition, is an example of an essential predication of Y to X. Where essential predication obtains, the rule 'If Y is predicated of X (essentially), and X is predicated of Z (essentially), then Y is predicated of Z.' may be used to make inferences, but not where accidental predication is involved. From these considerations, it is clear that theoretical science will be based upon essential predications and predicates which belong to the category *substance*.

Essential Predication

Restricting consideration of predication to essential predication makes it clear that predications can be arranged in a kind of hierarchy. To begin with, the following diagram might be chosen to represent the example of predications about Socrates given earlier. In this diagram, an arrow will signify that what stands at the point of the arrow is what is predicated of what stands at the nock:

Animal

↑

Man

↑

Socrates

Ways of expanding this hierarchy are obvious. It might be rapidly expanded to the following:

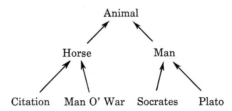

Animal

Horse   Man

Citation   Man O' War   Socrates   Plato

This is reminiscent of the way in which classification of living things is undertaken in biology, and it well might be so reminiscent, since the classificatory scheme of biology is derived from biologists who were familiar with Aristotelian notions of classification. Problems of biological classification may be thought of as problems for this kind of classification in general. One problem is whether or not everything can be brought into the

69

classification. For Aristotelians, the answer is affirmative, since each individual belongs to a natural kind, and the structure may be developed from the necessary properties associated with each natural kind. Acceptance of the Aristotelian outlook may be traced to this problem: Is the lack of a completely suitable biological classification a proof that the Aristotelian notion of natural kinds and an associated hierarchy is mistaken? Not necessarily. To an Aristotelian, it may indicate that the necessary properties of individuals have not all been isolated yet.

Adopting the Aristotelian viewpoint that a complete hierarchy is possible, there are still problems to be faced:

1. What will be at the bottom places in the hierarchy?
2. What will be at the top places in the hierarchy?
3. Are there levels in the hierarchy such as those assumed in our fragment?
4. If (3) is answered in the affirmative, will the bottom places in the hierarchy be at the same level?
5. If (3) is answered in the affirmative, will the top places in the hierarchy be at the same level?
6. Will there be a finite or infinite number of places in the hierarchy?
7. Can anything occur in more than one place in the hierarchy?

Although this is obviously not a complete listing of such problems, the questions raised here represent the kind of problem that Aristotle and Aristotelians must deal with. Actually, the Aristotelian position that the hierarchy is possible means that (6) must be answered by saying that there are only a finite number of places in the hierarchy. Aristotle argues that an infinite number of places is impossible because then knowledge of the hierarchy would be impossible. This argument is not conclusive since it shows only that philosophy and science may not attain complete understanding of the hierarchy if there are an infinite number of places in it, but that in some sense may be the case. However, it can be shown (although Aristotle probably did not know this) that a finite hierarchy follows from the assumption that no individual has more than a finite number of properties that are necessary, as well as the assumption that the hierarchy can be consistently described.

The answer to (1) is that *primary* substances stand in the bottom places of the hierarchy. Because a primary substance is defined to be anything of which things may be predicated, but which are predicated of nothing, this follows from the characterization of a primary substance. From examples which are given by Aristotle, the answers to both (3) and (4) appear to be affirmative. On the other hand, the answers to (2) and (5) prove difficult. There is some evidence that the answer to (2) is *substance,* in which case (5) is trivially answered in the affirmative, since there will be only one top place in the hierarchy. *Substance,* of course, was also the first category, so that some discussion of *substance* is required to distinguish this kind of substance from primary substance. Further, we may ask whether what is at any place in the hierarchy exists, and if so in what sense.

Primary substances are the only things which can be said to exist in a fundamental sense, precisely in the sense that nothing could be said to exist if they did not. This marks an important distinction between Plato and Aristotle. Where the ideas are said to *exist*, they are also conceived in a fashion which apparently makes their existence independent of the existence of objects of sense experience. The idea of red refers to an entity which exists independently of any object in the world of becoming. In Aristotelian philosophy, however, the possible truth of any sentence of the form '*X* is red.' is not dependent on a relationship between *X* and objects in a world of being. Thus, a universal like *red* is defined to be *that which is common* to a number of objects, with no suggestion that the universal is a separately existing thing. The reason that a universal may be predicated of any of a number of things is that it may be predicated of any of the things which have that universal in common. A universal is simply a predicate that might be applied to any arbitrary object. For Aristotle, only the individuals of sense experience *exist*, which means that all other affirmations of an '*X* is *Y*.' kind and all human knowledge is dependent on primary substances which are objects of sense experience.

What may prove initially surprising is that knowledge (theoretical science) is not knowledge *of* primary substances but of something else which is developed from an analysis of primary substances. If primary substances are the objects of sense experience, Aristotle's point can be gathered from his observations that sense experience is not knowledge. On this point, although not on its significance, Aristotle and Plato agree. In an interesting argument which occurs at the beginning of the *Metaphysics*, Aristotle notes that all men have the power of sense experience and that indeed they may share this with other animals. Yet knowledge is so unevenly distributed among human beings that it cannot be equivalent to sense experience. Memory must be added to sense experience, as well as *experience* in a broader sense, which enables man (unlike the other animals) to profit by noting similarities between remembered sense experiences and present sense experiences, in effect making present sense experience more sophisticated than it would otherwise be. This point is supported by the generally superior judgments of humans compared with the judgments that we may impute to animals. Even this kind of human experience, however, is not equivalent to knowledge, for the ability of men to perform effective action is more evenly distributed than the ability to assimilate theoretical knowledge. The point here is that two men may be equally good artisans of some kind but quite unequal in the degree in which they can explain their art. Knowledge is really the ability to understand and explain why things are as they are, and knowledge must be knowledge, not of the things themselves, but of the causes, principles, etc., which account for the way things are. Knowledge is thus knowledge of the difference, say, between the accidental and essential properties of something. Clearly two men may be able to deal with Socrates's actions with roughly equal practical success, while only one of them can explain Socrates and his actions in terms of Socrates's accidental and essential properties, as well as in terms of the relations of these properties to the properties of other individuals. Thus it is not surprising in Aristotle that the individual is not the subject of knowledge, even though only individuals are said to exist. The individual can be known only by comparing its properties with the properties of other things. But this is knowing essential properties, since it is through essential properties that things are compared.

The result of this Aristotelian scheme is that what exists is dependent on individuals, or primary substances, at the bottom of the hierarchy described earlier. Knowledge, however, is not knowledge of these primary substances, but knowledge is about the hierarchy, that is, the essential properties that link individuals to other individuals. Aristotelianism, if successful, avoids one difficulty, that of explaining how Red (as a unique idea or form) can be shared by many particulars because it *defines* red to be what is shared by a certain class of particulars. But Aristotelianism has its own problems, among them that of explaining how similarities are noted and of presenting a methodology to ensure that the similarities that are used to construct the hierarchy are in fact based on essential properties.

Further, there is the problem that not all 'X is Y.' statements true of the hierarchy are such that X refers to a primary substance. Some 'X is Y.' statements are true of higher levels of the hierarchy; for example, our repeated fragment contains the statement "A man is an animal.". The subject of this statement is not an individual (What man could be referred to?). Aristotelians call the subjects of these higher level statements 'secondary substances', but the question is how is it possible to explain knowledge about secondary substances in terms of the fundamental primary substances.

Finally, it should be clear that the answer to (7) must be negative. We do not want to have both 'X is Y.' and 'Y is X.' true of the *hierarchy* unless X and Y are identical. The appearance of such statements would destroy the levels structure of the hierarchy, and Aristotle takes time to demonstrate that no essential predication could occur along with its converse predication within the structure of human knowledge.

From what has been said about Aristotle it may be possible to obtain some clues about the Aristotelian treatment of change. Where Plato had taken all change to be without the realm of knowledge, Aristotle argued that objects in the world of sense experience changed but that there was an invariant, nonchanging aspect of these objects which might be the object of knowledge about them. Thus, any object of sense experience could be considered the member of a natural kind, in so far as it is intelligible, whose essence or form could be known and could serve as the basis of knowledge about the object. Apparent change in an object, where one accidental property of it became replaced by another accidental property, is as far from being known through theoretical science as it is through the theory of ideas.

Readings from Aristotle

The relationship between Socrates, Plato, and Aristotle is easy to remember. Plato was a student of Socrates's and Aristotle was a student of Plato's. *Student,* however, does not mean the same thing in each case. Plato, as a young man, heard Socrates discoursing on the streets of Athens and learned from him by absorbing what must have been the substance of a group of speeches delivered on haphazard topics as they were raised to Socrates for consideration. Aristotle was a student in Plato's *Academy* and as a result was no doubt exposed to a systematic treatment of Plato's philosophical positions. In turn, Alexander the Great was tutored in King Philip of Macedonia's court by Aristotle. This sequence of three teacher-student relationships is contemporaneous with the last one hundred years of the Greek intellectual achievements that proved influential for the Western philosophical tradition.

For Aristotle, the problem of textual interpretation is particularly acute. Not all of Aristotle's writings are consistent, and they are usually made coherent by putting them into a sequence which is supposed to represent his early acceptance of the theory of ideas which he learned in the Academy and his gradual achievement of a distinctively Aristotelian epistemology which is inconsistent with the theory of ideas. This hypothesis is developed in *Aristotle: Fundamentals of the History of His Development* by Werner Jaeger. The chapters on Aristotle, as well as the selections which are here included, are taken from Aristotelian writings which represent more or less mature Aristotelian thought in that they explicitly argue against the theory of ideas and in favor of those doctrines that are thought to be the basis of Aristotle's developed philosophical position.

Aristotle's writings do not have the polish and literary elegance ascribed to the Platonic dialogues. Some commentators have felt that Aristotle wrote some literary works which could match Plato's in terms of elegance, but that they have not survived the vagaries of manuscript history. Certainly the manuscripts that are available represent compilations of what may have been lecture notes as well as rough manuscript which contains internal evidence that Aristotle intended to revise it. Some of the manuscript material is almost certainly lecture-note material not written by Aristotle, but taken down by one of his students. Out of all this montage, it is difficult to settle on particular statements that are *Aristotle's*, as opposed to being *Aristotelian*.

It is not obvious that sound philosophy must be elegantly written, as many scholars who compare Aristotle invidiously with Plato on this account seem to have assumed. Where Plato and Berkeley seem to have written important philosophy with a literary flair, Aristotle and Kant seem to have produced rather dull copy for their exciting philosophical ideas. It would take an extremely partisan historian to argue that philosophical importance lies primarily with those who can write elegant prose. There may, in fact, be a rather easily grasped relationship between the analytical approach of Aristotle to philosophy that is discussed in earlier chapters and the choppy construction of the manuscripts available to us that no editing could entirely remove. In fact, one might make an invidious comparison in the other direction by arguing that a literary style makes it easier to camouflage weakness of argument under a stylistic cover. It is important for the purposes of philosophical evaluation to keep considerations of style from influencing one's judgment of the cogency of the argument.

Three selections from Aristotle's epistemological writings have been reprinted here:

A.	*Categories*	Chapters 1–5:33, Greek 1–2^b.
B.	*Posterior Analytics*	Books 1–6:10, Greek 71^a–74^b.
C.	*Metaphysics*	Book 7:1–7:7, Greek 1028^a–1032^a.

These selections are reprinted from the Oxford translation of *The Works of Aristotle*, edited by J. A. Smith and Sir W. D. Ross. Selections *A* and *B* are from volume I, and selection *C* is from volume VIII. They are reprinted here by kind permission of The Clarendon Press, Oxford. For those who can read classical Greek, *The Loeb Classical Library* editions have a facing English and Greek text.

The following bibliography consists of some secondary sources for the study of Aristotle:

Aaron, R. I.: *The Theory of Universals*, Oxford, 1952.
Allan, D. J.: *The Philosophy of Aristotle*, London, 1952.
Anton, J. P.: *Aristotle's Theory of Contrariety*, New York, 1957.
During, I., and G. E. L. Owen (eds.): *Aristotle and Plato in the Mid-fourth Century*, Göteborg, 1960.
Hamlyn, D. W.: "Aristotle on Predication," *Phronesis*, vol. 6, pp. 110–127, 1961.
*Jaeger, W.: *Aristotle: Fundamentals of the History of His Development*, Oxford, 1960. (Oxford Paperbound.)

Joseph, H. W. B.: *An Introduction to Logic*, Oxford, 1916.

Lukasiewicz, J.: *Aristotle's Syllogistic from the Standpoint of Modern Formal Logic*, Oxford, 1957.

*Mure, G. R. G.: *Aristotle*, Oxford, 1935. (Oxford Paperbound.)

Owens, J.: *The Doctrine of Being in the Aristotelian* Metaphysics, Toronto, 1957.

*Randall, J. H. Jr.: *Aristotle*, New York, 1960. (Columbia Paperbound.)

*Ross, W. D.: *Aristotle*, New York, 1956. (Meridian Paperbound.)

Sellars, Wilfrid: "Substance and Form in Aristotle," *The Journal of Philosophy*, vol. 54, pp. 688–699, 1957.

*Taylor, A. E.: *Aristotle*, New York, 1955. (Dover Paperbound.)

Zeller, E.: *Aristotle and the Earlier Peripatetics*, New York, 1962.

A From the CATEGORIES

1°   Things are said to be named 'equivocally' when, though they have a common name, the definition corresponding with the name differs for each. Thus, a real man and a figure in a picture can both lay claim to the name 'animal'; yet these are equivocally so named, for, though they have a common name, the definition corresponding with the name differs for each.

5   For should any one define in what sense each is an animal, his definition in the one case will be appropriate to that case only.

On the other hand, things are said to be named 'univocally' which have both the name and the definition answering to the name in common. A man and an ox are both 'animal', and these are univocally so named, inasmuch as not only the name, but also the definition, is the same in both

10   cases: for if a man should state in what sense each is an animal, the statement in the one case would be identical with that in the other.

Things are said to be named 'derivatively', which derive their name from some other name, but differ from it in termination. Thus the gram-

15   marian derives his name from the word 'grammar', and the courageous man from the word 'courage'.

Forms of speech are either simple or composite. Examples of the latter are such expressions as 'the man runs', 'the man wins'; of the former 'man', 'ox', 'runs', 'wins'.

20   Of things themselves some are predicable of a subject, and are never present in a subject. Thus 'man' is predicable of the individual man, and is never present in a subject.

By being 'present in a subject' I do not mean present as parts are present in a whole, but being incapable of existence apart from the said subject.[1]

25   Some things, again, are present in a subject, but are never predicable of a subject. For instance, a certain point of grammatical knowledge is present in the mind, but is not predicable of any subject; or again, a certain

1

2

whiteness may be present in the body (for colour requires a material basis), yet it is never predicable of anything.[2]

Other things, again, are both predicable of a subject and present in a subject. Thus while knowledge is present in the human mind, it is predicable of grammar.[3]   1[b]

There is, lastly, a class of things which are neither present in a subject nor predicable of a subject, such as the individual man or the individual horse. But, to speak more generally, that which is individual and has the   5 character of a unit is never predicable of a subject. Yet in some cases there is nothing to prevent such being present in a subject. Thus a certain point of grammatical knowledge is present in a subject.[4]

3   When one thing is predicated of another, all that which is predicable   10 of the predicate will be predicable also of the subject. Thus, 'man' is predicated of the individual man; but 'animal' is predicated of 'man'; it will, therefore, be predicable of the individual man also: for the individual   15 man is both 'man' and 'animal'.

If genera are different and co-ordinate, their differentiae are themselves different in kind.[5] Take as an instance the genus 'animal' and the genus 'knowledge'. 'With feet', 'two-footed', 'winged', 'aquatic', are differentiae of 'animal'; the species of knowledge are not distinguished by the same differentiae. One species of knowledge does not differ from another in being 'two-footed'.

But where one genus is subordinate to another, there is nothing to   20 prevent their having the same differentiae: for the greater class is predicated of the lesser, so that all the differentiae of the predicate will be differentiae also of the subject.

4   Expressions which are in no way composite signify substance,   25 quantity, quality, relation, place, time, position, state, action, or affection. To sketch my meaning roughly, examples of substance are 'man' or 'the horse', of quantity, such terms as 'two cubits long' or 'three cubits long', of quality, such attributes as 'white', 'grammatical'. 'Double', 'half', 'greater', fall under the category of relation; 'in the market place', 'in the Lyceum',   2[a] under that of place; 'yesterday', 'last year', under that of time. 'Lying', 'sitting', are terms indicating 'position'; 'shod', 'armed', state; 'to lance', 'to cauterize', action; 'to be lanced', 'to be cauterized', affection.

No one of these terms, in and by itself, involves an affirmation; it is by the combination of such terms that positive or negative statements arise.   5 For every assertion must, as is admitted, be either true or false, whereas expressions which are not in any way composite, such as 'man', 'white', 'runs', 'wins', cannot be either true or false.   10

5   Substance, in the truest and primary and most definite sense of the word, is that which is neither predicable of a subject nor present in a subject; for instance, the individual man or horse. But in a secondary sense those things are called substances within which, as species, the primary

15 substances are included; also those which, as genera, include the species. For instance, the individual man is included in the species 'man', and the genus to which the species belongs is 'animal'; these, therefore—that is to say, the species 'man' and the genus 'animal'—are termed secondary substances.

20 It is plain from what has been said that both the name and the definition of the predicate must be predicable of the subject. For instance, 'man' is predicated of the individual man. Now in this case the name of the species 'man' is applied to the individual, for we use the term 'man' in describing the individual; and the definition of 'man' will also be predicated of the individual man, for the individual man is both man and animal. Thus, both the name and the definition of the species are predica-
25 ble of the individual.

With regard, on the other hand, to those things which are present in a subject, it is generally the case that neither their name nor their definition is predicable of that in which they are present. Though, however, the definition is never predicable, there is nothing in certain cases to prevent
30 the name being used. For instance, 'white' being present in a body is predicated of that in which it is present, for a body is called white: the definition, however, of the colour 'white' is never predicable of the body.[6]

Everything except primary substances is either predicable of a primary substance or present in a primary substance. This becomes evident
35 by reference to particular instances which occur. 'Animal' is predicated of the species 'man', therefore of the individual man, for if there were no individual man of whom it could be predicated, it could not be predicated
2[b] of the species 'man' at all. Again, colour is present in body, therefore in individual bodies, for if there were no individual body in which it was present, it could not be present in body at all. Thus everything except primary substances is either predicated of primary substances, or is present
5 in them, and if these last did not exist, it would be impossible for anything else to exist.

Of secondary substances, the species is more truly substance than the genus, being more nearly related to primary substance. For if any one should render an account of what a primary substance is, he would render a more instructive account, and one more proper to the subject, by stating
10 the species than by stating the genus. Thus, he would give a more instructive account of an individual man by stating that he was man than by stating that he was animal, for the former description is peculiar to the individual in a greater degree, while the latter is too general. Again, the man who gives an account of the nature of an individual tree will give a more instructive account by mentioning the species 'tree' than by mentioning the genus 'plant'.

15 Moreover, primary substances are most properly called substances in virtue of the fact that they are the entities which underlie everything else, and that everything else is either predicated of them or present in them.

Now the same relation which subsists between primary substance and everything else subsists also between the species and the genus: for the species is to the genus as subject is to predicate, since the genus is predi- 20 cated of the species, whereas the species cannot be predicated of the genus. Thus we have a second ground for asserting that the species is more truly substance than the genus.

Of species themselves, except in the case of such as are genera, no one is more truly substance than another. We should not give a more appropriate account of the individual man by stating the species to which 25 he belonged, than we should of an individual horse by adopting the same method of definition. In the same way, of primary substances, no one is more truly substance than another; an individual man is not more truly substance than an individual ox.

It is, then, with good reason that of all that remains, when we exclude primary substances, we concede to species and genera alone the name 'secondary substance', for these alone of all the predicates convey a 30 knowledge of primary substance. For it is by stating the species or the genus that we appropriately define any individual man; and we shall make our definition more exact by stating the former than by stating the latter. All other things that we state, such as that he is white, that he runs, and so 35 on, are irrelevant to the definition. Thus it is just that these alone, apart from primary substances, should be called substances.

B   *From the POSTERIOR ANALYTICS*

BOOK I

1   All instruction given or received by way of argument proceeds from 71ᵃ pre-existent knowledge. This becomes evident upon a survey of all the species of such instruction. The mathematical sciences and all other speculative disciplines are acquired in this way, and so are the two forms of dialectical reasoning, syllogistic and inductive; for each of these latter 5 makes use of old knowledge to impart new, the syllogism assuming an audience that accepts its premises, induction exhibiting the universal as implicit in the clearly known particular. Again, the persuasion exerted by rhetorical arguments is in principle the same, since they use either example, a kind of induction, or enthymeme, a form of syllogism.[7] 10

The pre-existent knowledge required is of two kinds. In some cases admission of the fact must be assumed, in others comprehension of the meaning of the term used, and sometimes both assumptions are essential. Thus, we assume that every predicate can be either truly affirmed or truly denied of any subject, and that 'triangle' means so and so; as regards 'unit' we have to make the double assumption of the meaning of the word and the existence of the thing. The reason is that these several objects are not 15 equally obvious to us. Recognition of a truth may in some cases contain as factors both previous knowledge and also knowledge acquired simultaneously with that recognition—knowledge, this latter, of the particulars actually falling under the universal and therein already virtually known. For example, the student knew beforehand that the angles of every triangle are equal to two right angles; but it was only at the actual moment at which he was being led on to recognize this as true in the instance before him that he came to know this figure inscribed in the semicircle to be a triangle. For some things (viz. the singulars finally reached which are not predicable of anything else as subject) are only learnt in this way, i.e. there is here no recognition through a middle of a minor term as subject to a major. Before he was led on to recognition or before he actually drew a conclusion, we should perhaps say that in a manner he knew, in a manner not.[8]

If he did not in an unqualified sense of the term *know* the existence of this triangle, how could he *know* without qualification that its angles were equal to two right angles? No: clearly he *knows* not without qualification but only in the sense that he *knows* universally. If this distinction is not drawn, we are faced with the dilemma in the *Meno*: either a man will learn nothing or what he already knows; for we cannot accept the solution which some people offer. A man is asked, 'Do you, or do you not, know that every pair is even?' He says he does know it. The questioner then produces a particular pair, of the existence, and so a *fortiori* of the evenness, of which he was unaware. The solution which some people offer is to assert that they do not know that every pair is even, but only that everything which they know to be a pair is even: yet what they know to be even is that of which they have demonstrated evenness, i.e. what they made the subject of their premiss, viz. not merely every triangle or number which they know to be such, but any and every number or triangle without reservation. For no premiss is ever couched in the form 'every number which you know to be such', or 'every rectilinear figure which you know to be such': the predicate is always construed as applicable to any and every instance of the thing. On the other hand, I imagine there is nothing to prevent a man in one sense knowing what he is learning, in another not knowing it. The strange thing would be, not if in some sense he knew what he was learning, but if he were to know it in that precise sense and manner in which he was learning it.

We suppose ourselves to possess unqualified scientific knowledge of   2
a thing, as opposed to knowing it in the accidental way in which the sophist knows, when we think that we know the cause on which the fact depends, as the cause of that fact and of no other, and, further, that the fact could not be other than it is. Now that scientific knowing is something of this sort is evident—witness both those who falsely claim it and those who actually possess it, since the former merely imagine themselves to be, while the latter are also actually, in the condition described. Consequently

the proper object of unqualified scientific knowledge is something which   15
cannot be other than it is.[9]

There may be another manner of knowing as well—that will be
discussed later. What I now assert is that at all events we do know by
demonstration. By demonstration I mean a syllogism productive of scientific
knowledge, a syllogism, that is, the grasp of which is eo *ipso* such knowledge. Assuming then that my thesis as to the nature of scientific knowing is
correct, the premisses of demonstrated knowledge must be true, primary,   20
immediate, better known than and prior to the conclusion, which is further
related to them as effect to cause. Unless these conditions are satisfied, the
basic truths will not be 'appropriate' to the conclusion. Syllogism there
may indeed be without these conditions, but such syllogism, not being
productive of scientific knowledge, will not be demonstration. The premisses must be true: for that which is non-existent cannot be known—we   25
cannot know, e.g., that the diagonal of a square is commensurate with its
side. The premisses must be primary and indemonstrable; otherwise they
will require demonstration in order to be known, since to have knowledge,
if it be not accidental knowledge, of things which are demonstrable,
means precisely to have a demonstration of them. The premisses must
be the causes of the conclusion, better known than it, and prior to it; its   30
causes, since we possess scientific knowledge of a thing only when we
know its cause; prior, in order to be causes; antecedently known,
this antecedent knowledge being not our mere understanding of the
meaning, but knowledge of the fact as well. Now 'prior' and 'better known'
are ambiguous terms, for there is a difference between what is prior and
better known in the order of being and what is prior and better known to   72°
man. I mean that objects nearer to sense are prior and better known to
man; objects without qualification prior and better known are those
further from sense.[10] Now the most universal causes are furthest from
sense and particular causes are nearest to sense, and they are thus exactly   5
opposed to one another. In saying that the premisses of demonstrated
knowledge must be primary, I mean that they must be the 'appropriate'
basic truths, for I identify primary premiss and basic truth. A 'basic truth'
in a demonstration is an immediate proposition. An immediate proposition
is one which has no other proposition prior to it. A proposition is either
part of an enunciation, i.e. it predicates a single attribute of a single
subject. If a proposition is dialectical, it assumes either part indifferently; if
it is demonstrative, it lays down one part to the definite exclusion of the   10
other because that part is true. The term 'enunciation' denotes either part
of a contradiction indifferently. A contradiction is an opposition which of
its own nature excludes a middle. The part of a contradiction which
conjoins a predicate with a subject is an affirmation; the part disjoining
them is a negation.[11] I call an immediate basic truth of syllogism a 'thesis'   15
when, though it is not susceptible of proof by the teacher, yet ignorance of

it does not constitute a total bar to progress on the part of the pupil: one which the pupil must know if he is to learn anything whatever is an axiom. I call it an axiom because there are such truths and we give them the name of axioms *par excellence*. If a thesis assumes one part or the other of an enunciation, i.e. asserts either the existence or the non-existence of a subject, it is a hypothesis; if it does not so assert, it is a definition. Definition *is* a 'thesis' or a 'laying something down', since the arithmetician lays it down that to be a unit is to be quantitatively indivisible; but it is not a hypothesis, for to define what a unit is is not the same as to affirm its existence.

Now since the required ground of our knowledge—i.e. of our conviction—of a fact is the possession of such a syllogism as we call demonstration, and the ground of the syllogism is the facts constituting its premisses, we must not only know the primary premisses—some if not all of them—beforehand, but know them better than the conclusion: for the cause of an attribute's inherence in a subject always itself inheres in the subject more firmly than that attribute; e.g. the cause of our loving anything is dearer to us than the object of our love. So since the primary premisses are the cause of our knowledge—i.e. of our conviction—it follows that we know them better—that is, are more convinced of them—than their consequences, precisely because our knowledge of the latter is the effect of our knowledge of the premisses.[12] Now a man cannot believe in anything more than in the things he knows, unless he has either actual knowledge of it or something better than actual knowledge. But we are faced with this paradox if a student whose belief rests on demonstration has not prior knowledge; a man must believe in some, if not in all, of the basic truths more than in the conclusion. Moreover, if a man sets out to acquire the scientific knowledge that comes through demonstration, he must not only have a better knowledge of the basic truths and a firmer conviction of them than of the connexion which is being demonstrated: more than this, nothing must be more certain or better known to him than these basic truths in their character as contradicting the fundamental premisses which lead to the opposed and erroneous conclusion. For indeed the conviction of pure science must be unshakable.

Some hold that, owing to the necessity of knowing the primary premisses, there is no scientific knowledge. Others think there is, but that all truths are demonstrable. Neither doctrine is either true or a necessary deduction from the premisses. The first school, assuming that there is no way of knowing other than by demonstration, maintain that an infinite regress is involved, on the ground that if behind the prior stands no primary, we could not know the posterior through the prior (wherein they are right, for one cannot traverse an infinite series): if on the other hand—they say—the series terminates and there are primary premisses, yet these are unknowable because incapable of demonstration, which according to them is the only form of knowledge. And since thus one cannot know the primary premisses, knowledge of the conclusions which follow from them is not pure scientific knowledge nor properly knowing at all, but rests on the mere supposition that the premisses are true. The other party agree with them as regards knowing, holding that it is only possible by demon- 15 station, but they see no difficulty in holding that all truths are demonstrated, on the ground that demonstration may be circular and reciprocal.

Our own doctrine is that not all knowledge is demonstrative: on the contrary, knowledge of the immediate premisses is independent of dem- onstration.[13] (The necessity of this is obvious; for since we must know 20 the prior premisses from which the demonstration is drawn, and since the regress must end in immediate truths, those truths must be indemonstrable.) Such, then, is our doctrine, and in addition we maintain that besides scientific knowledge there is its originative source which enables us to recognize the definitions.

Now demonstration must be based on premisses prior to and better 25 known than the conclusion; and the same things cannot simultaneously be both prior and posterior to one another: so circular demonstration is clearly not possible in the unqualified sense of 'demonstration', but only possible if 'demonstration' be extended to include that other method of argument which rests on a distinction between truths prior to us and truths without qualification prior, i.e. the method by which induction produces 30 knowledge. But if we accept this extension of its meaning, our definition of unqualified knowledge will prove faulty; for there seem to be two kinds of it. Perhaps, however, the second form of demonstration, that which proceeds from truths better known to us, is not demonstration in the unqualified sense of the term.

The advocates of circular demonstration are not only faced with the difficulty we have just stated: in addition their theory reduces to the mere statement that if a thing exists, then it does exist—an easy way of proving anything. That this is so can be clearly shown by taking three terms, for to 35 constitute the circle it makes no difference whether many terms or few or even only two are taken. Thus by direct proof, if A is, B must be; if B is, C must be; therefore if A is, C must be. Since then—by the circular proof—if A is, B must be, and if B is, A must be, A may be substituted for C above. 73ª Then 'if B is, A must be' = 'if B is, C must be', which above gave the conclusion 'if A is, C must be': but C and A have been identified. Conse- quently the upholders of circular demonstration are in the position of saying that if A is, A must be—a simple way of proving anything. More- 5 over, even such circular demonstration is impossible except in the case of attributes that imply one another, viz. 'peculiar' properties.

Now, it has been shown that the positing of one thing—be it one term or one premiss—never involves a necessary consequent: two premisses constitute the first and smallest foundation for drawing a conclusion at all 10 and therefore a fortiori for the demonstrative syllogism of science. If, then, A is implied in B and C, and B and C are reciprocally implied in one another and in A, it is possible, as has been shown in my writings on the syllogism, to prove all the assumptions on which the original conclusion

15   rested, by circular demonstration in the first figure. But it has also been shown that in the other figures either no conclusion is possible, or at least none which proves both the original premisses. Propositions the terms of which are not convertible cannot be circularly demonstrated at all, and since convertible terms occur rarely in actual demonstrations, it is clearly frivolous and impossible to say that demonstration is reciprocal and that

20   therefore everything can be demonstrated.

Since the object of pure scientific knowledge cannot be other than it   4 is, the truth obtained by demonstrative knowledge will be necessary. And since demonstrative knowledge is only present when we have a demonstration, it follows that demonstration is an inference from necessary premisses. So we must consider what are the premisses of demonstration—

25   i.e. what is their character: and as a preliminary, let us define what we mean by an attribute 'true in every instance of its subject', an 'essential' attribute, and a 'commensurate and universal' attribute. I call 'true in every instance' what is truly predicable of all instances—not of one to the exclusion of others—and at all times, not at this or that time only; e.g. if

30   animal is truly predicable of every instance of man, then if it be true to say 'this is a man', 'this is an animal' is also true, and if the one be true now the other is true now. A corresponding account holds if point is in every instance predicable as contained in line. There is evidence for this in the fact that the objection we raise against a proposition put to us as true in every instance is either an instance in which, or an occasion on which, it is not true. Essential attributes are (1) such as belong to their subject as ele-

35   ments in its essential nature (e.g. line thus belongs to triangle, point to line; for the very being or 'substance' of triangle and line is composed of these elements, which are contained in the formulae defining triangle and line): (2) such that, while they belong to certain subjects, the subjects to which they belong are contained in the attribute's own defining formula. Thus

40   straight and curved belong to line, odd and even, prime and compound,
73ᵇ   square and oblong, to number; and also the formula defining any one of these attributes contains its subject—e.g. line or number as the case may be.

Extending this classification to all other attributes, I distinguish those that answer the above description as belonging essentially to their respective subjects; whereas attributes related in neither of these two ways to their subjects I call accidents or 'coincidents'; e.g. musical or white is a 'coincident' of animal.

5   Further (a) that is essential which is not predicated of a subject other than itself: e.g. 'the walking [thing]' walks and is white in virtue of being something else besides; whereas substance, in the sense of whatever signifies a 'this somewhat', is not what it is in virtue of being something else

besides. Things, then, not predicated of a subject I call essential; things predicated of a subject I call accidental or 'coincidental'.[14]

In another sense again (b) a thing consequentially connected with anything is essential; one not so connected is 'coincidental'. An example of the latter is 'While he was walking it lightened': the lightning was not due to his walking; it was, we should say, a coincidence. If, on the other hand, there is a consequential connexion, the predication is essential; e.g. if a beast dies when its throat is being cut, then its death is also essentially connected with the cutting, because the cutting was the cause of death, not death a 'coincident' of the cutting.

So far then as concerns the sphere of connexions scientifically known in the unqualified sense of that term, all attributes which (within that sphere) are essential either in the sense that their subjects are contained in them, or in the sense that they are contained in their subjects, are necessary as well as consequentially connected with their subjects. For it is impossible for them not to inhere in their subjects—either simply or in the qualified sense that one or other of a pair of opposites must inhere in the subject; e.g. in line must be either straightness or curvature, in number either oddness or evenness. For within a single identical genus the contrary of a given attribute is either its privative or its contradictory; e.g. within number what is not odd is even, inasmuch as within this sphere even is a necessary consequent of not-odd. So, since any given predicate must be either affirmed or denied of any subject, essential attributes must inhere in their subjects of necessity.

Thus, then, we have established the distinction between the attribute which is 'true in every instance' and the 'essential' attribute.

I term 'commensurately universal' an attribute which belongs to every instance of its subject, and to every instance essentially and as such; from which it clearly follows that all commensurate universals inhere *necessarily* in their subjects. The essential attribute, and the attribute that belongs to its subject as such, are identical. E.g. point and straight belong to line essentially, for they belong to line as such; and triangle as such has two right angles, for it is *essentially* equal to two right angles.

An attribute belongs commensurately and universally to a subject when it can be shown to belong to any random instance of that subject and when the subject is the first thing to which it can be shown to belong. Thus, e.g., (1) the equality of its angles to two right angles is not a commensurately universal attribute of figure. For though it is possible to show that a figure has its angles equal to two right angles, this attribute cannot be demonstrated of any figure selected at haphazard, nor in demonstrating does one take a figure at random—a square is a figure but its angles are not equal to two right angles. On the other hand, any isosceles triangle has its angles equal to two right angles yet isosceles triangle is not the primary subject of this attribute but triangle is prior. So whatever can be shown to

40   have its angles equal to two right angles, or to possess any other attribute, in any random instance of itself and primarily—that is the first subject to which the predicate in question belongs commensurately and universally, and the demonstration, in the essential sense, of any predicate is the proof

74ᵃ   of it as belonging to this first subject commensurately and universally: while the proof of it as belonging to the other subjects to which it attaches is demonstration only in a secondary and unessential sense. Nor again (2) is equality to two right angles a commensurately universal attribute of isosceles; it is of wider application.

We must not fail to observe that we often fall into error because our   5

5   conclusion is not in fact primary and commensurately universal in the sense in which we think we prove it so. We make this mistake (1) when the subject is an individual or individuals above which there is no universal to be found: (2) when the subjects belong to different species and there is a higher universal, but it has no name: (3) when the subject which the demonstrator takes as a whole is really only a part of a larger whole; for

10   then the demonstration will be true of the individual instances within the part and will hold in every instance of it, yet the demonstration will not be true of this subject primarily and commensurately and universally. When a demonstration is true of a subject primarily and commensurately and universally, that is to be taken to mean that it is true of a given subject primarily and as such. Case (3) may be thus exemplified. If a proof were given that perpendiculars to the same line are parallel, it might be supposed that *lines thus perpendicular* were the proper subject of the demonstration because being parallel is true of every instance of them.

15   But it is not so, for the parallelism depends not on these angles being equal to one another because each is a right angle, but simply on their being equal to one another. An example of (1) would be as follows: if isosceles were the only triangle, it would be thought to have its angles equal to two right angles *qua* isosceles. An instance of (2) would be the law that proportionals alternate.[15] Alternation used to be demonstrated separately of numbers, lines, solids and durations, though it could have been proved

20   of them all by a single demonstration. Because there was no single name to denote that in which numbers, lengths, durations, and solids are identical, and because they differed specifically from one another, this property was proved of each of them separately. To-day, however, the proof is commensurately universal, for they do not possess this attribute *qua* lines or *qua* numbers, but *qua* manifesting this generic character which they are

25   postulated as possessing universally. Hence, even if one prove of each kind of triangle that its angles are equal to two right angles, whether by means of the same or different proofs; still, as long as one treats separately equilateral, scalene, and isosceles, one does not yet know, except sophistically, that triangle has its angles equal to two right angles, nor does one yet know that triangle has this property commensurately and universally,

30   even if there is no other species of triangle but these. For one does not

know that triangle as such has this property, nor even that 'all' triangles have it—unless 'all' means 'each taken singly': if 'all' means 'as a whole class', then, though there be none in which one does not recognize this property, one does not know it of 'all triangles'.

When, then, does our knowledge fail of commensurate universality, and when is it unqualified knowledge? If triangle be identical in essence with equilateral, i.e. with each or all equilaterals, then clearly we have unqualified knowledge: if on the other hand it be not, and the attribute belongs to equilateral *qua* triangle; then our knowledge fails of commen-   35 surate universality. 'But', it will be asked, 'does this attribute belong to the subject of which it has been demonstrated *qua* triangle or *qua* isosceles? What is the point at which the subject to which it belongs is primary? (i.e. to what subject can it be demonstrated as belonging commensurately and universally?)' Clearly this point is the first term in which it is found to inhere as the elimination of inferior *differentiae* proceeds. Thus the angles of a brazen isosceles triangle are equal to two right angles: but eliminate brazen and isosceles and the attribute remains.[16] 'But'—you may say—   74ᵇ 'eliminate figure or limit, and the attribute vanishes.' True, but figure and limit are not the first *differentiae* whose elimination destroys the attribute. 'Then what is the first?' If it is triangle, it will be in virtue of triangle that the attribute belongs to all the other subjects of which it is predicable, and triangle is the subject to which it can be demonstrated as belonging commensurately and universally.

6   Demonstrative knowledge must rest on necessary basic truths; for the   5 object of scientific knowledge cannot be other than it is. Now attributes attaching essentially to their subjects attach necessarily to them: for essential attributes are either elements in the essential nature of their subjects, or contain their subjects as elements in their own essential nature. (The pairs of opposites which the latter class includes are necessary because one member or the other necessarily inheres.) It follows from this   10 that premisses of the demonstrative syllogism must be connexions essential in the sense explained: for all attributes must inhere essentially or else be accidental, and accidental attributes are not necessary to their subjects.

C   From the *METAPHYSICS*

BOOK Z

1   There are several senses in which a thing may be said to 'be', as we   10 pointed out previously in our book on the various senses of words; for in one sense the 'being' meant is 'what a thing is' or a 'this', and in another sense it means a quality or quantity or one of the other things that are predicated as these are.[17] While 'being' has all these senses, obviously that which 'is' primarily is the 'what', which indicates the substance of the thing.   15

For when we say of what quality a thing is, we say that it is good or bad, not that it is three cubits long or that it is a man; but when we say *what* it is, we do not say 'white' or 'hot' or 'three cubits long', but 'a man' or 'a god'. And all other things are said to be because they are, some of them, quantities of that which *is* in this primary sense, others qualities of it, others
20   affections of it, and others some other determination of it.[18] And so one might even raise the question whether the words 'to walk', 'to be healthy', 'to sit' imply that each of these things is existent, and similarly in any other case of this sort; for none of them is either self-subsistent or capable of being separated from substance, but rather, if anything, it is that which
25   walks or sits or is healthy that is an existent thing. Now these are seen to be more real because there is something definite which underlies them (i.e. the substance or individual), which is implied in such a predicate; for we never use the word 'good' or 'sitting' without implying this. Clearly then it is in virtue of this category that each of the others also *is*. Therefore that which is primarily, i.e. not in a qualified sense but without qualification,
30   must be substance.

Now there are several senses in which a thing is said to be first; yet substance is first in every sense—(1) in definition, (2) in order of knowledge, (3) in time. For (3) of the other categories none can exist independently, but
35   only substance. And (1) in definition also this is first; for in the definition of each term the definition of its substance must be present. And (2) we think we know each thing most fully, when we know what it is, e.g. what man is
1028ᵇ   or what fire is, rather than when we know its quality, its quantity, or its place; since we know each of these predicates also, only when we know *what* the quantity or the quality *is*.[19]

And indeed the question which was raised of old and is raised now and always, and is always the subject of doubt, viz. what being is, is just the question, what is substance? For it is this that some assert to be one,
5   others more than one, and that some assert to be limited in number, others unlimited.[20] And so we also must consider chiefly and primarily and almost exclusively what that is which *is* in *this* sense.

Substance is thought to belong most obviously to bodies; and so we
10   say that not only animals and plants and their parts are substances, but also natural bodies such as fire and water and earth and everything of the sort, and all things that are either parts of these or composed of these (either of parts or of the whole bodies), e.g. the physical universe and its parts, stars and moon and sun. But whether these alone are substances, or
15   there are also others, or only some of these, or others as well, or none of these but only some other things, are substances, must be considered. Some think the limits of body, i.e. surface, line, point, and unit, are substances, and more so than body or the solid.[21]

Further, some do not think there is anything substantial besides sensible things, but others think there are eternal substances which are more in number and more real; e.g. Plato posited two kinds of substance—

2

the Forms and the objects of mathematics—as well as a third kind, viz. the   20
substance of sensible bodies.²² And Speusippus made still more kinds of
substance, beginning with the One, and assuming principles for each kind
of substance, one for numbers, another for spatial magnitudes, and then
another for the soul; and by going on in this way he multiplies the kinds of
substance.²³ And some say Forms and numbers have the same nature, and   25
the other things come after them—lines and planes—until we come to the
substance of the material universe and to sensible bodies.²⁴

Regarding these mattters, then, we must inquire which of the common
statements are right and which are not right, and what substances there
are, and whether there are or are not any besides sensible substances, and
how sensible substances exist, and whether there is a substance capable of   30
separate existence (and if so why and how) or no such substance, apart
from sensible substances; and we must first sketch the nature of substance.

3   The word 'substance' is applied, if not in more senses, still at least to
four main objects; for both the essence and the universal and the genus are
thought to be the substance of each thing, and fourthly the substratum.   35
Now the substratum is that of which everything else is predicated, while it
is itself not predicated of anything else. And so we must first determine the
nature of this; for that which underlies a thing primarily is thought to be in   1029ᵃ
the truest sense its substance. And in one sense matter is said to be of the
nature of substratum, in another, shape, and in a third, the compound of
these. (By the matter I mean, for instance, the bronze, by the shape the
pattern of its form, and by the compound of these the statue, the concrete   5
whole.) Therefore if the form is prior to the matter and more real, it will be
prior also to the compound of both, for the same reason.

We have now outlined the nature of substance, showing that it is that
which is not predicated of a stratum, but of which all else is predicated.
But we must not merely state the matter thus; for this not enough. The
statement itself is obscure, and further, on this view, *matter* becomes
substance. For if this is not substance, it baffles us to say what else is. When   10
all else is stripped off evidently nothing but matter remains. For while the
rest are affections, products, and potencies of bodies, length, breadth, and
depth are quantities and not substances (for a quantity is not a substance),
but the substance is rather that to which these belong primarily. But when   15
length and breadth and depth are taken away we see nothing left unless
there is something that is bounded by these; so that to those who consider
the question thus matter alone must seem to be substance. By matter I mean   20
that which in itself is neither a particular thing nor of a certain quantity nor
assigned to any other of the categories by which being is determined. For
there is something of which each of these is predicated, whose being is
different from that of each of the predicates (for the predicates other than
substance are predicated of substance, while substance is predicated of
matter). Therefore the ultimate substratum is of itself neither a particular
thing nor of a particular quantity nor otherwise positively characterized;

25   nor yet is it the negations of these, for negations also will belong to it only by accident.

If we adopt this point of view, then, it follows that matter is substance. But this is impossible; for both separability and 'thisness' are thought to belong chiefly to substance. And so form and the compound of form and

30   matter would be thought to be substance, rather than matter. The substance compounded of both, i.e. of matter and shape, may be dismissed; for it is posterior and its nature is obvious. And matter also is in a sense manifest. But we must inquire into the third kind of substance; for this is the most perplexing.[25]

Some of the sensible substances are generally admitted to be sub-

1029ᵇ   stances, so that we must look first among these. For it is an advantage to advance to that which is more knowable. For learning proceeds for all in this way—through that which is less knowable by nature to that which is

5   more knowable; and just as in conduct our task is to start from what is good for each and make what is without qualification good good for each, so it is our task to start from what is more knowable to oneself and make what is knowable by nature knowable to oneself. Now what is knowable and primary for particular sets of people is often knowable to a very small

10   extent, and has little or nothing of reality. But yet one must start from that which is barely knowable but knowable to oneself, and try to know what is knowable without qualification, passing, as has been said, by way of those very things which one does know.

1   Since at the start we distinguished the various marks by which we   4 determine substance, and one of these was thought to be the essence, we

13   must investigate this.[26] And first let us make some linguistic remarks about it. The essence of each thing is what it is said to be *propter se*. For being you is not being musical, since you are not by your very nature musical.

15   What, then, you are by your very nature is your essence.

Nor yet is the whole of this the essence of a thing; not that which is *propter se* as white is to a surface, because being a surface is not *identical* with being white. But again the combination of both—'being a white surface'—is not the essence of surface, because 'surface' itself is added. The formula, therefore, in which the term itself is not present but its

20   meaning is expressed, this is the formula of the essence of each thing. Therefore if to be a white surface is to be a smooth surface, to be white and to be smooth are one and the same.[27]

But since there are also compounds answering to the other categories

25   (for there is a substratum for each category, e.g. for quality, quantity, time, place, and motion), we must inquire whether there is a formula of the essence of each of them, i.e. whether to these compounds also there belongs an essence, e.g. to 'white man'. Let the compound be denoted by cloak.[28] What is the essence of cloak? But, it may be said, this also is not a *propter se* expression. We reply that there are just two ways in which a

predicate may fail to be true of a subject *propter se,* and one of these   30
results from the addition, and the other from the omission, of a determinant. One kind of predicate is not *propter se* because the term that is
being defined is combined with another determinant, e.g. if in defining
the essence of white one were to state the formula of white *man;* the *other*
because in the subject another determinant is combined with that which
is expressed in the formula, e.g. if 'cloak' meant 'white man', and one
were to define cloak as white; white man is white indeed, but its essence
is not to be white.

But is being-a-cloak an essence at all? Probably not. For the essence   1030ᵃ
is precisely what something *is;* but when an attribute is asserted of a subject other than itself, the complex is not precisely what some 'this' *is,* e.g.
white man is not precisely what some 'this' *is,* since thisness belongs only   5
to substances. Therefore there is an essence only of those things whose
formula is a definition. But we have a definition not where we have a
word and a formula identical in meaning (for in that case all formulae or
sets of words would be definitions; for there will be some name for any
set of words whatever, so that even the *Iliad* will be a definition), but
where there is a formula of something primary; and primary things are   10
those which do not imply the predication of one element in them of another element. Nothing, then, which is not a species of a genus will have
an essence—only species will have it, for these are thought to imply not
merely that the subject participates in the attribute and has it as an affection, or has it by accident; but for everything else as well, if it has a name,
there will be a *formula of its meaning*—viz. that this attribute belongs to   15
this subject; or instead of a simple formula we shall be able to give a
more accurate one; but there will be no definition nor essence.

Or has 'definition', like 'what a thing is', several meanings? 'What
a thing is' in one sense means substance and the 'this', in another one or   20
other of the predicates, quantity, quality, and the like. For as 'is' belongs
to all things, not however in the same sense, but to one sort of thing
primarily and to others in a secondary way, so too 'what a thing is' belongs in the simple sense to substance, but in a limited sense to the other
categories. For even of a quality we might ask what it is, so that quality
also is a 'what a thing is',—not in the simple sense, however, but just as,   25
in the case of that which is not, some say, emphasizing the linguistic form,
that that which is not *is*—not *is* simply, but *is* non-existent; so too with
quality.

We must no doubt inquire how we should express ourselves on each
point, but certainly not more than how the facts actually stand. And so
now also, since it is evident what language we use, essence will belong,
just as 'what a thing is' does, primarily and in the simple sense to substance, and in a secondary way to the other categories also,—not essence   30
in the simple sense, but the essence of a quality or of a quantity. For it

must be either by an equivocation that we say these *are*, or by adding to and taking from the meaning of 'are' (in the way in which that which is not known may be said to be known),—the truth being that we use the
35 word neither ambiguously nor in the same sense, but just as we apply the word 'medical' by virtue of a *reference* to one and the same thing, not
1030ᵇ *meaning* one and the same thing, nor yet speaking ambiguously; for a patient and an operation and an instrument are called medical neither by an ambiguity nor with a single meaning, but with reference to a common end. But it does not matter at all in which of the two ways one likes
5 to describe the facts; this is evident, that definition and essence in the primary and simple sense belong to substances. Still they belong to other things as well, only not in the primary sense. For if we suppose this it does not follow that there is a definition of every word which means the same as any formula; it must mean the same as a particular kind of formula; and this condition is satisfied if it is a formula of something which
10 is one, not by continuity like the *Iliad* or the things that are one by being bound together, but in one of the main senses of 'one', which answer to the senses of 'is'; now 'that which is' in one sense denotes a 'this', in another a quantity, in another a quality. And so there can be a formula or definition even of white man, but not in the sense in which there is a definition either of white or of a substance.

It is a difficult question, if one denies that a formula with an added   5
15 determinant is a definition, whether any of the terms that are not simple but coupled will be definable. For we *must* explain them by adding a determinant. E.g. there is the nose, and concavity, and snubness, which is compounded out of the two by the presence of the one in the other, and it is not by *accident* that the nose has the attribute either of concavity or
20 of snubness, but in virtue of its nature; nor do they attach to it as whiteness does to Callias, or to man (because Callias, who happens to be a man, is white), but as 'male' attaches to animal and 'equal' to quantity, and as all so-called 'attributes *propter se*' attach to their subjects.²⁹ And such attributes are those in which is involved either the *formula* or the *name* of the subject of the particular attribute, and which cannot be explained
25 without this; e.g. white can be explained apart from man, but not female apart from animal. Therefore there is either no essence and definition of any of these things, or if there is, it is in another sense, as we have said.

But there is also a second difficulty about them. For if snub nose and
30 concave nose are the same thing, snub and concave will be the same thing; but if snub and concave are not the same (because it is impossible to speak of snubness apart from the thing of which it is an attribute *propter se*, for snubness is concavity-*in-a-nose*), either it is impossible to say 'snub nose' or the same thing will have been said twice, concave-nose nose; for snub nose will be concave-nose nose. And so it is absurd that such

things should have an essence; if they have, there will be an infinite re-   35
gress; for in snub-nose nose yet another 'nose' will be involved.

Clearly, then, only substance is definable. For if the other categories   1031ª
also are definable, it must be by addition of a determinant, e.g. the
qualitative is defined thus, and so is the odd, for it cannot be defined apart
from number; nor can female be defined apart from animal. (When I say
'by addition' I mean the expressions in which it turns out that we are saying the same thing twice, as in these instances.) And if this is true, coupled   5
terms also, like 'odd number', will not be definable (but this escapes our
notice because our formulae are not accurate). But if these also are definable, either it is in some other way or, as we said, definition and
essence must be said to have more than one sense. Therefore in one sense   10
nothing will have a definition and nothing will have an essence, except
substances, but in another sense other things will have them. Clearly, then,
definition is the formula of the essence, and essence belongs to substances
either alone or chiefly and primarily and in the unqualified sense.

We must inquire whether each thing and its essence are the same   15
6   or different. This is of some use for the inquiry concerning substance; for
each thing is thought to be not different from its substance, and the essence
is said to be the substance of each thing.

Now in the case of accidental unities the two would be generally
thought to be different, e.g. white man would be thought to be different   20
from the essence of white man. For if they are the same, the essence of
man and that of white man are also the same; for a man and a white man
are the same thing, as people say, so that the essence of white man and
that of man would be also the same. But perhaps it does not follow that
the essence of accidental unities should be the same as that of the simple
terms. For the extreme terms are not in the same way identical with the
middle term.[30] But perhaps *this* might be thought to follow, that the ex-   25
treme terms, the accidents, should turn out to be the same, e.g. the
essence of white and that of musical; but this is not actually thought to be
the case.[31]

But in the case of so-called self-subsistent things, is a thing necessarily
the same as its essence? E.g. if there are some substances which have no
other substances nor entities prior to them—substances such as some assert   30
the Ideas to be?—If the essence of good is to be different from good-
itself, and the essence of animal from animal-itself, and the essence of
being from being-itself, there will, firstly, be other substances and entities   1031ᵇ
and Ideas besides those which are asserted, and, secondly, these others
will be prior substances, if essence is substance. And if the posterior substances and the prior are severed from each other, (α) there will be no
knowledge of the former, and (β) the latter will have no being. (By   5
'severed' I mean, if the good-itself has not the essence of good, and the
latter has not the property of being good.) For (α) there is knowledge of

each thing only when we know its essence. And (β) the case is the same for other things as for the good; so that if the essence of good is not good, neither is the essence of reality real, nor the essence of unity one. And all essences alike exist or none of them does; so that if the essence of reality is not real, neither is any of the others. Again, that to which the essence of good does not belong is not good.—The good, then, must be one with the essence of good, and the beautiful with the essence of beauty, and so with all things which do not depend on something else but are self-subsistent and primary. For it is enough if they are this, even if they are not Forms; or rather, perhaps, even if they are Forms. (At the same time it is clear that if there are Ideas such as some people say there are, it will not be substratum that is substance; for these must be substances, but not predicable of a substratum; for if they were they would exist only by being participated in.)[32]

Each thing itself, then, and its essence are one and the same in no merely accidental way, as is evident both from the preceding arguments and because to *know* each thing, at least, is just to know its essence, so that even by the exhibition of instances it becomes clear that both must be one.[33]

(But of an accidental term, e.g. 'the musical' or 'the white', since it has two meanings, it is not true to say that it itself is identical with its essence; for both that to which the accidental quality belongs, and the accidental quality, are white, so that in a sense the accident and its essence are the same, and in a sense they are not; for the essence of white is not the same as the man or the white man, but it is the same as the attribute white.)

The absurdity of the separation would appear also if one were to assign a name to each of the essences; for there would be yet another essence besides the original one, e.g. to the essence of horse there will belong a second essence. Yet why should not some things be their essences from the start, since essence is substance? But indeed not only are a thing and its essence one, but the formula of them is also the same, as is clear even from what has been said; for it is not by accident that the essence of one, and the one, are one. Further, if they are to be different, the process will go on to infinity; for we shall have (1) the essence of one, and (2) the one, so that to terms of the former kind the same argument will be applicable.[34]

Clearly, then, each primary and self-subsistent thing is one and the same as its essence. The sophistical objections to this position, and the question whether Socrates and to be Socrates are the same thing, are obviously answered by the same solution; for there is no difference either in the standpoint from which the question would be asked, or in that from which one could answer it successfully. We have explained, then, in what sense each thing is the same as its essence and in what sense it is not.

NOTES

1   The difficulties in reading Aristotle are amply illustrated by the preceding paragraphs. At first, Aristotle speaks about forms of speech, and then he seems to switch to consideration of things, rather than of words, in a somewhat confusing fashion. Perhaps Aristotle did not distinguish carefully between speaking about things and speaking about a language in which they are described. On the other hand, the word *thing* in this context may be taken as a neutral word like *entity*, since Aristotle clearly holds that a particular man exists in a different sense than the manhood which may be predicated of him. Note that while 'being present in an object' is explained somewhat by Aristotle, being 'predicable of a subject' is not. These two predicates, 'being present in a subject' and 'being predicable of a subject', allow a fourfold classification, depending on whether each of the predicates holds or does not hold. Aristotle proceeds to give examples of each possibility.

2   Why can a certain whiteness not be predicable of anything? Because it is not *common* to more than one object in terms of Aristotle's example.

3   Is this example puzzling? It could be that *knowledge* is used equivocally of the content of the mind and of one property of grammar.

4   Notice that the things belonging to this fourth division are apparently defined as primary substances in section 5 of the *Categories*.

5   To speak of them as coordinate, by reference to the notion of *subordinate* used below, seems to mean that one does not stand above the other in the hierarchy of predication discussed in chapter on Aristotle's hierarchy above.

6   Compare this remark with footnote 2. *White*, as a predicable, is not present in any subject. The particular color present in a subject, however, may be what we call *white*, so that *white* is predicable of the subject.

7   Induction will be considered later in the chapters on the philosophies of Hume and Peirce. Aristotle's notion of induction is quite different. In general, it is a way of proving a generalization like 'All *A*'s are *B*'s.' from an examination of cases of *A*. The premises of scientific syllogisms must be ultimately established by inductions, which are grounded in knowledge derived from particular objects. But Aristotle's treatment of induction seems contradictory and misleading. (See the discussion on pp. 24–37 of William Kneale's *Probability and Induction*, Oxford, 1949.) *Enthymeme* is now used by logicians to refer to an argument with suppressed premises, usually premises that are taken as obvious by the arguer. Aristotle meant a syllogism whose premises were either general truths (not true in every case) or particular facts. (See the discussion on pp. 350–351 of H. W. B. Joseph's *An Introduction to Logic*, Oxford, 1957.)

8   This discussion of knowledge in connection with a mathematical example is of interest in comparison to Plato's treatment. For Aristotle, prior knowledge is increased in learning some particular case which falls under it, while Plato would hold only that more was recollected. Aristotle's self-awareness of this difference is indicated by the reference immediately following to Plato's *Meno*, mentioned earlier in the footnotes to the Plato readings.

9   The necessity of what the possessor of scientific knowledge knows (theoretical science) is a rationalistic element that pervades Aristotle's thought.

10   Aristotle points out an essential ambiguity in *prior* and *better known*. Having explained this ambiguity, does he clarify his original formulation? Could *appropriate*, as used a few lines later, be used to indicate that either sense of the ambiguity may be correct in some specific demonstrations?

11   Given a predicate *P* and a subject *S*, an enunciation is of the form '*S* is *P* or *S* is not *P*.'. '*S* is *P*.' and '*S* is not *P*.' are propositions. A demonstrative proposition is simply the affirmation of the truth of one of these propositions. *S* is assumed to be single, which evidently indicates that *S* must have *P* or not *P*. Aristotle seems to assume here that *S* exists (otherwise neither demonstrative proposition obtained from the enunciation above need be true), which is an example of his tendency to talk about (existing) things, even where his philosophical point may appear to be about the language in which these things are described.

12   To many philosophers, this view would seem mistaken. It might at least be possible that we know the premises and conclusion of an argument equally well. And, in Peirce's abductive inference, which will be discussed later, a well-known conclusion, found to follow deductively from premises that we are not sure of, may increase our belief that these premises are true, but even this resulting belief may not be as strong as the belief that the conclusion is true.

13   Does this not suggest the self-evident principles of the first chapter in the text discussing Aristotle? If so, what are the consequences for the discussion referred to in footnote 10?

14   This paragraph requires close examination. Something predicated of a subject (see the discussion in the *Categories* in the first reading) must be common to that subject and other subjects. A definition of a subject *S* for Aristotle would be an attribute without which *S* would not be and which could not apply to anything other than *S*. If, however, a definition is a conjunction of more than one predicate, all the predicates are essentially predicated of *S*, since the absence of any of them means that *S* does not occur. Consequently, this discussion of essential attributes must be an illustration of a particular kind of essential attribute if consistency with other remarks is to be maintained. Is this kind of essential attribute what Aristotle calls a 'commensurately universal' attribute below?

15   The law that proportionals alternate is apparently the law that if '$a/b = c/d$', then also '$a/c = b/d$'. Aristotle's point is not dependent on the exact statement of this law but on the fact that it need not be proved for every domain in which the appropriate arithmetic is used. See Sir Thomas Heath, *Mathematics in Aristotle*, Oxford, 1949, pp. 41–44, for an interesting comment on this passage.

16   The word translated here as *brazen* also means *bronze*. Notice that Plato would not make a statement like this about a metal triangle, which would not, strictly speaking, exist in terms of his epistemology.

17   The reference to previous work is probably to the *Metaphysics*, V, vii. Here the primary substances are said to *be* in some fundamental sense, all other things having existence because they belong to some category and may be predicated of some primary substance.

18   This reference to the *Categories* should occur to the reader.

19 Some study of the last phrase is required. Qualities, quantities, etc., can be
considers *whats*, since they may be the subject of some attribute. Now this
passage could mean that we know these instances of various categories where
we predicate of them only when we know them as individuals. But since they
are not individuals, this interpretation involves some obscurities. On the other
hand, the passage could be read as saying that we know some quality (to take
an example) only when we know what has that quality, so that 'the quality or
the quantity' refers to whatever quality or quantity is being considered at some
given time.

20 Aristotle was conscious of his philosophical predecessors, and he refers often
to their views but not to their names. Evidently he used their views largely to
establish a systematic way of exploring a problem, while arguing for his own
solution. In this case, the three views referred to belong to the Milesians and
Eleatics, the Pythagoreans and Empedocles, and the Atomists and Anaxagoras,
respectively. For their detailed views, see G. S. Kirk and J. E. Raven, *The
Presocratic Philosophers*, Cambridge, 1957.

21 This may refer to the Pythagoreans. See Kirk and Raven, *op. cit.*

22 The view that only sensible entities exist was held by some Sophists and pre-
Socratics, certainly not by Plato.

23 Speusippus followed Plato as the head of the Platonic Academy. The Academy
was a place for philosophers to study that Plato established in the town of
Academe, near Athens. After Plato's death, the members of the Academy
seem to have spent much of their time arguing over *the* correct interpretation
of Plato's philosophy.

24 Xenocrates was the head of the Academy following Speusippus, and this
mathematization of Platonic forms is often attributed to him.

25 To summarize the preceding argument is difficult. Bodies were first taken to
be the most obvious candidates for primary substances. But Aristotelian
analysis elsewhere has taken any body to be a composite of form and matter.
The problem is to see whether primary substance can be identified with form
alone, matter alone, or the composite of the two. It cannot be identified with
matter since the properties of primary substance, among them separateness
and individuality (thisness), are *not* properties of matter. The composite of
form and matter is what is accidentally predicated of, since it is this intelligible
object which has accidental attributes, and hence it is a kind of substrate. But,
the form is prior to the composite, so that if the doctrine of priority is held
here, the form must, in some sense, be the primary substance of sensible objects.

26 This introduces an apparent turning point in the argument. Essence will now
be discussed, but as a way of understanding form. Any body will have a form,
but *form* is somewhat ambiguous. The important part of the form of anything
is its essence, as will be discussed. In this way, this change in topic carries out
the conclusion of the preceding section. Compare the introduction of essence
as a topic with the list—substratum, essence, genus, and universal—given
earlier.

27 From the standpoint of contemporary philosophy, this passage is very interesting. The essence of something is said to be given in the formula which expresses

its meaning. Many modern philosophers would reject the assumption made here that there is exactly one such formula, and with the rejection of this assumption the Aristotelian notion of essence becomes even less clear. An apparently hypothetical suggestion in the text, that to be a white surface means to be a smooth object, may originate in the views of the pre-Socratic Democritus that the color of a surface was a function of its texture.

28   *Cloak* here may be replaced by *X*, since it is used as an arbitrary but simple expression standing for *white man*.

29   Snubness is a *propter se* attribute of noses, because *snub* is said correctly only of noses. Concavity, on the other hand, may be found in all kinds of objects.

30   Aristotle says that man and the essence of man, since man is a substance, may be regarded as identical, but white man and essence of white man may not be regarded as identical. Since white man and man, if it is regarded as an accidental unity that the class of men and the class of white men are coextensive (because all men are white), do not as a result have the same essence, we cannot use the identity of man and white man to conclude that the essence of man and the essence of white man are identical. This later identity is not the same as the first, and such inferences are invalid.

31   This is a little puzzling. Aristotle seems to suggest that accidental identities might be validly combined in syllogisms, but it is not clear that this could be of any use.

32   The preceding paragraph is an attack on the Platonic theory of ideas, successful in so far as it shows the Platonic theory is not compatible with Aristotle's own theory of essences.

33   At this point the basic answer to the question of what substance is can be given.

34   By identifying essence and substance, the question of the essence of an essence is avoided. In view of the preceding remarks about the theory of ideas, perhaps Aristotle is pointing out that the kind of paradox discussed in connection with the Platonic theory of ideas cannot arise for the Aristotelian system.

PART 3

Descartes

(1596–1650)

Epistemological Individualism

A number of parallels may be drawn between the philosophy of Descartes and the philosophies of Plato and Aristotle. Like Plato, Descartes restricts knowledge to what is certain, and by doing this rejects any simpleminded view that knowledge is obtained through sense experience, since sense experience proves to be misleading. But, like Aristotle, Descartes is interested in bringing all the areas of natural science within the domain of knowledge, and he is interested in various problems of change. Further, he is interested in relating areas of scientific investigation, so that certain more specialized sciences will be dependent on general sciences, in the sense that the laws of the more general sciences will be true in the domains of the more specialized sciences.

Nevertheless, Descartes differs from both Plato and Aristotle in ways that have made him a distinct major philosopher. If we were to look for some single feature of Descartes's philosophical writings that distinguish them sharply from the works of Plato and Aristotle, we might well choose Descartes's emphasis upon the *individual* thinking man. Without attempting to define individualism, we may say that Descartes's philosophy is individualistic in that it attempts to answer the question of what *a* man may know, rather than what *men* may know. The difference is extremely important, and it accounts for the fact that Descartes is often referred to as the father of modern philosophy.

We have seen that Plato and Aristotle begin with the assumption that there is knowledge, and that an important philosophical activity is to study its nature, acquisition, and extent. To do so, Plato and Aristotle each start with paradigm cases of indisputable knowledge, and attempt to answer broader questions by extending whatever results they can get from an analysis of the relatively limited examples of knowledge that they start with. Descartes, on the other hand, while he is not a skeptic, begins his study by attempting to *prove* that there are examples of human knowledge, rather than by assuming instances of human knowledge, and he does this by telling a reader of his *Meditations* how he proved to *himself* that he knew something with a certainty that would survive any conceivable criticism. From this apparently meagre starting point, Descartes developed a philosophy which granted a great many mathematical, scientific, and religious statements the status of indubitable truths.

The importance of certainty in Descartes, as well as in other rationalists who followed him, is different from what it was for Plato or Aristotle. The hope of rationalist philosophers after Descartes was to find some set of *certain* statements that could serve as the axioms for a deductive system, both consistent and complete, the theorems of which would embody all human knowledge, or less ambitiously, at least some considerable development of knowledge in mathematics or ethics, for example. The notion of a deductive system, familiar to Descartes in such examples as the axiomatic development of Euclid's *Elements of Geometry*, is important background for seeing why he took the discovery of what he called *clear* and *distinct* ideas to be so important. These were the kinds of ideas that could be used to establish certain truths which could play the role of axioms in a deductive system of human knowledge.

The epistemological problem of individuality is also to be noted in some detail. It is an implicit assumption of Plato and Aristotle that the rational faculty in man is the same from individual to individual. But this is the kind of implicit assumption that requires further examination. To see some of the difficulties which may arise from thinking about these problems, the following example may prove instructive. Suppose that there are two human individuals, call them A and B, whose differences are unimportant for our immediate philosophical purposes save for the following: when A and B both look at something that they agree to call *red*, A's subjective color impression is different than B's, and this is also the case when they both look at something that they agree to call *yellow*. Let us suppose, in fact, that their color impressions on these two occasions are such that A's subjective red impression is really identical with B's subjective color impression of yellow. This difference is not silly, since it might play an important role in determining their responses to paintings, and arguments between them over which paintings are most beautiful might be complicated by this difference. Can A and B discover that there is such a difference between them? It appears doubtful, because of the rather simple observation that the only way for A and B to communicate their color impressions is by reference to objects, *about which they use the same vocabulary* even though they have differing subjective impressions. This is just another way of making the commonsense claim that no one of us can get inside the mind of another. Thus it is quite possible that we can communicate with our contemporaries without disagreement, and yet be living in subjective worlds which are quite different. When A and B agree that there is a red painting on the wall, they may have quite different internal impressions of it, and this can be true even if they have the same remarks to make about the painting in other contexts. They may, for example, both consider the painting beautiful in spite of these differences. This observation poses serious problems for the Platonic world of being, since the agreement that dialectic may force upon arguing philosophers is no guarantee that they do not differ from one another in the noncommunicable aspects of the forms. It thus appears that one human being may have knowledge that he cannot communicate to another human being, and it is this kind of observation that lies behind the problem of individualism in modern philosophy. Many modern philosophers are concerned to satisfy themselves of what they themselves know, leaving the problem (apparently more difficult) of what human beings may know in common as something to be solved after some sort of acceptable answer has been found to the former question.

Descartes's approach to the problem of what knowledge he could satisfy himself that he had has fascinated subsequent philosophers. Like many important arguments, it is essentially simple. In fact, it is of the form which mathematicians use quite frequently, and call the argument from *reductio ad absurdum*. The basic idea is this: if one wishes to prove that some proposition p is true, but can see no straightforward way of doing so, it is quite possible to prove p indirectly by assuming that p is false, and looking for an obviously false statement (preferably a contradiction) which follows from this assumption. By the definition of validity, if such a consequence can be found, it is equivalent to the assertion that 'p is false' is false, and this in turn is equivalent to the assertion that p is true. In such an argument, p or not-p (the latter being assumed as true if p is taken to be false) may be conjoined with other logically true statements. The fact that the other assumed statements are logically true means that if a contradiction is found, it may be blamed on either of p or not-p, whichever was assumed in addition. Descartes had observed, for reasons not much different from those that had convinced Plato and other earlier philosophers, that in many cases statements that had been thought to constitute knowledge would turn out to be uncertain or false under scrutiny. These examples were usually examples from sense-experience reports, but that is not crucial here. In order to show that human beings have some knowledge, so that they can obtain satisfactory axioms for a deductive system of human knowledge, it is necessary to show that not every case in which they believe themselves to possess knowledge is in fact uncertain or mistaken. The proof of the existence of one such piece of knowledge is sufficient to settle this question. Let p be "There is some human knowledge.". Its denial, not-p, is then "There is no human knowledge.". In both cases, *knowledge* is to be read in the technical sense of indubitable truth. To prove p, therefore, it is sufficient to show that not-p, if assumed, leads to an obvious falsehood. This, in effect, was the way that Descartes argued. It is clear that his argument is not *entirely* satisfactory, since in order to look for the consequences of some statement, according to the definition of deductive argument, one has to know how to look for consequences, and hence it is difficult to see how one might assume that he knows nothing, and then look for consequences which follow from that assumption. Nevertheless, it is of interest to see whether or not absurd consequences do follow from such an assumption as the one that there is no knowledge, using only logically valid steps of inference. We might suppose for the course of investigation that we are not human beings. Then, just as the natural scientist, who is not a fish, may think about fish, so we might imagine ourselves temporarily as higher beings who are scrutinizing human activity to see whether any of it might lead to knowledge. Descartes removes himself from the problem in such a manner by supposing that there is some evil power who has deceived him about everything. The question for Descartes is then whether or not the existence of such a power can be consistently held.

It turns out that if we question those beliefs which we have that we consider most secure by means of such a sweeping criticism, most of them seem *possibly* wrong or mistaken, which is sufficient to condemn them for any philosophy, like Descartes's or Plato's, that wishes to discover *certain* knowledge. We shall see that the empiricists will be different from the rationalists partly because they will question the propriety of considering *knowledge* to consist only of *certain* beliefs. But for the present, it would appear that Descartes could hold his view about the evil power without inconsistency.

There is no difficulty in showing that no knowledge obtained through the senses could be knowledge in Descartes's philosophical sense. An interesting argument that Descartes employed to indicate this is the argument from a seeming inability to determine whether or not we are awake. The distinction between being awake and being asleep, which may be clear enough to most of us most of the time, is open to potential confusion. Descartes, as well as most of us, occasionally mixed up some impressions from a dream with those from reality. Surely dreamers often experience terror and other emotions in their dreams, and it is clear that sometimes dreamers suppose that they are awake at the time of these experiences. If the dream state and the waking state are confused occasionally, how can it ever be known by someone with certainty that he is awake or dreaming at any given moment? It appears that he can never know for certain, since a sufficiently evil power might cause him to be confused about the distinction with great frequency. Descartes supposes that a distinction can be made, although perhaps he does so in a manner which is not entirely satisfactory. Empiricists will contend that even if one cannot know with certainty, there are ways of distinguishing the two states which are adequate for the purposes of scientific investigation, and hence derivatively adequate for philosophy.

But the results of assuming the existence of the evil power cut much deeper than obliterating the certain distinction between dreaming and being awake. The significance of being unable to make that distinction is largely that if sense experience is taken as the source of knowledge, and if sense experience does not occur during sleep and dreaming although one feels himself to be having sense experiences during dreams, then no feeling of having a sense experience can be taken as conclusive evidence that one is having a sense experience. The argument from the evil power is apparently sufficient to show that sense experience cannot be the origin of knowledge. But consider any statement of fact, that is, significant statement about the world, which is such that it seems to be certain. Clearly any such statement must refer to some past events, and its certainty must be related to some past observations, sense-experiential, or otherwise. To put this another way, a judgment of certainty rests upon previous knowledge that we have acquired, if for no other reason than that we need to have learned some language in order to express any judgment that we would like to make. But this view raises the question of the reliability of memory. If a present judgment or observation is to be certain, and it rests upon past judgments or observations, then there must be some *past* judgments which are certain if there are to be any present judgments or observations which are certainly true. But the conception of an evil power makes it clear at once that there can be no certain past. Whatever events we have memory of may be dream events which we have confused with reality. But even more importantly, it is possible, given everything that we think we know now, that there has been no past; in short, that the evil power created the world just yesterday or a few seconds ago. The objection to this is that we can think back to events which happened before yesterday or a few seconds ago. But how powerful is this objection? Suppose that we only dreamed about past events when we were created, and that we can dream about events in a couple of seconds which would stretch over long periods of time if they were memories of actual, experienced events. And, of course, we might have been created with full memories of past events which never happened. If memory, for example, is to be explained on the basis of some organic structure of the brain, then we might surely have been created with an organic structure which gives us the impression of past events which never happened. When memory is questioned, it would appear that most of our knowledge of sense-experienced events is of dubious quality. Note that if memory is questioned, the argument is not only against the view that sense experience is the origin of knowledge, since past intuitions have to be remembered to account for knowledge, but also against one view of any philosopher like Plato, whose view of the acquisition of knowledge depends upon the recollection of past intuitions.

The Cogito *Argument*

In spite of the apparent success of the argument from universal doubt in showing that most of the instances of purported knowledge that we might bring forward without reflection are dubious, that is, open to possible error under scrutiny, Descartes does find at least one proposition that he considers certain. This proposition is his specific counterexample to the argument that human beings may not possess any knowledge. It is the famous "Cogito, ergo sum.". We turn now to an analysis of this proposition to see whether Descartes's contention that it is indubitable is really satisfactory.

We shall consider this proposition in its English form, namely, "I think, therefore I am.". The occurrence of the word *therefore* is almost always a sign that some inference is being made. As a result, it is tempting to suppose that "I think, therefore I am." expresses a logical inference, and that Descartes takes the certainty of the logical inference in conjunction with the certainty that he is thinking to prove that he exists. Let us suppose that a stands for Descartes. 'Tx' might stand for the expression 'x thinks', which may be turned into a sentence by substituting someone's name for x. In this way, Descartes's proposition might be formulated in the expression 'Ta', as it would be by many modern logicians. The problem of finding some formulation or symbolic expression for the statement "Descartes exists." is much more difficult.

There is, of course, a superficial grammatical similarity between the two sentences "Descartes thinks." and "Descartes exists.". In both cases, a subject noun is followed by a verb. But a serious problem for philosophical analysis is that grammatical similarities can prove to be misleading. Consider the following two sentences:

    A. The wastepaper basket in this room is circular.
    B. The wastepaper basket in this room exists.

Suppose, in the first case, that there is a wastepaper basket (and only one) in the room. In this case, the first sentence is quite clearly true or false, under an appropriate definition of *circular,* but the second sentence seems somehow to be redundant, or to convey very little information. Certainly it is the kind of thing that one would rarely say. At the same time, if there is no wastepaper basket in the room, the second sentence may seem to be either false or peculiar, while the first sentence seems to be quite peculiar, in that it seems neither true nor false. Philosophers have been perplexed by problems like these concerning existence since Plato, whose philosophy requires some explanation for the existence of the forms or ideas which do not exist in the ordinary sense that cats and dogs and people and Chevrolet cars exist.

Briefly, some philosophers have wanted to maintain that every grammatical, meaningful, indicative sentence should be true or false, but not both. For these philosophers, it is usually the case that, if the wastepaper basket exists, sentence B is true and sentence A is true or false depending on its construction, while if the wastepaper basket does not exist, sentence A is false along with sentence B. But this view, although it is very neat and simple in that it makes every grammatically well-formed sentence either true or false, does entail some revision of what common English usage seems to suggest. Since this is so, other revisions have been looked for. It will not be required here to survey these issues nor the various solutions to the difficulties inherent in them which have been proposed in the literature.

For our purpose, we merely note that the existence of a problem about existence is sufficient to cause us to refrain from putting down the sentence "Descartes exists." as something with the form 'Ea' with any assurance that we are doing something equivalent to what was done in the formulation of 'Ta'. The problem, then, is this: Is there any plausible way of writing down "Descartes exists." so as to make the inference from "Descartes thinks." to "Descartes exists." valid in some logical system? The general answer is that this is quite possible, but that in all known cases it results in an inference which is trivial in a way that Descartes clearly did not intend. Thus, many logicians write down 'a exists.' as '$(Ex) (x = a)$', which may be read 'There is at least one thing x such that x is identical with a.'. This seems to be a satisfactory way of expressing the claim that a exists for reasons that are too complicated to summarize quickly. If this reading is taken, then the inference 'If Ta, then $(Ex)(x=a)$.' may be proved in many logical systems as a consequence of the logically true statement 'If Ta, then $(Ex) (x = a$ and $Tx)$.', which is provable in very simple logical systems. Therefore, if 'Ta' symbolizes a sentence which is both true and asserts that Descartes thinks, we can also prove the truth of a statement which asserts that Descartes exists.

The importance of these observations is considerably diminished, however, by a closer look at the logical systems in which the inference 'If Ta, then $(Ex)(x=a)$.' can be proved. To begin with, these systems tacitly presuppose that the symbols which stand for nouns in their syntax, symbols into which *Descartes*, for example, would be translated, denote existing individuals. Consequently, at any time that one can assert ⌜*Ta*⌝ in such a system, one can also assert that *a* exists, since *a* cannot be used as a symbol in the system unless it refers to an existing individual. This makes the inference in question vacuous in the sense that we must know that the conclusion is true in order to formulate the premise correctly. Although the logical points that need to be made here are quite subtle, it is possible to demonstrate quite easily that the general form of an argument that goes like the following, ⌜*Da*, therefore *a* exists.⌝, is invalid, where ⌜*Da*⌝ in the sentence expressing the inference stands for any complete sentence that tells us about some property (other than existence) that *a* has. Consider the following argument: Hamlet thinks, therefore Hamlet exists. Here the transition is made from a sentence that most of us might consider true if we were asked casually about it to one that most of us would consider false, which means that the inference is not valid if the sentences are interpreted in this way. Hamlet does, of course, *exist* in some sense in the English language, but it is clear that Descartes does not mean to establish that he exists in the same sense that Hamlet exists. Therefore, if we treat the inference about Hamlet as invalid, Descartes's argument appears to be invalid. If we treat the inference about Hamlet as valid (proving that Hamlet exists), there remains the difficulty of distinguishing Hamlet's kind of existence from Descartes's existence, so that the inference does not do the job that Descartes seems to take it to do.

Descartes's notion of existence will be at least as complicated as Plato's. The sense of existence in which we say that Hamlet exists poses a number of philosophical problems. Those philosophers who have discussed fictional existence have generally tried to show how the existence of fictional characters could be analyzed in terms of the existence of other kinds of experienced objects. But Descartes cannot suppose that he exists in the same sense that experienced objects exist. The existence of the demon demonstrated to Descartes that the objects of sense experience might all be illusory, and that the whole notion of a world of sense experience can be doubted. Since Descartes felt that his own existence could not be doubted, it is clear that he did not identify himself with an object of sense experience. Descartes does not refer to the existence of his body when he says "I exist.". He is saying that thinking substances (souls) exist in a fashion quite different than material or corporeal bodies. Descartes, like Plato, uses *exist* in at least two ways, both of which must receive attention in his total theory of knowledge.

It might be argued that the logical framework which has been constructed thus far is misleading in that by means of it "I think, therefore I am." is subtly changed into "Descartes thinks, therefore he exists.", which is somewhat different. Suppose, therefore, that we try to construe the *cogito* argument as an argument which is not valid in general, since one cannot know about the thoughts of others, but which is valid only for the person who is proposing the argument, somewhat along the lines that Descartes intended. The notion of personal validity is not countenanced by most logicians, but Descartes may have implicitly believed that there were some arguments that I could not give an interpretation for myself in which the premises were true and the conclusion false, even though I might be able to imagine such an interpretation of the argument for others. In other words, Descartes may have intended that no one could prove the existence of another human being from the fact that the other human being seemed to think, while he intended that the *cogito* argument could be used by an individual to prove his own existence. "I think, therefore I am." in this case is not a valid argument to me if someone else utters it of himself, but it is a valid argument to me if I utter it of myself.

Suppose that I argue as follows:*

If I am right in thinking that I exist, then I exist. If I err in thinking that I exist, then I exist, since I must exist in order to err. But either I am right in thinking that I exist or I err in thinking that I exist. Therefore, I exist.

The apparent plausibility of this argument to many people is a good reason for urging the study of logic. Suppose, for example, that someone in a fit of madness should suppose that everything in the Old Testament of the Bible was not literally true. In particular, suppose that he doubted the historical existence of Moses. Ordinarily, we might take the existence of any historical figure to be a matter of doubt. But an orthodox opponent might argue in the following fashion:

If Moses was a Jew, then he existed, since no one could be a Jew without existing. If Moses was a Gentile (someone other than a Jew), then he existed, since no one could be a Gentile without existing. But Moses was either a Jew or a Gentile. Therefore, Moses existed.

It would be interesting to inform historical scholars that all problems of the existence of historical figures could be solved without doing any research. Apparently, restricting the argument to the case of someone asserting it for himself will not avoid the problem that arguments proving existence are either invalid or beg the question, in that the conclusion must be known to be true for the premises to be appropriately formulated. That Descartes could not have seriously intended the argument to rest on its logical merits alone is clear from the fact that he rejects the argument "I sweat, therefore I am." for his existence, even though it seems to be of the same logical form, and hence valid or invalid with the argument from the property of thinking.

Nevertheless the force of Descartes's argument is related to the fact

* This argument, as well as some of the other illustrations in the discussion of the *cogito* argument, is to be found in an excellent article by Jaakko Hintikka, "*Cogito, Ergo Sum:* Inference or Performance?" *The Philosophical Review,* vol. 71, pp. 3–33, January, 1962.

that it is an individual who is making it, and this requires some further study. Consider the following two sentences:

1. Samuel Richardson says that Tom Jones is dead.
2. Tom Jones says that Tom Jones is dead.

The first sentence may be taken both literally and metaphorically, but the second is peculiar in that it can make sense only metaphorically. Dead men tell no tales, least of all the one that they are dead. That seems unthinkable, apart from science fiction and spiritualism, which will not be taken into account here. Therefore, although anyone but Descartes may consistently argue that Descartes does not exist or is dead (as it was once argued that Hitler was dead in spite of apparent evidence to the contrary), Descartes himself cannot take this line of argument. Descartes, if he argues at all about the matter, must argue that he exists, or be considered mad. None of these reflections shows that Descartes's *cogito* argument is a piece of certain knowledge, indeed they argue to the contrary, but the difficulties raised by Descartes's argument have directly or indirectly stimulated a great deal of the discussions of the significance of individual experience that have taken place among philosophers since his time.

For Descartes, the *cogito* argument established one indubitable truth, the existence of his self, and from this Descartes thought that he could ultimately establish the existence of God, and from the nature of God the certainty that mathematics and science, properly pursued, could establish indubitable truth about the world in which we live.

The *cogito* argument is not an argument that one accepts like a demonstration in geometry; it must be taken rather as Descartes's report of what happened when he followed the hypothesis of doubt to some of its consequences. Presumably, others who follow the regimen of doubt will all come to the conclusion that they exist. Descartes himself did not devote much attention to whether this might be true. Later philosophers have been considerably perplexed by the problem of proving the existence of other selves, even if one can establish by the *cogito* argument the existence of one's own. What thinks, doubts, imagines, etc., is not a body, but a mind. Since one person cannot always see another thinking (unless one accepts a very strong version of behaviorist psychology), the *cogito* argument cannot be extended to prove that other beings exist, and hence by itself cannot prove the existence of human knowledge which is accessible to more than one person.

The *cogito* argument shows the existence of the philosopher's mind, which has the ideas that give him knowledge. These ideas, unlike those of Plato, exist in the mind of the philosopher, not as entities to which different philosophers have equal access through dialectic. Knowledge which is not based on sense experience is in effect the grasp of these ideas and the entities which they represent. Some of these ideas are related to objects of sense experience in such a way as to lead to science, but it is through the ideas, and not through sense experiences, that these objects are known by scientists.

Although both Plato and Aristotle had drawn distinctions between bodies and souls, their more primary epistemological distinctions were drawn between the world of becoming and the world of being, or the difference between form and matter. Their problem had been the nature of things, with the account of human acquisition of knowledge of that nature somewhat secondary. In Descartes, mind and body, or mind and matter, is the fundamental epistemological distinction, and the acquisition of knowledge the fundamental epistemological problem. It has continued to be so for later philosophers.

Clearness and Distinctness

To come to an understanding of Descartes's full position, it would be necessary to examine his proofs of the existence of God, as well as his conclusions from the nature of God that certain statements are indubitably true. Still, day-to-day development of human knowledge is not dependent on constant examination of metaphysical foundations, and we may profitably look at Descartes's discussion of how ideas may be said to provide knowledge, independently of the connection between the origin of these ideas and God's nature in Descartes's full system.

It is true that there are innumerable difficulties in Descartes's conception of the mind as a kind of real, though immaterial, organ of perception. If we grant Descartes at least the possibility that the mind may exist as he describes it, we can find in Descartes a number of apparently convincing arguments that no explanation not involving such a mind could account for scientific information which is indubitable.

Descartes's most famous example is taken from information about a piece of wax, chosen because it might seem to be something which could be comprehended by the senses, if anything could be comprehended by them. The illustration involves a piece of wax all of whose sensed properties change over a short period of time. In spite of the change in *all* the sensed properties, it is still possible to know something about the wax, notably that it is the same piece of wax at both the beginning and end of the interval in which it is considered, in spite of the fact that there is no sensed property which it has both at the beginning and end of that period of time. This argument shows that if we can truly say that the wax is the same piece of wax at both times, we cannot explain this fact by appealing to our sense experiences of the wax. What we know in this case, and by extension in other cases like it, cannot be fully explained by an appeal to sense experience. It is important to notice that sense experience is not totally irrelevant, in that we may not be able to form the judgment that we are considering a piece of wax without some sense experiences, but it shows that what we can *know* about the piece of wax is not *reducible* to descriptions of sense experiences that we have. Thus, by an argument similar to those we considered earlier in connection with Plato's philosophy, Descartes seems to have established that *certain* knowledge cannot be satisfactorily justified or explained in terms of sense experience alone, although Descartes seems inclined to allow sense experience a more important role in leading us to this certain knowledge than Plato did.

In connection with the piece of wax, Descartes notes that when we *abstract* from the color, shape, etc., of the wax, we are left with the knowledge that the wax is something which is extended and movable. These properties, extension and motion, form the basic notions of Cartesian physics. It is the position of Descartes that the possible incorrectness of our attributions of particular sensed properties to objects, possibly incorrect because we observe that different sense properties may characterize the same object at different times, does not extend to extension and motion, which objects always have. For Descartes, extension and motion must be intuited of objects by the mind, but to show this it is necessary to show that they are not sensual properties.

Descartes takes it as clear that these properties are not *directly* sensed in an object, since we would sense both (if that were possible) by *comparison* of one object with another. But Descartes distinguishes a faculty that he calls imagination from the faculty of understanding, which is the result of the mind's comprehension of truth through ideas. Imagination is the result of combining parts of different particular sense experiences so as to frame a conception of something that it would be possible to experience. A mermaid, on this view, is a creature of imagination, since the conception of a mermaid results from combining parts of two or more particular sense experiences. In the case of the mermaid, the probability of experiencing this possible object of sense experience seems arbitrarily close to zero. Why cannot motion or extension in an object be the result of the operation of the imagination, that is, the combination in some fashion of a large number of particular sense experiences? Descartes's response that they cannot result from an exercise of imagination hinges on the fact that imagination can combine only a *finite* number of sense experiences (those that we have had), while an infinitude of motions and extensions seems possible. Knowledge of motion and extension, involving a conception of an infinite number of possibilities, cannot result solely from imagination. For Descartes, the more we know about wax, the more we know that our selves (minds) exist, and the more we know about our *selves*, since knowledge is not about sense-experienced objects.

Where Plato had provided arguments that seemed to show that mathematical knowledge could not be accounted for solely by sense experiences, Descartes provides arguments to show that this is true of scientific knowledge as well. This argument is one that cannot be lightly dismissed, even though one may wish to renounce the particular metaphysics that Descartes employs to prove it. The reason why the argument cannot be lightly dismissed is related to the growth of modern scientific *theory*, a phenomenon beginning to develop in Descartes's time, but almost totally unknown in Plato's time. The objects spoken of in fragments of scientific theory, such as ideal gases and frictionless surfaces, to take some examples, are often such that they could not be experienced. Almost any important subject of scientific theorizing in the last one hundred years, for example, *gene, electron, DNA*, etc., can hardly be construed as something which is sense-experienced.

The relationship of theoretical entities and sense experience is an extremely difficult one to interpret. To take a simple example, one which Descartes considered, the sun of astronomical theory has an average distance from the earth of some 93 million miles, although no one has experienced that distance. Further, the sun of astronomical theory is known to have a diameter of 865,000 miles, while the sun of sense experience is a small disk. Without multiplying examples unnecessarily, we can see that many, perhaps even all, of the things which science theorizes about are not to be confused with the objects of sense experience, for they have different properties. To say this is to raise the problem of the relationship between the objects of sense experience and the objects of scientific theorizing, a problem that neither Plato's nor Descartes's rationalism fully answers, although the arguments of Plato and Descartes for rationalism point up the difficulties which must be encountered in framing a satisfactory account of the relationship of theory to practice. What is important for Descartes is that *knowledge* is partly mathematical and scientific, and that sense experience cannot explain the certainty found in at least these areas of knowledge. It is assumed here that mathematical truths and truths of scientific theorizing are certain, a position which is obviously capable of a vigorous defense.

For Plato, the ideas constituting knowledge were those corresponding to the ideas or forms in the world of being. Descartes, not having a world of being, must depend on some other criterion for separating the sound ideas from unsound ideas which may occur to us. The Cartesian criterion is twofold: those ideas are sound, that is, capable of good use in developing knowledge, which are both *clear* and *distinct*. The impact of the notions of clearness and distinctness on subsequent philosophy calls for some closer attention to what Descartes meant.

Descartes notices that our thoughts (comprising everything that we may call an *idea* ordinarily) may be divided into ideas proper and judgments. The former are, simply, the images that appear in the mind without any reflection as to their significance. Judgments are decisions as to the significance of ideas proper, or perhaps as to the relationships between ideas. Ideas proper cannot be right or wrong; we simply have them. Judgments, on the other hand, may be right or wrong. Thus, we may experience some red, about which experience we cannot be mistaken, although we may be mistaken in judging that the red we experienced was part of a cardinal, for example, or that it was the particular red that we call scarlet. This kind of distinction occurs over and over in epistemology since Descartes, notoriously in the notion of sense data, which are like Cartesian ideas proper in that they are not capable of being false. Many philosophers have hoped that such sense data might be taken as a sound basis for the epistemological foundation of science.

The clear and distinct ideas involved in knowledge are not ideas proper, since they are things that we have reflected on. It may be less misleading to speak of clear and distinct thoughts. Here, a *clear* thought is one which may be the direct object of apprehension, and hence may be described as a thought which is not vague. This means that it may be considered by itself, without reference to other ideas or judgments.

On the other hand, a *distinct* thought is one which may be comprehended or understood by itself, that is, whose understanding does not depend on other thoughts. The clear and distinct thoughts that are useful for developing knowledge are such that the notion of distinctness conflates with the notion of simplicity. A simple thought is a thought which is pregnant or endlessly fruitful for the development of some line of thought. For example, the concepts of *group* and *limit* are simple in mathematics in this sense, for they may be used to understand and develop mathematical truth in seemingly endless particular contexts. *Simple* may contrast with *adventitious*, yet an adventitious idea may be clear, and in some sense distinct, without being fruitful. Adventitious ideas are chance ideas, or ideas forced upon us by the vagaries of sense experience. In contrast to group and limit, the concept of a chiliagon would be an adventitious idea in mathematics. A distinct thought is then a thought which may be comprehended by itself and which it is fruitful to contemplate. In thinking of clear and distinct ideas it may be helpful to note that distinct ideas are also necessarily clear ideas, but that an idea may be clear without being distinct.

The status of the thought "I think, therefore I am." is surely that of a clear and distinct idea for Descartes, which he finds fruitful in developing his later epistemological claims. This may explain why Descartes thought that so much could be based on it that cannot be *deduced* from it by the rules of formal logic. While clearness and distinctness are not themselves entirely clear and distinct, they have proved influential notions for the thinking of many later philosophers who were rationalists in epistemology, particularly with respect to the problem of distinguishing those ideas that might constitute human knowledge.

Readings from Descartes

The readings which are reprinted here consist of the first two medita-tions and part of the third from Descartes's *Meditations on the First Philos-ophy in Which the Existence of God and the Distinction between Mind and Body Are Demonstrated*. They are reprinted here from *The Philosophical Works of Descartes*, translated by E. S. Haldane and G. R. T. Ross. This reprinting is by kind permission of the Cambridge University Press. The Haldane and Ross translation has also been available as a Dover paper-bound.

Descartes's *Discourse on Method* and his *Meditations* are usually re-garded as his philosophical masterpieces. They should be studied along with the sets of *Objections* to the *Meditations* which are found in Des-cartes's complete works. A friend of Descartes, the Rev. Father Mersenne, circulated the *Meditations* among various theologians and philosophers who then sent their comments and criticisms to Descartes. Descartes re-plied to the objections and published the entire correspondence along with the *Meditations*. These so-called *Objections and Replies* constitute what is perhaps the most valuable commentary on the *Meditations*.

Descartes is one of the major philosophers who would be important in intellectual history even if his philosophical achievements had been entirely neglected. He deserves a place in mathematical history, for ex-ample, because of his contributions to geometry. A short biography and summary of his mathematical achievements may be found in E. T. Bell's *Men of Mathematics*, New York, 1937. His most important mathematical insight was the discovery of the method of coordinates which made analytic geometry possible. The method of coordinates proposed by Descartes is the familiar one of dividing the Euclidean mathematical plane into four quadrants by means of two intersecting straight lines called the ordinate and the abscissa. As is well known, any geometrical curve in the plane can then be defined as an *equation* which represents each point of the curve by means of its perpendicular distances to the ordinate and the abscissa. The importance of analytic geometry, which is the study of geometrical problems expressed as algebraic equations, is that many difficult geometrical problems can be quickly solved when they are *translated* into algebraic equations whose solution is a matter of routine.

It is characteristic of the life of Descartes that the method of coordinates should have occurred to him while he was lying in bed watching a housefly walk on the ceiling of his room. Descartes saw that the position of the fly could always be represented by its perpendicular distances to any two walls forming a corner of the room, and this observation may quickly be abstracted into the notion of coordinates.

The following bibliography contains some secondary-source material in English. A vast literature on Descartes is available in French to those students who can read that language, and French sources may be obtained by consulting the bibliographies of the books which are listed here.

Balz, A. G. A.: *Descartes and the Modern Mind*, New Haven, 1952.

Beck, L. J.: *The Method of Descartes, a Study of the Regulae*, Oxford, 1952.

Carney, James D.: *"Cogito, Ergo Sum* and *Sum Res Cogitans,"* The Philosophical Review, vol. 71, pp. 492–497, 1962.

Hintikka, Jaakko: *"Cogito, Ergo Sum:* Inference or Performance?" *The Philosophical Review*, vol. 71, pp. 3–33, 1962.

Smart, J. J. C.: "Descartes and the Wax," *Philosophical Quarterly*, vol. 1, pp. 50–57, 1950.

Smith, N. K.: *Studies in Cartesian Philosophy*, London, 1914.

_____: *New Studies in the Philosophy of Descartes*, London, 1952.

Versfeld, M.: *An Essay on the Metaphysics of Descartes*, London, 1940.

Weinberg, J. R.: *"Cogito, Ergo Sum:* Some Reflections on Mr. Hintikka's Article," *The Philosophical Review*, vol. 71, pp. 483–492, 1962.

Wright, J. N.: "Descartes and the Wax," *Philosophical Quarterly*, vol. 1, pp. 352–355, 1950.

From Descartes's *MEDITATIONS*

MEDITATION I: OF THE THINGS WHICH MAY BE BROUGHT WITHIN THE SPHERE OF THE DOUBTFUL

It is now some years since I detected how many were the false beliefs that I had from my earliest youth admitted as true, and how doubtful was everything I had since constructed on this basis; and from that time I was convinced that I must once for all seriously undertake to rid myself of all the opinions which I had formerly accepted, and commence to build anew from the foundation, if I wanted to establish any firm and permanent structure in the sciences. But as this enterprise appeared to be a very great one, I waited until I had attained an age so mature that I could not hope that at any later date I should be better fitted to execute my design. This reason caused me to delay so long that I should feel that I was doing wrong were I to occupy in deliberation the time that yet remains to me for action. Today, then, since very opportunely for the plan I have in view I have delivered my mind from every care (and am happily agitated by no passions) and since I have procured for myself an assured leisure in a peaceable retirement, I shall at last seriously and freely address myself to the general upheaval of all my former opinions.

Now for this object it is not necessary that I should show that all of these are false—I shall perhaps never arrive at this end. But inasmuch as reason already persuades me that I ought no less carefully to withhold my assent from matters which are not entirely certain and indubitable than from those which appear to me manifestly to be false, if I am able to find in each one some reason to doubt, this will suffice to justify my rejecting the whole. And for that end it will not be requisite that I should examine each in particular, which would be an endless undertaking; for owing to the fact that destruction of the foundations of necessity brings with it the downfall of the rest of the edifice, I shall only in the first place attack those principles upon which all my former opinions rested.

All that up to the present time I have accepted as most certain and true I have learned either from the senses or through the senses; but it is sometimes proved to me that these senses are deceptive, and it is wiser not to trust entirely to any thing by which we have once been deceived. But it may be that although the senses sometimes deceive us concerning things which are hardly perceptible, or very far away, there are yet many others to be met with as to which we cannot reasonably have any doubt, although we recognize them by their means. For example, there is the fact that I am here, heated by the fire, attired in a dressing gown, having this paper in my hands and other similar matters. And how could I deny that these hands and this body were mine, were it not perhaps that I compare myself to certain persons, devoid of sense, whose cerebella are so troubled and clouded by the violent vapors of black bile, that they constantly assure us that they think they are kings when they are really quite poor, or that they are clothed in purple when they are really without covering, or who imagine that they have an earthenware head or are nothing but pumpkins or are made of glass.[1] But they are mad, and I should not be any the less insane were I to follow examples so extravagant.

At the same time I must remember that I am a man, and that consequently I am in the habit of sleeping, and in my dreams representing to myself the same things or sometimes even less probable things, than do those who are insane in their waking moments. How often has it happened to me that in the night I dreamt that I found myself in this particular place, that I was dressed and seated near the fire, whilst in reality I was lying undressed in bed?[2] At this moment it does indeed seem to me that it is with eyes awake that I am looking at this paper; that this head which I move is not asleep, that it is deliberately and of set purpose that I extend my hand

and perceive it; what happens in sleep does not appear so clear nor so distinct as does all this. But in thinking over this I remind myself that on many occasions I have in sleep been deceived by similar illusions, and in dwelling carefully on this reflection I see so manifestly that there are no certain indications by which we may clearly distinguish wakefulness from sleep that I am lost in astonishment. And my astonishment is such that it is almost capable of persuading me that I now dream.

Now let us assume that we are asleep and that all of these particulars, e.g. that we open our eyes, shake our head, extend our hands, and so on, are but false delusions; and let us reflect that possibly neither our hands nor our whole body are such as they appear to us to be. At the same time we must at least confess that the things which are represented to us in sleep are like painted representations which can only have been formed as the counterparts of something real and true, and that in this way those general things at least, *i.e.* eyes, a head, hands, and a whole body, are not imaginary things, but things really existent. For, as a matter of fact, painters, even when they study with the greatest skill to represent sirens and satyrs by forms the most strange and extraordinary, cannot give them natures which are entirely new, but merely make a certain medley of the members of different animals; or if their imagination is extravagant enough to invent something so novel that nothing similar has ever before been seen, and that then their work represents a thing purely fictitious and absolutely false, it is certain all the same that the colors of which this is composed are necessarily real. And for the same reason, although these general things, to wit, (a body), eyes, a head, and such like, may be imaginary, we are bound at the same time to confess that there are at least some other objects, yet more simple and more universal, which are real and true; and of these just in the same way as with certain real colors, all these images of things which dwell in our thoughts, whether true and real or false and fantastic, are formed.

To such a class of things pertains corporeal nature in general, and its extension, the figure of extended things, their quantity or magnitude and number, as also the place in which they are, the time which measures their duration, and so on.[3]

That is possibly why our reasoning is not unjust when we conclude from this that Physics, Astronomy, Medicine and all other sciences which have as their end the consideration of composite things, are very dubious and uncertain; but that Arithmetic, Geometry, and other sciences of that kind which only treat of things that are very simple and very general, without taking great trouble to ascertain whether they are actually existent or not, contain some measure of certainty and an element of the indubitable.[4] For whether I am awake or asleep, two and three together always form five, and the square can never have more than four sides, and it does not seem possible that truths so clear and apparent can be suspected of any falsity (or uncertainty).

Nevertheless I have long had fixed in my mind the belief that an all-powerful God existed by whom I have been created such as I am. But how do I know that He has not brought it to pass that there is no earth, no heaven, no extended body, no magnitude, no place, and that nevertheless (I possess the perceptions of all these things and that) they seem to me to exist just exactly as I now see them ? And, besides, as I sometimes imagine that others deceive themselves in the things which they think they know best, how do I know that I am not deceived every time that I add two and three, or count the sides of a square, or judge of things yet simpler, if anything simpler can be imagined ? But possibly God has not desired that I should be thus deceived, for He is said to be supremely good. If, however, it is contrary to His goodness to have made me such that I constantly deceive myself, it would also appear to be contrary to His goodness to permit me to be sometimes deceived, and nevertheless I cannot doubt that He does permit this.[5]

There may indeed be those who would prefer to deny the existence of a God so powerful, rather than believe that all other things are uncertain.[6] But let us not oppose them for the present, and grant that all that is said of God is a fable; nevertheless in whatever way they suppose that I have arrived at the state of being that I have reached—whether they attribute it to fate or to accident, or make out that it is by a continual succession of antecedents, or by some other method—since to err and deceive oneself is a defect, it is clear that the greater will be the probability of my being so imperfect as to deceive myself ever, as is the Author to whom they assign my origin the less powerful. To these reasons I have certainly nothing to reply, but at the end I feel constrained to confess that there is nothing in all that I formerly believed to be true, of which I cannot in some measure doubt, and that not merely through want of thought or through levity, but for reasons which are very powerful and maturely considered; so that henceforth I ought not the less carefully to refrain from giving credence to these opinions than to that which is manifestly false, if I desire to arrive at any certainty (in the sciences).

But it is not sufficient to have made these remarks, we must also be careful to keep them in mind. For these ancient and commonly held opinions still revert frequently to my mind, long and familiar custom having given them the right to occupy my mind against my inclination and rendered them almost masters of my belief; nor will I ever lose the habit of deferring to them or of placing my confidence in them, so long as I consider them as they really are, *i.e.* opinions in some measure doubtful, as I have just shown, and at the same time highly probable, so that there is much more reason to believe than to deny them. That is why I consider that I shall not be acting amiss, if, taking of set purpose a contrary belief, I allow myself to be deceived, and for a certain time pretend that all these opinions are entirely false and imaginary, until at last, having thus balanced my former prejudices with my latter (so that they cannot divert my opinions more to one side than to the other), my judgment will no longer be dominated by bad usage or turned away from the right knowledge of the truth. For I am assured that there can be neither peril nor error in this course, and that I cannot at present yield too much to distrust, since I am not considering the question of action, but only of knowledge.[7]

I shall then suppose, not that God who is supremely good and the fountain of truth, but some evil genius not less powerful than deceitful, has employed his whole energies in deceiving me; I shall consider that the heavens, the earth, colors, figures, sound, and all other external things are nought but the illusions and dreams of which this genius has availed himself in order to lay traps for my credulity; I shall consider myself as having no hands, no eyes, no flesh, no blood, nor any senses, yet falsely believing myself to possess all these things; I shall remain obstinately attached to this idea, and if by this means it is not in my power to arrive at the knowledge of any truth, I may at least do what is in my power (i.e. suspend my judgment), and with firm purpose avoid giving credence to any false thing, or being imposed upon by this arch deceiver, however powerful and deceptive he may be. But this task is a laborious one, and insensibly a certain lassitude leads me into the course of my ordinary life. And just as a captive who in sleep enjoys imaginary liberty, when he begins to suspect that his liberty is but a dream, fears to awaken, and conspires with these agreeable illusions that the deception may be prolonged, so insensibly of my own accord I fall back into my former opinions, and I dread awakening from this slumber, lest the laborious wakefulness which should follow the tranquillity of this repose should have to be spent not in daylight, but in the excessive darkness of the difficulties which have just been discussed.

MEDITATION II: OF THE NATURE OF THE HUMAN MIND; AND THAT IT IS MORE EASILY KNOWN THAN THE BODY

The Meditation of yesterday filled my mind with so many doubts that it is no longer in my power to forget them. And yet I do not see in what manner I can resolve them; and, just as if I had all of a sudden fallen into very deep water, I am so disconcerted that I can neither make certain of setting my feet on the bottom, nor can I swim and so support myself on the surface. I shall nevertheless make an effort and follow anew the same path as that on which I yesterday entered, i.e. I shall proceed by setting aside all that in which the least doubt could be supposed to exist, just as if I had discovered that it was absolutely false; and I shall ever follow in this road until I have met with something which is certain, or at least, if I can do nothing else, until I have learned for certain that there is nothing in the world which is certain. Archimedes, in order that he might draw the terrestrial globe out of its place, and transport it elsewhere, demanded only that one point should be fixed and immovable; in the same way I shall have the right to conceive high hopes if I am happy enough to discover one thing only which is certain and indubitable.[8]

I suppose, then, that all the things that I see are false; I persuade myself that nothing has ever existed of all that my fallacious memory represents to me. I consider that I possess no senses; I imagine that body, figure, extension, movement and place are but the fictions of my mind. What, then, can be esteemed as true ? Perhaps nothing at all, unless that there is nothing in the world which is certain.[9]

But how can I know that there is not something different from those things which I have just considered, of which one cannot have the slightest doubt ? Is there not some God, or some other being by whatever name we call it, who puts these reflections into my mind ? That is not necessary, for is it not possible that I am capable of producing them myself ? I myself, am I not at least something ? But I have already denied that I had senses and body. Yet I hesitate, for what follows from that ? Am I so dependent on body and senses that I cannot exist without these ? But I was persuaded that there was nothing in all the world, that there was no heaven, no earth, that there were no minds, nor any bodies; was I not then likewise persuaded that I did not exist ? Not at all; of a surety I myself did exist since I persuaded myself of something (or merely because I thought of something). But there is some deceiver or other, very powerful and very cunning, who ever employs his ingenuity in deceiving me. Then without doubt I exist also if he deceives me, and let him deceive me as much as he will, he can never cause me to be nothing so long as I think that I am something. So that after having reflected well and carefully examined all things, we must come to the definite conclusion that this proposition: I am, I exist, is necessarily true each time that I pronounce it, or that I mentally conceive it.[10]

But I do not yet know clearly enough what I am, I who am certain that I am; and hence I must be careful to see that I do not imprudently take some other object in place of myself, and thus that I do not go astray in respect of this knowledge that I hold to be the most certain and most evident of all that I have formerly learned. That is why I shall now consider anew what I believed myself to be before I embarked upon these last reflections; and of my former opinions I shall withdraw all that might even in a small degree be invalidated by the reasons which I have just brought forward, in order that there may be nothing at all left beyond what is absolutely certain and indubitable.

What then did I formerly believe myself to be ? Undoubtedly I believed myself to be a man. But what is a man ? Shall I say a reasonable animal ? Certainly not; for then I should have to inquire what an animal is, and what is reasonable; and thus from a single question I should insensibly fall into an infinitude of others more difficult; and I should not wish to waste the little time and leisure remaining to me in trying to unravel subtleties like these.[11] But I shall rather stop here to consider the thoughts which of themselves spring up in my mind, and which were not inspired by anything beyond my own nature alone when I applied myself to the consideration of my being. In the first place, then, I considered myself as having a face, hands, arms, and all that system of members composed of bones and flesh as seen in a corpse which I designated by the name of body. In addition to this I considered that I was nourished, that I walked, that I felt, and that I thought, and I referred all these actions to the soul: but I did not stop to consider what the soul was, or if I did stop, I imagined that it was something extremely rare and subtle like a wind, a flame, or an ether, which was spread throughout my grosser parts. As to body I had no manner of doubt about its nature, but thought I had a very clear knowledge of it; and if I had desired to explain it according to the notions that I had then formed of it, I should have described it thus: By the body I understand all that which can be defined by a certain figure: something which can be confined in a certain place, and which can fill a given space in such a way that every other body will be excluded from it; which can be perceived either by touch, or by sight, or by hearing, or by taste, or by smell: which can be moved in many ways not, in truth, by itself, but by something which is foreign to it, by which it is touched (and from which it receives impressions): for to have the power of self-movement, as also of feeling or of thinking, I did not consider to appertain to the nature of body: on the contrary, I was rather astonished to find that faculties similar to them existed in some bodies.

But what am I, now that I suppose that there is a certain genius which is extremely powerful, and, if I may say so, malicious, who employs all his powers in deceiving me? Can I affirm that I possess the least of all those things which I have just said pertain to the nature of body? I pause to consider, I resolve all these things in my mind, and find none of which I can say that it pertains to me. It would be tedious to stop to enumerate them. Let us pass to the attributes of soul and see if there is any one which is in me? What of nutrition or walking (the first mentioned)? [12] But if it is so that I have no body it is also true that I can neither walk nor take nourishment. Another attribute is sensation. But one cannot feel without body, and besides I have thought I perceived many things during sleep that I recognized in my waking moments as not having been experienced at all. What of thinking? I find here that thought is an attribute that belongs to me; it alone cannot be separated from me. I am, I exist, that is certain. But how often? Just when I think; for it might possibly be the case if I ceased entirely to think, that I should likewise cease altogether to exist. I do not now admit anything which is not necessarily true: to speak accurately I am not more than a thing which thinks, that is to say a mind or soul, or an understanding, or a reason, which are terms whose significance was formerly unknown to me.[13] I am, however, a real thing and really exist; but what thing? I have answered: a thing which thinks.

And what more? I shall exercise my imagination (in order to see if I am not something more). I am not a collection of members which we call the human body: I am not a subtle air distributed through these members, I am not a wind, a fire, a vapor, a breath, nor anything at all which I can imagine or conceive; because I have assumed that all these were nothing. Without changing that supposition I find that I only leave myself certain of the fact that I am somewhat. But perhaps it is true that these same things which I supposed were non-existent because they are unknown to me, are really not different from the self which I know. I am not sure about this, I shall not dispute about it now; I can only give judgment on things that are known to me. I know that I exist, and I inquire what I am, I whom I know to exist. But it is very certain that the knowledge of my existence taken in its precise significance does not depend on things whose existence is not yet known to me; consequently it does not depend on those which I can feign in imagination. And indeed the very term *feign* in imagination proves to me my error, for I really do this if I imagine myself a something, since to imagine is nothing else than to contemplate the figure or image of a corporeal thing. But I already know for certain that I am, and that it may be that all these images, and, speaking generally, all things that relate to the nature of body are nothing but dreams (and chimeras). For this reason I see clearly that I have as little reason to say, "I shall stimulate my imagination in order to know more distinctly what I am," than if I were to say, "I am now awake, and I perceive somewhat that is real and true: but because I do not yet perceive it distinctly enough, I shall go to sleep of excess purpose, so that my dreams may represent the perception with greatest truth and evidence." And, thus, I know for certain that nothing of all that I can understand by means of my imagination belongs to this knowledge which I have of myself, and that it is necessary to recall the mind from this mode of thought with the utmost diligence in order that it may be able to show its own nature with perfect distinctness.

But what then am I? A thing which thinks. What is a thing which thinks? It is a thing which doubts, understands, (conceives), affirms, denies, wills, refuses, which also imagines and feels.[14]

Certainly it is no small matter if all these things pertain to my nature. But why should they not so pertain? Am I not that being who now doubts nearly everything, who nevertheless understands certain things, who affirms that one only is true, who denies all the others, who desires to know more, is averse from being deceived, who imagines many things, sometimes indeed despite his will, and who perceives many likewise, as by the intervention of the bodily organs? Is there nothing in all this which is as true as it is certain that I exist, even though I should always sleep and though he who has given me being employed all his ingenuity in deceiving me? Is there likewise any one of these attributes which can be distinguished from my thought, or which might be said to be separated from myself? For it is so evident of itself that it is I who doubts, who understands, and who desires, that there is no reason here to add anything to explain it. And

I have certainly the power of imagining likewise; for although it may happen (as I formerly supposed) that none of the things which I imagine are true, nevertheless this power of imagining does not cease to be really in use, and it forms part of my thought. Finally, I am the same who feels, that is to say, who perceives certain things, as by the organs of sense, since in truth I see light, I hear noise, I feel heat. But it will be said that these phenomena are false and that I am dreaming. Let it be so; still it is at least quite certain that it seems to me that I see light, that I hear noise and that I feel heat. That cannot be false; properly speaking it is what is in me called feeling; and used in this precise sense that is no other thing than thinking.

From this time I begin to know what I am with a little more clearness and distinction than before; but nevertheless it still seems to me, and I cannot prevent myself from thinking, that corporeal things, whose images are framed by thought, which are tested by the senses, are much more distinctly known than that obscure part of me which does not come under the imagination. Although really it is very strange to say that I know and understand more distinctly these things whose existence seems to me dubious, which are unknown to me, and which do not belong to me, than others of the truth of which I am convinced, which are known to me and which pertain to my real nature, in a word, than myself. But I see clearly how the case stands: my mind loves to wander, and cannot yet suffer itself to be retained within the just limits of truth. Very good, let us once more give it the freest rein, so that, when afterwards we seize the proper occasion for pulling up, it may the more easily be regulated and controlled.

Let us begin by considering the commonest matters, those which we believe to be the most distinctly comprehended, to wit, the bodies which we see and touch; not indeed bodies in general, for these general ideas are usually a little more confused, but let us consider one body in particular. Let us take for example, this piece of wax: it has been taken quite freshly from the hive, and it has not yet lost the sweetness of the honey which it contains; it still retains somewhat of the odor of the flowers from which it has been culled; its color, its figure, its size are apparent; it is hard, cold, easily handled, and if you strike it with the finger, it will emit a sound.[15] Finally all the things which are requisite to cause us distinctly to recognize a body, are met within it. But notice that while I speak and approach the fire what remained of the taste is exhaled, the smell evaporates, the color alters, the figure is destroyed, the size increases, it becomes liquid, it heats, scarcely can one handle it, and when one strikes it, no sound is emitted. Does the same wax remain after this change? We must confess that it remains; none would judge otherwise.[16] What then did I know so distinctly in this piece of wax? It could certainly be nothing of all that the senses brought to my notice, since all these things which fall under taste, smell, sight, touch, and hearing, are found to be changed, and yet the same wax remains.

Perhaps it was what I now think, viz. that this wax was not that sweetness of honey, nor that agreeable scent of flowers, nor that particular whiteness, nor that figure, nor that sound, but simply a body which a little before appeared to me as perceptible under these forms, and which is now perceptible under others. But what, precisely, is it that I imagine when I form such conceptions? Let us attentively consider this, and, abstracting from all that does not belong to the wax, let us see what remains. Certainly nothing remains excepting a certain extended thing which is flexible and movable. But what is the meaning of flexible and movable? Is it not that I imagine that this piece of wax being round is capable of becoming square and of passing from a square to a triangular figure? No, certainly it is not that, since I imagine that it admits of an infinitude of similar changes, and I nevertheless do not know how to compass the infinitude by my imagination, and consequently this conception which I have of the wax is not brought about by the faculty of imagination.[17] What now is this extension? Is it not also unknown? For it becomes greater when the wax is melted, greater when it is boiled, and greater still when the heat increases; and I should not conceive (clearly) according to truth what wax is, if I did not think that even this piece we are considering is capable of receiving more variations in extension than I have ever imagined. We must then grant that I could not even understand through the imagination what this piece of wax is, and that it is my mind alone which perceives it. I say this piece of wax in particular, for as to wax in general it is yet clearer. But what is this piece of wax which cannot be understood excepting by the (understanding or) mind? It is certainly the same that I see, touch, imagine, and finally it is the same which I have always believed it to be from the beginning. But what must be particularly observed is that its perception is neither an act of vision, nor of touch, nor of imagination, and has never been such although it may have appeared formerly to be so, but only an intuition of the mind, which may be imperfect and confused as it was formerly, or clear and distinct as it is at present, according as my attention is more or less directed to the elements which are found in it, and of which it is composed.

Yet in the meantime I am greatly astonished when I consider (the great feebleness of mind) and its proneness to fall (insensibly) into error; for although without giving expression to my thoughts I consider all this in my own mind, words often impede me and I am almost deceived by the terms of ordinary language. For we say that we see the same wax, if it is present, and not that we simply judge that it is the same from its having the same color and figure. From this I should conclude that I knew the wax by means of vision and not simply by the intuition of the mind; unless by chance I remember that, when looking from a window and saying that I see men who pass in the street, I really do not see them, but infer that what I see is men, just as I say that I see wax. And yet what do I see from the window but hats and coats which may cover automatic machines? Yet I judge these to be men. And similarly solely by the faculty of judgment which rests in my mind, I comprehend that which I believed I saw with my eyes.[18]

A man who makes it his aim to raise his knowledge above the common should be ashamed to derive the occasion for doubting from the forms of speech invented by the vulgar; I prefer to pass on and consider whether I had a more evident and perfect conception of what the wax was when I first perceived it, and when I believed I knew it by means of the external senses or at least by the common sense as it is called, that is to say by the imaginative faculty, or whether my present conception is clearer now that I have most carefully examined what it is, and in what way it can be known. It would certainly be absurd to doubt as to this. For what was there in this first perception which was distinct? What was there which might not as well have been perceived by any of the animals? But when I distinguish the wax from its external forms, and when, just as if I had taken from it its vestments, I consider it quite naked, it is certain that although some error may still be found in my judgment, I can nevertheless not perceive it without a human mind.[19]

But finally what shall I say of this mind, that is, of myself, for up to this point I do not admit in myself anything but mind? What then, I who seem to perceive this piece of wax distinctly, do I not know myself, not only with much more truth and certainty, but also with much more distinctness and clearness? For if I judge that the wax is or exists from the fact that I see it, it certainly follows much more clearly that I am or that I exist myself from the fact that I see it. For it may be that what I see is not really wax, it may also be that I do not possess eyes with which to see anything; but it cannot be that when I see, or (for I no longer take account of the distinction) when I think I see, that I myself who think am nought. So if I judge that the wax exists from the fact that I touch it, the same thing will follow, to wit, that I am; and if I judge that my imagination, or some other cause, whatever it is, persuades me that the wax exists, I shall still conclude the same. And what I have here remarked of wax may be applied to all other things which are external to me (and which are met with outside of me). And further, if the (notion or) perception of wax has seemed to me clearer and more distinct, not only after the sight or the touch, but also after many other causes have rendered it quite manifest to me, with how much more (evidence) and distinctness must it be said that I now know myself, since all the reasons which contribute to the knowledge of wax, or any other body whatever, are yet better proofs of the nature of my mind! And there are so many other things in the mind itself which may contribute to the elucidation of its nature, that those which depend on body such as these just mentioned, hardly merit being taken into account.

But finally here I am, having insensibly reverted to the point I desired, for, since it is now manifest to me that even bodies are not properly speaking known by the senses or by the faculty of imagination, but by the understanding only, and since they are not known from the fact that they are seen or touched, but only because they are understood, I see clearly that there is nothing which is easier for me to know than my mind. But because it is difficult to rid oneself so promptly of an opinion to which one was accustomed for so long, it will be well that I should halt a little at this point, so that by the length of my meditation I may more deeply imprint on my memory this new knowledge.

MEDITATION III: OF GOD: THAT HE EXISTS

I shall now close my eyes, I shall stop my ears, I shall call away all my senses, I shall efface even from my thoughts all the images of corporeal things, or at least (for that is hardly possible) I shall esteem them as vain and false; and thus holding converse only with myself and considering my own nature, I shall try little by little to reach a better knowledge of and a more familiar acquaintanceship with myself. I am a thing which thinks, that is to say, that doubts, affirms, denies, that knows a few things, that is ignorant of many (that loves, that hates), that wills, that desires, that also imagines and perceives; for as I remarked before, although the things which I perceive and imagine are perhaps nothing at all apart from me and in themselves, I am nevertheless assured that these modes of thoughts that I call perceptions and imaginations, inasmuch only as they are modes of thought, certainly reside (and are met with) in me.

And in the little that I have just said, I think that I have summed up all that I really know, or at least all that hitherto I was aware that I knew. In order to try to extend my knowledge further, I shall now look around more carefully and see whether I cannot still discover in myself some other things which I have not hitherto perceived. I am certain that I am a thing which thinks; but do I not then likewise know what is requisite to render me certain of a truth? Certainly in this first knowledge there is nothing that assures me of its truth, excepting the clear and distinct perception of that which I state, which would not indeed suffice to assure me that what I say is true, if it could ever happen that a thing which I conceived so clearly and distinctly could be false; and accordingly it seems to me that already I can establish as a general rule that all things which I perceive very clearly and distinctly are true.

At the same time I have before received and admitted many things to be very certain and manifest, which yet I afterwards recognized as being dubious. What then were these things? They were the earth, sky, stars and all other objects which I apprehended by means of the senses. But what did I clearly (and distinctly) perceive in them? Nothing more than that the ideas or thoughts of these things were presented to my mind. And not even now do I deny that these ideas are met with in me. But there was yet another thing which I affirmed, and which, owing to the habit which I had formed of believing it, I thought I perceived very clearly, although in truth I did not perceive it at all, to wit, that there were objects outside of me from which these ideas proceeded, and to which they were entirely similar. And it was in this that I erred, or, if perchance my judgment was correct, this was not due to any knowledge arising from my perception.

But when I took anything very simple and easy in the sphere of arithmetic or geometry into consideration, e.g. that two and three together made five, and other things of the sort, were not these present to my mind so clearly as to enable me to affirm that they were true? Certainly if I judged that since such matters could be doubted, this would not have been so for any other reason than that it came into my mind that perhaps a God might have endowed me with such a nature that I may have been deceived even concerning things which seemed to me most manifest. But every time that this preconceived opinion of the sovereign power of a God presents itself to my thought, I am constrained to confess that it is easy to Him, if He wishes it, to cause me to err, even in matters in which I believe myself to have the best evidence. And, on the other hand, always when I direct my attention to things which I believe myself to perceive very clearly, I am so persuaded of their truth that I let myself break out into words such as these: Let who will deceive me, He can never cause me to be nothing while I think that I am, or some day cause it to be true to say that I have never been, it being true now to say that I am, or that two and three make more or less than five, or any such thing in which I see a manifest contradiction. And certainly, since I have no reason to believe that there is a God who is a deceiver, and as I have not yet satisfied myself that there is a God at all, the reason for doubt which depends on this opinion alone is very slight, and so to speak metaphysical. But in order to be able altogether to remove it, I must inquire whether there is a God as soon as the occasion presents itself; and if I find that there is a God, I must also inquire whether He may be a deceiver; for without a knowledge of these two truths I do not see that I can ever be certain of anything.

And in order that I may have an opportunity of inquiring into this in an orderly way (without interrupting the order of meditation which I have proposed to myself, and which is little by little to pass from the notions which I find first of all in my mind to those which I shall later on discover in it) it is requisite that I should consider in which of these kinds there is, properly speaking, truth or error to be found. Of my thoughts some are, so to speak, images of the things, and to these alone is the title 'idea' properly applied; examples are my thought of a man or of a chimera, of heaven, of an angel, or (even) of God. But other thoughts possess other forms as well. For example in willing, fearing, approving, denying, though I always perceive something as the subject of the action of my mind, yet by this action I always add something else to the idea which I have of that thing; and of the thoughts of this kind some are called volitions or affections, and others judgments.[20]

Now as to what concerns ideas, if we consider them only in themselves and do not relate them to anything else beyond themselves, they cannot properly speaking be false; for whether I imagine a goat or a chimera, it is not the less true that I imagine the one than the other. We must not fear likewise that falsity can enter into will and into affections, for although I may desire evil things, or even things that never existed, it is not the less true that I desire them. Thus there remains no more than the judgments which we make, in which I must take the greatest care not to deceive myself. But the principal error and the commonest which we may meet with in them, consists in my judging that the ideas which are in me are similar or conformable to the things which are outside me; for without doubt if I considered the ideas only as certain modes of my thoughts, without trying to relate them to anything beyond, they could scarely give me material for error.

But among these ideas, some appear to me to be innate, some adventitious, and others to be formed (or invented) by myself; for, as I have the power of understanding what is called a thing, or a truth, or a thought, it appears to me that I hold this power from no other source than my own nature.[21] But if I now hear some sound, if I see the sun, or feel the heat, I have hitherto judged that these sensations proceeded from certain things that exist outside of me; and finally it appears to me that sirens, hippogryphs, and the like, are formed out of my own mind. But again I may possibly persuade myself that all these ideas are of the nature of those which I term adventitious, or else they are all innate, or all fictitious: for I have not yet clearly discovered their true origin.

And my principal task in this place is to consider, in respect to those ideas which appear to me to proceed from certain objects outside me, what are the reasons to think them similar to these objects. It seems indeed in the first place that I am taught this lesson by nature; and secondly, I experience in myself that these ideas do not depend on my will nor therefore on myself—for they often present themselves to my mind in spite of my will. Just now, for instance, whether I will or whether I do not will, I feel heat, and thus persuade myself that this feeling, or at least this idea of heat, is produced in me by something which is different from me, *i.e.*, by the heat of the fire near which I sit. And nothing seems to me more obvious than to judge that this object imprints its likeness rather than anything else upon me.

Now I must discover whether these proofs are sufficiently strong and convincing. When I say that I am so instructed by nature, I merely mean a certain spontaneous inclination which impels me to believe in this connection, and not a natural light which makes me recognize that it is true.[22] But these two things are very different; for I cannot doubt that which the natural light causes me to believe to be true, as, for example, it has shown me that I am from the fact that I doubt, or other facts of the same kind. And I possess no other faculty whereby to distinguish truth from falsehood, which can teach me that what this light shows me to be true is not really true, and no other faculty that is equally trustworthy. But as far as (apparently) natural impulses are concerned, I have frequently remarked, when I had to make active choice between virtue and vice, that they often enough led me to the part that was worse; and this is why I do not see any reason for following them in what regards truth and error.

And as to the other reason, which is that these ideas must proceed from objects outside me, since they do not depend on my will, I do not find it any more convincing. For just as these impulses of which I have spoken are found in me, notwithstanding that they do not always concur with my will, so perhaps there is in me some faculty fitted to produce these ideas without the assistance of any external things, even though it is not yet known by me; just as, apparently, they have hitherto always been found in me during sleep without the aid of any external objects.

And finally, though they did proceed from objects different from myself, it is not a necessary consequence that they should resemble these. On the contrary, I have noticed that in many cases there was a great difference between the object and its idea. I find, for example, two completely diverse ideas of the sun in my mind; the one derives its origin from the senses, and should be placed in the category of adventitious ideas; according to this idea the sun seems to be extremely small; but the other is derived from astronomical reasonings, *i.e.*, is elicited from certain notions that are innate in me, or else it is formed by me in some other manner; in accordance with it the sun appears to be several times greater than the earth. These two ideas cannot, indeed, both resemble the same sun, and reason makes me believe that the one which seems to have originated directly from the sun itself, is the one which is most dissimilar to it.

All this causes me to believe that until the present time it has not been by a judgment that was certain (or premeditated), but only by a sort of blind impulse that I believed that things existed outside of, and different from me, which, by the organs of my senses, or by some other method whatever it might be, conveyed these ideas or images to me (and imprinted on me their similitudes).[23]

NOTES

1   The reference to black bile is an indication of the longevity of Greek ideas in Western culture. Greek physicians (notably Hippocrates and Galen) had developed a view due to the pre-Socratics, that all things were composed of some combination of four elements—earth, air, fire, and water. Further combinations of these four elements, taken two at a time, were supposed to produce the so-called four humours of human physiology. These were called blood, phlegm, black bile, and yellow bile. These liquids were balanced in quantity in a healthy individual. An excess of any of the four was thought to cause disease; an excess of black bile, for example, causing melancholy. These ancient speculations about the origins of certain human diseases were still widely accepted in Descartes's time.

2   Bertrand Russell points out in his *A History of Western Philosophy*, New York, 1945 that pyjamas and nightshirts had not been invented in Descartes's time.

3   What class of things is Descartes referring to? Is he saying that time and number with respect to corporeal things are manufactured by the imagination from parts of actual experiences? Apparently this is what he is saying, but confirmation of this requires development of his rather unusual views on these topics. With respect to time, for example, Descartes seems to have held that it is non-continuous, and composed of discrete instants. Descartes seemed to have thought that if a body existed continuously, it could be self-existent, but he wanted to hold that there must be some external cause for what we commonly call the continued existence of bodies. He imagined that in the absence of such a cause, bodies might pass inexplicably in and out of existence. Finally, he concluded that God causes existence, and causes the existence of any body at every instant when it exists. In this passage, then, he is literally saying that all of our knowledge of corporeal or experienced nature is the result of (possibly mistaken) amplification of our experiences by the imagination.

4   Physics, Astronomy, and Medicine are taken to be the study of composite things, but the objects of Arithmetic and Geometry can hardly be the simple things from which the subject matter of the former sciences is built up. This can be seen because the conclusions of mathematics are taken by Descartes to be indubitable. We might interpret this sentence by supposing that Descartes is here appealing to a commonsense recognition of the simplicity of Arithmetic, and intends his phrase "without taking . . . existent or not" to defer an examination of the exact nature of mathematical objects.

5   God permits us to be sometimes mistaken (we *are* sometimes mistaken, and Descartes's view of God is such that nothing can occur without his consent), which is contrary to what might be our initial view of his goodness, so that for the sake of argument we can suppose ourselves to be always deceived, without at this point compromising our view of God's goodness.

6   One way out of the coming difficulties is to deny the existence of such a God, since holding that some things are certain besides the existence of a God deceiving us at every turn implies that such a God does not exist. Descartes will want to hold that the existence of such a God is not possible, so that this doubt is merely hypothetical—consequently he defers argument on this point in the next sentence. The phrase 'a continual succession of antecedents' apparently refers to an error in reasoning which has no clear premises. The phrase itself is too obscure to be definitely explained otherwise. One argument Descartes suggests should be kept in mind for the time being is that the mere denial of the existence of the deceiving God may increase the possibility that I deceive myself. A full consideration of God's nature later indicates that this self-deception is not possible in the fully developed Cartesian philosophy.

7   The distinction between action and knowledge invoked at this point is apparently designed, as are some other passages, to quiet orthodox religious objections. Since a false hypothesis is being adopted only to test its intellectual consequences so that mistaken belief can be corrected, there is no danger of an evil act being performed on the false hypothesis, the consequences of which could be irrecoverable.

8   Archimedes was a Greek mathematician and scientist who, among other things,

is credited with discovering laws of the lever, and proving that an arbitrary weight might be lifted or moved by application of a lever whose length could be determined by mathematical calculation. This is the origin of his legendary claim to be able to move the earth if given a lever long enough, and a suitable fixed point for a fulcrum. Use of this analogy indicates how important Descartes took the discovery of a single indubitable truth to be.

9   Perhaps the statement that nothing is certain is the only true claim that we can make. This relates to an old philosophical problem. If I say "Everything is uncertain.", do I mean to say that this statement is also uncertain? If so, then something may be certain, contrary to what I intend to express. Consequently, it would seem that I must exempt the claim itself when I mean to say that everything is uncertain.

10 St. Augustine had used a similar line of reasoning in the fourth century. In his *The City of God*, XI, 26, translation by M. Dods, Edinburgh, 1872, he argues as follows:

> I am not at all afraid of the arguments of the Academicians, who say, What if you are deceived? For if I am deceived, I am. For he who is not, cannot be deceived; and if I am deceived, by this same token I am. And since if I am deceived, how am I deceived in believing that I am? for it is certain that I am if I am deceived. Since, therefore, I, the person deceived, should be, even if I were deceived, certainly I am not deceived in this knowledge that I am. And, consequently, neither am I deceived in knowing that I know. For, as I know that I am, so I know this also, that I know.

In spite of some apparent equivocation at the end of this passage, this argument by Augustine is very similar to Descartes's argument. Historical questions of precedence have been largely omitted from consideration in this book. Here, the passage in Augustine is incidental to Augustine's main argument, but Descartes's argument is crucial for his epistemology. The modern interest in the question is due almost entirely to Descartes's formulation.

11 Man was defined as *rational animal* in the Aristotelian tradition. Descartes rejects this definition as verbal and uninformative, since it then raises the question of the meaning of 'rational' and 'animal'. For Descartes, then, knowledge is not gained by verbal formulations, but by direct insight or intuition. In other words, some intuition must precede any meaningful verbal formulation, so that the verbal formulation is epistemologically unnecessary.

12 These are mentioned above, along with feeling and thought, as attributes of the soul. The soul *causes* change in the body, since the body cannot cause itself to change. Immediately following, sensation or feeling, along with nutrition and walking, are dismissed as part of Descartes (or anyone following the argument), since they involve the body which has been rejected for the purposes of this argument.

13 It may be hard to reconcile all Descartes's remarks on *reason, understanding, imagination, sense,* and *memory*. The soul is involved in all of these, depending on what type of object the *understanding* or *reason* is directed to. This explains why Descartes can go on to say that he is nothing that he can imagine, since imagination only analyzes and combines sense experiences, which are ruled out in this context by the fact that the deceiver renders the existence of my body a subject of doubt.

14   All of these things are ways in which thought can occur! At first, it might seem that feeling and imagination, in view of what has been said above, do not belong in this list. Yet Descartes includes a specific defense of their occurrence here in the next paragraph. In short, although what I imagine and feel may not correspond to anything, yet I cannot doubt that I do imagine and feel, or at least *seem* to, and hence their place is secure. Not every expression in this description of thought is argued for later. Willing, for example, is listed without later comment. Since the will is mentioned elsewhere as accounting for human error, perhaps its inclusion here is to be defended along similar lines as those which defend the inclusion of feeling. One might wish, however, for more extended treatment. Although 'I think' may seem proved, it is surprising to find Descartes including so many activities as sanctioned by this conclusion.

15   The translation *figure* here may prove misleading. It is helpful to read *shape* for *figure*, which approximates Descartes's meaning more closely.

16   This looks like an appeal to common sense, which seems out of place in Descartes. Surely the fact that we would all admit that it is the same piece of wax does not show that it is the same piece of wax. Descartes must mean that our intuitions will yield this knowledge, or he has slipped into using the notion of substance without arguing for it.

17   By the description of imagination, it can only combine previous sense experiences, or parts of them. But no one can experience infinitely many distinct objects, so that the infinite is beyond the grasp of the imagination. God's perfections, being infinite according to Descartes, are also beyond the grasp of the imagination, and must be known through the understanding.

18   It is interesting to notice how many passages in Descartes anticipate problems that later empiricists have to deal with. Here, Descartes notices that when I say "I see a man.", I cannot mean what the sentence may seem to suggest, but only that I see something which I take to be a man. Thus an inference seems to be involved in the simplest reports of observation, an inference which may be mistaken. Rationalists, accepting the conclusion, in some cases, of such inferences, must *know* the conclusion on some other basis than simply the sense experiences involved. Empiricists, on the other hand, must try to make do without such inferences. Clearly the rationalist comes closer to capturing what we intend to express in most observation reports.

19   Note Descartes's sharp distinction between human perception and the perception of animals. This is a reflection of his conception of soul, which he does not ascribe to animals (exclusive of man). Empiricists, who do not claim a special faculty peculiar to man as compared to animals for the acquisition of knowledge, will be more likely to suppose that the perception of some animals and that of men differs only in degree, and not in kind.

20   This is a good place to notice some differences between Plato's ideas and Descartes's ideas. An idea, for Plato, existed apart from any particular human mind, and common knowledge was explained by common intuition of the same ideas. Knowledge of ideas was the goal of human inquiry. In Descartes, ideas occur in individual minds, and are psychological entities. They represent, in important cases, some other kind of being, which we may come to know through the representing ideas. Thus God is known, not directly, but through the idea of God which exists in the mind. Ideas are not what is known in Descartes, but

they are what we use to acquire knowledge about what can be known. Although the use of *idea* in Berkeley's philosophy will be different from its use in either Plato or Descartes, it will be like Plato's usage in that it will be *ideas* that Berkeley says are known, and they will not be taken to represent something else, save possibly with the exception of the idea of God.

21   Adventitious ideas are those added to the mind, particularly those added as a result of sense experience.

22   The natural light may be taken to be the same as intuition or understanding. *Lumen naturale*, the expression here translated as *natural light*, was in common use among philosophers in Descartes's time. By its use, one might suggest how the mind was thought to illuminate truth. One might compare Plato's discussion of light in the Allegory of the Cave by way of indicating the antiquity of metaphors or analogies involving light in connection with knowledge.

23   Descartes goes on to establish God's existence, and the indubitable character of much of natural science. Ultimately, the existence of a benevolent God guarantees a correspondence between certain sense impressions and innate ideas which yield knowledge of the primary qualities of bodies, enabling Descartes to construct a rationalistic philosophy of science. (For primary qualities, see the first Berkeley chapter.) Descartes was one of the first to draw an epistemological distinction between various qualities of bodies, supposing that only some of them could be the source of knowledge of bodies, although the idea may have developed from the Aristotelian notion of essence.

PART 4

Berkeley

(1685–1753)

Science and Epistemology

It is not too surprising in retrospect that important philosophers before the seventeenth century, including all of the philosophers that we have so far considered, should have proposed epistemological systems which were largely rationalistic. Some qualification of this remark might be due Aristotle, who did study some beliefs that would now be considered scientific beliefs, as opposed to philosophical beliefs, and attempted a justification for them in his theory of knowledge. The point is this: if either mathematical systems or religious statements are taken as the test cases or paradigm cases of human knowledge that an adequate philosophy should have to explain, then it is a quite natural development that any philosopher working out an epistemological system should settle ultimately on some form of rationalism. Certainly there are good grounds for believing that mathematical objects are not experienced by the senses, as we have seen in connection with Plato. And it is quite obviously the case that objects of religious thought and study, such as God, are not known through sense experience; at least very few philosophers have thought them to be known through sense experience. If God and the square root of two, to take examples, are not known through sense experience, they must be known in some other way, and the faculty of intuition which rationalism introduces is an obvious candidate. Thus rationalism, if true, may provide an explanation of the way in which we acquire knowledge of mathematical and spiritual entities.

The seventeenth century is often cited as the century in which what is called modern science began to develop into a comprehensive, integrated system. Modern astronomy, for example, was largely shaped by Galileo and Newton, among others, who did their work in this one-hundred-year span. Before the seventeenth century, the only integrated systems of human thought were either mathematical or religious. After the seventeenth century, many philosophers began to take scientific knowledge as the test case for an adequate philosophical epistemology.

The publication of Sir Isaac Newton's *Principia* in 1686 made available to philosophers a complete scientific system which in its intuitive appeal was clearly the equal, if not the superior, of any mathematical or religious system of its time. An interesting feature of the *Principia* is that in it Newton completely ignores philosophical speculation, and simply supposes certain commonplace observations to be *facts* which he *explains* by appealing to certain other states of affairs which he assumes *must* be the case if the *facts* are to be explained in a convincing way. What is meant by saying that his system is the equal or superior of any system of its time may perhaps best be explained by noting that it is both *objective,* and that it deals with publicly observable objects. Numbered among these objects are the sun, the moon, and so forth, which are apparently sense-experienced objects, in that we check on the truth of some statement about them by making an observation, or a series of observations. The scientists who insisted that this was so had apparently not mastered Descartes, who, as we have seen, makes an observation a fairly different event than so-called common sense might suggest. Nevertheless, the report of scientists that sense observations constitute the test of a scientific statement (or at least of a wide class of testable scientific statements), has prejudiced many philosophers who have tried to justify scientific knowledge towards adopting an empiricistic epistemology.

What is meant by saying that scientific systems are objective is difficult to analyze. It is not enough for objectivity that the statements of some system be either true or false, but not both. Presumably the statements of religion, mathematics, or even astrology would all be objective in the sense that crucial sentences in these disciplines could not be both true and false, or neither true nor false. Objectivity is related primarily to the method for determining the truth or falsity of statements. Suppose that Newton's system predicts an eclipse of the sun at some place at some time. To test to see whether this statement is true, one goes to that place at that time and looks at the sun. (We assume that the weather permits.) The intuitive appeal of such observational tests is overwhelming. They seem conclusive in that almost universal agreement about what observation is to be made during the test can be obtained, and we can readily understand someone's report of his observations while making such a test. By comparison, religious statements are not nearly so objective, if they are objective at all. There are simply no commonly available observational tests for determining the truth or falsity of many religious statements. This remark may be justified by a comparative study of the history of the two kinds of systems.

While early scientists did their work without probing philosophical questions, philosophers were none the less interested in finding some explanation for the apparently objective results which scientists were able to reach in their practice. As science has become more and more comprehensive and useful, this justification has become almost imperative, so that most contemporary philosophers suppose that an adequate philosophy must *at least* justify scientific knowledge, and *then* religious knowledge, for example, depending on whether or not the philosopher wishes to give religious knowledge significance apart from science. Mathematical knowledge has by now been taken by empiricists as *part* of scientific knowledge, and it is not generally treated as a kind of knowledge distinct from scientific knowledge, in spite of sound rationalistic arguments to the contrary.

There are a number of fairly obvious problems which an empiricistic philosophy must face if it is to provide a justification for scientific knowledge. Some of these are philosophical problems that working scientists can often afford to ignore. One is the problem of making a transition from *personal* observations to the objective statements of science. The scientist may pretend that this problem does not exist, by treating observers as interchangeable, although it is clear that philosophers after Descartes cannot simply accept this move as a methodological principle which needs no justification. We might, however, suppose that these problems are separable, in that scientists may assume (not necessarily explicitly) that observers are interchangeable, while philosophers hunt for the justification of this assumption. The scientific discoveries based on such an assumption would then become epistemologically acceptable when such a justification was found.

A number of interesting philosophical problems occur as part of scientific inquiry. Two important questions will be mentioned here. One of them concerns the role of mathematics in science. If, as we have seen, mathematics seems to require a rationalistic justification, while scientific information distinct from mathematics is to be empirically justified, does this not require that a complete philosophy, justifying both, be neither a pure rationalistic system, nor an empiricistic system, but some compromise between the two? This point seems to hold against scientists who may wish to say that science can be justified by commonsense observations, in that the truth of the mathematics that they use cannot be so justified. Another question concerns the role of theoretical concepts in science. Early science, dealing with readily identifiable objects, raised this question only implicitly. In the twentieth century this question has caused a crisis for epistemology, since such concepts as that of *atom, gene, perfect gas,* etc., which abound in science, do not seem to be directly related to anything that is observed, at least in the sense that such terms do not seem to designate anything which is identifiable on the basis of ordinary sense experiences. Indeed, some of these entities seem as inaccessible to sense experience as the objects of mathematical inquiry. A serious problem for an empirical philosophy is that of showing how statements involving these terms can be related to observations in a way that will explain the objectivity reached by the application of scientific method.

The early attempts at an empirical philosophy which would justify modern science are well represented in the philosophy of John Locke, who preceded Berkeley. Locke's arguments against rationalism are not crushing refutations. He merely noted that there were strong common-sense grounds for doubting it, and then contended that since sense-experiential knowledge was necessary for scientific knowledge, and hence a necessary foundation for scientific knowledge in any adequate philosophical epistemology, and since all of the functions which innate ideas and intuition had performed in rationalistic philosophies could be handled in an empiricistic philosophy, that it was possible to demonstrate that rationalism was superfluous. Attention to Locke's position focuses on the question of whether or not he can demonstrate his claim that scientific knowledge may be satisfactorily justified on an empirical basis.

Locke's approach was to adopt a kind of commonsense theory of knowledge similar to that which many scientists of his time implicitly adopted. This commonsense theory is no doubt the commonsense theory of many people (including some scientists) at present, although it was not common sense in Locke's time. The fact that it has become something like the commonsense view is a result of the practical success of scientific inquiry. As an illustration, this theory finds three elements in any simple observation report, say the report of John that he sees a table: a thing, independent of John in some sense, transmission of light rays from the thing to John's retina where they form a pattern, and John's resulting idea or sensation or perception of the table. On this view there is a relationship between the table and John's seeing it, in that the table *causes* the seeing by virtue of the fact that it reflects light rays into John's eyes. Locke attempted to get from the unsatisfactory quality of private seeings, touchings, etc., to the objective domain of science, by supposing that our experiences were of two kinds of qualities, primary and secondary. The domain of science is concerned only with the former, and the vagaries of individual experience are to be explained by the presence of the latter. It is instructive to consider the differences between these two kinds of quality. Primary qualities include solidity, extension, motion, and number. Secondary qualities include colors, sounds, and tastes. It seems that we may be more easily mistaken about the presence of some particular secondary quality than about the presence of some primary quality. This is the point of the distinction which is explained by saying that primary qualities of things produce sensations in the mind which are in some sense accurate copies of themselves, while secondary qualities are *powers* of things to influence human perception which may vary with time or with respect to different observers. Thus Locke attempts to avoid the difficulties of earlier empirical philosophies which attempted to draw a distinction between false and veridical *experiences*, by drawing rather a distinction between false and veridical *parts* of any given experience. An experience of sensing a table is thus taken as a complex, rather than as a simple, in that the experience may be divided into false and veridical segments by philosophical analysis. These segments are not directly experienced but may be separated in any experience by a trained mind. An important consequence of this point of view is that we do not know the objects of experience directly but know their effects on us, which we call sensations, or ideas. Whether or not this foundation can justify science is not important here, since Berkeley successfully attacked the foundation, partly by claiming (as a close reader should suspect) that the distinction between primary and secondary qualities cannot itself be made on an empiricistic basis.

Perception in Empiricism

Berkeley took as one of his most important tasks that of refuting the theories of knowledge of ordinary people and of past philosophers and scientists. He contended that the refutation of these theories would result in the rejection of false views (those that he did not like, although this is irrelevant to our study of his philosophy) about various claims of religion and science.

The theory of knowledge that Berkeley imputed to ordinary people, and which might be called the commonsense view of his time in this connection, is difficult to formulate in a way that can lead to a direct refutation. This is due to the fact that ordinary people, whoever they are (philosophers have a tendency to impute views that they wish to reject to ordinary people, or 'the vulgar', in spite of a complete absence in most of their writings of any research into the matter of what a majority or plurality of people can reasonably be said to have as an implicit epistemological position), are not likely to hold self-conscious views about how they come to know what they profess to be aware of. In order to construct a commonsense view, it would be necessary to raise a theory about what theory of knowledge is implicit in ordinary behavior and ordinary conversation. There is the pitfall in this that if we could find an ordinary man and should start to ask him questions about epistemology and his implicit epistemological views, or even questions designed to reveal this information quite subtly, we might quickly turn him into a not-so-ordinary man, who would be responding from an increased sensitivity to problems that our questions had suggested.

We do want to say, however, that ordinary men know something, and that Berkeley was correct in pointing out that we must explain this knowledge in a manner compatible with what the ordinary man might reasonably be said to have at his command in the way of acquired knowledge. A good test case would be a young child who knows certain facts, but who could hardly be said to know anything about epistemology. Such a child may know that a book is red, for example, without being able to enunciate a theory as to what *red means* in sentences about the book's color. Berkeley's willingness to insist that such cases be discussed by philosophers is, in effect, construing knowledge much more broadly than Plato, Aristotle, or Descartes did. Plato, Aristotle, and Descartes might all say that the child does not *truly* know anything, and that the task of philosophy is to explicate the knowledge that the most informed people have, who do not consider themselves to know something until they understand why that something is what is to be known, and not something else. Berkeley argues that philosophy must explain the case of the knowledge of the young child, who typifies *common sense* in being unreflective. In this sense, Berkeley considered himself a *champion* of common sense.

An example may prove helpful. Suppose the question is asked how we may know that a given object *A* is further away than a given object *B*. One explanation is that the angle α shown in the diagram is greater than the angle β, which may be shown by investigation into the way in which the two eyes must converge in order to focus on the objects *A* and *B*. Although this is true, the size of the angles α and β cannot be the explanation of our seeing the object *A* as farther away than object *B*.

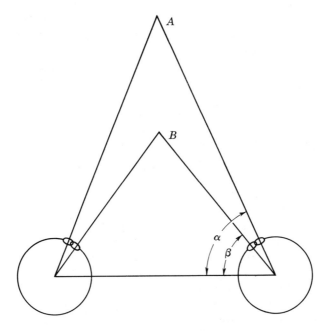

It is true that angle α is greater than angle β, but as we do not *see* the angles, we cannot compare them to make assessments of distance. Certainly the young child, who knows nothing of geometry or optics, is unaware of the angles α and β in any sense, but may still make distance judgments as accurately as the rest of us. To explain distance assessments in terms of α and β is to commit a fallacy of oversophistication. Berkeley, in an extremely important book (*The New Theory of Vision*), attempted to explain distance judgments in a manner compatible with the experiences of anyone who is in a position to make good distance judgments. Berkeleian objections to this pseudo-explanation are not a refutation of commonsense views, since he holds that an adequate philosophy must explain at least the more obvious and correct views of ordinary men in a manner compatible with their acquired knowledge and experiences.

The Berkeleian objection to commonsense views is largely that ordinary men confuse what they see with what they infer or judge to be true on the basis of what they see. Berkeley felt that this could easily be shown by analysis of ordinary experiences. Often two men, looking at the same object (what they would agree to be the same object), will say that they are looking at quite different things. Let us suppose that two men look at a painting in an art gallery, but that their past experiences with paintings are quite different. If we ask each of them "What are you looking at?", one might well say "Duchamp's *Nude Descending the Stairs*.", while the other would be at a loss to say what he was looking at, or could only describe it in terms of size, color, etc., as a painting on the wall. This situation repeats itself endlessly. What is a familiar object to one person may be mysterious or unrecognizable to another. Yet they still *see* the same object in another sense. In terms of our example, it might be awkward to deny that the two men are looking at the same painting.

The key to the resolution of the claim that the two men see and do not see the same thing is to be found in an ambiguity of the word *see*. Both men *see* the same thing in a primary sense which we may call *seeing*$_1$. Both men, that is, observe the same light and colors (or at least virtually identical light and colors—the differences are inessential at this point), or have the same *ideas* in Berkeley's sense. In our vocabulary they both *see*$_1$ the same thing, or have the same sensations, in the case of our example a rectangle of a certain size filled with colors that they might describe in common by means of a topological map. At the same time, one man sees that what he *sees*$_1$ is in fact Duchamp's *Nude Descending the Stairs*. In this sense he *sees*$_2$ that he sees *Nude Descending the Stairs*. Berkeley argues that this is an inference or judgment based on what he *sees*$_1$. There are two important aspects of this inference. The fact that one man makes it and the other does not is conveniently explained by the past experiences of the one. The man who sees the painting as *Nude Descending the Stairs* may be an art student, while the man who sees only colors in a rectangle may be someone unschooled in art history whose wife has commanded his presence in front of the painting. The inference that the painting is a Duchamp may obviously be mistaken, in that the painting may be misidentified through a mistake (in which case it may be quite unlike Duchamp's painting), or thought to be Duchamp's painting when in fact it is a sufficiently clever fake to fool him. We might say that the inference expresses the claim that what is *seen*$_1$ would yield certain other *ideas* in different circumstances. Sufficient repetition of a set of circumstances, or associated ideas, leads us to expect this repetition when some of the set of circumstances is repeated.

The distinction between $seeing_1$ and $seeing_2$ may also be drawn in the other senses. Then $seeing_1$, $touching_1$, $hearing_1$, $tasting_1$, etc., form the common foundation of human knowledge. Ordinary men often fail to observe this distinction. As a matter of fact, there is no proof that it must be made to explain their pronouncements about what they know, so that Berkeley has clearly lapsed into philosophy in his discussion. The proper objects of sight for Berkeley are what is $seen_1$. When a person sees something as outside his body, what he has done is *judged* or *inferred* that it is outside on the basis of what he $sees_1$, though he ambiguously reports that he *sees* it as outside his body. When one says "I see a red book on the table.", one really means that he $sees_1$ some red patch, etc., which he judges to be a book that is red which is on the table. In this analysis of seeing, the fact that one $sees_1$ red is relatively (perhaps completely) unassailable, although the fact that there is a red book on the table may be false because of illusion, the lighting of the table surface, one's emotional state at the time, and so on. For these reasons, Berkeley dismisses many commonsense knowledge reports as *inferences* from ideas, a fact which philosophers may discover by analysis. This, in effect, grounds Berkeley's epistemology in knowledge of ideas in this technical sense of $seeing_1$, $touching_1$, $hearing_1$, etc., experiences.

Berkeley's analysis, as well as others like it, runs into the problem that the inferences or judgments based on ideas are not always, indeed they are rarely, consciously performed. An empiricist may argue that these judgments or inferences become habitual, but this raises difficulties about whether or not the inference is to be taken as self-conscious at an early age, as well as the difficulty of explaining why certain habits are formed by human beings rather than other habits, solely in terms of an empiricistic epistemology.

The view of philosophers concerning the proper objects of sight which Berkeley opposed was already developed by Locke, who explicitly bears the brunt of many Berkeleian attacks. This view, which we have already summarized, is that there are objects independent of our thinking of them which *cause* ideas in the mind as a result of the transmission of light waves (ideas of sight), sound waves (ideas of hearing), etc. Objects independent of our thinking are known collectively as *matter* and are taken to be the objects of scientific thinking and theorizing. Now a result of scientific theorizing is that the scientist and the ordinary man find themselves in a position similar to the two art-gallery patrons that were discussed earlier. The scientist and the ordinary man, both looking at the sun, see_1 a bright, yellowish disk. The scientist also sees a star, composed of gas at high temperatures, some 93 million miles away, etc., so that he $sees_2$ the sun as something else, namely, the astronomical body that is at one focus of the elliptical orbit of the earth. On the other hand, the ordinary man may *see*₂ no more than he *sees*₁ or may simply *see*₂ the sun as a hot sphere some distance away, depending on the amount of astronomical information that he has assimilated.

Berkeley's concern is that the scientist should not allow his scientific view to contradict his ideas, since on Berkeley's view, the whole purpose of science is to explain why we observe certain repeatable congeries of ideas (what we call objects) as well as successions of ideas in some definite patterns. Science must not do this at the expense of impugning the ideas that it is developed to explain.

It is clear that Berkeley's approach to the whole problem determines that the answer to the question "Does matter exist?", when matter is construed as referring to objects obeying scientific laws that we do not directly experience, must be in the negative. There is nothing to be known except our ideas, that is, perceptions of the *seeing*₁, *hearing*₁, etc., kind. Consequently, there can be no matter that we can know about, discourse intelligently about, and make the object of scientific theorizing. Berkeley felt that those who fell into the trap of speaking seriously about nonexperienced entities also fell into talking nonsense.

The program that Berkeley has left for other empirical philosophers, that of building up from ideas our commonsense view of the world, as well as the body of knowledge called science, is referred to as *phenomenalism*. A phenomenalist tries to complete the kind of program that Berkeley argues is possible; namely, to analyze objects into congeries of, and regular sequences of, *ideas* in Berkeley's technical sense. No such program has been completely successful, although it is clear that the successful completion of such a program would establish the basic empiricistic claim that human knowledge does not require more than human experience organized in some appropriate way.

The Problem of Abstraction

An interesting fact about the history of philosophy is that Berkeley has often been held to support doctrines that a careful reading of his writings shows that he explicitly condemns. We have noted that his purpose in identifying the foundation of knowledge with what he calls *ideas* is to save commonsense views against the oversophistication to be found in some scientific theorizing. In spite of this, the notion of matter which he attacked seems to have become so well entrenched that his views have often been taken as representative of a philosophy at wide variance with the judgments of common sense.

This may be a result of mistaken inferences from capsulated versions of Berkeley's statements about *ideas*. These capsulated versions usually quote the phrase "esse est percipi." as a summary of Berkeley's views, translating this as "To be is to be perceived.". It seems to follow that what is not perceived does not exist. Unfortunately, there are important ambiguities in this inference. Caricatures of Berkeley take this to mean 'If *x* is not perceived now, then *x* does not exist now.', which is perhaps at variance with what may be deduced from "esse est percipi.". For example, one might just as well conclude 'If *x* is not perceived *at some time*, then *x* does not exist.', which is quite different from the earlier statement.

From the earlier statement, it has been argued that when one turns his back on something, it no longer exists because he is not perceiving it. But this does not follow from Berkeley's philosophical position. What does follow is that if I turn my back on something, then *if no one is perceiving it*, it does not exist. If we understand that saying that it does not exist here means that no one has present knowledge of it, the remark is a truism, since any statement about its current properties is an inference or judgment based on *what was known* about it. On the other hand, the feeling of absurdity that may accompany contemplation of this view is no doubt a feature of the fact that it conflicts with an entrenched, but on the Berkeleian view false, theory about matter.

Berkeley, like Descartes, introduces God at important places in his philosophy. In Berkeley's philosophy, God may play the role of a perceiver whose perceptions of ideas keep the world of experience as orderly and stable as we think it to be. Nevertheless, as with Descartes, we shall be concerned to examine the consequences of the philosophy without resort to invoking a divine being to help support weak places in the argument. A difficulty, which might as well be mentioned, is that it is not easy to see how Berkeley's God can be *known* within the framework of his empiricism. Evidently there are no direct *ideas* of God, who is not *seen*$_1$, *touched*$_1$, etc. A consistent Berkeleian empiricism must then find some way of admitting God as the result of an inference or judgment based on *ideas*, but for empiricists this is equivalent to admitting that God's existence is not certain, *contra* the position of most traditional theologians.

Berkeley's argument about existence is more properly summarized in another way. The *esse* (of a sensible object) is *percipi* (to be perceived), and the *esse* (of a perceiver—particularly a human being) is *percipere* (to perceive). Berkeley's universe consists of perceivers and what they know, i.e., their ideas. What can neither be labeled an idea or a perceiver cannot be *known* to exist, and by a tacit use of simplicity (we do not affirm the existence of what we do not know to exist), is said not to exist. In order to preserve the distinction between hallucination and veridical perception, we cannot *identify* what we think we perceive with what exists, but only what we do perceive with what exists.

The Berkeleian idea is *not mental* in the sense that its being mental suggests that it is not real. We do not invent or compose the world in our minds since our minds have ideas independently of our desires and wishes. It is important to realize that Berkeley is opposed to *matter* but convinced that all our views about the permanence of various objects (congeries of certain *ideas* for Berkeley) and casual sequences may be kept intact in a philosophy which repudiates the notion of matter. Reflection on the claim that this must be so because we can know only ideas, and not unperceived, obscure causes of them, if such causes existed, is so persuasive that some view like Berkeley's must constitute the basis of a respectable empiricism. In order to reinforce this, two sections (8, 38) of Berkeley's *Of the Principles of Human Knowledge* will be quoted here. Any suitable interpretation of Berkeley must be consistent with these passages, which deserve careful scrutiny.

Section 8 argues the plausibility of ideas as the foundation of human knowledge:

> But, say you, though the ideas themselves do not exist without the mind, yet there may be things *like* them, whereof they are copies or resemblances, which things exist without the mind in an unthinking substance. I answer, an idea can be like nothing but an idea; a color or figure can be like nothing but another color or figure. If we look but ever so little into our thoughts, we shall find it impossible for us to conceive a likeness except only between our ideas. Again,

> I ask whether those supposed originals or external things, of which our ideas are the pictures or representations, be themselves perceivable or no? If they are, then they are ideas and we have gained our point; but if you say they are not, I appeal to anyone whether it be sense to assert a color is like something which is invisible; hard or soft, like something which is intangible; and so of the rest.

Section 38 attempts to make clear the relation between what are ordinarily called *things*, and Berkeley's *ideas*.

> But, after all, say you, it sounds very harsh to say we eat and drink ideas, and are clothed with ideas. I acknowledge it does so; the word 'idea' not being used in common discourse to signify the several combinations of sensible qualities which are called 'things'; and it is certain that any expression which varies from the familiar use of language will seem harsh and ridiculous. But this doth not concern the truth of the proposition, which in other words is no more than to say, we are fed and clothed with those things which we perceive immediately by our senses. The hardness or softness, the color, taste, warmth, figure, or such-like qualities, which combined together constitute the several sorts of victuals and apparel, have been shown to exist only in the mind that perceives them; and this is all that is meant by calling them 'ideas'; which word if it was as ordinarily used as 'things' would sound no more harsher nor more ridiculous than it. I am not for disputing about the propriety, but the truth of the expression. If therefore you agree with me that we eat and drink and are clad with the immediate objects of sense, which cannot exist unperceived or without the mind, I shall readily grant it is more proper or conformable to custom that they should be called things rather than ideas.

To this point we have emphasized Berkeley's program of replacing matter with *ideas* in his technical sense. Now given the fact that the foundation of human knowledge consists in ideas, one might well wonder why it is not possible to infer the existence of matter in some legitimate fashion from this foundation. Berkeley is not opposed in general to inferences or judgments based on ideas. He is, however, opposed to the inference that matter exists. To block this inference, he subsumes the inference that matter exists under the general heading of abstractive inference, all of which inferences to *abstract* ideas he condemns as contradictory or meaningless. In order to complete an introduction to Berkeley's philosophy, it is important to consider why Berkeley felt that *abstract* ideas were not possible. Although Berkeley's reasoning on this point contains difficulties, much of it embodies conceptions about language that are now thought to be quite sophisticated.

Berkeley does not deny that abstract *words* are used in communicating knowledge. But, where Plato and other philosophers had assumed that these words have meaning because they stand for abstract ideas (note that Plato's ideas are quite unlike Berkeley's), Berkeley argues that there are no abstract ideas for them to correspond to. Berkeley's program, consequently, has two parts: he must show that abstract ideas are not possible, and he must account for the significance of abstract words by some means other than by letting them correspond to abstract ideas. To understand Berkeley's points, the example of the abstract word *triangle* can be used, since, as we have seen, it is the kind of abstract word that would receive significance in Plato's philosophy, and in most rationalistic philosophies, through its correspondence to an idea or form. Now it is possible, according to Berkeley, to abstract or generalize somewhat from ideas. Looking at an automobile, we can consider just the fender of the automobile, since it is a part of our original idea. Further, we may be able to consider Chevrolets as a group, since they possess some distinguishing part, such as the Chevrolet ornament. But this kind of abstracting must stop at a very low level, because it is probably not possible to find an *idea* which is part of every idea of an automobile. In the case of triangles, we may be able to understand the notion of scalene triangle, equilateral triangle, and so forth, because of ideas which the members of such classes have in common (such as equal sides). This indicates that Berkeley felt that the primary sense of *triangle* is that of actual figures drawn on blackboards, etc., while the problem is to understand the general case. This is the reverse of Plato's problem. A problem analogous to Plato's problem of participation occurs in Berkeley's problem of abstraction. Participation proved a difficult notion because the diverse properties of actual objects made it difficult to understand how they might be said to all participate in the same idea. On Berkeley's view, the diverse properties of ideas means that an abstracted idea must have contradictory properties, which seems unintelligible. *Triangle*, for example, must include both scalene and equilateral triangles, but one cannot understand how there can be an idea which has and has not equal angles. An abstract idea on any very high level must have contradictory properties; and on Berkeley's construal of *idea* this must be absurd. He therefore concludes that abstract ideas are not possible.

It is interesting to observe that Berkeley's rejection of abstract ideas makes him a nominalist. In this connection, a nominalist may be defined as someone who rejects the idea that abstract words can have meaning by referring to some abstract idea, as in Plato.

Now we may ask if the Platonic objection that actual triangles cannot be judged triangles without a standard is not sufficiently crushing to eliminate Berkeley's epistemology from serious consideration. But Berkeley is not open to a direct refutation by means of this observation. The Platonic objection holds cogently against empiricist theories which take objects, or resemblances between objects, as their starting point. Berkeleian ideas fare somewhat differently. We may take some idea, better, a class of ideas, and give it a name that we will use whenever this idea or class of ideas is repeated. Whenever this method runs into trouble, it will be because an idea must be added or subtracted from an experienced class in order to make some distinction that we are interested in. When that happens, we may change names or add names to our language. This seems to avoid direct confrontation of Plato's objection, but at severe cost, since (apart from problems about the mental mechanism for identifying classes) our experiences are so limited that the number of such classes that we would be able to distinguish may well be much smaller than common sense indicates that it should be. Thus, we have not experienced any idea common to all the objects which we have called *triangle*. The problem is whether or not Berkeley can find some way of explaining our use of words like *triangle* and *automobile* in terms of the relatively limited congeries of ideas to which we give direct names.

Berkeley's answer to this is the position that abstract words stand for less abstract *words*, not for any idea which might be correlated to them. Admittedly, this notion is not entirely clear in Berkeley's writing, but it adumbrates (as suggested earlier) a view that is now widely received about the meaning of at least some words: that a word has meaning not because of what it refers to, but because of how it is used in a language. An abstract word is a kind of placeholder for any of a number of particular words whose meaning *is* grounded in reference to particular ideas. Thus, a sentence about *triangles*, for example, "Every triangle has the sum of its interior angles equal to 180°." is simply construed (Caution: philosophers before the twentieth century meant every plane Euclidean triangle was such that . . .) as a compendious way of saying "Every scalene triangle has the sum of its interior angles equal to 180° and every equilateral triangle has the sum of its interior angles equal to 180° and every . . .".

This suggestion, ingenious as it is, is only *programmatic* in the sense that Berkeley's contention can only be shown to be true by an exhibition of a satisfactory way of writing out every sentence involving an abstract word in terms of sentences involving only nonabstract words whose meanings are appropriately grounded in particular ideas. No empiricist has been able to provide a successful algorithm for writing out sentences involving abstract words in terms of sentences not involving such words, along the lines that Berkeley suggests, but the program has been so attractive that a great many have worked on the problem. There are a number of reasons why rationalists are convinced that the program cannot succeed. One reason is an interesting variant of Plato's objection, cited earlier, that seems to apply directly to this program. The objection is that there does not seem to be any hope for an empiricist criterion for deciding which particular words are to be subsumed under a given abstract word. For example, labeling things *scalene triangle* and *equilateral triangle* yields a common element (the word *triangle*) that provides a natural candidate for abstraction. But why are these particular triangles so universally abstracted into the same abstract class, and not into two abstract classes corresponding to some different classification? If the two classes were called *gubs* and *migs*, no prejudice would appear in the naming, but the abstractive process becomes correspondingly obscure. The empiricist can reply that our abstractive classifications are due to convenience or perhaps to the satisfaction of certain human purposes, but as yet no empiricist has made this completely plausible. Berkeley's significance is that he first provides an empiricistic program that, if completed, could avoid some of the more persuasive arguments of the rationalists that empiricism is *necessarily* defective.

Readings from Berkeley

Two selections are reprinted here from Berkeley's *Three Dialogues between Hylas and Philonous the Design of Which Is Plainly to Demonstrate the Reality and Perfection of Human Knowledge, the Incorporeal Nature of the Soul, and the Immediate Providence of a Deity in Opposition to Sceptics and Atheists:*

    A. From *The First Dialogue between Hylas and Philonous*
    B. From *The Third Dialogue between Hylas and Philonous*

The text is Fraser's edition, and it is reprinted here by kind permission of the Clarendon Press, Oxford.

As in Plato, these dialogues are a discussion between two philosophers, Hylas and Philonous, about the existence of material substance and the nature of the soul. Philonous represents the Berkeleian position, and Hylas the positions which are to be refuted. This is obvious from a consideration of Berkeley's philosophy and the fact that *Hylas* and *Philonous* are constructed from Greek roots and might be translated *Materialist* and *Lover of the Mind*, respectively. The positions discussed here in dialogue form are exposited in a more didactic fashion in Berkeley's *A Treatise concerning the Principles of Human Knowledge*, which should be studied after the *Dialogues. An Essay towards a New Theory of Vision* is also an important work for students of Berkeley to consider.

Berkeley has an interesting moment in American history. In January, 1729, he landed in Newport, Rhode Island, in order to buy land for the support of the college of St. Paul, which was to have been located in the Bermudas, a college which he had conceived and won a charter for from the House of Commons. The college was never built, but Berkeley's stay in the United States influenced American academic life. Rent from the Rhode Island farm he occupied goes to support Berkeleian scholars at Yale University, and the famous Berkeleian Library at Yale was begun by a gift of about a thousand books that Berkeley sent from England. Berkeley also influenced Samuel Johnson, an important early American philosopher.

The following bibliography lists some secondary sources of interest to the student of Berkeley's philosophy.

Armstrong, D. M.: *Berkeley's Theory of Vision*, Melbourne, 1960.

Berkeley, George: *The Works of George Berkeley, Bishop of Cloyne*, T. E. Jessop and A. A. Luce (eds.), 8 vol., London, 1948–1956.

Bracken, H. F.: *The Early Reception of Berkeley's Immaterialism*, The Hague, 1959.

Grey, Denis: "The Solipsism of Bishop Berkeley," *Philosophical Quarterly*, vol. 2, pp. 338–349, 1952.

Hicks, G. D.: *Berkeley*, London, 1932.

Turbayne, C. M.: "Berkeley and Molyneux on Retinal Images," *The Journal of the History of Ideas*, vol. 16, pp. 339–355, 1955.

*Warnock, G. J.: *Berkeley*, Harmondsworth, 1953. (Pelican Paperbound.)

Van Steenburgh, E. W.: "Berkeley Revisited," *The Journal of Philosophy*, vol. 60, pp. 85–89, 1963.

A   From Berkeley's *FIRST DIALOGUE*

Hyl. Pardon me: the case of colours is very different. Can anything be plainer than that we see them on the objects?

Phil. The objects you speak of are, I suppose, corporeal Substances existing without the mind?

Hyl. They are.

Phil. And have true and real colours inhering in them?

Hyl. Each visible object hath that colour which we see in it.

Phil. How! is there anything visible but what we perceive by sight?

Hyl. There is not.

Phil. And, do we perceive anything by sense which we do not perceive immediately?

Hyl. How often must I be obliged to repeat the same thing? I tell you, we do not.

Phil. Have patience, good *Hylas;* and tell me once more, whether there is anything immediately perceived by the senses, except sensible qualities. I know you asserted there was not; but I would now be informed, whether you still persist in the same opinion.[1]

Hyl. I do.

Phil. Pray, is your corporeal substance either a sensible quality, or made up of sensible qualities?

Hyl. What a question that is! who ever thought it was?

Phil. My reason for asking was, because in saying, *each visible object hath that colour which we see in it,* you make visible objects to be corporeal substances; which implies either that corporeal substances are sensible qualities, or else that there is something beside sensible qualities perceived by sight: but, as this point was formerly agreed between us, and is still maintained by you, it is a clear consequence, that your corporeal substance is nothing distinct from sensible qualities.

Hyl. You may draw as many absurd consequences as you please, and endeavour to perplex the plainest things; but you shall never persuade me out of my senses. I clearly understand my own meaning.

Phil. I wish you would make me understand it too. But, since you are unwilling to have your notion of corporeal substance examined, I shall urge that point no farther. Only be pleased to let me know, whether the same colours which we see exist in external bodies, or some other.[2]

Hyl. The very same.

Phil. What! are then the beautiful red and purple we see on yonder clouds really in them ? Or do you imagine they have in themselves any other form than that of a dark mist or vapour ?

Hyl. I must own, *Philonous*, those colours are not really in the clouds as they seem to be at this distance. They are only apparent colours.

Phil. Apparent call you them ? how shall we distinguish these apparent colours from real ?

Hyl. Very easily. Those are to be thought apparent which, appearing only at a distance, vanish upon a nearer approach.

Phil. And those, I suppose, are to be thought real which are discovered by the most near and exact survey.

Hyl. Right.

Phil. Is the nearest and exactest survey made by the help of a microscope, or by the naked eye ?

Hyl. By a microscope, doubtless.

Phil. But a microscope often discovers colours in an object different from those perceived by the unassisted sight. And, in case we had microscopes magnifying to any assigned degree, it is certain that no object whatsoever, viewed through them, would appear in the same colour which it exhibits to the naked eye.

Hyl. And what will you conclude from all this ? You cannot argue that there are really and naturally no colours on objects: because by artificial managements they may be altered, or made to vanish.

Phil. I think it may evidently be concluded from your own concessions, that all the colours we see with our naked eyes are only apparent as those on the clouds, since they vanish upon a more close and accurate inspection which is afforded us by a microscope. Then, as to what you say by way of prevention: I ask you whether the real and natural state of an object is better discovered by a very sharp and piercing sight, or by one which is less sharp ?

Hyl. By the former without doubt.

Phil. Is it not plain from *Dioptrics* that microscopes make the sight more penetrating, and represent objects as they would appear to the eye in case it were naturally endowed with a most exquisite sharpness?[3]

Hyl. It is.

Phil. Consequently the microscopical representation is to be thought that which best sets forth the real nature of the thing, or what it is in itself. The colours, therefore, by it perceived are more genuine and real than those perceived otherwise.

Hyl. I confess there is something in what you say.

Phil. Besides, it is not only possible but manifest, that there actually are animals whose eyes are by nature framed to perceive those things which by reason of their minuteness escape our sight. What think you of those inconceivably small animals perceived by glasses? must we suppose they are all stark blind? Or, in case they see, can it be imagined their sight hath not the same use in preserving their bodies from injuries, which appears in that of all other animals? And if it hath, is it not evident they must see particles less than their own bodies, which will present them with a far different view in each object from that which strikes our senses? Even our own eyes do not always represent objects to us after the same manner. In the *jaundice* every one knows that all things seem yellow. Is it not therefore highly probable those animals in whose eyes we discern a very different texture from that of ours, and whose bodies abound with different humours, do not see the same colours in every object that we do? From all which, should it not seem to follow that all colours are equally apparent, and that none of those which we perceive are really inherent in any outward object?

Hyl. It should.

Phil. The point will be past all doubt, if you consider that, in case colours were real properties or affections inherent in external bodies, they could admit of no alteration without some change wrought in the very bodies themselves: but, is it not evident from what hath been said that, upon the use of microscopes, upon a change happening in the humours of the eye, or a variation of distance, without any manner of real alteration in the thing itself, the colours of any object are either changed, or totally disappear? Nay, all other circumstances remaining the same, change but the situation of some objects, and they shall present different colours to the eye. The same thing happens upon viewing an object in various degrees of light. And what is more known than that the same bodies appear differently coloured by candle-light from what they do in the open day? Add to these the experiment of a prism which, separating the heterogeneous rays of light, alters the colour of any object, and will cause the whitest to appear of a deep blue or red to the naked eye. And now tell me whether you are still of opinion that every body hath its true real colour inhering in it; and, if you think it hath, I would fain know farther from you, what certain distance and position of the object, what peculiar texture and formation of the eye, what degree or kind of light is necessary for ascertaining that true colour, and distinguishing it from apparent ones.[4]

Hyl. I own myself entirely satisfied, that they are all equally apparent, and that there is no such thing as colour really inhering in external bodies, but that it is altogether in the light. And what confirms me in this opinion is that in proportion to the light colours are still more or less vivid; and if there be no light, then are there no colours perceived. Besides, allowing there are colours on external objects, yet, how is it possible for us to perceive them? For no external body affects the mind, unless it acts first on our organs of sense. But the only action of bodies is motion; and motion cannot be communicated otherwise than by impulse. A distant object therefore cannot act on the eye, nor consequently make itself or its properties perceivable to the soul. Whence it plainly follows that it is immediately some contiguous substance, which, operating on the eye, occasions a perception of colours: and such is light.

Phil. How! is light then a substance?

Hyl. I tell you, *Philonous*, external light is nothing but a thin fluid substance, whose minute particles being agitated with a brisk motion, and in various manners reflected from the different surfaces of outward objects to the eyes, communicate different motions to the optic nerves; which, being propagated to the brain, cause therein various impressions; and these are attended with the sensations of red, blue, yellow, &c.[5]

Phil. It seems then the light doth no more than shake the optic nerves.

Hyl. Nothing else.

Phil. And, consequent to each particular motion of the nerves, the mind is affected with a sensation, which is some particular colour.

Hyl. Right.

Phil. And these sensations have no existence without the mind.

Hyl. They have not.

Phil. How then do you affirm that colours are in the light; since by *light* you understand a corporeal substance external to the mind?

Hyl. Light and colours, as immediately perceived by us, I grant cannot exist without the mind. But, in themselves they are only the motions and configurations of certain insensible particles of matter.[6]

Phil. Colours then, in the vulgar sense, or taken for the immediate objects of sight, cannot agree to any but a perceiving substance.

Hyl. That is what I say.

Phil. Well then, since you give up the point as to those sensible qualities which are alone thought colours by all mankind beside, you may hold what you please with regard to those invisible ones of the philosophers. It is not my business to dispute about them; only I would advise you to bethink yourself, whether, considering the inquiry we are upon, it be prudent for you to affirm—*the red and blue which we see are not real colours, but certain unknown motions and figures, which no man ever did or can see, are truly so.* Are not these shocking notions, and are not they

subject to as many ridiculous inferences, as those you were obliged to renounce before in the case of sounds?

Hyl. I frankly own, *Philonous*, that it is in vain to stand out any
longer.[7] Colours, sounds, tastes, in a word all those termed *secondary
qualities*, have certainly no existence without the mind. But, by this ac-
knowledgment I must not be supposed to derogate anything from the
reality of Matter or external objects; seeing it is no more than several
philosophers maintain, who nevertheless are the farthest imaginable from
denying Matter. For the clearer understanding of this, you must know
sensible qualities are by philosophers divided into *primary* and *secondary*.
The former are Extension, Figure, Solidity, Gravity, Motion, and Rest. And
these they hold exist really in bodies. The latter are those above enumer-
ated; or, briefly, all sensible qualities beside the Primary, which they
assert are only so many sensations or ideas existing nowhere but in the
mind. But all this, I doubt not, you are apprised of. For my part, I have
been a long time sensible there was such an opinion current along philosophers, but was never thoroughly convinced of its truth until now.

Phil. You are still then of opinion that *extension* and *figures* are inherent in external unthinking substances?

Hyl. I am.

Phil. But what if the same arguments which are brought against
Secondary Qualities will hold good against these also?

Hyl. Why then I shall be obliged to think, they too exist only in the
mind.

Phil. Is it your opinion the very figure and extension which you perceive by sense exist in the outward object or material substance?

Hyl. It is.

Phil. Have all other animals as good grounds to think the same of
the figure and extension which they see and feel?

Hyl. Without doubt, if they have any thought at all.

Phil. Answer me, *Hylas*. Think you the senses were bestowed upon
all animals for their preservation and well-being in life? or were they
given to men alone for this end?

Hyl. I make no question but they have the same use in all other
animals.

Phil. If so, is it not necessary they should be enabled by them to perceive their own limbs, and those bodies which are capable of harming
them?

Hyl. Certainly.

Phil. A mite therefore must be supposed to see his own foot, and
things equal or even less than it, as bodies of some considerable dimension; though at the same time they appear to you scarce discernible, or at
best as so many visible points?

Hyl. I cannot deny it.

Phil. And to creatures less than the mite they will seem yet larger?

Hyl. They will.

Phil. Insomuch that what you can hardly discern will to another extremely minute animal appear as some huge mountain?

Hyl. All this I grant.

Phil. Can one and the same thing be at the same time in itself of different dimensions?

Hyl. That were absurd to imagine.

Phil. But, from what you have laid down it follows that both the extension by you perceived, and that perceived by the mite itself, as likewise all those perceived by lesser animals, are each of them the true extension of the mite's foot; that is to say, by your own principles, you are led into an absurdity.

Hyl. There seems to be some difficulty in the point.

Phil. Again, have you not acknowledged that no real inherent property of any object can be changed without some change in the thing itself?

Hyl. I have.

Phil. But, as we approach to or recede from an object, the visible extension varies, being at one distance ten or a hundred times greater than at another. Doth it not therefore follow from hence likewise that it is not really inherent in the object?

Hyl. I own I am at a loss what to think.

Phil. Your judgment will soon be determined, if you will venture to think as freely concerning this quality as you have done concerning the rest. Was it not admitted as a good argument, that neither heat nor cold was in the water, because it seemed warm to one hand and cold to the other?

Hyl. It was.

Phil. Is it not the very same reasoning to conclude, there is no extension or figure in an object, because to one eye it shall seem little, smooth, and round, when at the same time it appears to the other, great, uneven, and angular?

Hyl. The very same. But does this latter fact ever happen?

Phil. You may at any time make the experiment, by looking with one eye bare, and with the other through a microscope.[8]

Hyl. I know not how to maintain it, and yet I am loath to give up *extension*, I see so many odd consequences following upon such a concession.

Phil. Odd, say you? After the concessions already made, I hope you will stick at nothing for its oddness. But, on the other hand, should it not seem very odd, if the general reasoning which includes all other sensible qualities did not also include extension? If it be allowed that no idea nor anything like an idea can exist in an unperceiving substance, then surely it follows that no figure or mode of extension, which we can either perceive or imagine, or have any idea of, can be really inherent in Matter; not to mention the peculiar difficulty there must be in conceiving a material substance, prior to and distinct from extension, to be the *substratum* of extension. Be the sensible quality what it will—figure, or sound, or colour; it seems alike impossible it should subsist in that which doth not perceive it.

Hyl. I give up the point for the present, reserving still a right to retract my opinion, in case I shall hereafter discover any false step in my progress to it.

Phil. That is a right you cannot be denied. Figures and extension being despatched, we proceed next to *motion*. Can a real motion in any external body be at the same time both very swift and very slow?

Hyl. It cannot.

Phil. Is not the motion of a body swift in a reciprocal proportion to the time it takes up in describing any given space? Thus a body that describes a mile in an hour moves three times faster than it would in case it described only a mile in three hours.

Hyl. I agree with you.

Phil. And is not time measured by the succession of ideas in our minds?

Hyl. It is.

Phil. And is it not possible ideas should succeed one another twice as fast in your mind as they do in mine, or in that of some spirit of another kind?

Hyl. I own it.

Phil. Consequently, the same body may to another seem to perform its motion over any space in half the time that it doth to you. And the same reasoning will hold as to any other proportion: that is to say, according to your principles (since the motions perceived are both really in the object) it is possible one and the same body shall be really moved the same way at once, both very swift and very slow. How is this consistent either with common sense, or with what you just now granted?

Hyl. I have nothing to say to it.

Phil. Then as for *solidity*; either you do not mean any sensible quality by that word, and so it is beside our inquiry: or if you do, it must be either hardness or resistance. But both the one and the other are plainly relative to our senses: it being evident that what seems hard to one animal may appear soft to another, who hath greater force and firmness of limbs. Nor is it less plain that the resistance I feel is not in the body.

Hyl. I own the very sensation of resistance, which is all you immediately perceive, is not in the *body*; but the cause of that sensation is.

Phil. But the causes of our sensations are not things immediately perceived, and therefore not sensible. This point I thought had been already determined.

Hyl. I own it was; but you will pardon me if I seem a little embarrassed: I know not how to quit my old notions.

Phil. To help you out, do but consider that if *extension* be once acknowledged to have no existence without the mind, the same must necessarily be granted of motion, solidity, and gravity—since they all evidently suppose extension. It is therefore superfluous to inquire particularly concerning each of them. In denying extension, you have denied them all to have any real existence.

Hyl. I wonder, Philonous, if what you say be true, why those philosophers who deny the Secondary Qualities any real existence, should yet attribute it to the Primary. If there is no difference between them, how can this be accounted for?

Phil. It is not my business to account for every opinion of the philosophers. But, among other reasons which may be assigned for this, it seems probable that pleasure and pain being rather annexed to the former than the latter may be one. Heat and cold, tastes and smells, have something more vividly pleasing or disagreeable than the ideas of extension, figure, and motion affect us with. And, it being too visibly absurd to hold that pain or pleasure can be in an unperceiving Substance, men are more easily weaned from believing the external existence of the Secondary than the Primary Qualities. You will be satisfied there is something in this, if you recollect the difference you made between an intense and more moderate degree of heat; allowing the one a real existence, while you denied it to the other.[9] But, after all, there is no rational ground for that distinction; for, surely an indifferent sensation is as truly a *sensation* as one more pleasing or painful; and consequently should not any more than they be supposed to exist in an unthinking subject.

Hyl. It is just come into my head, Philonous, that I have somewhere heard of a distinction between absolute and sensible extension. Now, though it be acknowledged that *great* and *small*, consisting merely in the relation which other extended beings have to the parts of our own bodies, do not really inhere in the Substances themselves; yet nothing obliges us to hold the same with regard to *absolute extension*, which is something abstracted from *great* and *small*, from this or that particular magnitude or figure. So likewise as to motion; *swift* and *slow* are altogether relative to the succession of ideas in our own minds. But, it doth not follow, because those modifications of motion exist not without the mind, that therefore absolute motion abstracted from them doth not.[10]

Phil. Pray what is it that distinguishes one motion, or one part of extension, from another? Is it not something sensible, as some degree of swiftness or slowness, some certain magnitude or figure peculiar to each?

Hyl. I think so.

Phil. These qualities, therefore, stripped of all sensible properties, are without all specific and numerical differences, as the schools call them.[11]

Hyl. They are.

Phil. That is to say, they are extension in general, and motion in general.

Hyl. Let it be so.

Phil. But it is a universally received maxim that *Everything which exists is particular.* How then can motion in general, or extension in general, exist in any corporeal Substance? [12]

Hyl. I will take time to solve your difficulty.

Phil. But I think the point may be speedily decided. Without doubt you can tell whether you are able to frame this or that idea. Now I am content to put our dispute on this issue. If you can frame in your thoughts a distinct abstract idea of motion or extension; divested of all those sensible modes, as swift and slow, great and small, round and square, and the like, which are acknowledged to exist only in the mind, I will then yield the point you contend for. But, if you cannot, it will be unreasonable on your side to insist any longer upon what you have no notion of.

Hyl. To confess ingenuously, I cannot.

Phil. Can you even separate the ideas of extension and motion from the ideas of all those qualities which they who make the distinction term *secondary?*

Hyl. What! is it not an easy matter to consider extension and motion by themselves, abstracted from all other sensible qualities? Pray how do the mathematicians treat of them?

Phil. I acknowledge, *Hylas,* is is not difficult to form general propositions and reasonings about those qualities, without mentioning any other; and, in this sense, to consider or treat of them abstractedly. But, how doth it follow that, because I can pronounce the word *motion* by itself, I can form the idea of it in my mind exclusive of body? Or, because theorems may be made of extension and figures, without any mention of *great* or *small,* or any other sensible mode or quality, that therefore it is possible such an abstract idea of extension, without any particular size or figure, or sensible quality, should be distinctly formed, and apprehended by the mind? Mathematicians treat of quantity, without regarding what other sensible qualities it is attended with, as being altogether indifferent to their demonstrations. But, when laying aside the words, they contemplate the bare ideas, I believe you will find, they are not the pure abstracted ideas of extension.

Hyl. But what say you to *pure intellect?* May not abstracted ideas be framed by that faculty?

Phil. Since I cannot frame abstract ideas at all, it is plain I cannot frame them by the help of *pure intellect;* whatsoever faculty you understand by those words. Besides, not to inquire into the nature of pure intellect and its spiritual objects, as *virtue, reason, God,* or the like, thus much seems manifest—that sensible things are only to be perceived by sense, or represented by the imagination. Figures, therefore, and extension, being originally perceived by sense, do not belong to pure intellect: but, for your farther satisfaction, try if you can frame the idea of any figure, abstracted from all particularities of size, or even from other sensible qualities.

Hyl. Let me think a little——I do not find that I can.

Phil. And can you think it possible that should really exist in nature which implies a repugnancy in its conception?

Hyl. By no means.

Phil. Since therefore it is impossible even for the mind to disunite the ideas of extension and motion from all other sensible qualities, doth it not follow, that where the one exist there necessarily the other exist likewise?

Hyl. It should seem so.

Phil. Consequently, the very same arguments which you admitted as conclusive against the Secondary Qualities are, without any farther application of force, against the Primary too. Besides, if you will trust your senses, is it not plain all sensible qualities coexist, or to them appear as being in the same place? Do they ever represent a motion, or figure, as being divested of all other visible and tangible qualities?

Hyl. You need say no more on this head. I am free to own, if there be no secret error or oversight in our proceedings hitherto, that all sensible qualities are alike to be denied existence without the mind.

B *From Berkeley's THIRD DIALOGUE*

Phil. Now, if you can prove that any philosopher hath explained the production of any one idea in our minds by the help of *Matter*, I shall for ever acquiesce, and look on all that hath been said against it as nothing; but, if you cannot, it is vain to urge the explication of phenomena. That a Being endowed with knowledge and will should produce or exhibit ideas is easily understood. But, that a Being which is utterly destitute of these faculties should be able to produce ideas, or in any sort to affect an intelligence, this I can never understand. This I say—though we had some positive conception of Matter, though we knew its qualities, and could comprehend its existence—would yet be so far from explaining things, that it is itself the most inexplicable thing in the world. And yet, for all this, it will not follow that philosophers have been doing nothing; for, by observing and reasoning upon the connexion of ideas, they discover the laws and methods of nature, which is a part of knowledge both useful and entertaining.

Hyl. After all, can it be supposed God would deceive all mankind? Do you imagine He would have induced the whole world to believe the being of Matter, if there was no such thing?

Phil. That every epidemical opinion arising from prejudice, or passion, or thoughtlessness may be imputed to God, as the Author of it, I believe you will not affirm. Whatsoever opinion we father on Him, it must be either because He has discovered it to us by supernatural revelation; or because it is so evident to our natural faculties, which were framed and given us by God, that it is impossible we should withhold our assent from it.[13] But where is the revelation? or where is the evidence that extorts the belief of Matter? Nay, how does it appear, that Matter, taken for something distinct from what we perceive by our senses, is thought to exist by all mankind; or, indeed, by any except a few philosophers, who do not know what they would be at? Your question supposes these points are clear; and, when you have cleared them, I shall think myself obliged to give you another answer. In the meantime let it suffice that I tell you, I do not suppose God has deceived mankind at all.

Hyl. But the novelty, *Philonous,* the novelty! There lies the danger. New notions should always be discountenanced; they unsettle men's minds, and nobody knows where they will end.

Phil. Why the rejecting a notion that hath no foundation, either in sense, or in reason, or in Divine authority, should be thought to unsettle the belief of such opinions as are grounded on all or any of these, I cannot imagine. That innovations in government and religion are dangerous, and ought to be discountenanced, I freely own.[14] But, is there the like reason why they should be discouraged in philosophy? The making anything known which was unknown before is an innovation in knowledge: and, if all such innovations had been forbidden, men would have made a notable progress in the arts and sciences.[15] But it is none of my business to plead for novelties and paradoxes. That the qualities we perceive are not on the objects: that we must not believe our senses: that we know nothing of the real nature of things, and can never be assured even of their existence: that real colours and sounds are nothing but certain unknown figures and motions: that motions are in themselves neither swift nor slow: that there are in bodies absolute extensions, without any particular magnitude or figure: that a thing stupid, thoughtless, and inactive, operates on a spirit: that the least particle of a body contains innumerable extended parts:— these are the novelties, these are the strange notions which shock the genuine uncorrupted judgment of all mankind; and being once admitted, embarrass the mind with endless doubts and difficulties. And it is against these and the like innovations I endeavour to vindicate Common Sense. It is true, in doing this, I may perhaps be obliged to use some *ambages,* and ways of speech not common.[16] But, if my notions are once thoroughly understood, that which is most singular in them will, in effect, be found to amount to no more than this:—that it is absolutely impossible, and a plain contradiction, to suppose any unthinking being should exist without being perceived by a mind. And, if this notion be singular, it is a shame it should be so at this time of day, and in a Christian country.

Hyl. As for the difficulties other opinions may be liable to, those are out of the question. It is your business to defend your own opinion. Can anything be plainer than that you are for changing all things into ideas?

You, I say, who are not ashamed to charge me with *scepticism*.[17] This is so plain, there is no denying it.

Phil. You mistake me. I am not for changing things into ideas, but rather ideas into things; since those immediate objects of perception, which, according to you, are only appearances of things, I take to be the real things themselves.

Hyl. Things! you may pretend what you please; but it is certain you leave us nothing but the empty forms of things, the outside only which strikes the senses.

Phil. What you call the empty forms and outside of things seem to me the very things themselves. Nor are they empty or incomplete, otherwise than upon your supposition—that Matter is an essential part of all corporeal things. We both, therefore, agree in this, that we perceive only sensible forms: but herein we differ, you will have them to be empty appearances, I real beings. In short, you do not trust your senses, I do.

Hyl. You say you believe your senses; and seem to applaud yourself that in this you agree with the vulgar. According to you, therefore, the true nature of a thing is discovered by the senses. If so, whence comes that disagreement? Why, is not the same figure, and other sensible qualities, perceived all manner of ways? And why should we use a microscope the better to discover the true nature of a body, if it were discoverable to the naked eye?[18]

Phil. Strictly speaking, *Hylas*, we do not see the same object that we feel; neither is the same object perceived by the microscope which was by the naked eye. But, in case every variation was thought sufficient to constitute a new kind or individual, the endless number or confusion of names would render language impracticable. Therefore, to avoid this as well as other inconveniences which are obvious upon a little thought, men combine together several ideas, apprehended by divers senses, or by the same sense at different times, or in different circumstances, but observed, however, to have some connexion in nature, either with respect to co-existence or succession—all which they refer to one name, and consider as one thing. Hence, it follows that when I examine by my other senses a thing I have seen, it is not in order to understand better the same object which I had perceived by sight—the object of one sense not being perceived by the other senses. And, when I look through a microscope, it is not that I may perceive more clearly what I perceived already with my bare eyes; the object perceived by the glass being quite different from the former. But, in both cases, my aim is only to know what ideas are connected together; and the more a man knows of the connexion of ideas, the more he is said to know of the nature of things. What, therefore, if our ideas are variable; what if our senses are not in all circumstances affected with the same appearances? It will not thence follow they are not to be trusted, or that they are inconsistent either with themselves or anything else; except it be with your preconceived notion of (I know not what) one single, unchanged, unperceivable, real nature, marked by each name: which prejudice seems to have taken its rise from not rightly understanding the common language of men, speaking of several distinct ideas as united into one thing by the mind. And, indeed, there is cause to suspect several erroneous conceits of the philosophers are owing to the same original: while they began to build their schemes not so much on notions as words, which were framed by the vulgar, merely for conveniency and dispatch in the common actions of life, without any regard to speculation.

Hyl. Methinks I apprehend your meaning.

Phil. It is your opinion the ideas we perceive by our senses are not real things, but images or copies of them. Our knowledge, therefore, is no farther real than as our ideas are the true representations of those originals. But, as these supposed originals are in themselves unknown, it is impossible to know how far our ideas resemble them; or whether they resemble them at all. We cannot, therefore, be sure we have any real knowledge. Farther, as our ideas are perpetually varied, without any change in the supposed real things, it necessarily follows they cannot all be true copies of them: or, if some are and others are not, it is impossible to distinguish the former from the latter.[19] And this plunges us yet deeper in uncertainty. Again, when we consider the point, we cannot conceive how any idea, or anything like an idea, should have an absolute existence out of a mind: nor consequently, according to you, how there should be any real thing in nature. The result of all which is that we are thrown into the most hopeless and abandoned Scepticism. Now, give me leave to ask you, First, Whether your referring ideas to certain absolutely existing unperceived substances, as their originals, be not the source of all this Scepticism? Secondly, whether you are informed, either by sense or reason, of the existence of those unknown originals? And, in case you are not, whether it be not absurd to suppose them? Thirdly, Whether, upon inquiry, you find there is anything distinctly conceived or meant by the *absolute or external existence of unperceiving substances*? Lastly, Whether, the premises considered, it be not the wisest way to follow nature, trust your senses, and, laying aside all anxious thought about unknown natures or substances, admit with the vulgar those for real things which are perceived by the senses?

Hyl. For the present, I have no inclination to the answering part. I would much rather see how you can get over what follows. Pray are not the objects perceived by the senses of one, likewise perceivable to others present? If there were a hundred more here, they would all see the garden, the trees, and flowers, as I see them. But they are not in the same manner affected with the ideas I frame in my imagination. Does not this make a difference between the former sort of objects and the latter?

Phil. I grant it does. Nor have I ever denied a difference between the objects of sense and those of imagination. But what would you infer from thence? You cannot say that sensible objects exist unperceived, because they are perceived by many.

Hyl. I own I can make nothing of that objection: but it hath led me into another. Is it not your opinion that by our senses we perceive only the ideas existing in our minds?

Phil. It is.

Hyl. But the same idea which is in my mind cannot be in yours, or in any other mind. Doth it not therefore follow, from your principles, that no two can see the same thing? And is not this highly absurd?

Phil. If the term *same* be taken in the vulgar acceptation, it is certain (and not at all repugnant to the principles I maintain) that different persons may perceive the same thing; or the same thing or idea exist in different minds. Words are of arbitrary imposition; and, since men are used to apply the word *same* where no distinction or variety is perceived, and I do not pretend to alter their perceptions, it follows that, as men have said before, *several saw the same thing,* so they may, upon like occasions, still continue to use the same phrase, without any deviation either from propriety of language, or the truth of things. But, if the term *same* be used in the acceptation of philosophers, who pretend to an abstracted notion of identity, then, according to their sundry definitions of this notion (for it is not yet agreed wherein that philosophic identity consists), it may or may not be possible for divers persons to perceive the same thing. But whether philosophers shall think fit to call a thing the *same* or no, is, I conceive, of small importance. Let us suppose several men together, all endued with the same faculties, and consequently affected in like sort by their senses, and who had yet never known the use of language; they would, without question, agree in their perceptions. Though perhaps, when they came to the use of speech, some regarding the uniformness of what was perceived, might call it the *same* thing: others, especially regarding the diversity of persons who perceived, might choose the denomination of *different* things. But who sees not that all the dispute is about a word? to wit, whether what is perceived by different persons may yet have the term *same* applied to it? Or, suppose a house, whose walls or outward shell remaining unaltered, the chambers are all pulled down, and new ones built in their place; and that you should call this the *same,* and I should say it was not the *same* house:—would we not, for all this, perfectly agree in our thoughts of the house, considered in itself? And would not all the difference consist in a sound? If you should say, We differ in our notions; for that you superadded to your idea of the house the simple abstracted idea of identity, whereas I did not; I would tell you, I know not what you mean by the *abstracted idea of identity;* and should desire you to look into your own thoughts, and be sure you understood yourself.[20] Why so silent, *Hylas?* Are you not yet satisfied men may dispute about identity and diversity, without any real difference in their thoughts and opinions, abstracted from names? Take this farther reflection with you—that whether Matter be allowed to exist or no, the case is exactly the same as to the point in hand. For, the Materialists themselves acknowledge what we immediately perceive by our senses to be our own ideas. Your difficulty, therefore, that no two see the same thing, makes equally against the Materialists and me.

Hyl. Ay, *Philonous*, But they suppose an external archetype, to which referring their several ideas they may truly be said to perceive the same thing.

Phil. And (not to mention your having discarded those archetypes) so may you suppose an external archetype on my principles;—*external*, I mean, to your own mind; though indeed it must be supposed to exist in that mind which comprehends all things; but then, this serves all the ends of *identity*, as well as if it existed out of a mind.[21] And I am sure you yourself will not say it is less intelligible.

Hyl. You have indeed clearly satisfied me—either that there is no difficulty at bottom in this point; or, if there be, that it makes equally against both opinions.

Phil. But that which makes equally against two contradictory opinions can be a proof against neither.

Hyl. I acknowledge it. But, after all, *Philonous*, when I consider the substance of what you advance against *Scepticism*, it amounts to no more than this:—We are sure that we really see, hear, feel; in a word, that we are affected with sensible impressions.

Phil. And how are we concerned any farther? I see this *cherry*, I feel it, I taste it: and I am sure *nothing* cannot be seen, or felt, or tasted: it is therefore real.[22] Take away the sensations of softness, moisture, redness, tartness, and you take away the *cherry*. Since it is not a being distinct from sensations; a *cherry*, I say, is nothing but a congeries of sensible impressions, or ideas perceived by various senses: which ideas are united into one thing (or have one name given them) by the mind;—because they are observed to attend each other. Thus, when the palate is affected with such a particular taste, the sight is affected with a red colour, the touch with roundness, softness, &c. Hence, when I see, and feel, and taste, in sundry certain manners, I am sure the *cherry* exists, or is real; its reality being in my opinion nothing abstracted from those sensations. But if, by the word *cherry*, you mean an unknown nature, distinct from all those sensible qualities, and by its *existence* something distinct from its being perceived; then, indeed, I own, neither you nor I, nor any one else, can be sure it exists.

Hyl. But, what would you say, *Philonous*, if I should bring the very same reasons against the existence of sensible things in a mind, which you have offered against their existing in a material *substratum*?

Phil. When I see your reasons, you shall hear what I have to say to them.

Hyl. Is the mind extended or unextended?

Phil. Unextended, without doubt.

Hyl. Do you say the things you perceive are in your mind?

Phil. They are.

Hyl. Again, have I not heard you speak of sensible impressions?

Phil. I believe you may.

Hyl. Explain to me now, O *Philonous!* how it is possible there should be room for all those trees and houses to exist in your mind. Can extended things be contained in that which is unextended? Or, are we to imagine impressions made on a thing void of all solidity? You cannot say objects are in your mind, as books in your study: or that things are imprinted on it, as the figure of a seal upon wax. In what sense, therefore, are we to understand those expressions? Explain me this if you can: and I shall then be able to answer all those queries you formerly put to me about my *substratum*.[23]

Phil. Look you, *Hylas*, when I speak of objects as existing in the mind, or imprinted on the senses, I would not be understood in the gross literal sense—as when bodies are said to exist in a place, or a seal to make an impression upon wax. My meaning is only that the mind comprehends or perceives them; and that it is affected from without, or by some being distinct from itself. This is my explication of your difficulty; and how it can serve to make your tenet of an unperceiving material *substratum* intelligble, I would fain know.

Hyl. Nay, if that be all, I confess I do not see what use can be made of it. But are you not guilty of some abuse of language in this?

Phil. None at all. It is no more than common custom, which you know is the rule of language, hath authorized: nothing being more usual, than for philosophers to speak of the immediate objects of the understanding as things existing in the mind. Nor is there anything in this but what is conformable to the general analogy of language; most part of the mental operations being signified by words borrowed from sensible things; as is plain in the terms *comprehend, reflect, discourse,* &c., which, being applied to the mind, must not be taken in their gross original sense.

NOTES

[1] In reading Berkeley, it is necessary to pay close attention to the ambiguity involved in the use of certain English words. In the preceding lines, Philonous has used the word *immediately.* As it is used here, the Berkeleian position is tacitly granted by Hylas. There might be more difficulty in the argument for Philonous if Hylas were to insist that we do perceive things other than sensible qualities immediately, physical objects, for example.

[2] That is, the same color as we see in it? The question is rhetorical, because Hylas has already said that he means the same color.

[3] Dioptrics is the scientific study of the refraction of light.

[4] A theory occasionally invoked in empiricist epistemology is the theory that the true qualities of objects can be sensed by a *standard* observer under *standard*

conditions. The problem with such a criterion is that unless the notion of a standard observer and standard conditions is to be arbitrary, from which the true qualities can hardly follow, some nonempiricistic rule must be invoked in order to determine what is standard. Hylas, however, goes on to admit that no such device as a *standard* observer in *standard* conditions can work.

5   It is hardly necessary to recapitulate scientific theories of Berkeley's time, one of which is alluded to here. The argument would seemingly apply under any explanation of how vision took place, where one aspect of the explanation involved light moving over some finite length of time from the object seen to the retina of the eye.

6   What is the meaning of *without* that Hylas intends? Notice that the phrase 'in themselves' is not clear, but Philonous takes this to mean that colors are to be identified with the motions of particles. The reader might notice that if Hylas's description of vision is accepted, it is difficult to locate the color of an object in the everyday sense as being *anywhere*, for an opponent can raise serious objections to every possibility. Berkeley avoids the difficulty by denying the existence of material objects, so that color does not have to be located either *in* the mind or *outside* of it. When one brings in the problem of the relationship of the mind to the brain, these questions prove to be extremely complicated.

7   Why does Hylas stop arguing? Apparently because he has identified colors with certain motions of matter, but these cannot be known by reasons of various arguments that he can now anticipate from Philonous. On the other hand, we do perceive colors.

8   As a matter of fact, persons who have astigmatism may see an object as having a different shape with each eye.

9   Earlier in the dialogue, Hylas has distinguished two kinds of heat, making greater heat identical with pain and lesser heat not necessarily identical with any sensation. Pain, obviously, is something perceived, so that greater heat must exist in a mind, according to Philonous. On the other hand, Hylas maintained that lesser heat could exist in material objects. Philonous's summary here is not entirely accurate, since his refutation of Hylas's view was not complete. In the next sentence, Hylas could mean that an indifferent sensation is *no* sensation, but Philonous might then argue that we could not *know* of such a sensation.

10   Here is an example of the ambiguous use of *without*. Does 'not without the mind' mean 'in the mind'? Or does the plausibility of this sentence rest on reading 'not without the mind' as meaning that without the reaction of some mind to its ideas, events could not move *swiftly* or *slowly*, but simply at whatever pace they moved. Usually the swiftness or slowness of events is related to what we are desiring at the time when the events are noticed. '*A* occurs without *B*.' can mean that *A* occurs spatially outside of *B*, or that *A* occurs when *B* does not, or even that *B* is not a cause of *A* in that *A* does not always follow *B*.

11   This remark is in reference to the traditional (Aristotelian) logic taught in the universities at Berkeley's time. Differences were required to explain how two objects could belong to different species within the same genus. A difference is consequently an appropriate property that the one object has that the other object does not have. If a property is abstracted from all sensible properties (there are no non-sensible properties for Philonous), then no difference can be

found between an object having the property and one that does not, so that Berkeley seems to be suggesting that abstraction is fruitless because we could not distinguish *different* abstract properties.

12 The basic tenet of nominalism, that only individuals or particulars exist, is simply assumed here without debate as a universally received maxim. In a live debate, Hylas might want to argue this. Still, the (scientific) view of matter which Hylas is representing is often taken to be consistent with this principle.

13 Notice the reference to supernatural revelation, not mentioned in earlier discussions of how we might know the existence of matter. Once again, this need not be a loophole that Hylas would want to explore if he represents scientific thought, since he has maintained that we can know matter through perception.

14 This incidental remark is a clue to Berkeley's religious and political conservatism.

15 What Berkeley appears to mean here seems to call for the addition of a *not* after *would*, although for some reason this emendation does not occur in any of Berkeley's revisions of the *Three Dialogues.*

16 *Ambages* are roundabout or circular ways.

17 Early in the first dialogue, Hylas and Philonous agreed to call a skeptic anyone who denied the reality of sensible things, meaning by sensible things those things immediately perceived by the senses. Hylas's doctrine of matter makes sensible things less intelligible (because of obscurities in this doctrine) than Philonous's view, according to Philonous. From this the charge of skepticism arises.

18 This is one of the best points allotted to Hylas in the dialogue. Note the circumspection with which Philonous replies, and the interesting point on which his reply depends, namely, that the object perceived through a microscope, for example, and the object of direct perception are never the same object. Hylas might have Philonous in difficulty if he were to explore the consequences of maintaining that the book one sees with the naked eye, and the book one sees when he puts his spectacles on are not the same object.

19 Is this point cogent? Could you argue that an unchanging object might have differing perspectives? Imagine a circle of people slowly walking around a statue, for example.

20 There is some question as to whether this argument is cogent. Philonous has distinguished between *sameness* and *identity*, but it would seem that his account of difficulties in the notion of identity leads us away from difficulties in sameness. If two people argue as to whether they see the same thing, how can the argument be resolved on empiricists' grounds?

21 The Mind in question is, of course, related to Berkeley's views about God.

22 Berkeley elsewhere claims to be able to distinguish hallucination from true perception in terms of the coherence of the sensations of the latter. At this point, however, it would seem that Berkeley is brushing over problems of hallucination.

23 Another good point for Hylas. Although Philonous protests that Hylas is taking him too literally (has he been guilty of taking Hylas too literally?) and denies the spatial suggestion of *in*, his positive point seems to be somewhat obscure.

In terms of the preceding argument, can he maintain that what he means is that the mind comprehends what is affected from without? Actually, he can because he supposes the affectation to be a consequence of mental substance, rather than material substance. Hume argues later that arguments against the existence of material substance could be supplemented by arguments against the existence of mental substance.

PART 5

Hume

(1711–1776)

The Association of Ideas

David Hume, like Berkeley, could not accept a rationalistic philosophy but accepted the view that an adequate philosophy would have to be built upon ordinary sense impressions. In accepting the empirical theory of the origins of knowledge, however, he drew conclusions more stringent than those which were drawn by Locke and Berkeley. Where Berkeley had taken empiricism to refute the existence of matter, or material substance, Hume took empiricism to be inconsistent with the existence of material *and* spiritual substances. For Hume, sense impressions do not yield knowledge of *any* kind of substance, which is sufficient warning that Hume will prove to be more skeptical than any of the philosophers that we have considered.

One fruitful way of looking at this skepticism is to observe that Hume believed that impressions could only give us probable knowledge, but that probable knowledge was a sufficient grounding (being the only grounding) for any significant knowledge that human beings might ordinarily be said to be capable of having. Thus Hume is the first important philosopher that we have considered to suppose that *certain* knowledge was not only a misleading goal for philosophy, but in fact an unobtainable goal. It is the position that *certain* knowledge is not possible that distinguishes modern empiricism and to some extent explains Hume's importance in the history of philosophy. The rationalistic philosophers have been right in holding that certain knowledge is not attainable through sense experience, but an adequate empiricistic counter to this must be, not that *parts* of sense experience are certain, but that we have *no* certain knowledge, so that the philosophical quest for certainty must end in failure. The problem for the empiricist thus becomes that of demonstrating that science does not require certain knowledge for its attainments. The severe difficulty facing such a program is provision of an empirical analysis of mathematical truth that can avoid Platonic objections that the certainty of mathematical truths which are re-

177

quired for scientific theorizing cannot be explained in terms of uncertain sense experiences.

Hume begins with a reformulation of the empiricistic account of ideas. He contends that everyone will, upon reflection, admit that there is an important qualitative difference between experiences at the time of their original occurrence, and at some time when they are either remembered or anticipated by the imagination. This difference is characterized as being one of *vividness.* An *impression,* which is after this point a technical term of Hume's philosophy, is similar to a Berkeleian idea in that it is the vivid and forceful mental occurrence that accompanies what might be called a present sensation. *Ideas,* in Hume's technical sense, are the result of the mind's analysis and combining of remembered impressions or parts thereof. Like Berkeley and Descartes, Hume takes the position that the powers of the human mind to form ideas are not unlimited but are bounded by the ability of the mind to analyze and combine whatever impressions it has had in the past. This position about the origin of ideas is taken by Hume to be obvious upon reflection, but he buttresses it with the empirical argument that wherever impressions of some sort are impossible to a person, the formation of ideas involving impressions of this sort is not possible. A congenitally blind man, for example, cannot form those ideas which are the result of analyzing and combining impressions of sight.

A Humean *impression* and a Berkeleian *idea* cannot be identified. One of Hume's major contributions to empiricism was to notice that simple sensations of sight, touch, hearing, etc., are obviously too meagre a basis on which to construct an adequate general theory of human knowledge. The simple fact is that all felt human emotion, as well as moral and aesthetic valuation, is completely unaccounted for in an empiricism which supposes that sensations are the result of sense-organ activity in terms of what is outside of the body. A feeling of anger, for example, is not analogous to a sight of blue in that the anger is clearly felt as my anger, but the blue as the blue of some object. Hume wished to include emotional impressions, as well as impressions of moral and aesthetic worth, as *basic* ingredients of empiricism, since there seems to be no way of obtaining an explanation of these experiences by the analysis and combination of sights, sounds, touches, etc. Consequently the kind of direct observation equivalent to an impression in Hume's sense is considerably more complicated than it appears to be in Berkeley's philosophy. For any philosopher who wishes to include the range of moral, emotional, and aesthetic experiences within an empiricistic account of human knowledge, Humean impressions will be a great advance over Berkeleian ideas. At the same time, there is a corresponding difficulty in that Hume should give an account of how we have impressions of this wider class, since a feeling of anger is not presumably seen with the eyes, heard with the ears, and so forth. Yet our understanding that we have these impressions is a straightforward consequence of an examination of our feelings. Ideas, on the other hand, must be understood because of the way in which we come to develop them. When we are unclear as to what the significance of an idea is, we can remove unclarity only by analyzing the idea into the impressions whose analysis and combination led to the formation of the idea. The basis for this is empirical, in the sense that Hume makes no claims as to the origins of impressions (we simply have them), but he claims that the distinction between ideas and impressions in terms of liveliness or vividness is presumably one that may be empirically verified.

To explain how various impressions are analyzed and combined to form an idea, Hume invokes the notion of association. Various impressions may be associated to form an idea, and various ideas may in turn be associated to form a complex idea. These associations must be explained, in Hume's philosophy, in terms that will permit a satisfactory account of the knowledge of common sense. The problem is to find some empiricistic account of association which will be comprehensive enough to explain why human beings seem to associate the same ideas, as witnessed by their success in communicating through language. Berkeley's account, as we have seen, resulted in the difficulty that there was no cogent explanation of the fact that general words stood for certain ideas but not for others. Hume's philosophy must tackle an analogous difficulty.

An explanation of the operation of association is given by Hume which utilizes the notions of resemblance, of contiguity, and of cause and effect. These he called natural relations between ideas. We shall consider resemblance in particular. The terminology 'natural relations between ideas' seems to suggest that *ideas* is being used here in a looser, more colloquial sense than the technical usage of *ideas* as opposed to *impressions,* since remarks made by Hume in his discussion indicate that impressions may resemble one another. At first sight it might be supposed that resemblance could be explained as the natural relation holding between any two things which had some parts in common. Thus, an object A consisting of the parts $a, b, c, d,$ and an object B consisting of the parts a, c, d, f might be said to resemble one another because they have the parts a, c, d in common. Throughout this discussion it will have to be assumed that the parts described are simple or ultimate in some sense, so that no part of one object is considered nonidentical with any part of the other, because the parts of one object are not analyzed finely enough. In terms of impressions, then, two experiences of objects would resemble one another if there were an impression as part of one experience identical (so far as can be remembered) with an impression which is part of the other. Even so, the account is obviously defective in that two objects A and B, consisting respectively of the parts a, b, c, d and e, f, g, h might be said to resemble one another in ways other than sharing parts. For example, the four parts of each may be arranged in some similar way, so that A and B resemble each other even though there is no part of A identical with any part of B. The four parts of each object, to make this perfectly clear, might be arranged as the corners of a square of similar size. Hume does not discuss this problem, perhaps because he holds that one would not be said to have an impression of a relation. One may see something he calls *red* but not something that he would call *on top of*. Hume does mention explicitly the fact that the simple ideas of blue and green resemble one another more than the simple ideas of blue and scarlet. If this is true, it cannot be because the impressions which give rise to the ideas of blue and green have identical parts more numerous than these in the impressions giving rise to the ideas of blue and scarlet. Exactly how Hume meant to explain this comparison of resemblances remains obscure.

It is interesting to note that even if resemblance could be defined in terms of the identity of common parts, there seems to be no way of construing identity in terms of resemblance. A theory of knowledge utilizing resemblance as a primitive or basic notion may not be able to account for the identity of objects, raising the interesting question of whether or not scientific theories may be constructed in terms of the resemblance of objects, without introducing a notion of the identity of objects as an additional primitive term.

An important feature of Hume's account is that he does not explain *why* ideas are associated, but attempts merely to *describe how* ideas are associated. By introspection, he discovers those ideas which are associated, and finds that they are in fact associated because they resemble one another or because they are related by contiguity or the cause-and-effect relationship. There is some apparent difficulty involved here in that at times objects are spoken of as resembling one another, and at other times ideas related to these objects by experience are said to resemble one another. As a result, the notion of resemblance does not help very much in the analysis of the association of ideas.

The fact that Hume explicitly rejects all explanations of *why* various ideas are in fact associated rather than others calls for some comment. To begin with, Hume has no explanation as to why, when a given idea occurs, some other idea is related to it by, for example, cause and effect, rather than by contiguity or resemblance. In other words, as a succession of ideas occurs to us, the sequence may be ordered by any one of the three natural relations, and it does not seem possible to predict, once an idea has occurred to us, which of the three natural relations will hold between it and the next idea which occurs to us. These associations are not logically necessary, but they are the result of custom or habit, according to Hume. The philosopher's job is to observe the associations and describe them: it cannot legitimately be to explain why they occur, because this is impossible.

The impossibility of this latter task is related to Hume's acceptance of scientific method as practiced by Newton. Newton took as his task not to explain *why* objects fall to the earth, etc., but to *describe how* they fell, that is, to give a formula describing the rate of their fall under specified conditions, the direction of their fall, and so forth. In an analogous fashion,

Hume took as his task not to explain *why* certain ideas are associated, but to describe how they are associated. The primitive, unexplained term *association* in Hume's theory of knowledge corresponds to the primitive, unexplained term *gravity* in Newton's theory of gravitation. How things fall is explained in terms of gravity, and how ideas are associated is explained in terms of association. Why things fall the way they do rather than some other way is not a significant problem for Newton, just as the problem of why ideas are associated the way they are rather than in other combinations is not a significant problem for Hume.

In taking this position, both Hume and Newton accepted views which have come to play an important role in contemporary empiricism. The basis of these views is sole reliance on observation, which comes to mean both ordinary experience *and* deliberate experimental observation as the test of the worth of any generalization. Metaphysics is simultaneously condemned. Hume's reason for this condemnation is precisely that metaphysical speculation is not subject to the check of observation, in that *any* observation would be compatible with most metaphysical theories.

We may see what an empiricist like Hume considers a metaphysical idea by discussion of the Humean reaction to the notion of substance. Hume argues that watching something change over a period of time is quite similar to watching something that does not change, in the sense that we see it throughout as one object. If, at the end of the change, we compare our memory of the object at the start with the object now, we see that the object may be quite different, as in Descartes's example of the piece of wax. To reconcile our contrary feelings that the object is the same and yet different, we invent or phantasize 'something unknown and invisible' which remains identical throughout the change. We call this substance. This tendency of the imagination to construct unobserved entities to explain sequences of impressions ought not to be accepted by philosophers because no experiment can demonstrate or refute the existence of substance or other metaphysical notions, since they are by their construction compatible with every observation. A metaphysical idea cannot be analyzed into impressions and is consequently either useless or meaningless. The point could be made in a more contemporary fashion by saying that since a metaphysical idea would have to be related to *every* impression, no way of *distinguishing* metaphysical ideas is possible. Consequently metaphysical ideas cannot serve as contributions to human knowledge. This feature of Hume's empiricism has proved very influential on contemporary empiricists, but as we shall see later, the Humean-Newtonian doctrine that any sound scientific generalization must *follow from* observation turned out to be entirely too restrictive.

Mathematical Truth and Skepticism

To this point, we have seen that impressions, as well as ideas derived from impressions, constitute the foundation for human knowledge in Hume's epistemology. But it is clear that we say that we know more than is legitimately entailed by our narrow range of impressions. Hume vacillates on the question of whether or not our impressions constitute knowledge. We have them, and they form the foundation of knowledge, but it is seemingly awkward to say either that they are certain or uncertain. What seems to be relatively certain or uncertain are the various opinions or judgments that are based on the impressions which we cannot doubt but which we do not *know* either.

The certainty of mathematics Hume takes cognizance of by holding that mathematical knowledge is really a special kind of comparison of the names of ideas which is undertaken by thought alone. When Hume says that mathematical knowledge is not dependent on what exists, he must be taken to mean that mathematical truths, being the mental comparison of ideas, cannot be subject to empirical check, since it is *ideas* which are being compared, and their relationships are not to be determined by scientific experiment. In another sense, of course, we would not have ideas without prior ordinary experience. All Hume's remarks on this topic are compact, and we learn little more than what has just been said, as well as that the nonempirical test of a mathematical truth is that its negation must result in contradiction; that is, we cannot consistently imagine its negation. If we imagine that the squares of the legs of a right triangle are not equal to the square of the hypotenuse, we can quickly find a contradiction in the system of which this statement is a theorem.

It is difficult to reconcile Hume's claims about the certainty of true mathematical statements with his obvious opinion that human knowledge is based solely on impressions. A reconciliation may be effected by drawing a distinction between significant and nonsignificant statements, and then claiming that *significant* statements (which make a nontrivial claim about our experiences) are never certain, while certain statements are never significant. In this way, statements of mathematics may be said to be nonsignificant in that their acquisition never increases our significant knowledge about the world, although it may enable us to organize this significant knowledge in some more convenient way. Then it could be claimed that mathematical knowledge is certain only in the sense that significant statements cannot controvert it. The Pythagorean theorem is true but not significant because we choose to apply the word *triangle* only to those ideas of which the Pythagorean theorem is true. If *triangle* is applied to something of which the Pythagorean theorem is not true, we take this as a discovery that the word *triangle* has been misapplied, and not as a proof that the theorem is false after all. Although this attempt at a reconciliation of Hume's remarks is compatible with what Hume says, there is no resolution of the status of mathematical truth in Hume's extant works, at least no clear resolution, and so we can take any such attempt at helping Hume out as but a charitable way of reading him to preserve his important empiricistic insight that certainty may not be required of scientific knowledge.

Hume's skepticism is a result of the fact that he limits certain knowledge in a rigorous sense to demonstrable mathematical truth. Whatever else we know, and this includes all our significant information, we know only probably. This second and more important kind of knowledge has been called *belief* by empiricists. Belief comprises probable opinion in experimental science, morality, political philosophy, and aesthetics. The application of association to impressions and ideas cannot result in certain knowledge. That two ideas are such that they resemble one another, or that they are contiguous, or that one is the cause of the other cannot be a necessary result of the nature of the ideas, but can only be some function of the way in which experience causes us to frame the ideas. This point assumes special significance in connection with cause and effect since cause and effect is the only relation of the three which could enable us to reason to existences and objects (to possible impressions) which we have not experienced. Resemblance and contiguity simply hold or do not hold between ideas that we already have. The relation of cause and effect, however, might enable us to say something about the unexperienced, thus enabling us to predict future events and otherwise discourse intelligibly about topics not entirely circumscribed by our meagre store of past experiences.

It is clear that we do assume cause-and-effect relationships, and it is also clear that they are used (as they were in the science of Hume's day) to predict the future and hence provide the basis for rational action. What Hume demonstrated is that reasoning involving cause and effect cannot be demonstrative; that is, the result of such reasoning is never a certain prediction, but only a probable one.

The argument that reasoning involving cause and effect is not demonstrative is based on two arguments. Experience with such reasonings indicates that they often fail. We can also see that such reasonings will fail by experimental introspection. Given some object, Hume argues that a man cannot determine any of its causes or effects with certainty. This seems a little strong, but it is clear that there are, say, effects which some objects in certain situations have that could not be guessed by inspection of the object in the lack of any more extended experience with it. Simple examples suffice to indicate that we cannot estimate with much accuracy the effects of some strange piece of apparatus under certain conditions. This argument to the probable nature of inferences of cause and effect is based on observation. Hume further argues that if cause-and-effect reasonings were demonstrative, then imagination of the negation of any correct statement of causal inference would be contradictory. We can, however, imagine two or more incompatible effects following from some given event or object taken as cause, so that reasoning from cause to effect violates the condition of contradiction placed on the negations of statements of demonstrable inference, which are certain. Given that something is X, the only way to investigate its effects is to observe X experimentally.

These arguments are not overwhelming in spite of their apparent plausibility. Part of their failure stems from the way in which we may be said to conceive the contradictory of a statement. Conception of a contradiction is at least implicitly a mark of the difference between the demonstrable truths of mathematics (whose contradictories are not conceivable) and the probable statements of the sciences. Nevertheless, it is possible to imagine the truth of either of a pair of contradictory statements in mathematics, unless the notion of 'conceiving a contradiction' is considerably sharpened. An example is *Fermat's Last Theorem* and its negation. Assuming again that we are dealing with plane triangles only, we can ask the following question: For $n \geqslant 3$, are there any three positive numbers x, y, and z which satisfy the relationship $x^n + y^n = z^n$? The negative answer to this question is called *Fermat's Last Theorem* among mathematicians, after the mathematician who advanced the claim. In spite of great effort, no one has been able to find a proof or disproof of *Fermat's Last Theorem*. Consequently, we might say that it is conceivable that either *Fermat's Last Theorem* or its negation may be a demonstrable truth of mathematics. Clearly not both can be true, but if one is true, then its negation is not obviously contradictory, or we would have a proof available as to which of the two is true. Consequently we cannot take the conceivability of contradiction in holding the negation of a claim X to be a test that X (if it is a mathematical statement) is a mathematical truth, since some mathematical truths will fail this test. Persons knowing little of mathematics may find it equally conceivable that either of two statements (for one of which there is a satisfactory proof that it is a mathematical truth) is a mathematical truth. And by the same token, scientists have reported that either of two effects might conceivably follow from some cause that is under experimental investigation. In order to make Hume's remarks effective, some further study of when a statement may be said to be contradictory is required.

Further, Hume's empirical proofs require some supplementation. Some arguments may be deductive in spite of the fact that the statements of the argument are about probabilities. Thus, it is a valid argument within the probability calculus to argue that if two independent events each have a probability of $\frac{1}{6}$, their joint occurrence has a probability of $\frac{1}{6}$ times $\frac{1}{6}$, or $\frac{1}{36}$. On the other hand, many philosophers have suggested that there may be legitimate nondeductive arguments (inductive arguments) holding between statements that are either true or false, in the sense that it is not known which value the statements have. For example, if I have observed 1,000,000 A's, and 998,567 of them have also been B's, I may argue that a new arbitrary A will be a B, assuming that I have no further information available that might influence the probabilities. Now, although the premises of such an argument may all be true while the conclusion is false, so that the argument is not deductively valid, one may also argue reasonably that the truth of the conclusion is more likely than the truth of its negation. If it is possible to construct an inductive logic, Hume's proof may be misleading. In other words, if either of two contradictory statements may both follow from some statement, this is still compatible with the possibility that the probability of the truth of one is much greater than the probability of the other. We may, however, take Hume to be arguing correctly that any analysis which *justifies* an assignment of probabilities cannot be based solely on our impressions.

Hume felt that there was no *certain* way of assigning probabilities. The acceptance of probabilities rests on psychological considerations, but we cannot know that these are reasonable. The occurrence of any event cannot establish a probability claim, since the occurrence of an event does not prove that the event is a probable or improbable event. We experience both.

Hume's skepticism is really his insistence that impressions cannot enable us to frame certain knowledge of the world. When this is coupled with the rejection of any rationalist methods, the result is that no empiricism based solely on impressions and immediate generalizations thereon can yield *any* certain knowledge. This is a strong claim which later empiricists have been forced to accept.

An interesting feature of this interpretation of Hume is that he does not seem to have considered himself a skeptic. While he felt that scientific practice could not be established on the basis of impressions alone without bringing in custom or habit, as we shall see in the next chapter, he seems to have developed his skeptical position in order to show that scientific methodology has no theoretical advantage over moral and political methodology. He apparently wished to become a Newton in the moral sciences (political theory, economics, and ethics) by using association and habit to demonstrate that moral questions might be as satisfactorily resolved as scientific questions. What his analysis accomplishes is that scientific methodology cannot be established on the basis of experience alone, contrary to the contention of some of the philosophers and to some of the implicit methodological assumptions of the scientists of his day.

The Cause-and-effect Relationship

Hume's analysis of the cause-and-effect relationship enables us to see how an analysis of an idea into impressions for the purposes of clarification is actually carried out. Throughout this discussion, Hume speaks of the constant conjunction of *objects*, which must be taken as a reference to what we ordinarily call objects, even though Hume's explicit consideration of what an object is does not involve a material substance anymore than Berkeley's consideration does. The analysis assumes that a relationship between cause and effect is intuitively known, and that in some sense this intuitive relationship is such that cause and effect are *necessarily* related. Thus, if we say that an event *a* is the cause of an event *b*, we would ordinarily say that *a must* be followed by *b* or is necessarily followed by *b*. Hume takes the analysis of this necessary connection to be an important problem.

Suppose that two events or objects thought to be in the causal relationship are examined. Hume speaks only of objects being in the causal relationship, but we often think of events as being in this relationship, and both shall be spoken of here, leaving open the question of how an object is to be distinguished from an event. It is immediately clear that the cause is taken to precede the effect and that the two are taken to be contiguous in space and time. The status of these two observations is quite different. That causes precede effects seems to be a trivial consequence of the way in which we define *cause* and *effect*, although this does not detract from what Hume says, since that is obviously true in virtue of our definitions. Contiguity proves more difficult to discuss. The fact that Hume uses this expression indicates that he was thinking about everyday occurrences, such as his examples of billiard balls striking one another. That cause and effect must be *separated* in space and time is surely the case, since this seems a necessary condition of our distinguishing *two* objects or events to be called, respectively, the cause and the effect. If they are definitely separated, the requirement of contiguity suggests that they are not to be separated by very much. Actually, although this view of the cause-and-effect relationship is perhaps true, it requires considerable augmentation to handle cases of causal laws in science. For one thing, it is not required in scientific cases that a cause be contiguous to one of its effects, but only that any cause and effect be related by a series of objects or events such that each object or event in this series be contiguous to the object or event preceding it and following it; and such that each event or object in the series is the effect of the object or event preceding it, and the cause of the object or event following it. In this way we may speak of *causal chains* connecting two events in the relationship of cause and effect which are not, considered in themselves, contiguous. Nevertheless, Hume's analysis could be extended if it were otherwise satisfactory to include such pairs of events.

A more serious question is that of relating two contiguous events. It is tempting to suppose that what we call cause and effect are simply two locations in some *continuous* causal chain. For Hume, the view that between any two instants of time or points in some body, another instant of time or another point in the body may be found, is excluded by his atomistic views of space and time. He would argue that we can have no *experience* of such a causal chain, which would involve experience of an infinite number of bodies or events, but that we can experience only disparate and finite sequences of bodies or events.

Contiguity and precedence of cause are all that we can determine of the causal relationship by examination of a single cause and effect. By considering several instances of cause and effect, a new feature comes into consideration. Let A-B, C-D, E-F, etc., be instances of cause and effect, such that A, C, and E resemble one another in some quality. Because of what we have said about identity, we cannot treat the sequences just mentioned as the same sequence of cause and effect. Still, we tend to regard objects which closely resemble one another as identical. Let us consider A, C, and E to be R-like objects in virtue of their resemblance, and B, D, and F to be S-like objects in virtue of their resemblance. To say that R-like objects cause S-like objects, we must have observed in every case that an R-like object is followed by an S-like object. Hume says that R-like objects, or simply R's (treating them as though they were identical in some respect) must be constantly conjoined with S-like objects, or S's. As a constant conjunction of R's and S's is repeated, Hume suggests that we come to expect that an S will follow an R, and finally that an S must follow an R. For Hume, the intuitive necessity that an effect must follow its cause is simply a result of the custom or habit that we acquire of expecting S's to follow R's when they have been uniformly noticed to do so in the past. This analysis accomplishes a grounding of the idea of the cause-and-effect relationship *in experience*.

After completing this analysis, Hume offers two distinct definitions of the relation of cause and effect. Defined as a philosophical relation, we may say that a cause is:

an object precedent and contiguous to another, and where all the objects resembling the former are placed in like relations of precedence and contiguity to those objects that resemble the latter.

On the other hand, as a natural relation, we may say that a cause is:

an object precedent and contiguous to another, and so united with it, that the idea of the one determines the mind to form the idea of the other, and the impression of the one to form a more lively idea of the other.

Why should Hume offer *two* definitions? An answer to this question may enable us to grasp the difference between a philosophical problem and a psychological problem. A natural relation is one which holds between ideas by virtue of their association. As we have seen, the natural relations are resemblance, contiguity in time and place, and causality. Natural relations are the relations of association which explain all unreflective belief. In analyzing a natural relation, we are discovering how people do, in fact, come to associate ideas. This question is not, strictly speaking, a philosophical question—but a question of psychology, or an empirical question. Hume's answer to these questions may not be an adequate account of how people do associate ideas (*if* they associate ideas, so that the general associationist account of knowledge is plausible), but even if it is false, its falsity does not mean that Hume's definition of the philosophical relation must also be rejected.

The first definition, in more contemporary terms, may be taken as an answer to the question "What do we mean by the words *cause, effect,* and *causal relationship?*". By Hume's theory of meaning, this should be traced solely to impressions and cannot incorporate *feelings* or *beliefs,* as the second definition does. This problem of meaning can be taken as a philosophical question. We might *mean* by a cause-effect relationship a constant union of various kinds of objects or events, but come to apply this relationship correctly in practice, not because of Hume's associationist account in terms of custom, but because of the *Intuition* of the rationalists or through some other means. Thus, it appears plausible that the question of what a word means can be separated in theory from the question of when we can apply a word correctly or know that the criteria giving its meaning are satisfied in some particular case. These problems of meaning are philosophical and are the result of reflection. A person has natural relationships between his ideas, and as a result may use and apply *cause, effect,* etc., correctly, even though he may be unaware of why the objects or events he calls *causes* can be grouped together. To return to a previous example, most of us can use the words *table, chair,* etc., without difficulty, at least well enough to communicate successfully to others, even though we would be unable to define *chair* in a philosophically adequate manner.

We can now see that a cause-and-effect relationship holds between *R*-like and *S*-like objects if and only if they are constantly conjoined; that is, a particular *R*-like object is always followed by a particular *S*-like object when they are contiguous in place and time, and this is taken to be what we mean by cause and effect. But we never experience *all* these constant conjunctions, or at least we cannot be sure that we have experienced all of them. Consequently the definition does not enable us to determine *which* of the constant unions we have observed in the past can be appropriately projected into the future as a causal relationship. It might be thought that Hume would argue that we must wait to see when the *feeling* arises to make a projection. But this is not so. The philosophical analysis of the cause-and-effect relationship enables us to determine rules (Hume cites eight), satisfaction of which we may take to lead to the custom or habit that the conjunction be projected as a cause-and-effect relationship. This projection is then at least partly justified because the projected cause-and-effect relationship can be shown to have properties which are given by the philosophical *analysis* of the relationship of cause and effect.

The first three of these rules are an immediate result of the earlier analysis, namely, that the cause and effect which is projected must be contiguous in space and time, that the cause must precede the effect, and that a constant conjunction must be observed between cause and effect. The rest of the rules provide the test of the occurrence of *resemblance* postulated in the definition to hold between the particular causes and the particular effects of any cause-and-effect relationship. Hume's fourth rule is that the same cause has the same effect and that an effect always arises from some one cause. An apparent exception to this could arise if some range of causes preceded the same effect, but Hume's fifth rule stipulates that this occurrence signals some common quality in the range of apparent causes which is the true cause of the effect. Similarly, if two apparently similar causes have different effects, this signals at least one quality in which the causes must differ. This is Hume's rule six. An example of the application of this rule would be two chemicals which might look alike, but behave quite differently. We can conclude that their behavior is *not* a function of their appearance. The seventh rule tells us that if some cause is increased or decreased, the effect will be increased or decreased accordingly; and the eighth rule is that if something thought to be a cause should occur, and the supposed effect not follow, the supposed cause may not be a *complete* cause. These eight rules enable one to design more effective tests of observed conjunctions in order to determine which may be validly projected. The relative sophistication of contemporary experimental design by comparison to these simple rules is an indication that Hume's rules are inadequate as they stand. Still, Hume has the historical merit of pointing out that the philosophical problem is not one of finding a necessary connection leading to *true* prediction of the future, but that of analyzing the successful predictions of the past in an effort to obtain rules that would enable our projections into the future to be more systematic and orderly than they might otherwise be.

Readings from Hume

The selection from Hume consists of sections II through IV and part of section V of Hume's *An Enquiry concerning Human Understanding*. Hume's *Enquiry* is readily available in reasonably priced editions, such as the version in *The English Philosophers from Bacon to Mill* (E. A. Burtt, editor) published by Random House, Inc. in *The Modern Library*. This edition is reprinted here. The *Enquiry concerning Human Understanding* is Hume's restatement in a somewhat more popular form of the first part of his *Treatise of Human Nature,* to which it should be compared. Hume was disappointed at the reception of the *Treatise* (1739) by the literary world, and he wrote the *Enquiry* (1748) to promote an interest in, and understanding of, the important ideas which had been proposed in the *Treatise.* This situation, the existence of a major epistemological work and an introduction to it in a somewhat less convoluted style, is not uncommon in the history of philosophy. A troubling question when this occurs is that of deciding whether or not any discrepancy between the two versions is due to a reconsideration of issues which should affect a reading of the major work, or whether it is due to a desire to keep less important issues and distinctions from distracting a reader of the introduction. These problems are most acute when the introductory or popular work was written after the supposed major work, as in the case of Hume.

In the *Treatise,* for example, Hume attempted to distinguish between arithmetic and geometry on the grounds that we had a perfect assurance of the truths of arithmetic, making them *certain,* while geometrical propositions failed of this precision and were *informative* about the world without being certain. In the *Enquiry,* on the other hand, Hume seems to have argued that geometrical *and* arithmetical propositions represent certain truths. Many later empiricists have supposed that Hume was confused about the distinction between pure and applied mathematics which has been considerably clarified since his time. With the use of this distinction, we may say that the inferences in pure Euclidean geometry are as certain

191

as they are in arithmetic, but that when we identify *light ray* with *straight line*, etc., to get an applied geometry, we turn pure geometrical assertions into assertions about the world which may well turn out to be false. These empiricists would then hold that Hume's position in the *Enquiry* was really the superior one, and the one that Hume's philosophical insight later led him to prefer, on the grounds that geometry and arithmetic should both be considered first as pure calculi, or formal systems. But it is possible to hold that Hume never made up his mind, or that he really preferred the version in the *Treatise* and tried to simplify his discussion of mathematics for the general reader when he came to write the *Enquiry*.

Hume has achieved a considerable reputation as a man of letters for contributions to literature other than his primarily philosophical works. He wrote a *History of England*, for example, that made him famous both in France and in England during his own lifetime. His philosophical reputation is so great among philosophers that it is sometimes a surprise for philosophers to discover that in England he may be better known as David Hume the historian, than as David Hume the philosopher.

The following secondary sources may prove useful to the reader of the *Enquiry* and the *Treatise*.

Aaron, R. I.: *The Theory of Universals*, Oxford, 1952.
Aschenbrenner, Karl: "Psychologism in Hume," *Philosophical Quarterly*, vol. 11, pp. 28–38, 1961.
*Basson, A. H.: *David Hume*, Harmondsworth, 1958. (Pelican Paperbound.)
Church, R. W.: *Hume's Theory of the Understanding*, London, 1935.
Flew, A. G. N.: *Hume's Philosophy of Belief: A Study of His Inquiry*, New York, 1961.
Passmore, John: *Hume's Intentions*, London, 1952.
Price, H. H.: *Hume's Theory of the External World*, Oxford, 1940.
Smith, N. K.: *The Philosophy of David Hume*, London, 1960.
Zabeeh, F.: *Hume: Precursor of Modern Empiricism*, The Hague, 1960.

From Hume's *ENQUIRY*

SECTION II   OF THE ORIGIN OF IDEAS

Everyone will readily allow that there is a considerable difference between the perceptions of the mind, when a man feels the pain of excessive heat, or the pleasure of moderate warmth, and when he afterwards recalls to his memory this sensation, or anticipates it by his imagination.[1] These faculties may mimic or copy the perceptions of the senses; but they never can entirely reach the force and vivacity of the original sentiment.[2] The utmost we say of them, even when they operate with greatest vigor, is, that they represent their object in so lively a manner, that we could *almost* say we feel or see it: But, except the mind be disordered by disease or madness, they never can arrive at such a pitch of vivacity, as to render these perceptions altogether undistinguishable. All the colors of poetry, however splendid, can never paint natural objects in such a manner as to make the description be taken for a real landscape. The most lively thought is still inferior to the dullest sensation.

We may observe a like distinction to run through all the other perceptions of the mind. A man in a fit of anger, is actuated in a very different manner from one who only thinks of that emotion. If you tell me, that any person is in love, I easily understand your meaning, and form a just conception of his situation; but never can mistake that conception for the real disorders and agitations of the passion. When we reflect on our past sentiments and affections, our thought is a faithful mirror, and copies its objects truly; but the colors which it employs are faint and dull, in comparison of those in which our original perceptions were clothed. It requires no nice discernment or metaphysical head to mark the distinction between them.[3]

Here therefore we may divide all the perceptions of the mind into two classes or species, which are distinguished by their different degrees of force and vivacity.[4] The less forcible and lively are commonly denominated *thoughts* or *ideas*. The other species want a name in our language, and in most others; I suppose, because it was not requisite for any, but philosophical purposes, to rank them under a general term or appellation. Let us, therefore, use a little freedom, and call them *impressions;* employing that word in a sense different somewhat from the usual. By the term *impression*, then, I mean all our more lively perceptions, when we hear, or see, or feel, or love, or hate, or desire, or will. And impressions are distinguished from ideas, which are the less lively perceptions, of which we are conscious, when we reflect on any of those sensations or movements above mentioned.

Nothing, at first view, may seem more unbounded than the thought of man, which not only escapes all human power and authority, but is not even restrained within the limits of nature and reality. To form monsters, and join incongruous shapes and appearances, costs the imagination no more trouble than to conceive the most natural and familiar objects. And while the body is confined to one planet, along which it creeps with pain and difficulty; the thought can in an instant transport us into the most distant regions of the universe; or even beyond the universe, into the unbounded chaos, where nature is supposed to lie in total confusion. What never was seen, or heard of, may yet be conceived; nor is anything beyond the power of thought, except what implies an absolute contradiction.

But though our thought seems to possess this unbounded liberty, we shall find, upon a nearer examination, that it is really confined within very narrow limits, and that all this creative power of the mind amounts to no more than the faculty of compounding, transposing, augmenting, or diminishing the materials afforded us by the senses and experience.[5] When we think of a golden mountain, we only join two consistent ideas, *gold,* and *mountain,* with which we were formerly acquainted. A virtuous horse we can conceive; because, from our own feeling, we can conceive virtue; and this we may unite to the figure and shape of a horse, which is an animal familiar to us. In short, all the materials of thinking are derived either from our outward or inward sentiment: the mixture and composition of these belongs alone to the mind and will. Or, to express myself in philosophical language, all our ideas or more feeble perceptions are copies of our impressions or more lively ones.

To prove this, the two following arguments will, I hope, be sufficient. First, when we analyze our thoughts or ideas, however compounded or sublime, we always find that they resolve themselves into such simple ideas as were copied from a precedent feeling or sentiment. Even those ideas, which, at first view, seem the most wide of this origin, are found, upon a nearer scrutiny, to be derived from it. The idea of God, as meaning an infinitely intelligent, wise, and good Being, arises from reflecting on the operations of our own mind, and augmenting, without limit, those qualities of goodness and wisdom.[6] We may prosecute this inquiry to what length we please; where we shall always find, that every idea which we examine is copied from a similar impression.[7] Those who would assert that this position is not universally true nor without exception, have only one, and that an easy method of refuting it; by producing that idea, which, in their opinion, is not derived from this source. It will then be incumbent on us, if we would maintain our doctrine, to produce the impression, or lively perception, which corresponds to it.

Secondly. If it happen, from a defect of the organ, that a man is not susceptible of any species of sensation, we always find that he is as little susceptible of the correspondent ideas. A blind man can form no notion of colors; a deaf man of sounds. Restore either of them that sense in which he is deficient; by opening this new inlet for his sensations, you also open an inlet for the ideas; and he finds no difficulty in conceiving these objects. The case is the same, if the object, proper for exciting any sensation, has never been applied to the organ. A Laplander or Negro has no notion of the relish of wine. And though there are few or no instances of a like deficiency in the mind, where a person has never felt or is wholly incapable of a sentiment or passion that belongs to his species; yet we find the same observation to take place in a less degree. A man of mild manners can form no idea of inveterate revenge or cruelty; nor can a selfish heart easily conceive the heights of friendship and generosity. It is readily allowed, that other beings may possess many senses of which we can have no conception; because the ideas of them have never been introduced to us in the only manner by which an idea can have access to the mind, to wit, by the actual feeling and sensation.

There is, however, one contradictory phenomenon, which may prove that it is not absolutely impossible for ideas to arise, independent of their correspondent impressions. I believe it will readily be allowed, that the several distinct ideas of color, which enter by the eye, or those of sound, which are conveyed by the ear, are really different from each other; though, at the same time, resembling. Now if this be true of different colors, it must be no less so of the different shades of the same color; and each shade produces a distinct idea, independent of the rest. For if this should be denied, it is possible, by the continual gradation of shades, to run a color insensibly into what is most remote from it; and if you will not allow any of the means to be different, you cannot, without absurdity, deny the extremes to be the same. Suppose, therefore, a person to have enjoyed his sight for thirty years, and to have become perfectly acquainted with colors of all kinds except one particular shade of blue, for instance, which it never has been his fortune to meet with. Let all the different shades of that color, except that single one, be placed before him, descending gradually from the deepest to the lightest; it is plain that he will perceive a blank, where that shade is wanting, and will be sensible that there is a greater distance in that place between the contiguous colors than in any other. Now I ask, whether it be possible for him, from his own imagination, to supply this deficiency, and raise up to himself the idea of that particular shade, though it had never been conveyed to him by his senses ? I believe there are few but will be of opinion that he can: and this may serve as a proof that the simple ideas are not always, in every instance, derived from the correspondent impressions; though this instance is so singular, that it is scarcely worth our observing, and does not merit that for it alone we should alter our general maxim.[8]

Here, therefore, is a proposition, which not only seems, in itself, simple and intelligible; but, if a proper use were made of it, might render every dispute equally intelligible, and banish all that jargon, which has so long taken possession of metaphysical reasonings, and drawn disgrace upon them. All ideas, especially abstract ones, are naturally faint and obscure: the mind has but a slender hold of them: they are apt to be confounded with other resembling ideas; and when we have often employed any term, though without a distinct meaning, we are apt to imagine it has a determinate idea annexed to it. On the contrary, all impressions, that is, all sensations, either outward or inward, are strong and vivid: the limits between them are more exactly determined: nor is it easy to fall into any error or mistake with regard to them. When we entertain, therefore, any suspicion that a philosophical term is employed without any meaning or idea (as is but too frequent), we need but inquire, *from what impressions is that supposed idea derived* ? And if it be impossible to assign any, this will serve to confirm our suspicion.[9] By bringing ideas into so clear a light we may reasonably hope to remove all dispute, which may arise, concerning their nature and reality.

SECTION III   OF THE ASSOCIATION OF IDEAS

It is evident that there is a principle of connection between the different thoughts or ideas of the mind, and that, in their appearance to the memory or imagination, they introduce each other with a certain degree of method and regularity. In our more serious thinking or discourse this is so observable that any particular thought, which breaks in upon the regular tract or chain of ideas, is immediately remarked and rejected. And even in our wildest and most wandering reveries, nay in our very dreams, we shall find, if we reflect, that the imagination ran not altogether at adventures, but that there was still a connection upheld among the different ideas, which succeeded each other. Were the loosest and freest conversation to be transcribed, there would immediately be observed something which connected it in all its transitions. Or where this is wanting, the person who broke the thread of discourse might still inform you, that there had secretly revolved in his mind a succession of thought, which had gradually led him from the subject of conversation. Among different languages, even where we cannot suspect the least connection or communication, it is found, that the words, expressive of ideas, the most compounded, do yet nearly correspond to each other: a certain proof that the simple ideas, comprehended in the compound ones, were bound together by some universal principle, which had an equal influence on all mankind.

Though it be too obvious to escape observation, that different ideas are connected together; I do not find that any philosopher has attempted to enumerate or class all the principles of association; a subject, however, that seems worthy of curiosity. To me, there appear to be only three principles of connection among ideas, namely, *resemblance, contiguity* in time or place, and *cause or effect*.

That these principles serve to connect ideas will not, I believe, be much doubted. A picture naturally leads our thoughts to the original:[10] the mention of one apartment in a building naturally introduces an inquiry or discourse concerning the others:[11] and if we think of a wound, we can scarcely forbear reflecting on the pain which follows it.[12] But that this enumeration is complete, and that there are no other principles of association except these, may be difficult to prove to the satisfaction of the reader, or even to a man's own satisfaction. All we can do, in such cases, is to run over several instances, and examine carefully the principle which binds the different thoughts to each other, never stopping till we render the principle as general as possible.[13] The more instances we examine, and the more care we employ, the more assurance shall we acquire, that the enumeration, which we form from the whole, is complete and entire.

SECTION IV   SCEPTICAL DOUBTS CONCERNING THE OPERATIONS OF THE UNDERSTANDING

PART I

All the objects of human reason or enquiry may naturally be divided into two kinds, to wit, *Relations of Ideas*, and *Matters of Fact*. Of the first kind are the sciences of Geometry, Algebra, and Arithmetic; and in short, every affirmation which is either intuitively or demonstratively certain. *That the square of the hypotenuse is equal to the square of the two sides,* is a proposition which expresses a relation between these figures. *That three times five is equal to the half of thirty,* expresses a relation between these numbers. Propositions of this kind are discoverable by the mere operation of thought, without dependence on what is anywhere existent in the universe. Though there never were a circle or triangle in nature, the truths demonstrated by Euclid would for ever retain their certainty and evidence.

Matters of fact, which are the second objects of human reason, are not ascertained in the same manner; nor is our evidence of their truth, however great, of a like nature with the foregoing. The contrary of every matter of fact is still possible; because it can never imply a contradiction, and is conceived by the mind with the same facility and distinctness, as if ever so conformable to reality. *That the sun will not rise tomorrow* is no less intelligible a proposition, and implies no more contradiction than the affirmation, *that it will rise.* We should in vain, therefore, attempt to demonstrate its falsehood. Were it demonstratively false, it would imply a contradiction and could never be distinctly conceived by the mind.

It may, therefore, be a subject worthy of curiosity, to enquire what is the nature of that evidence which assures us of any real existence and matter of fact, beyond the present testimony of our senses, or the records of our memory. This part of philosophy, it is observable, has been little cultivated, either by the ancients or moderns; and therefore our doubts and errors, in the prosecution of so important an enquiry, may be the more excusable; while we march through such difficult paths without any guide or direction. They may even prove useful, by exciting curiosity, and destroying that implicit faith and security, which is the bane of all reasoning and free enquiry. The discovery of defects in the common philosophy, if any such there be, will not, I presume, be a discouragement, but rather an excitement, as is usual, to attempt something more full and satisfactory than has yet been proposed to the public.

All reasonings concerning matter of fact seem to be founded on the relation of *Cause and Effect.* By means of that relation alone we can go beyond the evidence of our memory and senses. If you were to ask a man, why he believes any matter of fact, which is absent; for instance, that his friend is in the country, or in France; he would give you a reason; and this reason would be some other fact; as a letter received from him, or the knowledge of his former resolutions and promises. A man finding a watch or any other machine in a desert island, would conclude that there had once been men on that island. All our reasonings concerning fact are of the same nature. And here it is constantly supposed that there is a con-nexion between the present fact and that which is inferred from it. Were there nothing to bind them together, the inference would be entirely precarious. The hearing of an articulate voice and rational discourse in the dark assures us of the presence of some person: Why? because these are the effects of the human make and fabric, and closely connected with it. If we anatomize all the other reasonings of this nature, we shall find that they are founded on the relation of cause and effect, and that this relation is either near or remote, direct or collateral. Heat and light are collateral effects of fire, and the one effect may justly be inferred from the other.

If we would satisfy ourselves, therefore, concerning the nature of that evidence, which assures us of matters of fact, we must enquire how we arrive at the knowledge of cause and effect.

I shall venture to affirm, as a general proposition, which admits of no exception, that the knowledge of this relation is not, in any instance, attained by reasonings *a priori*; but arises entirely from experience, when we find that any particular objects are constantly conjoined with each other. Let an object be presented to a man of ever so strong natural reason and abilities; if that object be entirely new to him, he will not be able, by the most accurate examination of its sensible qualities, to discover any of its causes or effects.[14] Adam, though his rational faculties be supposed, at the very first, entirely perfect, could not have inferred from the fluidity and transparency of water that it would suffocate him, or from the light and wamth of fire that it would consume him. No object ever discovers, by the qualities which appear to the senses, either the causes which produced it, or the effects which arise from it; nor can our reason, unassisted by experience, ever draw any inference concerning real existence and matter of fact.

This proposition, that causes and effects are discoverable, *not by reason but by experience,* will readily be admitted with regard to such ob-jects, as we remember to have once been altogether unknown to us; since we must be conscious of the utter inability, which we then lay under, of foretelling what would arise from them. Present two smooth pieces of marble to a man who has no tincture of natural philosophy; he will never discover that they will adhere together in such a manner as to require great force to separate them in a direct line, while they make so small a resistance to lateral pressure. Such events, as bear little analogy to the common course of nature, are also readily confessed to be known only by experience; nor does any man imagine that the explosion of gunpowder, or the attraction of a loadstone, could ever be discovered by arguments *a priori*. In like manner, when an effect is supposed to depend upon an intricate machinery or secret structure of parts, we make no difficulty in attributing all our knowledge of it to experience. Who will assert that he can give the ultimate reason, why milk or bread is proper nourishment for a man, not for a lion or a tiger?

But the same truth may not appear, at first sight, to have the same evidence with regard to events, which have become familiar to us from our first appearance in the world, which bear a close analogy to the whole course of nature, and which are supposed to depend on the simple qualities of objects, without any secret structure of parts. We are apt to imagine that we could discover these effects by the mere operation of our reason, without experience. We fancy, that were we brought on a sudden into this world, we could at first have inferred that one Billiard-ball would communicate motion to another upon impulse; and that we needed not to have waited for the event, in order to pronounce with certainty concerning it. Such is the influence of custom, that, where it is strongest, it not only covers our natural ignorance, but even conceals itself, and seems not to take place, merely because it is found in the highest degree.

But to convince us that all the laws of nature, and all the operations of bodies without exception, are known only by experience, the following reflections may, perhaps, suffice. Were any object presented to us, and were we required to pronounce concerning the effect, which will result from it, without consulting past observation; after what manner, I beseech you, must the mind proceed in this operation? It must invent or imagine some event, which it ascribes to the object as its effect; and it is plain that this invention must be entirely arbitrary. The mind can never possibly find the effect in the supposed cause, by the most accurate scrutiny and observation. For the effect is totally different from the cause, and consequently can never be discovered in it. Motion in the second Billiard-ball is a quite distinct event from motion in the first; nor is there anything in the one to suggest the smallest hint of the other. A stone or piece of metal raised into the air, and left without support, immediately falls: but to consider the matter *a priori*, is there anything we discover in this situation which can beget the idea of a downward, rather than an upward, or any other motion, in the stone or metal?

And as the first imagination or invention of a particular effect, in all natural operations, is arbitrary, where we consult not experience; so must we also esteem the supposed tie or connexion between the cause and effect, which binds them together, and renders it impossible that any other effect could result from the operation of that cause. When I see, for instance, a Billiard-ball moving in a straight line towards another; even suppose motion in the second ball should by accident be suggested to me, as the result of their contact or impulse; may I not conceive, that a hundred different events might as well follow from that cause? May not the first ball return in a straight line, or leap off from the second in any line or direction? All these suppositions are consistent and conceivable. Why then should we give preference to one, which is no more consistent or conceivable than the rest? All our reasonings a *priori* will never be able to show us any foundation for this preference.

In a word, then, every effect is a distinct event from its cause. It could not, therefore, be discovered in the cause, and the first invention or conception of it, a *priori*, must be entirely arbitrary. And even after it is suggested, the conjunction of it with the cause must appear equally arbitrary; since there are always many other effects, which, to reason, must seem fully as consistent and natural. In vain, therefore, should we pretend to determine any single event, or infer any cause or effect, without the assistance of observation and experience.

Hence we may discover the reason why no philosopher, who is rational and modest, has ever pretended to assign the ultimate cause of any natural operation, or to show distinctly the action of that power, which produces any single effect in the universe. It is confessed, that the utmost effort of human reason is to reduce the principles, productive of natural phenomena, to a greater simplicity, and to resolve the many particular effects into a few general causes, by means of reasonings from analogy, experience, and observation. But as to the causes of these general causes, we should in vain attempt their discovery; nor shall we ever be able to satisfy ourselves, by any particular explication of them. These ultimate springs and principles are totally shut up from human curiosity and enquiry. Elasticity, gravity, cohesion of parts, communication of motion by impulse; these are probably the ultimate causes and principles which we shall ever discover in nature; and we may esteem ourselves sufficiently happy, if, by accurate enquiry and reasoning, we can trace up the particular phenomena to, or near to, these general principles. The most perfect philosophy of the natural kind only staves off our ignorance a little longer: as perhaps the most perfect philosophy of the moral or metaphysical kind serves only to discover larger portions of it. Thus the observation of human blindness and weakness is the result of all philosophy, and meets us at every turn, in spite of our endeavors to elude or avoid it.

Nor is geometry, when taken into the assistance of natural philosophy, ever able to remedy this defect, or lead us into the knowledge of ultimate causes, by all that accuracy of reasoning for which it is so justly celebrated. Every part of mixed mathematics proceeds upon the supposition that certain laws are established by nature in her operations; and abstract reasonings are employed, either to assist experience in the discovery of these laws, or to determine their influence in particular instances, where it depends upon any precise degree of distance and quantity. Thus, it is a law of motion, discovered by experience, that the moment or force of any body in motion is in the compound ratio or proportion of its solid contents and its velocity; and consequently, that a small force may remove the greatest obstacle or raise the greatest weight, if, by any contrivance or machinery, we can increase the velocity of that force, so as to make it an overmatch for its antagonist.[15] Geometry assists us in the application of this law, by giving us the just dimensions of all the parts and figures which can enter into any species of machine; but still the discovery of the law itself is owing merely to experience, and all the abstract reasonings in the world could never lead us one step towards the knowledge of it. When we reason *a priori*, and consider merely any object or cause, as it appears to the mind, independent of all observation, it never could suggest to us the notion of any distinct object, such as its effect; much less, show us the inseparable and inviolable connexion between them. A man must be very sagacious who could discover by reasoning that crystal is the effect of heat, and ice of cold, without being previously acquainted with the operation of these qualities.

PART II

But we have not yet attained any tolerable satisfaction with regard to the question first proposed. Each solution still gives rise to a new question as difficult as the foregoing, and leads us on to farther enquiries. When it is asked, *What is the nature of all our reasonings concerning matter of fact?* the proper answer seems to be, that they are founded on the relation of cause and effect. When again it is asked, *What is the foundation of all our reasonings and conclusions concerning that relation?* it may be replied in one word, Experience. But if we still carry on our sifting humour, and ask, *What is the foundation of all conclusions from experience?* this implies a new question, which may be of more difficult solution and explication. Philosophers, that give themselves airs of superior wisdom and sufficiency, have a hard task when they encounter persons of inquisitive dispositions, who push them from every corner to which they retreat, and who are sure at last to bring them to some dangerous dilemma. The best expedient to prevent this confusion, is to be modest in our pretensions; and even to discover the difficulty ourselves before it is objected to us. By this means, we may make a kind of merit of our very ignorance.

I shall content myself, in this section, with an easy task, and shall pretend only to give a negative answer to the question here proposed.[16] I say then, that, even after we have experience of the operations of cause and effect, our conclusions from that experience are *not* founded on reasoning, or any process of the understanding. This answer we must endeavour both to explain and to defend.

It must certainly be allowed, that nature has kept us at a great distance from all her secrets, and has afforded us only the knowledge of a few superficial qualities of objects; while she conceals from us those powers and principles on which the influence of those objects entirely depends. Our senses inform us of the colour, weight, and consistence of bread; but neither sense nor reason can ever inform us of those qualities which fit it for the nourishment and support of a human body. Sight or feeling conveys an idea of the actual motion of bodies, but as to that wonderful force or power, which would carry on a moving body for ever in a continued change of place, and which bodies never lose but by communicating it to others; of this we cannot form the most distant conception. But notwithstanding this ignorance of natural powers and principles, we always presume, when we see like sensible qualities, that they have like secret powers, and expect that effects, similar to those which we have experienced, will follow from them. If a body of like colour and consistence with that bread, which we have formerly eaten, be presented to us, we make no scruple of repeating the experiment, and foresee, with certainty, like nourishment and support. Now this is a process of the mind or thought, of which I would willingly know the foundation. It is allowed on all hands that there is no known connexion between the sensible qualities and the secret powers; and consequently, that the mind is not led to form such a conclusion concerning their constant and regular conjunction, by anything which it knows of their nature. As to past *Experience*, it can be allowed to give *direct* and *certain* information of those precise objects only, and that precise period of time, which fell under its cognizance: but why this experience should be extended to future times, and to other objects, which for aught we know, may be only in appearance similar; this is the main question on which I would insist. The bread, which I formerly ate, nourished me; that is, a body of such sensible qualities was, at that time, endued with such secret powers: but does it follow, that other bread must also nourish me at another time, and that like sensible qualities must always be attended with like secret powers? The consequence seems nowise necessary. At least, it must be acknowledged that there is here a consequence drawn by the mind; that there is a certain step taken; a process of thought, and an inference, which wants to be explained. These two propositions are far from being the same, *I have found that such an object has always been attended with such an effect*, and *I foresee, that other objects, which are, in appearance, similar, will be attended with similar effects*. I shall allow, if you please, that the one proposition may justly be inferred from the other: I know, in fact, that it is always inferred. But if you insist that the inference is made by a chain of reasoning, I desire you to produce that chain of reasoning. The connexion between these propositions is not intuitive. There is required a medium, which may enable the mind to draw such an inference, if indeed it be drawn by reasoning and argument. What that medium is, I must confess, passes my comprehension; and it is incumbent on those to produce it, who assert that it really exists, and is the origin of all our conclusions concerning matter of fact.

This negative argument must certainly, in process of time, become altogether convincing, if many penetrating and able philosophers shall turn their enquiries this way and no one be ever able to discover any connecting proposition or intermediate step, which supports the understanding in this conclusion. But as the question is yet new, every reader may not trust so far to his own penetration, as to conclude, because an argument escapes his enquiry, that therefore it does not really exist. For this reason it may be requisite to venture upon a more difficult task; and enumerating all the branches of human knowledge, endeavour to show that none of them can afford such an argument.

All reasonings may be divided into two kinds, namely, demonstrative reasoning, or that concerning relations of ideas, and moral reasoning, or that concerning matter of fact and existence. That there are no demonstrative arguments in the case seems evident; since it implies no contradiction that the course of nature may change, and that an object, seemingly like those which we have experienced, may be attended with different or contrary effects. May I not clearly and distinctly conceive that a body, falling from the clouds, and which, in all other respects, resembles snow, has yet the taste of salt or feeling of fire? Is there any more intelligible proposition than to affirm, that all the trees will flourish in December and January, and decay in May and June? Now whatever is intelligible, and can be distinctly conceived, implies no contradiction, and can never be proved false by any demonstrative argument or abstract reasoning *a priori*.

If we be, therefore, engaged by arguments to put trust in past experience, and make it the standard of our future judgment, these arguments must be probable only, or such as regard matter of fact and real existence, according to the division above mentioned. But that there is no argument of this kind, must appear, if our explication of that species of reasoning be admitted as solid and satisfactory. We have said that all arguments concerning existence are founded on the relation of cause and effect; that our knowledge of that relation is derived entirely from experience; and that all our experimental conclusions proceed upon the supposition that the future will be conformable to the past. To endeavour, therefore, the proof of this last supposition by probable arguments, or arguments regarding existence, must be evidently going in a circle, and taking that for granted, which is the very point in question.

In reality, all arguments from experience are founded on the similarity which we discover among natural objects, and by which we are induced to expect effects similar to those which we have found to follow from such objects. And though none but a fool or madman will ever pretend to dispute the authority of experience, or to reject that great guide of human life, it may surely be allowed a philosopher to have so much curiosity at least as to examine the principle of human nature, which gives this mighty authority to experience, and makes us draw advantage from that similarity which nature has placed among different objects. From causes which appear *similar* we expect similar effects. This is the sum of all our experimental conclusions. Now it seems evident that, if this conclusion were formed by reason, it would be as perfect at first, and upon one instance, as after ever so long a course of experience. But the case is far otherwise. Nothing so like as eggs; yet no one, on account of this appearing similarity, expects the same taste and relish in all of them. It is only after a long course of uniform experiments in any kind, that we attain a firm reliance and security with regard to a particular event. Now where is that process of reasoning which, from one instance, draws a conclusion, so different from that which it infers from a hundred instances that are nowise different from that single one? This question I propose as much for the sake of information, as with an intention of raising difficulties. I cannot find, I cannot imagine any such reasoning. But I keep my mind still open to instruction, if any one will vouchsafe to bestow it on me.

Should it be said that, from a number of uniform experiments, we *infer* a connexion between the sensible qualities and the secret powers; this, I must confess, seems the same difficulty, couched in different terms. The question still recurs, on what process of argument this *inference* is founded? Where is the medium, the interposing ideas, which join propositions so very wide of each other? It is confessed that the colour, consistence, and other sensible qualities of bread appear not, of themselves, to have any connexion with the secret powers of nourishment and support. For otherwise we could infer these secret powers from the first appearance of these sensible qualities, without the aid of experience; contrary to the sentiment of all philosophers, and contrary to plain matter of fact. Here, then, is our natural state of ignorance with regard to the powers and influence of all objects. How is this remedied by experience? It only shows us a number of uniform effects, resulting from certain objects, and teaches us that those particular objects, at that particular time, were endowed with such powers and forces. When a new object, endowed with similar sensible qualities, is produced, we expect similar powers and forces, and look for a like effect. From a body of like colour and consistence with bread we expect like nourishment and support. But this surely is a step or progress of the mind, which wants to be explained. When a man says, *I have found, in all past instances, such sensible qualities conjoined with such secret powers:* And when he says, *Similar sensible qualities will always be conjoined with similar secret powers,* he is not guilty of a tautology, nor are these propositions in any respect the same. You say that the one proposition is an inference from the other. But you must confess that the inference is not intuitive; neither is it demonstrative: Of what nature is it, then? To say it is experimental, is begging the question. For all inferences from experience suppose, as their foundation, that the future will resemble the past, and that similar powers will be conjoined with similar sensible qualities. If there be any suspicion that the course of nature may change, and that the past may be no rule for the future, all experience becomes useless, and can give rise to no inference or conclusion. It is impossible, therefore that any arguments from experience can prove this resemblance of the past to the future; since all these arguments are founded on the supposition of that resemblance. Let the course of things be allowed hitherto ever so regular; that alone, without some new argument or inference, proves not that, for the future, it will continue so. In vain do you pretend to have learned the nature of bodies from your past experience. Their secret nature, and consequently all their effects and influence, may change, without any change in their sensible qualities. This happens sometimes, and with regard to some objects: Why may it not happen always and with regard to all objects? What logic, what process of argument secures you against this supposition? My practice, you say, refutes my doubts. But you mistake the purport of my question. As an agent, I am quite satisfied in the point; but as a philosopher, who has some share of curiosity, I will not say scepticism, I want to learn the foundation of this inference. No reading, no enquiry has yet been able to remove my difficulty, or give me satisfaction in a matter of such importance. Can I do better than propose the difficulty to the public, even though, perhaps, I have small hopes of obtaining a solution? We shall at least, by this means, be sensible of our ignorance, if we do not augment our knowledge.

I must confess that a man is guilty of unpardonable ignorance who concludes, because an argument has escaped his own investigation, that therefore it does not really exist. I must confess that, though all the learned, for several ages, should have employed themselves in fruitless search upon any subject, it may still, perhaps, be rash to conclude positively that the subject must, therefore, pass all human comprehension. Even though we examine all the sources of our knowledge, and conclude them unfit for such a subject, there may still remain a suspicion, that the enumeration is not complete, or the examination not accurate. But with regard to the present subject, there are some considerations which seem to remove all this accusation of arrogance or suspicion of mistake.

It is certain that the most ignorant and stupid peasants—nay infants, nay even brute beasts—improve by experience, and learn the qualities of natural objects, by observing the effects which result from them. When a child has felt the sensation of pain from touching the flame of a candle, he will be careful not to put his hand near any candle; but will expect a similar effect from a cause which is similar in its sensible qualities and appearance. If you assert, therefore, that the understanding of the child is led into this conclusion by any process of argument or ratiocination, I may justly require you to produce that argument; nor have you any pretence to refuse so equitable a demand. You cannot say that the argument is abstruse, and may possibly escape your enquiry; since you confess that it is obvious to the capacity of a mere infant. If you hesitate, therefore, a moment, or if, after reflection, you produce any intricate or profound argument, you, in a manner, give up the question, and confess that it is not reasoning which engages us to suppose the past resembling the future, and to expect similar effects from causes which are, to appearance, similar. This is the proposition which I intended to enforce in the present section. If I be right, I pretend not to have made any mighty discovery. And if I be wrong, I must acknowledge myself to be indeed a very backward scholar; since I cannot now discover an argument which, it seems, was perfectly familiar to me long before I was out of my cradle.

SECTION V   SCEPTICAL SOLUTION OF THESE DOUBTS

PART I

The passion for philosophy, like that for religion, seems liable to this inconvenience, that, though it aims at the correction of our manners, and extirpation of our vices, it may only serve, by imprudent management, to foster a predominant inclination, and push the mind, with more determined resolution, towards that side which already *draws* too much, by the bias and propensity of the natural temper. It is certain that, while we aspire to the magnanimous firmness of the philosophic sage, and endeavour to confine our pleasures altogether within our own minds, we may, at last, render our philosophy like that of Epictetus, and other *Stoics*, only a more refined system of selfishness, and reason ourselves out of all virtue as well as social enjoyment.[17] While we study with attention the vanity of human life, and turn all our thoughts towards the empty and transitory nature of riches and honours, we are, perhaps, all the while flattering our natural indolence, which, hating the bustle of the world, and drudgery of business, seeks a pretence of reason to give itself a full and uncontrolled indulgence. There is, however, one species of philosophy which seems little liable to this inconvenience, and that because it strikes in with no disorderly passion of the human mind, nor can mingle itself with any natural affection or propensity; and that is the Academic or Sceptical philosophy. The academics always talk of doubt and suspense of judgment, of danger in hasty determinations, of confining to very narrow bounds the enquiries of the understanding, and of renouncing all speculations which lie not within the limits of common life and practice. Nothing, therefore, can be more contrary than such a philosophy to the supine indolence of the mind, its rash arrogance, its lofty pretensions, and its superstitious credulity. Every passion is mortified by it, except the love of truth; and that passion never is, nor can be, carried to too high a degree. It is surprising, therefore, that this philosophy, which, in almost every instance, must be harmless and innocent, should be the subject of so much groundless reproach and obloquy. But, perhaps, the very circumstance which renders it so innocent is what chiefly exposes it to the public hatred and resentment. By flattering no irregular passion, it gains few partizans: By opposing so many vices and follies, it raises to itself abundance of enemies, who stigmatize it as libertine, profane, and irreligious.

Nor need we fear that this philosophy, while it endeavours to limit our enquiries to common life, should ever undermine the reasonings of common life, and carry its doubts so far as to destroy all action, as well as speculation. Nature will always maintain her rights, and prevail in the end over any abstract reasoning whatsoever. Though we should conclude, for instance, as in the foregoing section, that, in all reasonings from experience, there is a step taken by the mind which is not supported by any argument or process of the understanding; there is no danger that these reasonings, on which almost all knowledge depends, will ever be affected by such a discovery. If the mind be not engaged by argument to make this step, it must be induced by some other principle of equal weight and authority; and that principle will preserve its influence as long as human nature remains the same. What that principle is may well be worth the pains of enquiry.

Suppose a person, though endowed with the strongest faculties of reason and reflection, to be brought on a sudden into this world; he would, indeed, immediately observe a continual succession of objects, and one event following another; but he would not be able to discover anything farther. He would not, at first, by any reasoning, be able to reach the idea of cause and effect; since the particular powers, by which all natural operations are performed, never appear to the senses; nor is it reasonable to conclude, merely because one event, in one instance, precedes another, that therefore the one is the cause, the other the effect. Their conjunction may be arbitrary and casual. There may be no reason to infer the existence of one from the appearance of the other. And in a word, such a person, without more experience, could never employ his conjecture or reasoning concerning any matter of fact, or be assured of anything beyond what was immediately present to his memory and senses.

Suppose, again, that he has acquired more experience, and has lived so long in the world as to have observed familiar objects or events to be constantly conjoined together; what is the consequence of this experience? He immediately infers the existence of one object from the appearance of the other. Yet he has not, by all his experience, acquired any idea or knowledge of the secret power by which the one object produces the other; nor is it, by any process of reasoning, he is engaged to draw this inference. But still he finds himself determined to draw it: And though he should be convinced that his understanding has no part in the operation, he would nevertheless continue in the same course of thinking. There is some other principle which determines him to form such a conclusion.

This principle is Custom or Habit. For wherever the repetition of any particular act or operation produces a propensity to renew the same act or operation, without being impelled by any reasoning or process of the understanding, we always say, that this propensity is the effect of *Custom*. By employing that word, we pretend not to have given the ultimate reason of such a propensity. We only point out a principle of human nature, which is universally acknowledged, and which is well known by its effects. Perhaps we can push our enquiries no farther, or pretend to give the cause of this cause; but must rest contented with it as the ultimate principle, which we can assign, of all our conclusions from experience. It is sufficient satisfaction, that we can go so far, without repining at the narrowness of our faculties because they will carry us no farther. And it is certain we here advance a very intelligible proposition at least, if not a true one, when we assert that, after the constant conjunction of two objects—heat and flame, for instance, weight and solidity—we are determined by custom alone to expect the one from the appearance of the other. This hypothesis seems even the only one which explains the difficulty, why we draw, from a thousand instances, an inference which we are not able to draw from one instance, that is, in no respect, different from them.[18] Reason is incapable of any such variation. The conclusions which it draws from considering one circle are the same which it would form upon surveying all the circles in the universe. But no man, having seen only one body move after being impelled by another, could infer that every other body will move after a like impulse. All inferences from experience, therefore, are effects of custom, not of reasoning.[19]

Custom, then, is the great guide of human life. It is that principle alone which renders our experience useful to us, and makes us expect, for the future, a similar train of events with those which have appeared in the past. Without the influence of custom, we should be entirely ignorant of every matter of fact beyond what is immediately present to the memory and senses. We should never know how to adjust means to ends, or to employ our natural powers in the production of any effect. There would be an end at once of all action, as well as of the chief part of speculation.

But here it may be proper to remark, that though our conclusions from experience carry us beyond our memory and senses, and assure us of matters of fact which happened in the most distant places and most remote ages, yet some fact must always be present to the senses or memory, from which we may first proceed in drawing these conclusions. A man, who should find in a desert country the remains of pompous buildings, would conclude that the country had, in ancient times, been cultivated by civilized inhabitants; but did nothing of this nature occur to him, he could never form such an inference. We learn the events of former ages from history; but then we must peruse the volumes in which this instruction is maintained, and thence carry up our inferences from one testimony to another, till we arrive at the eyewitnesses and spectators of these distant events. In a word, if we proceed not upon some fact, present to the memory or senses, our reasonings would be merely hypothetical; and however the particular links might be connected with each other, the whole chain of inferences would have nothing to support it, nor could we ever, by its means, arrive at the knowledge of any real existence. If I ask why you believe any particular matter of fact, which you relate, you must tell me some reason; and this reason will be some other fact, connected with it. But as you cannot proceed after this manner, *in infinitum*, you must at last terminate in some fact, which is present to your memory or senses; or must allow that your belief is entirely without foundation.

What, then, is the conclusion of the whole matter? A simple one; though, it must be confessed, pretty remote from the common theories of philosophy. All belief of matter of fact or real existence is derived merely from some object, present to the memory or senses, and a customary conjunction between that and some other object. Or in other words; having found, in many instances, that any two kinds of objects—flame and heat, snow and cold—have always been conjoined together; if flame or snow be present anew to the senses, the mind is carried by custom to expect heat or cold, and to *believe* that such a quality does exist, and will discover itself upon a nearer approach. This belief is the necessary result of placing the mind in such circumstances. It is an operation of the soul, when we are so situated, as unavoidable as to feel the passion of love, when we receive benefits; or hatred, when we meet with injuries. All these operations are a species of natural instincts, which no reasoning or process of the thought and understanding is able either to produce or to prevent.

NOTES

1   This appeal to introspection seems to have been taken by the empiricists as a method of proof of their theories. Philonous, in Berkeley's *Dialogues*, challenged Hylas to frame an abstract idea. Hume is also constantly challenging the reader to introspect, for example, to understand differences in vividness between ideas and impressions. It may be asked whether these challenges by empiricists are entirely fair, since it is not clear how one could introspect and find the claims of the empiricists to be mistaken. An empiricist might always inform a recalcitrant introspector that he was not introspecting carefully enough. As a result, the introspective tests mentioned by Berkeley and Hume are not really convincing experiments. It is interesting to consider whether any mental image of any particular thing, no matter how familiar we might be with it in the ordinary sense, could be clear enough that we could answer all of the questions which might be asked about the particular thing by some philosophical adversary.

2   *Sentiment*, as used by Hume, might be translated into *feeling* or *awareness* in order to capture his meaning. The point is that Hume's *sentiment* is not as subjective as *sentiment* may be now in such contexts as "He expressed his sentiments about the book.".

3   *Nice* is a word which has received outrageous treatment in ordinary discourse, having come to be applied to almost everything which is at least mildly agree-

able. Hume's *nice* might be replaced as you read by *precise* or *discriminating*, either of which would be close to his meaning.

4   *Perception* has a multitude of philosophical uses. Here it occurs in the phrase 'perceptions of the mind', where it suggests whatever the mind is conscious of. By a kind of philosophical convention, the word *idea* is used to describe whatever is presented to the mind (This is true in Plato, Descartes, and Berkeley, as we have seen.), but Hume wants to make a crucial distinction between kinds of mental presentations in terms of vivacity. If the distinction is legitimate, how could Berkeley have maintained it?

5   Apparently, what Hume calls thought is what Descartes called imagination. See the discussion of imagination in the *First Meditation.*

6   The example of God seems a poor choice to illustrate Hume's point. Surely many theists would argue that the concept of God is a perfect illustration that not all ideas can be derived from sense experience, and Descartes explicitly took this view. Further, the notion of augmenting qualities without limit used by Hume in this sentence seems to be a stronger mental operation than empiricism can readily admit, even though Hume uses the word *augment* above in describing mental operations. We might legitimately request that Hume expand his explanation of augmentation.

7   That is, any idea that we have must be copied from impressions having qualities involved in the idea. The use of *copied* here seems much weaker than the *augmentation* allowed in the case of the idea of God.

8   This entire paragraph can be met only with astonishment. Hume has proposed a rule that ideas can always be resolved into impressions, a rule that he claims must *always* hold. Then he produces a counterexample, accepts it, but says that it is scarcely worth observing, and retains his general rule. What can we make of this? Perhaps Hume took the formation of the idea of this shade of blue to be such a small augmentation of impressions that it could be ignored, but this approach has severe consequences with respect to the purpose of his division of perceptions of the mind into two sharp classes. It might also be suggested that Hume should just change his mind on this point in order to preserve consistency, although it is awkward with respect to common sense. There are some grounds for supposing that Hume never became entirely clear in his own mind as to a distinction between using certain words correctly and being able to frame ideas corresponding to them. A blind man, for example, might not be able to have mental images of color (although even this does not seem logically impossible), even though he may be able to use color words like *red* correctly. Similarly, a person not acquainted with the missing shade of blue of the example might be able to say true things about it. Rationalists would explain this by means of abstract ideas which are not available to Hume. Perhaps Hume should distinguish between correct verbal behavior and the ability to frame images. But then a Humean rejoinder might be that correct verbal usage requires knowledge of syntactical regularities that could be stated only by inductive inference from observed language samples. On the other hand, these regularities might be syntactical *conventions,* but the topic is too difficult to treat here.

9   (The following footnote is Hume's.) It is probable that no more was meant by those, who denied innate ideas, than that all ideas were copies of our impres-

sions; though it must be confessed, that the terms, which they employed, were
not chosen with such caution, nor so exactly defined, as to prevent all mistakes
about their doctrine. For what is meant by *innate?* If innate be equivalent to
natural, then all the perceptions and ideas of the mind must be allowed to be
innate or natural, in whatever sense we take the latter word, whether in opposition to what is uncommon, artificial, or miraculous. If by innate be meant,
contemporary to our birth, the dispute seems to be frivolous; nor is it worth
while to inquire at what time thinking begins, whether before, at, or after our
birth. Again, the word *idea,* seems to be commonly taken in a very loose sense,
by Locke and others; as standing for any of our perceptions, our sensations and
passions, as well as thoughts. Now in this sense, I should desire to know, what
can be meant by asserting, that self-love, or resentment of injuries, or the passion between the sexes is not innate?

By admitting these terms, *impressions* and *ideas,* in the sense above explained, and understanding by *innate,* what is original or copied from no
precedent perception, then we may assert that all our impressions are innate
and our ideas not innate.

To be ingenuous, I must own it to be my opinion, that Locke was be-
trayed into this question by the schoolmen, who, making use of undefined
terms, draw out their disputes to a tedious length, without ever touching the
point in question. A like ambiguity and circumlocution seem to run through
that philosopher's reasonings on this as well as most other subjects.

10   (The following footnote is Hume's.) Resemblance.

11   (The following footnote is Hume's.) Contiguity.

12   (The following footnote is Hume's.) Cause and effect.

13   (The following footnote is Hume's.) For instance, *contrast* or *contrariety* is also
a connection among ideas but it may, perhaps, be considered as a mixture of
causation and *resemblance.* Where two objects are contrary, the one destroys
the other; that is, the cause of its annihilation and the idea of the annihilation
of an object implies the idea of its former existence.

14   The defensibility of this claim is considerably helped by the locution 'entirely
new to him'. It is not clear what an entirely new object would be, or even if one
could be noticed, unless we define it as an object whose causes and effects we
could not discover, making the claim true by definition. What Hume is concerned to establish, however, seems to follow from the *surprising* causes and
effects we come to discern in some new objects of experience.

15   To the scientifically trained reader, Hume's remarks about force and momentum will not make good sense, since his description of the formulas is not quite
right when read in terms of present-day scientific vocabulary. His underlying
point, that laws of motion were discovered experimentally, is entirely sound.
There is, however, a problem in his remark that the discovery of the law owes
merely to experience (see the next sentence), since experiment *suggested* the
laws, historically, but experiment (because of error) must be conceptually
simplified and analyzed if its results are to be equivalent to consequences of the
relevant law. Further, once a law is adopted, it is not treated simply as a generalization from experience. For these topics, see Norwood Russell Hanson's
Patterns of Discovery, Cambridge, 1958, and R. B. Braithwaite's *Scientific Explanation,* Cambridge, 1955.

16   Why does Hume say that he will *pretend* only to give a negative answer? Because he later proposes that consideration of custom or habit will enable a solution of the problem.

17   Epictetus and the Stoics believed that involvement in the affairs of others, or too much desire in pursuit of our own ends, was certain to end in failure, frustration, and unhappiness. This followed from their view that events were completely determined, and hence one could only accept what would happen anyway. Consequently they counseled diminution of desire as much as possible, and contemplation of the determined universe as a philosophical goal and as a means of avoiding unhappiness. Hume points out that consistently following Stoical principles is a form of selfishness (in so far as avoidance of personal unhappiness is a goal), and a kind of behavior that removes all chance of moral action.

18   How may a thousand instances all be the same as some one instance? Although it seems a natural principle that our belief in some regularity should increase as observed instances of it increase, the number of observed instances is not, in some cases, as important as the differences between the instances. If some number of instances widely varying in spatio-temporal location and other features all confirm some regularity, we may believe the regularity to hold more strongly than some regularity whose confirming instances are greater in number, but much more similar in terms of spatio-temporal location, etc. These features of the confirmation of a regularity by consideration of instances of it are not adequately treated by Hume.

19   (The following footnote is Hume's.) Nothing is more useful than for writers, even, on *moral, political,* or *physical* subjects, to distinguish between *reason* and *experience,* and to suppose, that these species of argumentation are entirely different from one another. The former are taken for the mere result of our intellectual faculties, which, by considering *a priori* the nature of things, and examining the effects, that must follow from their operation, establish particular principles of science and philosophy. The latter are supposed to be derived entirely from sense and observation, by which we learn what has actually resulted from the operation of particular objects, and are thence able to infer, what will, for the future, result from them. Thus, for instance, the limitations and restraints of civil government, and a legal constitution, may be defended, either from *reason,* which reflecting on the great frailty and corruption of human nature, teaches, that no man can safely be trusted with unlimited authority; or from *experience* and history, which inform us of the enormous abuses, that ambition, in every age and country, has been found to make of so imprudent a confidence.

    The same distinction between reason and experience is maintained in all our deliberations concerning the conduct of life; while the experienced statesman, general, physician, or merchant is trusted and followed; and the unpracticed novice, with whatever natural talents endowed, neglected and despised. Though it be allowed, that reason may form very plausible conjectures with regard to the consequences of such a particular conduct in such particular circumstances; it is still supposed imperfect, without the assistance of experience, which is alone able to give stability and certainty to the maxims, derived from study and reflection.

    But notwithstanding that this distinction be thus universally received, both in the active and speculative scenes of life, I shall not scruple to pronounce, that it is, at bottom, erroneous, at least, superficial.

If we examine those arguments, which, in any of the sciences above mentioned, are supposed to be the mere effects of reasoning and reflection, they will be found to terminate, at last, in some general principle or conclusion, for which we can assign no reason but observation and experience. The only difference between them and those maxims, which are vulgarly esteemed the result of pure experience, is, that the former cannot be established without some process of thought, and some reflection on what we have observed, in order to distinguish its circumstances, and trace its consequences: Whereas in the latter, the experienced event is exactly and fully familiar to that which we infer as the result of any particular situation. The history of a Tiberius or a Nero makes us dread a like tyranny, were our monarchs freed from the restraints of laws and senates. But the observation of any fraud or cruelty in private life is sufficient, with the aid of a little thought, to give us the same apprehension; while it serves as an instance of the general corruption of human nature, and shows us the danger which we must incur by reposing an entire confidence in mankind. In both cases, it is experience which is the foundation of our inference and conclusion.

There is no man so young and unexperienced, as not to have formed, from observation, many general and just maxims concerning human affairs and the conduct of life; but it must be confessed, that, when a man comes to put these in practice, he will be extremely liable to error, till time and farther experience both enlarge these maxims, and teach him their proper use and application. In every situation or incident, there are many particular and seemingly minute circumstances, which the man of greatest talent is, at first, apt to overlook, though on them the justness of his conclusions, and consequently the prudence of his conduct, entirely depend. Not to mention, that, to a young beginner, the general observations and maxims occur not always on the proper occasions, nor can be immediately applied with due calmness and distinction. The truth is, an unexperienced reasoner could be no reasoner at all, were he absolutely unexperienced; and when we assign that character to anyone, we mean it only in a comparative sense, and suppose him possessed of experience, in a smaller and more imperfect degree.

PART 6

Kant

(1724–1804)

Kant's Synthesis

It is time to reflect momentarily on the status of rationalism and empiricism as they have been developed by the philosophers we have studied to this point. This is true because the history of philosophy indicates that the corrosive effects of Hume's empirical skepticism, as well as the limitations of rationalism in accounting for scientific statements that were obviously to be considered part of human knowledge, but which apparently lacked the *certainty* or *necessity* of rationalistic knowledge, resulted in a temporary impasse for philosophical epistemologists after the publication of Hume's *Treatise.* If scientific knowledge is to be plausibly justified, it is apparent that neither rationalism nor empiricism, as they have been characterized so far, can accomplish the task. Our simplified versions of the philosophers we have studied have concealed tensions and problems indicated in their writings which yield the suspicion that most of the great philosophers at least *suspected* that difficulties would force abandonment of either program if it was developed with uncompromising rigor. In fact, the writings of most philosophers contain elements of both rationalism and empiricism, although the major attempts to construct complete theories of knowledge before Kant had been along either of the two incompatible lines that have previously been indicated. By the eighteenth century, problems of philosophical epistemology, coupled with two centuries of accumulating scientific success *in spite of* no sound philosophical justification for the commonsense procedures adopted by most scientists, made it clear that a new approach to epistemology would have to be tried. The next two philosophers that we shall study, Kant and Peirce, represent modified rationalistic and empiricistic epistemologies, respectively, in that they attempted to adapt sound features of rationalism and empiricism to the problem of developing a theory of knowledge that would justify burgeoning scientific theory. Although the problem of developing such a theory of knowledge will not be pursued into contemporary issues, we may note that there is a severe contemporary problem in that scientists in such areas as nuclear

217

physics and astrophysics are now dealing with objects and distances so small or so large, that the commonsense methodological rules of the theories of knowledge of the past have turned out to be decidedly inadequate. Extrapolations from observations of objects with which we can deal easily because of their sizes and distances to submicroscopic and intergalactic events have proved spectacular failures. In quantum physics, scientists themselves are concerned with their methodological inability to choose between conflicting interpretations of submicroscopic events. In astronomical theory, they are concerned with their inability to choose between steady-state and evolutionary theories of the universe. These controversies have led some scientists to realize that problems of justifying methodology are not simply a philosopher's pastime, in that normative methodological problems may be encountered in scientific theorizing at very crucial moments. To some extent, this has resulted in a *rapprochement* between philosophers concerned with justifying current scientific knowledge in terms of some epistemology, and those scientists concerned with improving their understanding of the ways in which methodology may be justified.

An obvious approach to the difficulty suggested above, that both rationalism and empiricism are inadequate, is to try to *combine* them. We might suppose that we could *synthesize* rationalism and empiricism by accepting a rationalistic epistemology to justify the mathematical knowledge required by science, and an empiricistic epistemology to explain scientific observations. Kant's importance to the history of philosophy was in seeing that a profoundly *new* methodology was required, not merely a combination of the two older ones. It is true that Kant speaks of his philosophy as a synthesis of rationalism and empiricism, but this does not indicate that scientific knowledge consists of bits and pieces each of which can be accounted for either in terms of pre-Kantian rationalism or of pre-Kantian empiricism. Kant's point is that all important instances of scientific knowledge are the result of observation *and* thought, empiricistic *and* rationalistic elements, *neither of which is intelligible without the other.* In a way, this may remind you of Aristotle's position, to which Kant owes some historical indebtedness. But where Aristotle took *experience* to be analyzable into material and formal aspects, and hence into empiricistic and rationalistic components, Kant took the different position that no observation could make *sense* or be *meaningful* unless prior thought not based on experience is presupposed. Instead of analyzing *primitive* experience into differing empiricistic and rationalistic components, Kant takes experience to be what it is because of the way we interpret it by means of the concepts that we bring to our experiences. Our experimental experiences do not simply exhibit order; they are orderly because we look for the order in them. We can *understand* them only by means of a prior conceptual framework which is built up out of a mental comprehension of order. We may take this conception of an interaction between experience and thought to be Kant's major contribution to epistemology. Kant's position is here taken to be a modified rationalism rather than a modified empiricism because he holds that the prior concepts we bring to experience may have the certainty and necessity that rationalists before him had attributed to what they called *knowledge*.

Kant's notion of an experience is considerably more complex than the notion of an experience which the empiricists before him had used. If we consider the illustration of two men standing in front of a painting, we have seen that there is a sense in which they can both be said to see_1 the same thing, but another sense in which they see_2 quite different things. Empiricism before Kant had a tendency to make sense perceptions like $seeing_1$ the foundation of human knowledge. This foundation was a kind of lowest common denominator of sense perception. The difficulty in this view was that the empiricist was then required to explain $seeing_2$ differences in terms of other sense experiences. As we have seen, this problem proves difficult in view of the commonsense observation that three people, A, B, and C, may be such that A and B see_2 something more similarly than A and C or B and C, even though the $seeing_1$ histories of A and C are more similar than the $seeing_1$ histories of A and B or B and C. This may be true if A and C are identical twins brought up in a similar environment while B is a stranger to both. The problem of accounting for differences in $seeing_2$ experiences proves refractory for empiricism. On the other hand, by making the foundation of scientific knowledge $seeing_2$ sense experiences and perceptions like it, Kant eliminates this difficulty while gaining the advantage of making his account fit our common observation that a trained observer and a tyro are said to be different because they *see* things differently. But these advantages are purchased at the cost of making perception a rationalistic experience that can no longer serve as an empirical primitive notion since perception now essentially involves, not just sense experience, but knowledge gained through judgment which is based on concepts developed prior to sense experiences.

To see how Kant took experience to be shaped by prior concepts, we may consider the problem of individuation. A general method for answering problems of individuation must enable us to tell in any case whether or not x and y (construed as two names or descriptions of objects) refer to the same individual object or not. Strictly speaking, it would appear that empiricism must hold that x and y refer to the same individual if and only if x and y may be analyzed as standing for the same tastes, colors, and so forth. According to Kant, this method is defective. Two objects might have all their empirically sensed properties so similar as to be indistinguishable, yet they might clearly be *different* objects because they occupied different spatial or temporal regions. Kant held that the two conditions, space and time, were necessary for individuating all objects of experience, and yet empiricists had never provided a way of directly experiencing a difference in space or in time. Since empiricists had provided no adequate justification for space and time as they are used in science (this seems largely true as an historical observation), and as many previous philosophers (some rationalists) had not included space and time as part of the complete description of objects, Kant's analysis of the importance of adequate concepts of space and time is a valuable insight. Kant's view is that space and time are not seen or heard like other empirical properties, and he holds that they are not abstracted from immediate sense experiences; he contends instead that immediate sense experience would be meaningless unless space and time are presupposed to be known in immediate sense experience. We do not see space or time, we see things in space and time. We could not, in fact, imagine what it would be like to see something that was not in space and time. This indicates that we must know space and time prior to experiencing objects in them.

Kant employs a distinction between the form and matter of experienced objects which is derived from the Aristotelian analysis. The matter of an object of experience is whatever appearances sense experience presents to the mind. The matter of an experience is thus its highly variable sensual content. Space and time, being present in every such experience in that we cannot experience or imagine objects without assigning them a location in space and time (Be careful! This means that although we may not imagine centaurs as living in some place and at some time, we cannot imagine a centaur as taking up *no* space or time.), are the *form* of sensed objects. Although any specified sense property may be *missing* in a given sense experience, *all* sense experiences have spatial and temporal properties. An observation of nothing but a uniform red field and an observation of nothing but a blue field would have the same spatial *form*, but different empirical content or matter.

Space is what Kant calls the form of outer intuitions, time the form of inner intuitions. *Intuition* is used here in a sense quite different than the sense suggested earlier in defining *rationalism*. *Intuition* was used in that connection to refer to the faculty invoked by rationalists to account for *certain* knowledge about non-sense-experienced objects. Kant uses *intuition* as almost synonymous with *sensation*, in that it suggests an immediate awareness of something. But it must also be observed that what Kant calls *empirical intuition* corresponds more strictly to *sensation*, since Kant held that we can have *pure intuitions* (immediate awarenesses) of the a priori particulars space and time.

Kantian space cannot be a concept abstracted from experience for a variety of reasons. Indeed, as we ordinarily say that we experience objects as outside us, Kant argues that this notion itself would not be possible unless a distinction between *outer* and *inner*, i.e., a *spatial* distinction, were itself presupposed. Kant further suggests that space cannot be abstracted from objects and the relations between objects because we can represent to ourselves space as empty of all objects. This argument appeals to introspection in that it holds that we can consistently conceive of empty space. It is correspondingly open to the usual arguments against introspective proof.

According to Kant, we know space by a *pure intuition* as a kind of object. Kant argues that space is a kind of object or particular on the grounds that there is only *one* space, and that when one speaks of diverse spaces, different parts of space is all that can be meant. Space is thus not a property of things but our manner of experiencing them. Similar arguments purport to show that time is presupposed in experience (in all experience, since temporal succession is perceived in inner experiences as well as outer), and that it is an object of pure intuition. We may then take space and time to be presupposed in perception. Kant's view that space and time are presupposed in perception needs modification in that some views that he took to be *indubitable* with respect to space and time as well as consequences of these views would have to be modified in the light of more recent mathematical and scientific views of space and time, particularly the theory of space-time of relativity, in which space and time are not so neatly separable as they are on the commonsense view.

A problem for Kantian epistemology is raised by consideration of Berkeley's point that a theory of knowledge must account for the knowledge of children who are able to know the relevant area of knowledge in that they can apparently use it. This raises some question as to what it may mean to say that space and time are presupposed in perception, since knowledge of space and time may not be held in any straightforward sense by many human beings who seem able to make accurate reports of their other perceptions. Kant replied to this by supposing that commonsense space and time underlie ordinary perceptions. The difficulty with this reply is that the necessity that Kant takes to characterize some judgments about space and time are not necessary for commonsense notions of space and time, since scientific research and theorizing occasionally change the nature of our commonsense conceptions about space and time. This is exactly what has happened since Kant, making the *necessity* of the propositions about Euclidean space, as they are characterized in Kant's philosophy, extremely dubious. In any current version of the Kantian system the various *spaces* considered by scientists would have to be allowed for by some revision of Kant's notion of *necessity* for geometrical propositions.

To this point, we have seen that what Kant calls sensibility or intuition he regards as a faculty of humans to apprehend particular objects as given in space and time. The matter of these apprehensions is given by empirical intuition of the sensible appearances of things. Sensibility, then, provides us with perceptions. But perceptions do not constitute knowledge. Even the pure intuition of space and time (which contains no sensible element) does not give us scientific knowledge. Knowledge arises when *judgments* about sense objects as given in space and time are made by the *understanding*, a distinct faculty of human beings, which provides knowledge through objects which are *thought*, by means of the concepts used to think them. To see what this means, we must examine Kant's analysis of *judgment*, which had great impact on the rationalistic philosophers who followed him.

The Synthetic A Priori

The central concept involved in grasping Kant's theory of judgment is his twofold classification of judgments into a priori–a posteriori and analytic-synthetic dichotomies. Any subject-predicate proposition asserted by someone which fits into these classifications may be considered a judgment, and all judgments may be analyzed in terms of these classifications.

Judgments are a priori if and only if they are absolutely independent of all experience. We have had examples of such judgments in the case of mathematical statements whose truth or falsity is independent of experience because these mathematical statements are not about experienced objects. The independence involved is logical independence. In order to make statements about truths of mathematics, we must have had enough experience to have mastered a language capable of handling these statements, but this is not what is in question. As we have seen in connection with Plato, no statement or set of statements about experienced objects can contradict a statement about mathematical objects. On the other hand, if a judgment may be contradicted by statements about experienced objects, that judgment is a posteriori. Kant gives necessary and sufficient conditions for a judgment to be a priori. If a judgment is thought as *necessary*, or if a judgment is thought as *universal*, then the judgment is a priori. The converse cases hold also. Now it is not clear what the distinction between *necessary* and *universal* is in this connection: they both seem to suggest, in qualifying an argument, that the judgment can have no exceptions. This criterion, it should be noted, is rationalistic in that its basis is whether or not exceptions to a judgment can be *thought*.

The other dichotomy of judgments involves a relationship between the subject and predicate of the judgment. Either the predicate is *contained* in the subject concept, or it is not. In the former case, the judgment is said to be analytic; otherwise it is said to be synthetic. There are a number of restatements of this definition in terms other than those of containment. We might say that if an analysis of the subject term of a judg-

223

ment can break it down into parts, one of which is the predicate, then the judgment is analytic, so that an analytic judgment has a relationship of identity holding between some part of the subject and the predicate. It should be remembered that "7 + 5 = 12" is explicitly cited as *synthetic,* not analytic, and that the requisite notion of identity is thus a problem for considerably greater analysis than Kant provides. The notion that seems to be at stake here is the notion of informativeness. A synthetic judgment is one that tells us something new, or informative, about the relationship between its subject and its predicate. An analytic judgment, since the relationship is always one of containment, is uninformative, save that it may enable us to note clearly that some such relationship is trivial, where we had mistakenly thought it to be of some informative importance.

The two dichotomies, if they are *distinct,* give rise to four possible forms of judgment: analytic a priori judgment, synthetic a priori judgment, analytic a posteriori judgment, and synthetic a posteriori judgment. No judgments would be considered analytic a posteriori judgments. An a posteriori judgment is dependent on experience, and hence gives us information, which an analytic judgment, being uninformative, does not. Synthetic a posteriori judgments are simply informative judgments about concepts derived from experienced objects which may be proved false by future experience. None of these judgments constitutes certain knowledge in the older rationalistic sense, since they rest upon experience and are to some extent problematic. On the other hand, the triviality of analytic a priori judgments, although they are certain, insures that they cannot give us knowledge, or add to what we already know. Knowledge, for Kant, consists primarily of synthetic a priori judgments, which are informative because they are synthetic, yet certain because they are a priori and cannot be contradicted by experience. The importance of synthetic a priori judgments in their role of principles of scientific and mathematical knowledge constitutes one of the claims upon which the adequacy of Kantian philosophy must be taken to rest.

What judgments are to be found among the synthetic a priori judgments? Synthetic a priori judgments are found in mathematics, natural science, legitimate metaphysics, and ethical theory, according to Kant's total philosophy, but only the first two cases concern us here. Except for certain analytic a priori statements of logic ($a = a$), Kant took all of the statements of mathematics to be synthetic a priori judgments. "7 + 5 = 12," for example, is both necessary (a priori) and yet synthetic, since Kant felt that the concept of putting seven and five together expressed by '7 + 5' was not equivalent to the concept of the number twelve. In addition, Kant took all of the principles on which he thought scientific laws to depend as synthetic a priori judgments, notably the statement of the causal principle "All alterations occur in accordance with the law of the connexion of cause and effect."

There are three traditional objections to Kant's definition and discussion of synthetic a priori judgments. To begin with, he does not *prove* that there are synthetic a priori judgments; he *assumes* that certain mathematical and scientific statments are both informative and necessary, and then proceeds to the problem of discussing how we come to form such judgments on the supposition that we do form them. By adopting such a procedure, Kant does not *refute* Humean skepticism; he simply begins by taking it to be a false or misleading basis for justifying those mathematical and scientific statements that common sense takes to be necessary. Kant takes Hume's failure to find this necessity in anything but custom a consequence of his incorrect epistemology. This objection to Kant, that he begins by assuming the existence of synthetic a priori knowledge, is not crushing since most philosophers take their epistemological question to be that of justifying what they initially take to constitute human knowledge. And a good case can be made that mathematical statements are not trivial. While "7 + 5 = 12" may strike us as so obvious as to be uninformative, so that Kant's position that it is synthetic seems mistaken, one can see that "512,367 + 31,274 = 543,641" is hardly obvious to the person who has not been trained in rapid addition.

The other philosophical objections are that the notion of containment used in defining analytic judgments is vague, and that Kant's dependence on the subject-predicate form of proposition led him astray. While both of these objections hold against Kant's formulations, the question is really one of whether these formulations might be improved so as to avoid these objections. Containment is vague because although we may speak of one box *containing* another and understand what this means, subjects and predicates or subject and predicate concepts are not physical objects to which this paradigm case of containment may apply. At the same time, the statement "If $a < b$, then $b > a$." is presumably *a priori*, and yet it does not have subject-predicate form. A great deal of effort has been expended by philosophers after Kant in an attempt to find some formulation of the a priori–a posteriori, analytic-synthetic dichotomies that is not open to objections of this kind.

There is, however, a further objection that deserves some close scrutiny. This objection is a variant of the historical argument against rationalism, namely, that Kant's assurance about the *necessity* of much of his scheme has been proved premature in the light of later scientific and mathematical developments. Kant believed that he had found a *complete* list of synthetic a priori judgments in the sense that he believed that all of the synthetic a priori judgments necessary for a justification of scientific knowledge could be deduced from his list. In view of the fact that Kant's list could be considered adequate for developing Newtonian physics, but not for contemporary nuclear physics or relativity theory, this belief is mistaken. Further, the Kantian position that Euclidean geometry is the only accurate description of space was proved wrong with the discovery of non-Euclidean geometries in the nineteenth century. Indeed, this is a special case of the remark made above, in that Newtonian physics is usually taken to presuppose a Euclidean geometry assigning space zero curvature, while relativity theory is usually taken to presuppose a Riemannian geometry assigning space positive curvature. The point of these remarks is that inability to conceive failure of universality cannot be taken by itself as a reliable index that some judgment is a priori, or synthetic a priori, if a criterion for being a synthetic judgment is added to it.

The supposition that there are synthetic a priori judgments, and that they constitute some kind of necessary knowledge, is reasonably distinctive of modified rationalism after Kant. Modified empiricists, as we shall see, take the position that the analytic-synthetic, a priori–a posteriori dichotomies divide all judgments or statements the same way, so that they are really two versions of the same principle of division. On this view, in connection with which the analytic-synthetic vocabulary is most often employed, synthetic statements are both informative and about the objects of experience. Analytic statements are then construed as statements which are immune to falsification by confrontation with true statements about experience. Analytic statements are adopted by convention to provide a convenient framework for organizing the information expressed in synthetic statements. Kant's classification of synthetic a priori judgments is then emptied into these two groups. The most important are the mathematical statements. They are interpreted by later empiricists as analytic. Most of the rest of the judgments that Kant took to be synthetic a priori are then declared to be either synthetic and hence not necessary, or meaningless, in which case they are dropped from the consideration of philosophers. In this connection, it should be noted that Kant did not create the analytic-synthetic distinction. There are foreshadowings of it in earlier philosophers, for example, in Hume's distinction between relations of ideas and matters of fact, even though Hume's treatment of this distinction construed as an insight into the analytic-synthetic distinction is quite cursory. Kant's importance to the history of philosophy was to attempt a rigorous treatment of the distinction, as well as to indicate a way in which it need not be construed as giving empiricists an impregnable position from which they could pass off the claims of the rationalists to certain knowledge as complete nonsense.

The Transcendental Deduction

From what has been said to this point, it should be obvious that Kant makes a good case for both intuition (sensibility) and understanding as contributing to our stock of knowledge, largely because of difficulties with the empiricist point of view. It may be nearly as obvious that the major difficulty in Kant's program is to provide a satisfactory account of how the intuition and the understanding influence one another.

Since synthetic a posteriori judgments are not necessary, the interaction between intuition and the understanding must obviously be some way in which the active understanding operates upon the results of intuition. This operation is one of judgment. The understanding, by means of a priori concepts, is able to make judgments on the basis of the perceptions which intuition provides.

These judgments may be made clearer by considering the difference between perceptual judgments (or subjective empirical judgments) and objective empirical judgments. The difference between these two judgments is illustrated by the difference in force between "This shirt seems to be red." and "This shirt is red.". A perceptual judgment is a judgment which, if true, is true for some observer by virtue of some relation between intuitions which he has had. On the other hand, an objective empirical judgment is about some object, and it does not mention, either explicitly or implicitly, any special observer of this object. If an objective empirical judgment is true, it is true for everybody.

Kant does not question the existence of objective empirical judgments. We make them, and some of them must be true. After taking the existence of these judgments as an obvious fact, Kant takes his problem to be that of explaining the objectivity of these judgments. In other words, Kant takes the problem to be that of explaining where objective empirical judgments get their objective reference and general validity.

Assuming the legitimacy of objective empirical judgments has far-reaching consequences for Kant's epistemology. Since objective empirical judgments are about objects which háve properties that one cannot experience, the assumption seems to generate a world of objects much like the assumption of a material world against which Berkeley had violently argued. But instead of taking the disastrous position (as Hylas did in the *Dialogues*) that these objects can be directly known or experienced, Kant takes a position compatible with Berkeley's strictures on this point by denying that we can have sensible knowledge of these things-in-themselves. Indeed, we may take Berkeley and Kant to agree that if there are material objects, they cannot be the objects of sense-experiential knowledge. But where Berkeley construed the notion of *material object* to be that of an *unperceived* object, and hence a contradictory notion, Kant construed *material object* to be something that, if it did exist, could not be known as it was through human perception because of the interaction between the human perceptual apparatus and the object perceived. Berkeley supposed any apparent order in the world could be accounted for by regular sequences of ideas. But Kant felt that there were more regular sequences in experience than Berkeley's theory could account for. Kant would agree with Berkeley's strictures against an assumption of material bodies on an epistemological basis of passively received ideas that are organized in fairly mechanical ways by the mind. But Kant further argues that this account of human nature is too poor; when an *active* mind is coupled with sense experience, however, we may rationally suppose that there may be legitimate grounds for the assertion of objective empirical judgments.

In a procedure reminiscent of certain analyses of Aristotle, Kant tries to list all the *forms* of objective empirical judgments. He felt, in fact, that he had produced a complete list. The *form* of an objective empirical judgment, say "This shirt is red.", constitutes such features as that it is affirmative, about a particular object, etc., and hence has the same form as the judgment "This book is blue.".

Suppose we take any particular objective empirical judgment and consider its form. We might also consider any perceptual judgment of the same form except that the words 'it seems to me' are added. For example, "This shirt is red." and "This shirt is red—it seems to me." might be the subject of comparison. In the second judgment, the words 'it seems to me' subtract somewhat from the force of "This shirt is red.". We might well ask exactly what is subtracted. In the subjective empirical judgment we are referring only to certain sense impressions—and suggesting that there might be an actual red shirt which accounts for them. The objective empirical judgment is that there is a shirt in which the property redness inheres. Kant supposes that the application of the a priori category of substance with qualities inhering constitutes the difference between a subjective empirical judgment and an objective empirical judgment. To each of the forms of objective empirical judgment, therefore, one may relate an a priori concept which Kant calls a category (in obvious reference to the Aristotelian term), the application of which accounts for the objective reference and general validity of the related judgment. When the category is not applied, only subjective empirical judgments can be made. One of these categories, incidentally, is cause and effect, and by its application Kant thought that he had avoided the subjectivism of Hume's analysis.

We may take our everyday use of objective empirical judgments to prove that they are in fact made. The Kantian analysis of the ground of such judgments in terms of the categories suggests that we do in fact apply the categories to our experiences in judgments. An obvious question, which Kant faces next, is whether or not the categories may be *legitimately* employed in this way. Kant's attempt to show that they may be legitimately employed is called the *Transcendental Deduction of the Pure Concepts of the Understanding*. 'The Pure Concepts of the Understanding' are simply the categories. *Transcendental* indicates that the use of the categories is to be justified for *every* area of human knowledge, not by means of sense experience, but by the means of showing that unless the Pure Concepts of the Understanding and their application is presupposed, sense experiences and the synthetic empirical judgments of science would not be possible. By a deduction, Kant means a justification, not a formally valid deductive argument.

Now the objects mentioned in an objective empirical judgment are not *generalizations* from experience, even though experience yields information about them. They are thus objects which are *thought*, and the real problem of the Transcendental Deduction may be taken to be that of showing that the applicability of the categories is a necessary condition of any objective experience of objects in so far as they are experienceable. Because of this the Transcendental Deduction contains considerable probing into the nature of thought, probing which at times becomes extremely complicated and somewhat obscure.

Suppose we take all the sense impressions available to us at any time. Some of these impressions we put together according to certain synthetic a priori rules in order to obtain an impression of an object. We may thus put together in terms of such a rule some color, a place, etc., and call it a shirt. The empiricists had held that we do this because certain impressions repeatedly occur together. But so many impressions are available to us that Kant supposes that we must have some way of unifying certain impressions independently of repeated association. It is clear that repeated association can lead us into error. If we had experienced only brown dogs up to a point, we might erroneously conclude that all dogs are brown. We do ascribe unity to groups of sense impressions and even to all our sense impressions (they are *our* sense impressions). This unity is an act of the understanding which synthesizes our impressions. That the unity of impressions must be due to the understanding follows from the passive character of sense intuition. We may call this unity *synthesis,* to signify that it is the synthetic connection of impressions into a unified representation which has been synthesized according to a rule of thought.

A unified manifold (field) of sense impressions suggests that a unified subject experiences it. The reason for this is that a unified manifold would otherwise exist which is not related to any understanding. But understanding is a necessary condition of unifying. Grasp by some understanding of a unified manifold of sense impressions is what Kant calls pure apperception, to contrast it with the contingent and uncertain self-awareness which may accompany some impressions, such as pain. This position reflects the general Kantian position of interdependence between mind and perception.

Knowledge of an object is then the consistent judgment that a category is applicable to the object synthesized out of various impressions. An unperceived object, for example, a unicorn, cannot be known because the empirical element is absent. The total argument shows that the knowledge of objects presupposes a unified understanding which employs categories to make objective judgments about synthesized impressions. Both the concepts (for the judgments) and the impressions (to be synthesized) must occur prior to knowledge. A full analysis of objective empirical judgments requires attention to some problems, of which we shall mention one. Kant's critique of the empiricistic view of the role of mind in knowledge is impressive, and at the very least it shows that some active or spontaneous mental activity seems to be required to explain the recognition of natural regularities. Still, it does not follow logically from this that the regularities are *manufactured* by this mental activity, which Kant comes close to accepting. Perhaps no reasonable alternative is available, but Kant's development is not entirely persuasive. An interesting problem for Kantian philosophy is that of explaining the similarity of categories which all minds develop. Some philosophers have attempted to explain this similarity in terms of physiological resemblances between human brains, but this seems to make the a priori concepts too arbitrary in that we could imagine that alternative physiological structures exist; but on the Kantian view we cannot imagine that alternative a priori concepts could exist. The Kantians, of course, are free to assume a similarity in the conceptual apparatus of different human beings, but non-Kantians who desire conversion may well ask for some account of it that is not explicitly available in Kant's treatment.

Readings from Kant

The obscurity of Kant's German prose is legendary. It may safely be said that of the seven philosophers discussed in this book, it is most difficult to support claims made for Kant's philosophy because of the fact that it is so difficult to find unambiguous texts supporting these claims. Even where this seems possible, it is not always possible to find texts that do not clash with texts that appear elsewhere.

As with Hume's *Treatise* and *Enquiry*, one is again confronted with a major epistemological work (the *Critique of Pure Reason*) and a more easily read introduction to it (the *Prolegomena to Any Future Metaphysics*). The interpretive situation discussed in connection with Hume's *Treatise* and *Enquiry* arises again because of the fact that the *Critique* (1781) was written before the *Prolegomena* (1783). But in this case there is a very important revision of the *Critique* which incorporates extensive changes over the first edition that appears four years after the publication of the *Prolegomena*. It thus seems possible to suppose that by comparing the two editions of the *Critique* with the *Prolegomena* we can ferret out Kant's *maturest* epistemological positions.

Unfortunately, it is not easy to *introduce* Kant through his maturest positions because of their difficulty. In many cases, the arguments of the *Prolegomena* are clear and convincing without being the arguments that Kant saw fit to accept as the foundation of his philosophy in the second edition of the *Critique*. For example, the distinction between subjective and objective empirical judgments which is discussed in the chapters on Kant and in the *Prolegomena* as an argument for the necessity of the application of the Pure Concepts of the Understanding to provide an epistemology adequate for justifying scientific knowledge is not presented as an explicit argument in the second edition of the *Critique*. Similarly, the arguments for the existence of things-in-themselves as material objects not known to us in perception as they really are, which are presented in the *Prolegomena*, do not occur in the Second Analogy of the second edition of the *Critique*, where one might expect to find them. For these reasons, it is exceptionally difficult to select readings from Kant which are both introductory and yet representative of the epistemological reasoning that has made him such an important figure in the Western philosophical tradition.

The readings attempt to present a crucial early line of reasoning from the *Prolegomena* which is obviously one of the major *insights* into the critical philosophy that Kant formulated. In addition, they present some passages from the *second* edition of the *Critique of Pure Reason* which exhibit some of the Kantian positions that have already been discussed. Marginal notations such as 'B 9' in the selections from the *Critique* refer to the fact that the material in the text is the translation of the 9th paragraph of the second edition of the *Critique*. 'A 9' is used by scholars to refer to the ninth paragraph of the first edition.

Very little has been said in these notes about the editions of the works of the philosophers being considered. This information is not as important for the other six philosophers as it is for Kant. There are many fine editions of Plato's various dialogues, for example, and the student may be reasonably sure that recent editions that he finds in the library contain at least defensible translations from the Greek. This is not true for Kant's works. Because of the convolutions and obscurities of Kant's style, good English translations of his German that are philosophically defensible have not appeared until relatively recently, when the translations have been undertaken by men such as Professor Beck and Professor Kemp Smith, who have been able to make sound judgments of the philosophical importance and consistency of the translated material.

The Kant selections consist of the following passages:

A. Sections 17, 18, 19, and 20 of the Second Part of the Main Transcendental Problem from the *Prolegomena to Any Future Metaphysics*. From Immanuel Kant: *Prolegomena to Any Future Metaphysics*, translated by Lewis White Beck, copyright 1951 by the Liberal Arts Press, Inc., reprinted by permission of the Liberal Arts Press Division of the Bobbs-Merrill Company, Inc.

B. Sections I through V and part of VI of the Introduction to the second edition of the *Critique of Pure Reason*.

C. Section I of Chapter I of the Analytic of Concepts from the second edition of the *Critique of Pure Reason*.

D. Chapter II of the Analytic of Concepts from the second edition of the *Critique of Pure Reason*.

E. Part 22 of section 2 of the Deduction of the Pure Concepts of the Understanding from the second edition of the *Critique of Pure Reason*.

F. Parts 26 and 27 of section 2 of the Deduction of the Pure Concepts of the Understanding from the second edition of the *Critique of Pure Reason*.

Selections *B* through *F* are reprinted from Immanuel Kant's *Critique of Pure Reason*, translated by Norman Kemp Smith. Reprint rights have been given by kind permission of Macmillan and Company, Ltd., and St Martin's Press, Inc.

The secondary source material for Kant's philosophy is very extensive. There is, in fact, a journal (*Kant-Studien*) devoted exclusively to the study of Kant's philosophy. A few recent secondary sources which discuss in some detail the arguments of the *Critique of Pure Reason* and the *Prolegomena* are all that will be listed here.

Bird, Graham: *Kant's Theory of Knowledge*, New York, 1962.

Cassirer, H. W.: *Kant's First Critique*, London, 1954.

Ewing, A. C.: *A Short Commentary on Kant's Critique of Pure Reason*, Chicago, 1950.

*Körner, S.: *Kant*, Harmondsworth, 1955. (Pelican Paperbound.)

Paton, H. J.: *Kant's Metaphysic of Experience*, 2 vol., New York, 1936.

Smith, A. H.: *Kantian Studies*, Oxford, 1947.

Smith, N. K.: *A Commentary to Kant's 'Critique of Pure Reason,'* 2d ed., New York, 1962.

Weldon, T. D.: *Kant's Critique of Pure Reason*, 2d ed., Oxford, 1958.

Wolff, R. P.: *Kant's Theory of Mental Activity*, Cambridge, 1963.

A From the *PROLEGOMENA*

§ 17. The formal aspect of nature in this narrower sense is therefore the conformity to law of all the objects of experience and, so far as it is known *a priori*, their *necessary* conformity. But it has just been shown that the laws of nature can never be known *a priori* in objects so far as they are considered, not in reference to possible experience, but as things in themselves. And our inquiry here extends, not to things in themselves (the properties of which we pass by), but to things as objects of possible experience, and the complex of these is what we here properly designate as nature. And now I ask, when the possibility of knowledge of nature *a priori* is in question, whether it is better to arrange the problem thus: "How can we know *a priori* that things as objects of experience necessarily conform to law?" or thus: "How is it possible to know *a priori* the necessary conformity to law of experience itself as regards all its objects generally?"

Closely considered, the solution of the problem represented in either way amounts, with regard to the pure knowledge of nature (which is the point of the question at issue), entirely to the same thing. For the subjective laws, under which alone an empirical knowledge of things is possible, hold good of these things as objects of possible experience (not as things in themselves, which are not considered here). It is all the same whether I say: "A judgment of perception can never rank as experience without the law that, whenever an event is observed, it is always referred to some antecedent, which it follows according to a universal rule," or: "Everything of which experience teaches that it happens must have a cause."

It is, however, more suitable to choose the first formula. For we can *a priori* and prior to all given objects have a knowledge of those conditions on which alone experience of them is possible, but never of the laws to which things may in themselves be subject, without reference to possible experience. We cannot, therefore, study the nature of things *a priori* otherwise than by investigating the conditions and the universal (though subjective) laws, under which alone such a cognition as experience (as to mere form) is possible, and we determine accordingly the possibility of things as objects of experience. For if I should choose the second formula and seek the *a priori* conditions under which nature as an object of experience is possible, I might easily fall into error and fancy that I was speaking of nature as a thing in itself, and then move round in endless circles, in a vain search for laws concerning things of which nothing is given me.

Accordingly, we shall here be concerned with experience only and the universal conditions of its possibility, which are given *a priori*. Thence we shall define nature as the whole object of all possible experience. I think it will be understood that I here do not mean the rules of the observation of a nature that is already given, for these already presuppose experience. Thus I do not mean how (through experience) we can study the laws of nature, for these would not then be laws *a priori* and would yield us no pure science of nature; but [I mean to ask] how the conditions *a priori* of the possibility of experience are at the same time the sources from which all universal laws of nature must be derived.

§ 18. In the first place we must state that, while all judgments of experience are empirical (that is, have their ground in immediate sense-perception), all empirical judgments are not judgments of experience; but, besides the empirical, and in general besides what is given to the sensuous intuition, special concepts must yet be superadded—concepts which have their origin wholly *a priori* in the pure understanding, and under which every perception must be first of all subsumed and then by their means changed into experience.

Empirical judgments, so far as they have objective validity, are *judgments of experience,* but those which are only subjectively valid I name mere *judgments of perception.* The latter require no pure concept of the understanding, but only the logical connection of perception in a thinking subject. But the former always require, besides the representation of the sensuous intuition, special *concepts originally begotten in the understanding,* which make possible the objective validity of the judgment of experience.

All our judgments are at first merely judgments of perception; they hold good only for us (that is, for our subject) and we do not till afterward give them a new reference (to an object) and desire that they shall always hold good for us and in the same way for everybody else; for when a judgment agrees with an object, all judgments concerning the same object must likewise agree among themselves, and thus the objective validity of the judgment of experience signifies nothing else than its necessary universal validity. And conversely when we have ground for considering a judgment as necessarily having universal validity (which never depends upon perception, but upon the pure concept of the understanding under which the perception is subsumed), we must consider that it is objective also—that is, that it expresses not merely a reference of our perception to a subject, but a characteristic of the object. For there would be no reason for the judgments of other men necessarily agreeing with mine if it were not the unity of the object to which they all refer and with which they accord; hence they must all agree with one another.

§ 19. Therefore objective validity and necessary universality (for everybody) are equivalent terms, and though we do not know the object in itself, yet when we consider a judgment as universal, and hence necessary, we thereby understand it to have objective validity. By this judgment we know the object (though it remains unknown as it is in itself) by the universal and necessary connection of the given perceptions. As this is the case with all objects of sense, judgments of experience take their objective validity, not from the immediate knowledge of the object (which is impossible), but from the condition of universal validity of empirical judgments, which, as already said, never rests upon empirical or, in short, sensuous conditions, but upon a pure concept of the understanding. The object in itself always remains unknown; but when by the concept of the understanding the connection of the representations of the object, which it gives to our sensibility, is determined as universally valid, the object is determined by this relation, and the judgment is objective.

To illustrate the matter: when we say, "The room is warm, sugar sweet, and wormwood bitter," we have only subjectively valid judgments. I do not at all expect that I or any other person shall always find it as I now do; each of these sentences only expresses a relation of two sensations to the same subject, that is, myself, and that only in my present state of perception; consequently they are not valid of the object. Such are judgments of perception. Judgments of experience are of quite a different nature. What experience teaches me under certain circumstances, it must always teach me and everybody; and its validity is not limited to the subject nor to its state at a particular time. Hence I pronounce all such judgments objectively valid. For instance, when I say the air is elastic, this judgment is as yet a judgment of perception only; I do nothing but refer two of my sensations to each other. But if I would have it called a judgment of experience, I require this connection to stand under a condition which makes it universally valid. I desire therefore that I and everybody else should always connect necessarily the same perceptions under the same circumstances.

§ 20. We must consequently analyze experience in general in order to see what is contained in this product of the senses and of the understanding, and how the judgment of experience itself is possible. The foundation is the intuition of which I become conscious, that is, perception (*perceptio*), which pertains merely to the senses. But in the next place, there is judging (which belongs only to the understanding). But this judging may be twofold: first, I may merely compare perceptions and connect them in a consciousness of my particular state; or, secondly, I may connect them in consciousness in general. The former judgment is merely a judgment of perception, and hence is of subjective validity only; it is merely a connection of perceptions in my mental state, without reference to the object. Hence it does not, as is commonly imagined, suffice for experience that perceptions are compared and connected in consciousness through judgment; thence arises no universal validity and necessity by virtue of which alone consciousness can be objectively valid, that is, can be called experience.

Quite another judgment therefore is required before perception can become experience. The given intuition must be subsumed under a concept which determines the form of judging in general relatively to the intuition, connects empirical consciousness of intuition in consciousness in general, and thereby procures universal validity for empirical judgments. A concept of this nature is a pure *a priori* concept of the understanding, which does nothing but determine for an intuition the general way in which it can be used for judgments. Let the concept be that of cause; then it determines the intuition which is subsumed under it, for example, that of air, relative to judging in general—namely, the concept of air in respect to its expansion serves in the relation of antecedent to consequent in a hypothetical judgment. The concept of cause accordingly is a pure concept of the understanding, which is totally disparate from all possible perception and only serves to determine the representation subsumed under it, with respect to judging in general, and so to make a universally valid judgment possible.

Before, therefore, a judgment of perception can become a judgment of experience, it is requisite that the perception should be subsumed under some such concept of the understanding; for instance, air belongs under the concept of cause, which determines our judgment about it in respect to its expansion as hypothetical. Thereby the expansion of the air is represented, not as merely belonging to the perception of the air in my present state or in several states of mine, or in the perceptual state of others, but as belonging to it necessarily. The judgment, "Air is elastic," becomes universally valid and a judgment of experience only because certain judgments precede it which subsume the intuition of air under the concept of cause and effect; and they thereby determine the perceptions, not merely with respect to one another in me, but with respect to the form of judging in general (which is here hypothetical), and in this way they render the empirical judgment universally valid.

If all our synthetical judgments are analyzed so far as they are objectively valid, it will be found that they never consist of mere intuitions connected only (as is commonly believed) by comparison into a judgment; but that they would be impossible were not a pure concept of the understanding superadded to the concepts abstracted from intuition, under which concept these latter are subsumed and in this manner only combined into an objectively valid judgment. Even the judgments of pure mathematics in their simplest axioms are not exempt from this condition. The principle, "A straight line is the shortest distance between two points," presupposes that the line is subsumed under the concept of magnitude, which certainly is no mere intuition, but has its seat in the understanding alone and serves to determine the intuition (of the line) with regard to the judgments which may be made about it, in respect to their quantity, that is, to plurality (as *judicia plurativa*). For under them it is understood that in a given intuition there is contained a plurality of homogeneous parts.

B   From the CRITIQUE

INTRODUCTION

B 1

1. THE DISTINCTION BETWEEN PURE AND EMPIRICAL KNOWLEDGE

There can be no doubt that all our knowledge begins with experience. For how should our faculty of knowledge be awakened into action did not objects affecting our senses partly of themselves produce representations, partly arouse the activity of our understanding to compare these representations, and, by combining or separating them, work up the raw material of the sensible impressions into that knowledge of objects which is entitled experience? In the order of time, therefore, we have no knowledge antecedent to experience, and with experience all our knowledge begins.

But though all our knowledge begins with experience, it does not follow that it all arises out of experience. For it may well be that even our empirical knowledge is made up of what we receive through impressions and of what our own faculty of knowledge (sensible impressions serving merely as the occasion) supplies from itself. If our faculty of knowledge makes any such addition, it may be that we are not in a position to distinguish it from the raw material, until with long practice of attention we have become skilled in separating it.

This, then, is a question which at least calls for closer examination, and does not allow of any off-hand answer:—whether there is any knowledge that is thus independent of experience and even of all impressions of the senses. Such knowledge is entitled *a priori*, and distinguished from the *empirical*, which has its sources *a posteriori*, that is, in experience.[1]

The expression '*a priori*' does not, however, indicate with sufficient precision the full meaning of our question. For it has been customary to say, even of much knowledge that is derived from empirical sources, that we have it or are capable of having it *a priori*, meaning thereby that we do not derive it immediately from experience, but from a universal rule—a rule which is itself, however, borrowed by us from experience. Thus we would say of a man who undermined the foundations of his house, that he might have known *a priori* that it would fall, that is, that he need not have waited for the experience of its actual falling. But still he could not know this completely *a priori*. For he had first to learn through experience that bodies are heavy, and therefore fall when their supports are withdrawn.

In what follows, therefore, we shall understand by *a priori* knowledge, not knowledge independent of this or that experience, but knowledge absolutely independent of all experience. Opposed to it is empirical knowledge, which is knowledge possible only *a posteriori*, that is, through experience. *A priori* modes of knowledge are entitled pure when there is no admixture of anything empirical. Thus, for instance, the proposition, 'every alteration has its cause', while an *a priori* proposition, is not a pure proposition, because alteration is a concept which can be derived only from experience.

2. WE ARE IN POSSESSION OF CERTAIN MODES OF *A PRIORI* KNOWLEDGE, AND EVEN THE COMMON UNDERSTANDING IS NEVER WITHOUT THEM

What we here require is a criterion by which to distinguish with certainty between pure and empirical knowledge. Experience teaches us that a thing is so and so, but not that it cannot be otherwise. First, then, if we have a proposition which in being thought is thought as *necessary*, it is an *a priori* judgment; and if, besides, it is not derived from any proposition except one which also has the validity of a necessary judgment, it is an absolutely *a priori* judgment.[2] Secondly, experience never confers on its judgments true or strict, but only assumed and comparative *universality*, through induction. We can properly only say, therefore, that, so far as we have hitherto observed, there is no exception to this or that rule. If, then, a judgment is thought with strict universality, that is, in such manner that no exception is allowed as possible, it is not derived from experience, but is valid absolutely *a priori*. Empirical universality is only an arbitrary extension of a validity holding in most cases to one which holds in all, for instance, in the proposition, 'all bodies are heavy'.[3] When, on the other hand, strict universality is essential to a judgment, this indicates a special source of knowledge, namely, a faculty of *a priori* knowledge. Necessity and strict universality are thus sure criteria of *a priori* knowledge, and are inseparable from one another. But since in the employment of these criteria the contingency of judgments is sometimes more easily shown than their empirical limitation, or, as sometimes also happens, their unlimited universality can be more convincingly proved than their necessity, it is advisable to use the two criteria separately, each by itself being infallible.[4]

Now it is easy to show that there actually are in human knowledge judgments which are necessary and in the strictest sense universal, and which are therefore pure *a priori* judgments. If an example from the sciences be desired, we have only to look to any of the propositions of mathematics; if we seek an example from the understanding in its quite ordinary employment, the proposition, 'every alteration must have a cause', will   B5
serve our purpose. In the latter case, indeed, the very concept of a cause so manifestly contains the concept of a necessity of connection with an effect and of the strict universality of the rule, that the concept would be altogether lost if we attempted to derive it, as Hume has done, from a repeated association of that which happens with that which precedes, and from a custom of connecting representations, a custom originating in this repeated association, and constituting therefore a merely subjective necessity. Even without appealing to such examples, it is possible to show that pure *a priori* principles are indispensable for the possibility of experience, and so to prove their existence *a priori*. For whence could experience derive its certainty, if all the rules, according to which it proceeds, were always themselves empirical, and therefore contingent?[5] Such rules could hardly be regarded as first principles. At present, however, we may be content to have established the fact that our faculty of knowledge does have a pure employment, and to have shown what are the criteria of such an employment.

Such *a priori* origin is manifest in certain concepts, no less than in judgments. If we remove from our empirical concept of a body, one by one, every feature in it which is [merely] empirical, the colour, the hardness or softness, the weight, even the impenetrability, there still remains the space which the body (now entirely vanished) occupied, and this cannot be removed. Again, if we remove from our empirical concept of any   B6
object, corporeal or incorporeal, all properties which experience has taught us, we yet cannot take away that property through which the object is thought as substance or as inhering in a substance (although this concept of substance is more determinate than that of an object in general).[6] Owing, therefore, to the necessity with which this concept of substance forces itself upon us, we have no option save to admit that it has its seat in our faculty of *a priori* knowledge.

3. PHILOSOPHY STANDS IN NEED OF A SCIENCE WHICH SHALL DETERMINE THE POSSIBILITY, THE PRINCIPLES, AND THE EXTENT OF ALL *A PRIORI* KNOWLEDGE

But what is still more extraordinary than all the preceding is this, that certain modes of knowledge leave the field of all possible experiences and have the appearance of extending the scope of our judgments beyond all limits of experience, and this by means of concepts to which no corresponding object can ever be given in experience.

It is precisely by means of the latter modes of knowledge, in a realm beyond the world of the senses, where experience can yield neither guidance nor correction, that our reason carries on those enquiries which owing to their importance we consider to be far more excellent, and in their purpose far more lofty, than all that the understanding can learn in the field of appearances. Indeed we prefer to run every risk of error rather than desist from such urgent enquiries, on the ground of their dubious character, or from disdain and indifference. These unavoidable problems set by pure reason itself are *God, freedom,* and *immortality.* The science which, with all its preparations, is in its final intention directed solely to their solution is metaphysics; and its procedure is at first dogmatic, that is, it confidently sets itself to this task without any previous examination of the capacity or incapacity of reason for so great an undertaking.[7]

Now it does indeed seem natural that, as soon as we have left the ground of experience, we should, through careful enquiries, assure ourselves as to the foundations of any building that we propose to erect, not making use of any knowledge that we possess without first determining whence it has come, and not trusting to principles without knowing their origin. It is natural, that is to say, that the question should first be considered, how the understanding can arrive at all this knowledge *a priori,* and what extent, validity, and worth it may have. Nothing, indeed, could be more natural, if by the term 'natural' we signify what fittingly and reasonably ought to happen. But if we mean by 'natural' what ordinarily happens, then on the contrary nothing is more natural and more intelligible than the fact that this enquiry has been so long neglected. For one part of this knowledge, the mathematical, has long been of established reliability, and so gives rise to a favourable presumption as regards the other part, which may yet be of quite different nature. Besides, once we are outside the circle of experience, we can be sure of not being *contradicted* by experience.[8] The charm of extending our knowledge is so great that nothing short of encountering a direct contradiction can suffice to arrest us in our course; and this can be avoided, if we are careful in our fabrications — which none the less will still remain fabrications. Mathematics gives us a shining example of how far, independently of experience, we can progress in *a priori* knowledge. It does, indeed, occupy itself with objects and with knowledge solely in so far as they allow of being exhibited in intuition. But this circumstance is easily overlooked, since this intuition can itself be given *a priori,* and is therefore hardly to be distinguished from a bare and pure concept. Misled by such a proof of the power of reason, the demand for the extension of knowledge recognises no limits. The light dove, cleaving the air in her free flight, and feeling its resistance, might imagine that its flight would be still easier in empty space. It was thus that Plato left the world of the senses, as setting too narrow limits to the understanding, and ventured out beyond it on the wings of the ideas, in the empty space of the pure understanding. He did not observe that with all his efforts he made no advance—meeting no resistance that might, as it were, serve as a support upon which he could take a stand, to which he could apply his powers, and so set his understanding in motion. It is, indeed, the common fate of human reason to complete its speculative structures as speedily as may be, and only afterwards to enquire whether the foundations are reliable. All sorts of excuses will then be appealed to, in order to reassure us of their solidity, or rather indeed to enable us to dispense altogether with so late and so dangerous an enquiry. But what keeps us, during the actual building, free from all apprehension and suspicion, and flatters us with a seeming thoroughness, is this other circumstance, namely, that a great, perhaps the greatest, part of the business of our reason consists in analysis of the concepts which we already have of objects. This analysis supplies us with a considerable body of knowledge, which, while nothing but explanation or elucidation of what has already been thought in our concepts, though in a confused manner, is yet prized as being, at least as regards its form, new insight. But so far as the matter or content is concerned, there has been no extension of our previously possessed concepts, but only an analysis of them. Since this procedure yields real knowledge *a priori*,   B 10 which progresses in an assured and useful fashion, reason is so far misled as surreptitiously to introduce, without itself being aware of so doing, assertions of an entirely different order, in which it attaches to given concepts others completely foreign to them, and moreover attaches them *a priori*. And yet it is not known how reason can be in position to do this. Such a question is never so much as thought of. I shall therefore at once proceed to deal with the difference between these two kinds of knowledge.

4. THE DISTINCTION BETWEEN ANALYTIC AND SYNTHETIC JUDGMENTS

In all judgments in which the relation of a subject to the predicate is thought (I take into consideration affirmative judgments only, the subsequent application to negative judgments being easily made), this relation is possible in two different ways.[9] Either the predicate B belongs to the subject A, as something which is (covertly) contained in this concept A; or B lies outside the concept A, although it does indeed stand in connection with it. In the one case I entitle the judgment analytic, in the other synthetic. Analytic judgments (affirmative) are therefore those in which the connection of the predicate with the subject is thought through identity; those in which this connection is thought without identity should be entitled synthetic. The former, as adding nothing through the predicate to the concept   B 11 of the subject, but merely breaking it up into those constituent concepts that have all along been thought in it, although confusedly, can also be entitled explicative. The latter, on the other hand, add to the concept of the subject a predicate which has not been in any wise thought in it, and which no analysis could possibly extract from it; and they may therefore be entitled ampliative. If I say, for instance, 'All bodies are extended', this is an analytic judgment. For I do not require to go beyond the concept which I connect with 'body' in order to find extension as bound up with it. To meet with this predicate, I have merely to analyse the concept, that is, to become conscious to myself of the manifold which I always think in that concept. The judgment is therefore analytic. But when I say, 'All bodies are heavy', the predicate is something quite different from anything that I think in the mere concept of body in general; and the addition of such a predicate therefore yields a synthetic judgment.

Judgments of experience, as such, are one and all synthetic. For it would be absurd to found an analytic judgment on experience. Since, in framing the judgment, I must not go outside my concept, there is no need to appeal to the testimony of experience in its support. That a body is ex-

B 12   tended is a proposition that holds a *priori* and is not empirical. For, before appealing to experience, I have already in the concept of body all the conditions required for my judgment. I have only to extract from it, in accordance with the principle of contradiction, the required predicate, and in so doing can at the same time become conscious of the necessity of the judgment—and that is what experience could never have taught me. On the other hand, though I do not include in the concept of a body in general the predicate 'weight', none the less this concept indicates an object of experience through one of its parts, and I can add to that part other parts of this same experience, as in this way belonging together with the concept. From the start I can apprehend the concept of body analytically through the characters of extension, impenetrability, figure, etc., all of which are thought in the concept. Now, however, looking back on the experience from which I have derived this concept of body, and finding weight to be invariably connected with the above characters, I attach it as a predicate to the concept; and in doing so I attach it synthetically, and am therefore extending my knowledge. The possibility of the synthesis of the predicate 'weight' with the concept of 'body' thus rests upon experience. While the one concept is not contained in the other, they yet belong to one another, though only contingently, as parts of a whole, namely, of an experience which is itself a synthetic combination of intuitions.[10]

B 13   But in a *priori* synthetic judgments this help is entirely lacking. [I do not here have the advantage of looking around in the field of experience.] Upon what, then, am I to rely, when I seek to go beyond the concept A, and to know that another concept B is connected with it? Through what is the synthesis made possible? Let us take the proposition, 'Everything which happens has its cause'. In the concept of 'something which happens', I do indeed think an existence which is preceded by a time, etc., and from this

concept analytic judgments may be obtained. But the concept of a 'cause' lies entirely outside the other concept, and signifies something different from 'that which happens', and is not therefore in any way contained in this latter representation. How come I then to predicate of that which happens something quite different, and to apprehend that the concept of cause, though not contained in it, yet belongs, and indeed necessarily belongs, to it? What is here the unknown = X which gives support to the understanding when it believes that it can discover outside the concept A a predicate B foreign to this concept, which it yet at the same time considers to be connected with it? It cannot be experience, because the suggested principle has connected the second representation with the first, not only with greater universality, but also with the character of necessity, and therefore completely *a priori* and on the basis of mere concepts. Upon such synthetic, that is, ampliative principles, all our *a priori* speculative knowledge must ultimately rest; analytic judgments are very important, and indeed necessary, but only for obtaining that clearness in the concepts   B 14
which is requisite for such a sure and wide synthesis as will lead to a genuinely new addition to all previous knowledge.

5. IN ALL THEORETICAL SCIENCES OF REASON SYNTHETIC A *PRIORI* JUDGMENTS ARE CONTAINED AS PRINCIPLES

1. *All mathematical judgments, without exception, are synthetic.* This fact, though incontestably certain and in its consequences very important, has hitherto escaped the notice of those who are engaged in the analysis of human reason, and is, indeed, directly opposed to all their conjectures. For as it was found that all mathematical inferences proceed in accordance with the principle of contradiction (which the nature of all apodeictic certainty requires), it was supposed that the fundamental propositions of the science can themselves be known to be true through that principle. This is an erroneous view. For though a synthetic proposition can indeed be discerned in accordance with the principle of contradiction, this can only be if another synthetic proposition is presupposed, and if it can then be apprehended as following from this other proposition; it can never be so discerned in and by itself.

First of all, it has to be noted that mathematical propositions, strictly so called, are always judgments a priori, not empirical; because they carry with them necessity, which cannot be derived from experience. If this be   B 15
demurred to, I am willing to limit my statement to *pure* mathematics, the very concept of which implies that it does not contain empirical, but only pure *a priori* knowledge.

We might, indeed, at first suppose that the proposition $7 + 5 = 12$ is a merely analytic proposition, and follows by the principle of contradiction from the concept of a sum of 7 and 5. But if we look more closely we find that the concept of the sum of 7 and 5 contains nothing save the union of the two numbers into one, and in this no thought is being taken as to what that single number may be which combines both. The concept of 12 is by no means already thought in merely thinking this union of 7 and 5; and I may analyse my concept of such a possible sum as long as I please, still I shall never find the 12 in it. We have to go outside these concepts, and call in the aid of the intuition which corresponds to one of them, our five fingers, for instance, or, as Segner does in his *Arithmetic*, five points, adding to the concept of 7, unit by unit, the five given in intuition. For starting with the number 7, and for the concept of 5 calling in the aid of the fingers of my hand as intuition, I now add one by one to the number 7 the units

B 16   which I previously took together to form the number 5, and with the aid of that figure [the hand] see the number 12 come into being. That 5 should be added to 7, I have indeed already thought in the concept of a sum = 7 + 5, but not that this sum is equivalent to the number 12. Arithmetical propositions are therefore always synthetic. This is still more evident if we take larger numbers. For it is then obvious that, however we might turn and twist our concepts, we could never, by the mere analysis of them, and without the aid of intuition, discover what [the number is that] is the sum.

Just as little is any fundamental proposition of pure geometry analytic. That the straight line between two points is the shortest, is a synthetic proposition. For my concept of *straight* contains nothing of quantity, but only of quality. The concept of the shortest is wholly an addition, and cannot be derived, through any process of analysis, from the concept of the

B 17   straight line. Intuition, therefore, must here be called in; only by its aid is the synthesis possible. What here causes us commonly to believe that the predicate of such apodeictic judgments is already contained in our concept, and that the judgment is therefore analytic, is merely the ambiguous character of the terms used. We are required to join in thought a certain predicate to a given concept, and this necessity is inherent in the concepts themselves. But the question is not what we *ought* to join in thought to the given concept, but what we *actually* think in it, even if only obscurely; and it is then manifest that, while the predicate is indeed attached necessarily to the concept, it is so in virtue of an intuition which must be added to the concept, not as thought in the concept itself.

Some few fundamental propositions, presupposed by the geometrician, are, indeed, really analytic, and rest on the principle of contradiction. But, as identical propositions, they serve only as links in the chain of method and not as principles; for instance, $a = a$; the whole is equal to itself; or $(a + b) > a$, that is, the whole is greater than its part.[11] And even these propositions, though they are valid according to pure concepts, are only admitted in mathematics because they can be exhibited in intuition.

2. *Natural science (physics) contains a priori synthetic judgments as principles.* I need cite only two such judgments: that in all changes of the material world the quantity of matter remains unchanged; and that in all

communication of motion action and reaction must always be equal.[12] Both propositions, it is evident, are not only necessary, and therefore in their origin *a priori*, but also synthetic. For in the concept of matter I do not think its permanence, but only its presence in the space which it occupies. I go outside and beyond the concept of matter, joining to it *a priori* in thought something which I have not thought *in* it. The proposition is not, therefore, analytic, but synthetic, and yet is thought *a priori;* and so likewise are the other propositions of the pure part of natural science.

B 18

3. *Metaphysics,* even if we look upon it as having hitherto failed in all its endeavours, is yet, owing to the nature of human reason, a quite indispensable science, and *ought to contain* a priori *synthetic knowledge.* For its business is not merely to analyse concepts which we make for ourselves *a priori* of things, and thereby to clarify them analytically, but to extend our *a priori* knowledge. And for this purpose we must employ principles which add to the given concept something that was not contained in it, and through *a priori* synthetic judgments venture out so far that experience is quite unable to follow us, as, for instance, in the proposition, that the world must have a first beginning, and such like. Thus metaphysics consists, at least *in intention,* entirely of *a priori* synthetic propositions.

6. THE GENERAL PROBLEM OF PURE REASON

B 19

Much is already gained if we can bring a number of investigations under the formula of a single problem. For we not only lighten our own task, by defining it accurately, but make it easier for others, who would test our results, to judge whether or not we have succeeded in what we set out to do. Now the proper problem of pure reason is contained in the question: How are *a priori* synthetic judgments possible?

That metaphysics has hitherto remained in so vacillating a state of uncertainty and contradiction, is entirely due to the fact that this problem, and perhaps even the distinction between analytic and synthetic judgments, has never previously been considered. Upon the solution of this problem, or upon a sufficient proof that the possibility which it desires to have explained does in fact not exist at all, depends the success or failure of metaphysics. Among philosophers, David Hume came nearest to envisaging this problem, but still was very far from conceiving it with sufficient definiteness and universality. He occupied himself exclusively with the synthetic proposition regarding the connection of an effect with its cause (*principium causalitatis*), and he believed himself to have shown that such an *a priori* proposition is entirely impossible. If we accept his conclusions, then all that we call metaphysics is a mere delusion whereby we fancy ourselves to have rational insight into what, in actual fact, is borrowed solely from experience, and under the influence of custom has taken the illusory semblance of necessity. If he had envisaged our problem in all its universality, he would never have been guilty of this statement, so de-

B 20

structive of all pure philosophy. For he would then have recognised that, according to his own argument, pure mathematics, as certainly containing a *priori* synthetic propositions, would also not be possible; and from such an assertion his good sense would have saved him.

In the solution of the above problem, we are at the same time deciding as to the possibility of the employment of pure reason in establishing and developing all those sciences which contain a theoretical *a priori* knowledge of objects, and have therefore to answer the questions:

How is pure mathematics possible?
How is pure science of nature possible?

Since these sciences actually exist, it is quite proper to ask *how* they are possible; for that they must be possible is proved by the fact that they exist. But the poor progress which has hitherto been made in metaphysics, and the fact that no system yet propounded can, in view of the essential purpose of metaphysics, be said really to exist, leaves everyone sufficient ground for doubting as to its possibility.

B 21

C *From the CRITIQUE*

THE TRANSCENDENTAL CLUE TO THE DISCOVERY OF ALL PURE CONCEPTS OF THE UNDERSTANDING

Section 1   THE LOGICAL EMPLOYMENT OF THE UNDERSTANDING

The understanding has thus far been explained merely negatively, as a non-sensible faculty of knowledge. Now since without sensibility we cannot have any intuition, understanding cannot be a faculty of intuition. But besides intuition there is no other mode of knowledge except by means of concepts. The knowledge yielded by understanding, or at least by the human understanding, must therefore be by means of concepts, and so is not intuitive, but discursive.[13] Whereas all intuitions, as sensibile, rest on affections, concepts rest on functions. By 'function' I mean the unity of the act of bringing various representations under one common representation. Concepts are based on the spontaneity of thought, sensible intuitions on the receptivity of impressions. Now the only use which the understanding can make of these concepts is to judge by means of them. Since no representation, save when it is an intuition, is in immediate relation to an object, no concept is ever related to an object immediately, but to some other representation of it, be that other representation an intuition, or itself a concept.[14] Judgment is therefore the mediate knowledge of an object, that is, the representation of a representation of it. In every judgment there is a concept which holds of many representations, and among them of a given representation that is immediately related to an object. Thus in

B 93

the judgment, 'all bodies are divisible', the concept of the divisible applies to various other concepts, but is here applied in particular to the concept of body, and this concept again to certain appearances that present themselves to us. These objects, therefore, are mediately represented through the concept of divisibility. Accordingly, all judgments are functions of unity among our representations;[15] instead of an immediate representation, a *higher* representation, which comprises the immediate representation and various others, is used in knowing the object, and thereby much possible knowledge is collected into one. Now we can reduce all acts of the understanding to judgments, and the *understanding* may therefore be represented as a *faculty of judgment*. For, as stated above, the understanding is a faculty of thought. Thought is knowledge by means of concepts. But concepts, as predicates of possible judgments, relate to some representation of a not *yet* determined object. Thus the concept of body means something, for instance, metal, which can be known by means of that concept. It is therefore a concept solely in virtue of its comprehending other representations, by means of which it can relate to objects. It is therefore the predicate of a possible judgment, for instance, 'every metal is a body'. The functions of the understanding can, therefore, be discovered if we can give an exhaustive statement of the functions of unity in judgments.

B 94

D   *From the CRITIQUE*

ANALYTIC OF CONCEPTS
Chapter 2   THE DEDUCTION OF THE PURE CONCEPTS OF UNDERSTANDING

Section 1   § 13   THE PRINCIPLES OF ANY TRANSCENDENTAL DEDUCTION

Jurists, when speaking of rights and claims, distinguish in a legal action the question of right (*quid juris*) from the question of fact (*quid facti*); and they demand that both be proved. Proof of the former, which has to state the right or the legal claim, they entitle the *deduction*. Many empirical concepts are employed without question from anyone. Since experience is always available for the proof of their objective reality, we believe ourselves, even without a deduction, to be justified in appropriating to them a meaning, an ascribed significance. But there are also usurpatory concepts, such as *fortune, fate*, which, though allowed to circulate by almost universal indulgence, are yet from time to time challenged by the question: *quid juris*. This demand for a deduction involves us in considerable perplexity, no clear legal title, sufficient to justify their employment, being obtainable either from experience or from reason.[16]

B 117

Now among the manifold concepts which form the highly complicated web of human knowledge, there are some which are marked out for pure *a priori* employment, in complete independence of all experience; and their right to be so employed always demands a deduction. For since empirical proofs do not suffice to justify this kind of employment, we are faced by the problem how these concepts can relate to objects which they yet do not obtain from any experience. The explanation of the manner in which concepts can thus relate *a priori* to objects I entitle their transcendental deduction; and from it I distinguish empirical deduction, which shows the manner in which a concept is acquired through experience and through reflection upon experience, and which therefore concerns, not its legitimacy, but only its *de facto* mode of origination.[17]

B 118   We are already in possession of concepts which are of two quite different kinds, and which yet agree in that they relate to objects in a completely *a priori* manner, namely, the concepts of space and time as forms of sensibility, and the categories as concepts of understanding. To seek an empirical deduction of either of these types of concept would be labour entirely lost. For their distinguishing feature consists just in this, that they relate to their objects without having borrowed from experience anything that can serve in the representation of these objects. If, therefore, a deduction of such concepts is indispensable, it must in any case be transcendental.

We can, however, with regard to these concepts, as with regard to all knowledge, seek to discover in experience, if not the principle of their possibility, at least the occasioning causes of their production. The impressions of the senses supplying the first stimulus, the whole faculty of knowledge opens out to them, and experience is brought into existence. That experience contains two very dissimilar elements, namely, the *matter* of knowledge [obtained] from the senses, and a certain *form* for the ordering of this matter, [obtained] from the inner source of the pure intuition and thought which, on occasion of the sense-impressions, are first brought into action and yield concepts. Such an investigation of the first strivings of our faculty of knowledge, whereby it advances from particular percep-
B 119   tions to universal concepts, is undoubtedly of great service. We are indebted to the celebrated Locke for opening out this new line of enquiry. But a *deduction* of the pure *a priori* concepts can never be obtained in this manner; it is not to be looked for in any such direction. For in view of their subsequent employment, which has to be entirely independent of experience, they must be in a position to show a certificate of birth quite other than that of descent from experiences. Since this attempted physiological derivation concerns a *quaestio facti*, it cannot strictly be called deduction; and I shall therefore entitle it the explanation of the *possession* of pure knowledge.[18] Plainly the only deduction that can be given of this knowledge is one that is transcendental, not empirical. In respect to pure *a priori* concepts the latter type of deduction is an utterly useless enterprise which can be engaged in only by those who have failed to grasp the quite peculiar nature of these modes of knowledge.

But although it may be admitted that the only kind of deduction of pure *a priori* knowledge which is possible is on transcendental lines, it is not at once obvious that a deduction is indispensably necessary. We have already, by means of a transcendental deduction, traced the concepts of space and time to their sources, and have explained and determined their *a priori* objective validity. Geometry, however, proceeds with security in knowledge that is completely *a priori*, and has no need to beseech philosophy for any certificate of the pure and legitimate descent of its fundamental concept of space. But the concept is employed in this science only in its reference to the outer sensible world—of the intuition of which space is the pure form—where all geometrical knowledge, grounded as it is in a *priori* intuition, possesses immediate evidence. The objects, so far as their form is concerned, are given, through the very knowledge of them, *a priori* in intuition. In the case of the *pure concepts of understanding*, it is quite otherwise; it is with them that the unavoidable demand for a transcendental deduction, not only of themselves, but also of the concept of space, first originates. For since they speak of objects through predicates not of intuition and sensibility but of pure *a priori* thought, they relate to objects universally, that is, apart from all conditions of sensibility. Also, not being grounded in experience, they cannot, in a *priori* intuition, exhibit any object such as might, prior to all experience, serve as ground for their synthesis. For these reasons, they arouse suspicion not merely in regard to the objective validity and the limits of their own employment, but owing to their tendency to employ the *concept of space* beyond the conditions of sensible intuition, that concept also they render ambiguous; and this, indeed, is why we have already found a transcendental deduction of it necessary. The reader must therefore be convinced of the unavoidable necessity of such a transcendental deduction before he has taken a single step in the field of pure reason. Otherwise he proceeds blindly, and after manifold wanderings must come back to the same ignorance from which he started. At the same time, if he is not to lament over obscurity in matters which are by their very nature deeply veiled, or to be too easily discouraged in the removal of obstacles, he must have a clear foreknowledge of the inevitable difficulty of the undertaking. For we must either completely surrender all claims to make judgments of pure reason in the most highly esteemed of all fields, that which transcends the limits of all possible experience, or else bring this critical enquiry to completion.

We have already been able with but little difficulty to explain how the concepts of space and time, although *a priori* modes of knowledge, must necessarily relate to objects, and how independently of all experience they make possible a synthetic knowledge of objects. For since only by means of such pure forms of sensibility can an object appear to us, and so be an object of empirical intuition, space and time are pure intuitions which contain *a priori* the condition of the possibility of objects as appearances, and the synthesis which takes place in them has objective validity.

B 120

B 121

B 122

The categories of understanding, on the other hand, do not represent the conditions under which objects are given in intuition. Objects may, therefore, appear to us without their being under the necessity of being related to the functions of understanding; and understanding need not, therefore, contain their *a priori* conditions. Thus a difficulty such as we did not meet with in the field of sensibility is here presented, namely, how *subjective conditions of thought* can have *objective validity*, that is, can furnish conditions of the possibility of all knowledge of objects. For appearances can certainly be given in intuition independently of functions of the understanding. Let us take, for instance, the concept of cause, which signifies a special kind of synthesis, whereby upon something, A, there is posited something quite different, B, according to a rule. It is not manifest *a priori* why appearances should contain anything of this kind (experiences cannot be cited in its proof, for what has to be established is the objective validity of a concept that is *a priori*); and it is therefore *a priori* doubtful whether such a concept be not perhaps altogether empty, and have no object anywhere among appearances. That objects of sensible intuition must conform to the formal conditions of sensibility which lie *a priori* in the mind is evident, because otherwise they would not be objects for us. But that they must likewise conform to the conditions which the understanding requires for the synthetic unity of thought, is a conclusion the grounds of which are by no means so obvious. Appearances might very well be so constituted that the understanding should not find them to be in accordance with the conditions of its unity. Everything might be in such confusion that, for instance, in the series of appearances nothing presented itself which might yield a rule of synthesis and so answer to the concept of cause and effect. This concept would then be altogether empty, null, and meaningless. But since intuition stands in no need whatsoever of the functions of thought, appearances would none the less present objects to our intuition.

If we thought to escape these toilsome enquiries by saying that experience continually presents examples of such regularity among appearances and so affords abundant opportunity of abstracting the concept of cause, and at the same time of verifying the objective validity of such a concept, we should be overlooking the fact that the concept of cause can never arise in this manner. It must either be grounded completely *a priori* in the understanding, or must be entirely given up as a mere phantom of the brain. For this concept makes strict demand that something, A, should be such that something else, B, follows from it *necessarily and in accordance with an absolutely universal rule*. Appearances do indeed present cases from which a rule can be obtained according to which something usually happens, but they never prove the sequence to be *necessary*. To the synthesis of cause and effect there belongs a dignity which cannot be empirically expressed, namely, that the effect not only succeeds upon the

B 123

B 124

cause, but that it is posited *through* it and arises *out of* it. This strict universality of the rule is never a characteristic of empirical rules; they can acquire through inducton only comparative universality, that is, extensive applicability. If we were to treat pure concepts of understanding as merely empirical products, we should be making a complete change in [the manner of] their employment.

§ 14   TRANSITION TO THE TRANSCENDENTAL DEDUCTION OF THE CATEGORIES

There are only two possible ways in which synthetic representations and their objects can establish connection, obtain necessary relation to one another, and, as it were, meet one another. Either the object alone must make the representation possible, or the representation alone must make the object possible. In the former case, this relation is only empirical, and the representation is never possible *a priori*. This is true of appearances, as regards that [element] in them which belongs to sensation. In the latter case, representation in itself does not produce its object in so far as *existence* is concerned, for we are not here speaking of its causality by means of the will. None the less the representation is *a priori* determinant of the object, if it be the case that only through the representation is it possible to *know* anything *as an object*. Now there are two conditions under which alone the knowledge of an object is possible, first, *intuition*, through which it is given, though only as appearance; secondly, *concept*, through which an object is thought corresponding to this intuition. It is evident from the above that the first condition, namely, that under which alone objects can be intuited, does actually lie *a priori* in the mind as the formal ground of the objects. All appearances necessarily agree with this formal condition of sensibility, since only through it can they appear, that is, be empirically intuited and given. The question now arises whether *a priori* concepts do not also serve as antecedent conditions under which alone anything can be, if not intuited, yet thought as object in general. In that case all empirical knowledge of objects would necessarily conform to such concepts, because only as thus presupposing them is anything possible as *object of experience*. Now all experience does indeed contain, in addition to the intuition of the senses through which something is given, a *concept* of an object as being thereby given, that is to say, as appearing. Concepts of object in general thus underlie all empirical knowledge as its *a priori* conditions.[19] The objective validity of the categories as *a priori* concepts rests, therefore, on the fact that, so far as the form of thought is concerned, through them alone does experience become possible. They relate of necessity and *a priori* to objects of experience, for the reason that only by means of them can any object whatsoever of experience be thought.

The transcendental deduction of all *a priori* concepts has thus a principle according to which the whole enquiry must be directed, namely,

B 125

B 126

that they must be recognised as a *priori* conditions of the possibility of experience, whether of the intuition which is to be met with in it or of the thought. Concepts which yield the objective ground of the possibility of experience are for this very reason necessary. But the unfolding of the experience wherein they are encountered is not their deduction; it is only their illustration. For on any such exposition they would be merely accidental. Save through their original relation to possible experience, in which all objects of knowledge are found, their relation to any one object would be quite incomprehensible.

The illustrious Locke, failing to take account of these considerations, and meeting with pure concepts of the understanding in experience, deduced them also from experience, and yet proceeded so *inconsequently* that he attempted with their aid to obtain knowledge which far transcends all limits of experience. David Hume recognized that, in order to be able to do this, it was necessary that these concepts should have an a *priori* origin. But since he could not explain how it can be possible that the understanding must think concepts, which are not in themselves connected in the understanding, as being necessarily connected in the object, and since it never occurred to him that the understanding might itself, perhaps, through these concepts, be the author of the experience in which its objects are found, he was constrained to derive them from experience, namely, from a subjective necessity (that is, from *custom*), which arises from repeated association in experience, and which comes mistakenly to be regarded as objective. But from these premisses he argued quite consistently. It is impossible, he declared, with these concepts and the principles to which they give rise, to pass beyond the limits of experience. Now this *empirical* derivation, in which both philosophers agree, cannot be reconciled with the scientific a *priori* knowledge which we do actually possess, namely, *pure mathematics* and *general science of nature*; and this fact therefore suffices to disprove such derivation.

B 128

While the former of these two illustrious men opened a wide door to *enthusiasm*—for if reason once be allowed such rights, it will no longer allow itself to be kept within bounds by vaguely defined recommendations of moderation—the other gave himself over entirely to *scepticism*, having, as he believed, discovered that what had hitherto been regarded as reason was but an all-prevalent illusion infecting our faculty of knowledge. We now propose to make trial whether it be not possible to find for human reason safe conduct between these two rocks, assigning to her determinate limits, and yet keeping open for her the whole field of her appropriate activities.

But first I shall introduce a word of explanation in regard to the categories. They are concepts of an object in general, by means of which the intuition of an object is regarded as determined in respect of one of the logical functions of judgment. Thus the function of the categorical judgment is that of the relation of subject to predicate; for example, 'All bodies

are divisible'. But as regards the merely logical employment of the understanding, it remains undetermined to which of the two concepts the function of the subject, and to which the function of predicate, is to be assigned.   B 129
For we can also say, 'Something divisible is a body'. But when the concept
of body is brought under the category of substance, it is thereby determined that its empirical intuition in experience must always be considered as subject and never as mere predicate. Similarly with all the
other categories.

E From the *CRITIQUE*

§ 22   THE CATEGORY HAS NO OTHER APPLICATION IN KNOWL-
EDGE THAN TO OBJECTS OF EXPERIENCE

To *think* an object and to *know* an object are thus by no means the same
thing. Knowledge involves two factors: first, the concept, through which
an object general is thought (the category); and secondly, the intuition,
through which it is given. For if no intuition could be given corresponding
to the concept, the concept would still indeed be a thought, so far as its
form is concerned, but would be without any object, and no knowledge of
anything would be possible by means of it. So far as I could know, there
would be nothing, and could be nothing, to which my thought could be
applied. Now, as the Aesthetic has shown, the only intuition possible to
us is sensible; consequently, the thought of an object in general, by means
of a pure concept of understanding, can become knowledge for us only in
so far as the concept is related to objects of the senses. Sensible intuition   B 147
is either pure intuition (space and time) or empirical intuition of that
which is immediately represented, through sensation, as actual in space
and time. Through the determination of pure intuition we can acquire *a*
priori knowledge of objects, as in mathematics, but only in regard to their
form, as appearances; whether there can be things which must be intuited
in this form, is still left undecided. Mathematical concepts are not, therefore, by themselves knowledge, except on the supposition that there are
things which allow of being presented to us only in accordance with the
form of that pure sensible intuition. Now *things in space and time* are
given only in so far as they are perceptions (that is, representations accompanied by sensation)—therefore only through empirical representation. Consequently, the pure concepts of understanding, even when they
are applied to *a priori* intuitions, as in mathematics, yield knowledge only
in so far as these intuitions—and therefore indirectly by their means the
pure concepts also—can be applied to empirical intuitions. Even, therefore, with the aid of [pure] intuition, the categories do not afford us any
knowledge of things; they do so only through their possible application
to *empirical intuition*. In other words, they serve only for the possibility of
empirical knowledge, and such knowledge is what we entitle experience.

B 148   Our conclusion is therefore this: the categories, as yielding knowledge of *things*, have no kind of application, save only in regard to things which may be objects of possible experience.

F From the CRITIQUE

We have now to explain the possibility of knowing *a priori*, by means of *categories*, whatever objects may *present themselves to our senses*, not indeed in respect of the form of their intuition, but in respect of the laws of their combination, and so, as it were, of prescribing laws to nature,

B 160   and even of making nature possible. For unless the categories discharged this function, there could be no explaining why everything that can be presented to our senses must be subject to laws which have their origin *a priori* in the understanding alone.

First of all, I may draw attention to the fact that by *synthesis of apprehension* I understand that combination of the manifold in an empirical intuition, whereby perception, that is, empirical consciousness of the intuition (as appearance), is possible.

In the representations of space and time we have *a priori forms* of outer and inner sensible intuition; and to these the synthesis of apprehension of the manifold of appearance must always conform, because in no other way can the synthesis take place at all. But space and time are represented *a priori* not merely as *forms* of sensible intuition, but as themselves *intuitions* which contain a manifold [of their own], and therefore are represented with the determination of the *unity* of this manifold (*vide* the

B 161   Transcendental Aesthetic).[20] Thus *unity of the synthesis* of the manifold, without or within us, and consequently also a *combination* to which everything that is to be represented as determined in space or in time must conform, is given *a priori* as the condition of the synthesis of all *apprehension*—not indeed in, but with these intuitions. This synthetic unity can be no other than the unity of the combination of the manifold of a given *intuition in general* in an original consciousness, in accordance with the categories, in so far as the combination is applied to our *sensible intuition*. All synthesis, therefore, even that which renders perception possible, is subject to the categories; and since experience is knowledge by means of connected perceptions, the categories are conditions of the possibility of experience, and are therefore valid *a priori* for all objects of experience.

B 162   When, for instance, by apprehension of the manifold of a house I make the empirical intuition of it into a perception, the *necessary unity* of space and of outer sensible intuition in general lies at the basis of my apprehension, and I draw as it were the outline of the house in conformity with this synthetic unity of the manifold in space. But if I abstract from the form of space, this same synthetic unity has its seat in the understanding, and is the category of the synthesis of the homogeneous in an intuition in general, that is, the category of *quantity*. To this category, therefore, the synthesis of apprehension, that is to say, the perception, must completely conform.[21]

When, to take another example, I perceive the freezing of water, I apprehend two states, fluidity and solidity, and these as standing to one another in a relation of time. But in time, which I place at the basis of the appearance [in so far] as [it is] inner *intuition,* I necessarily represent to myself synthetic *unity* of the manifold, without which that relation of time could not be given in an intuition as being *determined* in respect of time-sequence. Now this synthetic unity, as a condition *a priori* under which I combine the manifold of an *intuition in general,* is—if I abstract from the constant form of *my* inner intuition, namely, time—the category of *cause,* by means of which, when I apply it to my sensibility, I determine *everything that happens* in accordance with the relation which it prescribes, and I do so *in time in general.* Thus my apprehension of such an event, and therefore the event itself, considered as a possible perception, is subject to the concept of the *relation* of *effects* and *causes,* and so in all other cases.

B 163

Categories are concepts which prescribe laws *a priori* to appearances, and therefore to nature, the sum of all appearances (*natura materialiter spectata*). The question therefore arises, how it can be conceivable that nature should have to proceed in accordance with categories which yet are not derived from it, and do not model themselves upon its pattern; that is, how they can determine *a priori* the combination of the manifold of nature, while yet they are not derived from it. The solution of this seeming enigma is as follows.

That the *laws* of appearances in nature must agree with the understanding and its *a priori* form, that is, with its faculty of *combining* the manifold in general, is no more surprising than that the appearances themselves must agree with the form of *a priori* sensible intuition. For just as appearances do not exist in themselves but only relatively to the subject in which, so far as it has senses, they inhere, so the laws do not exist in the appearances but only relatively to this same being, so far as it has understanding. Things in themselves would necessarily, apart from any understanding that knows them, conform to laws of their own. But appearances are only representations of things which are unknown as regards what they may be in themselves. As mere representations, they are subject to no law of connection save that which the connecting faculty prescribes. Now it is imagination that connects the manifold of sensible intuition; and imagination is dependent for the unity of its intellectual synthesis upon the understanding, and for the manifoldness of its apprehension upon sensibility. All possible perception is thus dependent upon synthesis of apprehension, and this empirical synthesis in turn upon transcendental synthesis, and therefore upon the categories. Consequently, all possible perceptions, and therefore everything that can come to empirical consciousness, that is, all appearances of nature, must, so far as their connection is concerned, be

B 164

B 165

subject to the categories. Nature, considered merely as nature in general, is dependent upon these categories as the original ground of its necessary conformity to law (*natura formaliter spectata*). Pure understanding is not, however, in a position, through mere categories, to prescribe to appearances any a priori laws other than those which are involved in a *nature in general*, that is, in the conformity to law of all appearances in space and time. Special laws, as concerning those appearances which are empirically determined, cannot in their specific character be *derived* from the categories, although they are one and all subject to them. To obtain any knowledge whatsoever of these special laws, we must resort to experience; but it is the a priori laws that alone can instruct us in regard to experience in general, and as to what it is that can be known as an object of experience.

§ 27   OUTCOME OF THIS DEDUCTION OF THE CONCEPTS OF UNDERSTANDING

We cannot think an object save through categories; we cannot *know* an object so thought save through intuitions corresponding to these concepts. Now all our intuitions are sensible; and this knowledge, in so far as

B 166   its object is given, is empirical. But empirical knowledge is experience. *Consequently, there can be no a priori knowledge, except of objects of possible experience.*[22]

But although this knowledge is limited to objects of experience, it is not therefore all derived from experience. The pure intuitions [of receptivity] and the pure concepts of understanding are elements in knowledge, and both are found in us a priori. There are only two ways in which we can account for a *necessary* agreement of experience with the concepts of its objects: either experience makes these concepts possible or these concepts make experience possible. The former supposition does

B 167   not hold in respect of the categories (nor of pure sensible intuition); for since they are a priori concepts, and therefore independent of experience, the ascription to them of an empirical origin would be a sort of *generatio aequivoca*. There remains, therefore, only the second supposition—a system, as it were, of the *epigenesis* of pure reason—namely, that the categories contain, on the side of the understanding, the grounds of the possibility of all experience in general. How they make experience possible, and what are the principles of the possibility of experience that they supply in their application to appearances, will be shown more fully in the following chapter on the transcendental employment of the faculty of judgment.

A middle course may be proposed between the two above mentioned, namely, that the categories are neither *self-thought* first principles a priori of our knowledge nor derived from experience, but subjective dispositions of thought, implanted in us from the first moment of our existence, and so ordered by our Creator that their employment is in complete harmony with the laws of nature in accordance with which experience proceeds—a kind of *preformation-system* of pure reason. Apart, however, from the objection that on such an hypothesis we can set no limit to the assumption of predetermined dispositions to future judgments, there is this decisive objection against the suggested middle course, that the necessity of the categories, which belongs to their very conception, would then have to be sacrificed. The concept of cause, for instance, which expresses the necessity of an event under a presupposed condition, would be false if it rested only on an arbitrary subjective necessity, implanted in us, of connecting certain empirical representations according to the rule of causal relation. I would not then be able to say that the effect is connected with the cause in the object, that is to say, necessarily, but only that I am so constituted that I cannot think this representation otherwise than as thus connected. This is exactly what the sceptic most desires. For if this be the situation, all our insight, resting on the supposed objective validity of our judgments, is nothing but sheer illusion; nor would there be wanting people who would refuse to admit this subjective necessity, a necessity which can only be felt. Certainly a man cannot dispute with anyone regarding that which depends merely on the mode in which he is himself organised.

B 168

NOTES

1   It seems here that Kant makes pure knowledge (see the heading of this section) and a priori knowledge equivalent. At other times Kant distinguishes pure a priori knowledge from a priori knowledge which is not free from empirical elements, in other words, synthetic a priori knowledge. In this case, pure a priori knowledge is restricted to analytic a priori knowledge, as in the discussion immediately following. Apparently the difficulty is to be resolved by holding that a priori knowledge can be had about appropriate concepts derived partly from experience, in which case the knowledge may be said to be independent of experience.

2   The criterion of being *thought* as *necessary* is rationalistic.

3   This example seems puzzling, partly because of the use of the word *heavy*. If *are heavy* is replaced by *have weight*, then the statement may seem to be strictly universal, but then it is not an example of *empirical* universality. Consequently, *heavy* must be taken in some other sense. Other candidates, 'heavier than an equivalent volume of air', for example, run the risk of making the statement false (consider balloons filled with hydrogen as objects), so that the example is not very convincing.

4   One wishes that Kant had provided some examples of cases in which the one criterion could settle the a priori character of some judgment more quickly than the other. Since both criteria are criteria for the applicability of the same concept, and consequently when one is satisfied, the other must be also, it is not easy to understand what distinction Kant had in mind when he spoke of them as different criteria.

5   The two preceding sentences make interesting claims. One makes it an assumption of Kantian philosophy that some experiences are certain. This assumption is preceded by the claim that the a priori can be shown necessarily (a priori) to be indispensable for experience. As we can hardly doubt that we have experience, this purports to make the proof of a priori judgments indubitable.

6   Notice the distinction between (merely) empirical properties of an object, and concepts related to the concept of an object which experience has taught us. Some concepts taught by experience will not be directly experienced in any object.

7   In this context, *science* means broadly *branch of knowledge*. This section defines metaphysics as the study of certain specified problems, a definition that will be referred to later.

8   At several points in the discussion of Kant's philosophy, rationalistic elements are emphasized. This passage, which adumbrates the Kantian rejection of much of metaphysics on the grounds that it cannot be contradicted or controlled by experience, emphasizes the empirical element that experience should at least *potentially* be capable of conflicting with metaphysics, and should establish the fact that Kant's philosophy must be taken as a synthesis of the rationalisms and empiricisms which preceded his epistemological investigations.

9   The application to negative judgments requires some care. One cannot say that a negative analytic judgment holds if the predicate B is not contained in the subject concept A, since this would make negative analytic judgments synthetic. Presumably a negative analytic judgment is one in which the predicate complementary to B (*not-B*) is contained in the subject concept A.

10   Compare this passage with the passage connected with footnote 3. In footnote 3 it was deliberately suggested that "All bodies have weight." seemed *necessary*. Did it? Here Kant informs us that it is not necessary, indicating that the concept of body may not be a priori intelligible.

11   Here is an example indicating that Kant's intuition could not have the qualities of necessity which he supposed it to have. Contemporary mathematicians reject the general applicability of the rule that the whole is greater than any of its parts. The reasons for rejecting this rule derive from discoveries about the properties of infinite sets which were not made clear until after Kant's time. An exception to the rule based on the properties of infinite sets will be briefly sketched. Mathematicians say that two collections of things are of equal cardinality (intuitively, have the same number of things in them) when they may be placed in a one-to-one correspondence with each other. A one-to-one correspondence is a function which assigns each member of one collection a unique member of the other collection, and vice versa. Consider the set of all positive integers, $(1, 2, 3, 4, 5, \ldots)$, which can be called set A. From A, we could imagine ourselves removing all of the odd numbers, leaving the set of even numbers, $(2, 4, 6, 8, \ldots)$, which we could call set B. Intuitively, in view of the rule that the whole is greater than any of its parts, we would expect that A is larger than B, since B seems to have only some of the members of A. Yet a one-to-one correspondence may be established between A and B. If x is an arbitrary member of A, let $2x$ be the (unique) member of B correlated to x by the correspondence, and vice versa. By the rule discussed previously, A and B are in one-to-one correspondence and have the same cardinality, indicating

that the rule that a whole is greater than any of its parts does not *necessarily* hold in infinite collections.

12   Again, the first of these claims is now vitiated by the discovery of physicists that matter may be converted to energy. These critical comments show, not that Kantian philosophy needs to be rejected, but that the concept of a priori requires further analysis.

13   *Discursive* is *not* equivalent to *analytic*. *Discursive* is opposed to *intuitive*, and means *dealing with concepts*. Consequently, some discursive thought is synthetic a priori, and not analytic.

14   This sentence begins Kant's discussion of the relationship between concepts and objects. Since objects are not known directly or intuited directly, concepts must be related not to the object, but to its representation as a result of intuition, or to a concept of a kind of object formed by an intellectual synthesis which unifies a number of intuitions of similar objects.

15   The use of *function* here is puzzling. Kant means to say that a judgment is a unification of ideas. Apparently *function*, which is *defined* a few sentences later, indicates that a judgment unifies concepts in a manner analogous to the way in which diverse intuitions are unified into the concept of an object.

16   Clearly no legal title is available from experience. But the remark that it is not available from reason requires scrutiny. Reasoning will show us that these concepts are legitimate, but there is no prima facie case that they are, for the mere fact of reasoning does not show that we are reasoning *about* something. What is needed is a proof that these concepts can be applied in judgments about experience, particularly in judgments of objects not yet experienced.

17   Notice Kant's distinction between a transcendental and an empirical deduction. This distinction is similar to the distinction often made between the context of discovery and the context of justification of a theory in the philosophy of science. In rough terms, once a theory has been proposed, its acceptability may be judged (context of justification) without knowledge of how it came to be discovered (context of discovery). We may, for example, take a theory to be acceptable or unacceptable without knowing anything about the biography of the man who proposed it. Students sometimes suppose that the fact that we must acquire a language (through experience) in order to *express* our knowledge means that all knowledge is based on experience. But what is expressed (mathematical truth), for example, may well be true independently of our means of expressing it, indeed true if we never express it. Kant points out that the universality and necessity of a priori judgments means that the concepts employed cannot be *derived* from our limited experience, even though our experience may indicate that they can be successfully employed to develop knowledge.

18   Read *psychological* for *physiological*. Kant refers to an attempted empirical deduction from a history of someone's past experiences.

19   Notice that this is a succinct statement of Kant's crucial insight. We could not legitimately make judgments about *trees*, for example, based simply on sense experiences, since the stability, etc., of trees cannot *follow* from sense experience. Judgments about trees are based on the concept of a tree which results from the category of substance and accident as applied to certain of our sense experiences. Thus the category is an a priori condition of our being able to give

our sense experiences the significance that can result in human knowledge of a scientific kind.

20 (The following footnote is Kant's.) Space, represented as *object* (as we are required to do in geometry), contains more than mere form of intuition; it also contains *combination* of the manifold, given according to the form of sensibility, in an *intuitive* representation, so that the *form of intuition* gives only a manifold, the *formal intuition* gives unity of representation. In the Aesthetic I have treated this unity as belonging merely to sensibility, simply in order to emphasize that it precedes any concept, although, as a matter of fact, it presupposes a synthesis which does not belong to the senses but through which all concepts of space and time first become possible. For since by its means (in that the understanding determines the sensibility) space and time are first *given* as intuitions, the unity of this *a priori* intuition belongs to space and time, and not to the concept of the understanding.

21 (The following footnote is Kant's.) In this manner it is proved that the synthesis of apprehension, which is empirical, must necessarily be in conformity with the synthesis of apperception, which is intellectual and is contained in the category completely *a priori*. It is one and the same spontaneity, which in the one case, under the title of imagination, and in the other case, under the title of understanding, brings combination into the manifold of intuition.

22 (The following footnote is Kant's.) Lest my readers should stumble at the alarming evil consequences which may over-hastily be inferred from this statement, I may remind them that *for thought* the categories are not limited by the conditions of our sensible intuition, but have an unlimited field. It is only the *knowledge* of that which we think, the determining of the object, that requires intuition. In the absence of intuition, the thought of the object may still have its true and useful consequences, as regards the subject's *employment of reason*. The use of reason is not always directed to the determination of the object, that is, to knowledge, but also to the determination of the subject and of its volition —a use which cannot therefore be dealt with here.

PART 7

Peirce

(1839–1914)

Abductive Inference

We have seen that Kant's philosophy attempts to avoid difficulties in older forms of rationalism and empiricism by working out a synthesis or compromise incorporating the strong points of each. Now it should be noted that compromise solutions are not *necessarily* better than any of the solutions which they compromise among. If three doctors recommend, respectively, 50, 100, and 150 cubic centimeters of some drug to a patient afflicted with some disease, there is no way of proving that 100 cubic centimeters is the best amount to administer. Indeed, we can imagine cases in which one amount will cure, and the others will not, even though the curing amount is any one of the three. Nevertheless, at least one of Kant's insights in making a compromise, the insight that knowledge is not given in experience, but is at least partly a contribution of the knower in organizing his experiences, seems to be required for a theory of knowledge if awkward consequences of more traditional rationalism and empiricism are to be avoided. The details of Kant's epistemology indicate that the knower's contribution to knowledge is in some sense *necessary*, so that knowledge in Kant carries a distinctly rationalistic flavor in his compromise. It is clear that a more empiricistic compromise between traditional rationalism and empiricism will require a weakening of the knower's mental contribution to knowledge to a contribution which does not have the necessity of synthetic a priori judgments. Such a compromise, in which the knower's presuppositions determine partly what he comes to know without these presuppositions being necessary is represented by the philosophy known as pragmatism.

Pragmatism is the only major philosophical position in epistemology that has been developed largely by American philosophers. Except for some historical influences not equivalent to pragmatism in spirit, pragmatism is first formulated in the writings of the American philosopher Charles Peirce. Unfortunately, the history of pragmatism is complicated

263

by the fact that Peirce's formulation was adopted by William James and John Dewey, who influenced (one might almost say caused) the wide acceptance of pragmatism by empiricists, even though they seem to have misunderstood Peirce on some technical points. Pragmatism was formulated by Charles Peirce at one stage in his philosophical development, and this formulation was adapted into an empiricistic compromise in spite of the fact that Peirce himself was not nearly so empiricistic as the philosophers who called themselves pragmatists later. Thus, although we shall talk about Peirce, we shall also pay less attention to his actual views than we have to the views of previous philosophers that we have considered and pay correspondingly greater attention to the empiricistic compromise that develops out of his original work in epistemology.

Interestingly enough, Peirce's pragmatism developed out of Peirce's study of Kant's *Critique of Pure Reason* in response to slowly accumulating difficulties that Peirce found in Kant's treatment. Briefly, Peirce found major difficulties in the fact that Kant's table of the kinds of judgments made by the understanding was incomplete, and this seemed to Peirce to entail a complete revision of the categories. From this attempted revision Peirce's views about inference developed. This development led to the view that neither the results of observation nor the relationships of concepts could be considered certain and beyond revision, a key insight in the formulation of pragmatism.

The most important of Peirce's new logical views for the development of pragmatism was his contention that he had developed a new form of inference, which he called retroduction or abduction. This form of inference is now commonly called the method of hypothesis. Peirce contrasts abduction with induction. Induction is also of great importance for pragmatism, particularly when inductive inference is used to test the truth of a general statement. Suppose a statement says that three-fourths of all guinea pigs are white. Nothing about any particular guinea pig may be deduced from this statement, since a particular guinea pig's being white is compatible with this statement as well as a particular guinea pig's not being white. By contrast, if the statement said that all guinea pigs are white, then it can be deduced from that statement that any particular guinea pig is white. Consequently, a particular guinea pig's being black *refutes* the claim that all guinea pigs are white. The difficulty with induction, as Peirce clearly saw, is that *any* observations are compatible with the statement that three-fourths of all guinea pigs are white, since observation of fifty black ones may only indicate that a poor sample has been taken. We expect that the proportion of white guinea pigs among all guinea pigs will closely correspond to the proportion of white guinea pigs in a *fair* sample of guinea pigs, and Peirce takes a major problem of induction to be that of specifying rules for taking *fair* samples. This is an extremely complicated problem, which we shall leave at this point, noting only that Peirce's view of induction is similar to many modern views.

Abduction is quite different from either deduction or induction, and has the following form:

The surprising fact, *C,* is observed.
But if *A* were true, *C* would be a matter of course.
Hence, there is reason to suspect that *A* is true.

This argument is not a deduction since it does not claim that its conclusion *must* be true if its premises are true. On the other hand, it is not inductive since the statement referred to in the conclusion is not tested by sampling. The difference between abduction and induction is that the latter tells us that a statement, true in some observed cases, is likely to be true in un-observed cases, while the former allows us to conclude the likelihood of a fact totally unlike anything which is observed. Abduction allows us to explain things, and it allows us to infer *new* knowledge in a sense that is not possible through the use of deductive inference and possible in a very weakened sense in the use of inductive inference.

Peirce relates abduction to both induction and deduction. The hypothesis *A,* abductively inferred, must be such that *C* is deducible from it. (Here, since deduction holds between statements, it is meant that a statement describing *C* is deducible from some statement of *A.*) At the same time, *A* should be such that it may be inductively tested by *C* as well as by other facts.

In a way, abductive inference is the key to pragmatism. Although such inferences had been made before Peirce, the explicit analysis of them by Peirce as an integral part of scientific method allows the epistemological position of pragmatism to be formulated. By abductive inference we may accept hypotheses that are not known to be true, because they would, if true, explain some observed fact or range of facts. This fact, called *C* in the exhibited form of abductive inference, is characterized by pragmatists as a *surprising* fact. Presumably, an event or fact is surprising because we may have no current explanation for it, or because we were not expecting it in terms of the beliefs which we held at the time of its appearance.

Repeated application of abductive inference may led to continued revision of our hypotheses. For exmple, suppose that I accept a hypothesis, call it *A,* which I accepted in order to explain *C.* A new fact, *C',* may occur which is inexplicable in terms of *A.* At this point I may abductively infer a new hypothesis *A',* such that both *C* and *C'* are explained by it. In principle, I may imagine myself continuing to formulate new hypotheses *A', A'', A''',* etc., to explain any new surprising facts which occur. The formulation of each new hypothesis eliminates the surprising quality of the fact which it is invoked to explain, for the reason that after a hypothesis is abductively inferred to explain it, I psychologically tend to expect similar occurrences in the future.

Pragmatism is the extension of the possibility of revising hypotheses to all our knowledge. Pragmatists believe that all our important knowledge has the tentative status of a hypothesis, and that any part of it may require revision as a result of confrontation with experience. It is in this way that pragmatists feel that the rationalistic flavor of Kant's philosophy may be circumvented. Experience and understanding do influence one another. In some sense, however, experience is still primary in that none of the concepts brought by understanding to experience are necessary; indeed any of them may be revised when they conflict with experience, or when they fail to explain some experience, or even when they do not seem to be the most convenient explanation of some experience.

Pragmatism has some surprising consequences. To begin with, a pragmatist need not hold that we have any *certain* knowledge whatsoever. On the scheme of revising hypotheses, we only know that we are *improving* our hypotheses over a period of time, but never that we have one that will not be revised later. This view fits well with the history of science, in that it may explain the continual rejection and adoption of hypotheses in the history of science as a function of the way in which they explain or fail to explain scientific observation.

Further, this scheme of explaining improvement in understanding seems to entirely expunge human knowledge construed as certain information and to replace it by human *belief.* Many philosophers feel that some certainty is required if an epistemology is to be acceptable. The pragmatist avoids any requirement of certainty because of his novel view of man, a view in which the active powers of human understanding are secondary to man's goal-seeking behavior. A man, according to pragmatists, values beliefs only in so far as they are useful for attaining his goals. This rather novel view of man will be discussed in the next chapter.

There are two major and fairly obvious objections to pragmatism as it has been outlined. One objection is that while the pragmatic view seems to require that it is always possible to perform abductive inference in the face of surprising facts, this possibility cannot be explained solely on pragmatic grounds. This objection maintains that the view that abductive inference will always be possible is a rationalistic or mystical *belief* held as a fundamental tenet by the pragmatist, since it cannot itself be the conclusion of a deductive, abductive, or inductive inference about human experiences. Peirce himself recognized this and called the pragmatic belief that revision was always, in principle, possible a *hope,* although succeeding pragmatists have not always been so frank. It would seem that the pragmatist's best defense may be that this hope represents the smallest rationalistic segment possible in any compromise philosophy recognizing Kant's arguments for the inadequacy of traditional rationalism and traditional empiricism.

Another problem raised by pragmatism which is often cited as an objection is that more than one hypothesis may be abductively inferred anytime that a suitable C occurs. For example, two hypotheses A and A' may both be such that if they were true, C would be a matter of course.

Both of these hypotheses may also be compatible with our other past beliefs. The difficulty then is to choose between A and A', since it is clear that if they are *different* hypotheses, they could not both be *true* claims. Where more than two hypotheses are abductively inferred, the problem may be taken as comparing all possible pairs of such hypotheses, so that the problem of comparing *two* hypotheses is sufficient for raising the general objection to pragmatism. Pragmatism has trouble in framing a decision method for such a problem of choice, and we shall turn to this difficulty in the last chapter.

The Pragmatic Account of Ideas

The pragmatic dependence upon acceptable belief rather than certain knowledge for the consideration of epistemological problems may be illustrated by an example. Suppose one has as a problem to determine the temperature of some body of liquid. Ignoring the complication that the liquid may have no single temperature because it has different temperatures at different points, the problem is still quite indeterminate for a pragmatist. Traditional epistemologists would have supposed that there was such a property of the liquid as its temperature. Pragmatists would hold that such a property is somewhat vague until a *purpose* for discovering the temperature of the liquid is known, and they would hold that the liquid's temperature is always determined inexactly by measurement. On this latter point they are in agreement with rationalism. Pragmatists, however, would go on to hold that the temperature may be determined accurately enough for any given *purpose*, even though the temperature as determined by any measurement is not the precise temperature assigned to the liquid by older theories of knowledge. Thus, if the body of liquid is someone's bath, he is (normally) concerned to determine the temperature of the bath only to within several degrees. The big toe of his foot may well serve as an adequate gauge of the water's temperature for this purpose. If the body of liquid is being used to develop photographic film, determination of temperature may be more important, and chemical thermometers may be required to measure the temperature with sufficient accuracy to spell the difference between successful and unsuccessful development. Even greater accuracy may be required in sensitive chemical experiments, where special thermocouples may be required to measure temperatures. This indicates that we do not always need the most accurate estimate of the temperature which is possible or even the actual (theoretical) temperature, but only a determination *accurate enough* for a given purpose.

By extension, an acceptable answer to any question of fact is to be determined by reference to what is at stake in giving the answer. We need only consider answers that make a difference to us.

This account of human action seems well supported by observations of our behavior. Where an answer matters a great deal, we are likely to spend correspondingly greater time in obtaining it. As a result, pragmatists are able to view scientific method as an extension of common sense. In both cases, a common pattern of inquiry is adopted. Scientific inquiry is distinguished from ordinary inquiry largely by the importance with which its questions are treated, and the care with which the scientist formulates alternative hypotheses and accumulates observations to discriminate between them. Further, the scientist's inquiry is controlled to a greater extent by his self-conscious understanding of the pattern of inquiry.

By giving an account of abductive inference in terms of the psychological states which accompany it, this pattern of inquiry can be made reasonably explicit. The occurrence of an unexpected or unexplained event C is accompanied by doubt, in view of the fact that our previously accepted beliefs have broken down, and this doubt irritates thought into action. Thought's function is to find a belief or hypothesis A to account for the occurrence of C. Thought, of course, may provide more than one hypothesis that would explain C, so that some investigation may be required to choose a hypothesis that is acceptable. When an adequate hypothesis is found, belief is obtained again, and the organism is directed by the newly accepted beliefs or habits along with old beliefs and habits which are retained until fresh doubt occurs.

The essential importance of facts of an empirical kind in pragmatism is reflected in Peirce's description of fact as immediately known, while belief is mediately known and is abductively inferred from the facts. A belief is a habit of thought causing us to expect certain further events to occur, subject to continual revision. Now this account is not entirely clear until we understand in what way further events are expected.

This account must be distinguished, for example, from Humean induction. There, if A's have always been followed by B's, in an appropriate way, we may form the habit of expecting a B whenever an A occurs. Pragmatic belief is a much wider concept. Having found that my electric drill will make a suitable hole in ¼-inch steel plate for some immediate purpose, I may form the habit of expecting that the drill will perform suitably on later occasions. This situation is complicated. It is not possible, given this experience, to describe an event which I expect to be *invariably* followed by some other event. My habit or rule of action cannot be formulated as the rule "Always use an electric drill to make holes in ¼-inch steel plate.", or even as the directive "If you want to make holes in ¼-inch steel plate, an electric drill will do the job.". Instead, my habit may be formulated as the rule "If you should want to drill holes in ¼-inch steel plate, an electric drill is a good tool to try.". When such a habit is reinforced by repeated success in drilling ¼-inch steel plate with an electric drill whenever the problem of providing holes in such plate arises, the habit becomes strengthened to a *belief*. My belief may be looked at as a disposition to act in a certain way, namely, to use an electric drill if faced with ¼-inch steel plate that I want to drill holes into.

This account of belief has the consequence of tying pragmatic inquiry very closely to purposes and ends, rather than to the disinterested search for certain knowledge characteristic of earlier philosophies. The account of pragmatists may be extended to provide an explanation of animal behavior, particularly as the pragmatists argue that beliefs may be followed and even formed without self-conscious thought about the fact that a belief is being followed or formulated. The difference between a dog, an ordinary person, and a scientist then becomes one of degree, centering about the critical self-awareness with which these three creatures formulate their beliefs and adhere to them.

Habit and belief, on this view, are different names for the same kind of rule of action, depending on the degree of entrenchment with which the rule is applied. An event conflicting with a habit would not be as surprising as an event conflicting with a belief. Another way to put this would be to say that beliefs are those rules of action that we would tend to preserve in the face of doubt, while habits are those rules of action that we would first revise or attempt to revise. Clearly one man's habit may be another man's belief, depending on the subjective order with which they have faced personal doubts and resolved them. This subjective element in pragmatism is thought by pragmatists to be entirely acceptable, since they feel that over long periods of time, the same rules of action will become beliefs for all interested human beings. This follows from their supposition that repeated confrontation with experience will cause defective habits to be rejected and similar or common beliefs to be retained.

There remains the particular case of our conceptions of objects. As might be expected, we do not know objects directly but know about them because we have beliefs about them, and these beliefs exhaust our conception of objects. To make our idea or conception of an object clear, we consider those practical effects it can conceivably have and *identify* our idea of the object with these effects. Peirce takes this definition to be an improvement upon the criteria of clearness and distinctness proposed by Descartes. He argues that it does little good to urge adoption of clear and distinct ideas, since we will in fact adopt ideas which appear clearly and distinctly to us. The problem is to decide when we are mistaking a seeming clearness and distinctness for true clearness and distinctness. This point reiterates our earlier objection to traditional rationalism, since it is in effect pointing out that if two people claim to have clear and distinct ideas which conflict, no satisfactory methodology for removing the conflict is available in the epistemological tradition of rationalism. By making an idea of an object coincident with our conception of its practical effects, however, a methodology seems to be provided, for conflicting ideas may then be resolved by studying which of the conflicting practical effects are found to obtain. If those of the one obtain, but not those of the other, the first idea is preferred as a conception of the object. In practice, it may happen that both ideas are defective, so that some new conception is called for as a synthesis of the initial ideas. Ideas are not absolutely clear and distinct for the pragmatists but relatively clear and distinct with respect to given ends.

An interesting feature of Peirce's account of the conception of an object is the way in which his account disposes of the controversy between rationalists and empiricists over the status of material objects. An empiricism which proposes to reduce our knowledge of an object to our experiences of it wreaks havoc with our intentions in speaking about an object, as we have seen. On the other hand, adoption of a rule specifying what is true of an object when it is not experienced involves a concession to rationalism. If belief is simply the practical effects of an object, then when that object is not being put to a practical test of its effects, we are simply not concerned about the object and may say anything that we like, because belief is not involved. To take Peirce's example, our experiences with a diamond indicate that, among other things, it will scratch most other solid objects. Our conception of a diamond then involves the practical effect that if we want to scratch glass, marble, or whatever, a diamond is a good tool for the purpose. Our disposition to use the diamond in these contexts exhausts our beliefs about it. When its practical effects are not being considered or tested, the diamond might be considered either hard or soft. Both views are compatible with our other beliefs, and neither can cause a genuine doubt. Peirce says that truth is not involved, and by this he means that supposition about a diamond's hardness which has no practical consequence is not a matter of belief. Since speculation about the diamond's hardness when it is not being tested or used has no practical consequences, we are free to invent any view about it that suits our convenience or aesthetic taste. It is not, in short, a genuine irritation or a genuine problem.

The Choice of Hypotheses

The material in the preceding chapters on Peirce should enable us to make clear two of the expressions commonly used in discussing various features of pragmatism: critical common-sensism and fallibilism. Both of these expressions apply primarily to Peirce's treatment of scientific inquiry. Critical common-sensism expresses the view that scientific inquiry is a self-aware and sophisticated version of commonsense inquiry. Fallibilism expresses the view that no statement of fact or hypothesis can be taken to be absolutely certain. For the pragmatist, all human beliefs confront experience simultaneously, and he is willing to reject any currently held belief in the face of some surprising fact, although he may well expect that certain beliefs will be more likely to be rejected than others.

Pragmatists make the synthetic a priori statements of Kant synthetic, except for many statements of mathematics, which are considered analytic. In theory, it would seem that pragmatists must treat all statements as synthetic, and many of them do. On the other hand, statements of logic and mathematics seem so immune to revision (we cannot imagine the surprising fact that would cause us to give them up) that many pragmatists in practice have insisted that these statements can safely be treated as analytic, or immune to revision. The pragmatic movement has not been entirely consistent on this issue, although modern empirical philosophers have spent much time *reducing* areas of uncertainty in logic and mathematics, and hence increasing the plausibility that these statements are conveniently considered to be analytic.

This reduction has been accomplished by the development of *formal* logic and *formal* systems. Formal logic, in this sense, is the restriction of inference to operations on symbols, which may be viewed as a kind of conservatism in logic. A valid deductive inference is one in which the premises could not be interpreted as true while the conclusion was interpreted as false. Descartes took this condition to be met when he could not *conceive* of the premises being true and the conclusion false. But the difficulty with conception is that simple inability to conceive the truth of the premises and the falsity of the conclusion may not *prove* the argument invalid but may only show that the powers of conceiving are weak. Further, some rules of procedure which have been accepted for a long time may turn out to be defective. For example, it was thought for thousands of years that everything could always be consistently divided into two large classes by means of any well-defined property. To the one class would belong everything having that property, and to the other class would belong everything not having that property. Thus, the concept that everything belonged either to the class of red things or to the class of things which are not red seemed to be perfectly straightforward. Nonetheless, it was discovered in the early twentieth century that this rule of procedure is defective. Suppose we consider everything, *including all classes.* Now we will define a class which we shall call W. The property of non-self-membership is used to define W. By way of background for this property, let *Troy* be some dog. Then Troy is a member of the class of all dogs, which we will designate as the class D. Now is D itself a member of D? Obviously not, since all members of the class D are dogs, and the class D is not itself a dog, but a collection of dogs. D is therefore not a member of itself. Let us define the class W mentioned above as the class of all things which are not members of themselves, and put everything else into the class $\widetilde{W}$ of things which are members of themselves. (You will probably not be able to think of an example of a member of $\widetilde{W}$, but this does not affect the validity of the argument.) What about the class W? Since it is something, it must be a member of W or of $\widetilde{W}$. But to say that W is a member of W is to say also that W is not a member of itself, or not a member of W, in view of the way in which W is defined. To avoid this contradiction, W must be taken as a member of $\widetilde{W}$, but this means that W is a member of itself, because if it were not, it would be a member of W. But we have already seen that if W is taken as a member of W, a contradiction results. Consequently, we conclude that W cannot be a member of either W or $\widetilde{W}$. This means that the general principle that all things may consistently be divided into two classes by any well-defined property is not a generally useful rule. Some philosophers have taken this to prove that the notion of a class is inherently contradictory, while others have supposed either that the class W cannot be consistently investigated, or that classes must be structured in infinitely many levels of generality, so that not everything can be considered at once.

The discovery of this defect in a previously accepted rule of procedure (which has far-reaching implications for mathematical systems), as well as other paradoxes in the accepted reasoning of the nineteenth century, led to the development of formal systems in which the rules of procedure are so restricted that they avoid paradox of this kind. Formal systems are such that the symbols of a formal system are not taken to have meaning but are treated quite objectively as *objects* which may be operated on by simple and unambiguous rules.

An example of a formal rule could be the following: "If P is a sentence and Q is a sentence, and P *and* Q represents their conjunction, then if P *and* Q is a premise in an argument, P may be asserted as the conclusion of the argument." This is a very cautious rule which is perfectly valid, as one can easily see by taking some examples of sentences in English. Let P be the sentence "John hit Mary." and Q be the sentence "Mary went to the hospital.". Now consider the following argument:

John hit Mary and Mary went to the hospital.
Therefore, Mary was hit by John.

This would normally be thought to be a valid argument, but it is not sanctioned by our formal rule, since to construe "John hit Mary." and "Mary was hit by John." as the *same* sentence, so that either expression can be substituted for P, is to smuggle in an assumption that these two sentences have the same meaning, which is nowhere expressed in the formal rule. Considered as *objects*, "John hit Mary." and "Mary was hit by John." are two *different* things. One of them has a 'J' as its leftmost part, and the other has an 'M'. This is sufficient to show that they are different, and that they cannot both replace P in one application of the cited rule. This illustrates the point of formal systems, which attempt to be so conservative in the rules that they allow that no unnoticed assumptions or unconscious presuppositions can be smuggled into an argument to affect its validity.

We may invent all the formal systems that we care to and interpret and use them in any way that is convenient. If they are interpreted in some way, and they lead to awkward consequences, we say not that the formal system is defective, but merely that it is not useful to interpret it in this fashion.

Modern empirical philosophers (including, of course, pragmatists) usually treat most mathematical statements in this fashion. Their answer to Kant would be that the statement "$7+5=12$" is a statement in a formal system used quite frequently which may be transformed into an obvious identity as follows: $7+5=12$, which is equivalent to $(1+1+1+1+1+1+1) + (1+1+1+1+1) = (1+1+1+1+1+1+1+1+1+1+1+1)$, is equivalent to the following identity using an associative law on the left hand side: $(1+1+1+1+1+1+1+1+1+1+1+1) = (1+1+1+1+1+1+1+1+1+1+1+1)$. If we interpret this statement such that what is taken to be seven objects is added to five objects and twelve objects do not result, we conclude that this formal system, arithmetic, is not conveniently applied to these objects. For example, if 7 cubic centimeters of water are added to 5 cubic centimeters of alcohol, 12 cubic centimeters of liquid do not result, but an amount of liquid somewhat less than 12 cubic centimeters. In the face of this fact, we do not reject the arithmetic statement "$7+5=12$" as false but conclude that it is not the right formal system for describing the addition of water to alcohol.

Thus it is possible to limit the analytic to statements which are posited to be true by virtue of their form. Notice that the combination of a formal system, and some interpretation of it, may lead to the rejection of both if some statement interpreted as true in the formal system under the interpretation is found in experience to be false. Then a new system *and* a new interpretation may have to be found. Although such an approach limits statements to analytic and synthetic statements, emptying Kant's synthetic a priori category of its content, it has the consequence that it is extremely difficult to find satisfactory rules for accepting or rejecting scientific hypotheses on the basis of observed fact.

To see this, consider the following diagram:

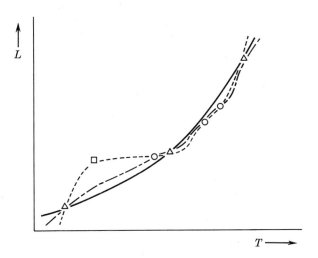

This diagram could represent the relationship between two observed properties *L* and *T* of some object, say the temperature and length of an iron bar, although we will take the diagram to represent the gathering of any scientific data and the fitting of those data to hypotheses. Let the symbols (△,○,□) in the diagram stand for observed facts, and the three lines (—, — - —, - -) stand for abducted hypotheses from the facts. A close study of this diagram will illustrate most of the problems associated with the acceptance or rejection of hypotheses on the basis of a pragmatic epistemology.

Suppose those facts represented by △ to be already accepted. Now let the theory represented by the line — be the result of an abductive inference, and let further facts be represented by ○ and □.

The basic problem is to avoid either one of two types of errors: we do not want to accept hypotheses that are false and we do not want to reject hypotheses which are true. Since hypotheses will never be conclusively shown to be true or false, we may revise this to say that we do not want to reject hypotheses that will have to be believed later, and we do not want to believe hypotheses that will have to be rejected later. Doubt forces us to accept some hypothesis. An interesting feature of pragmatism is that failure to choose between hypotheses is also taking an action and accepting a hypothesis whose risk must be evaluated along with the other alternatives. Once a genuine doubt assails us, some belief must be found to assuage our difficulty and make experience coherent, or we could consider ourselves *insane* in that we were not adjusting to empirical reality.

Fallibilism has several consequences for our diagram. Since an observation of fact will never be certain (because of the inherent error of observation), we can at best take our data points to be approximate. At the same time, since any of several abductive inferences may be possible from the data, we are faced with the difficulty of choosing from among many possible alternative hypotheses. In fact, through any number of finite points on a diagram like that above, an infinite number of distinct possible lines representing different hypotheses may be drawn. This is sufficient to indicate that the problem is complex: we are to choose some hypothesis from an infinite number of possibilities to fit data which are at best approximate. The pragmatic problem is to reduce this decision problem to manageable proportions.

What factors influence the decision? At least three have been commonly recognized in contemporary pragmatic thought: cost, simplicity, and evidential fit. The last is most familiar. We do not want to accept a hypothesis that conflicts with the data. Still, since the data are approximations, we could in principle accept any hypothesis on any data if we were willing to stretch the approximation involved sufficiently. Consider all the data represented by the symbols △, ○, and □ in the diagram. The datum represented by □ is most troublesome. Intuitively, we might suppose that it was a mistake, and take the datum again, because it differs so widely from any reasonably smooth line passing through the other data. It is a difficult problem to decide how often a problematic datum must be verified before we are willing to accept it as true, and revise our hypotheses accordingly.

Simplicity is a characteristic of hypotheses which may seem to make them so intuitively acceptable if they are sufficiently simple that we would be willing to stretch the approximation of the data before decisively rejecting an intuitively simple hypothesis. If we ignore the datum represented by □, both the hypothesis represented by — and the hypothesis represented by — - — might be said to satisfy the criterion of evidential fit. Nevertheless, most writers would agree that the hypothesis represented by — is *simpler* than the hypothesis represented by — - — . A satisfactory criterion of simplicity in this sense and an argument for using the criterion in the selection of hypotheses is still to be devised, although observation of successful scientific practice seems to indicate that some such factor may be important in the selection of hypotheses.

Cost is an interesting factor that has only recently been consciously explored. We might look at the cost of accepting a hypothesis as the amount of revision in our accepted beliefs which would be entailed by its adoption. The more our accepted beliefs conflict with a given hypothesis, the less likely we are to adopt it because the cost of its adoption is high. Where cost plays an important role, we may delay the adoption of a hypothesis until evidential fit can be very closely ascertained.

The point of this introduction of evidential weight, simplicity, and cost is that these factors do not seem to lead to any definite acceptance of certain hypotheses in certain situations. Indeed, by appropriately weighing these three factors, almost any decision might be pragmatically defended. Until pragmatism can explain some procedure for weighing evidential fit, simplicity, and cost in order to explain less intuitive applications of the criteria, the pragmatic account of scientific knowledge cannot be considered entirely adequate.

Readings from Peirce

The readings from Peirce are collected into three passages. Each of these is identified by its location in the *Collected Papers of Charles Sanders Peirce* through the use of the numbering system that is now used by Peirce scholars. For example, '5.189,' means that the reprinted passage may be found in volume 5 of the *Collected Papers* as the paragraph numbered 189.

    A. This selection represents fragments 6.522–6.528, 5.189, 1.71–1.74, and 6.477 from the *Collected Papers*. These paragraphs were arranged in this fashion in a section called "Abduction and Induction" in Justus Buchler's collection of Peirce's writings called *Philosophical Writings of Peirce*, New York, 1955.

    B. This selection is the first part of Peirce's essay "How to Make Our Ideas Clear," and is found as paragraphs 5.388–5.403 in the *Collected Papers*.

    C. This selection consists of paragraphs 1.135–1.149 of the *Collected Papers*.

These paragraphs are reprinted here from the *Collected Papers of Charles Sanders Peirce*, edited by Charles Hartshorne and Paul Weiss. Reprinting rights have been given by kind permission of the Belknap Press of Harvard University Press.

    Peirce spent much of his life in the employ of the U. S. Geodetic Survey doing experimental work on such problems as that of the density of the earth. Although his training and philosophical writings fitted him to an academic post, he found himself unable to hold such a post because of inability to get along with university administrators and professors. He was an exceedingly brilliant but eccentric man, and it is very difficult to obtain a sound biographical estimate of his personality. Pragmatism was really inaugurated as a philosophical movement by William James, and then later by John Dewey. James was quick to see the importance of Peirce's discoveries, but in characteristic fashion, Peirce quarreled with

278

James over events in which James seems to have been entirely considerate of Peirce. The events surrounding early American pragmatism and the personalities of Peirce and James make interesting intellectual history that the student should explore through some of the secondary sources which are now listed.

*Buchler, Justus: *Philosophical Writings of Peirce*, London, 1940. (Dover Paperbound.)

Feibleman, James: *An Introduction to Peirce's Philosophy Interpreted as a System*, London, 1960.

*Gallie, W. B.: *Peirce and Pragmatism*, Harmondsworth, 1952. (Pelican Paperbound.)

Goudge, T. A.: *The Thought of C. S. Peirce*, Toronto, 1950.

Murphey, M. G.: *The Development of Peirce's Philosophy*, Cambridge, 1961.

*Thompson, M.: *The Pragmatic Philosophy of C. S. Peirce*, Chicago, 1953. (University of Chicago Paperbound.)

Wiener, Philip, and Frederic Young: *Studies in the Philosophy of Charles Sanders Peirce*, Cambridge, 1952.

A From the COLLECTED PAPERS OF CHARLES SANDERS PEIRCE

I

All our knowledge may be said to rest upon *observed facts*. It is true that there are psychological states which antecede our observing facts as such. Thus, it is a fact that I see an inkstand before me; but before I can say that I am obliged to have impressions of sense into which no idea of an inkstand, or of any separate object, or of an 'I', or of seeing, enter at all; and it is true that my judging that I see an inkstand before me is the product of mental operations upon these impressions of sense. But it is only when the cognition has become worked up into a proposition, or judgment of a fact, that I can exercise any direct control over the process; and it is idle to discuss the 'legitimacy' of that which cannot be controlled.[1] Observations of fact have, therefore, to be accepted as they occur.

But observed facts relate exclusively to the particular circumstances that happened to exist when they were observed. They do not relate to any future occasions upon which we may be in doubt how we ought to act. They, therefore, do not, in themselves, contain any practical knowledge.

Such knowledge must involve additions to the facts observed. The making of those additions is an operation which we can control; and it is evidently a process during which error is liable to creep in.

Any proposition added to observed facts, tending to make them applicable in any way to other circumstances than those under which they were observed, may be called a hypothesis. A hypothesis ought, at first, to be entertained interrogatively.[2] Thereupon, it ought to be tested by experiment so far as practicable. There are two distinct processes, both of which may be performed rightly or wrongly. We may go wrong and be wasting time in so much as entertaining a hypothesis, even as a question. That is a subject for criticism in every case. There are some hypotheses which are of such a nature that they never can be tested at all. Whether such hypotheses ought to be entertained at all, and if so in what sense, is a serious question; but it hardly concerns our present inquiry.[3] The hypotheses with which we shall have in this paper to deal are capable of being put to the test. How this is to be done is a question of extreme importance; but my intention is to consider it only in a very cursory manner, at present. There are, moreover, many hypotheses in regard to which knowledge already in our possession may, at once, quite justifiably either raise them to the rank of opinions, or even positive beliefs, or cause their immediate rejection. This also is a matter to be considered. But it is the first process, that of entertaining the question, which will here be of foremost importance.

Before we go further, let us get the points stated above quite clear. By a *hypothesis*, I mean, not merely a supposition about an observed object, as when I suppose that a man is a Catholic priest because that would explain his dress, expression of countenance, and bearing, but also any other supposed truth from which would result such facts as have been observed, as when van't Hoff, having remarked that the osmotic pressure of one percent solutions of a number of chemical substances was inversely proportional to their atomic weights, thought that perhaps the same relation would be found to exist between the same properties of any other chemical substance.[4] The first starting of a hypothesis and the entertaining of it, whether as a simple interrogation or with any degree of confidence, is an inferential step which I propose to call *abduction* (or *retroduction*). This will include a preference for any one hypothesis over others which would equally explain the facts, so long as this preference is not based upon any previous knowledge beating upon the truth of the hypotheses, nor on any testing of any of the hypotheses, after having admitted them on probation.[5] I call all such inference by the peculiar name, *abduction*, because its legitimacy depends upon altogether different principles from those of other kinds of inference.

Long before I first classed abduction as an inference it was recognized by logicians that the operation of adopting an explanatory hypothesis—which is just what abduction is—was subject to certain conditions. Namely, the hypothesis cannot be admitted, even as a hypothesis, unless it be supposed that it would account for the facts or some of them. The form of inference, therefore, is this:

> The surprising fact, C, is observed;
> But if A were true, C would be a matter of course,
> Hence, there is reason to suspect that A is true.

Thus, A cannot be abductively inferred, or if you prefer the expression, cannot be abductively conjectured until its entire content is already present in the premiss, "If A were true, C would be a matter of course."

The operation of testing a hypothesis by experiment, which consists in remarking that, if it is true, observations made under certain conditions ought to have certain results, and then causing those conditions to be fulfilled, and noting the results, and, if they are favourable, extending a certain confidence to the hypothesis, I call *induction*. For example, suppose that I have been led to surmise that among our coloured population there is a greater tendency toward female births than among our whites. I say, if that be so, the last census must show it.[6] I examine the last census report and find that, sure enough, there was a somewhat greater proportion of female births among coloured births than among white births in that census year. To accord a certain faith to my hypothesis on that account is legitimate. It is a strong induction. I have taken all the births of that year as a sample of all the births of years in general, so long as general conditions remain as they were then. It is a very large sample, quite unnecessarily so, were it not that the excess of the one ratio over the other is quite small. All induction whatever may be regarded as the inference that throughout a whole class a ratio will have about the same value that it has in a random sample of that class, provided the nature of the ratio for which the sample is to be examined is specified (or virtually specified) in advance of the examination. So long as the class sampled consists of units, and the ratio in question is a ratio between counts of occurrences, induction is a comparatively simple affair. But suppose we wish to test the hypothesis that a man is a Catholic priest, that is, has all the characters that are common to Catholic priests and peculiar to them. Now characters are not units, nor do they consist of units, nor can they be counted, in such a sense that one count is right and every other wrong. Characters have to be estimated according to their significance. The consequence is that there will be a certain element of guess-work in such an induction; so that I call it an *abductory induction*. I might say to myself, let me think of some other character that belongs to Catholic priests, beside those that I have remarked in this man, a character which I can ascertain whether he possesses or not. All Catholic priests are more or less familiar with Latin pronounced in the Italian manner. If, then, this man is a Catholic priest, and I make some remark in Latin which a person not accustomed to the Italian pronunciation would not at once understand, and I pronounce it in that way, then if that man is a Catholic priest he will be so surprised that he cannot but betray his understanding of it. I make such a remark; and I notice that he does understand it. But how much weight am I to attach to that test? After all, it does not touch an essential characteristic of a priest or even of a Catholic. It must be acknowledged that it is but a weak confirmation, and all the more so, because it is quite uncertain how much weight should be attached to it. Nevertheless, it does and ought to incline me to believe that the man is a Catholic priest. It is an induction, because it is a test of the hypothesis by means of a prediction, which has been verified. But it is only an abductory induction, because it was a sampling of the characters of priests to see what proportion of them this man possessed, when characters cannot be counted, nor even weighed, except by guess-work. It also partakes of the nature of abduction in involving an original suggestion; while typical induction has no originality in it, but only tests a suggestion already made.

In induction, it is not the fact predicted that in any degree necessitates the truth of the hypothesis or even renders it probable. It is the fact that it has been predicted successfully and that it is a haphazard specimen of all the predictions which might be based on the hypothesis and which constitute its practical truth. But it frequently happens that there are facts which, merely as facts, apart from the manner in which they have presented themselves, necessitate the truth, or the falsity, or the probability in some definite degree, of the hypothesis. For example, suppose the hypothesis to be that a man believes in the infallibility of the Pope. Then, if we ascertain in any way that he believes in the immaculate conception, in the confessional, and in prayers for the dead, or on the other hand that he disbelieves all or some of these things, either fact will be almost decisive of the truth or falsity of the proposition. Such inference is *deduction.* So if we ascertain that the man in question is a violent partisan in politics and in many other subjects. If, then, we find that he has given money toward a Catholic institution, we may fairly reason that such a man would not do that unless he believed in the Pope's infallibility. Or again, we might learn that he is one of five brothers whose opinions are identical on almost all subjects. If, then, we find that the other four believe in the Pope's infallibility or all disbelieve it, this will affect our confidence in the hypothesis. This consideration will be strengthened by our general experience that while different members of a large family usually differ about most subjects, yet it mostly happens that they are either all Catholics or all Protestants. Those are four different varieties of deductive considerations which may legitimately influence our belief in a hypothesis.

These distinctions are perfectly clear in principle, which is all that is necessary, although it might sometimes be a nice question to say to which class a given inference belongs. It is to be remarked that, in pure abduction, it can never be justifiable to accept the hypothesis otherwise than as an interrogation. But as long as that condition is observed, no positive falsity is to be feared; and therefore the whole question of what one out of a number of possible hypotheses ought to be entertained becomes purely a question of economy.[7]

II

Mill denies that there was any reasoning in Kepler's procedure.[8] He says it is merely a description of the facts. He seems to imagine that Kepler had all the places of Mars in space given him by Tycho's observations;

and that all he did was to generalize and so obtain a general expression for them. Even had that been all, it would certainly have been inference. Had Mill had even so much practical acquaintance with astronomy as to have practised discussions of the motions of double stars, he would have seen that. But so to characterize Kepler's work is to betray total ignorance of it. Mill certainly never read the *De Motu* (*Motibus*) *Stellae Martis,* which is not easy reading. The reason it is not easy is that it calls for the most vigorous exercise of all the powers of reasoning from beginning to end.

What Kepler had given was a large collection of observations of the apparent places of Mars at different times. He also knew that, in a general way, the Ptolemaic theory agrees with the appearances, although there were various difficulties in making it fit exactly. He was furthermore convinced that the hypothesis of Copernicus ought to be accepted. Now this hypothesis, as Copernicus himself understood its first outline, merely modifies the theory of Ptolemy so far as (to) impart to all the bodies of the solar system one common motion, just what is required to annul the me. n motion of the sun. It would seem, therefore, at first sight, that it ought not to affect the appearances at all. If Mill had called the work of Copernicus mere description he would not have been *so very far* from the truth as he was. But Kepler did not understand the matter quite as Copernicus did. Because the sun was so near the centre of the system, and was of vast size (even Kepler knew its diameter must be at least fifteen times that of the earth), Kepler, looking at the matter dynamically, thought it must have something to do with causing the planets to move in their orbits. This retroduction, vague as it was, cost great intellectual labour, and was most important in its bearings upon all Kepler's work. Now Kepler remarked that the lines of apsides of the orbits of Mars and of the earth are not parallel; and he utilized various observations most ingeniously to infer that they probably intersected in the sun. Consequently, it must be supposed that a general description of the motion would be simpler when referred to the sun as a fixed point of reference than when referred to any other point. Thence it followed that the proper times at which to take the observations of Mars for determining its orbit were when it appeared just opposite the sun—the true sun—instead of when it was opposite the *mean* sun, as had been the practice. Carrying out this idea, he obtained a theory of Mars which satisfied the longitudes at all the oppositions observed by Tycho and himself, thirteen in number, to perfection. But unfortunately, it did not satisfy the latitudes at all and was totally irreconcilable with observations of Mars when far from opposition.

At each stage of his long investigation, Kepler has a theory which is approximately true, since it approximately satisfies the observations (that is, within 8′, which is less than any but Tycho's observations could decisively pronounce an error), and he proceeds to modify this theory, after the most careful and judicious reflection, in such a way as to render it more rational or closer to the observed fact. Thus, having found that the centre of the orbit bisects the eccentricity, he finds in this an indication of the falsity of the theory of the equant and substitutes, for this artificial device, the principle of the equable description of areas. Subsequently, finding that the planet moves faster at ninety degrees from its apsides than it ought to do, the question is whether this is owing to an error in the law of areas or to a compression of the orbit. He ingeniously proves that the latter is the case.

Thus, never modifying his theory capriciously, but always with a sound and rational motive for just the modification he makes, it follows that when he finally reaches a modification—of most striking simplicity and rationality—which exactly satisfies the observations, it stands upon a totally different logical footing from what it would if it had been struck out at random, or the reader knows not how, and had been found to satisfy the observation. Kepler shows his keen logical sense in detailing the whole process by which he finally arrived at the true orbit. This is the greatest piece of Retroductive reasoning ever performed.

III

Modern science has been builded after the model of Galileo, who founded it, on *il lume naturale*.[9] That truly inspired prophet had said that, of two hypotheses, the *simpler* is to be preferred; but I was formerly one of those who, in our dull self-conceit fancying ourselves more sly than he, twisted the maxim to mean the *logically* simpler, the one that adds the least to what has been observed, in spite of three obvious objections: first, that if so there was no support for any hypothesis; secondly, that by the same token we ought to content ourselves with simply formulating the special observations actually made; and thirdly, that every advance of science that further opens the truth to our view discloses a world of unexpected complications. It was not until long experience forced me to realize that subsequent discoveries were every time showing I had been wrong, while those who understood the maxim as Galileo had done, early unlocked the secret, that the scales fell from my eyes and my mind awoke to the broad and flaming daylight that it is the simpler Hypothesis in the sense of the more facile and natural, the one that instinct suggests, that must be preferred; for the reason that, unless man have a natural bent in accordance with nature's, he has no chance of understanding nature at all.[10]

B   From the COLLECTED PAPERS OF CHARLES SANDERS PEIRCE

I

Whoever has looked into a modern treatise on logic of the common sort, will doubtless remember two distinctions between *clear* and *obscure* conceptions, and between *distinct* and *confused* conceptions.[11] They have lain in the books now for nigh two centuries, unimproved and unmodified, and are generally reckoned by logicians as among the gems of their doctrine.

A clear idea is defined as one which is so apprehended that it will be recognized wherever it is met with, and so that no other will be mistaken for it. If it fails of this clearness, it is said to be obscure.

This is rather a neat bit of philosophical terminology; yet, since it is clearness that they were defining, I wish the logicians had made their definition a little more plain. Never to fail to recognize an idea, and under no circumstances to mistake another for it, let it come in how recondite a form it may, would indeed imply such prodigious force and clearness of intellect as is seldom met with in this world. On the other hand, merely to have such an acquaintance with the idea as to have become familiar with it, and to have lost all hesitancy in recognizing it in ordinary cases, hardly seems to deserve the name of clearness of apprehension, since after all it only amounts to a subjective feeling of mastery which may be entirely mistaken. I take it, however, that when the logicians speak of "clearness," they mean nothing more than such a familiarity with an idea, since they regard the quality as but a small merit, which needs to be supplemented by another, which they call *distinctness*.

A distinct idea is defined as one which contains nothing which is not clear. This is technical language; by the *contents* of an idea logicians understand whatever is contained in its definition. So that an idea is *distinctly* apprehended, according to them, when we can give a precise definition of it, in abstract terms. Here the professional logicians leave the subject; and I would not have troubled the reader with what they have to say, if it were not such a striking example of how they have been slumbering through ages of intellectual activity, listlessly disregarding the enginery of modern thought, and never dreaming of applying its lessons to the improvement of logic.[12] It is easy to show that the doctrine that familiar use and abstract distinctness make the perfection of apprehension has its only true place in philosophies which have long been extinct; and it is now time to formulate the method of attaining to a more perfect clearness of thought, such as we see and admire in the thinkers of our own time.

When Descartes set about the reconstruction of philosophy, his first step was to (theoretically) permit scepticism and to discard the practice of the schoolmen of looking to authority as the ultimate source of truth. That done, he sought a more natural fountain of true principles, and professed to find it in the human mind; thus passing, in the directest way, from the method of authority to that of a priority, as described in my first paper.[13] Self-consciousness was to furnish us with our fundamental truths, and to decide what was agreeable to reason. But since, evidently, not all ideas are true, he was led to note, as the first condition of infallibility, that they must be clear. The distinction between an idea *seeming* clear and really being so, never occurred to him. Trusting to introspection, as he did, even for a knowledge of external things, why should he question its testimony in respect to the contents of our own minds? But then, I suppose, seeing men, who seemed to be quite clear and positive, holding opposite opinions upon fundamental principles, he was further led to say that clearness of ideas is not sufficient, but that they need also to be distinct, *i.e.*, to have nothing unclear about them.[14] What he probably meant by this (for he did not explain himself with precision) was, that they must sustain the test of dialectical examination; that they must not only seem clear at the outset, but that discussion must never be able to bring to light points of obscurity connected with them.

Such was the distinction of Descartes, and one sees that it was precisely on the level of his philosophy. It was somewhat developed by Leibnitz.[15] This great and singular genius was as remarkable for what he failed to see as for what he saw. That a piece of mechanism could not do work perpetually without being fed with power in some form, was a thing perfectly apparent to him; yet he did not understand that the machinery of the mind can only transform knowledge, but never originate it, unless it be fed with facts of observation.[16] He thus missed the most essential point of the Cartesian philosophy, which is, that to accept propositions which seem perfectly evident to us is a thing which, whether it be logical or illogical, we cannot help doing. Instead of regarding the matter in this way, he sought to reduce the first principles of science to formulas which cannot be denied without self-contradiction, and was apparently unaware of the great difference between his position and that of Descartes. So he reverted to the old formalities of logic, and, above all, abstract definitions played a great part in his philosophy. It was quite natural, therefore, that on observing that the method of Descartes labored under the difficulty that we may seem to ourselves to have clear apprehensions of ideas which in truth are very hazy, no better remedy occurred to him than to require an abstract definition of every important term. Accordingly, in adopting the distinction of *clear* and *distinct* notions, he described the latter quality as the clear apprehension of everything contained in the definition; and the books have ever since copied his words. There is no danger that his chimerical scheme will ever again be overvalued. Nothing new can ever be learned by analyzing definitions. Nevertheless, our existing beliefs can be set in order by this process, and order is an essential element of intellectual economy, as of every other. It may be acknowledged, therefore, that the books are right in making familiarity with a notion the first step towards clearness of apprehension, and the defining of it the second. But in omitting all mention of any higher perspicuity of thought, they simply mirror a philosophy which was exploded a hundred years ago. That much-admired "ornament of logic"—the doctrine of clearness and distinctness—may be pretty enough, but it is high time to relegate to our cabinet of curiosities the antique *bijou*, and to wear about us something better adapted to modern uses.

The very first lesson that we have a right to demand that logic teach us is, how to make our ideas clear; and a most important one it is, depreciated only by minds who stand in need of it. To know what we think, to be masters of our own meaning, will make a solid foundation for great and weighty thought. It is most easily learned by those whose ideas are meagre and restricted; and far happier they than such as wallow helplessly in a rich mud of conceptions. A nation, it is true, may, in the course of generations, overcome the disadvantage of an excessive wealth of language and its natural concomitant, a vast, unfathomable deep of ideas. We may see it in history, slowly perfecting its literary forms, sloughing at length its metaphysics, and, by virtue of the untirable patience which is often a compensation, attaining great excellence in every branch of mental acquirement. The page of history is not yet unrolled which is to tell us whether such a people will or will not in the long run prevail over one whose ideas (like the words of their language) are few, but which possesses a wonderful mastery over those which it has. For an individual, however, there can be no question that a few clear ideas are worth more than many confused ones. A young man would hardly be persuaded to sacrifice the greater part of his thoughts to save the rest; and the muddled head is the least apt to see the necessity of such a sacrifice. Him we can usually only commiserate, as a person with a congenital defect. Time will help him, but intellectual maturity with regard to clearness comes rather late, an unfortunate arrangement of Nature, inasmuch as clearness is of less use to a man settled in life, whose errors have in great measure had their effect, than it would be to one whose path lies before him. It is terrible to see how a single unclear idea, a single formula without meaning, lurking in a young man's head, will sometimes act like an obstruction of inert matter in an artery, hindering the nutrition of the brain, and condemning its victim to pine away in the fullness of his intellectual vigor and in the midst of intellectual plenty. Many a man has cherished for years as his hobby some vague shadow of an idea, too meaningless to be positively false; he has, nevertheless, passionately loved it, has made it his companion by day and by night, and has given to it his strength and his life, leaving all other occupations for its sake, and in short has lived with it and for it, until it has become, as it were, flesh of his flesh and bone of his bone; and then he has waked up some bright morning to find it gone, clean vanished away like the beautiful Melusina of the fable, and the essence of his life gone with it.[17] I have myself known such a man; and who can tell how many histories of circle-squarers, metaphysicians, astrologers, and what not, may not be told in the old German story?[18]

II

The principles set forth in the first of these papers lead, at once, to a method of reaching a clearness of thought of a far higher grade than the "distinctness" of the logicians. We have there found that the action of thought is excited by the irritation of doubt, and ceases when belief is attained; so that the production of belief is the sole function of thought. All these words, however, are too strong for my purpose. It is as if I had described the phenomena as they appear under a mental microscope. Doubt and Belief, as the words are commonly employed, relate to religious or other grave discussions. But here I use them to designate the starting of any question, no matter how small or how great, and the resolution of it. If, for instance, in a horse-car, I pull out my purse and find a five-cent nickel and five coppers, I decide, while my hand is going to the purse, in which way I will pay my fare. To call such a question Doubt, and my decision Belief, is certainly to use words very disproportionate to the occasion. To speak of such a doubt as causing an irritation which needs to be appeased, suggests a temper which is uncomfortable to the verge of insanity. Yet, looking at the matter minutely, it must be admitted that, if there is the least hesitation as to whether I shall pay the five coppers or the nickel (as there will be sure to be, unless I act from some previously contracted habit in the matter), though irritation is too strong a word, yet I am excited to such small mental activity as may be necessary to deciding how I shall act. Most frequently doubts arise from some indecision, however momentary, in our action. Sometimes it is not so. I have, for example, to wait in a railway-station, and to pass the time I read the advertisements on the walls, I compare the advantages of different trains and different routes which I never expect to take, merely fancying myself to be in a state of hesitancy, because I am bored with having nothing to trouble me. Feigned hesitancy, whether feigned for mere amusement or with a lofty purpose, plays a great part in the production of scientific inquiry. However the doubt may originate, it stimulates the mind to an activity which may be slight or energetic, calm or turbulent. Images pass rapidly through consciousness, one incessantly melting into another, until at last, when all is over—it may be in a fraction of a second, in an hour, or after long years —we find ourselves decided as to how we should act under such circumstances as those which occasioned our hesitation. In other words, we have attained belief.

In this process we observe two sorts of elements of consciousness, the distinction between which may best be made clear by means of an illustration. In a piece of music there are the separate notes, and there is the air. A single tone may be prolonged for an hour or a day, and it exists as perfectly in each second of that time as in the whole taken together; so that, as long as it is sounding, it might be present to a sense from which everything in the past was as completely absent as the future itself. But it is different with the air, the performance of which occupies a certain time, during the portions of which only portions of it are played. It consists in an orderliness in the succession of sounds which strike the ear at different times; and to perceive it there must be some continuity of consciousness which makes the events of a lapse of time present to us. We certainly only perceive the air by hearing the separate notes; yet we cannot be said to directly hear it, for we hear only what is present at the instant, and an orderliness of succession cannot exist in an instant. These two sorts of object, what we are *immediately* conscious of and what we are *mediately* conscious of, are found in all consciousness. Some elements (the sensations) are completely present at every instant so long as they last, while others (like thought) are actions having beginning, middle, and end, and consist in a congruence in the succession of sensations which flow through the mind.[19] They cannot be immediately present to us, but must cover some portion of the past or future. Thought is a thread of melody running through the succession of our sensations.

We may add that just as a piece of music may be written in parts, each part having its own air, so various systems of relationship of succession subsist together between the same sensations. These different systems are distinguished by having different motives, ideas, or functions. Thought is only one such system, for its sole motive, idea, and function, is to produce belief, and whatever does not concern that purpose belongs to some other system of relations. The action of thinking may incidentally have other results; it may serve to amuse us, for example, and among *dilletanti* it is not rare to find those who have so perverted thought to the purposes of pleasure that it seems to vex them to think that the questions upon which they delight to exercise it may ever get finally settled; and a positive discovery which takes a favorite subject out of the arena of literary debate is met with ill-concealed dislike. This disposition is the very debauchery of thought. But the soul and meaning of thought, abstracted from the other elements which accompany it, though it may be voluntarily thwarted, can never be made to direct itself toward anything but the production of belief. Thought in action has for its only possible motive the attainment of thought at rest; and whatever does not refer to belief is no part of the thought itself.

And what, then, is belief? It is the demicadence which closes a musical phrase in the symphony of our intellectual life. We have seen that it has just three properties: First, it is something that we are aware of;[20] second, it appeases the irritation of doubt; and, third it involves the establishment in our nature of a rule of action, or, say, for short, a *habit*. As it appeases the irritation of doubt, which is the motive for thinking, thought relaxes, and comes to rest for a moment when belief is reached. But, since belief is a rule for action, the application of which involves further doubt and further thought, at the same time that it is a stopping-place, it is also a new starting-place for thought. That is why I have permitted myself to call it thought at rest, although thought is essentially an action. The *final* upshot of thinking is the exercise of volition, and of this thought no longer forms a part; but belief is only a stadium of mental action, an effect upon our nature due to thought, which will influence future thinking.

The essence of belief is the establishment of a habit, and different beliefs are distinguished by the different modes of action to which they give rise. If beliefs do not differ in this respect, if they appease the same doubt by producing the same rule of action, then no mere differences in the manner of consciousness of them can make them different beliefs, any more than playing a tune in different keys is playing different tunes. Imaginary distinctions are often drawn between beliefs which differ only in their mode of expression;—the wrangling which ensues is real enough, however. To believe that any objects are arranged as in Fig. 1, and to believe that they are arranged (as) in Fig. 2, are one and the same belief; yet it is conceivable that a man should assert one proposition and deny the other.[21] Such false distinctions do as much harm as the confusion of beliefs really different, and are among the pitfalls of which we ought

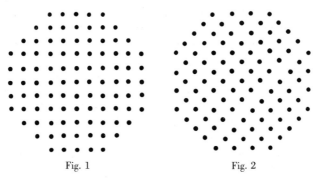

Fig. 1   Fig. 2

constantly to be aware, especially when we are upon metaphysical ground. One singular deception of this sort, which often occurs, is to mistake the sensation produced by our own unclearness of thought for a character of the object we are thinking. Instead of perceiving that the obscurity is purely subjective, we fancy that we contemplate a quality of the object which is essentially mysterious; and if our conception be afterward presented to us in a clear form we do not recognize it as the same, owing to the absence of the feeling of unintelligibility. So long as this deception lasts, it obviously puts an impassable barrier in the way of perspicuous thinking; so that it equally interests the opponents of rational thought to perpetuate it, and its adherents to guard against it.

Another such deception is to mistake a mere difference in the grammatical construction of two words for a distinction between the ideas they express. In this pedantic age, when the general mob of writers attend so much more to words than to things, this error is common enough. When I just said that thought is an *action*, and that it consists in a *relation*, although a person performs an action but not a relation, which can only be the result of an action, yet there was no inconsistency in what I said, but only a grammatical vagueness.

From all these sophisms we shall be perfectly safe so long as we reflect that the whole function of thought is to produce habits of action; and that whatever there is connected with a thought, but irrelevant to its purpose, is accretion to it, but no part of it. If there be a unity among our sensations which has no reference to how we shall act on a given occasion, as when we listen to a piece of music, why, we do not call that thinking. To develop its meaning, we have, therefore, simply to determine what habits it produces, for what a thing means is simply what habits it involves. Now, the identity of a habit depends on how it might lead us to act, not merely under such circumstances as are likely to arise, but under such as might possibly occur, no matter how improbable they may be. What the habit is depends on *when* and *how* it causes us to act. As for the *when*, every stimulus to action is derived from perception; as for the *how*, every purpose of action is to produce some sensible result. Thus, we come down to what is tangible and conceivably practical, as the root of every real distinction of thought, no matter how subtle it may be; and there is no distinction of meaning so fine as to consist in anything but a possible difference of practice.

To see what this principle leads to, consider in the light of it such a doctrine as that of transubstantiation. The Protestant churches generally hold that the elements of the sacrament are flesh and blood only in a tropical sense; they nourish our souls as meat and the juice of it would our bodies.[22] But the Catholics maintain that they are literally just that; although they possess all the sensible qualities of wafer-cakes and diluted wine. But we can have no conception of wine except what may enter into a belief, either—

1. That this, that, or the other is wine; or,
2. That wine possesses certain properties.

Such beliefs are nothing but self-notifications that we should, upon occasion, act in regard to such things as we believe to be wine according to the qualities which we believe wine to possess. The occasion of such an action would be some sensible perception, the motive of it to produce some sensible result. Thus our action has exclusive reference to what affects the senses, our habit has the same bearing as our action, our belief the same as our habit, our conception the same as our belief; and we can consequently mean nothing by wine but what has certain effects, direct or indirect, upon our senses; and to talk of something as having all the sensible characters of wine, yet being in reality blood, is senseless jargon. Now, it is not my object to pursue the theological question; and having used it as a logical example I drop it, without caring to anticipate the theologian's reply. I only desire to point out how impossible it is that we should have an idea in our minds which relates to anything but conceived sensible effects of things. Our idea of anything *is* our idea of its sensible effects; and if we fancy that we have any other we deceive ourselves, and mistake a mere sensation accompanying the thought for a part of the thought itself. It is absurd to say that thought has any meaning unrelated to its only function. It is foolish for Catholics and Protestants to fancy themselves in disagreement about the elements of the sacrament, if they agree in regard to all their sensible effects, here or hereafter.

It appears, then, that the rule for attaining the third grade of clearness of apprehension is as follows: Consider what effects, which might conceivably have practical bearings, we conceive the object of our conception to have.[23] Then, our conception of these effects is the whole of our conception of the object.

III

Let us illustrate this rule by some examples; and, to begin with the simplest one possible, let us ask what we mean by calling a thing *hard*. Evidently that it will not be scratched by many other substances. The whole conception of this quality, as of every other, lies in its conceived effects. There is absolutely no difference between a hard thing and a soft thing so long as they are not brought to the test. Suppose, then, that a diamond could be crystallized in the midst of a cushion of soft cotton, and should remain there until it was finally burned up. Would it be false to say that that diamond was soft? This seems a foolish question, and would be so, in fact, except in the realm of logic. There such questions are often of the greatest utility as serving to bring logical principles into sharper relief than real discussions ever could. In studying logic we must not put them aside with hasty answers, but must consider them with attentive care, in order to make out the principles involved. We may, in the present case, modify our question, and ask what prevents us from saying that all hard bodies remain perfectly soft until they are touched, when their hardness increases with the pressure until they are scratched. Reflection will show that the reply is this: there would be no *falsity* in such modes of speech. They would involve a modification of our present usage of speech with regard to the words hard and soft, but not of their meanings. For they represent no fact to be different from what it is; only they involve arrangements of facts which would be exceedingly maladroit. This leads us to remark that the question of what would occur under circumstances which do not actually arise is not a question of fact, but only of the most perspicuous arrangement of them. For example, the question of free-will and fate in its simplest form, stripped of verbiage, is something like this: I have done something of which I am ashamed; could I, by an effort of the will, have resisted the temptation, and done otherwise? The philosophical reply is, that this is not a question of fact, but only of the arrangement of facts. Arranging them so as to exhibit what is particularly pertinent to my question— namely, that I ought to blame myself for having done wrong—it is perfectly true to say that, if I had willed to do otherwise than I did, I should have done otherwise. On the other hand, arranging the facts so as to exhibit another important consideration, it is equally true that, when a temptation has once been allowed to work, it will, if it has a certain force, produce its effect, let me struggle how I may. There is no objection to a contradiction in what would result from a false supposition. The *reductio ad absurdum* consists in showing that contradictory results would follow from a hypothesis which is consequently judged to be false. Many questions are involved in the free-will discussion, and I am far from desiring to say that both sides are equally right. On the contrary, I am of opinion that one side denies important facts, and that the other does not. But what I do say is, that the above single question was the origin of the whole doubt; that, had it not been for this question, the controversy would never have arisen; and that this question is perfectly solved in the manner which I have indicated.

C From the *COLLECTED PAPERS OF CHARLES SANDERS PEIRCE*

Upon this first, and in one sense this sole, rule of reason, that in order to learn you must desire to learn, and in so desiring not be satisfied with what you already incline to think, there follows one corollary which itself deserves to be inscribed upon every wall of the city of philosophy:

Do not block the way of inquiry.

Although it is better to be methodical in our investigations, and to consider the economics of research, yet there is no positive sin against logic in *trying* any theory which may come into our heads, so long as it is adopted in such a sense as to permit the investigation to go on unimpeded and undiscouraged. On the other hand, to set up a philosophy which barricades the road of further advance toward the truth is the one unpardonable offence in reasoning, as it is also the one to which metaphysicians have in all ages shown themselves the most addicted.

Let me call your attention to four familiar shapes in which this venomous error assails our knowledge.

The first is the shape of the absolute assertion. That we can be sure of nothing in science is an ancient truth. The Academy taught it. Yet science has been infested with overconfident assertion, especially on the part of the third-rate and fourth-rate men, who have been more concerned with teaching than with learning, at all times. No doubt some of the geometries still teach as a self-evident truth the proposition that if two straight lines in one plane meet a third straight line so as to make the sum of the internal angles on the one side less than two right angles those two lines will meet on that side if sufficiently prolonged. Euclid, whose logic was more careful, only reckoned this proposition as a Postulate, or arbitrary Hypothesis. Yet even he places among his axioms the proposition that a part is less than its whole, and falls into several conflicts with our most modern geometry in consequence. But why need we stop to consider cases where some subtilty of thought is required to see that the assertion is not warranted when every book which applies philosophy to the conduct of life lays down as positive certainty propositions which it is quite as easy to doubt as to believe?

The second bar which philosophers often set up across the roadway of inquiry lies in maintaining that this, that, and the other never can be known. When Auguste Comte was pressed to specify any matter of positive fact to the knowledge of which no man could by any possibility attain, he instanced the knowledge of the chemical composition of the fixed stars; and you may see his answer set down in the *Philosophie Positive*.[24] But the ink was scarcely dry upon the printed page before the spectroscope was discovered and that which he had deemed absolutely unknowable was well on the way of getting ascertained. It is easy enough to mention a question the answer to which is not known to me today. But to aver that that answer will not be known tomorrow is somewhat risky; for oftentimes it is precisely the least expected truth which is turned up under the plowshare of research. And when it comes to positive assertion that the truth will never be found out, that, in the light of the history of our time, seems to me more hazardous than the venture of Andrée.[25]

The third philosophical stratagem for cutting off inquiry consists in maintaining that this, that, or the other element of science is basic, ultimate, independent of aught else, and utterly inexplicable—not so much from any defect in our knowing as because there is nothing beneath it to know. The only type of reasoning by which such a conclusion could possibly be reached is *retroduction*. Now nothing justifies a retroductive inference except its explanation of the facts. It is, however, no explanation at all of a fact to pronounce it *inexplicable*. That, therefore, is a conclusion which no reasoning can ever justify or excuse.

The last philosophical obstacle to the advance of knowledge which I intend to mention is the holding that this or that law or truth has found its last and perfect formulation—and especially that the ordinary and usual course of nature can never be broken through. "Stones do not fall from heaven," said Laplace, although they have been falling upon uninhabited ground every day from the earliest times.[26] But there is no kind of inference which can lend the slightest probability to any such absolute denial of an unusual phenomenon.

All positive reasoning is of the nature of judging the proportion of something in a whole collection by the proportion found in a sample. Accordingly, there are three things to which we can never hope to attain by reasoning, namely, absolute certainty, absolute exactitude, absolute universality. We cannot be absolutely certain that our conclusions are even approximately true; for the sample may be utterly unlike the unsampled part of the collection. We cannot pretend to be even probably exact; because the sample consists of but a finite number of instances and only admits special values of the proportion sought. Finally, even if we could ascertain with absolute certainty and exactness that the ratio of sinful men to all men was as 1 to 1; still among the infinite generations of men there would be room for any finite number of sinless men without violating the proportion.[27] The same is the case with a seven legged calf.

Now if exactitude, certitude, and universality are not to be attained by reasoning, there is certainly no other means by which they can be reached.

Somebody will suggest *revelation*. There are scientists and people influenced by science who laugh at revelation; and certainly science has taught us to look at testimony in such a light that the whole theological doctrine of the "Evidences" seems pretty weak.[28] However, I do not think it is philosophical to reject the possibility of a revelation. Still, granting that, I declare as a logician that revealed truths—that is, truths which have nothing in their favour but revelations made to a few individuals—constitute by far the most uncertain class of truths there are. There is here no question of universality; for revelation is itself sporadic and miraculous. There is no question of mathematical exactitude; for no revelation makes any pretension to that character. But it does pretend to be *certain*; and against that there are three conclusive objections. First, we never can be absolutely certain that any given deliverance really is inspired; for that can only be established by reasoning. We cannot even prove it with any very high degree of probability. Second, even if it is inspired, we cannot be sure, or nearly sure, that the statement is true. We know that one of the commandments was in one of the Bibles printed without a *not* in it. All inspired matter has been subject to human distortion or colouring. Besides we cannot penetrate the counsels of the most High, or lay down anything as a principle that would govern his conduct. We do not know his inscrutable purposes, nor can we comprehend his plans. We cannot tell but he might see fit to inspire his servants with errors. In the third place, a truth which rests on the authority of inspiration only is of a somewhat incomprehensible nature; and we can never be sure that we rightly comprehend it. As there is no way of evading these difficulties, I say that revelation, far from affording us any certainty, gives results less certain than other sources of information. This would be so even if revelation were much plainer than it is.

But, it will be said, you forget the laws which are known to us *a priori*, the axioms of geometry, the principles of logic, the maxims of *causality*, and the like. Those are absolutely certain, without exception and exact. To this I reply that it seems to me there is the most positive historic proof that innate truths are particularly uncertain and mixed up with error, and therefore *a fortiori* not without exception.[29] This historical proof is, of course, not infallible; but it is very strong. Therefore, I ask *how do you know* that *a priori* truth is certain, exceptionless, and exact? You cannot know it by *reasoning*. For that would be subject to uncertainty and inexactitude. Then, it must amount to this that you know it *a priori*; that is, you take *a priori* judgments at their own valuation, without criticism or credentials. That is barring the gate of inquiry.

Ah! but it will be said, you forget direct experience. Direct experience is neither certain nor uncertain, because it affirms nothing—it just *is*. There are delusions, hallucinations, dreams. But there is no mistake that such things really do appear, and direct experience means simply the appearance. It involves no error, because it testifies to nothing but its own appearance. For the same reason, it affords no certainty. It is not *exact*, because it leaves much vague; though it is not *inexact* either; that is, it has no false exactitude.

All this is true of direct experience at its first presentation. But when it comes up to be criticized it is past, itself, and is represented by *memory*. Now the deceptions and inexactitude of memory are proverbial.

. . . On the whole, then, we cannot in any way reach perfect certitude nor exactitude. We never can be absolutely sure of anything, nor can we with any probability ascertain the exact value of any measure or general ratio.

This is my conclusion, after many years study of the logic of science; and it is the conclusion which others, of very different cast of mind, have come to, likewise. I believe I may say there is no tenable opinion regarding human knowledge which does not legitimately lead to this corollary. Certainly there is nothing new in it; and many of the greatest minds of all time have held it for true.

Indeed, most everybody will admit it until he begins to see what is involved in the admission—and then most people will draw back. It will not be admitted by persons utterly incapable of philosophical reflection. It will not be fully admitted by masterful minds developed exclusively in the direction of action and accustomed to claim practical infallibility in matters of business. These men will admit the incurable fallibility of all opinions readily enough; only, they will always make exception of their own. The doctrine of fallibilism will also be denied by those who fear its consequences for science, for religion, and for morality. But I will take leave to say to these highly conservative gentlemen that however competent they may be to direct the affairs of a church or other corporation, they had better not try to manage science in that way. Conservatism—in the sense of a dread of consequences—is altogether out of place in science —which has on the contrary always been forwarded by radicals and radicalism, in the sense of the eagerness to carry consequences to their extremes. Not the radicalism that is cocksure, however, but the radicalism *that tries experiments.* Indeed, it is precisely among men animated by the spirit of science that the doctrine of fallibilism will find supporters.

Still, even such a man as that may well ask whether I propose to say that it is not quite certain that twice two are four—and that it is even not probably quite exact! But it would be quite misunderstanding the doctrine of fallibilism to suppose that it means that twice two is probably not exactly four. As I have already remarked, it is not my purpose to doubt that people can usually *count* with accuracy. Nor does fallibilism say that men cannot attain a sure knowledge of the creations of their own minds. It neither affirms nor denies that. It only says that people cannot attain absolute certainty concerning questions of fact. Numbers are merely a system of names devised by men for the purpose of counting. It is a matter of real fact to say that in a certain room there are two persons. It is a matter of fact to say that each person has two eyes. It is a matter of fact to say that there are four eyes in the room. But to say that *if* there are two persons and each person has two eyes there *will be* four eyes is not a statement of fact, but a statement about the system of numbers which is our own creation.

NOTES

1   In order to assess the claim made in the text chapters that Kant's synthesis between traditional empiricism and rationalism is primarily a rationalistic synthesis, and that Peirce's synthesis is empiricistic, this paragraph can be compared with similar remarks made by Kant. Where Kant said that knowledge *begins* with experience, Peirce says that knowledge *rests upon* experience. The difference is not unimportant. From the rest of this paragraph, we can see that Peirce is sensitive to the interplay of sense impressions and mental operations. But where Kant makes certain mental operations antecedent to *meaningful* experience, Peirce takes mental operations to *add* to what is observed or to judge the significance of what is observed. This allows observations to have a distinct character of their own, in some sense independent of our conceptual schemes, in that we cannot control what we observe by mental operations (although we can look to see what happens in some circumstances that particularly interest us). Kant and Peirce differ, not as Descartes and Hume, but in a much more subtle way that is worth thinking about.

2   That is, we should first ask ourselves what the consequences of adopting it are.

3   This remark conceals serious problems. From Peirce's immediately preceding remarks, one might suppose that a hypothesis which had no practical consequences could not be considered. To say that a hypothesis cannot be tested is not quite the same thing as to say that it has no practical consequences. Some hypotheses might be confirmed by any observation, and others might be so unclear that we could not determine what observations would confirm them. Two plausible broad rules of acceptance and rejection of hypotheses are possible. On the one hand, we might decide that we could accept only hypotheses that have not decisively *failed* an experimental test. On the other hand, we might decide to accept only those hypotheses that have been confirmed by some experiment which, if quite different results had been obtained, would have led to the rejection (by disconfirmation) of the hypothesis. The significance of the difference between these two rules is that all Kant's metaphysical hypotheses (such as the existence of God) would be *rejected* by the second rule

but accepted by the first rule. (Why?) Peirce, as well as other early pragmatists, wanted to accept the hypothesis of the existence of God, and hence he implicitly used a rule of acceptance more like the first rule just described. Later empiricists, who considered themselves more hardheaded (Peirce might argue that they were), wanted to reject all hypotheses that were not confirmed by an *experimentum crucis*, that is, an experimental test whose results would either disconfirm or strongly confirm the hypothesis for which it was designed. Many contemporary empiricists, wanting to accept some, but not all, of the hypotheses which are compatible with past experiment but which have not survived an *experimentum crucis* (there may not be one which can be readily performed), have tried to find some compromise rule between the two proposed above. The existence of God, construed as a hypothesis, would be taken by many theologians as having no *experimentum crucis* (It is compatible with any observation.), while other theologians have held that the *experimentum crucis* is to be performed after death, which is an example of an experiment that is not readily performed. Peirce restricts himself in the following passages to hypotheses for which a convenient *experimentum crucis* is available. It might also be noticed that rejection and acceptance of hypotheses is not an all-or-nothing operation for Peirce, since some are strongly held beliefs and others are only opinions or hunches. This calls for some complication of any extensive treatment of the issues raised in this footnote.

4 Van't Hoff was a contemporary of Peirce who first proposed some important generalizations about the laws of chemical solutions. His work is reviewed in most moderately technical surveys of chemical theory. The interesting point here is that van't Hoff's generalizations are inferences of the kind called *inductions* by many people and discussed earlier in the third chapter on Hume. Van't Hoff argued that because certain chemicals in solution had a certain property, all chemicals capable of being dissolved in the same circumstances would also exhibit this property. Because an inference of this sort is commonly called an induction, it is important to notice that Peirce calls it an abduction, reserving the use of *induction* for another purpose.

5 Unfortunately, Peirce does not discuss how one might legitimately prefer one hypothesis over another by abduction, where both hypotheses explain the facts.

6 There are some hidden problems in Peirce's example. One question is the formulation of the hypothesis as a *tendency*. It would be compatible with a tendency that the proportion of births in the populations be the same in any given census; consequently the *must* in the last sentence is too strong. (Anyone annoyed with the social implications of the example may substitute some other hypothesis about relative ratios in two populations.) All of these objections are saved by Peirce's formulation of an induction as essentially involving the hypothesis that random samples of a population will exhibit about the same statistics as the whole population. The difficulties in understanding what is meant by *random* and 'about the same' tend to make the formulation trivial. (Why?)

7 Compare this remark with footnote 5. Does the notion of economy solve the problem?

8 No exposition of Peirce's extended example from astronomy will be given

here. The interested reader may consult Norwood Russell Hanson's *Patterns of Discovery*, Cambridge, 1958 for a discussion of Kepler's reasoning from the standpoint of the philosophy of science. John Stuart Mill was an empiricist who lived after Hume, and who attempted a kind of total empiricism which made even mathematical statements empiricistic. What Peirce's example illustrates is what should be known independently of the example, that what Peirce calls abductive reasoning is an important aspect of scientific theorizing.

9   The *il lume naturale* is an expression equivalent to Descartes's *natural light*. See footnote 22 to the Descartes reading.

10   It is interesting to speculate on the relationship between simplicity, as it is discussed here, and the economy mentioned earlier (see footnote 7). Simplicity has always been cited since Copernicus as a criterion by which hypotheses of equal explanatory power can be discriminated. See the remarks on simplicity in Nelson Goodman's *The Structure of Appearance*, Cambridge, 1951 for clarification of a way in which economy and simplicity can be usefully distinguished.

11   The reader who does not think of Descartes at this point may turn to page 1 and start over.

12   This passage marks Peirce's correct observation that the philosophical methodology of his time was entirely inadequate to scientific inquiry.

13   The first paper referred to is one called "The Fixation of Belief," which was published before "How to Make Our Ideas Clear" in the *Popular Science Monthly* of 1878.

14   Several passages in this essay suggest that Peirce felt that a separate criterion for distinctness was unnecessary. Further, his own contribution is directed solely to the problem of making our ideas clear. Where he speaks of distinctness, as here, he either reduces distinctness to clearness, or *conjectures* what distinctness might mean. Clearly Peirce felt that his single rule for clearness was a considerable gain in simplicity for scientific inquiry, as well as in fruitfulness, by comparison to the older Cartesian doctrine of clearness *and* distinctness.

15   Leibnitz was a rationalistic philosopher who lived shortly after Descartes.

16   Leibnitz knew that a perpetual motion machine was impossible, because a moving machine requires work to be performed in order to sustain its motion, and no infinite source of energy to enable such continual work to be performed is available. Peirce suggests an analogy between a perpetual motion machine and the mind, which he argues cannot work perpetually without being fed information from the outside in the form of facts.

17   Melusina was the principal character of a story in which she was condemned to turn into a serpent every Saturday (for the day) from the waist down. She married a man named Raymond under the condition that he would not visit her on Saturday. When he broke this promise, Melusina disappeared.

18   A circle-squarer is someone who believes that he can, with ruler and compass (more properly, straightedge and compass, since no length can be measured under the stipulations of the problem), construct a square equal in area to an arbitrary circle. This problem, a live issue in Greek geometry, is now known to be impossible of solution, a fact which can be proved in an appropriate

algebraic system. In spite of this, many persons still propose solutions to the problem! A history of some of these attempts is found in Augustus DeMorgan's *Budget of Paradoxes.*

19   Whether sensations are completely present at every instant so long as they last raises the intriguing question of whether or not there is an instant at which they begin and an instant at which they end. Similar questions may be raised with respect to thought.

20   Are there unconscious beliefs? We must be aware of belief as it appeases the irritation of doubt, on Peirce's view. But a habit established by belief may be performed unconsciously until it breaks down in the face of some conflicting fact.

21   These two arrangements (Notice that Peirce takes the belief that the dots are arranged in such and such a way as his subject.) are similar, except for a rotation about their center. Any human purpose for which the one arrangement is suitable is also a purpose for which the other is suitable, *as long as they may both be freely manipulated.* This is Peirce's point, in that an apparent difference may be no real difference. Still, although Fig. 1 and Fig. 2 are identical except for their orientation, their orientation makes them different for purposes of communication in English. Peirce's example needs some amplification to take care of the significance (in some cases) of arrangement.

22   *Tropical* may mean *figurative.*

23   Peirce distinguishes three grades of clearness which are not to be thought of as degrees of the same concept. The first grade of clearness of an idea is familiarity with it, and the second grade of clearness is a satisfactory definition of it. These grades had been discussed before Peirce. The third grade of clearness is the significance of an idea with respect to its real consequences, or nonabstract consequences. It might be noted that the first two grades need not enable us to know whether two ideas can be distinguished.

24   Auguste Comte was a philosopher who maintained that metaphysical speculation (in Kant's sense) should be avoided and knowledge limited to the definite results of science. The example shows that Comte did not fare very well in his anticipations of future scientific thought.

25   Andrée attempted to fly over the polar regions in a balloon in the late nineteenth century, but he did not make it. It was a hazardous venture.

26   The striking fact about this example is that Laplace was one of the great mathematical astronomers.

27   Compare these remarks with the discussion in footnote 6.

28   William Paley wrote a book called *View of the Evidences of Christianity* in which he tried to ground Christian doctrine on natural science. Many of his arguments appear invalid.

29   This proof is simply that history records that many statements thought at one time to represent innate truths have proved false or misleading.

INDEX

A priori, 200–203, 212n.
    and a posteriori judgments, Kant on, 223–226, 233, 234, 237–243, 249
Abstraction, 113, 149–154, 172n., 173n., 195
Accidental predication, 65–68, 72, 73, 85, 92, 94
Actuality, 58
Adventitious ideas, 130, 135n.
Allegory of the cave, 46–50, 52n., 53n., 135
Apprehension, synthesis of, 254, 260n.
Aristotle, 3, 5, 54–98, 101, 102, 111, 133n., 135, 139, 145, 218, 220, 228
    on accidental predication, 65–73, 85, 92, 94
    on the categories, 63–65, 77, 89, 90, 96n.
    definition of knowledge, 57–62
    the development of his thought, 74, 75
    on essential predication, 66–73, 84, 85
    form and matter in, 58, 60, 89, 90, 97n., 111
    on knowledge, 57–62, 71–73
    on metaphysics, 61
    substance in, 58, 64, 68, 70, 71, 77, 87, 88, 98n.
    views on sense experience, 71–73
Association, 179–181, 189, 196
Attribute, 65, 66, 82, 91, 96n.
    commensurately universal, 84–87, 96n.

Beck, L. W., 232
Belief, in empiricism, 183, 189, 209

Belief (cont.), pragmatist's notion of, 266, 268–271
    (See also Opinion)
Berkeley, 135, 137–174, 177, 178, 187, 209, 210n., 221, 228
    on abstract ideas, 149–154, 164, 165, 169–171
    dialogue form in, 155
    on ideas, 148–151, 169–171
    on knowledge, 150, 151, 168, 169
    matter in, 147–151, 161, 165–167, 173n., 228
    mind in, 150, 151, 159, 164, 165, 168, 171
    nominalism of, 152–154
    phenomenalism of, 148
    on popular theories of knowledge, 143–148
    substance in, 159
    views on sense experience, 166

Categorical statements, 59
Categories, in Aristotle, 63–65, 77, 89, 90, 96n.
    in Kant, 228–230, 251–257
Causation, 51n., 58, 81, 85, 142, 224, 229, 245
    Hume's account of, 179, 180, 183, 184, 187–190, 196–198, 200–209, 211n.
Certainty, 2, 14, 15, 19, 24, 57, 61, 67, 101, 102, 104, 121, 122, 128, 177, 182, 191, 263, 266
    Descartes on, 101–105
City-states, 13, 14

301

Classification as a methodological tool, 59, 60, 63, 84

Clearness of ideas (*see* Ideas, clearness and distinctness of)

Commensurately universal attributes, 84–87, 96*n.*

Common sense, 142, 144–149, 166, 179

Concept of containment, 225

Constant conjunction, 189, 190, 202, 208

Contiguity, 179, 180, 183, 187–189

Cost, 276, 277

Custom, 185–188, 207–209, 270

Deductive inference, 96*n.*, 102–104, 106–110, 115, 185, 229, 265, 272, 273, 282

(*See also* Syllogistic inference)

Definition, 61, 62, 65–67, 76, 78, 82, 88, 91–93, 96*n.*, 286

Demonstration, 81–84, 86, 87, 96*n.*, 184, 197, 203

Descartes, 24, 101–135, 140, 145, 150, 178, 210*n.*, 285, 286, 297*n.*

on certainty, 101–105

cogito argument of, 106–111, 122

definition of knowledge, 103, 104, 115

on doubt, 120, 122

on empiricism, 112, 113, 125–127

on the faculty of understanding, 130, 131

on ideas, 112–115, 129, 130

imagination in, 113, 119, 123, 124, 126, 127, 130, 134*n.*

on knowledge, 104, 110, 111

mind in, 110, 111, 125, 127

views on sense experience, 104, 105, 112–114, 118

Dewey, John, 264, 278

Dialectic, 29, 37, 45, 46, 103

Dialogue form, in Berkeley, 155

in Plato, 30, 31

Differentia, 65–67, 77, 87

Distinction between knowledge and opinion, 1, 2, 9, 20, 21, 57

Distinctness of ideas (*see* Ideas, clearness and distinctness of)

Doubt, Descartes on, 120, 122

pragmatist's view of, 269, 275

Dreaming, 104, 105, 118, 119

Empiricism, 24, 27, 104, 134, 140, 141.

Empiricism, (*cont.*) 148, 150, 152–154, 177, 181, 183, 209, 217–219, 226, 229, 230

Epistemology, 1–3, 8, 9, 13, 15, 62, 96*n.*, 102, 115, 139, 140, 143, 152, 217, 231

Equivocal names, 76

Eristics, 14, 40

Essence, 66, 89, 91–94, 97*n.*, 98*n.*

Essential predication, 66–73, 84, 85

Ethics, 3, 4, 20, 178

Evidential fit, 276, 277

Experimentum crucis, 297*n.*, 298*n.*

Extension, 113, 142, 160–164, 166

Facts, 140, 141, 279

Fermat's last theorem, 184

Form and matter, in Aristotle, 58, 60, 89, 90, 97*n.*, 111

in Kant, 220, 221, 228

Formal systems, 106–108, 273, 274

Forms, 18, 22, 23, 25–27

(*See also* Ideas, Plato on)

General knowledge, 8, 80

Genus, 65–67, 77–79, 85, 89, 91

God, 110, 112, 120–122, 128–135, 139, 150, 165, 166, 173*n.*, 194, 210*n.*, 240

Habit, 185–188, 207–209, 270

Haldane, E. S., 116

Hartshorne, Charles, 278

Hintikka, Jaako, 109, 117

Hume, 95*n.*, 177–213, 217, 225, 229, 231, 239, 245, 252, 297*n.*

association in, 179–181

on causation, 187–190, 197–209

on custom or habit, 185, 186, 207–209

definition of knowledge, 182–185

on ideas and impressions, 178–182, 187, 192–197, 210*n.*, 211*n.*

imagination in, 181, 193, 195, 196, 199

on knowledge, 182, 197

on mathematical knowledge, 182, 183, 197

matters of fact in, 197, 198, 201, 203, 207, 209

on metaphysics, 181, 195

mind in, 192–196, 202, 210*n.*

relations of ideas in, 197, 203

rules for causation in, 190, 200, 201

skeptical position of, 183–185, 201–205

Hume (*cont.*), substance in, 177, 181
    views on sense experience, 198, 199,
    201, 202
Hypotheses, 45, 46, 132*n*., 264–267, 272–
    277, 279–284, 293, 297*n*., 298*n*.

Ideas, clearness and distinctness of, 102,
        112–115, 125, 270, 284–287, 300*n*.
    Berkeley on, 146, 149–153, 166–171
    Descartes on, 110–115, 129–131, 134,
        135
    Hume on, 178, 179, 187, 192–196,
        210*n*., 211*n*.
    Peirce on, 270, 271
    Plato on, 18, 21–27
    theory of, 18, 21–29, 31, 32, 44–50,
        51*n*., 58, 61, 98*n*.
Imagination, in Descartes, 113, 119, 123,
        124, 126, 127, 130, 134*n*.
    in Hume, 181, 193, 195, 196, 199
    in Kant, 255, 260*n*.
Impressions in Hume's epistemology, 178–
        182, 187, 193–195, 211*n*.
Individualism, 4, 5, 101–103
Individuation, problem of, 219, 220
Inductive inference, 83, 95*n*., 185, 264,
        265, 281, 282, 298
Intuition, 8, 18, 24, 105, 113, 189, 202
    Kant's notion of, 220, 221, 227, 236,
        237, 242, 251–256, 258*n*., 260*n*.

Jaeger, Werner, 74, 75
James, William, 263, 278, 279
Jowett, Benjamin, 30
Judgment, 5, 114, 115, 146, 147, 222–229,
        234, 235, 241–245

Kant, 236–260, 263, 264, 266, 272, 274,
        275, 297*n*.
    on a priori and a posteriori judgments,
        223–226, 233, 234, 237–243, 249
    on analytic and synthetic judgments,
        223–226, 236–238, 242, 243, 250,
        251, 258*n*., 259*n*., 274
    categories in, 228–230, 251–257
    definition of knowledge, 237–241, 253
    on empirical knowledge, 236–238, 242,
        243, 254, 255
    on the faculty of understanding, 222,
        227, 246–250, 260*n*.

Kant (*cont.*), form and matter in, 58, 60,
        89, 90, 97*n*., 111
    imagination in, 255, 260*n*.
    on mathematical knowledge, 243, 244,
        249, 252, 253, 258*n*., 259*n*.
    on metaphysics, 240, 245
    notion of intuition, 220, 221, 227, 236,
        237, 242, 251–256, 258*n*., 260*n*.
    philosophy of, synthesis in, 229, 230
    space and time in, 219–221, 254, 255
    substance in, 228, 239, 253
    synthesis of rationalism and empiricism
        in, 217–222
    on synthetic a priori judgments, 223–
        226, 242–245, 272, 275
    views on sense experience, 219–222,
        229, 230
Kemp Smith, N., 232, 233
Knowledge, Aristotle on, 57–62, 71–73
    Berkeley on, 150, 151, 168, 169
    definition of, 1, 2, 9, 61, 62
        Aristotle's, 57–62
        Descartes's, 103, 104, 115
        Hume's, 182–185
        Kant's, 237–241, 253
        Plato's, 13–16, 20, 21, 24, 37
    Descartes on, 104, 110, 111
    Hume on, 182, 187

Leibnitz, 286, 299*n*.
Linguistic uniformity, 22, 23
Locke, John, 141, 142, 147, 177, 210*n*.,
    248, 252
Lumen naturale, 135, 284, 299

Mathematical knowledge, 5–9, 14–17, 20,
        21, 61, 79, 80, 113, 114, 119, 129,
        132*n*., 139, 141, 182, 183, 191, 192,
        197, 200, 201, 225, 226, 274, 275
    Kant on, 243, 244, 249, 252, 253, 258*n*.,
        259*n*.
Matter, in Berkeley, 147–151, 161, 165–
        167, 173*n*., 228
    (*See also* Form and matter)
Matters of fact in Hume, 197, 198, 201,
    203, 207, 209
Memory, 71, 104, 105, 133, 181, 196, 197
Metaphysics, 113
    Aristotle on, 61
    Hume on, 181, 195
    Kant on, 240, 245

Mind, in Berkeley, 150, 151, 159, 164, 165, 168, 171
    in Descartes, 110, 111, 125, 127
    in Hume, 192–196, 202, 210n.
    in Plato, 17, 18, 20, 22
Motion, 113, 142, 159, 160–164, 166

Natural kinds, 67, 70, 78, 79, 88, 91
Natural relations, 180, 189
Necessary property, 66–73, 84, 85
Newton, Sir Isaac, 139, 140, 180, 181, 185, 225
Nominalism, 152, 173n.

Objective empirical judgment, 227–231
Opinion, definition of, 2, 3, 9
    Plato's view about, 13, 20–24, 35–38, 41

Participation, 22, 26, 28, 29, 31, 39–42, 52n., 63, 152
Peirce, 95n., 96n., 217, 261–300
    on abduction, 96n., 264–269, 280–284, 298n., 299n.,
    on fallibilism, 272, 276, 296, 297
    on the nature, of habits, beliefs, and ideas, 268–271, 288–292, 300n.
    of hypotheses, 279–284
Perceptual judgment, 227, 230
Phenomenalism, 148
Philosophical relation, 188, 189
Plato, 3, 5, 13–63, 72, 74, 88, 96n., 97n., 98n., 101–103, 105, 108, 111, 114, 134, 135, 139, 145, 151–153, 155, 177, 210n., 232
    definition of knowledge, 13–16, 20, 21, 24, 37
    dialogue form in, 30, 31
    on ideas, clearness and distinctness of, 18, 21–27
    on knowledge, 13–16, 20, 21, 24, 37
    mind in, 17, 18, 20, 22
    on the nature of man, 17–20, 31–34
    on opinion, 13, 20–24, 35–38, 41
    relations of ideas in, 28, 29
    on sense experience, 15–19, 32–34, 41– 46, 51n.
    theory of ideas in, 18, 21–29, 31, 32, 41, 42, 44–50, 51n., 52n., 61, 98n.
Plato's Academy, 74, 97n., 293
Potentiality, 58

Powers, 142, 201, 202, 204, 207
Practical science, 57, 58
Pragmatism, 263–269, 272, 276
    (*See also* Peirce)
Predicables, 64–66, 76, 77, 95n.
Predicate, 63, 78, 79, 88, 89, 91, 96n.
Prediction, 15, 140, 183, 190, 197, 198, 208, 209
Primary qualities, 135, 142, 143, 160, 163, 165
Primary substance, 70–72, 77–79, 89–93, 97n.
Psychological problems as distinct from philosophical, 189
Pythagorean theorem, 5–7, 8, 14, 183

Rationalism, 24, 28, 29, 95n., 102, 114, 115, 134, 139, 141, 154, 177, 185, 189, 217, 218, 220, 223, 225, 226, 258n., 263, 268, 270, 271, 297n.
Reason, 4, 5, 46, 133, 208, 212n.
Recollection, 17, 18, 31, 34–38, 51n., 105
Reductio ad absurdum argument, 103
Relations of ideas, in Hume, 197, 203
    in Plato, 28, 29
Resemblance, 179, 180, 183, 189, 190, 196, 211n.
Ross, G. R. T., 116
Ross, W. D., 75
Russell, Bertrand, 132

St. Augustine on deception, 133
Scientific knowledge, 69, 70, 84, 113, 114, 117, 119, 139–143, 147, 148, 199, 200, 211n.–213n., 217, 218, 225
Secondary qualities, 142, 143, 160, 163, 165
Seeing, an analysis of, 145–148, 156–160
Self-evident principles, 58, 96
Self-predication of ideas, 27, 28, 51n.
Sensation, 162, 163, 192, 195, 210n., 220, 289, 300
Sense data, 115
Sense experience, 101, 103, 140, 142, 143, 172n., 219
    Aristotle's views on, 71–73
    Berkeley's views on, 166
    Descartes's views on, 104, 105, 112– 114, 118
    Hume's views on, 198, 199, 201, 202
    Kant's views on, 219–222, 229, 230

Sense experience (*cont.*), Plato's views on, 15–19, 32–34, 41–46, 51*n.*
Simple thought, 115
Simplicity, 115, 276, 277, 284
Skepticism, 15, 58, 101, 168–170, 185
Smith, J. A., 75
Socrates, 30, 31, 74
Sophists, 14, 40
Soul, 17, 20, 33, 38, 40, 46, 49, 50, 51*n.*, 123
    (*See also* Mind, in Plato)
Space and time, in Descartes, 119
    in Kant, 219–221, 254, 255
Species, 67, 70, 78, 79, 88, 91
Standard observer, 171*n.*, 172*n.*
Stoicism, 206, 212
Substance, in Aristotle, 58, 64, 68, 70, 71, 77, 87, 88, 98*n.*
    in Berkeley, 159
    in Hume, 177, 181
    in Kant, 228, 239, 253
    primary, in Aristotle, 70–72, 77–79, 89–94, 95*n.*–97*n.*
Substratum, 58, 89, 90, 162, 171*n.*

Syllogistic inference, 59, 60, 79–84, 87, 95*n.*, 98*n.*
    (*See also* Demonstration)
Synthesis, of apprehension, 254, 260*n.*
    in Kant's philosophy, 229, 230

Theoretical science, 57, 58, 61, 73
Theory of ideas, 18, 21–29, 31, 32, 44–50, 51*n.*, 52*n.*, 58, 61, 98*n.*
Theory of knowledge, 3, 23, 31, 63, 64, 139
Things-in-themselves, 231, 233, 255
Transmigration, 17
Transubstantiation, 291, 292

Univocal names, 76

Weiss, Paul, 278
World, of becoming, 18, 21, 22, 50, 67, 111
    of being, 18, 21, 46, 71, 103, 111, 114

HIEBERT LIBRARY

3 6877 00172 7360

BD
161
.A33
1965